The DEFINITIVE GUIDE to

FISHING

Northern
CALIFORNIA

D0754041

by: Chris Shaffer

Extremely Important! You must read this.

While all of us love and cherish the great outdoors, at all times we must remember that many vast dangers are found on our precious lands. Many sites in this book require hiking on trails, places where there is no trail or the trail is no longer maintained. Many of these trails require stream crossings that are simple and very complex, as well as treks through snow, climbs over mountains with stable and loose structures. Although we have strived to our greatest ability to point out the dangers you'll encounter, the author and publisher of this book urge you to use the highest respect of carefulness while being in the outdoors, and does not assume liability or responsibility for any loss due to injury and or death that occur in the outdoors or while traveling to, or visiting any site in the book. Keep in mind rivers, creeks and lakes fluctuate in an instant. Unstable and unsafe weather, water and road conditions can create harmful and deadly hazards. Hikers and anglers drown or are seriously injured due to the use of poor judgment and because they over estimate their human capabilities. Jumping, diving, sliding off rocks and walking the streambed can be dangerous. You are responsible for checking the depth of the water and locating submerged structures. Please use extreme caution at all times. In certain locations in this book the line between public and private property can be very vague. Do your best to respect all private property and obey all no trespassing signs.

With all this in mind, please have a great time, be safe and please remember to catch and release.

This book could not have been done without the help and support of several people. In addition to my parents Ernie and Carole and Uncle Ron Shaffer, who became my No. 2 dad for five years during this project, a special thank you goes out to Dan and Cheryl Lezak for their tremendous support, both personally and financially. Without them, this book would be just an idea. Also, thanks to Tony Abel, Blake Lezak, Big Todd McLean, Scott Wiessner, Brandi Koerner and Brett Ross for assisting me on many of the long and extensive trips required to complete this book. To the California Department of Fish and Game employees who gathered information to help make this book a success, specifically biologists Paul Chappell, Larry Hanson, John Hiscox, Stafford Lehr, Ivan Paulsen, Rick Macedo, Dave Lentz and Bill Summer, your help and thoughts are priceless have helped make this project a success. Nicole Shaffer, you did a fantastic job editing this book. Gary Dobyns, Sep and Marilyn Hendrickson, Steve Vaughn, Jean Rodgers, Mick Thomas, Wally Johnson, Tim King, Greg Squires, John Gray, Gary Mirales, Steve Carson, Terry Knight, Guy Ives, Mike Nielsen, Chuck Self, Randy Pringle, Pete Alexander, Jack Findleton and the hundreds of other anglers who helped educate me on Northern California fishing, your work and contributions will benefit the fishing community for decades.

Printed in Asia

Edited by Nicole Shaffer

Book Design, Maps and Production by Chris Shaffer

Send all questions and comments to Shafdog Publications by email to: cshaffer@californiawaterfalls.com or visit us on the web @ www.californiawaterfalls.com or www.fishingcalifornia.net

All photos Copyright Chris Shaffer except: Cover by Joel Shangle P. 99 Ron Babbini, P. 135 Brandi Koerner, P. 174 Mark Delnero, P. 375 JeanRodgers, P. 551 Steve Carson, P. 555, 581, 585, 586 Blake Lezak, P. 758 Mike Nielsen, P. 759 Steve Marugg

It was 2 p.m. I had just walked off the Southwest jet in Sacramento, on a Sunday afternoon. The 45-minute flight from Burbank had replaced the five-hour drive from my home in Southern California. There was no time for rest. I booked a rental car on this dry, warm, sunny, breezy fall day and began the routine drive up Interstate 80 to Lake Tahoe. It was 5 p.m. when I met Tahoe Topliners guide Mike Nielsen at the dock in the Tahoe Keys. Nielsen a Pautzke, Rebel, Bomber and Silver Thread Pro Staffer had fished the lake exclusively for more than 25 years. He knew it as well as anyone.

"It's up to you," Nielsen said, wrapped in a heavy winter coat. The boat struggled to remain still. The wind was so strong it churned up waves even in well protected marinas. "I don't think it's going to let down. I hope you haven't eaten anything in the last few hours."

Guide JD Richey and an American Shad

This was my 44th time with Nielsen since 1999. We had scheduled the trip to test new products and learn how to target Tahoe's trophy rainbows and browns. Despite the red flag warning, we fished the harsh, unforgiving ocean-like conditions in the name of research. As expected, we were the only boat on the lake. Most sane folks drove by and asked, "I thought Tahoe was a lake. Lakes have waves?"

Blake Lezak (Left) and Christian Perez with a Shasta bow

I left Tahoe at roughly 9 p.m., heading down the hill to Sacramento to try for a few hours of sleep before meeting bass pro Gary Dobyns at 4 a.m. Reaching Sac Town at 11:30 p.m., I grabbed my laptop, downloaded our photos and scribbled my half legible notes onto a notepad. Now 1 a.m., there was a chance for two-and-a-half hours of sleep. I took them, so I thought. An hour-and-a-half had passed when I woke up remembering more data from our trip.

There was no time for sleep or a shower. Instead, I headed to the truck stop near I-5 and I-80, asked for ice-tea, crispy bacon, eggs over easy, dry toast with strawberry jelly and hash browns and began to catalog more notes.

Dobyns arrived early, as always. The guy is not only one of the most successful bass fishermen in the West; he puts roosters to shame on a daily basis. Dobyns knew the drill. He was an integral part in the research and exploration for this unprecedented project.

"You are a sick dude," he said. "You've been doing this everyday for five years now?"

Here, drink this. He spared the bass gossip long enough to give me a Monster energy drink. Dobyns was nervous for the first time since I'd known him. We were heading to Salt Springs Valley Reservoir, a place he'd never heard of, or fished. What better way to learn a lake for your audience than to fish with the all-time leading bass fishing money winner in the West?

Still no more sleep. It was 8 p.m.

Time to travel again. I reached Redding about 11 p.m. when my wariness escalated. My girlfriend, at the time, did a good job of keeping me awake the last few hours, but once I hit Whiskeytown Reservoir on Highway 299, cell service was lost. A cute voice wasn't going to help me now. I was on my own. It was time for another Monster.

I twisted my way over Buckhorn Summit, the windy, dangerous pass between Redding and Weaverville. The brakes were surely tired. Shortly after reaching the turnoff for Lewiston Reservoir and Trinity Lake and while trying to focus on staying alert and awake, I saw flashing red lights ahead. Fortunately ok, paramedics were attending to a man and his son. They had flipped their car several times. The consensus? The driver had fallen asleep at the wheel.

I struggled enough over the next 45 minutes to know it was time to take a nap. Now 1 a.m., I had to meet professional steelhead guide Tim King in three hours. It was our third trip on the lower Trinity River. The focus was to teach anglers to catch more steelhead early in the run when waters were clear and low. King met me on the side of the road at 4 a.m.

"You've been doing this no sleep thing for three days now?" he said.

"No Tim, five years," I replied.

This routine is only a partial account of three-days of a five-year journey critiqued to design and accomplish a feat that was laughed upon by many opponents when the idea first circulated. The dream was the most comprehensive destination driven fishing

(Left) Randy Pringle with a pair of Delta stripers

Casey Kelley with a fat rainbow trout taken on Balls O' Fire salmon eggs

guide ever complied on one particular region. In spite of the, "No way, it can't be done," comments, my determination to prove critics wrong was eternal.

The real success stems from the research. This book, the fourth in the series of *Definitive Guides*, wasn't compiled in an air conditioned room, while sitting in a leather chair and waiting for phone calls from hundreds of marinas, guides and tackle shops. We, on the other hand, went to them. We queried the top guides, tackle shop owners, Forest Service and BLM employees, Fish and Game biologists, writers, tackle reps, tackle manufactures and locals who knew the most about each water and invited them to be a part of the *Definitive Guide to Fishing Northern California*. After all, these are the folks who know the waters best.

The *Definitive Guide* is a compilation of facts, stories, tales, hints,

Christopher Crawley with a pair of rainbows

recommendations and dos and don'ts taken from a half-decade of on the water research achieved in conjunction with those who know it best. This was not a one-man team, rather an effort by the masses to provide Northern California residents and those who are fortunate enough to fish our vast region, with the most up-to-date, thorough and exclusive information deemed necessary to help anglers better understand the waters and become more successful in improving their ability to catch fish.

As you read on, you'll meet hundreds of folks who make Nor Cal fishing what it is. These folks did their best to express and portray their secrets of how they get the fish to bite. None were compensated whatsoever. They donated their time, daily wages and sometimes meals, a bed and a warm cup a tea in the middle of the night as the studies drug on. I owe many thanks to those who were a part of transforming this dream book into reality.

Throughout the process Mother Nature wasn't always on our side; However, there was no time to wait for ideal conditions. We plowed through snow on the launch ramp at Lake Siskiyou one morning, Mc Cloud the next. Uncle Ron Shaffer and I brought shovels to Ice House Reservoir to clear the launch ramp so we could fish. Hail pounded bass guide John Gray and I as we darted across Trinity Lake at 30 mph trying to escape a late summer thunderstorm. Sleet met guide Mick Thomas and I on the Smith River, while fishing for a state record steelhead. High winds send us scurrying to get our boat on the trailer at Medicine Lake, 118 degree heat forced Big Todd McLean and I to take cover on our backcountry tour of the Caribou

Chris Cocoles with a Tahoe lake trout

Wilderness. Guide Captain Jack Findleton and I braved zero visibility on the Delta near Sherman Island for a shot at sturgeon. Striper guide Greg Squires managed to catch fish on the Sacramento River near Colusa on a day where flood levels were approaching, the barometer was falling and river levels were rising. These events are a minute part of 1,825 days of research. It was a journey even the most exquisite adventurer would be proud of.

After more than 100,000 miles in three years on what was purchased as a new Excursion midway through the project, thousands of miles on rental cars, 30,000 miles on a Suburban that we sunk in Lake Tahoe under harsh conditions, hundreds of miles in canoes and float tubes, another few hundred in laced up boots surveying the backcountry and several hundred more in jet, drift and other power boats, this dream has finally bloomed.

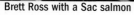
Brett Ross with a Sac salmon   David Rush with a pair of Oroville spotted bass

    More than 300 44 gallon tanks of gas later, countless cases of Monsters and Red Bulls, thousands of new contact email addresses, cell and house phone numbers, references and lifelong friends, the ultimate, most inclusive, broad and thorough guide is complete. Stuffed with more than 525 lakes, rivers, streams, ponds, brooks, reservoirs, canals and bays, *The Definitive Guide to Fishing Northern California* is a must have for every angler who plans to cast a line in Northern California.

    The guide was premeditated to be gold for hardcore anglers, pros, kids, first timers and weekend warriors. We've gathered a lifetime of experiences, memories, friends and destinations through the progression of this fishing marathon. It's time to turn the fun and excitement over to you. Enjoy!

Chris Shaffer
Author

How to use this book

This book has been designed to help anglers choose their desired fishing location by geographical region. The book is broken into 27 geographical regions, all located in Northern California. After selecting your desired region, go to the map preceding the section about that particular region. It will list all of the lakes, rivers and streams in that area. Then, it's as simple as choosing your ideal fishing spot and flipping to the corresponding page to learn more about it.

If you already know which body of water you want to fish, open to the table of contents and turn to the page with your favorite fishing hole. Once you've chosen a location, the rest is easy. Each article is written and structured in a user-friendly format that provides you with quick, fun and easy reading.

The book is set up with 10 categories containing all the information you could ever want to know about each lake, river or stream. The structure is as follows:

Name of fishing hole
Rating
Species present
Fish Stocked
Facilities
Contact Information
Lake Information
Tips For Making the Trip
Nearby Attractions
Directions

Name of the Fishing Hole

Rating:

Trinity Lake guide John Gray and a smallmouth bass

The ratings are based upon a comparison of more than 1,050 fishing spots covered in *The Definitive Guide to Fishing in Southern California, Central California and Northern California,* not just in Northern California. A "ten" is the best possible score and "one" is the worst. A "one" means there are no gamefish present and a "ten" qualifies it as one of the top 20 fisheries in the state.

Ratings are based on ideal weather and fishing conditions. Keep in mind, fishing conditions can change in an instant: skies can darken, bites can shut off, fish can die when water becomes too warm, cold or due to dissolved oxygen levels. The ratings are based on a number of factors, including, but not limited to, catch rates, the amount of fish in the body of water and the quantity of trophy fish.

Outdoor Writer Steve Carson with a salmon

Species:

Just below the rating is a list of all the species of catchable fish inhabiting the waters. Species include: American shad; yellow perch; golden, cutthroat, rainbow, brown, lake, redband and brook trout; channel, blue and white catfish; largemouth, smallmouth, mule, red eye, striped and spotted bass; green and red ear sunfish; carp; bluegill; warmouths; crappie; black and brown bullhead; steelhead; sturgeon; kokanee, coho and chinook salmon. Non-game fish such as shad and minnows are not listed, but may be present.

Stocks:

Both trout and catfish are stocked in many Northern California lakes, rivers and streams. Stocking numbers are provided in pounds, which usually differs greatly from the actual number of fish planted. For example, in most places in Northern California, the California Department of Fish and Game stocks half-pound trout; for every pound, typically, two fish are stocked. Fish are also planted as three-to-four-inch fingerlings and five-to-six-inch sub-catchables. To find the actual number of fish stocked in any particular place, consult the "Lake Information" section of its write-up.

Stocking information totals are from 2003. Each year, the amount of fish stocked can change. Places can be added to, or deleted, from the stocking list. Also, poor water quality, low water levels and high water levels can affect the number of fish planted. Check the "Lake Information" section for the times of the year that plants take place.

In many waters trout are purchased from other vendors aside from the CA DFG by private business and agencies to increase recreational opportunities for anglers. Those fish farms include Mt. Lassen Trout Farms, Calaveras Trout Farm, Donaldson Trout from Lake Amador Resort, the American Trout and Salmon Company and a few others.

Fish stocked by the CA DFG in the Motherlode region come from the Moccasin Fish Hatchery and American River Hatchery. The greater Sierra high country is planted mostly by the American River Hatchery, while waters on the Modoc Plateau and in most waters of Shasta, Lassen and Plumas County come from Darrah Springs and the Crystal Lake Hatchery. The Mt. Shasta Fish Hatchery handles most waters north of Redding on both sides of Interstate 5 and also many waters in Trinity County. The Silverado Planting Base in

Yountville is responsible for the Bay Area, Clear Lake region and most North Coast waters. The fish that come from the DFG are rainbow trout, brown trout, brook trout, cutthroat trout, kokanee, chinook salmon and golden trout. Steelhead and/or chinook salmon are also raised at the Iron Gate Hatchery on the Klamath River, the Trinity River Hatchery on the Trinity River, the Feather River Hatchery on the Feather River, the Nimbus Hatchery on the American River, Warm Springs Hatchery on the Russian River and the Mokelumne River Hatchery on the Mokelumne River.

Jack Findleton with a Delta striped bass

As for catfish, the CA DFG does stock them, but they don't raise them. To decide where the CA DFG purchases the cats a closed bidding is held. The breeder with the lowest bid gets to stocks the fish. Bidders are located across the state. The number of pounds of catfish planted is listed, however a total number of fish is not tallied. Almost all catfish planted are channel cats. The catfish generally range from one-to-three pounds.

Facilities:

Listed in the "Facilities" section are the services provided at the various lakes, rivers and streams. Services in the surrounding communities are not discussed in that section, however they are sometimes mentioned elsewhere. Services listed are as follows: Fish Cleaning Stations, Ranger Stations, Restrooms, Launch Ramps, Gas, General Stores, Campgrounds, RV Hookups, Snack Bars, Restaurants, Boats, Canoes and Kayaks Rentals, Lodging, Picnic Areas, Recreation Areas, Fishing Piers, Playgrounds, Horseshoe Pits, Visitor Centers, Boat Tours, Marinas and Bait & Tackle Shops.

Contact Information:

The "Contact" section is dedicated to providing phone numbers to help you plan your trip. This section includes numbers to check on the latest weather and fishing conditions and to find lodging, tourist information and the best fishing guides at your destination.

All of the fishing guides written about in this book have been thoroughly checked to ensure they are qualified, well mannered, certified, courteous, knowledgeable, fair and will provide you with an enjoyable fishing experience.

Lake Information:

The "Lake Information" section can be found in the body of each write-up. It tells you everything you need to know about fishing your favorite lake, river or stream. It includes information about how to catch the fish, where to find the fish and which baits and lures are best to use. In addition, the surrounding area and its wildlife are often described. In an attempt to help bring these exciting destinations to life, I sometimes tell about interesting and humorous personal experiences.

Tips For Making the Trip:

One of the most helpful sections is called "If You Plan to Make the Trip." This covers the "plan ahead" stage where you are warned of obstacles and/or hazards you might want to prepare for prior to visiting these various destinations. For example, in the winter some destinations may require chains; fishing and day-use fees may be charged; some streams dry-up by summer; and roads to certain locations are often closed by heavy rains, snow or torrential flows. Other questions that might arise are also answered. Are there special regulations? Are only electric boat motors allowed? Where can you buy supplies? Do you need to keep an eye out for rattlesnakes? If four-wheel drive is required or if the roads are poorly maintained, that information will also be discussed. Is this destination sometimes closed to fishing? All this and more is covered in this section.

Mike Nielsen with a Lake Tahoe brown trout

Nearby Attractions:

Perhaps you want to spend a whole day at your destination instead of just a few hours and you want to bring the family along. No problem. Listed in the "Also Nearby" section are ideas for places to take your family, including amusement parks, other fishing sites, waterfalls, hiking trails, historic sites, shopping and more.

Directions:

To make accessing some of these remote locations easy, all of the directions tell you how to get to your desired destination from a major city.

11 Siskiyou County 263

17 **Lakes Basin** **488**

Region   1   Del Norte County

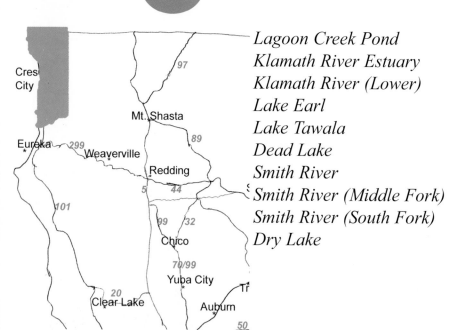

Lagoon Creek Pond
Klamath River Estuary
Klamath River (Lower)
Lake Earl
Lake Tawala
Dead Lake
Smith River
Smith River (Middle Fork)
Smith River (South Fork)
Dry Lake

LAGOON CREEK POND

Rating: 3

Species: Rainbow Trout

Stocks: None

Facilities: Restrooms

Need Information?
Contact: Redwood
National and State
Parks (707) 464-6101

Prior to 2003, Lagoon Creek Pond was one of the easiest spots on the North Coast for anglers to catch trout. The California Department of Fish and Game used to plant trout every other week from December through May in the one-acre pond only a quarter-mile from the Pacific Ocean. With easy, drive to access, catching 10-inch rainbow trout with spinners or spoons is easy.

However, in May of 2003 the CA DFG discovered high dioxins in the mud on the base of the pond and called off fish plants until further notice. The pond rests on a former mill site. According to the CA DFG, it is unsure when and if stocking will resume. For now, trout will not be planted, but hopefully this may change in the future.

If plants resume, catching trout will be a synch. Casting any shallow running spoon or spinner is effective. The pond can get weedy so you won't want to fish anything that's going to sink much. Floating bait off the bottom is another way to entice trout.

If you plan to make the trip, supplies are available in Klamath and Crescent City.

Also nearby is the Klamath River.

Directions: *From Crescent City, drive south on Highway 101 for roughly 15 miles to Lagoon Creek Pond on the right side of the road. (The pond is located at the signed rest area.) Or, drive 6.6 miles north of the Klamath River Bridge near Klamath.*

Lagoon Creek Pond

KLAMATH RIVER ESTUARY

Rating: 5

Species: Silver Salmon, Steelhead and King Salmon

Stocks: None

Facilities: Campgrounds, General Store, Gas, Restrooms, Boat Launches and a Restaurant

When it comes to catching salmon and steelhead in the Klamath River Estuary anglers take a backseat to seals, sea lions and Native Americans. At times, you have to work hard to catch fish in the estuary. Seal lions and seals cruise through the shallow water nabbing salmon. This can be entertaining to many anglers. These mammals don't eat the fish in one bite, rather chomp them into pieces and eat large chunks at a time. The scene is something you'd expect to see on the Discovery Channel. A sea lion rises to the surface after biting the salmon in half and throws pieces of the fish into the air as dozens of seagulls harass the sea lion for scrubs.

The natives, on the other hand, are a nuscience to many anglers. Compared to modern day anglers, their methods are unorthodox and virtually a slap in the face. (This is a matter of my personal opinion. To me, it's commercial fishing in a river system. But, seeing thousands of dead wasted salmon doesn't seem right.) While they were given the right by US courts to gillnet on tribal lands, the practice isn't approved by locals and out-of-town anglers.

When salmon and steelhead are entering the mouth of the river and leaving the crashing waves of the Pacific Ocean, they must first break through lines of gillnets. Regulations prohibit Natives from completely closing the outlet off with nets. They must have an opening for the salmon to swim upriver. I've personally been there when the mouth was completely closed off by nets though. One thing to consider is that we aren't talking about one or two nets, rather several dozen at a time. The beach, inlet and boat launch will be full of gill nets. Anglers are advised not to confront those with gill nets despite their feelings. You must remember this is an Indian reservation.

The estuary can yield excellent results. All the salmon and steelhead that enter the Trinity, Klamath and Scott rivers cross through the estuary. The Klamath River Estuary runs from the Highway 101 Bridge to the Pacific. While gillnets litter the water near the mouth, they are far less evident near the Highway 101 Bridge. Fortunately, anglers can successfully evade the nets to catch salmon and steelies.

Trolling spinners is your best option. Trolling allows you to cover more ground and locate aggressive fish, yet it can be frustrating to battle with more seaweed, weeds and grass than salmon. To keep the spinner off the surface, a 1 1/2 -2-ounce weight is recommended. Fish the main channel which can slice a different path each year. If you are successful finding the channel, vertical mooching sardines and anchovies can be productive. It's best to fish outgoing tides. Most salmon enter the river on high tide.

Trip info for Klamath River (Lower) also applies to Klamath River Estuary.

Directions: *From Highway 101 in Eureka, drive north to the town of Klamath Glen.*

KLAMATH RIVER (LOWER)

Rating: 8

Species: Chinook Salmon, Silver Salmon and Steelhead

Stocks: None

Facilities: RV Parks, Lodging, Restaurant, Bait & Tackle, Restrooms, Boat Launches and Campgrounds

Need Information? Contact: Fishing Guide Wally Johnson of Seiad Valley Guide Service (530) 496-3291, California Department of Fish and Game (707) 445-6493

The Lower Klamath River is one of the North Coast's most productive rivers. The Klamath system is the largest system on the North Coast, but not all the fish caught in the Lower Klamath are Klamath River fish. The Klamath fishery benefits from several major tributaries, including the Trinity, Salmon and Scott. Fih headed to these tributaries must swim through the Klamath. Two hatcheries, Iron Gate on the Klamath and Trinity River Fish Hatchery on the Trinity River, also play a part in bringing fish through the system.

In addition to hatchery fish, the Klamath River harbors many wild fish. Fishing the Lower Klamath allows anglers the chance to pick off fish headed into the many tributaries. All fish heading into rivers, streams or creeks that are part of the web of Klamath all must pass through the Lower river. Thus, angling can be excellent at times.

In recent years, anglers have seen promising numbers of fish in the system. However, salmon and steelhead populations struggled for what seemed like eternity to many longtime Klamath anglers. Locals blame over harvesting by offshore foreign commercial fleets, which some say nearly destroyed runs of steelhead and salmon. Drift nets killed everything with fins. On record, at one time authorities found more than 30,000 steelhead and some salmon dead on one boat.

Fortunately, the US government stepped in several years ago, implementing laws prohibiting foreign boats to commercial fish within 300 miles of the US coastline. The absence of the nets coupled with several wet winters helped bring the runs back. Recently, better management, more water and fewer fish being killed by commercial boats has the Klamath fishing the way it was in the Seventies when anglers from all over the state flocked here during the late summer and fall.

May and June are slow months. You have some springers blasting through the lower river, but they can be tough to catch. July is better as some salmon creep into the system. August brings more and bigger fish. While some salmon or steelhead

Guide Wally Johnson with a Klamath River steelhead caught near Happy Camp.

can be found in the Lower Klamath most of the year, September and October are the best months. Strong numbers of both species occupy the river during this period. November and December don't bring salmon, rather steelhead, while file into the system through March. Steelhead that don't have a long trip up the Klamath, like the Blue Creek fish, wait until February or March to enter the system.

The downside to the Klamath is that the salmon aren't large. Steelhead average three-to-six pounds with a few to 12 pounds. Salmon run 10-15 pounds, some to 40 pounds are landed each year. Anglers, nonetheless, don't fish the Lower Klamath for size, rather numbers and its surroundings. While it can be sweltering at nearby Sacramento Valley waters, the Klamath keeps anglers comfortable with mild temperatures.

For many anglers the Lower K is much easier to fish than the fast flowing Sacramento. The Klamath is gin clear in the fall and brimming with salmon and steelhead. Locating fish is straightforward. Salmon can be spotted in deep holes with a little bit of current or those with fresh water coming in. Steelhead are best targeted in six-to-10 foot deep holes or riffle-like water.

While salmon and steelhead can be found in the same holes, there are several different ways to target each species. Most anglers, however, do nothing but boondoggle. A good setup is a reel filled with 15-pound test and a 10-pound leader. On the Klamath, three-eights to half-ounce slinky weights are best. Fish either a puff ball or roe. Back bouncing roe or a Luhr Jensen K-13 or K-14 Kwikfish and casting Panther Marin spinners is also productive.

For those who insist on other methods, fly fishing can yield consistent action. Using a floating line with a nine-to-12-foot leader and wet flies, target the same areas you would boondoggling. Others use a sink tip or sinking line and size six or eight bead head assassins, silver hiltons and brindle bugs. Anglers please remember the river is governed by special regulations implemented to protect the fishery. Only barbless hooks may be used.

Much of the lower river runs through the Hoopa Indian Reservation. Gill netting operations are common in the estuary, but less likely above the Highway 101 Bridge near the town of Klamath. Upriver you'll find gravel bars, long runs, deep holes, lots of riffle water and tailouts.

Whether in a drift boat, jet boat, tossing bait from shore or fishing the river in full body waders, there is a spot for all anglers to enjoy the action. For

Lower Klamath River

our purposes we are going to concentrate on the river from Johnson's Bar to the estuary. This is what's we've destined the Lower River.

For anglers planning on fishing from shore, access can be found from the Highway 101 Bridge to Blake's Riffle, which is located a few miles upriver from the bridge. Unless you have access to private property or a boat, very little access can be found upriver between Blake's Riffle and Johnson's Bar.

For boaters, Johnson's Bar is a place to launch from the upper stretch of the lower river. There is no paved launch ramp in this area, just a gravel bar. Four ramps can be found in the lower section: in the town of Requa, the Old Town Ramp located in Klamath, the Klamath Glen Launch Ramp and a gravel ramp at The Riffle RV Park.

Several areas traditionally produce salmon and steelhead. However, few spots can match the Blue Creek inlet, and the holes just downriver. Blue Creek is the largest tributary to the Klamath between the Pacific Ocean and the Trinity River. The creek brings cold water into the system.

Prior to the first big rains, which oftentimes occur in late October or early November, both salmon and steelies stage near Blue Creek and take in the fresh cold water while waiting for increased flows and more cold water to bring them upriver. Releases from Iron Gate Reservoir and Trinity Lake can also help the fish push upriver. Other fish hold in the estuary for increased flows.

While boat traffic can be an issue on the Klamath, the scenery cools your frustrations from the inconsiderate jet boat that blew by at 35 mph while you were battling a steelhead. The river is lined with redwoods, dominated by osprey and the occasional bald eagle, as well as mink, river otter and bears.

It's also loaded with fish. Anglers who choose to catch and release

between September and October can bank on 20-30 fish days between four anglers if you know how to boondoggle and have roe. The river is conducive to boondoggling. In fact, few other techniques are practiced from a boat.

If you plan to make the trip, supplies are available in Klamath and Klamath Glen. Only barbless hooks are permitted. Check sportfishing regulations. Bag limits and quotas change each year.

Also nearby is the Mad River and Smith River.

Directions: *From Eureka, drive north on Highway 101 to the town of Klamath. The river crosses under Highway 101.*

Brett Ross caught this late August salmon on the Lower Klamath River with roe.

LAKE EARL

Rating: 7

Species: Cutthroat Trout, Chinook Salmon and Steelhead

Stocks: None

Facilities: Gravel Boat Launch

Lake Earl is one of California's most intriguing waters. Situated on the North Coast a few miles north of Crescent City and 15 minutes south of the Oregon border, Lake Earl is a fishery with several micro fisheries inside its' sand lined retainer walls. The lake is within rock throwing distance of the Pacific Ocean and while several creeks run into the lake, it has no year-round outlet. Salt water does, in fact, seep through the sand into the lake.

Lake Earl is the largest shallow freshwater lagoon in the continental western US. Earl is fed by two streams: Jordan and Yonkers Creek. When the natural lake begins to fill and retain more water many of the locals get worried. The water backs up and flood roads, farmlands and some homes. For decades, Del Norte County used equipment to breach the lake and allow the flood waters to recede. Flooding is a natural effect that occurred as the lake rose in the past. However, with homes now on the land, Earl won't be allowed to breach on its own in fear of destroying property.

Recently, there have been arguments regarding when Earl should be breached. Battles between the county, farmers, environmentalists and state agencies have erupted. No one can agree on the best level to breach the lake. What ends up happening is farmers do it on their own in the middle of the night and ignore the red tape. Good move guys.

Breaching Lake Earl is a good thing. Without it, many of the fish present would die or not be able to complete their lifespan. When the lake is breached, the flow of water into the Pacific attracts cutthroat, steelhead and if available in December when the spawn occurs, Chinook salmon as well. All three species spawn in the creeks that feed the lake. If the breached area isn't opened when they choose to return to the Pacific, they end up staying in the system. They mill around until their next chance to return to the salt, or they become resident fish.

While fishing was known to be much better decades ago, Lake Earl is still a great place to catch wild sea-run cutthroat trout. No fish stockings take place. Cutthroat to 15 pounds have been caught, however, most cutts run 12-18 inches.

The best place to catch them is in the narrow channel between Lake Earl and Lake Talawa, which are connected. This is the deepest part of the lake and bodes well for shoreline anglers tossing Panther Martins or trollers dragging small FlatFish. Fly anglers see success casting towards the reeds in the channel.

Directions *and trip info for Lake Tawala also apply to Lake Earl.*

LAKE TAWALA

Rating: 7

Species: Steelhead, Chinook Salmon and Cutthroat Trout

Stocks: None

What's the difference between Lake Earl and Lake Tawala? To be honest, there really isn't one, but if you consult a map each has their own name. Lake Earl is much larger than Tawala, however, both are connected. A fish could swim freely between the lakes. There's a small, yet fairly deep channel roughly 50 yards long that separates the two.

The importance of Tawala is that when the lake is breached, it's done on the Tawala side. Therefore, steelhead, Chinook salmon and sea-run cutthroat swim through Tawala's water first and then move on to Earl. That doesn't mean the fishing is better though. The best action is found in the channel between the two lakes. Bring along a spinner or spoons and cast the channel for your best bet at fish. Try tossing night crawlers soaked in Pautzke Liquid Krill near the tules.

When you're at Tawala, keep an eye out for river otters. There are a few monsters that from a distance look as big as a seal. Don't worry, they aren't known to grab spinners.

Directions: From Crescent City on Highway 101, drive north to King Valley Road and turn left. Continue one-tenth of a mile to a stop sign. Drive straight (now on Morehead) for 1.8 miles to Lower Lake Road. Turn right and drive one-tenth of a mile to Kellogg Road. Turn left and drive seven-tenths of a mile to Tell Road. Turn left and drive 1.7 miles to the lake.

River Otter at Lake Tawala

Lake Tawala

DEAD LAKE

Rating: 4

Species: Catfish and Largemouth Bass

Stocks: None

Facilities: A Dirt Launch Ramp

Need Information? Contact: Lunker Fish Trips Bait and Tackle (707) 458-4704

In a sense Dead Lake is now dead. Several decades ago, Dead Lake was a happening place; at least for business. The lake was used as a mill pond. There were two mills around the lake and locals will tell you that there was far more lumber floating on the surface than there were fish swimming in it. The lumber operations have since ceased. Nevertheless, there's plenty of reminders to keep the memories, namely tons of lumber resting on the bottom.

With lumber operations gone, Dead Lake has become a recreational fishery, at least that's what some may call it. Located near the Crescent City Airport, I visited several times to watch anglers try their luck. Every time I go there is one car with a young man and women in it. Never have I seen anyone actually down at the shore. I guess it's become a good spot to "watch planes."

As for the fishing, Dead Lake doesn't offer much. A while back largemouth bass were introduced, but they haven't taken well yet. It's fair to say the population will never boom in this rusty color water. There are a few catfish to target, but not enough to warrant a full day fishing. Let's cut to the chase: I think there are far too many great fisheries around for anglers to spend time trying to catch small warmwater fish at Dead Lake. Heck, there's a state record steelhead swimming only a few miles away.

Directions: *From Crescent City, drive north on Highway 101 to Washington Blvd. Exit the highway and make a left, driving over the freeway. Continue 1.8 miles to Riverside and turn right. Continue nine-tenths of a mile to the end of the road.*

Dead Lake

SMITH RIVER

Rating: 10

Species: Steelhead, Chinook Salmon and Cutthroat Trout

Stocked with 4,765 pound of fingerling chinook salmon and 13,524 pounds of fingerling steelhead.

Facilities: RV Hookups, Boat Launches, Restrooms, Campgrounds, Picnic Areas, Restaurants, General Store, Bait and Tackle, Lodging and Boat Launches

Need Information? Contact: Steelhead Fishing Guide Greg Squires (800) 551-3984, Steelhead Fishing Guide Wally Johnson (530) 496-3291, Salmon, Steelhead and Cutthroat Fishing Guide Mick Thomas (707) 458-4704, Lunker Fish Trips Bait and Tackle and Shuttle Service (707) 458-4704, For Lodging: Ship Ashore in Smith River (800) 487-3141

The year was 1972, and like many teenagers in Del Norte County, Mick Thomas spent much of his time fishing when he wasn't in school. To him, few concepts were more important than chasing after sea-run cutthroat trout, salmon and steelhead. It was a cold December morning when Thomas' father dropped him off at the Smith River Estuary. Thomas hooked his usual limit of salmon, gilled and gutted his catch and headed home.

"That's a nice steelhead," Thomas' father said to him.

Mick laughed.

"Dad, that's not a steelhead. That's a salmon," Mick was positive. Gutted and gilled, the scale put the fish at 25 pounds.

That Christmas Vacation day passes through Thomas' mind everyday as he guides anglers from all over the West on the world famous Smith River. Now a full-time guide and owner of Lunker Fish Trips Bait and Tackle, it was determined that his fish was in fact a steelhead: a sure state record.

Thomas has lived his life on the banks of and in a drift boat on top of the majestic waters of the Smith River. Despite what you might read elsewhere, know this: the Smith may be one of California's shortest systems, but it's also one of the best, if not the best. The state record steelhead – a Dec 22, 1976 fish that went 27.4-pounds – was taken here. It's likely that record will be broken on this magnificent fishery.

Nonetheless, the Smith isn't kind to beginners. Because of technicalities, the Smith can be an emotionally draining system. Uttermost concentration is needed to maximize success. With all the pressure that exists, the competition to succeed can be too much for many anglers to face. The Smith can humble the world's best anglers. On the other hand, the rewards are first class.

The Smith is arguably the prettiest and most prestigious river in California. This gem flows through the North Coast's renowned redwood groves, cuts through pristine canyons and winds through some of the most charming, clear water on the West Coast.

The Smith is the first river on the North Coast to clear and the last to be blown out, but that's only part of the reason it been the most popular steelhead system in California for decades. Each year, many fish come close to setting a new state record. So far, it hasn't happened, but it's inevitable.

The Smith kicks out both wild and hatchery raised steelhead. These fish are big, bright and don't play games. When you hook up, you'll know it. Smith River steelhead never come easy; once hooked it's a battle to the finish. They pull line off your reel, leap out of the water, make exhilarating runs one direction and then turn on a dime and burst the other direction without showing signs of weakness.

Guide Mick Thomas with a 15-pound Smith River steelhead.

Landing steelhead isn't a given. If you are fortunate enough to hook three fish in a day, be happy with one to the net. This is real steelhead fishing. These steelhead have room to run and aren't impressed by even the world's priciest gear. Steelhead aren't guaranteed on the Smith.

Until you fish the river seven days a week for decades, you'll be humbled daily, and even then, there will be plenty of days Smith River steelies will get the best of you. Unlike most rivers, these fish are in a different spot daily and can be rattled by factors you have no control over. Oftentimes, seals swim into the system to feed on steelhead. When this occurs, even the brightest anglers won't catch fish. Your best bet is to move downriver a few holes and get away from the seal.

Unfortunately, when it comes to fishing the Smith, you are always taking a chance. It's much different from the Trinity and Klamath fisheries where guides can guarantee fish. Trusting fish reports in papers can also be sketchy. Use caution reading what the papers are reporting in regards to how fishing has been. Remember, these publications are only as good as their source.

Unfortunately, many of the publications in the state only take reports from fishing guides who advertise with them, which sometimes may, but doesn't always give you the best and most reliable sources. Also, that news is several weeks old. At the Smith, conditions change by the minute.

Make sure you are getting your information from a reliable guide. Some guides exaggerate fishing reports on the Smith to stir up business. Please be wary of that. Contact the guide, ask for references and check them out before fishing with them. Many of these guides aren't experienced on the Smith. There are many local guides who have been fishing the river for decades and know every hole, gravel bar and rock in the system. Those are the guides that can help make your trip the most memorable. The guides I've listed in the need information section of this write-up are some of the best on the system. I stand behind their legitimacy 100 percent, but there are many more guides who are as good as them. Unfortunately, I didn't have a chance to fish with all of them. There are more than 50 guides on the river.

Many are based in California, others in Southern Oregon. Do your homework before calling them. If they are the cheapest, it doesn't mean they are the best. My personal experience is that if a guide tells you fishing is going to be excellent and tries to sell you on catching a half-dozen or more steelhead on the Smith, than he probably isn't telling the truth.

The Smith is a humbling system. It puts the best guides in the West to the test everyday. It's true, some days a boat will catch six or seven fish, but that's a fantastic day. The reality is many top notch anglers get skunked one day, catch one the next, three the day after and may hook up with a half dozen once a week. Guides who talk of hooking 15, or more, fish per trip are either the world's best guides or are trying to put money in their pockets.

Another aspect to take into consideration is how much time you allot to fish the Smith. Unfortunately, this isn't a one day deal. For most folks, it's a half-day drive to the Smith. Depending on where you live in the Bay Area, you are looking at a six-to-eight hour drive. The same goes from the Sacramento and Stockton regions. It's the better of four hours from Redding and a few hours from Medford, Oregon. There is no easy way to get to the Smith. While it may be longer in miles, it's often quicker for Sacramento, East/South Bay and Redding area residents to shoot up Interstate 5 and take Highway 199 through Grants Pass to the river. This route allows you to drive much faster than taking the slow, winding 101 or Highway 299.

When you arrive during steelhead season, don't expect sunny days.

The Forks of the Smith River

The weather is unpredictable. It can be snowing one minute, raining the next, windy for a few hours and clear all in one morning. Be prepared to fish in t-shirts and in blizzard conditions. There's no way to tell what's going to happen in this northern most section of the California coast.

It's best to plan on being in the region for at least two, if not more, days. The logic is understandable. If it rains hard, which it often does on the North Coast in the winter, it could possibly push the river to unfishable levels. It can take anywhere from one to three days to clear (barring a massive blast of precipitation). If you only plan to fish one day, you may be out of luck. On the other hand, if the long term forecast calls for light rain or fair conditions, you won't have a problem only planning to fish one day. Nonetheless, winter weather and stability get along as well as cats and dogs in this northwest corner of California.

The Smith drainage is like a massive toilet bowl. Because much of the landscape surrounding the drainage is rock, the system drains fast and stays clear when most other rivers are muddy. When it rains the system flushes out quickly.

If you are fishing the Smith as a beginner, it's best to fish with a guide first, especially if you plan to fish from a drift boat. Unlike most California rivers, if you aren't tuned in to how to position your boat and approach each run, you'll spook fish easily and upset many other anglers. The Smith isn't a beginner's river. It can be more productive to learn the river from an experienced angler and then venture out on your own.

Guide Greg Squires with a Smith River steelhead.

Steelhead fishing can heat up as early as November. Steelhead creep into the Smith in late November when the first major rain lifts the low flow closure. Prior to this, the Smith looks more like a stream. Steelhead can be found in the Smith through the closure; however, action tends to dip by mid-March.

Some steelhead spawn in the main stem of the Smith. Others head up the South and Middle Fork of the Smith and other tributaries. Each year, the privately funded Rowdy Creek Fish Hatchery releases 87,883 fingerling steelhead.

For drift boats, the action is concentrated from The Forks down to the estuary. Knowing how to approach the system in high and low water is important.

When the water is high, you want to fish high. Steelhead recognize the high water as a sign that it's time to head upriver to spawn. When the water is high, fish from the Hiouchi Bridge to The Forks. If you are fishing from a drift boat it's not a good idea to fish the lower section in high water because anglers have to contend with sunken willows and plunkers.

When the water is high, the lower river is more spread out than normal and can be tougher to fish. Bank fishermen, on the other hand, see success in the lower river when the water is high. Plunkers do well because they are patient enough to keep their bait in one place and let the fish come to them.

Following USGS gauges on the internet before you head to the river can increase catch rates. There are two gauging stations. The upper mark can be found at Jed Smith State Park. When the gauge is at seven feet or lower, the river can be tough to drift. Anglers may need to get out and drag their boat across some of the riffles. You'll also have a problem with clear water. Ideally, you are looking for the gauge to run between nine and 10.5. If the gauge rises to 15-17 or above, the river can be too high to fish.

For drift boats, the Smith is user friendly. Only under high water does the river create a problem for first time drift boaters. If you are a newcomer, use caution when the upper gauge rises above 16 feet. The river can develop major back eddies and whirlpools that could suck a drift boat down in these conditions.

Smith River

The Lower mark is found at the 101 Bridge. Fishing is ideal when the gauge reads between 15-17 feet here. If the gauge is higher than 20-21 feet, the river will be too tough to fish.

In spite of what you may have read, locals will tell you that the fly fishing is tough on the Smith. Some of the world's best fly anglers have had great difficultly getting steelhead to cooperate. Success is limited on spoons and spinners as well. However, this could be because few anglers try to use them. Roe and running plugs are far more popular.

The color of the Smith plays an important role in how anglers choose to fish the system. When the water is high and slightly colored, fishing is much easier than when the system is low and clear. When visibility is low, it allows anglers to use heavier line and be less cautious. When the water is low and clear, the fish are spooked easily. Under these conditions anglers have to be careful not to run drift boats over the top of them. If the water is tainted, you can run your boat over the fish or drop bait down on top of them and you still won't spook them.

When the Smith is low and clear, you may need to run six-pound test, or risk decreasing catch rates. Also, downscale. Use smaller baits. Eight-pound test on the main line with a six-pound leader is standard. When the water is high, it's safe to use 10-pound test.

Early on in the steelhead season, roe is a mainstay. Most anglers in the know soak their roe in Pautzke Liquid Krill for a few days before fishing the river. This keeps your roe in tact longer and adds a natural and effective scent to your bait. Later on in the season, traditionally around late-February and into March, plugs work phenomenal. Plugs work best in clear water. Luhr Jensen Hot Shots in size 30 are best. Try silver with a black bill, silver prism with a black scale and black and silver glitter.

Here's a lift of drifts on the Smith. There is excellent public access for bank anglers and drift boaters. A good map of the river is recommended.

The first access can be found at The Forks, where the Middle and South Fork of the Smith meet. This isn't a great shore fishing spot, rather a put-in for drift boats. The next good access for both shore and boat anglers is at Jed Smith State Park. Heading downriver, Pyramid Hole, Pink Rock, Picnic Ground Hole, The Outhouse and Society Hole are prime spots. Moving on, Stout Grove offers access on the south side of the river. Don't discount the Mill Creek inlet, Grey Rock and White Horse.

Next is the Hiouchi Bridge, which offers access to both sides of the river. Rip Rap and Simpson Bar are two popular holes in this area. Access downriver can be found along North Bank Road and at Van Simpson Park. Peacock Bar is a long run popular to boaters and bait dunkers. Then you have Stump Hole, Rock Garden and Walker Hole.

Ruby Van Deventer County Park gives anglers a half-mile of public access before you come to the Highway 101 Bridge and the Water Tower. No power boats are permitted upriver of the tower. There are two more access points: Smith River Outfitters, Serrania Road and the estuary.

The Smith can also be fished from shore. Plunking is the best method. It's normally most effective during high water, for instance when the water exceeds 12-14 feet on the upper gauge. If the gauge is running at 12 feet or below, you are better off side drifting roe. On average, one steelhead is caught per five anglers (when you are talking about inexperienced anglers). The guys who know where to fish can nab at least one or more fish per day.

Native sea-run cutthroat are also in the system. They come in small numbers during the steelhead season. Then, you'll see a push of fish in March and April when steelhead season slows. Unfortunately, the bulk of the cutthroat run isn't available to anglers because the river closes to fishing on April 31 after sundown. Cutthroat spend the summer spawning in tributaries, prior to returning to sea. They tend to push out with the first rains in fall. These

Walter Fowler and a Smith steelie

carnivorous creatures eat crawdads and juvenile steelhead.

Chinook salmon make a fall run into the Smith River, but the window to catch them is short. By the third week of August you'll find small numbers of salmon entering the system. Anglers will catch some of these fish casting Little Cleos and Kastmasters from shore in the estuary. Then in September, you'll have some salmon push up to the Early Hole. It isn't until October that you'll find salmon all the way to The Forks and above.

Sadly, many anglers can't fish a bulk of the salmon run because of a low flow closure designed to protect the fish. When the low flow closure is in effect, you can only fish from the mouth of the Smith to the confluence with Rowdy Creek. This means angling is concentrate in the Rowdy Creek Hole, Piling Hole and Sand Hole. Back trolling KwikFish is standard.

Salmon season heats up with the first big rain in the fall. After the rain, the low closure is lifted and salmon bust into the system. This can occur in September, October, November and even December, depending on when the first big rain is. When the rain comes, the run is short and sweet. The prime season to catch them can only last a few weeks.

Salmon can be quite large. While they average 25-30 pounds, it's not uncommon to land 40-50 pound fish. The river also sees a small run of springers in late March and April.

There is no hatchery system run by the California Department of Fish and Game on the Smith River. A great deal of the success anglers experience on the Smith stems from work done at Rowdy Creek Fish Hatchery. This privately funded hatchery raises steelhead and chinook salmon that are released into the Smith each year. It's estimated that 27 percent of the steelhead caught each year are hatchery raised. Nearly one-half million salmon and steelhead are released each year.

If you plan to make the trip, supplies are available in Hiouchi. Don't leave your car on the bank alongside the river. If there is a storm, the river can rise quickly. It's not uncommon to see cars swept downriver.

Also nearby are Lake Earl, Dry Lake and Lake Tawala.

Directions: *From the San Francisco Bay Area, drive north on Highway 101 to Crescent City. Continue north on Highway 101 to either North Bank Road or South Bank Road. Access is available in many places.*

Guide Wally Johnson used roe soaked in Pautzke Liquid Krill on the Smith River.

43

SMITH RIVER (MIDDLE FORK)

Rating: 7

Species: Chinook Salmon, Sea-Run Cutthroat Trout and Steelhead

Stocks: None

Facilities: Lodging, Restaurants, Picnic Areas, Restrooms, RV Hookups and Campgrounds

Need Information? Contact: Six Rivers National Forest (707) 457-3131, Lunker Fish Trips Bait and Tackle (707) 458-4704

The Middle Fork of the Smith River differs greatly from the South Fork. The biggest differences are the Middle Fork carries more volume, sees more fishing pressure and has much better access for anglers. While a lot of the water on the Middle Fork is hard water, there are plenty of runs and holes to fish.

Highway 199 parallels and crosses the Middle Fork several times and provides good access. Most anglers choose to ignore the Class IV and V water from Slant Bridge to the Middle Fork Gorge River Access. Once you reach this point your options are endless. Treat the Middle Fork like a hit and run system. Fish a certain hole with roe and a Puff Ball for 15 minutes and if you don't get anything, move on. There are dozens of great holes to fish. When action slows on the main stem in March there are traditionally tons of fish in the Middle Fork spawning.

Here's a list of a few you'll not want to pass up before the town of Gasquet: RH Mine Hole, Cooper Flat Hole and Hard Scrabble Hole. (There's a good map of the river with all these holes listed that is sold everywhere where fishing supplies are found.) Once you reach Gasquet, hang a left on Middle Fork Road. Most anglers blast by this turnoff. Nonetheless, it's a good idea to stop. This is where the North Fork enters the Middle Fork, and better yet, a place where tons of steelhead pass through. Upriver you'll find good water and great access near Panther Flat and Patrick Creek. Remember, you can't fish for steelhead above Patrick Creek. Patrick Creek is 17.3 miles from the junction of Highways 199 and 197.

Trip info for Smith River (South Fork) also apply to Smith River (Middle Fork.)

Directions: *From Smith River, drive south on Highway 101 and turn left on North Bank Road (Highway 197). Drive 6.6 miles to Highway 199 and turn left. Continue 2.8 miles to South Fork Road. Access is available from this point for the next 12 miles.*

Smith River (Middle Fork)

SMITH RIVER (SOUTH FORK)

Rating: 6

Species: Chinook Salmon, Sea-Run Cutthroat Trout and Steelhead

Stocks: None

Facilities: Picnic Areas, Restrooms and Campgrounds

Need Information? Contact: Six Rivers National Forest (707) 457-3131, Lunker Fish Trips Bait and Tackle (707) 458-4704

The South Fork of the Smith River is a stream set aside for hard core steelhead fishermen. This isn't a beginner's river. Some of the areas my be easy for anglers to read under low water conditions, but when the rains, come the South Fork swells and can be unfishable in many areas. This does pose an interesting fact: when this occurs you'll only have two kinds of water: hard and soft. Don't fish the hard water. All the steelhead will be in the soft water.

What sets the South Fork apart from easy to approach rivers is access. Most of the fishable section of the South Fork is located in a deep, narrow canyon, with little drive to access. Located in the Six Rivers National Forest, the land adjacent to the river is mostly public, but tough to get to. Stemming from the beginning of South Fork Road, the first possible access point is a bridge over the South Fork. From here you'll come to Craigs Beach, which is well signed. Then, you'll cross three more bridges before coming to Steven Memorial Bridge. This is an important point. Slightly upriver is Jones Creek. No fishing is permitted above this point.

Far fewer anglers fish the South Fork than the Middle Fork. The rewards, on the other hand, are plentiful. The same sought after steelhead that venture into the Smith River, come into this system. There are some big boys to be caught. Unfortunately, there is no drift boat access, only bank fishing. There are a ton of good holes, but mostly only locals know how to reach them. Here's a list of spots you'll want to fish. The first spot to key in on is Coon Creek Hole. Then, to pay attention to where Rock Creek enters, and finally Stevens Creek Hole at Steven Memorial Bridge. If you veer off of South Fork Road towards Big Flat Campground you'll have the option to fish two more great holes before the closure: Goose Creek Hole and Hurdy Gurdy Creek Hole.

To fish the South Fork you'll likely need at least intermediate steelhead skills. If you know how to read water you'll do fine. There's a lot of heavy water, few slow runs. Side drifting roe or yard is best

If you plan to make the trip, supplies are available in Hiouchi. Check sport fishing regulations for bag limits, gear restrictions and closures.

Also nearby is Dry Lake.

Directions: *From Smith River, drive south on Highway 101 and turn left on North Bank Road (Highway 197). Drive 6.6 miles to Highway 199 and turn left. Continue 2.8 miles to South Fork Road. Turn right. The road follows the river for the next 14 miles.*

DRY LAKE

Rating: 4

Species: Rainbow Trout, Channel Catfish and Bullhead

Stocked with 3,750 pounds of rainbow trout.

Facilities: Primitive Campsites

Need Information? Contact: Six Rivers National Forest (707) 457-3131

Dry Lake is a lake fit for locals. Located a few miles from the South Fork of the Smith River, this pond is too small to attract tourists and well enough hidden at 1,330 feet in the Six Rivers National Forest that most sightseers wouldn't find it without being told to go there. The small lake is located in the Hurdy Gurdy Creek Drainage. A two-foot high stone dam was built on its' shoreline to allow the pond to retain more water, though it wasn't very effective.

For it being only three acres, Dry Lake can be a tough place to fish. The problem lies in the abundance of weeds and other vegetation. Not only do anglers have to complete with hang-ups, but insect life as well. Trout aren't always willing to suck on Power Bait because of all the food available. Bobbers are best, especially fished from a float tube or canoe. Some sort of watercraft would allow you to fish open pockets of water and stay out of the weeds. Nonetheless, a trail that loops around the lake gives anglers a decent shot at one of the 5,415 trout that are planted annually.

After turning off South Fork Road, a dirt road takes you to Dry Lake. This isn't dry country though. In fact, if you come during the winter you'll see the road department trimming the trees and roadside vegetation. They do this once a year. If they didn't the road would be covered and impassible. The region receives a ton of rainfall in the winter and is warm during the summer. The plants grow like weeds.

If you plan to make the trip, supplies are available in Hiouchi.

Also nearby is the South Fork of the Smith River, Middle Fork of the Smith River and the Smith River.

Directions: *From Crescent City, drive north on Highway 101 for roughly three miles to the right turnoff for Highway 199. Turn right, drive past Hiouchi and make a right on South Fork Road. Drive 14.1 miles to Big Flat Road. Turn left and drive 5.1 miles to the unsigned left turnoff for the lake. Turn left to the parking area.*

Dry Lake

Region

Humboldt County/ Mendocino Coast

Trinity River (Lower)
Eel River (South Fork)
Stone Lagoon
Big Lagoon
Redwood Creek
Freshwater Lagoon
Mattole River
Van Duzen River
Eel River
Mad River
Ten Mile River
Cleone Lake
Noyo River
Albion River
Navarro River
Garcia River
Gualala River

TRINITY RIVER (LOWER)

Rating: 8

Species: Steelhead, Chinook Salmon and Silver Salmon

Stocks: None

Facilities: Picnic Areas, Campgrounds, RV Hookups, Restrooms, Lodging, Restaurants, Gas, General Store and Bait and Tackle

Need Information? Contact: Tim King's Guide Service (530) 623-3438

The differences between fishing the Lower Trinity and the Upper Trinity are vast. While the upper section is pounded by anglers, the lower section remains relatively quiet and holds more, and oftentimes, larger fish. The lower river is more of a natural system.

The Lower Trinity can be described as the section which runs from Del Loma to the confluence with the Klamath River. This beautiful, scenic river flows along Highway 299 and Highway 96, offering good access in many places and none in others. Some spots you'd have to be a bighorn sheep to reach.

Fishing the Lower Trinity has many perks. Anglers who fish the Upper Trinity miss out on salmon and steelhead that spawn in the New River, South and North Forks of the Trinity, Canyon Creek and other waters below the upper stretch. Fishing this lower stretch not only boasts fewer anglers, but rewards anglers with a shot at catching those fish headed for the tributaries, not just the hatchery fish headed to the Trinity River Fish Hatchery in Lewiston. Many of the fish caught on the upper stretch are destined for the hatchery.

Traditionally, Lower Trinity fish are in much better shape. Fish found in the Upper Trinity have busted through Burnt Ranch Falls, Grey's Falls and many rapids that beat them up. The Lower Trinity fish have a fairly easy route from the Pacific.

Springers (chinook salmon) arrive in June/July. Then you have a small gap, which is filled by a run of fall fish from August through mid-November. Many anglers ignore the Lower Trinity until mid-November and instead concentrate on the Lower Klamath in September and October when the fish are stacked up as they come into the river. The Trinity is a tributary to the Klamath.

While steelhead creep into the system in July, you'll find that most trickle in from early October into March. Starting in December, you'll find down streamers. For steelhead, the early season isn't always as advertised. Prior to the first major downpour (which tends to occur in late-October or early November) gin clear water makes steelhead skittish and less aggressive. Increased flows bring more fish upriver from the Klamath.

Steelhead are fooled by size 50 Hot Shots. For salmon, fish a K-15 Kwikfish with a sardine wrap or back bounce roe.

The Lower Trinity possesses a different contour than its' upper counterpart. Sand bars and open shorelines are common, rather than the trees you find on the upper stretch. This makes for great fly fishing water. Pack golden stoneflies with a bead headed nymph, black rubber legs and egg imitations for winter steelhead. By March, when the water warms, dry fly action and spinners with black blades take a good share of fish. The Lower Trinity offers great shoreline access, but is even better for drift boats. There are five major drifts in this section.

The first is an overnight trip beginning at Hawkins Bar and terminating at Willow Creek. The run takes roughly 18 hours and is recommended for advanced rowers, not beginners. There's a lot of challenging whitewater including Suzy Q, a nasty rapid that tests even veterans. There's little shoreline access on the upper portion of this stretch. You will, however, find more access on the bottom end near Willow Creek.

The second run somewhat overlaps the first, yet can be done in a day. This normal eight-hour drift has no rough sections. However, anglers have to put in roughly one-mile up the South Fork. In the fall the river can be low, requiring one person to row the boat down to the confluence with the Trinity and pick the other anglers up there.

Drift three is another section that poses a threat to anglers with little rowing experience. The Sugar Bowl, or T-Bone, as some locals call it, tests the skill of even long time rowers. Again, there's little public access.

The fourth drift takes you on Indian reservation land for the first time. The put-in is found at Tish Tan Campground. The take out: Red Rock. This drift should last all day if you take time to fish the river thoroughly. This is an excellent fall, winter and spring run.

Number five runs from Red Rock to Weitchpec. Once you put in there is no take out until the confluence with the Klamath River. This section is a narrow canyon with almost no public access, except for a few roads which lead to homes on the reservation. This is a fall drift. Come winter or spring and the water runs too high to permit safe passageways for drift boats. There's one portion of water, called The Smokers, that anglers need to be wary of. Otherwise, the run is fairly straightforward.

The Canyon is a well-known section that is heavily fished by guides. Unfortunately, competition to battle for position has grown. Many guides have to hit the river hours before sunrise so they can be the first to drift through or risk battling for position the rest of the day. By mid winter, rain pushes this section to levels not navigable by boaters.

The section of the river through Hoopa isn't for everyone. Some anglers will have their patience pushed to the brink. Not all Hoopa are bad. Not by any means. They do, in the eyes of many, have a bad rap. However, like everything else, a few bad apples spoil the bunch. Traditionally, a few bad apples have created issues for the tribe through confrontations with anglers, but it's no different than gangs in LA or terrorists in foreign countries.

For instance, fishing guide Tim King and I floated through an excellent stretch of water almost always occupied by several steelhead. King sighed as we cruised around the turn and a red Chevy Suburban stood on a flat above the river. A man of the tribe, with a rod in one hand and a cigarette in the other, stood on the hill, 15 feet above the river. He ran down to the river before we got there and cast toward a rock in the middle of the 50-foot wide section. With a spinner that had hooks large enough to snag a shark, he began to reel slow before yanking back with all his force. You guessed it; he snagged an eight-pound steelhead in the side, reeled it in, smiled and threw it on the dirt.

The man laughed with his buddies and screamed at us as we attempted to slide by the hole, roughly 20 yards from where he was snagging. He wanted us to wait until he had snagged and killed every fish in the hole. We moved past and set the anchor 40 yards downriver from where he worked. He still wasn't satisfied and proceeded to yell. King, looking to avoid confrontation, properly moved downriver. Not all encounters aren't this smooth.

Sadly, the Hoopa aren't forced to abide by the Fish and Game codes that we are. They are allowed to snag and gillnet fish, amongst other methods that would earn us hefty fines. Don't expect to feel comfortable at all times either. If you fish near the confluence of the Trinity and Klamath rivers, expect to find a group of Hoopa drunk and holding rifles, another exception to the otherwise heart warming and caring people who reside on the reservation. They usually don't bother anyone. Nonetheless, it's not a sight many anglers aren't used to seeing.

Injecting Liquid Krill under the skirt of jigs is effective when fishing for steelhead .

Fishing Kwikfish are a staple on the Trinity.

Another pet peeve of many anglers is the use of gillnets. The idea of gillnetting is that by practicing this method, the Hoopa can sell the fish as a source of income. Nonetheless, many throw gillnets and leave them overnight, which spoils the fish. To successfully run a gillnet operation, the nets need to be watched closely, as they are on the Lower Klamath. When the fish are trapped they need to be moved immediately and put on ice, rather than sitting in the nets and spoiling.

If you want to be realistic, traditionally only those who engage in confrontations find trouble. You may find a broken window in your car or flattened tires. However, the Hoopa issues are far lighter than in the past. The tribe welcomes anglers now. The idea is more anglers=more voice=more water.

Unlike the Upper Trinity, the Lower Trinity isn't regulated and acts more like a natural watershed that rises and falls with the level of its' tributaries. The course of the river also changes annually. Mother Nature stirs up new gravel bars each year to keep the river healthy.

Unfortunately, the South Fork can be a burden if a heavy rainstorm sweeps through the drainage. A few years back, a mudslide up the South Fork caused the river to mud up with passing storms. It may take a week to clear. However, upriver from the South Fork the river clears fast. Fish above the South Fork when the river muddies.

If you plan to make the trip, supplies are available in Weaverville, Willow Creek and Weitchpec. This section of the Trinity River is closed to fishing from April 1 to the fourth Saturday in May. Only barbless hooks may be used. Check sportfishing regulations for quotas and limits.

Also nearby are the South Fork of the Trinity River, Upper Canyon Creek and the Mad River.

Directions: *From Redding at the junction of Interstate 5 and Highway 299, drive west on Highway 299 for 54.3 miles to the right turnoff for Highway 96. Turn right and continue to the river. There are several access points along the road.*

The confluence of the Trinity and the Klamath River

EEL RIVER (SOUTH FORK)

Rating: 9

Species: Chinook
Salmon, Silver Salmon
and Steelhead

Stocks: None

Facilities:
Campgrounds, RV
Hookups, Picnic Areas,
Boat Launches,
Restaurants, General
Store, Bait and Tackle,
Lodging and Gas

Need Information?
Contact: Fishing Guide
John Pizza (707) 539-
0440, Brown's Sporting
Goods (707) 923-2533

It may sound kooky, but anglers who know how good the South Fork of the Eel River can be pray for droughts. Unknown by most Western anglers, the South Fork of the Eel is one of the best steelhead rivers in the state, possibly the best. However, several factors play a part in the downplay of the system. The South Fork suffers from poor planning that occurred years ago. Basically mudslides, silt buildup, culverts that were constructed when a population boom struck the region and logging (which doesn't occur much anymore) have made the South Fork a pain in the butt for anglers.

The South Fork muddies as fast as any river in the state and can take what seems like ages to clear. Fortunately, it clears quicker than the nearby Mattole and the main stem of the Eel.

Locals waste no time joking about the river's silt problems. Decades ago, the real old-timers remember having to walk down to the river. Now hinting at how bad the river has silted up, they say it's a flat walk from the road. Nonetheless, the going joke in town is that in a few years anglers will have to walk up the banks to the river because the silt will be so bad. Silt is a natural occurrence in many waters. However, some of the problem can be attributed to the removal of the Benbow Dam in the late Eighties.

A rare 20-pound South Fork of the Eel steelhead

Prior to the mid-Seventies, Benbow Dam hurt the South Fork's steelhead and salmon fishery. The dam was installed to generate electricity for the Benbow Area. Unfortunately, it negatively affected the coldwater fishery. While there was a fish ladder, few fish could surmount it. To create a free passageway upriver, the dam was removed and a weir was put in place. Now, instead of fish stacking up at the base of the dam in the wintertime, fish are able to continue upriver to spawn.

Shortly after the dam was removed, fishing improved in the early Eighties as more fish were able to reproduce. The dam is now put in place in the summer months for recreation and removed during spawning times. The removal of the dam created a better steelhead fishery, yet it also dumped tons of silt into the river below.

In the late Seventies, the South Fork saw a rapid decline in the steelhead fishing. In response, in 1979-80, the Garberville Rotary Club had a meeting to discuss options to restore the runs. According to the locals, the California Department of Fish and Game didn't pay attention to their needs. Therefore, the club decided to begin a rearing program.

The first efforts took place at the mouth of Sprowel Creek where wash out ponds were constructed to harbor juvenile steelhead. The project was expanded in its' third year when more wash out ponds were constructed at Piercy and Chimney Tree on Omen Creek. Doughboy pools were installed at Bull Creek and the mouth of Cedar Creek near Leggett.

Although a relatively cheap and simple operation, the doughboy pools were deemed a success for the most part. Roughly 3,000-5,000 steelhead could be reared in each pond/pool and raised to six-to-nine inches before being released. The fry weren't taken directly from the river, but trucked in from the Mad River and Yountville Fish Hatcheries. They were put in the holding ponds in January and released in June.

It's estimated that prior to 1988, more than 70,000 steelhead were raised in these ponds/pools and released into the South Fork. Amongst other folks, former owner of the Garberville Motel, John Mc Grath, was primarily responsible for these operations. Shortly after, the hatchery moved to Little Sprowel Creek. The program ran out of steam as some failure rates, fewer volunteers and word from the CA DFG that a permit would not be issued any longer prompted the end of hatchery operations.

Other similar operations also took place. There was a successful silver salmon operation at Cedar Creek. However, that was demolished in the 1955 flood. Two locals – Bill Eastwood and Harry Vaughn - were instrumental in the Redwood Creek Hatchery. In existence since 1983 the Redwood Creek operation took eggs from chinook salmon, fertilized them and raised the salmon at Redwood Creek. Roughly 30-50,000 fish were released per year. The success rate is roughly 88-90 percent. The hatchery tried to raise steelhead in the mid-Eighties, but little success kept that idea a one year plan. This hatchery is funded under the salmon stamp program. They reapply every five years. Sadly, the CA DFG may pull the plug on the program soon.

Another successful program is the Hollow Tree Creek Hatchery, where silver salmon and chinook are processed. It's also run under the salmon stamp program and sport fish restoration funds and has been around since the Seventies. While it was at one time, the South Fork isn't a prolific salmon river. The best run of salmon comes in November when fish that average 10-16 pounds enter the system. Salmon fishing is catch and release.

For steelhead, the South Fork is catch and release only. There is no current hatchery

The scenic South Fork of the Eel River 53

for steelhead on the system. Nonetheless, steelhead are available. The average fish runs eight-to-12 pounds, but you can land a lot of 10-15 pound fish. A few 20-plus fish are caught each year. The river is open to fishing from the confluence with the main stem of the Eel to Rattlesnake Creek. The road parallels the river for more than 55 miles.

Steelhead enter the system with the first rain in late fall. After the low closure is lifted, they can be found in the system through April. However, the river closes to fishing on March 31. In March, you'll catch half downstreamers and the rest fresh fish. If conditions allow, you'll want to fish as close to the forks as possible. Because many steelhead leave the South Fork and swim up tributaries to spawn, there are fewer steelhead the further upriver you fish.

Longtime guides, like John Pizza, use several factors to determine when fishing will be best, but none are more important than Pizza's best recommendation: fish the river when the water is just below the willows. For some reason when this occurs the bite couldn't be better. The easiest way to accomplish fishing more productive areas is to start high and move downriver daily as the river clears. The South Fork clears from the top downriver. This gives you more time on the water if you start high and move down as water becomes available.

This tributary to the Eel flows through dozens of redwood groves and parallels Highway 101 most of the way. There is better than 55 miles of roadside water to fish. An interesting note is the river flows south to north. Shore fishing can be good. There's excellent access from Cooks Valley to Philipsville, along the Avenue of the Giants and around Miranda. Look for long gravel bars. Try to fish the inside corner either with roe, spinners or a fly.

For the drift boater, there are more than 25 drifts to learn. Here's a list of seven quality drifts: Leggett to Bell Glen, Cooks Valley to Bear Pen, Benbow

Guide John Pizza with a trophy South Fork steelhead taken on roe.

Lodge to Garberville, Garberville to Philipsville, Sylvandale to Miranda, Landsdale to Williams Grove and Williams Grove to The Forks. These are day long drifts and can be broken down into many smaller drifts.

Darren Brown, owner of Browns Sporting Goods in Garberville, has lived through much of the history on the South Fork. Timing the system right is important to him. Here are a few basic rules to follow: If two inches of rain fall in Garberville, it could take four-to-five days for the river to clear. If the river reaches a height of 13 feet, it will take seven days or more to become fishable. If there are any mudslides we are talking several weeks of unfishable water.

The trick is fishing above the massive slide on the East Branch of the South Fork of the Eel. This tributary muddies the system in a hurry. Water upriver of this branch clears much quicker than below it. For example, the Leggett area, which is upriver of the slide, may clear in three days. Here's what to look for when we are talking about river levels: eight feet is ideal at both Leggett and Miranda.

The South Fork can be approached many ways. Side drifting roe and Puff Balls is the most common method, however, boondoggling, tossing spinners and running plugs are effective. Fluorescent, silver and red and silver and green size 30 and 35 Hot Shots are best.

Whether on a drift boat or from shore, picking out gravel bars is a smart approach. If you are standing on the sand bar, keep in mind the deep water and the slot that is holding the fish will be on the other side. If you come across an area with a gravel bar on both sides fish the middle. South Fork steelhead love to hang in areas with deep water and surface chop.

The water on the South Fork goes from green to clear. Green is much easier to fish. Once it becomes clear the fish are easily spooked and anglers need to employ stealth like techniques. Here's a rule of thumb: look for perfect water and then fish one drift below it.

If you plan to make the trip, supplies are available in several towns along the river. Garberville is the only one with major services though. The South Fork of the Eel River is open to fishing from Rattlesnake Creek to its' confluence with the main stem Eel River. All fishing is catch and release only. From the fourth Saturday in May through September 30, only artificial lures with barbless hooks may be used. From October 1 through March 30, only barbless hooks may be used.

Also nearby is the Mattole River.

Directions: From Santa Rosa drive north on the 101 Freeway to Leggett. Access is available from this point for at least the next 70 miles.

Chad Glover with a South Fork steelie

STONE LAGOON

Rating: 5

Species: Steelhead, Chinook Salmon and Cutthroat Lake

Stocks: None

Facilities: Boat Launch, Restrooms and a Visitor Center

Need Information? Contact: Lunker Fish Trips (707) 458-4704

The future on Stone Lagoon's cutthroat fishery rests of the shoulders of the tidewater goby. The goby was placed on the endangered species list in 1994, forcing the California Department of Fish and Game to cease stocking cutthroat trout in Stone. Prior to the listing of the goby, Stone Lagoon was managed as a wild trout fishery by the CA DFG and was actively planted with cutthroat to create a flourishing, trophy fishery. Unfortunately, Stone doesn't have big tributaries for the cutthroat to spawn in.

The project was a great success until stocking ceased to protect the goby. The fishery has gone downhill ever since. Nonetheless, there is talk of delisting the goby altogether. If this occurs, cutthroat will again be stocked and it's likely the fishery will rebound. Most cutthroat average six-to-10 inches.

There are still cutthroat available, but their numbers are down. Cutthroat are native to the lagoon, which rests along the North Coast, only a short drive from Eureka. A narrow strip of sand separates the lagoon from the Pacific Ocean. Traditionally in January, the lagoon breaches, allowing cutthroat and steelhead to enter the lagoon. They proceed to spawn in Stone's tributaries before being landlocked until breaching occurs again.

Boats are permitted, which aids anglers in fishing the tules and main channel for the cuts and steelhead. Depending on what time of year breaching occurs, it's possible to have chinook and Coho salmon enter, but it's not likely. All species can be taken on spinners, spoons and flies. No bait is permitted.

If you plan to make the trip, supplies are available in Orick. Only artificial lures with barbless hooks may be used. There is a two-fish limit. Each fish must be 14 inches or larger to keep. All salmon and steelhead must be released.

Also nearby is Big Lagoon.

Directions: *From the junction of Highway 299 and 101 in Arcata, drive north on Highway 101 for 26.2 miles to the lagoon on the left.*

Stone Lagoon at sunset

BIG LAGOON

Rating: 5

Species: Steelhead, Coho Salmon, Chinook Salmon and Cutthroat Trout

Stocks: None

Facilities: Boat Launch, Restrooms and Campgrounds

Need Information? Contact: Lunker Fish Trips (707) 458-4704

What's the difference between Big and Stone Lagoon? Both are freshwater coastal lagoons along the North Coast that maintain populations of steelhead and cutthroat trout. However, Big Lagoon isn't actively managed by the California Department of Fish and Game. Whereas Stone at one time received plants of cutthroat trout to supplement the fishery, Big relies solely on natural reproduction. Big has sufficient tributaries for coldwater fish to spawn in.

Big Lagoon typically breaches between late December and early February, allowing groups of cutthroat and steelhead to enter the large lagoon. According to the CA DFG, reproduction takes place on steelhead and cutthroat, but only 10 percent return to the Pacific. There is a low survival rate on both species. In fact, there is almost no return to sea for adults.

Big Lagoon, unlike Stone, has a paved launch ramp and a campground, providing anglers the convenience of being able to fish for cutthroat and steelhead and then walk across the break and swim in the ocean the rest of the day. Also, anglers are permitted to use bait, spinners and flies, providing they are barbless. Winter and spring provide the best action on steelhead. It's best to target the fishery when breaching occurs and fresh fish are moving into the system. Try casting a gold or orange Little Cleo or Panther Martin in the main channel. Cutthroat are best pursued with night crawlers dipped in Pautzke Liquid Krill. Most cutts run 10-14 inches, but fish to 20 inches aren't uncommon.

If you plan to make the trip, supplies are available in Orick. Only barbless hooks may be used. There is a two-fish limit. Each fish must be 10 inches or larger to keep. All salmon and steelhead must be released.

Also nearby is Big Lagoon.

Directions: *From the junction of Highway 299 and 101 in Arcata, drive north on Highway 101 for 19.4 miles to the Big Lagoon turnoff on the left. Turn left and drive four-tenths of a mile to Big Lagoon Park Road. Turn right and follow the signs for six-tenths of a mile to the day-use and boat launch area.*

Big Lagoon (Note the break between the lagoon and ocean.) 57

REDWOOD CREEK

Rating: 5

Species: Steelhead and
Cutthroat Trout

Stocks: None

Facilities: Restrooms

Need Information?
Contact: Little Rays
Bait & Tackle
(707) 482-7725

Redwood Creek is a coastal fishery that needs to be timed perfectly to catch fish. While the creek receives a fair run of steelhead, arriving at a time when the creek is fishable can be a chore. Redwood is a small stream that runs high and muddy after a storm and low and clear when there hasn't been recent precipitation. The key is to arrive on one of the few days when the system is in perfect shape. The only way to find out when the creek will fish best is by making phone calls to local tackle shops and watching creek levels on the internet.

Redwood's steelhead traditionally enter the system from November through April. Most of these fish are native, although a few may be derived from the Prairie Creek Hatchery. This hatchery closed around 1990 and was found on Lost Man Creek, a tributary to Redwood.

Redwood is a fishery that must be tackled from shore. The creek is too small to fish from a drift boat. There isn't much pressure on the fishery, but action can be steady for anglers fishing spinners, yarn and Glo Bugs during the first couple of days of partially clear water.

If you plan to make the trip, supplies are available in Orick. Check updated sportfishing regulations for updated gear restrictions, bag limits and closures.

Also nearby are Smith River, Freshwater Lagoon, Stone Lagoon and Big Lagoon.

Directions: *From the junction of Highway 299 and 101 in Arcata, drive north on Highway 101 for 33.3 miles to the right turnoff for Bald Rock Road. Turn right, drive four-tenths of a mile and veer right at the Redwood Creek Trailhead turnoff. Continue four-tenths of a mile to the parking area.*

Redwood Creek

FRESHWATER LAGOON

Rating: 5
Species: Rainbow Trout and Smallmouth Bass
Stocked with 9,800 pounds of rainbow trout.
Facilities: Gravel Boat Launch
Need Information? Contact: California Department of Fish and Game (707) 445-6493

Redwood National Park is one of the most heavily visited tourist traps on the California Coast. Unfortunately, for anglers arriving in the summer months there aren't many great fishing opportunities for the park to promote. It's too late for steelhead and until late summer or early fall, there aren't many salmon hanging around nearby rivers.

Located within rock throwing distance of the Pacific Ocean, Freshwater Lagoon offers anglers the unique opportunity of fishing for trout in freshwater while listening to waves crash on the white sandy beach across Highway 101. This coastal lagoon rests at five feet above sea level, stems 245 acres and is stocked with a total of 15,675 trout! That's a ton for such a small lake. Freshwater Lagoon is the most heavily planted coastal trout water north of Bon Tempe Reservoir in Marin County. The fish are planted from December through May.

Freshwater Lagoon's trout can be taken from shore or boat. There's a gravel boat launch to allow trollers a good shot at these planted fish. Standard trout techniques are effective. Troll slow. I'd run a Needlefish, Thomas Buoyant, Hum-Dinger or a Sep's Pro Flasher in front of a worm. From shore, you'll want to either soak night crawlers or cast Panther Martins. Make sure to fish during winter and spring. A plethora of weed growth can make summertime angling tough. Ironically, this is the time when salmon and steelhead are gone.

If you plan to make the trip, supplies are available in Orick.

Also nearby is Redwood Creek.

Directions: *From the junction of Highway 101 and 299 in Arcata, drive north on Highway 101 for 29 miles to the lake on the right.*

Freshwater Lagoon

MATTOLE RIVER

Rating: 7

Species: Steelhead,
Chinook Salmon and
Coho Salmon

Stocks: None

Facilities:
Campgrounds,
Restrooms and Lodging

Need Information?
Contact: The Mattole
Salmon Group (707)
629-3433, Lunker Fish
Trips (707) 458-4704,
Mattole River Resort
(800) 845-4607

Overlapping Humboldt and Mendocino Counties, the Mattole River is part of a 305-square mile watershed in the King Range. Reports show that in this drainage logging has left fewer than nine-percent of the old growth forest intact and that salmon runs have declined to less than 10 percent of historical levels. Despite the decline in the salmon fishery, the Mattole is still an excellent steelhead river.

On the other hand, it's not always a great place for out-of-towners to fish. There are a few small communities (Honeydew and Petrolia) along the river and some locals aren't friendly for several reasons. Most folks live out here to get away from the rest of the world. Others grow marijuana and don't want people stumbling on their crops. In any case, the Mattole is a free flowing river that offers superb scenery.

The Mattole is a great place to fish when conditions apply. The Mattole is a low lying, small, meandering coast stream, set amidst dope growing hills populated with turkey, deer and pretty rolling hills. Unlike the Smith, which has a rocky base, the Mattole is comprised of loose soil. Many folks will tell you it's from the logging. Others argue it's simply the composition of the system.

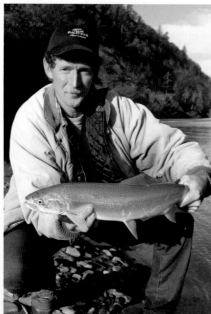

There are dozens of mudslides and hillsides that affect the river. The biggest culprit is below Honeydew. The slightest rainfall can plug mud into the river in seconds and leave it unfishable for a week to a few weeks. It's a major problem, but there's nothing we can do about it. It's nature. Also, the river sits on a fault line, so the soil is always loose and moving. At any moment, half the hillside can drop into the Mattole. It's best to plan to fish from late February through March when traditionally the rainy season slows down and the river clears.

The Mattole can be fished from boat or shore. There are no paved launch ramps though, yet there are plenty of spots you can get a boat in. Here's a list of the drifts: Honeydew to Hadley Bridge, a five-mile drift, Hadley Bridge to A.W. Way State Park, a five-mile drift, A.W. Way State Park to the Gauge Hole, an eight-mile drift, the Gauge Hole to the North Fork of the Mattole, a five-mile run and from the North Fork to the mouth, a two-mile section.

The Mattole is open to fishing from Jan. 1 to March 31 and is catch and release only. No bait or scent can be used either, only artificial lures or flies with barbless hooks. No stocks take place anywhere on the system. All fish are wild and average eight to 11 pounds, although it's not uncommon to catch a steelhead in the high teens. Most angling is done with yarn and a Puff Ball, corkies and yarn, flies, size 30 Hot Shots, spoons and spinners.

The Mattole goes through drastic changes during the year. For example, in the rainy season it can flow at 20,000 cfs. In summer, flows drop to 50 cfs. When this happens the Mattole doesn't flow into the Pacific Ocean. Traditionally, the mouth closes from May through July and opens again in November. Each year, a small run of summer steelhead get trapped when the mouth closes. These fish stay in the river and spawn in the winter with the winter run of steelhead. In 2003, snorkel surveys by the Mattole Salmon Group showed that nine adults and 21 half pounders came in the summer run. These fish range from 17 to 22 inches.

Mattole's salmon aren't doing as well as the steelhead. Historically, the Mattole harbored a good run of salmon. In a report issued in the 1960's by the US Fish & Wildlife Service, it was thought that 7,900 pairs of king salmon, 10,000 pairs of Coho and 10,000 pairs of steelhead could spawn each year.

Unfortunately, in 2002 only 300 pairs of Coho and 750 pairs of chinook spawned. Since 1981, the Mattole Salmon Group and several other groups have been determined to prevent the salmon run from going extinct. The group isn't trying to bring the numbers of salmon up, rather prohibit the run from extinction. They temporarily rear naturally spawned fish and have returned a total of 400,000 juvenile salmon to the Mattole.

If you plan to make the trip, supplies are available in Eureka and Garberville. For updated bag limits, closures and gear restrictions, consult sportfishing regulations.

Also nearby is the South Fork of the Eel River and the Eel River.

Directions: From Eureka on Highway 101, drive south to the right turnoff for Honeydew. Turn right and drive 22 miles to Honeydew or 35 miles to Petrolia.

The Mattole River

VAN DUZEN RIVER

Rating: 5

Species: Steelhead and Chinook Salmon

Stocks: None

Facilities: Picnic Areas and Campgrounds

Need Information?
Contact: Fishing Guide
John Klar (707)
442-1867, Fishing
Guide Brice Dusi
(707) 444-2189

There are dozens of rivers on the North Coast that get overlooked. The Van Duzen is definitely one of them. Since fishing conditions are usually more favorable on the Smith River and at the South Fork of the Eel River, many anglers don't attempt to overcome the obstacles at the Van Duzen. The Duzen does fish better than many of the small coastal streams in Mendocino County, though.

A tributary to the Eel, the Van Duzen can be a pain in the butt to fish due to water conditions. It can muddy with a little as a half-inch of rain, and can take a week to clear even if no more rain falls. If a strong storm moves through, it can take several weeks for the river to clear and become fishable again. For the most part, the Van Duzen is either too high and muddy or too low and clear to fish. There is normally a small window of opportunity for anglers, with the exception being drought years where runoff is not an issue at all.

When the weather is stable, usually in late February and March, the river can be a great place to fish for steelhead. The Van Duzen sees a nice run of steelhead that tent to average seven-to-10 pounds. While some anglers fish roe from the shore, others target the lower stretch of the river from drift boats. From a drift boat, size 50 Hot Shots are best.

If you plan to make the trip, supplies are available in Fortuna. Check sportfishing regulations for updated closures, bag limits and gear restrictions.

Also nearby is the South Fork of the Eel River, Eel River, Mattole River and Mad River.

Directions: *From Fortuna on Highway 101, drive west on Highway 36. The road parallels the river for the next 24 miles.*

EEL RIVER

Rating: 4

Species: Chinook
Salmon, Silver Salmon
and Steelhead

Stocks: None

Facilities: Boat
Launches, Bait & Tackle,
Campgrounds, Picnic
Areas, RV Hookups,
Restaurants, Lodging and
Restrooms

Need Information?
Contact: Fishing Guide
Frank Humphrey (707)
923-3643, Brown's
Sporting Goods
(707) 923-2533

I can honestly say the main stem of the Eel River is the only water in this book that I haven't cast a line in. It wasn't by choice, though. In 2003-04, I desperately tried to fish the river for steelhead between January and March, but unfortunately was unsuccessful. The Eel River is one of the toughest in the state to time right. Because of logging and other human interaction in the Humboldt National Forest, most of the soils in the Eel River Drainage are unstable. Every time the region gets even just a little rain, the river muddies up and can take weeks to clear. I had dozens of dates scratched off the calendar by guides because of inclement conditions.

In rainy years, anglers may have less than one week of optimal conditions to fish the Eel. Regardless of the conditions, steelhead are available. The Eel still receives a quality run of wild steelhead. Keep in mind there is no hatchery on this system. Steelhead spawn in the Eel itself in addition to using the river as a highway to reach other systems, including the South Fork of the Eel River and its' other braches. Even though conditions may be horrid, a good run of steelies will pass through the river each year.

Muddy runoff will frustrate anglers for most of the open season. On the other hand, if the river clears long enough to warrant angling, the Eel has the potential to yield one of your best steelhead days ever. The bulk of the action takes place from the confluence with the South Fork down. There is excellent fishing above this spot as well, but private property and poor access tends to keep most anglers from venturing upriver.

There are several excellent drifts from the confluence down, however many anglers remain at the confluence where they try to pick off steelhead heading up the South Fork. Another plus to this spot is that you'll likely have clear water coming down the South Fork. Fishing the mud line often produces high catch rates for anglers employing roe soaked in Liquid Krill or running plugs such as Hot Shots. There is also a great deal of shoreline access in this area, so if there's a long enough window of opportunity, don't pass on it. You may find some of the best fishing available on the North Coast. The best conditions usually arise in March when winter storms taper off.

If you plan to make the trip, supplies are available in Garberville and Fortuna. Check sportfishing regulations for bag limits, gear restrictions and closures.

Also nearby is Ruth Lake and the Mattole River.

Directions: *From Fortuna, drive south on Highway 101. The Eel River parallels the road for much of the way.*

MAD RIVER

Rating: 6

Species: Chinook
Salmon, Rainbow
Trout, Coho Salmon,
Steelhead and
Cutthroat Trout

Stocked with 125,000
steelhead smolts.

Facilities: Bait and
Tackle, Lodging, Gas,
Restaurants, Picnic
Areas, Campgrounds,
Boat Launch and
Restrooms

Need Information?
Contact: Mad River
Outfitters
(707) 826-7201

The chopping block has been busy in California over the last decade. Sadly, with the California Department of Fish and Game being forced to continue cutting back more and more, the Mad River Hatchery fell under in 2004 when the CA DFG's funds to operate its' grounds dried up.

Located a few miles north of Eureka, the Mad River has been famous for its' ability to produce great returns of hatchery raised steelhead. Those numbers will be cut back, but don't except the Mad's fishery to crumble. The Friends of the Mad River Fish Hatchery have taken over operations in attempt to keep steelhead runs in place. This non-profit organization plans to stay afloat on $120,000 each year as long as donations keep flowing in. If not, the Mad is in dire danger. The Friends estimate they'll kick out 150,000 steelhead smolts a year, 100,000 less than they CA DFG did. No salmon will be reared.

Unfortunately, no fish were planted in 2004. However, if funds are available, fish will be released in 2005 and thereafter. It's expected that the closure will effect the 2006 season most. Steelhead spend between one to three years in the ocean before returning to spawn. The bulk of those that would have been planted in 2004 would likely return in 2006, so return will be low. Keep in mind though, there are wild steelhead in the system that will enter the Mad to spawn.

The Mad also receives a run of summer steelhead. In June and early July, you'll find mostly four-to-six-pound fish. It's recommended you fish early in the day though. Because the water is so clear, once the sun hits it can be tough to get fish to bite. These fish will hold in the same areas as winter fish and can be caught on spinners. (Bait isn't allowed this time of year.) In July, these fish stack up in the Mad River Canyon, but don't spawn until the fall.

The Mad River has a rich history. In 1971 when the Mad River Hatchery opened, steelhead were taken from the San Lorenzo River in Santa Cruz and the South Fork of the Eel River to develop a brood fish program where eggs could be taken. The Eel fish were flown in via helicopters. The hatchery fish in the system were derived from these fish.

The Mad River is a prime spot for anglers who bank fish. It offers high catch rates, even in poor conditions. The Mad is too small for drift boats. There are a few areas where you could try to get a drift boat on the water, but you'd probably come away with dents in your boat, or head, from angry shoreline anglers throwing rocks. This is a true bank anglers' home and those fishermen aren't afraid to keep it that way.

Angler success has been wonderful on the Mad. Nonetheless, this is a direct reflection of the hatchery program. With less stocking taking place it's still unclear if the Friends of the Mad River will be able to maintain the Mad's great reputation. It's estimated that at least 80 percent of all Mad River fish are hatchery fish. It's known that after 2005, the number of returning fish will decrease because 100,000 fewer fish, or more, won't be reared.

When fishing the Mad River, the old Mad River Hatchery is the first place you need to find on a map. This is where most of the steelhead are caught, as they return here to spawn. The best fishing is found in the two-mile section from the Blue Lake Bridge to the Hatchery.

Another notable aspect of the Mad is that even when the river is high and muddy, anglers catch fish. Kevin Mellegers of Mad River Outfitters recalls days where the river was stained like brown coffee with heavy cream in it and he and other anglers still found success. Another positive is that despite its' mud-like waters, the river is never unfishable, although it does fish best at 1,700 cfs and below.

The Mad River isn't for everyone though. While it's possible to catch fish in the mud, which traditionally lasts from December through February, most anglers catch their fish by "lining", which is known as a legal form of snagging. The fish don't bite when the water is milky. When the water carries a green tint, the fish bite well on Corkys and yarn.

Depending on how much rain falls and how high the river was before the rain, the Mad needs roughly a week to lose its' milky tint. On rainy years you may never see green, but on dry years green is a common color. From December through March, steelhead can be found in abundance from the hatchery to the mouth, roughly an eight-mile stretch. The main concentration of fish will be from the Blue Lake Bridge to the hatchery, but the lower section also holds fish as they have to move through this section to get to the hatchery and other spawning areas.

Hatchery fish can be taken on roe dipped in Pautzke Liquid Krill and a Fish Pill under clear water conditions. With almost no drift boat access on the lower section, running plugs isn't an option. Fly fishing isn't popular, but success can be had with Popsicles (size 2 or 4), Flame Bunny Leeches and Polar Shrimp or fishing indicators with Glo Bugs.

The upper stretches of the Mad (closer to Ruth Lake) offer fishing for resident rainbow trout. These fish are best taken on small spinners. Look for deeper holes, riffles and the heads of runs.

If you plan to make the trip, supplies are available in Blue Lake and Arcata. For updated closures, bag limits and gear restrictions, consult sport fishing regulations.

Also nearby is Ruth Lake.

Directions: *From Highway 101 in Eureka, drive north to the Highway 299 east turnoff. The river can be accessed at several points along the highway and in Blue Lake.*

TEN MILE RIVER

Rating: 4

Species: Coho Salmon, Chinook Salmon and Steelhead

Stocks: None

Facilities: None

Need Information?
Contact: California Department of Fish and Game (707) 964-0739

Ten Mile River is a small coastal system on the North Coast near the city of Mendocino. Because of its' remoteness from metropolitan areas, coupled with the fact that there are dozens of more productive systems in the region to fish, few anglers spend much time fishing Ten Mile.

Ten Mile receives a small run of chinook in the fall, and a decent run of coho and steelhead in late fall and winter. There was a small private salmon and steelhead hatchery on Ten Mile River, nonetheless, that operation has been closed for some time. All fish are wild.

Ten Mile River

Steelhead offer the best action. The run traditionally takes place from November to March, but can vary depending on weather. The downfall to Ten Mile is that access isn't great. There is access at the Highway 101 Bridge. Unfortunately, this brings you to brackish water, rather than prime steelhead spawning areas. The better access upriver is pretty much closed off the public, unless you know someone who owns land in the area. Some anglers are successful with spinners and jigs dipped in Pautzke Gel Krill, but few spend much time fishing this system.

If you plan to make the trip, supplies are available in Mendocino. Check updated sport fishing regulations for bag limits, gear restrictions and closures.

Also nearby is Cleone Lake.

Directions: *From the Bay Area, drive north on the 101 Freeway to the Highway 116 west exit. Continue west for 33.5 miles to Highway 1 and turn right. Continue north on Highway 1 for roughly 103.3 miles to the Ten Mile River bridge.*

CLEONE LAKE

Rating: 4

Species: Rainbow Trout and Largemouth Bass

Stocked with 1,750 pounds of rainbow trout.

Facilities: Campgrounds, RV Hookups, Showers, Restrooms and Picnic Areas

Need Information? Contact: MacKerricher State Park (707) 964-9112

Cleone Lake is one of the rare coastal trout fisheries in California. A lot like Freshwater Lagoon located 100 or so miles north, and El Estero Lake a few hundred miles south in Monterey, Cleone is within rock throwing distance of salt water, yet is a freshwater lake. Cleone rests entirely within the boundaries of MacKerricher State Park and is a viable option for folks camping in the park who opt to spend time trout fishing.

Cleone isn't a great fishery by any means. The 3,000 half-pound rainbows planted by the California Department of Fish and Game in this 25-acre pond do provide a sport for day users and campers though. Rainbows can live in the lake all year, but are only planted between April and June.

Cleone is a shallow lake and isn't a sure thing when it comes to catching trout. You need patience to find success for the most part. Bait fishing is best. Spinners and spoons can be effective, but it's the angler who tosses out a juicy night crawler and waits that often gets more bites.

Cleone is more popular with bird watchers than anglers. Formally a tidewater lagoon, Cleone is frequented by more than 90 species of birds and attracts bird watchers from across the state.

If you plan to make the trip, supplies are available in Fort Bragg.

Also nearby is Ten Mile River.

Directions: *From Fort Bragg on Highway 1, drive north for three miles to Mill Creek Road. Turn left and drive one-mile to the lake.*

Cleone Lake

NOYO RIVER

Rating: 4

Species: Coho Salmon,
Chinook Salmon and
Steelhead

Stocks: None

Facilities: None

Need Information?
Contact: California
Department of Fish and
Game (707) 964-0739,
Ruble Fish Bait and
Tackle (707) 964-3000

The Noyo River can be an excellent steelhead river for anglers who live on the Mendocino Coast and know the back roads around town. On the other hand, the Noyo isn't a place for an out-of-towner to come for the day and try to learn how to approach this small, coastal system.

Chances are, if you don't know your way around you'll have a rough fishing experience. While steelhead may be prevalent in the winter, finding ways to catch them is a chore for the average angler. Much of the Noyo Drainage rests on private property or lands that are inaccessible to anyone other than a mountain goat. Only the lower section of the river, which is comprised of brackish water, offers good access. Unfortunately, steelhead blow through this section and are tough to catch. This lower section is for tourists, not anglers.

For the few anglers who know the river well, there are plenty of steelhead to be caught further upriver. Several techniques, including drifting jigs, casting medium size Panther Martin spinners and spoons like Little Cleos are effective. On the other hand, keep in mind that you tend to catch smaller steelhead in the Noyo than you would in larger coastal systems like the Mattole, Eel and Smith. Fortunately, most anglers catch and release, but one steelhead can be taken.

Coho salmon are also part of the mixed bag. The California Department of Fish and Game operates the Noyo Egg Collection Station which takes Coho eggs out of the Noyo, rears them offsite and returns the fish to the system when they are older and have a better chance of survival. No coho can be kept.

If you plan to make the trip, supplies are available in Mendocino. Check updated sport fishing regulations for bag limits, gear restrictions and closures.

Also nearby is Cleone Lake.

Directions: From the Bay Area, drive north on the 101 Freeway and exit west on Highway 116. Continue west for 33.5 miles to Highway 1 and turn right. Drive north on Highway 1 for roughly 94.3 miles to North Harbor Drive. Turn right and continue a half-mile to the parking area.

ALBION RIVER

Rating: 3

Species: Coho Salmon,
Chinook Salmon,
Steelhead and Perch

Stocks: None

Facilities:
Campgrounds, General
Store, Picnic Areas,
Restrooms, Boat
Launch and RV
Hookups

Need Information?
Contact: Albion River
Campground
(707) 937-0606

The Albion River is one of the least known rivers in California. Hidden on the Mendocino Coast, the Albion rests between the Navarro and Noyo Rivers and goes unnoticed to most anglers. In fact, if you polled 10,000 Nor Cal anglers, chances are less than one percent would say they have ever heard of the Albion.

The Albion is a small coastal system that sees runs of chinook and coho salmon in the fall, as well as steelhead in the winter. Unfortunately, poor access makes for difficult fishing. There's access to the lower portion off of Highway 1, but sadly this section isn't comprised of holding water for salmon and steelhead. These fish race through this part of the river. It's possible for anglers to kayak upriver from here, but few do, not with so many other great rivers nearby.

This lower stretch is comprised of brackish water and is popular with surf perch anglers in the spring. Nonetheless, still few anglers take advantage of this fishery.

The Albion River near the mouth of the Pacific Ocean

If you plan to make the trip, supplies are available in Mendocino. Check sportfishing regulations for updated bag limits, gear restrictions and closures.

Also nearby is the Noyo River and Navarro River.

Directions: *From the Bay Area, drive north on the 101 Freeway to the Highway 116 west exit. Continue west for 33.5 miles to Highway 1 and turn right. Continue north on Highway 1 for roughly 79.3 miles to the right turnoff just after crossing a bridge over the Albion River. Turn right to the campground.*

NAVARRO RIVER

Rating: 5

Species: Steelhead, Chinook Salmon and Silver Salmon

Stocks: None

Facilities: Restrooms, Picnic Areas and Campgrounds

Need Information? Contact: Outdoor Pro Shop (707) 588-8033

As with all the smaller coastal river systems, the Navarro River has to be timed perfectly if you want to do well. The Navarro is a productive system for anglers in the know, but can be a humbling experience for anglers attempting to learn the system for the first time. The Navarro does receive an impressive run of winter steelhead and offers the chance at trophy fish, but there isn't much information available to folks who want to learn how to fish the river. On the other hand, locals and longtime anglers with knowledge of the river see no need to travel elsewhere to fish. Unfortunately these folks keep the secrets of the river locked away. Information isn't available to many.

Most folks stumble upon the Navarro when driving up Highway 1. This section of the river can be deceiving to anglers. More of an estuary, this isn't where you want to fish. You can troll spinners through the estuary for limited success. On the other hand, your productivity will increase if you fish where the river breaks into the estuary. Trolling spinners or flies in this area is effective because you'll have steelhead positioning themselves to head upriver when flows increase.

For anglers interested in traditional steelhead fishing with yarn, roe, spinners and Glo Bugs, there is plenty of access available through Navarro River Redwoods State Park. Access is available off Highway 128, although fishing pressure is typically light. Most folks fish more popular waters where more fishing information is available to anglers.

If you plan to make the trip, supplies are available in Boonville and Navarro. Check sportfishing regulations for updated bag limits, gear restrictions and closures.

Also nearby are the Noyo River, Albion River and Garcia River.

Directions: *From the Bay Area, drive north on the 101 Freeway to the Highway 116 west exit. Continue west for 33.5 mile to Highway 1 and turn right. Continue north on Highway 1 for roughly 75.7 miles to Highway 128 Bridge over the Navarro River.*

The Navarro River at Highway 1

GARCIA RIVER

Rating: 6

Species: Chinook
Salmon, Coho Salmon
and Steelhead

Stocks: None

Facilities: None

Need Information?
Contact: Outdoor Pro
Shop (707) 588-8033

While many steelhead rivers in California are flooded with drift boats on the weekends, the little Garcia River is one that is unofficially reserved for shoreline anglers. This small coastal system is better fit for fly anglers and those casting Glo Bugs and yarn rather than anglers running plugs out of drift boats. The Garcia is a great river to fish spinners in as well. A No. 4 or 5 Mepps spinner property swept along the current line can produce excellent action.

The Garcia receives a healthy run of winter steelhead, yet isn't overrun by anglers on a daily basis, partially because there's a lot of private property to overcome. Local landowners aren't keen on anglers trespassing and they wont be friendly if they catch you doing so. If you obey no trespassing signs you'll stay out of trouble and enjoy your fishing experience. Keep in mind only barbless hooks can be used. All wild fish must be released.

All in all though, you have to time everything right to fish the Garcia. Because it's such a short system, the river muddies fast, clears fast and becomes low and clear even faster. If you time it just right you can have a banner day, but if you end up fishing the system when it's low and clear you may ask yourself if there really are any fish in the system. Anglers from Santa Rosa live close enough to make trips to the coast and fish the Garcia when conditions are optimal.

The Garcia River can be challenging to fish when the river is low and clear as shown above.

If you plan to make the trip, supplies are available in Gualala. Check sportfishing regulations for updated bag limits, gear restrictions and closures.

Also nearby is the Noyo River and Navarro River.

Directions: From the Bay Area, drive north on the 101 Freeway to the Highway 116 west exit. Continue west for 33.5 miles to Highway 1 and turn right. Continue north on Highway 1 for roughly 55 miles to the Garcia River Bridge. Consult a detailed map for localized access.

GUALALA RIVER

Rating: 6

Species: Coho Salmon, Chinook Salmon and Steelhead

Stocks: None

Facilities: Campgrounds, General Store, Picnic Areas and Restrooms

Need Information? Contact: Outdoor Pro Shop (707) 588-8033

At 32 miles long and resting in a 300 square mile watershed, the Gualala River has suffered from 100 years of logging, yet still maintains fair steelhead runs. The rivers was one of California's purest at one time, but sediment buildup has helped raise water temperatures and has taken away prime fish structure in this scenic river. Nonetheless when conditions are ideal, steelhead anglers can find excellent action on wild fish.

The Gualala River isn't for everyone, though. The locals keep a close eye on this place. In fact, they aren't keen on outsiders coming in to fish their waters. Private property can make access though, especially for newcomers looking to learn the river. Being a coastal system, you need to be able to time the river perfect to attain success. Historically the river clears in three days, unless a strong winter storm moves though. The river rises fast, muddies and then within a few days can be low and clear. When it's low and clear action can be tough to achieve unless you know the river well.

As of late, fishing the river out of small pontoon boats has taken on popularity. The most common drift is from Twin Bridge to Switchville, roughly an eight-mile full day drift. Because the Gualala clears at least twice as fast as the Russian, many Santa Rosa area residents have made it a habit to spend their weekends on the Gualala. Crowds are much denser than they used to be, that's for sure. You'll need a local map to find the best access spots, but Annapolis Road, Gualala Road and other local roads will bring you to the river.

While most anglers believe the Gualala is a river that harbors only native fish, take into considering that many of the wild fish available are derived from hatchery fish. Between 1970 and 1990 more than 425,000 steelhead were planted here, in addition to nearly 350,000 coho planted between 1969 and 1999. While the coho are pretty much non-existent, steelhead remain available and tend to average five-to-15 pounds. They can be taken on roe, spinners, spoons and flies.

If you plan to make the trip, supplies are available in Gualala. Check sportfishing regulations for updated bag limits, gear restrictions and closures.

Also nearby is the Noyo River and Navarro River.

Directions: From the Bay Area, drive north on the 101 Freeway to the Highway 116 west exit. Continue west for 33.5 miles to Highway 1 and turn right. Continue north on Highway 1 for roughly 37.5 miles to the right turnoff for the Gualala River Redwood Park. Turn right and continue to the park where access is available.

Region

3

Clear Lake Ukiah Region

LAKE EMILY

Rating: 5

Species: Rainbow
Trout, Largemouth Bass
and Bluegill

Stocked with 4,800
pounds of rainbow
trout.

Facilities: Restrooms

Need Information?
Contact: Diamond Jim's
Sporting Goods
(707) 462-9741

If you don't live in the city of Willits, but know where Lake Emily is, you are definitely one in a million. Tiny Lake Emily isn't a prime destination for out-of-towners, rather a short trip for locals looking to catch a few small rainbow trout.

Lake Emily is a nine-acre reservoir that provides a portion of Willits' water supply. To local residents with recreation, the California Department of Fish and Game plants 7,400 half-pound trout from April through June. That's sounds like a heck of a lot of fish, but for some reason crowds don't get out of hand. This dinky lake is a well kept local secret.

Located in a well-forested area near Highway 101, trout fishing is fair for shoreline bait dunkers and spin casters looking to bring home fish for dinner. If you use a heavy enough spinner, you can almost cast across the lake. It's a good idea to bring a medium size spoon or spinner and walk the shoreline making cast after cast. Sooner than later you'll find a few willing fish. Otherwise, soak some bait and wait.

If you plan to make the trip, supplies are available in Willits.

Also nearby is the South Fork of the Eel River.

Directions: *From Highway 101 in Willits, turn left on Sherwood Road and continue 2.5 miles to Primrose Lane. Turn left and drive a half-mile to the lake on the right.*

MILL CREEK PONDS

Rating: 7

Species: Rainbow
Trout, Bluegill,
Largemouth Bass and
Channel Catfish

Stocked with 4,350
pounds of rainbow
trout.

Facilities: Picnic Areas
and Restrooms

Need Information?
Contact: Big 5
(707) 462-2870

Located only a short drive from Ukiah, Mill Creek Ponds are a great place to bring children to experience fishing for the first time. There are two small stocked ponds that always remain quiet and pose a quality family fishing atmosphere. The ponds are eight and three acres respectively, and are planted from April through June with 7,650 trout. That many half-pound trout in such small ponds keeps catch rates high.

There are two ponds that are planted. The upper pond is the most heavily stocked and provides the best access. There's plenty of room on the shoreline for chairs, but a float tube can definitely be helpful if you opt to fish deeper water. The lower pond is much smaller and poses only limited bank access.

There are largemouth bass, bluegill and catfish, but none in the trophy category which keeps most folks after the trout instead. Trout fishing couldn't be more traditional. You have three choices: to stand on the bank and cast spoons and spinners, soak night crawlers or Power Bait or fish fly and bubble combos in the evening. While it's odd to see a fish larger than one-pound caught, limits are common.

If you plan to make the trip, supplies are available in Ukiah.

Also nearby are Lake Mendocino, East Branch of the Russian River and the Russian River.

Directions: *From Highway 101 in Ukiah, exit Talmage Road and drive east for 1.5 miles to East Side Road. Turn south and drive four-tenths of a mile to Mill Creek Road. Turn east and drive 1.6 miles to the lake.*

Mill Creek Ponds

LAKE MENDOCINO

Rating: 8

Species: Largemouth
Bass, Smallmouth Bass,
Striped Bass, Crappie,
Bluegill, Channel
Catfish and Carp

Stocked with 1,000
pounds of striped bass.

Facilities: Boat Launch,
Restrooms, Picnic
Areas, Showers,
Campgrounds, RV
Hookups, Marina, Gas,
Bait & Tackle, Visitor
Center, Snack Bait and
General Store

Need Information?
Contact: Lake
Mendocino (707) 462-
7581, Lake Mendocino
Marina (707) 485-8644

Stripers aren't native to Lake Mendocino. Nonetheless, they've been a major part of the lake's ecosystem since 1967. In the early Sixties, Mendocino was overloaded with crappie and bluegill. The problem escalated to the point where the fish were so stunted they looked deformed. In order to crop the panfish population and pave the way for a healthier fish, the California Department of Fish and Game opted to introduce stripers in 1967.

The initial stocking consisted of more than 20,000 fish, many of which were trophy size. The stripers did their job, eating up most of the panfish, thus creating a healthy population of traditional size panfish. Stripers thrived for the first several years. It wasn't uncommon to catch 20-30-pound fish that were filled with crappie and bluegill. However, as the panfish population was minimized, stripers began to grow much slower. Currently, the average size fish is four-to-eight pounds. The CA DFG continued to plant stripers through 1992.

Some stripers reproduce here, but it's unclear how many. According to the CA DFG, under ideal conditions, stripers can spawn in the East Branch of the Russian River. Nonetheless, a stable population of stripers can only be kept up with adequate stocking, which the CA DFG says should be roughly 5,000 fish per year.

When the CA DFG stopped planting the lake, the Mendocino Striped Bass Chapter took over. At the present time, they purchase roughly 5,000 six-to-eight-inch stripers from Pro Aquaculture in Chico. It takes a striper three-to-four years to grow to legal size at Mendocino (which is 18 inches here).

For anglers who know the

Stripers like this pair caught by Danny Layne are common at Lake Mendocino.

scoop on 1,822-acre Mendocino, it's common to catch fish all year, except for the winter when stripers seem to enter a black hole. Once the rains begin, the bite shuts off. Fortunately, the stripers tend to emerge in February when trolling Cotton Cordel Red Fins and broken back Rebels in deep water produces consistent catch rates. The best trolling occurs in the middle of the lake for anglers running at least 3.5 mph.

From May through fall, the focus turns to the surface. Stripers round up balls of shad, push the shad to the surface and become venerable to anglers tossing topwater lures. Casting a solid chrome Super Spook, Pencil Popper or black and silver Pop-R can be deadly. Others cast Hair Raiser jigs.

Springtime is marked by a fair bite on small and largemouth bass. It's common to find bass near the East Branch of the Russian River inlet. When the water is high, you'll have a shoreline full of flooded willows that harbors many bass. Crappie Cove is another spot that shouldn't be overlooked. This cove has been blessed with artificial structure, grassy areas and is gently sloped. The rest of the lake has little structure. In the spring there are several creek inlets that will harbor bass. Find them and you'll do well.

Mendocino was constructed in 1958 and is overloaded with boaters during the summer when fishing suffers, except for anglers targeting early morning shad boils and the occasional youngster who brings along his rod to soak a worm at night for the chance at a channel catfish.

If you plan to make the trip, supplies are available in Ukiah.

Also nearby is the East Branch of the Russian River, Lake Pillsbury and Upper and Lower Blue Lakes.

Directions: From Highway 101 in Ukiah, drive north for 4.5 miles and exit east on Highway 20. Continue 2.2 miles to the marina or 3.2 miles to the recreation area.

Lake Mendocino

RUSSIAN RIVER (EAST BRANCH)

Rating: 8

Species: Rainbow Trout and Brown Trout

Stocked with 115 pounds of fingerling brown trout and 8,800 pounds of rainbow trout.

Facilities: Restrooms

Need Information? Contact: GI Joe's Outdoor Store (707) 468-8834

The East Branch of the Russian River is a tributary to Lake Mendocino and is the best stocked stream/river on the entire North Coast. In fact, from the Bay Area to the Oregon border, it's one of the last remaining stocked rivers. Most others are no longer planted because of concerns those fish would breed with steelhead.

Nonetheless, the East Branch of the Russian isn't in danger of losing its' plants. A three-mile stretch of water upriver of Mendocino is planted with roughly 13,500 half-pound rainbows each year. In 2003, 25,300 fingerling brown trout were also planted.

The great thing about the East Branch is that it can be approached by all types of anglers. Some anglers fly fish, but they are outnumbered by bait anglers and those fishing spinners. The river has some pools, but mostly riffles and faster moving water. It's not necessarily a great place to bring children to fish, but does provide superb opportunities for anglers who can read water well.

If you plan to make the trip, supplies are available in Ukiah. The East Branch of the Russian River is closed to fishing from November 16 to the last Saturday in April.

Also nearby is Lake Pillsbury, Upper and Lower Blue Lake and Clear Lake.

Directions: From Highway 101 in Ukiah, drive north roughly seven miles and exit east on Highway 20. Continue 4.7 miles to Potter Valley Road and turn left. Continue three-tenths of a mile to the stream.

East Branch of the Russian River

VAN ARSDALE RESERVOIR

Rating: 1

Species: Rainbow
Trout, Steelhead, Coho
Salmon and Chinook
Salmon

Stocks: None

Facilities: None

Need information?
Contact: Mendocino
National Forest
(530) 934-3316

In order to protect spawning salmon and steelhead in the Eel River, Van Arsdale Reservoir was closed to fishing of the latter years of the Nineties. Van Arsdale Dam is located 11 miles downriver of Scott Dam and Lake Pillsbury. The dam has been in place for nearly a century and is equipped with a fish ladder to create easy passage for salmon and steelhead to come up and spawn.

From the dam, cool water is sent down to the Eel River and the East Branch of the Russian River. There are resident rainbow trout, steelhead and salmon in the reservoir at certain times of the year, but no fishing is permitted. This dammed section of the Eel River, known as Van Arsdale Reservoir, is utilized by kayakers and swimmers. It's likely it will never be reopened to anglers.

Directions: *From Highway 101 in Ukiah, drive north for roughly five miles to the Highway 20 turnoff. Drive five miles east on Highway 20 to the left turnoff for Potter Valley Road. Turn left and drive 6.4 miles to Potter Valley. Turn right on Eel River Road and continue to the bridge over the Eel River.*

Van Arsdale Reservoir

PILLSBURY LAKE

Rating: 8

Species: Largemouth
Bass, Smallmouth Bass,
Bluegill, Channel
Catfish, Crappie and
Rainbow Trout

Stocked with 6,300
pounds of rainbow
trout.

Facilities:
Campgrounds, Boat
Launches, Picnic Areas,
Restrooms, Boat
Rentals, Lodging,
General Store, Showers
and RV Hookups

Need Information?
Contact: Lake Pillsbury
Resort (707) 743-1581

In the Sixties and Seventies, Pillsbury was one of the top trout fisheries in Northern California. In fact, catching limits of two-to-three-pound trout was fairly common. On the other hand, in the early Eighties squawfish became a big problem. The squawfish reportedly ate the trout and destroyed the coldwater fishery. It got so bad that in 1985 one of the local resorts offered a $100 reward for anyone who caught a trout during the summer months. Sadly, not one was brought in.

Thankfully, the California Department of Fish and Game took action. They opted to do two things: introduce adult bass and stock larger trout. In 1986, the CA DFG transferred 200 largemouth bass from Clear Lake to Pillsbury, hoping that the bass would help eat and minimize the squawfish population. The plan worked magnificently. The bass cropped down the squawfish population and the larger trout weren't being eaten anymore.

The bass have since stood tall. Pillsbury has become on of the better bass fisheries in the region. The lake poses an excellent topwater bite for anglers fishing a half-hour after sunset or a half-hour before the sun goes down. Your best bet is to fish at Oak Flat, Sunset Camp and the inlet. Most bass run

Pillsbury Lake

three-to-four pounds, but its not uncommon to catch fish up to 10 pounds.

While catfish are scarce, Pillsbury offers what many would consider the best bluegill fishing in the Northern California. It's not uncommon for bait fishermen tossing mealworms and red worms to nab bluegill up to 2.5 pounds.

At 2,280 acres, Pillsbury doubles as a great coldwater fishery. The lake is planted with 10,077 trout during the summer months and while many of those fish are caught by trollers working from the middle of the lake to the dam, others live through the winter and grow to two-to-three pounds by the following summer.

One downfall to Pillsbury is that in order to keep cold water flowing into the Eel River to protect anadromous runs of salmon and steelhead, the lake is drawn down to a minimal pool by the fall.

If you plan to make the trip, supplies are available in Ukiah and at Lake Pillsbury Resort. In winter, call ahead for road conditions. The road to the lake may be impassible due to muddy conditions. The final stretch of the road is dirt and can be rough in the winter and spring before the road is graded.

Also nearby are Van Arsdale Reservoir, Lake Mendocino and the East Fork of the Russian River.

Directions: From Highway 101 in Ukiah, drive north for roughly five miles to the Highway 20 turnoff. Drive five miles east on Highway 20 to the left turnoff for Potter Valley Road. Turn left and drive 6.4 miles to Potter Valley. Turn right on Eel River Road and drive 16.3 miles to Forest Road M-1. Turn left and drive 1.8 miles to the Fuller Grove turnoff. Continue a half-mile to the launch ramp.

Pillsbury Lake

UPPER BLUE LAKE

Rating: 8

Species: Rainbow Trout, Channel Catfish, Largemouth Bass, Bluegill and Crappie

Stocked with 12,500 pounds of rainbow trout.

Facilities: Fishing Docks, Bait & Tackle, General Store, Boat Launches, Restaurants, RV Hookups, Campgrounds, Restrooms, Lodging, Showers and Picnic Areas

Need Information? Contact: Lake County Visitor Center (800) 525-3743

Upper Blue Lake is an ideal family destination for folks in the Bay Area. This natural lake is similar to Pinecrest Lake near Sonora, Bass Lake near Yosemite, Gregory Lake in the San Bernardino National Forest and Bucks Lake near Quincy. It offers good trout fishing and amenities to keep even non-anglers happy.

Located along Highway 20 between Clear Lake and Ukiah, Upper Blue Lake is roughly 80 feet deep and is fed by natural springs which allow the California Department of Fish and Game to stock trout even when temperatures soar in the summer months. It's a pretty lake surrounded by private resorts, all with fishing docks, swimming areas and enough material items to make you feel at home.

The CA DFG plants roughly 19,000 rainbows into Upper Blue. These fish join thousands of holdovers from years past. Trollers and shoreline fishermen tackle the lake without much difficulty. There isn't a lot of public access. However, for $3 a day most resorts allow anglers to fish off their docks. Green Power Bait and night crawlers are the way to go. Others troll. Trolling depth varies depending on time of year, but trout never go too deep. You don't need to bring any specific lures. Any spoon with red and gold will work.

Don't discount the bass fishing. There's a fantastic bass fishery. In the spring and summer, experienced anglers can catch 25-30 bass per day and a five-fish, 25-pound limit isn't uncommon. Upper Blue is an exclusive drop-shotting lake. There is very little shallow water available. As soon as you step off the bank, you'll run into steep drop-offs. There is a lot of timber on the bottom of the lake. If you can locate structure and are comfortable drop-shotting, you'll do well. Upper Blue has fairly clear water and clouds of baitfish. Any deep running crankbait works well.

If you plan to make the trip, supplies are available at the lake. There is a day-use fee at most of the resorts and boat launch fee.

Also nearby is Lower Blue Lake, East Branch of the Russian River, Lake Mendocino and Clear Lake.

Directions: *From Highway 101 in Ukiah, drive north for roughly five miles to the Highway 20 turnoff. Drive five miles east on Highway 20 for 13 miles to Upper Blue Lake.*

LOWER BLUE LAKE

Rating: 7

Species: Channel Catfish, Largemouth Bass, Bluegill and Crappie

Stocks: None

Facilities: None

Need Information?
Contact: Lake County Visitor Center
(800) 525-3743

There are no trout in Lower Blue Lake, but for anglers who have access to a float tube or small car top boat, action couldn't be better for largemouth bass and crappie. Lower Blue Lake is the opposite of its' neighbor, Upper Blue. It has no resorts along its' shore, isn't planted with trout, nor is it one of the North State's premier summer destinations. Lower Blue is a small, seldom used lake that suffers from poor access.

To many anglers though, poor access is what makes Lower Blue such as great find. Lower Blue offers an excellent population of largemouth bass that aren't harassed by hundreds of anglers each week. The natural lake holds all largemouth bass and although the lake is small, it's not too uncommon for anglers to catch bass to 10 pounds. Bass average two-to-three pounds, but four-and-five-pound fish are common.

Lower Blue is an excellent Senko lake, but don't discount tossing white spinnerbaits. The lake is user friendly. With its' deepest section at 25 feet, the majority of the shoreline is five feet deep, making for easy water to read.

If you plan to make the trip, supplies are available at Upper Blue Lake.

Also nearby is Clear Lake.

Directions: *From Highway 101 in Ukiah, drive north for roughly five miles to the Highway 20 turnoff. Drive five miles east on Highway 20 for 13.7 miles to Lower Blue Lake.*

Lower Blue Lake

Rating: 10

Species: Largemouth Bass, Channel Catfish, White Catfish, Crappie, Bluegill and Carp

Stocks: None

Facilities: Restrooms, Picnic Areas, Campgrounds, Lodging, RV Hookups, Bait & Tackle, Restaurants, General Store, Fish Cleaning Stations, Boat Launches, Boat Rentals, Mooring and Gas

Clear Lake is one of the top bass lakes in the country. Conversely, as great as Clear Lake is, it can turn to one of the worst fisheries in a short period of time. Clear Lake is the largest natural lake that is entirely within California's borders. It averages 21 feet deep, is 18 miles long, seven miles wide and 2.5 million years old, harboring some of the biggest largemouth bass in Nor Cal.

Clear Lake hasn't always been a great bass lake though. For example, in the late sixties, bluegill and crappie made up 79 percent of the sport fish population. Bass only makes up one percent. On the other hand, by 1988, bass had grown to 67 percent of the sport fish biomass, whereas 21 percent was crappie and bluegill.

What caused such as drastic change? According to the California Department of Fish and Game, the answer centers on threadfin shad, which were first seen in 1985. Studies show the shad weren't legally introduced. Instead, they entered via a collapsed farm pond. Regardless, they have cast an enormous effect on Clear Lake's fishery.

In very little time the shad population exploded, creating a free buffet for adult bass. Additionally though, the shad themselves needed an unprecedented amount of food as well. Both juvenile bass and shad consume plankton as a major part of their diet. While the shad provide an excellent food source for adult bass, they also compete with juvenile bass.

Over the next several years there were a large number of big bass in Clear Lake, but far fewer juvenile fish. Basically, more big bass were being caught than ever before. Nonetheless, fewer bass were being caught overall. Shad had disrupted the ecological food chain.

Nature took its' own course to fix the problem. In January of 1991, a massive cold spell, known as the Arctic Express, blanketed the region causing Clear Lake's water temperature to plummet and killed off the shad. Consequently, the bass population was devastated. Shortly after the die-off, the bass

Editor's Note: Because of the large number of contacts for Clear Lake, we've listed all info numbers below in an easy to use format:

Fishing Tackle: Limit Out Bait and Tackle (707) 998-1006, Tackle It Bait and Tackle (707) 262-1233

Visitor Info:
Lake County Visitor Center (707) 525-3743, Konocti Harbor Resort (800) 660-LAKE, Lake County Parks (707) 262-1618, Red Bud Park (707) 994-8210, Edgewater Resorts (800) 396-6224, Clear Lake State Park (707) 279-2267, Konocti Vista Casino Resort and Spa (800) 386-1950, Clear Lake Chamber of Commerce (707) 994-3600, Lakeport Chamber of Commerce (866) 525-3767

fishery was almost non-existent. The fishery was horrendous. During the next several years, the CA DFG received pressure from the community, anglers and tourism agencies to reintroduce shad.

The CA DFG wasn't so gung ho to follow those recommendations. The CA DFG opted to follow a policy based on biological reasons, a plan that would last, rather than help to create a quick boom that would again result in another major die-off. It's no secret that reintroducing shad alters the traditional growing cycles of Clear Lake's bass. While there were more large bass in Clear Lake during the great shad bonanza, there were far fewer juvenile fish, which hinted that the population was soon going to suffer whether the die-off did or didn't occur. When the larger fish grew old and died there were few young fish coming up the ladder to replace them.

In addition, the shad out-competed all other bait sources and altered the natural balance of the lake. Shad compete for food with juvenile fish and baitfish. For adult bass, the shad aren't an issue. As long as bass can make it past their juvenile stage and grow to six-to-eight inches, they'll be large enough to eat shad. Barring disease or getting picked off by anglers or birds, they'll grow to trophy sizes at Clear Lake. Unfortunately, due to the immense competition during their juvenile stage, many bass don't make it to adult life.

As you can see, shad are good and bad for Clear Lake. Shad are again part of the lake's ecosystem as someone illegally put them back in Clear Lake in 1995. (Others will argue that they never fully died off.) If history repeats and we have another massive shad die- off, Clear Lake will again go from being the best bass lake to one of the worst.

Setting aside the shad, Clear Lake's productivity is amazing. While most agencies won't want you to read this stat, at one time nearly 50,000 septic lines ran into the lake. These lines bring in nutrients from broken down products from our waste. A combination of the broken down waste and agricultural runoff, there's an abundance of nitrates and phosphates in Clear Lake. In addition, the soil in Clear Lake's drainage is mineral rich and fertile which help fund an abundance of zooplankton and phytoplankton.

The abundance of zooplankton and phytoplankton causes huge blooms of green algae. This provides a primary food base for forage fish. Clear Lake is loaded

Bass pro Kent Brown used a spinnerbait in the spring to trick this 8-pound Clear Lake largemouth.

with forage fish. These include shad, Mississippi silver sides, hitch, crappie, bluegill and juvenile bass. With all this food for the forage fish, they in turn do well. Then, the adult bass feed on the forage fish and grow large fast.

Unfortunately, Clear Lake's ecosystem is a double edge sword. When the algae blooms are prolific, it ties up and sucks oxygen out of the lake causing fish die offs. The die offs usually look horrible, but they aren't necessarily all bad. This is a normal cycle in nature. Fish die, decompose and provide another nutrient base for a future population of fish.

Nevertheless the future is hard to predict. The lake seems to be on a three year cycle where old bass die and only a few fish take their place since the competition between shad and juvenile bass hampers recruitment. In the absence of a catastrophic event, shad could reach an equilibrium which would mean that bass that make it past the juvenile stage would continue to grow to monster sizes rapidly, yet the overall number of bass in Clear Lake could continue to fall. Again, it all depends on what happens with the shad.

Hands down, for now, Clear Lake is the best bass lake in Northern California. In fact, there's not even a close second. The lake is comprised of northern and Florida strain largemouth and has tons of forage, allowing bass to grow large quickly. Bass grow so fast in Clear Lake that it takes time for their head to catch up with their body.

There is tons of structure (coves, docks, piers and tules) for bass to hide in and enough food to pig out every night. There's a tremendous baitfish, panfish and crawdad population for the bass to utilize as growing pills. The only thing missing is planted trout.

Bass average two pounds at Clear Lake, but it takes a four-pound average to place in a tournament. A five-pound average won't put you in the money in the spring. There are so many two-to-three-pound fish it's unreal.

Fred Williams soaked minnows under a bobber to nab this Clear Lake seven pounder.

There are also a countless amount of four-to-six-pound fish and enough 10 pounders to consider them quite common. It needs to be a 12 or better to impress. For some reason, the bass peak near 12 pounds. You don't get many 15-20-pound fish like you would in Southern California.

Clear Lake offers great facilities and good public access. While much of the shoreline is taken up by private residences there are also tons of public parks, drive-to shoreline access on Highway 20 and several docks that can be fished. Nonetheless, Clear Lake is best approached from a vessel.

Although techniques differ by season, bass bite year-round. The toughest time to fish is from December through mid-February when Clear Lake's temperature falls. With 42-44 degree surface temperatures, you'll be forced to fish tight to structure, except for the guys who fish live minnows. Winter is when many of the largest fish are caught at Clear Lake.

The rock piles, reefs and islands on the south end tend to produce the best action, as well and the Red Bud and Rattlesnake Arm. Anglers will take lots of bass on jigs in the winter. A three-eights or half-ounce black or brown jig is best. Die-hards with endless patience will throw rip baits, but count on few strikes. Fortunately, the few bites you get will likely be bigger fish. Keep in mind, the water is cold. You have to rip very slow to find action. Bass pro Gary Dobyns makes his money tossing Lucky Craft Stacee 90's and Smithwick half-ounce Rattling Rogues in clown or black and silver.

The bite tends to change in mid-February to mid-April when water begins to warm to the sixties. During the beginning of this cycle, bass stage to spawn. This is the best time of the year to hook large bass. It's when big bass have no choice but to come to the bank. All fish are coming shallow to seek out spawning beds, especially on the north end. The south end tends to heat up a few weeks after the north end. There are an endless amount of spots on the north end that kick out bass, but Lakeport, the state park area, Nice, Lucerne and Rodman's Slough are always top producers.

There's no shortage of effective techniques during the pre-spawn period. Rip baits, swimbaits, spinnerbaits and flipping are all sure bets. The rip bait bite on the south end can be excellent for anglers who let their jerkbait sit for four-to-five seconds before twitching it again. Clear Lake's bass like a long pause.

Back to the north end, a lot of fish are taken on worms. Fishing breaks, docks and rock piles with a six-inch Robo worm or Yum worms in purple, neon, dark grape and oxblood can be highly effective.

The swimbait bite shouldn't be overlooked. Swimbaits work well on the north end because it's so shallow. Cast them around launch ramps and flats. A carp, hitch or rainbow trout pattern Megabait or Optimum will work, but ease up on throwing trout patterns. Since there are no rainbows in Clear Lake, the bass don't key in on them.

Flipping is effective in the sloughs and tules. Try and put your bait in heavy cover. Brush hogs, crawdad imitations, jigs and bulky plastics do the job for anglers who aren't afraid to cast baits deep into the tules and into thick

88 Nationally known bass pro Gary Dobyns flipped a spinnerbait under a dock to catch this 5-pounder at Clear Lake in early sping. Bass can be caught year round at Clear Lake.

vegetation. This is also prime season for spinnerbait fishing. You can catch fish anywhere on the north end with a spinnerbait this time of year. In fact, catching dozens of fish is common.

May is the main month bass spawn in Clear Lake. The spawn may continue into June, but it all depends on water temperature. The best possible bait in May and into June is a Senko. Try a five-or six-inch green pumpkin or watermelon Senko and make sure to fish shallow. This isn't the time of year to concentrate on structure.

From the end of June through August there's lots of grass. This is when white or black frogs come into play. Clear Lake yields a great summer bite to folks tossing frogs under docks, in the tules and around grass. Despite the sweltering temperatures, anglers still manage to catch fish in the summer months. If you aren't throwing a frog, jigging and fishing worms on structure will entice fish, but keep in mind that few big fish are caught during summer.

When September arrives, the water begins to cool and the crankbait bite gets better with each passing day. Also, you'll have a great bite on rattling baits and a topwater bite on frogs and Zara Super Spooks. In early September, a lot of the bass can be found in the grass. Fortunately, they move deeper as soon as the grass dies with the coming of winter. For anglers looking to fish structure, stay on the south end of Clear Lake. If it's grassy areas you are after, stay on the north end.

Not everyone at Clear Lake fishes with artificial lures. Many anglers choose to fish live bait. Clear Lake is one of the best lakes in the West to fish minnows in. For inexperienced anglers or those who simply aren't into tournament style fishing, a minnow can produce excellent catch rates. Shiners are best from November through March and can be fished under any dock, around the tules or on any piece of structure.

In the past, crappie have been an integral part of Clear Lake's fishery. In fact, the state record white crappie, a four-pound, eight-ounce fish, was caught here. Crappie aren't as prolific as they once were though. The downfall stems back to the early Seventies when inland silversides were introduced to get rid of gnats. At the time, the crappie population was exceptional. Unfortunately, juvenile crappie and the silversides feed on the same plankton and because the silversides outnumbered the crappie so much, they lost the battle. Another factor was overfishing. In the Seventies and Eighties, anglers left the lake with tubs of bluegill and crappie which decimated the population. It wasn't until a few years ago when a limit of 25 was implemented.

Crappie from time to time are still abundant. The population fluctuates vastly. Crappie begin to show in late winter when they can be found near dead and calm water, around structure and weeds in marinas. By spring, when crappie spawn, they'll start moving into the backs of sloughs and in the tules. Most anglers soak minnows and work crappie jigs. Crappie can run from four inches to 3.5 pounds.

Over the years, Clear Lake has also been known as one of the greatest catfish waters in the West. However, since the mid-Nineties, the population has plummeted. For example, for Clear Lake's annual catfish derby in the mid-Nineties when 500 applicants took part, several thousand fish were checked in. In 2004, with 1,500 entries, fewer than 300-400 catfish were checked in. Much of the decline can also be blamed on overfishing. While bass anglers release fish, during the peak of catfish action, it wasn't uncommon to see guys leave with 80-90 catfish. The population has never rebounded.

Clear Lake still kicks out quality catfish though. The average cat runs eight-to 14 pounds, but fish to 25-30 pounds aren't uncommon. Catfish are active year round if you know where to find them. In the summer, Horseshoe Bend, White Rock and Rattlesnake Island are best, but you can get them anywhere on crawdads and frozen cut baits.

Catfish action is prime in the winter when they are following schools of shad. The cats sit on the bottom under the schools of shad and as shad die they gobble them up. When they get under big schools of shad, they are very easy to catch with silver spoons or fresh dead shad. The schools of shad typically start near Rattlesnake Island. As the winter progresses, the school moves through The Narrows and towards Konocti Bay. You don't need a fish finder to locate these schools of shad. It's easier to follow the grebes and sea gulls on the surface that also feed on them.

In spring, you can sight fish for the catfish. The cats compete with the crappie and bass for spawning grounds and can be seen in shallow water. Try tossing night crawlers or crawdads. It's not uncommon for bass anglers to hook into huge cats.

If you plan to make the trip, supplies are available in several cities that border Clear Lake.

Also nearby is Highland Springs Reservoir.

Directions: From Sacramento, drive north on Interstate 5 to Williams and exit west on Highway 20. Continue roughly 37 miles to the junction with Highway 53. For the north shore, continue west on Highway 20 toward Upper Lake. For the east shore, drive south for four miles on Highway 53 to the town of Clear Lake. Access is available off Lakeshore Drive. From the Bay Area, Clear Lake can be reached via the 101 north freeway to Highway 20 east.

Spinnerbaits fished near docks are a great combination when targeting big bass at Clear Lake.

HIGHLAND SPRINGS RESERVOIR

Rating: 6

Species: Largemouth Bass, Bluegill, Crappie and Channel Catfish

Stocks: None

Facilities: Picnic Areas, Restrooms and Picnic Tables

Need Information?
Contact: Limit Out
Bait and Tackle
(707) 998-1006

Float tubing for bass is becoming increasingly popular in small waters across the United States. At Highland Springs Reservoir, near Lakeport, float tube fishing couldn't be better. The small reservoir has a good mix of bass, calm water, few crowds and offers a great worm bite most of the year.

Highland Springs is a short distance from Clear Lake, yet receives little fishing pressure likely because no gas-powered motors are permitted. There is no paved boat launch and few trophy bass are available. Nonetheless, float tube fishing can be excellent for anglers fishing plastics and Senkos along the tules in the spring. By June, weed growth can make for difficult angling conditions, requiring fishermen to fish near the dam where deeper water can be found and weeds are less prevalent. Regardless, fishing remains good throughout the warmer months.

Highland Springs has a fairly good distribution of bass. It's year classes of fish is conducive of a healthy bass lake and prove successful reproduction is occurring. If you caught 25 bass a day, chances are that 15 would be smaller than 12 inches, most others would run one-to-two-pounds and one fish might be better than three pounds. There are a few larger bass available, but they aren't a typical catch.

If you plan to make the trip, supplies are available in Lakeport. No gas-powered motors are permitted.

Also nearby is Clear Lake.

Directions: *From Lakeport, drive towards Kelseyville on Highway 29 and turn right on Highland Springs Road. Continue a few miles to the left turnoff for the reservoir.*

Outdoor Writer Terry Knight's Senko got whacked by a bluegill at Highland Springs Reservoir while fishing for bass.

Region

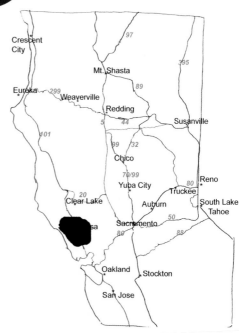

4

Santa Rosa
North Bay

Napa River
Sonoma Creek
Petaluma River
Novato Creek
Russian River
Lake Ralphine
Spring Lake
Lake Sonoma
Lake Hennessey
Phoenix Lake
Lagunitas Lake
Bon Tempe Reservoir
Alpine Lake
Kent Lake
Lagunitas Creek
Nicasino Reservoir
Stafford Reservoir

NAPA RIVER

Rating: 4

Species: Chinook
Salmon, Steelhead,
Striped Bass, Sturgeon,
Largemouth Bass and
Bluegill

Stocks: None

Facilities: Boat
Launches, Gas,
Lodging, Bait & Tackle,
General Store,
Restaurant and
Restrooms

Need Information?
Contact: Vallejo City
Marina (707) 648-4370,
Napa Valley Marina
(707) 252-8011

At 50 miles long, the Napa River extends from Mt. St. Helena to the San Pablo Bay. The Napa River has 47 tributaries and contains anadromous and freshwater fish, but isn't the ideal water to fish in the north Bay Area. The last 17 miles of the river are more like an estuary and is comprised of brackish water.

It's true that the Napa sees seasonal runs of stripers and sturgeon, but their numbers aren't convincing, as least not compared to some nearby sloughs and river systems. Sturgeon action varies year to year. If you hit the right tide and there are solid numbers of fish moving through the system, catching legal sturgeon on traditional baits is a definite possibility. However, also keep in mind that the Napa River is a place where even old-timers who have honey holes are humbled. There is no guarantee that you'll catch fish on the Napa. It's not a sure bet for sturgeon. On the other hand, it can also be a shocker, where know hows catch three-to-five sturgeon an outing, but don't count on it.

Stripers, on the other hand, can be easier to target than the sturgeon simply due to the number of fish available. The number of stripers in the Napa is much less than other nearby systems, but there are plenty of small stripers to go around. This isn't the place to come if you want to catch large fish, but smaller one-to-four-pound stripers are definitely on tap. It's best to anchor up and soak cut baits, although some anglers opt to troll broken-back Rebels. Shore fishing off points or where the river bends may be the most sufficient method.

The river sees a run of a few hundred adult steelhead and a few chinook salmon, but neither species are targeted. Their numbers are too few and the salmon are protected. The upper river harbors bass and panfish, but few anglers fish for them because of decreased access.

If you plan to make the trip, supplies are available in Vallejo. For updated bag limits, gear restrictions and closures please consult an updated sportfishing regulations booklet.

Also nearby are Sonoma Creek and the Petaluma River.

Directions: *Access is available at several points in Vallejo. Consult a more detailed map for exact locations.*

SONOMA CREEK

Rating: 5

Species: Bullhead, Channel Catfish, Sturgeon and Striped Bass

Stocks: None

Facilities: None

Need Information?
Contact: Leonard's
Bait & Tackle
(707) 762-7818

Sonoma Creek's correlation to San Pablo Bay gives it merit when it comes to fishing. San Pablo Bay is an excellent striper and sturgeon fishery. Sonoma Creek benefits because it's a tributary to the bay that stripers and sturgeon migrate up in the winter and early spring.

On the other hand, action fluctuates on the creek. At times, striper fishing can be strong. Other days bites are hard to come by. Traditionally, anglers use primarily cut baits to bag small stripers. Larger fish are tough to come by. Using scent is a must. Try soaking or injecting Pautzke's Liquid Krill into shad or anchovies. Because of the murky water, scent can give you the advantage needed to be successful.

There isn't a lot of drive-to public access on Sonoma Creek. However, this section (at the vista point) can be okay for sturgeon. The mouth of Sonoma Creek is only a few hundred yards downstream and is a common spot for migrating sturgeon to sift though. There are sturgeon in the system consistently, but seldom enough to warrant heavy pressure on them. Traditional methods and baits work.

If you plan to make the trip, supplies are available in Petaluma and Vallejo.

Also nearby are Novato Creek, Napa River and Petaluma River.

Sonoma Creek

Directions: *From the junction of Highway 29 and 37 in Vallejo, take Highway 37 towards San Raphael for 8.7 miles the right turnoff signed for "Vista Point." Park and follow the path to the creek.*

PETALUMA RIVER

Rating: 5

Species: Bullhead,
Stripers, Channel
Catfish and Sturgeon

Stocks: None

Need Information?
Contact: Petaluma
Marina (707) 778-4489

When it comes to striper fishing, there's opportunity to catch these fish in every tributary to the Delta. Of course, some spots offer better catch rates than others. A tributary to San Pablo Bay, the Petaluma River isn't one of the region's better striper fisheries, although it does offer the chance to catch small ones.

The Petaluma River doesn't see the same banner run that the Sacramento and San Joaquin River systems experience. Heck, even Sonoma Creek and the Napa River have more productive fishing. But, there are a few folks who like to troll the Petaluma with broken back Rebels and catch one-to-three-pound stripers. Others find it more productive to bank fish with anchovies. Nonetheless, the river sees little fishing pressure.

The Petaluma can be tough to conquer in the winter and spring when stripers are in the system. Oftentimes, the river is so clogged with mud that you need heavy scent just to have a chance at a bite. One thing to consider: the Petaluma will see a run of stripers every year. If luck is on your side you can catch stripers, but the opportunity is still greater at many other rivers.

The river is also home to a good seasonal sturgeon fishery. While it can have its' ups-and-downs, the Petaluma holds viable populations of sturgeon from late fall through early spring. Traditional sturgeon baits work well. Most anglers fish near the mouth of the river and the first mile or two upriver.

Petaluma River

If you plan to make the trip, supplies are available in Petaluma.

Also nearby are Novato Creek, Sonoma Creek and the Petaluma River.

Directions: From Santa Rosa, drive south on Highway 101 to the Highway 116 exit in Petaluma. Take Highway 116 towards Napa/Sonoma. Make a left off the freeway, drive under the overpass and make a quick right into Petaluma Marina. The river can also be accessed in downtown Petaluma, at Lakeville Marina and Port Sonoma.

NOVATO CREEK

Rating: 2

Species: Rainbow Trout

Stocks: None

Facilities: Restrooms

Need Information?
Contact: Outdoor Pro
Shop (707) 588-8033

Several years ago, Novato Creek was a great seasonal trout stream for anglers in the Novato area. During the spring and summer, the California Department of Fish and Game used to stock a few thousand rainbow trout in the small creek to provide an urban fishery for Marin County residents.

However, those plants will never take place again. The CA DFG chose to remove Novato Creek from the allotment sheet in order to protect the coastal steelhead, a member of the threatened species list. The concept was to make sure that hatchery raised rainbow trout didn't breed with wild steelhead, thus altering their wild genes.

Prior to this decision, rainbows were stocked at Sutro and Mi-Wok Park. Most of the trout were stocked at the bridge in Sutro Park where a dam was installed each spring and summer to back up the creek and create a small pond where youngsters could easily catch trout. Unfortunately, those days are long gone as are planted rainbow trout in the creek.

If you plan to make the trip, supplies are available in Novato.

Also nearby is the Napa River.

Directions: *From Highway 101 in Novato, exit west on San Marin Drive and go 2.6 miles to Novato Blvd. Continue through the intersection to where the creek crosses the road at Sutro Park.*

Novato Creek

RUSSIAN RIVER

Rating: 6

Species: Rainbow Trout, Steelhead, Chinook Salmon, Coho Salmon, Smallmouth Bass, Channel Catfish, Bullhead, Largemouth Bass and Bluegill

Stocked with fingerling chinook, coho and steelhead.

Facilities: Restrooms, Picnic Areas, Gas, Restaurants, Campgrounds, RV Hookups, Bait & Tackle, General Store, Lodging, Picnic Areas and Playgrounds

Need Information? Contact: Outdoor Pro Shop (707) 588-8033, Fishing Guide Ron Babbini (707) 431-0851, Russian River Chamber of Commerce (707) 877-644-9001

The Russian River isn't one of Northern California's prime waters for salmon or steelhead. However, for anglers who can time the system right, action can be excellent. The key variable is water flow. Water flow is necessary to bring steelhead into the system; nevertheless, too much of it can make fishing almost impossible. The Russian has a problem with runoff. A mere inch of rain (which is nothing for this wet portion of California) can muddy the river for several days. There are several culprits: natural muddy runoff from agricultural practices, muddy tributaries, releases from Lake Mendocino and Lake Sonoma and runoff from wineries in the region. Couple these with wintry conditions for a few days and you could be looking at roughly one-to-two weeks of unfishable conditions. Unfortunately, the Russian is one of the slowest clearing steelhead rivers is California.

So how is a person successful when it comes to steelhead fishing on the Russian? Hope for intermittent rain and scaled back releases. When the US Army Corps of Engineers try and dump water out of Lake Mendocino or Lake Sonoma things can go from bad to worse as swollen river levels are met by more dirty water from the lakes. Releases combined with rainfall can spell disaster for anglers.

Steelhead are the most sought after fish in the system. They arrive as early as November and some remain in the system through March. Most are hatchery bred fish. There are two hatcheries funded by the US Army Corps of Engineers as part of litigation when Lake Sonoma and Lake Mendocino were constructed. The Warm Springs Hatchery is found on Dry Creek and the Coyote Valley Fish Hatchery is located on the East Branch of the Russian River. The Russian and its' tributaries also maintain a population of wild steelhead that spawn in the river. The Russian has one of the longest lasting runs in the state as some fish spawn in the fall, others in the spring. Hatchery steelhead average eight-to-10 pounds. The largest recorded at the hatchery in the last decade is 20 pounds.

Steelhead can be taken by shore anglers and drift boaters. In recent years, floating pontoon boats have taken an unprecedented popularity because they allow more anglers to access portions of the river not accessible by foot. Public access is a major downfall to many sections of the Russian.

The Russian offers several sections of water, the first being the mouth, which mostly fly fishermen target. The lower section around Guerneville offers some roadside pullout access. Johnson's Beach is a popular access point. Prior to water being diverted off the Eel River by a tunnel built by PG&E, the Russian dried up each year in this section. Fortunately, that's no longer the case as water for humans and agricultural purposes keep the system with minimal flows in the summer.

The next section runs from Healdsburg to Steelhead Beach, where easy access can be found from Steelhead Beach in Healdsburg down to the Dry Creek area. Access is prime at Wohler Bridge and Steelhead Bridge. Hands down, the best shoreline access comes at the confluence of Dry Creek and the main stem of the Russian. While crowds are definitely an issue here, catch rates can be high for anglers' side drifting roe soaked in Pautzke Liquid Krill or casting Mepps and Panther Martin spinners. This area offers excellent conditions because all fish headed to the Warm Springs Fish Hatchery must pass through here.

Moving upriver, Alexander Valley offers prime steelhead water, but sadly most of it is protected by private access. There's at least two full day runs in this valley for anglers who know ranchers or have other means of getting a boat on the water. The same goes for the section from Geyserville to Cloverdale where there is no public access, except for the Geyserville Bridge and other spots where a road crosses over the river. If you are going to run a drift boat, side drifting roe and running Hot Shots is the best way to fish.

The next section stretches from Cloverdale to Hopland and offers drive-to access along Highway 101. However, this section can be too rough for drift boats. From Hopland to Ukiah you'll find more than 30 miles of private access, but little public access. Some access is found near Coyote Dam as well. Bait, spoons and spinners are all effective. Keep in mind, all hooks must be barbless.

Coho salmon were abundant in the Russian more than a half century ago. There numbers are now close to extinct. The California Department of Fish and Game began a last ditch effort to bring coho back. As part of a new program launched in 2001, teams are sent into the field to trap wild fingerling coho and bring them to the hatchery where they will remain in freshwater and not be allowed to return to the saltwater as their traditional lifestyle requires. Coho have a three-year lifespan. These fish are raised to brood fish size and spawned in captivity. In essence, the CA DFG is creating a safe spawning matrix where 300-400 brood fish are artificially spawned to yield 50,000 fingerling coho that are released in the wild in hope of reestablishing themselves in the Russian and its tributaries.

We know visible results wont show for at least a decade, if then. The CA DFG is aware that this is a last ditch effort to stop coho from becoming extinct in the watershed. The Russian has more than 1,000 tributaries and according to the CA DFG, it's likely that roughly 20 percent have had proper coho habitat. Recently though, only four streams in the Russian's web have harbored coho and just one of them had numerous year classes of coho.

Historically coho were available in many more streams. The success of the project won't be evident for a long time. On the other hand, the CA DFG knows that bringing coho in from another system isn't an option. Coho were taken from the Klamath River in 1981 and introduced to the Russian. Unfortunately they weren't able to adapt, and died.

The chinook population is also in limbo. For now, chinook can't be kept. All fishing is catch and release. While returns differ drastically some reports put the run at nearly 7,000 fish in 2004. Salmon enter the hatcheries in October and November.

The Russian is well known for its' smallmouth fishery. During the summer when adult trout, salmon and steelhead are in the Pacific Ocean, action shifts towards rafting, kayaking and bass fishing. Action is best during the warmer months when the water is low. Smallmouth fishing here isn't for everyone though. While you'll likely catch 20-30 fish a day, most of them will run just eight-to-12 inches. A one-to-two-pound fish is a big one, if you can believe that.

It can be a blast to fish the smallies on light tackle. Fly anglers fish poppers, while conventional fishermen pitch darterheads in deeper holes, toss topwater in shady areas and float night crawlers off rocky banks. The best action is had from Alexander Valley to Healdsburg.

Many folks utilize commercial outfitters to fish out of canoes and kayaks. This allows anglers to be shuttled back to their cars at the end of the day. The Alexander Valley Bridge to Memorial Bridge offers great smallmouth fishing. Look for deeper holes and shady pockets.

If you make the trip, supplies are available in several cities and towns along the river. Please respect no trespassing signs as there is a lot of private property along the bank. Consult sportfishing regulations for updated bag limits, gear restrictions and closures.

Also nearby is Lake Sonoma.

Directions: *The Russian River can be accessed from dozens of roads and highways along Highway 101 and 116. Consult a detailed map for accurate directions to your desired spot.*

(Left to Right) Ronnie Babbini, Ron Babbini and Jake Garzini show off a Russian River steelhead they caught and released.

LAKE RALPHINE

Rating: 5

Species: Rainbow Trout, Largemouth Bass, Bluegill and Channel Catfish

Stocked with 7,500 pounds of rainbow trout.

Facilities: Playground, Boathouse, Picnic Areas, Restrooms and a Fishing Pier

Need Information? Contact: Outdoor Pro Shop (707) 588-8033

Seasonally, Lake Ralphine can be a good put-and-take trout fishery for anglers residing in the Santa Rosa area. During the cooler months, the 26-acre lake is planted with 11,100 half-pound rainbow trout by the California Department of Fish and Game. Most of these trout are caught by anglers fishing dough baits and casting spinners. There are no trophy trout available.

Once the weather starts to warm in March, Ralphine can be a pain in the butt to fish. Because there is little water flow through the lake, weeds and algae grow to suffocating levels. When this occurs, anglers put away their trout rigs and concentrate on tossing bobbers with mealworms to catch palm size bluegill. There are a few bass available as well.

Anglers should understand that Ralphine isn't a wonderful fishery. Instead, it's a great, urban alternative for anglers looking to take their kids fishing for a few hours without having to veer far from home.

If you plan to make the trip, supplies are available in Santa Rosa.

Also nearby are the Russian River and Spring Lake.

Directions: *From Highway 101 in Santa Rosa, take Highway 12 towards Napa/Sonoma for 3.5 miles and turn right on Mission. Continue one-tenth of a mile and turn right on Montgomery. Drive another one-tenth of a mile and turn left on Summerfield. Continue three-tenths of a mile to the left turnoff for Howarth Park. Lake Ralphine is inside the park.*

Lake Ralphine

Spring Lake

Rating: 7

Species: Rainbow
Trout, Largemouth
Bass, Bluegill and
Channel Catfish

Stocked with 5,350
pounds of rainbow
trout.

Facilities: Boat Launch,
Campgrounds,
Restrooms, Picnic
Areas, Swimming
Lagoon an a
Concession Stand
(Seasonal)

Need Information?
Contact: Spring Lake
Regional Park
(707) 565-2041

At 75 acres, Spring Lake may be the most popular small bass lake in the world. Two anglers have petitioned for world record bass caught in this small regional park near Santa Rosa. The first came several years ago when a man caught a large bass, but didn't have the proper instrumentation to weigh it for a certified reading. Instead, he pulled a bathroom scale out of his car (as the newspapers reported) stood on the scale and weighed himself and the fish. Then he put the bass down and weighed himself without the fish, noting the difference in weight. Obviously, the International Fish and Game Commission didn't accept the reading.

In the winter of 2003-4 another scenario surfaced when a woman tried to apply for the world record with a 25-pound bass that again wasn't properly weighed. Yet pictures of the fish hinted it was in the mid teens. As you may have guessed, the application was denied. The moral of the story is, Spring Lake has a handful of large bass, but it's not a place where anglers can go and expect to catch lots of fish. In fact, the opposite is true.

For the most part, anglers have to work hard to catch three-to-four fish a day though. Spring is situated in a moderate coastal climate, therefore bass can grow year-round. There is a small population of Florida strain largemouth bass available. Bucketloads of nine-inch trout aid the growing process which creates a small population of a few big bass. Try fishing swimbaits or Senkos.

Spring was drained and bulldozed in 1986 to rid the lake of hydrilla. The lake was refilled and planted with adult largemouth bass and trout. Trout are a big hit. They are planted roughly 10 months out of the year, 8,650 in all. Outdoor writer Terry Knight estimates that nearly 60-70 percent of the trout are caught within a few days of the plants, leaving few holdover fish.

Most trout are small; 14 inches max. There are no shad to use as growing pills so growth is slow. Anglers do well casting spinners, spoons and bait.

If you plan to make the trip, supplies are available in Santa Rosa. There is a day-use fee. Gas powered boats are not permitted.

Also nearby are the Russian River and Lake Ralphine.

Directions: From Highway 101 in Santa Rosa, take Highway 12 towards Napa/Sonoma for 3.5 miles and turn right on Mission Street. Drive one-tenth of a mile and turn right on Montgomery. Continue one-tenth of a mile and turn left on Summerfield. Drive 1.3 miles to Hoen Avenue and turn left. Then, make an immediate right on Newanga and continue to Spring Lake Park.

LAKE SONOMA

Rating: 8

Species: Steelhead,
Largemouth Bass,
Smallmouth Bass,
Channel Catfish,
Crappie, Bluegill and
Carp

Stocks: None

Facilities: Boat-In
Campsites, Marina,
Gas, Launch Ramps,
Restrooms, Picnic
Areas, RV Hookups and
Campgrounds

Need Information?
Contact: Outdoor Pro
Shop (707) 588-8033,
Lake Sonoma Marina
(707) 433-2200,
Lake Sonoma
(707) 433-9483

Located only an hour north of the Bay Area, Lake Sonoma is a multiuse reservoir that offers excellent fishing and recreational opportunities. With 53 miles of shorelines and more than 2,500 acres, Sonoma is the only lake in Sonoma County that you can water-ski on. Fortunately, it's never too crowded to completely turn off the fishing.

For California standards, Sonoma is a fairly new reservoir. Warm Springs Dam was built in 1983 by the US Army Corps of Engineers. Despite not having any major tributaries, Sonoma manages to fill every year. (Dry Creek is the only year-round tributary.) Sonoma is located in one of the wettest portions of California. Some years, the drainage receives more than 100 inches of rain per year.

Lake Sonoma is similar to a lake you'd find back East. There's a lot of flooded timber and grass. The timber holds bass 365 days a year. The trick is knowing where in the water column to find them. Anytime of year, it's effective to throw a brown and black jig with an Uncle Josh pork trailer from the surface to 15 feet deep.

Smallmouth and largemouth bass are available. Largemouth are the

Shown above with a pair of Sonoma bass, Scott Green is one of Sonoma's best bass anglers.

dominant species. While there are no trout, pond smelt or silverside minnows to serve as growing pills for bass, panfish, shad and crawdads make for excellent meals and allow Sonoma's bass to grow to legal size and better. While a 15.37-pound lake record was established in 1997, few bass over 10 pounds are ever caught. Most largemouth run two-to-three pounds. One good thing about Sonoma is that it doesn't get fished anywhere near as heavily as many Nor Cal bass lakes. For example, in 2003 there were 97 tournaments on Clear Lake and three on Sonoma.

Sonoma boasts great structure for warmwater fish. Fortunately when Warm Springs Dam was built, they didn't clear cut the lake or alter the banks in any way, rather flooded standing timber. This left good spawning areas, grassy flats, deepwater access, standing timber, rock piles and creek channels, all ideal bass hideouts.

Bass action takes place all year. In January and February, the reservoir is traditionally full or overflowing. The water is cold and muddy, yet largemouth bite well. This is brass and glass time. Try shaking a jig with rattles on cover. Also, fish from the surface to 25 feet in creek channels, target breaks and transition areas from flats to deep water.

March and April are marked by tossing spinnerbaits on flats. If fish aren't shallow, you can throw a pig-and-jig in deeper water. For this technique, try Dry and Cherry Creek. Once mid-April arrives, many anglers sight fish. Split or drop-shotting is effective, however, many of the larger fish are found in deeper water. Clarity can also be a problem this time of year.

During the summer, tossing frogs in the weeds and on mats will put fish in the boat. Fishing deeper water is also effective. As the sun rises, the bass suspend near the trees for shade. Try working six-inch Robo worms in 10-30 feet of water. There's also a quality topwater bite.

Somona's timber is good bass water

In October and November, Rat-L-Traps are the choice bait on the main body and in creek channels. The wind will blow bait into the banks and anglers fishing primary and secondary points find consistent action. November and December are good months to throw swimbaits in creek channels because you'll have trout trying to spawn in these areas.

Smallmouth aren't the main focus, but are abundant in the marina, at the dam, launch ramp and rocky bluffs. Try throwing Zara Spooks on the dam in the summer or flipping night crawlers and crawdads in the rocks.

Lake Sonoma is also home to landlocked steelhead. Technically, they should be called rainbow trout, because while they did come from the ocean, they will never return. The population that remains spawns in the lake, which makes them a wild rainbow trout. Sonoma receives no stocks. These fish are descendants of steelhead that ran up Dry Creek prior to the completion of the dam. There are a fair amount of steelhead, yet they aren't overabundant. It's recommended that anglers catch and release to preserve the wild fish. On average, steelhead run 15-19 inches, with some to eight pounds caught.

In the fall and early winter, many anglers fish inlets with minnows as they try and pick off spawning steelhead. The rest of the year, steelhead are found in the thermocline, which is traditionally located 30-60 feet deep. Troll shad imitations, white trolling flies or a white Needlefish. There are two areas that tend to be consistent: from the dam to the no ski buoys and in front of Sheriff's Cove.

Spring is prime time to cash in on catfish action. When feeder creeks are pumping water into the lake, anglers fishing 15-20 feet deep with fresh cut mackerel on a sliding sinker rig can catch cats to 20 pounds. During the warmer months, anglers throwing cut baits off the campgrounds at night also find action.

Spring is also best for panfish. The crappie bite tends to turn on before the bluegill. March and April are best for anglers fishing 10-20 feet of water on brush piles. For bluegill, approach coves with a bobber and a red worm.

If you plan to make the trip, supplies are available in Healdsburg. There is a day-use fee.

Also nearby is the Russian River.

Directions: *From the 101 Freeway in Santa Rosa, drive north to Healdsburg and take the Dry Creek Road exit. Drive west for 11 miles to the lake.*

Gary Dobyns (Left) and Scott Green fishing on the same boat for the first time at Sonoma.

LAKE HENNESSEY

Rating: 5

Species: Rainbow Trout, Channel Catfish, Largemouth Bass, Smallmouth Bass, Crappie, Green Sunfish, Bluegill and Red Ear Sunfish

Stocked with 7,250 pounds of rainbow trout.

Facilities: Picnic Areas, Restrooms and a Boat Launch

Need Information? Contact: Sweeny's Sports 707-255-5544

Lake Hennessey is an 850-acre reservoir that was constructed to supply the city of Napa with water and is stocked heavily with California Department of Fish and Game trout. Hennessey is a great trout lake (11,000 or more half pounders are planted each year) for shore anglers and hardcore trout anglers who have small outboard or trolling motors. The downfall to the fishery is size: most of the trout are dinks, but they can fill a creel fast.

Trollers dragging a Sep's Pro Dodger in front of a nickel or chrome Needlefish or Dick Nite spoon and those running small Rebels do well catching small trout, just be sure to keep your lures off the bottom. Downriggers or leadcore line isn't necessary. It's best to fish for trout from late fall through spring. Fed by Sage, Moore and Chiles Creek, the lake fills almost every year.

When the weather warms, Hennessey provides a decent bass fishery. Largemouth and smallmouth are available to anglers tossing plastics, Persuader spinnerbaits or Doc Waters jigs into the tules. The lake doesn't hold an enormous amount of bass, but enough to keep anglers interested. Most of the fish are small, but good numbers are possible. It's a great lake to float tube for bass.

If you plan to make the trip, supplies are available in Napa. There is a boat launch fee.

Also nearby is Lake Berryessa.

Directions: *From the junction of Highway 29 and 121 in Napa, drive north on Highway 121 for 2.6 miles to the left turnoff for the Silverado Trail. Turn left, then make an immediate right to stay on the Silverado Trail. Drive 13.3 miles to the right turnoff for Highway 128. Turn right and drive three miles to the boat launch area.*

Lake Hennessey

PHOENIX LAKE

Rating: 5

Species: Rainbow
Trout, Largemouth Bass
and Bluegill

Stocked with 4,500
pounds of rainbow
trout.

Facilities: None

Need Information?
Contact: Marin County
Water District
(415) 945-1455

Natalie Coffin Greene Park isn't a place where fishing is the main attraction. As a matter of fact, it's likely that fewer than one percent of the park's visitors fish. Situated in a pretty, wooded section just out of sight of the city of Ross, the park is popular to bikers, joggers and families looking to take a relaxing walk in the wilderness. On any given day it's common to see several hundred locals exercising. The park has several trails for bike and foot traffic.

Fishing, on the other hand, isn't a big deal. The California Department of Fish and Game plants nearly 7,350 half-pound trout, yet action isn't always as good as you'd expect if you planted that many fish into a 23-acre lake. Phoenix Lake is mainly a trout fishery fit for locals. There are largemouth bass and bluegill the tules in the spring and summer, but they sure aren't the attraction.

Trout are best plucked by shoreline anglers fishing with Power Bait or inflating night crawlers off the bottom. Spinner fishing can be good for anglers tossing quarter-ounce Panther Martins and No. 3 Mepps spinners. Pay attention to if the trout are rising or down deep and you'll increase catch rates. One downfall to some anglers is that there is no drive-to access to the reservoir. A short walk up a dirt road takes roughly five minutes to reach the shoreline.

If you plan to make the trip, supplies are available in Ross. If planning a trip on the weekends you might want to show up early. There are limited parking spaces and they fill up early.

Also nearby are Lagunitas Lake and Bon Tempe Lake.

Directions: *From the 101 Freeway in San Raphael, exit west on Sir Francis Drake Blvd and drive 2.7 miles to Lagunitas Road. Turn left and drive 1.1 miles to the parking area at the end of the road.*

Phoenix Lake

LAGUNITAS LAKE

Rating: 6

Species: Rainbow Trout

Stocked with 125 pounds of fingerling rainbow trout and 3,650 pounds of rainbow trout.

Facilities: Restrooms

Management of Lagunitas Lake has changed drastically since 1988 when the Marin County Water District drew the lake down to a minimum pool to perform maintenance on the dam. When the lake was low they also removed all largemouth bass and with the help of Cal Trout installed an aerator unit to maintain a cool pool year-round. The concept was to create a self-sustaining trophy fishery.

Special regulations were also implemented. Anglers were forced to return all trout caught that were 14 inches or longer. The idea was to create a brood fishery and reduce fishing pressure by not allowing anglers to keep all fish caught. While fishing pressure was reduced, the overall plan didn't pan out as envisioned. Some spawning does occur, but for the most part the fishery is maintained through trout stocking by the California Department of Fish and Game. In addition to nearly 10,000 fingerling trout, 5,730 half-pound trout are also planted. There are holdover trout available, but most trout are fresh planters.

At 22 acres, Lagunitas is a small lake, but can yield good catch rates for anglers. On the other hand, bait fishermen aren't welcome. Only artificial lures with barbless hooks or barbless flies may be used. Anglers may keep two fish per day as long as they are 14 inches or smaller. Lagunitas isn't a drive to lake; however, the short five-minute walk from the parking area doesn't keep folks out. No matter what time of year, tossing a quarter-ounce Panther Martin or Kastmaster will do the trick.

Directions *and trip info for Bon Tempe Lake also apply to Lagunitas Lake.*

Lagunitas Lake

BON TEMPE RESERVOIR

Rating: 6

Species: Largemouth Bass, Rainbow Trout and Bluegill

Stocked with 17,150 pounds of rainbow trout.

Facilities: Picnic Areas and Restrooms

Need Information? Contact: Sky Oaks Ranger Station (415) 945-1181

Put a boat on Bon Tempe Reservoir and you'd have limits of trout before you could finish a crossword puzzle. Bon Tempe is a 140-acre lake that is stocked with more than 25,695 half-pound rainbow trout each year. The lake is set up perfectly for the troller as there are several points and coves in what would be a highly productive dam area. Unfortunately, trolling in any boat or launching personal watercraft is prohibited. Anglers are restricted to fishing from shore, much of which is also closed to fishing.

Despite the lack of access, there are trout to be caught. This is a sit-and-wait lake. Anglers find suitable access in a few areas, all of which are found near parking lots. There's access at Bon Tempe Dam, near the Lagunitas Creek Picnic Area and along two roadside pullouts. Trout can be taken several ways: fly and bubble combos, casting spoons and spinners and soaking bait. The key is to locate areas where there are sloped drop-offs, tapered banks, coves and points. These are common trout holding zones.

Most of the trout run between 10-12 inches, however, fish up to 16 inches are common. During the fall, winter and spring anglers find it intriguing to walk to the inlet from Lagunitas Reservoir. This creek, which feeds Bon Tempe, is loaded with rainbows attempting to spawn. A steep flume prohibits trout from swimming upstream, but dozens do try. Unfortunately, fishing is prohibited in this area.

Bon Tempe also harbors bass and bluegill that can be found in brushy areas in the spring and summer. Warm water fishing has never really taken shape though; however, there are fish available.

If you plan to make the trip, supplies are available in Fairfax. There is a day-use fee. No water contact or watercraft of any kind is permitted.

Also nearby are Alpine Lake and Lagunitas Reservoir.

Directions: From the 101 Freeway in San Raphael, exit Sir Francis Drake Blvd and drive west for 5.1 miles to Pacheco. Turn left, then make an immediate right on Broadway and drive one-tenth of a mile to Bolinas Road. Turn left, drive 1.5 miles and take a left at the sign for Bon Tempe/Lagunitas Reservoir. Drive eight-tenths of a mile to a split in the road. For the dam, stay right and drive four-tenths of a mile to the parking area and access road. Or, stay left and drive 1.3 miles to the main parking area.

ALPINE LAKE

Rating: 3

Species: Largemouth Bass, Rainbow Trout and Bluegill

Stocked with 520 pounds of fingerling rainbow trout.

Facilities: Picnic Areas and Restrooms

Need Information?
Contact: Sky Oaks Ranger Station
(415) 945-1181

Alpine Lake isn't your ideal trout fishing water in Marin County. There are several factors that contribute to this poor fishery, but access is the biggest obstacle. Alpine is a long, narrow reservoir with steep shorelines which can make for challenging fishing conditions. While part of the shoreline is completely inaccessible, the shoreline that parallels the highway is also difficult to tackle. A few trails allow anglers to hike down to the reservoir, but most of the banks are too steep to reach. The only exception is at the dam, where decent drive-to access can be found.

Another issue is action. Most anglers don't do well at Alpine. The lake is planted with 40,000 fingerling rainbow trout by the California Department of Fish and Game each year, but their survival rates aren't impressive. The reservoir is deep and cold enough to support a viable trout fishery, but biologist believe that many of the planted fish end up being food for larger fish or osprey and cormorants.

Nonetheless, for the patient angler willing to soak a night crawler all day or diligently work a Kastmaster or Krocodile from the shore, there is a chance at catching a trout, just don't arrive expecting to catch a limit. Alpine would be an excellent lake to troll. Unfortunately, no watercraft of any kind is permitted.

If you plan to make the trip, supplies are available in Fairfax.

Also nearby are Lagunitas Lake and Bon Tempe Reservoir.

Directions: *From the 101 Freeway in San Raphael, exit Sir Francis Drake Blvd and drive west for 5.1 miles to Pacheco. Turn left, then make an immediate right on Broadway and drive one-tenth of a mile to Bolinas Road. Turn left and drive 7.7 miles to Alpine Lake Dam.*

KENT LAKE

Rating: 4

Species: Largemouth Bass, Crappie, Channel Catfish and Rainbow Trout

Stocks: None

Facilities: None

Need Information? Contact: Sky Oaks Ranger Station (415) 945-1181

Prior to 1982, Kent Lake was a fairly decent trout lake. The lake was planted each year with fingerling rainbow trout by the California Department of Fish and Game. While you couldn't drive to the lake, there was a trail that provided easy access to anglers who chose to walk or ride a bike to the lake. Then in 1982, Kent Lake's dam was raised 45 feet. The new level inundated the trail. At the present time, anglers may fish anywhere around the lake, but unfortunately access is steep and uneasy. The exception is near the dam where a paved road leads anglers on a short walk from the parking area.

At the request of the Marin County Water District (MCWD), the 25,000-40,000 fingerling rainbow trout that were planted each year won't be stocked anymore. The MCWD told the CA DFG that they were afraid planted trout will get washed over Kent Dam during high water and breed with salmon and steelhead in Lagunitas Creek.

Since rainbows can spawn in Lagunitas Creek (the lake's inlet), Kent will continue to harbor trout, but their numbers won't be anything to boast about. Trout fishing has never been great and it's likely it will become poorer in the future. Fishing at Kent Lake isn't promising. You are better off fishing elsewhere because of access issues and the lack of plants.

If you plan to make the trip, supplies are available in Fairfax.

Also nearby is Lagunitas Creek.

Directions: *From the 101 Freeway in San Raphael, exit Sir Francis Drake Road and drive west for 13.5 miles to the left turnoff for Kent Lake and the Lagunitas Creek viewing area.*

Kent Lake

LAGUNITAS CREEK

Rating: 1

Species: Chum Salmon, Chinook Salmon, Coho Salmon and Steelhead

Stocks: None

Facilities: None

Lagunitas Creek is a rare opportunity for folks living in the North Bay area to witness salmon and steelhead spawning. Located downstream of Kent Lake, there is a special fish viewing area where you can see chinook, coho and chum salmon and steelhead spawning in Lagunitas Creek. During the spawning season, the creek tends to be clear so you shouldn't have a problem spotting fish. There is a paved road on both sides of the creek, which provides convenient walking access to the viewing area.

Historically, the creek harbored fair runs of salmon. However, diversion dams and other deterrents nearly spelt disaster for these anadromous fish. Extensive habitat work has aided the comeback of many of the runs. In early 2004, more than 1,000 coho salmon were counted. This was the best run in more than a decade. In addition, chinook and chum salmon were also spotted which is a great sign. Their numbers have been almost non-existent in previous years. The best time to see the salmon is between late October and early February, although the bulk of the run takes place between December and January. Steelhead also spawn in the creek in February.

To protect these runs, Lagunitas Creek is closed to fishing all year below Kent Dam. It's likely it will never be reopened in order to preserve this delicate run of fish.

Directions *and trip info for Kent Lake also apply to Lagunitas Creek.*

NICASINO RESERVOIR

Rating: 4

Species: Largemouth Bass, Crappie, Bluegill and Channel Catfish

Stocks: None

Facilities: None

Need Information? Contact: Sky Oaks Ranger Station (415) 945-1181

Nicasino Reservoir seems like the perfect place for a bass angler to fish from a float tube. There are dozens of coves to fish, fairly shallow water and good habitat for bass. Unfortunately, the Marin County Water District (MCWD) doesn't allow water contact of any kind at its' reservoirs, including Nicasino. Therefore, no boats, float tubes or wading is allowed.

Only shore fishing is permitted, yet few anglers take advantage of the warmwater fishery available at Nicasino, partly because no fish plants take place or ever will. The California Department of Fish and Game and the MCWD chose not to actively manage the lake. However, as many bass anglers know, sometimes the best management is no management at all.

The bass population here, along with some panfish and catfish is alive and well. There are trophy bass, but other than a few teenagers tossing swimbaits few anglers spend much time vying for the big boys. Anglers fishing Zara Super Spooks and Pop-R's from spring through fall in the morning and evenings can find consistent action on bass, mostly smaller than four pounds. Without a boat it can be tough to get the panfish at times, but hooking a catfish isn't out of the question for anglers willing to soak stink baits in coves.

If you plan to make the trip, supplies are available in Nicasino.

Also nearby is Stafford Reservoir.

Directions: *From Novato on Highway 101, exit Lucas Valley Road and drive 10.2 miles to a T intersection. Turn right at the sign for Nicasino and go 2.7 miles to the reservoir.*

STAFFORD LAKE

Rating: 4

Species: Largemouth Bass, Crappie, Bluegill and Channel Catfish

Stocks: None

Facilities: Restrooms and Picnic Areas

Need Information? Contact: Stafford Lake Park (415) 897-0618

Stafford Lake is the primary water source for the city of Novato and thus its' main purpose is to provide water, not recreation. While no fish plants take place there is a stable population of warmwater fish available to anglers who opt to fish from shore. Absolutely no water contact is allowed.

Stafford isn't a great fishery by any means. There are many bass that hang out near the tules, but since you can't fish from a boat, they can be tough to target. When you hook a bass, you'll have a tough time pulling the fish out of the weeds without breaking your line. Nonetheless, there can be a good summer topwater bite for anglers who fish during lowlight hours.

Stafford supports a fair catfish and panfish population, but fishing isn't the main attraction here. Most hardcore fishermen would rather make the drive to Clear Lake or Lake Sonoma, rather than sift through small fish at Stafford. Your best bet is to fish stink baits during the evening in the summer and fall.

If you plan to make the trip, supplies are available in Novato. There is a day use fee.

Also nearby is Novato Creek and Nicasino Reservoir.

Directions: *From Novato, drive west on Novato Blvd. for roughly 4.5 miles to the left turnoff for the reservoir.*

Scott Yates with a sturgeon caught and released near the mouth of the Napa River

Region ⑤ Bay Area

LOS VAQUEROS RESERVOIR

Rating: 7

Species: Largemouth
Bass, Channel Catfish,
White Catfish, Rainbow
Trout, Crappie, Green
Sunfish, Striped Bass,
Carp, Sacramento
Perch, Brown Bullhead
and Bluegill

Stocked with 9,500
pounds of rainbow
trout.

Facilities: Boat Rentals,
Bait & Tackle, General
Store, Fishing Piers,
Fish Cleaning Station,
Restrooms and a Picnic
Area

Need Information?
Contact: Los Vaqueros
Marina (925) 371-2628,
Los Vaqueros
Watershed Office
(925) 240-2360

When Los Vaqueros Reservoir first opened to the public in September of 2002, swarms of hype surrounded California's newest reservoir. However, the fiasco didn't last long. Los Vaqueros is a good fishery, nonetheless, one major factor keeps anglers from visiting. The lake doesn't allow any personal watercraft or private boats, which is disheartening to bass and trout anglers. The marina does offer boat rentals, but in this windy section of the Los Vaqueros Watershed they don't do the job when the winds kick up. Since the publicity wore off in 2002, the reservoir has become a shoreline bait dunker lake.

For residents of the Bay Area and greater Stockton and Sacramento metropolitan regions, Los Vaqueros is a diverse, year-round fishery that has yet to be explored. Once an old Spanish ranch set in the rolling hills between Livermore and Brentwood, the reservoir is now a quality warm and cold water fishery. The reservoir's construction was completed in November of 1997 and with the help of El Nino in early 1998, the lake was filled in December of 1998. It opened to the public four years later.

Endangered species usually create problems for fisheries, however, in this case, the threatened red-legged frog actually enhanced Los Vaqueros' fishery. In order to be granted approval for the construction of the lake, the Contra Costa Water District agreed to provide habitat and mitigation for the frogs, which are found in the lake's watershed. Better habitat meant draining stock and farm ponds in the lake's watershed to eradicate the frog's predators. When the ponds were drained, the fish from them were transported to the reservoir. Catfish to 12 pounds and largemouth bass to nine pounds were part of the mix. The California Department of Fish and Game managed the trout fishery a few years before the public was granted access to the 1,500-acre reservoir. In 2000 and 2001, the CA DFG planted more than 80,000 10-14 inch rainbow trout, which were known to grow quickly. Contra Costa County also planted more than 100,000 rainbow trout prior to the opener. The CA DFG plants roughly 15,800 rainbows each year in addition to trophy size fish stocked by the lake concessionaire.

For some reason, few anglers rent boats to troll the lake. If you do, target winter and spring and work the shorelines and dam area with red Cripplures, red and gold Thomas Buoyants and Needlefish. A Sep's Pro Flasher, Dodger or Sidekick and a night crawler also work. Most of the fishing for trout is done by shore anglers tossing bait off of fishing piers.

As for the bass fishery, it has yet to boom. However, all of the ingredients needed for giant bass are in place. There's cover, coves, submerged oak trees, creek channels and most importantly, food. Rainbow trout serve as rapid growing pills, and smaller forage such as threadfin shad, hitch, crawdads and hundreds of thousands of juvenile fish are also available. The bass fishery is widely ignored because bass anglers can't bring their own boats.

Kokanee were planted in the lake in spring of 2001, however, the lake has never materialized as a kokanee fishery. Because anglers can't bring their own boats equipped with downriggers, the fish aren't easy to target. Basically, the CA DFG planted 110,000-fingerling kokanee as a trial run of excess fish. Unless future plants are made, all the kokanee will have died off by fall of 2004.

Regardless of the species, all gamefish are known to thrive in Los Vaqueros. The equation is simple. Crawdads, hitch and threadfin shad provide forage. When you include inland silversides, Sacramento blackfish, carp, Sacramento sucker, prickly sculpin, three spined stickleback and mosquito fish that are pumped in from the Delta, you get even better productivity, thus allowing the fish to grow large fast. On the downside, stripers have also been pumped into the lake, but haven't established themselves.

Comprised of mostly tapered banks, shoreline access is great for anglers. Dunking Power Bait, floating night crawlers off the bottom and tossing traditional lures have produced the most consistent catch rates.

Currently, the east shoreline is closed to all human contact. Anglers have drive-to access on the south end and at the north end near the dam. Talks are underway to enlarge the reservoir, which could create an even better fishery, but nothing has been set in stone.

If you plan to make the trip, supplies are available in Livermore and Brentwood. There is a day-use and fishing fee. No private boats or personal watercraft is permitted. No frogs, clams, fish or dead animals are allowed as bait.

Also nearby is Contra Loma Reservoir and the Delta.

Los Vaqueros Reservoir

Directions: *From the junction of Interstate 5 and Highway 4 in Stockton, exit west on Highway 4 and drive 26.7 miles to Lone Tree Way. Turn left, drive 2.6 miles and turn left on the Highway 4 Bypass. Drive another 2.6 miles to Balfour. Turn left, drive two miles and turn right on Walnut. Drive for 2.5 miles to where Walnut breaks off the right. For the dam, stay right and continue to the lake. For the marina, stay left on Vasco Road and continue 12 miles to the Los Vaqueros Road. Turn right and continue to the lake.*

CONTRA LOMA RESERVOIR

Rating: 7

Species: Rainbow Trout, Largemouth Bass, White Catfish, Channel Catfish, Striped Bass, Crappie, Red Ear Sunfish and Bluegill

Stocked with 6,000 pounds of rainbow trout.

Facilities: Boat Launch, Restrooms, Picnic Area, Playground, Swimming Area, Snack Bar, Fishing Piers and Showers

Need Information? Contact: East Bay Regional Parks District (510) 562-7275

Contra Loma Reservoir is a small 80-acre park lake in the city of Antioch that offers local anglers a shot at warmwater and coldwater fish. The lake is heavily planted with trout during the cooler months and has viable populations of bass and catfish.

Stripers aren't planted, but that's not to say they aren't available. Stripers get pumped in from the Delta as juvenile fish and don't have a problem living here. Shad, inland silversides, rainbow trout and pan fish make for great meals. Try soaking anchovies near the dam or trolling trout imitation lures. The lake record is bigger than 44 pounds so if something big is tugging, it might not be a snag!

The lake is a good seasonal trout fishery. Contra Loma is stocked with trout from November through May. The California Department of Fish and Game plants more than 9,500 half-pound rainbows in addition to fish paid for by the East Bay Regional Parks District. The EBRPD plants pound-size and trophy trout. Action can be hot for trollers working small spoons and shoreline anglers fishing near the boat launch or off of the fishing piers .

Catfish are a big attraction in the summer and fall. Channel catfish are pumped in from the Delta. However, EBRPD plants channel cats in the warmer months. Fish low light hours with stink baits and you'll do well.

If you plan to make the trip, supplies are available in Antioch. No gasoline motors are permitted. All boat must be 17 feet or shorter. There is a day-use and fishing fee.

Also nearby is Los Vaqueros Reservoir.

Contra Loma Reservoir

Directions: *From Highway 4 in Antioch, exit Lone Tree Road and drive south for 1.5 miles to Golf Course Road. Turn right and drive seven-tenths of a mile to the park entrance. Continue 1.4 miles to boat ramp and lake.*

DEL VALLE RESERVOIR

Rating: 8

Species: Rainbow Trout, Chinook Salmon, Largemouth Bass, Smallmouth Bass, Striped Bass, Bluegill, Crappie, Channel Catfish and Carp

Stocked with 12,500 pounds of channel catfish and 61,350 pounds of rainbow trout.

Facilities: Restrooms, Showers, Swimming Beach, Picnic Areas, Campgrounds, Boat Launch, Marina, Boat Rentals, Bait and Tackle and RV Sites

Need Information? Contact: Del Valle Reservoir (925) 449-5201

Del Valle is one of the most diverse fisheries in the greater Bay Area. It boasts excellent trout angling from fall through spring and a good bite on an array of warmwater fish throughout the year. But, Del Valle offers more than just fishing opportunities. Located only a short drive from downtown Livermore, Del Valle is situated in a rolling foothill coastal setting. It's a great place for the family to spend a day or to get a quick getaway from urban life.

Whether trolling for trout with a Needlefish or drop-shotting for largemouth bass, it's not uncommon for anglers to be distracted by turkeys roaming the hillsides, bald eagles doing their own fishing or deer sipping water along the shoreline. This reservoir has a rural setting that rivals any lowland reservoir in the Bay Area or Stockton-Sacramento region.

For most anglers, rainbows are the main attraction. The CA DFG dumps more than 41,000 half-pound trout and 10,000 fingerling Chinook salmon. The East Bay Regional Parks District plants at least another 28,000 pounds of trout ranging from one-to-15 pounds from September through mid March.

Cooperative efforts between the CA DFG and EBRPD have made the reservoir a better trout fishery. Trout are now planted when cormorants are less likely to be in the lake. In 2003, the CA DFG said they would begin dumping only a few loads of small fish between mid-November and February, when plants wouldn't be smart because most of the trout would be eaten by the birds shortly after being planted. Instead, the bulk of the CA DFG fish will be planted from March through May and again in late September and October.

Those that aren't caught grow. There's an excellent source of food for trout, and other fish. In addition to shad, silverside minnows and zoo plankton provide a smorgasbord of food. A big part of the fishing centers around boaters who have no restrictions on what size or type of engine can be brought onto the lake. There is, fortunately, a 10 mph speed limit which keep things quiet.

Del Valle provides excellent access for bank anglers. Available is at least one-mile of drive-to shoreline where anglers can kick back in a lounge chair and cast towards willing trout. Bank anglers don't have trouble getting into trout. Weekly plants keep many trout in the vicinity of the marina and south end of the lake where bank anglers rule.

The south end is shallow and not conducive to trollers. It's dominated by shoreline anglers. Some trollers try to fish this area, but with water ranging from eight to 20 feet, anglers who don't watch their lines carefully find themselves catching more leaves and sticks than fish. Don't get me wrong, trollers can catch fish here, but it's more difficult because of the depth. Even using a light spoon, such as a Needlefish or Hum-Dinger, doesn't guarantee fish.

When fishing from shore you'll want to try fish the insides of bays and points. Oftentimes, trout will station themselves in these areas waiting to sabotage a school of shad or minnows. Other trout simply cruise across the points and through the coves looking for crawdads and other food sources.

Shore anglers have several choices, although most soak Power Bait on a sliding sinker rig. It's best to keep your bait a foot or two off the bottom. Others cast medium size spoons such as Cripplures, Thomas Buoyants, Krocodiles and Kastmasters off points.

In the spring, trolling can be done with downriggers, leadcore line or by simply top-lining. Traditionally, the largest fish are caught either by a guy soaking Power Bait from a boat or shore or by deepwater trolling. The ironic thing is that there isn't a top spot to troll at Del Valle. With the exception of the shallow south end, anything north of the boat launch is game.

At Del Valle you don't have to risk getting bored with the same scenery. It's a good idea to launch your boat, drop lines and begin paralleling the shoreline towards the dam. You have two options; stay 20 feet offshore or 30 yards. It makes no difference. You'll find some rainbows pinned to the shore and others out towards the middle of the channel, commonly referred to as "The Narrows".

Folks, this is easy trolling, perfect for beginners and hardcore trout anglers. Depending on your skill, anglers have the option of making things complex or keeping them simple. Either way, plan on being successful. There are so many trout planted in the lake that by following these rules of thumb, triumph is eminent.

The quickest way to a limit in the spring is varying your trolling depths. Anglers with downriggers or leadcore

Del Valle Reservoir

line and a second rod stamp can expect to catch limits in an hour or two. The idea is to place offerings towards each group of trout, namely those cruising the surface, others just below the surface and trout that are deep.

First, set your downriggers. I'd try a Needlefish on one side at 30-35 feet and either a Cripplelure, Kastmaster or Sep's Pro Grub on the other at roughly 22-30 feet. Then, release your top-lines. You'll want one side to fish deeper than the other. On this side, a small Countdown Rapala works great, followed by a red and gold Thomas Buoyant or gold Hot Rod with a red eye on the surface.

Chris "Pescado" Cocoles and a Del Valle bow

While the entire lake can kick out fish to trollers, the highest concentrations is in "The Narrows" and near the dam. The shoreline, within a quarter-mile of the dam, always holds fish. In the spring, anglers can also do well in this zone by trolling a night crawler behind a Sep's Pro Dodger or Pro Flasher.

Any cove between "The Narrows" and the dam is a great place to bait fish in a boat. The idea is not to station yourself in the cove, but at the mouth of the cove where the trout move into and out of the cove. Any bait will work.

Recently, Del Valle has added another aspect to its' coldwater fishery. Chinook salmon fingerlings are planted each year to provide anglers with an added incentive of another trophy fish. In the spring, chinook can be picked up employing the same methods used for trout. The chinook grow roughly 12 inches a year.

Del Valle doubles as a quality largemouth bass fishery. Florida strain largemouth were purchased from a private vendor and planted in the mid-Eighties. Tag recapture studies taken from the south end in 2001 showed 1,700 adult bass greater than 12 inches.

Smallmouth were introduced in 1969 and tend to hold tight to the steep areas. It's common to find younger smallmouth in the shallow habitat where you'll find largemouth. However, the larger smallies will be in deeper water.

Striped bass are also part of the mixed bag. The stripers have been pumped in from the Delta. Del Valle is a Department of Water Resources reservoir that was constructed for use as a transfer facility. Water is pumped in from the Delta and then out to the South Bay Aqueduct.

The stripers' size composition has changed. A decade ago the DWR would only pump water in from the Delta a few times a year or only a couple of years. This would create one class size of fish, all of which tended to grow large in a hurry. In recent years, water is pumped more frequently, allowing year classes of stripers and smaller fish in the lake. There's no indication that stripers are reproducing. Currently, there isn't a huge population of stripers, but they are available and are sometimes huge.

Catfish plants make sure that fishing for the bottom feeders is always good. Each year, thousands of cats are planted. Summer and fall evening and night fishing is best on cut baits. The lake does have a problem with carp, which also came in from the Delta. Funny thing is you never know what the Delta will bring. A few years back a 10-inch Flounder was caught!

If you plan to make the trip, supplies are available in Livermore. There is a day-use, boat launch and fishing fee.

Also nearby is Los Vaqueros Reservoir.

Directions: *From Interstate 580 east of Livermore, exit Vasco Road and drive 2.9 miles to Tesla Road. Turn west and drive eight-tenths of a mile to Mines Road. Turn left, drive 3.4 miles and veer right on Del Valle Road. Drive 3.1 miles to park entrance. Turn right and drive one-mile to the launch ramp.*

Del Valle Reservoir

SHADOW CLIFFS RESERVOIR

Rating: 7

Species: Rainbow
Trout, Channel Catfish,
Largemouth Bass,
Crappie and Bluegill

Stocked with 9,200
pounds of rainbow
trout.

Facilities: Swim Beach,
Picnic Areas, A
Waterslide, Restrooms,
Fishing Docks, Boat
Rentals and Bait &
Tackle

Need Information?
Contact: East Bay
Regional Parks District
(510) 562-7275

In Pleasanton, Shadow Cliffs Reservoir is a great put-and-take fishery that allows local residents to experience success at this urban fishing hole. Formerly a gravel quarry, similar operations take place at a plant behind the reservoir, yet the lake is nestled enough out of the way that the clear water keeps you from noticing the quarry operations.

Without a heavy stocking program, Shadow Cliffs wouldn't be a great fishing lake. Fortunately, rainbow trout are planted by the East Bay Regional Parks District and the California Department of Fish and Game. The CA DFG plants more than 13,500 trout. While trout don't reproduce, the lake is deep enough to support trout year-round.

One of the few downfalls is that only boats with electric trolling motors are permitted. On the other hand, trollers in small boats and canoes do well working the depths with Needlefish. This 80-acre lake is 45 feet deep and a great place to go when other nearby lakes are murky because of storm runoff. Shadow Cliffs has no natural inlet, therefore the water stays clear.

For East Bay anglers looking for a close, yet worthy fishing spot, Shadow Cliffs takes the bait. It's a great place for float tubers, shoreline anglers and anglers with small boats to fish. Bank fishermen have an excellent shot at trout by tossing floating baits off the fishing docks, near the Pumphouse (when it's on) and on the shoreline alongside Stanley Blvd.

The EBRPD plants channel catfish in the summer. However, the cats don't get the same wide-spread attention trout do. While largemouth bass and pan fish are available, they aren't heavily targeted.

If you plan to make the trip, supplies are available in Pleasanton. There is a fishing, boat launch and day-use fee. No boats larger than 17 feet are permitted.

Also nearby are Lake Elizabeth and Alameda Creek.

Directions: *From Interstate 680, 4.5 miles south of the junction with I-580, take the Pleasanton-Sunol Blvd exit. Turn left, drive 2.2 miles (Sunol becomes First St.) and turn right on Stanley. Continue 1.3 miles to the lake entrance on the right.*

Shadow Cliffs Reservoir 123

LAFAYETTE RESERVOIR

Rating: 7

Species: Rainbow Trout, Largemouth Bass, Crappie, Bluegill, Yellow Perch and Channel Catfish

Stocked with 14,500 pounds of rainbow trout.

Facilities: Boat Rentals, Restrooms, Boat Launch, Bait & Tackle and Picnic Areas

Need Information? Contact: Lafayette Reservoir (925) 284-9669

Lafayette Reservoir is a perfect spot for local anglers to plan a day-long or quick fishing trip without having to endure a long drive. This 111-acre reservoir, which is popular to joggers and walkers, is also a quality cold water fishery. The California Department of Fish and Game dumps more than 23,400 half-pound rainbows into the lake from October through June. The East Bay Municipal Utilities District also plants fish ensuring action for almost everyone.

Trout can be taken several ways; the best are bait fishing and trolling. The reservoir has several fishing piers that allow anglers good access to the water. Otherwise, the brushy shorelines would make it difficult for anglers to fish. Try dunking a night crawler or Power Bait. Trollers do well. You can't launch your own boat if it's on a trailer; however, car top boats and float tubes are permitted. Boat rentals are available. Slow trolling night crawlers or Needlefish behind a set of flashers is best.

The largemouth bass fishery isn't great, but 108 11-19 inch fish that were introduced in October of 2003 should help boost action. A 12-inch minimum size limit is in effect. The EBMUD also plants catfish in the summer months, keeping action consistent for anglers fishing bait in coves. Pan fish are on tap in the summer months. Bring along a carton of red worms.

If you plan to make the trip, supplies are available in Lafayette. There is a boat launch, fishing and day-use fee. No gas motors are permitted. No boats on a trailer can be launched. All boats must be on or in your vehicle when you drive through the gate.

Also nearby is Lake Anza and Lake Temescal.

Directions: *From Oakland, drive east on Highway 24 to Lafayette. Exit Acalanes Road and drive south for two-tenths of a mile to Mt. Diablo Road. Turn left, and drive eight-tenths of a mile to the right turnoff for the reservoir. Turn right and continue four-tenths of a mile to the parking area.*

Lafayette Reservoir

ALAMEDA CREEK

Rating: 3

Species: Steelhead, Coho Salmon, Chinook Salmon

Stocks: None

Facilities: None

Need Information? Contact: Alameda Creek Alliance (510) 845-2233

Alameda Creek was once a favorite spot for trout anglers. The California Department of Fish and Game would plant half-pound rainbows almost weekly and fish stacked up in pools, providing easy angling for fishermen in the South and East Bay areas. Things have changed drastically, however.

In response to the coastal steelhead joining the endangered species list, in the late Nineties, the CA DFG stopped planting rainbow trout. Due to the efforts to revive the once healthy steelhead run, trout are no longer stocked and will likely never be planted again.

Since 2000, Alameda Creek has seen coho, chinook and steelhead return in small numbers. While these runs are currently small, groups like The Friends of Alameda Creek and the Alameda Creek Alliance are working with government agencies to help restore fish populations to remove dams.

Their efforts have created better habitat to help revive the anadromous runs, but only time will tell how successful the efforts will be. Be sure of one thing: this isn't planter heaven anymore. But, being blessed with more than 700 miles of watershed, Alameda Creek is the largest watershed in the East Bay, offering good access along the highway and water that is easy to fish.

Alameda Creek

If you plan to make the trip, supplies are available in Niles.

Also nearby is Quarry Lakes.

Directions: From Interstate 680 near Sunol, exit west on Highway 84 (Niles Canyon Road) and drive 2.8 miles to the parking area on the left for the creek.

SANDY WOOL LAKE

Rating: 4

Species: Rainbow Trout, Largemouth Bass, Bluegill and Channel Catfish

Stocked with 6,100 pounds of rainbow trout.

Facilities: Picnic Areas, Restrooms and Fishing Piers

Need Information? Contact: Santa Clara County Parks (408) 355-2200, Ed Levin County Park (408) 262-6980

Resting inside Ed Levin County Park in the coastal mountains above Milpitas - and what feels like light-years away from the busy and crowded 680 and 880 Freeways - Sandy Wool Lake is a great place for a getaway from urban life that offers a chance to catch trout. While Sandy Wool isn't a good fishery, it accomplishes its purpose by providing a seasonal put-and-take fishery for rainbow trout.

In fact, this tiny 13-acre lake is planted with six tons of trout, equaling roughly 9,940 trout. Tossing Power Bait from shore, fly fishing from float tubes, or casting small spoons off the fishing piers all work well on half-pound fish in this shallow lake.

Catfish are planted in the summer and provide sport for anglers soaking stink baits or night crawlers. There is also a sprinkling of largemouth bass and bluegill that tend to stay around the tules.

If you plan to make the trip, supplies are available in Milpitas. There is a day-use parking fee. No power boats are permitted on the lake.

Also nearby are Spring Valley Lake and Elizabeth Lake.

Directions: From San Jose drive north on Interstate 880 and exit Calaveras Blvd (237). Drive east for 3.5 miles to Downing Road and turn left. Continue to El Levin County Park and Sandy Wool Lake.

Sandy Wool Lake

Spring Valley Pond

Rating: 3
Species: Rainbow Trout, Largemouth Bass, Channel Catfish and Bluegill
Stocked with 1,000 pounds of rainbow trout.
Facilities: Restrooms and a Picnic Area
Need Information? Contact: Ed Levin County Park (408) 262-6980

Spring Valley Pond is a good candidate for one of the poorest fisheries in the South Bay. It's dinky, shallow, silted, muddy, murky and no larger than a basketball court, yet it does have good qualities too. Spring Valley Pond isn't managed for adults. It's set aside for children ages 5-12 and is planted with 1,000 rainbow trout for the kids by the California Department of Fish and Game's "Fishing in the City" project.

You have to time your arrival just right though. Trout are only planted in the winter and early spring, and the numbers are so small that if you don't arrive shortly after a stock you'll be out of luck. When the water warms, small catfish, bluegill and a few bass enter the equation. Don't bother bringing lures, this is a bait play. Try Power Bait for the trout and worms for the warm water fish.

Spring Valley Pond is largely overshadowed by nearby Sandy Wool Lake and the golf course, however, nice picnic areas and shade make this a great family picnic destination with a chance at your child's first fish.

Trip info for Sandywool Lake also applies to Spring Valley Pond.

Directions: *From San Jose drive north on Interstate 880 and exit Calaveras Blvd (237). Drive east for 3.5 miles to Ed Levin County Park. Continue one-half mile to Spring Valley Pond.*

Spring Valley Pond

LAKE ELIZABETH

Rating: 3

Species: Rainbow Trout, Channel Catfish, Crappie, Green Sunfish, Carp, Pumpkinseed, Largemouth Bass and Sturgeon

Stocked with 500 pounds of channel catfish.

Facilities: Restrooms, Visitor Center, Boat Launch, Playground and Fishing Docks

Need Information? Contact: Fremont Parks and Recreation (510) 790-5541

Lake Elizabeth is a heavily used urban lake in the city of Fremont. Fishermen tend to be at the bottom of the chain. Fishing isn't great at this flood control catch basin, but it's good enough to excite a few locals to spend some time at the lake.

Nestled inside Central Park, the lake used to be part of the Fishing in the City program. However, budget cuts have since narrowed the scope on this shallow lake. While some catfish are still planted, trout are currently not on the allotment and are not expected to return.

The lake is fed by natural runoff from local mountains, yet when water is needed for recreation it can be pumped from a well. At full pool, Elizabeth's deepest hole reaches just 5.5 feet. Since the lake is used for flood control, it's often drained down to just four feet deep in the winter.

Fishing takes a backseat approach to playgrounds and normal park activities like playing catch and jogging. Row boats, sail boats and canoes are allowed on weekends and holidays. No motors are permitted.

Fished exclusively by Fremont residents, the lake is a self-maintaining warm water fishery. Electroshocked once in the Nineties, the largest bass to be seen is seven pounds. Fish from one-to-two pounds are realistic. Carp are the most abundant fish, with pan fish a close second. Carp to 30 pounds are common. There aren't a lot of bluegill, but some large crappie and a sprinkling of pumpkinseed. Evenings are dominated by bait fishermen tossing cut baits for catfish. A bizarre two sturgeon have been taken.

If you plan to make the trip, supplies are available in Fremont.

Also nearby are The Quarry Lakes and Alameda Creek.

Lake Elizabeth

Directions: *From Interstate 680 in San Jose, drive north to Fremont and exit Mission Blvd. (Highway 238). Turn left and continue 2.2 miles to Stevenson Blvd. and turn left. Drive 1.2 miles to Paseo Padre and turn left. Drive three-tenths of a mile to Sailway Drive and turn left to the lake.*

HORSESHOE LAKE

Rating: 5

Species: Rainbow
Trout, Largemouth Bass
and Crappie

Stocked with 7,500
pounds of rainbow
trout.

Facilities: Restrooms,
Picnic Area, Swim
Beach and a Boat
Launch

Need Information?
Contact: Quarry Lakes
Regional Recreation
Area (510) 795-4883

Located in what is known as the Quarry Lakes Regional Recreation Area, Horseshoe Lake is the largest in a chain of three lakes within park boundaries. It's also the only lake that is planted with rainbow trout. Trout are stocked by the California Department of Fish and Game and Mt. Lassen Trout Farm. The CA DFG stocks more than 11,000 trout. Horseshoe provides good access for shore anglers and a much needed urban fishery.

The lake is large enough for boat anglers to tackle, yet only electric trolling motors are permitted. Management is strict here. If you have any sort of gas motor on your boat, you will not be allowed through the gate. For the most part, only anglers with float tubes, canoes and small car top boats bring watercraft.

Fortunately, trout can survive year-round, even when temperatures soar into the Nineties. Horseshoe is the site of an old quarry pit, which means it's deep. At full pool, the pit is greater than 160 feet deep. For those still wondering, yes it is shaped like a Horseshoe. Even when the water is low, the depth is still 120 feet deep. Good thing for the trout. Trout fishing is a year-round thing and the primary reason to fish. Largemouth bass and crappie are present, yet make up only a small portion of the pool.

If you can get a boat on the water, trolling can be excellent, especially after June when the fish move deeper to seek cooler water. From late fall through spring, rainbows can be picked up from shore anywhere around the lake with Power Bait and night crawlers.

There are also a handful of cats worth targeting in the summer. A near 20-pound lake record keeps anglers after the fish on summer evenings. Fish rare flats on the lake. Most of the lake has steep shorelines which won't produce good catch rates.

If you plan to make the trip, supplies are available in Fremont. There is a day-use fishing and parking fee.

Also nearby is Alameda Creek.

Horseshoe Lake

Directions: *From I-880 in Fremont, take the Decoto Road (Hwy. 84) exit east. Turn right on Paseo Padre Parkway, then left on Isherwood Way. Proceed to the park entrance on the right.*

RAINBOW LAKE

Rating: 4

Species: Largemouth Bass and Channel Catfish

Stocks: None

Facilities: Restrooms and Picnic Areas

Quarry Lakes are proof that the East Bay Regional Parks District works its' tail off to try to provide Alameda County residents with as many recreational opportunities as possible. Quarry Lakes are four lakes that rest in Quarry Lakes Regional Recreation Area that were opened in 2001 after exhaustive efforts to prepare the lakes for recreation. Two others lakes, Lago Los Osos and Willow Slough, are on the property, but closed to fishing. Horseshoe and Rainbow are open though.

To give credit where it's due, the Alameda County Water District also worked diligently to make this ordeal happen. All the lakes are sites of old quarry pits. In order to fill these pits for recreation, water was diverted off Alameda Creek. Presently, the ponds are used for ground water recharge.

Rainbow Lake isn't stocked with rainbow trout, rather set aside for warm water fish. Currently, largemouth bass and channel catfish make up the composition of fish. Little fishing pressure occurs, most likely due to steep banks and a yet to thrive fishery. Because of steep shorelines (which are expected because of the quarries), access isn't great. Neither is the structure for bass or catfish. Recently, a local Boy Scout troop added Christmas Trees in the lake to attempt to help the bass. However, the success of that project won't be known for a few years. For now, few anglers will fish here until someone catches a big one. In 2002, 32 bass were stocked to help start a population.

Directions *and trip info for Horseshoe Lake also apply to Rainbow Lake.*

Rainbow Lake

JORDAN POND

Rating: 3

Species: Largemouth
Bass, Channel Catfish
and Bluegill

Stocked with 500
pounds of channel
catfish.

Facilities: A Fishing
Pier and Picnic Area

Need Information?
Contact: East Bay
Regional Parks District
(510) 562-7275

Jordan Pond isn't stocked with largemouth bass, however, somehow these fish end up here. Personally, I look at Jordan as a "pet fish" lake. You'll understand why in a second. Most likely, the bass are coming from a few "weekend biologists" trying to establish their own private fishery. In other words, anglers are catching fish from one lake and illegally transporting them to Jordan Pond. While by law this isn't a good thing, the practice fortunately gives the lake a few small "pet" bass.

Jordan Pond isn't a large lake. It's one of the smallest ponds you'll find, but the East Bay Regional Parks District gives you 250 reasons to come and fish each year. In summer, roughly 250 one-pound channel catfish are planted providing anglers dunking a night crawler a shot at a fish. There is also a sprinkling of bluegill.

Located inside Garin Regional Park, Jordan Pond isn't a drive-to destination. A short, 10-minute walk from the parking area brings you to the lake, which commonly keeps crowds low. There is plenty of open access to warrant your trip. Just think of it as a chance to get out of the house, rather than a great fishing pond.

Cut Baits work well for catfish at Jordan

If you plan to make the trip, supplies are available in Hayward. There is a day-use parking fee.

Also nearby is Don Castro Lake.

Directions: *From Interstate 680 near San Jose, exit Mission Blvd. (Highway 238) and turn right. Drive 9.1 miles to Garin Ave. Turn right and drive eight-tenths of a mile to parking area.*

DON CASTRO RESERVOIR

Rating: 4

Species: Largemouth Bass, Bluegill, Rainbow Trout and Channel Catfish

Stocked with 500 pounds of channel catfish and 2,000 pounds of rainbow trout.

Facilities: Restrooms, Swimming Pool, Picnic Area, Fishing Piers and a Bathhouse

Need Information? Contact: Don Castro Park (510) 538-1148

If you live near Castro Valley or Hayward and don't have more than a few hours to spare fishing, Don Castro Reservoir is a great destination for you. Don Castro is a small lake that is seasonally planted with catfish and trout. Don Castro's dam was constructed in 1964 to dam San Lorenzo Creek which makes up the lake's watershed.

At one time, Don Pedro Reservoir was heavily planted by the California Department of Fish and Game. Prior to the turn of the century, the small reservoir received more than 5,000 pounds of fish each year. However, resurgence in the cormorant population and poorer water quality has prompted the CA DFG to cut those numbers to 2,000 pounds of trout each year. Plants have also been scaled back because the lake has silted heavily in the recent flood years. The East Bay Regional Park District has talked of dredging it, but nothing has come as of yet.

Nonetheless, three months of the year (March-May) the lake offers good trout fishing for small rainbows. While the water quality may not always be great, the lake has a decent amount of water flowing in and the temperatures are cooperative. Trout tend to do well here through June. By summer though, action slows down and trout fishing becomes a thing of the past. Plants stop in the summer when the lake picks up a green tint as an algae bloom sets in.

Don Castro gets the smallest allotment of trout in the East Bay, but a tiny population of bass and bluegill still await as well as plentiful numbers of planted catfish. As long as you are patient, catfish can be easy to catch. Any cut baits work, but scent is a must. Try soaking baits in Pautzke Nectar or Liquid Krill.

If you plan to make the trip, supplies are available in Hayward. There is a day-use fishing fee.

Also nearby is Cull Canyon Reservoir.

Directions: From Interstate 580 in Castro Valley, take the Center St/Crow Canyon Road exit to Center Street. Turn right and drive one-half mile to Kelly St. Turn left and drive six-tenths of a mile to the Maud-Woodroe Ave intersection. Turn left and drive a half-mile to the park entrance.

CULL CANYON RESERVOIR

Rating: 4

Species: Largemouth Bass, Bluegill and Channel Catfish

Stocks: None

Facilities: Swimming Area, Restrooms and Picnic Areas

Need Information? Contact: East Bay Regional Parks District (510) 562-7275

Cull Canyon Reservoir isn't the Bay Area's prettiest reservoir by any means. In fact, it may offer the poorest scenery of the East Bay Regional Parks. Cull Canyon Reservoir will remind you of a catch basin which is used as flood control by containing debris. That debris prevents the California Department of Fish and Game from stocking this muddy reservoir that has low visibility.

Even with the poor water conditions, the reservoir manages a decent warmwater put-and-take fishery. While bass and bluegill may be tough to come by, catfish are often caught by anglers tossing cut baits from shore. The CA DFG hasn't planted fish in the lake since 1982. However, the East Bay Regional Parks District plants some fish each year. In 1963-4 black crappie, red ear sunfish and largemouth bass were planted by the CA DFG as well as channel catfish in 1978-9 and '82. This lake is dominated by shoreline fishing. No boats are permitted. Action is best from mid-spring through fall when anglers can pick up catfish all day at the dam or inlet.

San Francisco isn't far from Cull Canyon Reservoir

If you plan to make the trip, supplies are available in Castro Valley.

Also nearby are Don Castro Reservoir and Lake Chabot.

Directions: *From the intersection of Castro Valley Road and Crow Canyon Road in Castro Valley, turn left on Crow Canyon and drive one-half mile to Cull Canyon Road. Turn left on Cull Canyon Road and drive two-tenths of a mile to the parking area on the left.*

LAKE MERRITT

Rating: 3

Species: Steelhead, Chinook Salmon, Catfish and Striped Bass

Stocks: None

Facilities: Restrooms

Need Information?
Contact: Lake Merritt Institute
(510) 238-2290

Lake Merritt is a lot like Echo Park Lake in Los Angeles and Southside Park Pond in downtown Sacramento. It's in an urban area of a major city where local residents visit to escape the traffic, smog and the hustle of the city. Unfortunately, they end up finding the same dense conditions at the lake. Merritt is mobbed by joggers, runners, walkers, other folks taking naps on the grass, throwing Frisbees, etc. You get the point.

I, on the other hand, was there to fish. For some reason there wasn't a single person fishing, which was odd considering I had just finished reading the Bay Area's Fishing in the City brochure that listed Merritt as a quality warmwater fishery. I walked in to the park office, stood at the counter for 20 minutes and watched a half-dozen employees walk by. I must have been a ghost. Each person walked by making eye contact with me, yet ignoring me.

Finally, a woman who has passed by me three times stopped. "Do you need something," she said. Whoa, that was rude. I asked what kind of fish were in the lake. "Fish. Boy you better not be thinking about fishing out in my lake. There aint no fishing out there. That lake is polluted and loaded with crabs and fish from the Bay. You aren't allowed to fish."

She was pretty serious, obviously angry and was big enough to break me and my fishing pole in half. There was no room for dissent. I fled. My confusion grew as the California Department of Fish and Game assured me there were fresh and saltwater fish in the lake. They said it was open to fishing regardless of what the park district said. Further research assured me the lake was in fact open to fishing.

The lake is accompanied by mostly brackish water. However, studies by the CA DFG prove trout could survive. In the Nineties, the CA DFG's Fishing in the City team placed 200 trout in a protected cage in the lake to see how the trout would react. Fortunately, they survived and flourished. Unfortunately, the CA DFG couldn't relish any support from the Oakland City Parks and had to abandon the project.

Contrary to popular belief, there are fish in the lake. Steelhead enter the lake to spawn each year. It's not uncommon to see steelies up to 22 inches. The CA DFG was planning on planting sterile fish to avoid breeding between the rainbows and steelhead, but with the lack of interest from the park district, it never happened anyway. The 140-acre lake has 3.5 miles of shoreline and an average depth of eight to 10 feet.

Lake Merritt is heavily affected by tidal influences. It's a natural tidal lagoon that has been modified. Seasonally, striped bass and channel catfish can be found in the channel as well as sharks, rays, anchovies and smelt. At times, you'll find salmon and halibut as well.

Merritt's fishery would be better if tide gates were removed. Constructed in the Seventies to keep out the high tide for flood control, bars prohibit schools of larger fish from entering the lake. There is a movement, however, to remove the bars. Government funds are available for the project. Only time will tell.

If you plan to make the trip, supplies are available in Oakland.

Also nearby is Temescal Lake.

Directions: *From Interstate 580 in Berkeley, drive towards Oakland and exit Grand Avenue. Turn right and continue to Bellevue. Turn left to the lake.*

Although it would be a miracle to catch one this big, stripers are common at Lake Merritt.

LAKE TEMESCAL

Rating: 5

Species: Rainbow Trout, Channel Catfish, Largemouth Bass, Red Ear Sunfish and Bluegill

Stocked with 2,000 pounds of rainbow trout.

Facilities: Restrooms, Fishing Docks, Snack Bar, Swimming Beach and Picnic Areas

Need Information? Contact: East Bay Regional Parks District (510) 562-7275

When it comes to East Bay lakes, Lake Temescal is the prettiest in my mind, and while it may not provide the best fishing, it offers the opportunity to catch planted rainbow trout, channel catfish and an outside shot at bluegill and largemouth bass.

Located near Oakland, 10-acre Temescal is a family lake that caters to an array of outdoor enthusiasts. Soccer practices are held on the grassy knolls during part of the year, a swim beach is popular in the summer, trails make for running, biking and walking, and of course, there's fishing. The lake and park is well kept up and presents a cozy, safe feeling. It's a great place for a family to spend the day or a father and son to soak bait in hopes of catching fish.

Temescal's claim to fame is that the lake rests on the Hayward Fault. However, the earthquake fault doesn't seem to scare anglers away, not when trout and catfish are being stocked. Temescal isn't a great fishing lake. In fact, catch rates are typically low. However, the California Department of Fish and Game manages to plant nearly 3,300 half-pound rainbow trout each year. They can be caught by shoreline anglers soaking Power Bait and night crawlers. Trout fishing is best in the fall and spring. Since the water isn't always clear, it's a good idea to add some sort of scent to your bait.

Trout fishing is best shortly after fish are stocked. This is when they are concentrated and easier to catch. Within two-to-three days after they are stocked many of the trout have either been caught or a scattered all over the lake, which can make catching them a bit more challenging. If you aren't keen on soaking baits, casting spinners and spoons can be effective too. Try throwing an orange Cripplure or quarter-ounce Panther Martin.

Warm water species don't excel at Temescal. However, some pan fish, bass and catfish are available. Most catfish are caught from mid-afternoon to late evening by anglers dunking stink baits.

If you plan to make the trip, supplies are available in Oakland. There is a day-use parking fee.

Also nearby are Lake Anza, Lake Merritt and Lake Chabot.

Directions: *From Oakland, at the junction of I-580 and Highway 24, take Highway 24 east for roughly 2.5 miles to the Broadway exit. Exit, veer left off the ramp and drive east for seven-tenths of a mile to the park entrance on the right.*

LAKE ANZA

Rating: 5

Species: Steelhead and Largemouth Bass

Stocks: None

Facilities: Restrooms, Swimming Area and Picnic Area

Need Information?
Contact: Tilden Park
(510) 843-2137

Lake Anza rests in the middle of Tilden Park, one of California's best urban parks. In the hills that rise above Berkeley and the Bay and Golden Gate bridges, Tilden Park has something for everyone. I mean everyone. Hiking trails, horseback riding, swimming, picnicking, train rides and a merry-go-round make up a few of the advertised activities.

Anza isn't a great fishery, however it's rich with history. Anza rests on a dammed portion of Wildcat Creek. Prior to the dam being created, native steelhead runs occurred here. Native runs no longer take place below the lake because of two impassable dams. Nonetheless, there are still steelhead in the system. In 1983, steelhead were taken from a sister stream, Redwood Creek, which runs to the south of Wildcat and also is a member of the San Leandro Drainage. These fish were genetically proven to have steelhead genes and were planted above the Anza. While these fish do come in the lake, they aren't available in great numbers. It's recommended you catch and release all trout caught in the reservoir.

Bass, on the other hand, are fair game. Largemouth bass have lived in the reservoir for more than a half-century. In fact, up until the late Seventies, anglers caught some nice bass. Due to the competition of food, the East Bay Regional Parks District encourages anglers to catch and keep the bass to pave the way for better living conditions for trout.

If you plan to make the trip, supplies are available in Berkeley.

Also nearby are Lake Merritt, San Pablo Reservoir and Lake Temescal.

Directions: *From Highway 24 near Oakland, take the Fish Ranch Road exit east and drive uphill to Grizzly Peak Blvd. Turn right and continue to the Shasta Road entrance.*

Lake Anza

SAN PABLO RESERVOIR

Rating: 9

Species: Sturgeon, Channel Catfish, Rainbow Trout, Smallmouth Bass, Largemouth Bass, Crappie and Red Ear Sunfish

Stocked with 17,500 pounds of rainbow trout.

Facilities: Restrooms, Boat Launches, Bait & Tackle, Fish Cleaning Station, Boat Rentals, Picnic Areas, Restaurant and a Playground

Need Information? Contact: That Dam Company (510) 223-1661, Urban Park Concessionaires (925) 426-3060

Special Note: San Pablo Reservoir is closed from November 15 to February 12 to protect bird migration. Editor's Note: San Pablo will be closed for two years while work is done on the dam. Please contact the lake for updated info.

San Pablo Reservoir is one of the Bay Area's best trout fisheries. Only Del Valle and Chabot compete with it. It's also one of two Bay Area lakes where there are no boat restrictions. The lake is troller friendly and equally kind to shoreline anglers. Each year, the California Department of Fish and Game dumps more than 30,000 half-pound rainbows into the 866-acre lake. Those fish are joined by larger trout that are paid for directly by San Pablo Reservoir. Those fish total more than 108,000 pounds of fish, and while they average one-pound, 10 percent are five pounds and greater.

San Pablo is a good beginner's troller's lake. There are few snags and the ones that are present are visible. Plus, there aren't steep drop-offs or areas where you need to worry about losing a downrigger ball. With 14 miles of shoreline there's room for lots of trollers.

When trout are on the top it's a easy lake to troll. Basically, anywhere on the lake's entire shoreline, or down the middle, you'll be able to catch fish. Realistically, it doesn't matter what you troll with. There are so many trout just about anything works, although shad imitation lures seem to increase catch rates. I used a Yo-Zuri 3D Minnow.

Still, boat anglers do well with night crawlers and Power Bait. Any of the lake's coves are good. Station yourself at the mouth of the bay and trout will come to you. There's no drive-to access on the north shore. The south shore, on the other hand, is filled with shoreline access for bait dunkers. The lake boasts excellent facilities for anglers.

San Pablo doubles as a quality bass fishery. There are some smallmouth, but it's predominately a largemouth fishery. San Pablo isn't considered one of the best Nor Cal bass lakes, but it does put out some fish of size, including the lake record, a bass that pushed near 19 pounds. The lake receives far more pressure on its trout fishery than the bass fishery.

San Pablo is also stuffed with catfish. Each year spring and summer is highlighted with massive plants of cats. The fish in the three-to-five-pound range are realistic on cut baits. Often anglers soaking Power Bait on the bottom land cats or a fluke sturgeon which are a tiny portion of the mixed bag. The lake record, a 105-pound sturgeon, was caught in 2003. In December of 1986,

136 sturgeon between five and 12.5 pounds were planted.

If you plan to make the trip, supplies are available in Pinole. There is a day-use, boat launch and fishing fee. There is a 25 mph speed limit.

Also nearby is Lake Anza.

Directions: *From Interstate 80 in the Bay Area drive west to the city of Pinole and exit Apian Way. Turn south and drive 2.3 miles to San Pablo Dam Road. Turn east and drive 7.3 miles to the park entrance.*

Big Todd McLean used a red Hot Rod to catch this San Pablo bow.

MERCED LAKE (NORTH)

Rating: 4

Species: Rainbow Trout

Stocked with 9,700 pounds of rainbow trout.

Facilities: Restrooms

Need Information?
Contact: San Francisco
City Parks and
Recreation Department
(415) 831-2700

Both Merced Lake North and South get planted with trout, however, the north lake used to be an excellent trophy lake. At one time, the City of San Francisco took an active role in managing this lake. They used to purchase large rainbow trout, but budget issues and a lack of enthusiasm for the project ended Merced Lake North's tenure.

A few years back, the lake concessionaire was granted to a group who basically led it straight downhill. Now, young adults who return to the lake 15 years after they first pulled up to the bait and tackle shop, bought a pack of worms and sat in a rowboat with dad to catch a limit of trout, are devastated to see their childhood fishing hole no longer intact.

Memories of bobbers being yanked under by one-to-five-pound trout have been replaced by an old, beat up boat house, the absence of boat rentals and a smorgasbord of poop infested docks, seagulls and cormorants. The lake has a brown sugar tint, which can make for poor visibility and cut down on growing conditions. Local enthusiasm is also at an all-time low. I arrived the week the California Department of Fish and Game was slated to make a trout plant and there wasn't a sole fishing. They plant 17,650 trout each year.

There isn't a lot of shoreline access either. Much of the lake is bordered by tules and the fishing docks are occupied by birds, not anglers. The boathouse looks abandoned at best. Sadly, Merced isn't the great trout fishing lake that is has been historically.

If you plan to make the trip, supplies are available in San Francisco.

Also nearby is Brooks Falls.

Directions: *From the junction of Interstate 380 and 280, drive north on I-280 for 5.1 miles to the John Daly/West District. Exit and continue straight off the offramp for six-tenths of a mile to John Daly Blvd. Turn left and drive 1.3 miles to Skyline Blvd. Turn right and drive two miles to Lake Merced County Park on the right. Turn right to the lake. The north lake is on the left.*

Merced Lake North

MERCED LAKE (SOUTH)

Rating: 4

Species: Rainbow Trout

Stocked with 12,750 rainbow trout.

Facilities: Restrooms

Need Information? Contact: San Francisco City Parks and Recreation Department (415) 831-2700

At one time, there was a big difference between Merced Lake (North) and Merced Lake (South). Locals always knew the north lake as the trophy lake and the south lake as a place where the California Department of Fish and Game planted pan size rainbow trout. On the other hand, since the north's trophy program was dropped several years ago, there's no longer much difference between the fishing in each of the lakes. Both lakes offer small trout along with stained water.

The CA DFG and the city of San Francisco have taken a lassie faire attitude when it comes to managing the lake. Basically, the south lake is now managed as a put-and-take urban fishery. The CA DFG stocks 21,780 trout as anglers sit on the banks with dough baits and night crawlers waiting to cash in on the action. It's a basic fishery, but with clarity poor, you better apply lots of scent.

The lake is within sight of the zoo, a gun club and receives a maritime influence that allows trout to live year-round.

Directions *and trip info for Merced Lake (North) also applies to Merced Lake (South).*

Merced Lake South

For Donner Lake (pictured above) please refer to pages 591-592

Region

Motherlode

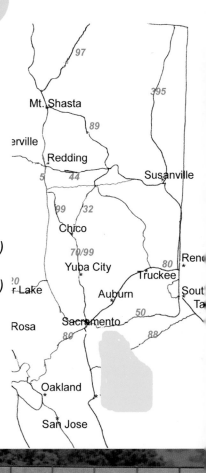

6

Lake Camanche
Lake Pardee
New Melones Reservoir
Salt Springs Valley Reservoir
New Hogan Reservoir
Angels Creek (Lower)
Angels Creek (Upper)
White Pines Lake
Stanislaus River (North Fork, Lower)
Beaver Creek
Stanislaus River (North Fork, Upper)
Mokelumne River
Consumnes River (Middle Fork)
Bear River Reservoir (Lower)
Schaads Reservoir
Tabeaud Reservoir
Tiger Creek Afterbay
Lake Amador

LAKE CAMANCHE

Rating: 9

Species: Kokanee, Rainbow Trout, Channel Catfish, Blue Catfish, Bluegill, Red Ear, Crappie, Largemouth Bass, Smallmouth Bass, Spotted Bass and Sturgeon

Stocked with 66,500 pounds of rainbow trout.

Facilities: Campgrounds, RV Hookups, Boat Launches, Picnic Areas, Restrooms, General Store, Bait & Tackle, Boat Rentals, Snack Bar, Lodging, Showers and Laundry Facilities

Need Information? Contact: Lake Camanche North Shore Marina (209) 763-5166, Lake Camanche South Shore Marina (209) 763-5915, Camanche Campground Reservations (209) 763-5178, North Shore Office (209) 763-5121

A lot can be said for great management of a fishery. Anglers familiar with Lake Camanche know the lake has become one of the best and most diverse fisheries in the state because it has been actively managed since 1990 when Urban Park Concessionaires took over operations.

Carefully monitoring fish populations, management, headed by Chris Cantwell, makes sure there are always enough rainbow trout, largemouth bass, bottom feeders and panfish available for anglers to have a successful fishing experience. Regardless of time of year, at least one species will provide excellent action for anglers, but fishing isn't the only incentive.

Camanche also offers some of the nicest facilities in Northern California. You could remain at the 7,700-acre reservoir for a week and stay clean, comfortable, well fed and have enough activities to keep you from getting bored. Nonetheless, most folks come for the fishing.

Camanche is one of the best lowland trout lakes in the state. The lake is planted with 60,000 pounds of privately stocked trout. These fish come in two classes: 90 percent are one-pound each and 10 percent are three pounds and better. The California Department of Fish and Game also plants 5,600 half-pound rainbows. These rainbows join holdovers from years past and some trout that have spawned in the reservoir.

Trout can be caught year round, but the best months are ironically when the fewest anglers are fishing. In December and January trout fishing can be amazing with limits coming easy to anglers working the surface with spoons and stickbaits.

In February, anglers can expect to catch trout toplining, but March through May can be questionable. Depending on weather patterns, trout may already be headed into deeper water. The best days to fish are when conditions are overcast and cloudy, as trout can be subsequently caught on the surface all day.

Camanche's trout traditionally go to two places: upriver or towards the lower lake near the dam. The middle is only good in the dead of winter. The upriver fishery relies on releases from Pardee Dam. When water is being released into Camanche (traditionally, this occurs from September through spring, but it varies year-to-year), you'll have trout moving towards the eastern end to cash in on food and cool water being brought in. The river canyon averages 30-60 feet deep and is an excellent area to troll.

From June through October, anglers will need deepwater trolling gear to be successful. During this time trout school up trout in deep water. Camanche's lake management publishes where the thermocline is so anglers always know what depth to troll.

Summertime trout fishing is often dictated by the Speece Cone. The Speece Cone was completed in 1994 to oxygenate the water by the dam. Prior to the installation of the cone, Camanche had poor water quality. Water that was released downriver into the Mokelumne River Fish Hatchery caused several fish kills prior to the cone's installation.

The cone sucks water in at the top of the tube, mixes it with oxygen and then spits liquid oxygen into the lake, creating cooler, more oxygenated water. It's beneficial to Camanche as well as the hatchery. The affects of the cone attracts coldwater species to the dam. Unfortunately, you can't fish directly above the cone for obvious safety reasons. While the cone is set behind the buoy line, it does influence the water around it for one-eighth to one-quarter of a mile. Anglers fishing the surrounding area typically find lots of willing trout. Usually, the cone is turned on in July and can stay on into October.

Camanche isn't a great panfish lake, but does offer good catfish action. The CA DFG told Camanche there are too many catfish in the lake and no plants are necessary. Despite these numbers anglers don't pay much attention to the species.

Camanche's catfish are traditionally done spawning by mid June. After they've spawned you can find them in the holes and around the cliffs in The Narrows protecting their young. Camanche catfish run four pounds on average, but fish to 10 pounds are common.

Summer action can be good in the evenings and early mornings for anglers fishing in the backs of coves with liver and mackerel. On the other hand, winter may provide the best action of the year. February and March are odd months for catfish anglers. Cats are commonly taken by trout trollers working 10-20 feet of water in rocky areas (The Narrows).

Other prime winter catfish areas are Cosway Cove and Rabbit Creek. If you really want action, head to Cosway Cove and fish in front of guardrail post 43. There is a culvert here that brings water in during the winter months and attracts loads of catfish.

While not heavily targeted, Camanche has an excellent population of bass. Largemouth bass are becoming more prevalent each year. In 1990, Camanche began a program to aid the progression of the largemouth fishery. The lake plants $15,000 of Florida-strain largemouth every year. Roughly 7,000 three-to-four-inch bass are planted to help strengthen the largemouth population.

Camanche is also a decent smallmouth bass lake. Smallies aren't the most abundant bass, but anglers fishing the Lancha Plana area can find one-to-five-pound fish targeting the cobble rock piles. It's effective to jig Luhr Jensen Crippled Herrings or throw crankbaits.

Spotted Bass were introduced in 1980 and are well accounted for. For its' size and the amount of bass available, Camanche's bass fishery goes sadly unnoticed. Most anglers arrive in the spring and sight fish in Cosway Cove and on the southeastern corner of the Camanche Arm. Almost no one bass fishes in the summer and fall.

Interestingly enough, in 1980, 100 40-inch sturgeon were planted, but few have been caught. There's no telling how big they are or how big they'll get, but one day a lucky angler will get tugged around the lake for a few hours by a big sturgeon.

Kokanee were last planted 1995, but no future plants are expected. The CA DFG is cautious about stocking kokanee due to the possibility of escapement into the Mokelumne River where endangered species might breed with the kokanee. Nonetheless, anglers mange to catch kokanee, which means they are successfully spawning in Camanche or being washed in from Pardee. When excess stock is available, inland chinook salmon are stocked, but this doesn't occur often.

If you plan to make the trip, supplies are available at the lake. There is a day-use, boat launch and fishing fee.

Also nearby are the Mokelumne River, Pardee Reservoir, New Hogan and Salt Springs Valley Reservoir.

Directions: *From Clements on Highway 12/88, drive east for one-half mile to a junction. For the north shore, take Highway 88 east for three miles to Camanche Parkway N. Turn east and drive seven miles to Camanche Road. Turn south and drive one-mile to the entrance. Or, for the south shore take Highway 12 east for four miles to Camanche Parkway S. Turn left and drive five miles to Pattison Road. Turn north and drive one-mile to the entrance.*

146 Spotted bass, like this one caught by Kent Brown, are common at Lake Camanche throughout the year.

LAKE PARDEE

Rating: 7

Species: Rainbow Trout, Brown Trout, Kokanee, Largemouth Bass, Smallmouth Bass, Crappie, Bluegill and Channel Catfish

Stocked with 208 pounds of fingerling kokanee and 9,000 pounds of rainbow trout.

Facilities: Boat Rentals, Bait & Tackle, Showers, General Store, Restaurant, Restrooms, Boat Launch, Campgrounds, Picnic Areas, RV Hookups, Marina and Gas

Need Information? Contact: Fishing Guide Shane Quimby of Jack-A-Lope Charters (209) 304-1800, Lake Pardee Marina (209) 772-1472

Lake Pardee is arguably the prettiest foothill lake in the Motherlode region and offers a diverse cold and warm water fishery. Pardee is a fishermen's lake. No water contact is permitted, which keeps water-skiers, waverunners and swimmers off the water. An added bonus is that the lake offers excellent facilities and great amenities. Pardee has been opened to the public since 1958. The 2,100-acre reservoir has 37 miles of shoreline, but only limited bank access.

Pardee isn't your normal reservoir. While most reservoirs in this region are open year-round, Pardee opens the first Saturday of February and closes the last Sunday in October. This arrangement was not set up by the California Department of Fish and Game, rather the lake concessionaire.

Pardee used to be recognized as the home of the record trout, but the status of the fishery has changed drastically since the mid-Nineties. At the present time, the concessionaire is planting fewer fish and smaller trout than they did in the past. No longer are truckloads of massive trout coming in weekly. It simply became too expensive. Nonetheless, plenty of trout are still planted. The CA DFG plants 13,000 trout each year averaging a half-pound, while the concessionaire plants fish that run one-to-two pounds.

Similar to Lake Berryessa and many other California reservoirs, Pardee lacks a good food source for trout. If the smaller planters aren't caught near the marina, many of them won't live through the following year because they can't find food on their own. There is no shad population or pond smelt, rather only a few minnows to go around. Kokanee is a major baitfish for the larger trout, but not the small planters.

Rainbow trout greatly outnumber browns. In the past, browns were more prevalent. However, over harvesting and a lack of plants has diminished the brown trout population. Another theory, this one courtesy of Shane Quimby of Jack-A-Lope Guide Service, is that the browns don't like boat traffic and stay upriver of the log jam where anglers can't target them. Quimby believes that browns wait until a lot of debris enters the lake after a storm before they swim below the log jam. He says they feel protected by the debris. Nevertheless and whatever the reason, there are still browns available.

From shore, the prime area to catch trout is in the marina. Locals refer to this area as the "Fish Bowl." All the planted trout enter here and provide good action to Power Baiters. No trolling is permitted in this area.

Trollers have an excellent chance at catching trout. One of the most promising areas to catch holdover trout is the river channel. The mouth of the Mokelumne River channel is a wide and deep area that gets narrower and shallower as you move upriver. The channel ranges from 20-150 feet deep and always harbors trout. It's in a trout's nature to find current. Therefore, many of the trout that are planted leave the main body and head up the river channel. Oftentimes trout caught at Pardee are holdovers in the river channel. Quimby fishes the river channel with Sep's Pro grubs and Uncle Larry's spinners behind Sep's Pro dodgers, but any spoon or stickbait will get the job done.

If you are going to troll the main body, it's necessary that you have a reliable depth finder. The main body is as deep as 350 feet and has several submerged islands. It can be tough to effectively troll if you aren't familiar with the lake though. The depth will jump from 100 feet to 30 feet in a matter of seconds. It's best to work these areas: the dam, spillway, the channel that runs north to south in the main body, the buoy line and the pumphouse.

Kokanee are a big deal in the summer. While they can be taken on small Sep's Pro sidekicks trolled in front of kokanee bugs in the top 20 feet in early spring, they'll head as deep as 125 feet in the summer. The water temperature dictates where they'll be. Traditionally, Pardee doesn't yield trophy kokanee, but fish to 17 inches are common.

Pardee doubles as a great warmwater fishery. Even more so in recent years, anglers are reporting excellent fishing for largemouth and smallmouth bass. For some reason, the tournament trail hasn't hit Pardee yet, which keeps many bassers off the water. On the other hand, trophy size fish in both species are available. There is no pressure on the bass fishery.

If you plan to make the trip, supplies are available in at the lake. There is a day-use, boat launch and fishing fee.

Also nearby is Salt Springs Valley Reservoir and Lake Amador.

Directions: *From the 99 Freeway in Sacramento, drive south to the Twin Cities Road exit. Exit east and drive 23 miles to Road 124. Turn right and drive 2.3 miles to Highway 88. Turn left and drive six-tenths of a mile to Buena Vista. Turn right and drive 4.7 miles to a "V" in the road. Veer left on Stoney Creek Road and continue nine-tenths of a mile to the right turnoff for Pardee Reservoir.*

148 Guide Shane Quimby and a three-pound Pardee bow taken from The Narrows in the early morning hours.

Rating: 8

Species: Red Eye Bass, Mule Bass, Largemouth Bass, Smallmouth Bass, Spotted Bass, Channel Catfish, Bullhead, Carp, Hitch, Rainbow Trout, Brown Trout, Kokanee, Red Ear Sunfish, Green Sunfish, Crappie and Bluegill

Stocked with 3,000 pounds of sub-catchable brown trout, 1,400 pounds of fingerling rainbow trout, 29,500 pounds of rainbow trout and 1,746 pounds of fingerling kokanee.

Facilities: Restrooms, Picnic Areas, Campgrounds, Bait & Tackle, General Store, Marinas, Gas, Houseboat Rentals, Boat Rentals, Fish Cleaning Stations, Hot Showers, RV Hookups and Swim Beach

Need Information? Contact: Glory Hole Sports (209) 736-43333, New Melones Lake Marina (209) 785-3300, New Melones Visitor Center (209) 536-9543, Bureau of Reclamation (209) 536-9094, Danny Layne of Fish'n Dan's Guide Service (209) 586-2383

In the heart of the Motherlode Region, New Melones is a large reservoir with a capacity of 2.4 million acre feet. The reservoir is located on the Stanislaus River roughly 60 miles upstream from the confluence with the San Joaquin River. Eighth in size to San Luis Reservoir, Clear Lake, Trinity, Berryessa, Lake Shasta, Oroville and Don Pedro, New Melones comprises 12,500 acres when full and has 100 miles of shoreline. Sadly though, full pool is almost never attained.

New Melones functions like a reservoir. Each spring the reservoir is allowed to fill (although it doesn't fill every year) before water is released from summer through fall into Tulloch Reservoir. When runoff isn't abundant, water levels can suffer. In fact, it's not uncommon to see draw-downs of more than 50-200 feet.

New Melones Reservoir is actually situated were Melones Reservoir once was. In 1926, the Oakdale and South San Joaquin Irrigation Districts constructed the 183-foot high New Melones dam that was inundated by the 625-foot dam that created New Melones Reservoir in 1983.

Melones is a multi use lake, perfect for houseboats, boaters and anglers. It provides an excellent warm and cold water fishery. Melones is an ideal destination for trollers looking to tap into kokanee, rainbows and browns, and offers great spotted and largemouth bass fishing in addition to reliable panfish and catfish action.

There are several strains of bass available, but largemouth and spotted bass are the only ones targeted by anglers. Smallmouth can be found, but are rare. A few smallmouth reside by the dam, but they aren't caught often. Red eye bass are abundant, however they don't make for much of a sport fish because rarely do they reach 12 inches. They average six-to-nine inches and can be found in the same areas as largemouth and spotted bass. Their growth to legal size is believed to be hindered because of competition for food with other species.

Currently there's a big battle brewing between largemouth and spots. Most experts will tell you the spots will prevail in time because typically spots spawn deeper and aren't affected by drastic draw downs as largemouth are. For now though, there will be largemouth and spots for all anglers to enjoy. Trophy sizes of each are available.

Regardless of the time of year, largemouth and spotted bass can be found. In the spring, you'll find the larger fish in the north end of Melones. Most of these bigger fish will be spots.

The fall bite can be excellent. During the afternoons, shad ball up and move into the flats where they are later ambushed by the bass. Drop-shotting here with four-inch shad colored worms or spooning with a 3/8 ounce silver or silver and blue Kastmaster works well. The

California Department of Fish and Game scientific aid Eric Guzmon with a Melones spotted bass taken electrofishing.

most important factor is locating offshore humps, breaks, sunken islands and flats. Many anglers are speeding by these areas so fast that they unaware of these submerged areas that exist and consequently overlook the best fishing.

This technique works through early December when the lake typically turns over.

During the winter traditionally you'll catch bigger fish, but the number of bass you catch will decrease. From mid-December through early February methods don't change from what works in fall, but you'll have to slow your retrieve and fish steeper areas to maintain success.

Spring is the easiest time to catch bass. Most fish are shallow and can be caught on worms, spinnerbaits, rip baits and

150 California Department of Fish and Game bioligist Jim Houk netted a white catfish while sampling New Melones Reservoir.

jigs. From late-June through September, night fishing is effective. Drop-shotting or Carolina rigging a Zoom black lizard with a bright blue tail, a Brush Hog or slow rolling a black spinnerbait can be deadly. Fish in roughly 20-25 feet of water or target points and sunken islands. During the day in the heat of summer, drop-shot with shad colored worms near steep drop-offs.

New Melones isn't just about bass and trout though. Bullhead grow unusually large. On my last electrofishing trip with the California Department of Fish and Game, we weighted several bullhead in the one-to-two-pound class. They have large heads and plump bodies. In many of the flats and coves they are more abundant than catfish. From April through November, expect bullhead to be in one-to-five feet of water in places where mud and silt are found. Look for the flattest coves you can find.

Catfish are also plentiful. Anglers fishing the backs of coves, island tops and near marinas from June through summer's end can find great action using cut baits soaked in Pautzke Liquid Krill or Nectar. Most cats run two-to-four pounds, however it's not uncommon to catch fish up to 15.

Hitch may be the least know species in the lake. Hitch are rarely caught by anglers, let alone targeted. Few even know they exist. Hitch aren't a gamefish. They look like a cross between a carp and a striper. In New Melones, they average one-to-three pounds, but aren't abundant. Hitch tend to school up and are most likely to be found in cover during the spring. Basically, locate them in the same places you'd expect to find bullhead. They are a native species to Melones and eat algae and insects.

Panfish are a vital part of the fishery, but not so much targeted by anglers. Bass and catfish feed heavily on the green sunfish, bluegill, crappie and

Former guide Tom Taylor with a group of New Melones bass.

red ears that are available. The key is finding a prime location. If you fish a steep bank, your success will be limited, but anglers who station themselves in the backs of coves off Highway 49 where trees and stumps can be found often find limits of half-pound crappie and as many bluegill as you want to catch.

New Melones is also an excellent trout fishery. The reservoir is heavily stocked with kokanee, rainbows and browns. Coho were planted in 1982 and chinook in 1982-83, though neither are still in the reservoir.

Sacramento Pike Minnow

Browns are definitely abundant, but they are the least common cold-water species caught at New Melones. This is most likely because they simply aren't targeted. Rainbows and kokanee are easier to catch. Nonetheless, browns are the largest coldwater species here, ranging from two-to-five pounds. Seldom are browns smaller than two pounds caught. Roughly 22,000 sub-catchable browns are planted each year.

Browns are best targeted from October through March. In the fall, they can be found staging to spawn in the creek channels and chasing kokanee. Here's the most likely locations you'll find them: Angels Creek, South Fork of the Stanislaus River, the Middle Fork of the Stanislaus River, Carson Creek and Bear Creek.

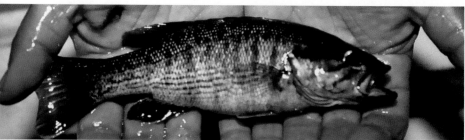
Red Eye Bass

Browns are caught on bait and lures. Guide Danny Layne says most of his browns are caught on dead shad. Slow trolling dead shad imitates a wounded baitfish. Trolling anchovies is also common. Whether trolling shad or anchovies, you'll need two hooks; a No. 4 treble hook in the spine and an egg hook in the nose. Other anglers run plugs and stickbaits. A rainbow trout pattern Rebel Minnow or Bomber Long A, a lighted J-Plug or Megabait Charlie

Hitch

swimbait are all effective. The browns can be found between 30-60 feet in the fall and then from the surface down 20 feet in the winter and early spring.

New Melones is loaded with rainbow trout, but since kokanee were introduced few anglers target the bows. The CA DFG plants 28,000 fingerling rainbow trout and 58,000 half-pound bows, but because the reservoir is so large, they can be scattered all over. Rainbows can be caught all year, but early spring is when they are easiest to catch. Toplining on the surface with Rebel Minnows, Cripplures and Thomas Buoyants on the south end is best, because here the wind pushes bait, luring the fish to follow. Other notable areas to troll are the Highway 49 Bridge, Carson Creek Arm and where the South Fork takes off from main branch of the Stanislaus. Rainbows are also available in the summer for anglers using shad imitation Luhr Jensen Mini Speed Traps 35-40 feet deep. Rainbows grow rapidly. In fact, most trout average two pounds.

Kokanee have become a major aspect of the fishery. Not only do they provide great forage for bass and trout, they are readily available to anglers with deepwater trolling gear. Kokanee are planted each year. While numbers fluctuate, to give you an idea 200,000 were planted in 2003. Size varies year by year, but it's safe to say that fish run 12-20 inches. Kokanee can be caught all

New Melones has abnormally large bullhead.

Spotted Bass

year, but the first consistent bite starts in April. Action generally starts in the Parrots Ferry Arm or Angel's Cove where toplining with Needlefish or a night crawler works well.

In June and July, the main body of New Melones tends to yield the best action. In June, kokanee are typically found in 40 feet of water and then move toward 80-90 feet in July. Several areas consistently harbor kokanee, but Rose Island, South Island, Glory Hole Point, the Spillway and Carson Cove are the most consistent producers. Running an Uncle Larry's pink Tiger, Uncle Larry's pink Triple Teaser, pink Hoochies and pink Apex is best, although you can't discount fishing a 4/0 Sep's copper Pro Dodger and corn dipped in Pautzke Nectar.

If you plan to make the trip, supplies are available in Angels Camp and Sonora.

Also nearby is Tulloch Reservoir.

Directions: *From the junction of Highway 4 and the 99 Freeway in Stockton, drive east on Highway 4 for 46.6 miles to the junction with Highway 49 in Angels Camp. Turn right and drive for 1.5 miles on Highway 4/49 to the turnoff for Highway 4 on the left. Stay on Highway 49 and drive south two miles to the right turnoff for the Glory Hole Recreation Area. Continue to the recreation area.*

A spreadsheet from the California Department of Fish and Game's electrofishing trip to New Melones Reservoir.

SALT SPRINGS VALLEY RESERVOIR

Rating: 7

Species: Crappie,
Bluegill, Largemouth
Bass and Channel
Catfish

Stocks: None

Facilities: Showers,
Restrooms, Picnic
Areas, Campgrounds,
Picnic Areas, Bait &
Tackle and a General
store

Need Information?
Contact: Salt Springs
Valley Reservoir
(209) 785-7787

Salt Springs Valley Reservoir reminds me of an enormous farm pond. It's is surrounded by gentle rolling hills, shallow, is fed by rain water, has no year-round inlet and is home to bass, panfish and catfish. The reservoir was constructed in 1856 for hydraulic mining and is used for water storage. The lake is privately run, but governed by California Department of Fish and Game regulations.

Bass is the main attraction. In the Seventies, the reservoir was overwhelmed by carp and other trash fish, however, in 1977 it dried up completely. The following year though, the CA DFG stocked Alabama strain largemouth bass. Bass are said to do well here. Nevertheless, in 2001 Salt Springs Valley Resort opted to plant Florida strain as well. Each year since, 500-1,000 fingerling bass have been planted.

Reports are sketchy when it comes to the bass fishery here. Some local anglers swear by it being the best fishery in the region. Others leave with a sour taste in their mouth. The reservoir does sport excellent cover for bass. In fact, from June through fall, weed growth can be so extensive your trolling motor can get clogged after going just a few feet. That cover protects bass and fry. On the other hand, there are some things that are questionable about the fishery.

I fished with bass pro Gary Dobyns. The first thing that crossed our minds was, "Why are there bullfrogs 30 yards from shore on mats." If there was a booming bass population, bullfrogs would refrain from venturing from shore. They obviously weren't worried about getting eaten, which doesn't say much for the bass population.

Some anglers report a two-to-three-pound average on bass. Conversely, the seven fish we caught looked to be stunted. They were long and slender. There are panfish and crawdads for bass to feed on, but no baitfish. Regardless, there are bass available. The reservoir has been governed by catch and release only fishing, but the resort lifted that in 2004 because they believed there were too many bass and the overall size was decreasing. Again, my experience was much different, but we could have just fished on a bad day.

Nonetheless, it's obvious where you should fish: there's the rocky dam, creek channels, weed beds, rocky points and several flooded chicken wire fences. Throwing topwater plugs in the morning or frogs on mats on hot days can yield bass if they are in the biting mood. Drop-shotting near the dam can be effective. For bait anglers, minnows aren't allowed, but you can soak night crawlers and crawdads.

In the spring, Salt Springs Valley is famous for its' panfish bite.

Anglers fishing in coves find that mealworms and jigs take quality fish.

If you plan to make the trip, supplies are available in Stockton. There is a day use and boat launch fee. Fishing is prohibited during duck season and three times a year when speed boat races take place. Call ahead to avoid these dates.

Also nearby are New Hogan Reservoir and New Melones Reservoir.

Directions: From Stockton on Highway 99, exit east on Highway 4 and drive roughly 30 miles to Copperopolis. Turn left on Rock Creek Road and go drive six miles to a "v" intersection. Turn left and drive two miles to the reservoir.

156 These bullfrogs grabbed artificial frogs near one of the inlets at Salt Springs Valley Reservoir. They were photographed and released. Bullfrogs are abundant in most portions of the reservoir.

NEW HOGAN RESERVOIR

Rating: 8

Species: Largemouth Bass, Striped Bass, Crappie, Bluegill and Channel Catfish

Stocks: None

Facilities: Boat Launches, Restrooms, Campgrounds, Picnic Areas, Swimming Areas, Showers and Fish Cleaning Station

Need Information? Contact: New Hogan Reservoir (209) 772-1343, Fishing Guide Danny Layne (209) 586-2383

Located roughly two hours from the Bay Area and Fresno, an hour from Sacramento and 30 minutes from Stockton, New Hogan Reservoir is a dammed portion of the Calaveras River that offers a good warmwater fishery. It's a place where anglers can have a great time, yet spend little money. The reservoir was created by the US Army Corps of Engineers and is managed as a traditional irrigation reservoir: it's allowed to fill and then is drawn down during the summer and fall when water is in demand.

Prior to 1980, New Hogan was a prime trout and bass fishery. It had a self-sustaining population of largemouth bass and saw plentiful stocks of rainbow trout from the California Department of Fish and Game. New Hogan was an excellent lake to troll and kicked out plump trout.

The fishery has since changed drastically, though. As an experiment in the early Eighties, the CA DFG introduced stripers. The stripers did better than anyone could ever have dreamed of. In what seemed like weeks, the stripers bred like rabbits and took over the lake. They ate all the trout and out-competed the largemouth bass.

New Hogan has become a top striper fishery in California, yet it's not your traditional striper reservoir. Unlike most striper waters, New Hogan only has one class size of fish. While most fisheries have trophy, average and below average fish, New Hogan's stripers all pretty much run two-to-five pounds.

Basically, Hogan's striper population has exploded. There are an enormous number of stripers, which is good and bad. Good because there are a ton of fish, yet bad since the abundance of stripers creates an overall smaller fish. The CA DFG and locals will tell you that if you are going to eat them, then take your limit of 10 stripers. If anglers can manage to reduce the number of stripers, we'll begin to see larger average size fish.

Striper fishing isn't difficult. Unfortunately, you need a boat to get in on the action. For starters, don't bother fishing from Thanksgiving through Memorial Day. While some fish can be found in deep water during that period, action is much better during the warmer months. June through August is the prime time. Concentrate on fishing in The Narrows and the main body. Downriggers can be helpful, however, many anglers simply run their lines 80 feet behind their boat with 1.5 ounces of weight to reach depths required to locate stripers. If you have a downrigger, try fishing 20-25 feet deep. It's best to run 1.2 mph. Shad and anchovies fished on a No. 2 hook and a 1/0 trail hook is best. Use a 15-pound test leader. While The Narrows can be productive, others work the area from the buoy line near the launch ramp to the south end of the dam and then over to Deer Flat.

Summer is also marked by topwater action. Anglers tossing Pencil Poppers and Zara Super Spooks in the shallows in lowlight conditions find fair action. Others simply await shad boils and toss Kastmasters and Hair Raiser jigs towards them.

If you plan to make the trip, supplies are available in Valley Springs. There is a day use fee. There's a limit of 10 stripers per day.

Also nearby are Lake Amador and Salt Springs Valley Reservoir.

Directions: *From Stockton, drive east on Highway 26 to Valley Springs. From Valley Springs, follow signs to New Hogan Reservoir. The route is well signed.*

Photo Caption (Right) Guide Danny Layne uses slow rolled shad and anchovies to catch stripers at New Hogan.

158 An average New Hogan striped bass.

ANGELS CREEK (LOWER)

Rating: 3

Species: Rainbow Trout

Stocked with 1,600 pounds of rainbow trout.

Facilities: None

Need Information?
Contact: Calaveras County Chamber of Commerce
(800) 225-3764

The town of Angels Creek is a tourist town with the contemporary retail stores and mom-and-pop shops that are common in the Motherlode. Angels Camp is a hot spot for visitors to the area; however, anglers might want to look elsewhere for a place to dip their lines. While rainbow trout are planted by the California Department of Fish and Game, Angels Creek runs right through Angels Camp's business district and access to the creek is subsequently the pits.

Decent access can be found just upstream of town in Tryon Park, but it is plagued by fast flowing water and swift currents. There is also a smidgen of public access where the stream crosses under Highway 4 in town, but overgrown berry bushes can make casting here sour. The best and most likely only way to catch the fish is with Balls 'O Fire eggs plucked under an overhanging bank.

The only advantage the lower section has over the upper section is that it's open year-round.

If you plan to make the trip, supplies are available in Angels Camp. There is a lot of private property along the stream. Please respect no tresspassing signs.

Also nearby are Angels Creek (Upper) and White Pines Lake.

Directions: *From the junction of Highway 4 and the 99 Freeway in Stockton drive east on Highway 4 for 46.6 miles to the junction with Highway 49. Turn right and drive for 1.5 miles on Highway 4/49 to the turnoff for Highway 4 on the left. Turn left and continue two-tenths of a mile to Tryon Park on the left.*

Angels Creek (Lower) is open to fishing all year.

Rating: 5

Species: Rainbow Trout

Stocked with 1,600 pounds of rainbow trout.

Facilities: Restrooms and a Playground

Need Information? Contact: Calaveras County Chamber of Commerce (800) 225-3764

What a difference a few miles make! The upper stretch of Angels Creek near Murphys is an angler's paradise compared to the section downstream in Angels Camp. The upper section is much calmer; the man-made rock walls provide great structure and good habitat for trout. And its pools are suitable for all types of angling.

Like its lower counterpart, this small, low gradient stream is also stocked within rock throwing distance of a business district, but this time located in the town of Arnold. However, this well maintained community park allows your mind to sway far away from Arnold's tourist-filled streets. Plants take place both above and below the bridge, yet the best catch rates are found directly in front of the local library. Both locals and out-of-towners fish here, therefore casting next to other anglers is a good possibility. As bait dunkers do best, white Captain America Power Bait is your best bet.

If you plan to make the trip, supplies are available in Arnold. Angels Creek (Upper) is closed to fishing from Nov. 16 to the last Saturday in April.

Also nearby are Angels Creek (Lower) and White Pines Lake.

Directions: *From the junction of Highway 4 and the 99 Freeway in Stockton drive east on Highway 4 for 46.6 miles to the junction with Highway 49. Turn right and drive for 1.5 miles on Highway 4/49 to the turnoff for Highway 4 on the left. Turn left and continue 8.2 miles to Main Street in Murphys. Turn left and drive a half-mile to Algiers Street. Turn left and continue one-tenth of a mile to Murphys Community Park.*

Angels Creek (Upper)

WHITE PINES LAKE

Rating: 5

Species: Rainbow Trout

Stocked with 2,750 pounds of rainbow trout.

Facilities: Restrooms, Picnic Area, Swimming Area and a Playground

Need Information? Contact: Calaveras County Chamber of Commerce (800) 225-3764

For families living in the Motherlode Region there are few places better than White Pines Lake to introduce kids to fishing. Situated near the town of Arnold in a heavily wooded area, the 26-acre lake is a year-round fishery with aspects of both cold and warm water fishing. The lake is planted with rainbow trout and also harbors catfish and bluegill. Bobber fishing can be exceptional for those fishing a worm down 18 inches from the surface. Weeds make spin fishing tough though.

This small, but exceptional family-style park offers an alternative to the stream fishing found at nearby Angels Creek. At 3,820 feet the pond has lots of tules, but there are also openings to allow for access. The dam area is a great spot. Formally an old mill site, the lake can become too warm for trout by August. Because no gas-powered motors are permitted the lake always stays quiet. Luckily, rowdies don't often come here.

If you plan to make the trip, supplies are available in Arnold.

Also nearby are Angels Creek (Upper and Lower).

Directions: *From the junction of Highway 4 and the 99 Freeway in Stockton, drive east on Highway 4 for 46.6 miles to the junction with Highway 49. Turn right and drive for 1.5 miles on Highway 4/49 to the turnoff for Highway 4 on the left. Turn left and continue 20.5 miles to Blagen Road. Turn left and drive one-tenth of a mile to White Pines Park on the left.*

White Pines Lake

Rating: 7

Species: Rainbow Trout
and Brown Trout

Stocked with 2,700
pounds of rainbow
trout.

Facilities: Restrooms
and Picnic Areas

Need Information?
Contact: Calaveras Big
Trees State Park
(209) 795-2334

Almost no one, outside of a few locals, comes to the Lower North Fork of the Stanislaus River only to fish. Oftentimes tourists who come to visit the giant sequoia trees take their children down to the river to fish. There are two areas of Big Trees State Park that hold sequoias: the heavily visited north grove and the overlooked south grove. The river is found near the south grove, so a day long trip jam packed with fishing and viewing the sequoias is an option. The river offers drive-to access and gorgeous swimming holes during the warmer months.

If you have children, it may be better to take them to nearby Beaver Creek where angling is much more suitable for youngsters. The Lower North Fork of the Stanislaus isn't a great place to introduce kids to fishing. The river is wide and flows fast and swift. Beaver is much calmer and more pool oriented.

There are many wild rainbow and brown trout in the river. However, fishing for them isn't for beginners. The California Department of Fish and Game dumps 5,320 rainbow trout in the river each year to give tourists an easy alternative to the harder to catch wild fish, yet many anglers who aren't experienced in reading water correctly still don't have a lot of success. Being such a large river with many deep holes, just about any technique works if you fish the right spots. Tossing Orange Deluxe salmon eggs behind large boulders, fly fishing and spin casting works well.

If you plan to make the trip, supplies are available in Arnold. There is a day use fee to enter the state park. The Lower North Fork of the Stanislaus River is closed to fishing from November 16 to the last Saturday in April. The river is also planted at Boards Crossing, which can be reached from Dorrington and off USFS Road #5N02 near Sourgrass. The road to the river closes in the winter.

Also nearby are White Pines Lake and Angels Creek.

Directions: *From the junction of Highway 4 and the 99 Freeway in Stockton, drive east on Highway 4 for 46.6 miles to the junction with Highway 49. Turn right and drive for 1.5 miles on Highway 4/49 to the turnoff for Highway 4 on the left. Turn left and continue 23.4 miles to the turnoff on the right for Calaveras Big Trees State Park. Turn right and drive 5.8 miles towards the south grove to the river crossing..*

BEAVER CREEK

Rating: 6

Species: Rainbow Trout and Brown Trout

Stocked with 1,100 pounds of rainbow trout.

Facilities: Restrooms, Primitive Campgrounds and Picnic Area

Need Information? Contact: Calaveras Big Trees State Park (209) 795-2334

If you live in the Motherlode Region and are looking for a small stream that maintains enough volume of water year-round to support the stocking of rainbow trout and you want to avoid crowds, Beaver Creek is your place. Located near the Lower North Fork of the Stanislaus River, Beaver Creek is situated in Calaveras Big Trees State Park and has all the attributes of a secret water hole.

Beaver Creek is one of the least fished waters along Highway 4 that gets planted by the California Department of Fish and Game. The creek is quite user friendly. Long, shallow runs make for high catch rates on more than 2,100 planted rainbow trout between a half-pound and three-quarters of a pound. Few larger fish are caught. For the best results, park at the end of the road and fish the vicinity of Beaver Picnic Area.

Beaver is also a good place to practice fly fishing. There's enough room along the bank to cast, while slow moving runs and shallow pools make for an easy presentation. Fishing bait can be deadly. Try using white Predator or Power Bait and you should catch a quick limit. Tossing small yellow and black or black and red Panther Martins is also worthy of some time. There are a few small pools perfect for drowning spinners.

If you plan to make the trip, supplies are available in Arnold. There is a day use fee to enter the state park. Beaver Creek is closed to fishing from November 16 to the last Saturday in April. The river is also planted off USFS Road #5N02 near Sourgrass. The road to the creek closes in the winter.

Also nearby are White Pines Lake and Angels Creek.

Directions: *From the junction of Highway 4 and the 99 Freeway in Stockton, drive east on Highway 4 for 46.6 miles to the junction with Highway 49. Turn right and drive for 1.5 miles on Highway 4/49 to the turnoff for Highway 4 on the left. Turn left and continue 23.4 miles to the turnoff on the right for Calaveras Big Trees State Park. Turn right and drive 9.2 miles to the end of the road.*

Beaver Creek

STANISLAUS RIVER (NORTH FORK, UPPER)

Rating: 7

Species: Rainbow Trout and Brown Trout

Stocked with 2,700 pounds of rainbow trout.

Facilities: Restrooms and Campgrounds

Need Information? Contact: Stanislaus National Forest (209) 795-2334

The Upper North Fork of the Stanislaus River may be nestled in a remote section of the Stanislaus National Forest, but many people still know about the river and also fish it. The river gets fished by both California and Nevada residents, most of which are on camping trips. Few people drive this far from civilization for day use purposes.

The Upper North Fork differs a lot from the Lower North Fork found downstream in Calaveras Big Trees State Park. This portion of the river has a much lower gradient, flows slower and is easier to fish. For starters, it's a great place to come for a weeklong camping trip. You can fish the river and make side trips to Spicer Meadow Reservoir, Elephant Rock Lake and Union and Utica Reservoirs.

The California Department of Fish and Game plants the river with 5,320 rainbows from the opener in April through mid August. After that, the water gets too low and warm to plant fish. As with most other waters in the region, this section of the river is planted with half-pound fish. Because the open area around the water the river is conducive to all types of fishing, and isn't difficult to fish. If you have children, break out a jar of Power Bait, Predator or drift a night crawler. More experienced anglers will take fish on nymphs and small silver or gold Panther Martins.

If you plan to make the trip, supplies are available at Alpine Lake. In early spring, call ahead for road conditions. The road may be closed due to snow. The Upper North Fork of the Stanislaus River is closed to fishing from November 16 to the last Saturday in April.

Also nearby are Alpine Lake, Calaveras Big Trees State Park and Mosquito Lakes.

Directions: *From the junction of Highway 4 and the 99 Freeway in Stockton, drive east on Highway 4 for 46.6 miles to the junction with Highway 49. Turn right and drive for 1.5 miles on Highway 4/49 to the turnoff for Highway 4 on the left. Turn left and continue 42.4 miles to Spicer Reservoir Road. Turn right and drive 3.1 miles to the river crossing.*

MOKELUMNE RIVER (MAIN STEM)

Rating: 7

Species: Kokanee, Rainbow Trout and Brown Trout

Stocked with 1,000 pounds of rainbow trout.

Facilities: Restrooms

Need Information? Contact: Bureau of Land Management (916) 985-4474

This lower section of the Mokelumne River isn't the kind of place you want to take a kid fishing. Closed from November 16 to the last Saturday in April, the river can be difficult to fish in the spring when snow runoff leaves the river full of rapids and nearly barren of pools and slow moving water. Every other week from April through July the California Department of Fish & Game stocks rainbow trout, totaling roughly 200 each plant.

When fishing the 50-100 foot wide river, make sure you aren't on private property. The Bureau of Land Management maintains the river upstream from the private lands. Though rainbows are planted, the majority of anglers fish for wild browns that swim up from Lake Pardee. By July, the river subsides enough to make fishing easier and pools clearly visible. Try casting white, red and black Panther Martins and silver and blue Kastmasters.

Catching kokanee is a possibility in the fall, though they aren't in a biting mood. Kokanee swim out of Pardee Reservoir and up the Mokelumne to spawn.

If you plan to make the trip, supplies are available in Jackson and Mokelumne Hill. The river is closed to fishing from November 16 to the last Saturday in April.

Also nearby are Rancho Seco Lake, Lake Amador, Tiger Creek Afterbay and Tabeaud Reservoir.

Directions: *From the junction of Interstate 5 and Highway 50 in Sacramento, drive east on Highway 50 for approximately five miles to Highway 16. Drive east on Highway 16 for roughly 32 miles to Highway 49. Turn right on Highway 49 and drive 8.4 miles to the junction with Highway 88. Turn left on Highway 49/88 and drive two miles to a stop sign. Highway 88 veers off to the left. Continue straight on Highway 49 and drive 3.7 miles to Electra Road. Turn left and drive 1.5 miles to the fishing area.*

The Mokelumne River above Lake Pardee

CONSUMNES RIVER (MIDDLE FORK)

Rating: 6

Species: Rainbow Trout and Brown Trout

Stocked with 900 pounds of rainbow trout.

Facilities: Restrooms, Picnic Area and Campgrounds

Need Information? Contact: El Dorado National Forest (530) 647-5314

The Middle Fork of the Consumnes River is one of the last streams in the Sierra that offers good fishing and isn't overloaded with anglers. While many fishermen pluck bait, fly fish and toss spinners in the Consumnes River at Pi Pi Campground, this section of the Middle Fork rarely gets to the point where there are too many anglers and too few fish.

The California Department of Fish and Game plants 1,660 rainbow trout in the Comsumnes which is located at 4,000 Feet in the El Dorado National Forest. It's roughly 30-45 minutes from Jackson. The river meanders through a heavily wooded area and offers riffles, small runs and pools. Amazingly enough, you'll find bait fishermen, fly anglers and spin casters fishing simultaneously.

To put things in perspective, there's only a quarter-mile long section of the Consumnes River that provides good fishing for planted trout. This has to do with where plants take place. If you stray too far up or downriver from the campground, you'll catch a few planters, but mostly smaller wild trout.

This section of the Consumnes River is best approached with bait. Spinners and spoons can be effective; on the other hand, many of the pools and runs aren't large enough to properly work them. A jar of Orange Deluxe Pautzke salmon eggs show up well on the river bottom, although many anglers choose to nymph under an indicator.

If you plan to make the trip, supplies are available in Jackson. The Consumnes River (Middle Fork) is closed to fishing from November 16 to the last Saturday in April. In winter and early spring, call ahead for road conditions. The road may be closed due to snow.

Also nearby are Tiger Creek Afterbay, Bear River Reservoir and Silver Lake.

Consumnes River (Middle Fork)

Directions: *From Jackson at the junction of Highway's 49-88, take Highway 88 east for 26.3 miles to Omo Ranch Road. Turn left and drive seven-tenths of a mile to the right turnoff for Pi Pi Road. Turn right and drive 5.5 miles to Pi Pi Campground.*

166

BEAR RIVER RESERVOIR (LOWER)

Rating: 8

Species: Rainbow Trout, Brown Trout and Lake Trout

Stocked with 9,000 pounds of rainbow trout and 3,000 pounds of brown trout.

Facilities: Restaurant, Restrooms, Campgrounds, Picnic Areas, General Store, Boat Launch, Gas, Showers, Playground, Bar, Boat Rentals and Lodging

Need Information? Contact: Bear River Reservoir Resort (209) 295-4868

Bear River Reservoir is a great place for anglers who enjoy having great fishing coupled with all the amenities. The reservoir is heavily planted with rainbow and brown trout, has a fair population of lake trout and also is equipped with a marina, general store, hot showers, campgrounds, a bar, restaurant and many other necessities that help to make a great camping trip.

Located off Highway 88 between Jackson and South Lake Tahoe, the 746-acre reservoir situated at 5,800 feet in the El Dorado National Forest is planted with 7,200 brown trout and 13,000 rainbow trout by the California Department of Fish and Game. Each year, Bear River Reservoir Resort also plants 2,000 pounds of three-to-nine-pound trout for their fishing derbies. Bear River Reservoir isn't known as a trophy fishery per say, yet it does offer the opportunity to catch large trout.

The great thing is that trollers and bank anglers can do well. While Bear River is not accessible in the winter and early spring, anglers topdining three-inch Rebel Holographic minnows, frog pattern Thomas Buoyants, a Sep's Pro dodger behind a night crawler or any Needlefish will do well. You'll catch a mix of rainbows and browns.

For shore anglers, the dam area, marina and just about any point or cove offers the chance to catch trout if you are casting red Cripplures, gold Krocodiles or floating dough baits or night crawlers off the bottom.

While the reservoir doesn't have an enormous population of lake trout, there are enough available for anglers to target. Many folks will jig Crippled Herrings and Megabait Live jigs in deep water. Others troll rainbow trout pattern Bomber Long A's or Diamond King spoons. Most of the lake trout are one-to-three pounds, but each year fish in the teens are caught.

If you plan to make the trip, supplies are available in at the lake.

Also nearby is Silver Lake.

Directions: *From the junction of Interstate 5 and Highway 50 in Sacramento, drive east for five miles to the Power Inn Road/Howe exit. Turn right off the freeway and drive one-tenth of a mile to Folsom Blvd. Turn left and drive six-tenths of a mile to Jackson Road. Turn right and continue 30.5 miles to Highway 49. Veer right and drive 10.7 miles to the Highway 88 turnoff in Jackson. Turn left on Highway 88 and drive 38.6 miles to the right turnoff for Bear River Reservoir Road. Drive two miles and turn left. Continue one-half mile to the resort.*

SCHAADS RESERVOIR

Rating: 5

Species: Rainbow Trout, Channel Catfish, Bluegill and Largemouth Bass

Stocked with 4,650 pounds of rainbow trout.

Facilities: Restrooms

Need Information?
Contact: El Dorado National Forest
(530) 647-5314

It was a warm summer day when I arrived at a locked gate near the entrance to Schaads Reservoir. The sign said the road was to be closed in the winter, yet open the remainder of the year. I was a little confused to find the gate closed, but still looked forward to a day of fishing, so I walked the half-mile to the reservoir and found a parking lot filled with boat trailers and cars. After catching and releasing a half-dozen trout, I walked back to my car when a man and his two kids pulled alongside me.

"Why are you walking?" he said. "Why didn't you just drive?"

I smiled, trying to not show I was an out-of-towner.

"The gate was locked," I said.

"Locked?" he laughed. "It's not locked. Just push it open."

The man's six-year old jumped out of the car to show me. Locked it was, but not latched. I guess you had to be a local to know the routine. The man said it keeps city slickers away.

Schadds Reservoir is a small, 55-acre reservoir near Plymouth. It's a marginal put-and-take fishery that takes a bit of pressure off some of the other larger reservoirs nearby. It's a place for locals to take their kids and troll a night crawler and a flasher and catch pan-size rainbow trout. Roughly 9,000 rainbow trout are planted by the California Department of Fish and Game each year. Rarely are trout better than one-pound caught. There's no need for a full size boat. Canoes, float tubes and car top boats are more than enough.

Shoreline fishing can also be effective for the angler who soaks Power Bait or inflates night crawlers off the bottom. In fact, if you fish a mini crawler below a bobber you'll have a fair chance at small bass and bluegill as well.

If you plan to make the trip, supplies are available in Jackson. The last half-mile of the road to the reservoir is closed in the winter. However, walk-in fishing is allowed. No gas-powered motors are permitted.

Also nearby is Tiger Creek Afterbay.

Schaads Reservoir

Directions: *From Jackson, drive south on Highway 26/49 for 7.2 miles to Mokelumne Hill. Turn left on Highway 26 and drive 14 miles to Associate Office Road. Turn right, drive a half-mile and turn right on Railroad Flat Road. Continue 1.1 miles and veer left on Blue Mountain Road. Continue 3.2 miles and turn left on Forest Service Road 6N03 (Schaad Road). Continue 1.6 miles to the right turnoff for the reservoir.*

TABEAUD RESERVOIR

Rating: 5

Species: Rainbow Trout

Stocked with 600 pounds of rainbow trout.

Facilities: Restrooms and Picnic Area

Need Information? Contact: Amador County Chamber of Commerce (209) 223-0350

With Highways 88 and 49 running directly through town, residents of Jackson hardly know what it feels like to live a day without thousands of tourists crowding their streets. There is one place locals can retreat to and escape out of town visitors: Tabeaud Reservoir. Hidden about six miles out of city limits, few tourists know about the little 44-acre reservoir. Most that do choose not to bother fishing it anyway. The reservoir is planted with 1,060 rainbow trout from April through July and doesn't hold any larger fish.

With boating and float tubing prohibited, coupled with the small allotment of trout, tourists leave the lake alone. But, those who take the time to fish do have a shot at doing well. The CA DFG tosses 100 fish a week in. The fish quickly scatter throughout the reservoir, but the patient angler soaking Power Bait or a juicy night crawler shouldn't have a problem catching a few.

If you plan to make the trip supplies are available in Jackson.

Also nearby are Rancho Seco Lake, Lake Amador, Tiger Creek Afterbay and Mokelumne River.

Directions: *From the junction of Interstate 5 and Highway 50 in Sacramento, drive east on Highway 50 for approximately five miles to Highway 16. Drive east on Highway 16 for roughly 32 miles to Highway 49. Turn right on Highway 49 and drive 8.4 miles to the junction with Highway 88. Turn left on Highway 49/88, drive two miles to a stop sign. Highway 88 veers off to the left. Continue straight on Highway 49 and drive six-tenths of a mile to Clinton Road. Turn left and drive 6.5 miles to the lake on the right.*

Tabeaud Reservoir

TIGER CREEK AFTERBAY

Rating: 6

Species: Rainbow Trout and Brown Trout

Stocked with 1,350 pounds of rainbow trout.

Facilities: Restrooms and Picnic Areas

Need Information? Contact: El Dorado National Forest (530) 644-6048

While only rainbow trout are planted at Tiger Creek Afterbay, surprisingly, anglers do better catching browns. No browns are stocked, but wild browns are abundant in the Mokelumne River, which is one of three water sources that feed Tiger Creek Afterbay.

Released from Salt Creek Reservoir, the Mokelumne feeds the Afterbay from the east. A pumping plant used to generate hydroelectric power releases water from the Tiger Creek Canal due north of the Mokelumne and Tiger Creek, and empties into the Afterbay north of the powerhouse.

The 70-acre Afterbay is restricted to shoreline fishing. No boats or float tubes are permitted. The steep reservoir has several access points: the dam, alongside Tiger Creek Road, at Tiger Creek Picnic Area and between the powerhouse and the Mokelumne. Acknowledging that most trout swim upriver after being stocked (and don't stay in the reservoir) the smartest anglers fish upstream of this rapid flowing area.

There is a trail that parallels the creek for at least a quarter-mile. Joining some wild rainbows, the California Department of Fish & Game plants 2,600 rainbows each spring in the Afterbay, most of which are caught on small Rapalas, Panther Martins and Kastmasters. The rainbows are a mere half-pound, whereas the browns range from one-to-four.

If you plan to make the trip, supplies are available in Pioneer.

Also nearby are Rancho Seco Lake, Lake Amador, Tabeaud Reservoir and Mokelumne River.

Tiger Creek Afterbay

Directions: *From the junction of Interstate 5 and Highway 50 in Sacramento, drive east on Highway 50 for approximately five miles to Highway 16. Drive east on Highway 16 for roughly 32 miles to Highway 49. Turn right on Highway 49 and drive 8.4 miles to the junction with Highway 88. Turn left on Highway 49/88, drive two miles and make a left on Highway 88 (stop sign). Continue 17 miles to Tiger Creek Road and turn right. Drive 2.1 miles and veer left at a "t" intersection. Continue eight-tenths of a mile to the Tiger Creek Day-Use area.*

LAKE AMADOR

Rating: 9

Species: Rainbow Trout, Channel Catfish, Blue Catfish, Crappie, Largemouth Bass, Smallmouth Bass, Carp and Bluegill

Stocked with 156,300 pounds of rainbow trout and 3,000 pounds of channel catfish.

Facilities: Campgrounds, Picnic Areas, Boat Launch, Bait & Tackle, General Store, Café, Boat Rentals, Fishing Piers, Restrooms, RV Hookups, Gas, Swimming Area, Waterslide, Showers and Lodging

Need Information? Contact: Lake Amador (209) 274-4739

What is the best trout fishery in the Sacramento and San Joaquin Valleys? Try Lake Amador, a 485-acre lake in the foothills between Stockton and Sacramento. What makes Amador such a fabulous fishing lake? Pure stocking numbers and the size of fish that are stocked easily outdo any other lake in the region. Amador ranks up there with the great pay lakes of Southern California, Laguna Niguel and Irvine Lake. Lake Amador Resort plants more than 150,000 pounds of a unique breed of trout called the Donaldson Trout.

To better appreciate the Donaldson Trout, here's how Amador acquired the strain. In 1944, a professor named Donaldson tried to produce the ultimate trout for a fly-fisherman to catch. After crossbreeding strains of trout, the professor thought he had come up with the ultimate trout. The Donaldson, a 50-percent rainbow, 30-percent cutthroat and 20-percent silver salmon, was a great fighter and could live in warmer water.

The hype of the trout lasted for a few years in the United States, but then seemed to die off. Over the years the Donaldson eggs were transported to Sweden and could no longer be found in the US. In the early Nineties, Lake Amador Resort operators began importing the eggs from overseas and raising Donaldson trout at a hatchery below the lake. Currently Amador no longer needs to import eggs. They now have their own strain of broodstocks.

The California Department of Fish & Game plants 9,800 rainbow trout, all under a pound. Lake Amador refuses to stock fish smaller than two pounds, and plants some up to 10 pounds. The lake record is slightly under 17 pounds. So what do these trout look like? Well, the males have hook jaws and resemble a brown trout, while the female's chrome gives her the likeness of a steelhead.

Trout fishing slows from June through September when temperatures soar into the 100's, but the trout can live year-round in the 200-feet deep lake run by the Jackson Valley Irrigation District and fed by the 52-square mile watershed of Jackson Creek. During the warmer months, the trout stay in 50-75 feet of water and can be caught by drifting Power Bait or slow trolling a night crawler behind a set of flashers. You want to keep the troll slow enough to where the blades barely turn.

As summer tapers off and temperatures cool, the trout regenerate into feeding mode. Fishing is exceptional from October through May. Trolling small orange Rapalas in the top 20 feet of the lake works well. However, the absolute best way to catch fish is trolling a white mini jig behind two-pound test at 2 mph. When is the best time to catch the Donaldson's? Either 8 a.m., noon, or 3 p.m. Why? Because that's when they are fed in the pens before they are released into the lake. You don't need a boat to catch fish at Amador. Anglers do well soaking Power Bait off the dam, in coves or casting from one of the fishing piers.

Amador isn't only a trout lake; all species thrive here, including bass. There are both large and smallmouth bass, as well as northern and Florida strain. The lake record largemouth is a tad more than 17 pounds, then again with such a great deal of forage in the lake, bigger ones will most likely be caught in the near future. Along with the trout that the CA DFG plants, there is an enormous population of threadfin shad for the bass to feed on. During the spawn use spinnerbaits, jigs and night crawlers in coves. Then as the spawning period ends in late April/early May, concentrate your efforts on points.

Only 3,000 pounds of catfish are planted each year, but a self-sustaining population of blue and channel cats keep nighttime fishing good during the warmer months. Cats from 20-40 pounds are caught regularly. Good pan fish action is also had. Red ear reach three pounds, crappie 4.5 and bluegill, two.

If you plan to make the trip, supplies are available at the lake. No water-skiing is permitted. There is a day-use and fishing fee.

Also nearby are Rancho Seco Lake, Tiger Creek Afterbay, Tabeaud Reservoir and Mokelumne River.

Directions: From the junction of Highways 50 and 99 in Sacramento, drive south on Highway 99 for 20 miles to the Jackson exit (Highway 104). Drive east on Highway 104 for 25.3 miles to the junction of Highway 104 and 88. Turn right on Highway 88 and drive less than one-tenth of a mile to Jackson Valley Road on the left. Turn left and continue two miles to a sign for Lake Amador. Turn left and drive one-mile to the lake.

Cannon downriggers can help anglers catch fish at Amador during the summer months.

Region The Delta

MONTEZUMA SLOUGH

Montezuma Slough historically has been known as one of the better sloughs for sturgeon in the Delta system. However, anglers who have been keeping tabs in recent years have noticed the system hasn't been as productive. According to the experts like Captain Jack Findleton and Mark Delnero who fish the slough daily, the problem is related to boat traffic. In 2002, a new boat launch on Montezuma opened the door for increased traffic. This slough is fairly shallow (even for the Delta) and with boats racing through the system the sturgeon are easily spooked. Nonetheless, for educated and lucky anglers, the slough can still yield good action.

Sturgeon are best fished in late winter and early spring when they wander through for food. Try to locating clam beds. You'll find sturgeon there for sure. Run through the water slow and keep a close eye on your meter looking for previously plotted known clam beds as well as hunting for new possibilities. Take this piece of advice from Delnero. "Clams are like wildflowers. They die and move to other areas."

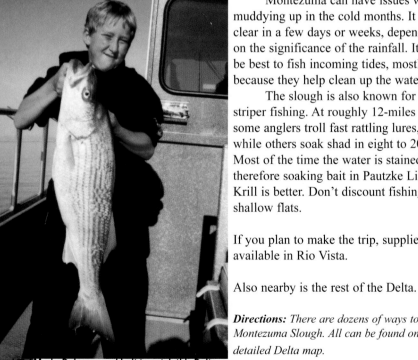

Montezuma can have issues with muddying up in the cold months. It can clear in a few days or weeks, depending on the significance of the rainfall. It can be best to fish incoming tides, mostly because they help clean up the water.

The slough is also known for its' striper fishing. At roughly 12-miles long, some anglers troll fast rattling lures, while others soak shad in eight to 20 feet. Most of the time the water is stained, therefore soaking bait in Pautzke Liquid Krill is better. Don't discount fishing shallow flats.

If you plan to make the trip, supplies are available in Rio Vista.

Also nearby is the rest of the Delta.

Directions: *There are dozens of ways to reach Montezuma Slough. All can be found on a detailed Delta map.*

174 Marky Delnero used bait to catch this Delta striper on shrimp during the winter.

Rating: 7

Species: Sturgeon, Stripers, Steelhead, Smallmouth Bass, Bullhead and Channel Catfish

Stocks: None

Facilities: Boat Launches

Need Information? Contact: Fishing Guide Jack Findleton of Sacramento Sportfishing (916) 487-3392

It's no secret that when you're talking pure numbers of fish, there is no better inland striper fishery than The Delta. However, the Delta is a big place, so for anglers to be successful, it's best to make sure you're fishing where stripers are sure to come through. Although some stripers are residents, the Sacramento River Deepwater Channel is an excellent place for anglers to target those swimming up the system to spawn in the Sacramento, American, Feather and Yuba Rivers.

Bait fishing is popular, but trolling may be the quickest way to put fish in the boat. Drag a six-inch DJ-30 series broken-back Rebel on 20-pound test. Some anglers, like fishing guide Jack Findleton of Sacramento Sportfishing, use a seven-inch Zoom Trick worm as a trailer on the Rebel to increase catch rates. Run the Rebels between 2-2.5 mph.

Trolling is best from February through May. Typically, fishing doesn't pick up until water temperatures increase after winter. By April, stripers are usually thick in this area. In May stripers are still attainable, but many of those fish will be downstreamers.

While most of the Sacramento River Deepwater Channel is deep, keep in mind that stripers don't key in on deep water. Fish shallow flats, sand bars and areas where current isn't strong. Stay out of fishing the main channel. I'm sure you'll spot many boats anchored in the middle, but those folks are likely fishing for sturgeon, not stripers.

Here's a list of hot spots. Beginning at the point where the San Joaquin and Sacramento Rivers meet, and working upstream concentrate on these areas; try Broad Slough, Sherman Island, Decker Island, Sandy Beach and The Old Dairy. The Old Dairy is a nice flat just below the Rio Vista Bridge, across from the Coast Guard Station. Above the bridge, your best bet is fishing in the area known as Cliffhouse Shoals, which is directly in front of the Cliffhouse Restaurant and Marina. Moving upstream, the mouth of the

A 15-pound striper was no match for Brandi Koerner and her broken-back Rebel.

175

Sacramento River is a good staging area for stripers.

Rain can be a pain. It can turn the water brown and muddy, and hurts fishing. When the conditions occur, you'll need to change tactics. Use a lure that rattles or live bait, and add some sort of fish attractant. Pautzke Liquid Krill is best. Essentially, it's always best to try and find the clearest water in the system.

Sturgeon fishing

There isn't much shoreline access, but some bank fishing areas can be found at Sherman Island, the Rio Vista fishing pier and along Sandy Beach. From shore, bait is the play. Shad, sardines, anchovies, shrimp, oriental gobies, bullhead and mudsuckers work best.

If you plan to make the trip, supplies are available in Rio Vista and Sacramento. A Delta Enhancement stamp is needed to fishing for stripers in The Delta.

Directions: *There are dozens of access points from Rio Vista to Sacramento. Please consult a map for the one that best suits your needs.*

Captain Jack Findleton and a 12-pound striper caught shallow water trolling.

SACRAMENTO RIVER DEEPWATER CHANNEL (DECKER AND SHERMAN ISLAND)

Rating: 8

Species: Chinook Salmon, Steelhead, Largemouth Bass, Channel Catfish, Crappie, Bluegill, Striped Bass and Sturgeon

Stocks: None

Facilities: Marinas, Boat Launches, Bait & Tackle, Gas, Restaurant and General Store

Need Information? Contact: Fishing Guide Captain Jack Findleton of Sacramento Sport Fishing Guides (800) 344-4871, Fin Addict Sportfishing Guide Mark Delnero (209) 367-4665

Many anglers confuse the Sacramento River with the Sacramento River Deepwater Channel. There is a big difference. The Sacramento River Deepwater Channel is a manmade waterway used by large ships, vessels and of course, fish. The section of the deepwater channel we are discussing is located downriver from the confluence of the Sacramento River and the Sacramento River Deepwater Channel. This area, adjacent to Sherman and Decker Island, is known as a highway for fish looking to reach their spawning areas.

The Sacramento River Deepwater Channel is one of the most productive areas to sturgeon fish in the Delta. All sturgeon who are planning on spawning in the Sacramento River or any of the sloughs above Rio Vista must pass through. The key is knowing where to fish. Unfortunately, there isn't a definitive answer.

Consider this analogy, courtesy of Captain Jack Findleton of Sacramento Sport Fishing Guides: *Someone from Sacramento wants to drive through the Central Valley to Southern California. There are several roads one could use to get there. You could take 99, 5 or a number of small side roads to accomplish your goal. The same goes for sturgeon. While there are places sturgeon are more likely to use as their highway, not all fish follow the same path. Just as we would stop and eat at a Burger King or Del Taco, the sturgeon veer off their path to feed.*

There are several theories as to where sturgeon are commonly caught, remember these can easily be broken. Some fish cruise flats, others stay in the channel and some hang out in deep holes, but no one is reliably consistent. Definitely though, there's no correct answer. There are three ways to catch sturgeon: 1) get lucky 2) see fish jumping and move into their path 3) fish in a channel or depression in the river. (Depressions are known to retain food that gets washed down the river.)

Sturgeon can be caught in this area year round. However, there is a definite season when action is best. When the leaves fall off trees, temperatures drop and heavy rainfall begins, you'll best be able to nab sturgeon. December through March is ideal. After March, many of the sturgeon move back into the bay or to saltwater to chase anchovies and sardines.

The area from Pittsburg to Cash Slough has one of the highest concentrations of fish in the Delta. Here's a list of the more consistent areas: Broad Slough, Sherman Lake, Sherman Island, Decker Island, Light 14,

Channel by the Old Dairy, Rio Vista Bridge, the holes off Cliffhouse Shoals and Cash Slough.

Standard gear consists of a seven-foot rod with a fast tip, rigged with 20-30 pound test on the main line, and a 50-pound or stainless steel leader. Several baits are noteworthy: ghost shrimp, lamprey, shad, bullhead, grass shrimp and mud shrimp.

Additionally, a trick to fishing for sturgeon is watching the weather. Storms, fog, wind and other wintry factors can keep anglers off the water for days, if not weeks at a time. Action is best when runoff is heavy, but not so heavy that the river is unfishable. It's also important to fish in moving tides. Moving tides stir up the bottom, revealing food deposits which cue the sturgeon into feeding mode.

If you plan to make the trip, supplies are available in Rio Vista. Only sturgeon between 46-72 inches can be kept. However, it is recommended that anglers catch and release all fish to preserve the fishery.

Also nearby is Montezuma Slough.

Directions: *There are dozens of access points along the Delta. Please consult a Delta map for your best options.*

Captain Mark Delnero and an undersize sturgeon.

FRANK'S TRACT

Rating: 8

Species: Steelhead, Chinook Salmon, Channel Catfish, Sturgeon, Striped Bass, Largemouth Bass, Crappie, Bluegill, Bullhead and Carp

Stocks: None

Facilities: None

Need Information? Contact: Randy Pringle of The Fishing Instructor Guide Service (209) 543-6260, Hook, Line & Sinker (925) 684-0668

The greater Delta region is full of opportunities to catch an array of cold and warm water species. However, there is so much water to learn it can take anglers a lifetime to fish it all. If you plan to do largemouth bass fishing, Frank's Tract is a good meter as to where to start.

What sets Frank's Tract aside from many other areas of the Delta is that Frank's offers good spawning grounds for bass. Ironically, the spawn doesn't take place in a familiar area. According to Delta bass expert and professional fishing guide Randy "The Fishing Instructor" Pringle, bass in Frank's Tract spawn roughly 300-400 yards offshore.

The criterion for a successful bass population is intact here and should remain for decades. You have calm water and a pebbly bottom, which is proper for bass eggs to be incubated. Most of the Delta's bottom is comprised of silt. Thankfully, that's not the case here. Frank's sand and pebble like bottom is conducive to a successful spawn.

Stemming off the San Joaquin River, Frank's Tract is roughly two miles wide and has more than 10 miles of shoreline. The area is dominated by shallow and flat contour. The shorelines are made up of levees comprised of rock walls, tules and lily pads.

The tract has a good mixture of bass. At times, you'll catch dozens of one-to-two-pound bass. Others times you'll find groups of six-to-10-pound fish. The ingredients for rapid growing conditions are in place; shad and crawdads are readily available.

From June through the first week of November, the early morning and late evening topwater bite can be excellent. The topwater bite shouldn't expire until the water temperatures drop below 60 degrees. Because it's a shallow water fishery, topwater is a mainstay.

Fishing during optimum tides is important. Low tide is best. When the water has receded, it enables anglers to fish the outside of weed lines more effectively. Try a Berkeley Frenzy or a Pop-R in a trout or shad pattern. Buzzbaits work well during this

Guide Randy Pringle with a Frank's Tract largemouth taken on a white spinnerbait.

period. Target the back of, on top of and inside the weed lines and in front of the tules.

Frank's Tract

From June through October bait is in moving water, which is where you'll find bass also. The back bay bite slows tremendously during the warmer months. On the other hand, when the water temperature drops below 60 degrees the bait moves into bays and flats and the fish follow.

Fall can yield an excellent bite. The Delta region doesn't have a true three month fall. A rapid transition between the summer and winter takes place in weeks. As water temperatures fall, bass sense that it's time to feed heavily in preparation for winter. They position themselves on eddies located out of the main current to ambush shad.

The fall bite typically is spectacular. However, anglers need to be aware of indications that a fall bite is near. Consistency of weather patterns is important. When the air temperature falls from the 90's in the afternoons to the 70's and cooler nights prevail, you'll see a sharp drop in water temperature. Traditionally, this occurs in early October. Speaking of water temperature, get your thermometers out. The magic number is 60 degrees. The fall bass bite is best in the low 60's to high 50's. Any colder and you can call it winter.

Crankbait fishing is promising in the fall. Use a No. 4 or 5 Strike King or half-ounce Frenzy. Nonetheless, if you can't find the strike zone, even a crankbait won't save the day. The strike zone in Frank's Tract differs from that in a lowland bass lake. The Delta has lots of dead water. The bass hold tight to a small zone. They stay roughly on the weed lines, rock walls and dikes. There's no structure to hold bass in the deeper water.

It's better to fish parallel to the weed lines rather than perpendicular. By fishing perpendicular you're only in the strikezone for a matter of seconds. Paralleling the weed line maintains a constant beat in the strike zone.

Wintertime isn't great for bass anglers. Bass move out of the current to follow bait and can be found in backwaters that are a few degrees warmer than the rest of the Tract. Winter normally lasts from late November through February. Throw worms, jigs, crawdad imitations and slow walk crankbaits. The fish aren't active. You'll need to slow down to entice a bite. Small bends in the rock wall with the least amount of tidal current will also hold fish. The key is to find the warmest water in any area of the Tract. Keep in mind, there are always fish in shallow water, yet you'll be able to find fish as deep as 20 feet.

By late February, bass go into a prespawn mode. Bass move into deeper water just off the weedline and flats and close to spawning grounds. Not all bass spawn at the same time, some spawn in March, April and May on flats will very little current. Current brings silt. Eggs don't fare well with silt.

During the spawn, fish six-inch plastics, lizards and crawdads. Try flipping or pitching a five-inch Mister Twister crawdad imitation into spawning areas. If you are fishing really shallow, go weightless. When the bass move into post spawn mode, throw trout, shad, bluegill and crawdad imitations.

Regardless of the season, low tide is your best chance at landing a big fish. In a sense, there are fewer places for bass to hide at low tide. As the water retreats, the outside edges of the weed lines become exposed. At low tide, target the outside of weedline just out of the current, eddies and lily pads near currents. For bass, use 20-pound test for topwater and flipping and 14-17-pound test for crankbaits, depending on water clarity.

Frank's Tract isn't just a bass fishery. Coldwater species frequent the waters as well. Salmon and steelhead don't spawn here, but decent numbers of fish can be found as they stop to rest or get lost. These fish can be common from October through December as they search for a route up the San Joaquin River system to spawn.

Stripers are resident and anadromous fish. While many small schoolie stripers are in the area throughout the year, once the water drops to 65 degrees or lower, you'll find larger stripers moving in. Larger eight-to-20-pound fish join the smaller two-to-four-pound yearlong residents.

From October through January, it's not uncommon to hook 50-60 stripers a day casting two-ounce silver spoons. Try to locate stripers working up shad and cast Hair Raiser jigs, Pop-R's, Zara Super Spooks and Pencil Poppers.

While not the most best area for sturgeon, some of the deeper holes do harbor them. Crappie and bluegill are also popular. In the spring, anglers can catch hundreds of them in the flats or behind the docks. In the winter, look for pan fish in calm water. Try seeking out deeper holes that are out of the current. Bullhead and channel catfish are also part of the mixed bag.

If you plan to make the trip, supplies are available in Stockton. There is no public shoreline access at Frank's Track. You need a boat to fish it. For directions on the water, consult a Delta map.

Also nearby is the rest of the Delta.

Directions: *There are several ways to reach Frank's Tract. There is no drive-to access. Consult a Delta map for the best route to Frank's Tract.*

Fishing with frogs can produce big bites at Frank's Tract

DISCOVERY BAY

Rating: 8

Species: Largemouth Bass, Crappie, Bluegill, Channel Catfish, Carp, Striped Bass, Sturgeon, Chinook Salmon and Steelhead

Stocks: None

Facilities: Boat Launch

Need Information? Contact: Bass Fishing Guide Randy Pringle (209) 543-6260, Hook, Line and Sinker (925) 625-2441

Discovery Bay isn't your average Delta fishery. In fact, there are few fisheries in the state that can parallel what the bay has to offer. Discovery Bay is one of the top spots to fish year-round in the Delta. On the other hand, it's also one of the finer places to live in Northern California. The bay is a community of beautiful homes set ashore in a ravishing, wealthy area.

While residents have backdoor access to some of the best warmwater fishing in the Delta, there is little access shoreline accress. A few anglers are wealthy enough to purchase a home in the bay, others have to enter via waterways. It's legal for anyone to fish this area from a boat.

A different species shines each season at Discovery Bay. However, the most sought after species is the striped bass. While some stripers can be found in the bay year-round, late fall and winter are most desirable because the fish come in large groups. Here's how it all pans out.

When the temperatures in Delta river systems fall to the lower sixties and upper fifties, stripers migrate into bays. There is warmer water in bays and the backs of sloughs. Stripers, however, aren't drawn in by warmer water, rather the movement of shad. Shad head into bays seeking warmer water. Being their main food source, stripers follow the shad. The first group of stripers that come into the bay are resident fish. Then, several runs of fish move into and out of Discovery Bay from mid-October through May.

Knowing that stripers are in Discovery Bay is common knowledge. Familiarizing yourself with their feeding patterns can greatly increase catch rates. Stripers practice different feeding patterns in Discovery Bay than they would in the San Joaquin River or any other river system. In rivers, stripers stage in the current, waiting for bait to swim past so they can ambush it. Yet, they aren't ambush oriented in the bay.

The bay isn't a current oriented system. It's true that Discovery Bay is in the realm of a tidal influence, but stripers don't position themselves the way they would in a river system. Instead, they pursue the shad by corraling them into bait balls and then work them up for a meal.

Playing the tides right increase your chance of catching fish. Action is best during tidal movement. At slack tide or when there is little wind, fishing can be slow. Shad don't move much in slack tide. They tend to sit in one place as they aren't being pushed around by stripers. On the other hand, when the tide comes in or goes out, the bite can be hot.

Shad are mainly plankton feeders. If there is wind or current, plankton

A Delta Striper

moves around, enticing shad to become more aggressive, with movements and feeding habits. As shad get more aggressive their movement makes the stripers more active. It's a chain reaction. This occurs with any movement of the tide.

When using the shad to catch stripers, there are several methods that can be employed. One of the most popular is spooning. A Hopkins or half-ounce silver Luhr Jensen Crippled Herring are standard jigs that imitate dying shad.

Knowing what a jig is attempting to imitate can aid anglers in learning how to properly use it. When stripers approach a bait ball of shad, they do so with force, swimming through the group of shad and injuring many. Then, they turn back around and eat the injured fish fluttering as they struggle to swim. The jigging motion imitates a dying shad. It's important to stay in touch with your line at all times. Try one foot lifts. If that doesn't work go with two foot lifts, but always feel your line when it's falling. Almost every fish you hook will be on the fall. Otherwise, you are illegally snagging fish.

Other important factors, such as line and hooks, should be taken into consideration. It's a good idea to use Superlines: 20-30-pound Spiderwire Stealth is low stretch and has a high sensitivity, perfect to jigging. Also, it's recommended to change out the factory hooks on the jigs. Use a stronger 2/0 hook, rather than the smaller hook that comes in the package.

Discovery Bay averages 20 feet deep; therefore jigging is applicable in nearly the whole tract. Locating shad is half the battle. If you find shad, you'll find stripers. Using your fish finder and preferably a trolling motor, mill around each bay looking for shad. Other indications of bait are birds and other anglers jigging in a concentrated area. When possible, try not to use a gas motor. They easily spook the shad and send them scurrying.

Jigging isn't the only way to fish. When stripers are boiling, try casting a Zara Super Spook or a Pencil Popper. Topwater can be excellent, as can casting jigs. Try a Hair Raiser or Rat-L-Trap. Bait takes a large number of stripers. On the other hand, Bobber fishing with minnows or shad is common, as is soaking anchovies. Every kind of angler can use his or her own favorite techniques to catch stripers here as long as you are positioned near the shad.

Largemouth bass fishing is top notch in the bay. Because it's tucked away from the cold moving river systems, the bay warms quicker than much of the Delta. This means that bass spawn earlier here than in other portions of the Delta.

The spawn is prime time to fish for bass. While there is tons of structure available for the bass, you'll find spawning fish where you see vegetation. Spawning occurs as early as late February and continues into June. Look for water to rise into the upper sixties for the first sign of spawning.

The largest bass caught in the Delta came from this bay. That fish weighed more than 18 pounds. In theory, the bay acts like a lake. Fish can feed all year and grow rapidly. Every home is equipped with dock and personal boat. There's a ton of structure available for bass, but time doesn't allow anglers to fish each dock. Look for different elements such as docks with more shade than others, docks with tules nearby, etc, and you'll find more bass.

In the spring and early summer plastics are the bait of choice. By mid summer, the water gets so warm that many bass flee the bay and head into cooler areas of the Delta. Summer is marked by partying on docks and lots of boat activity, which hurts fishing. However, this is prime time for crappie and catfish action.

If you plan to make the trip, supplies are available in Discovery Bay.

Also nearby is the rest of the Delta.

Directions: *From the junction of Interstate 5 and Highway 4 in Stockton, exit west on Highway 4 and continue to the right turnoff for Discovery Bay.*

Guide Randy Pringle utilizes his fish finder to locate schools of stripers in Discovery Bay. This is a prime location for fall stripers.

SAN JOAQUIN RIVER

Rating: 7

Species: Largemouth
Bass, Smallmouth Bass,
Striped Bass, Sturgeon,
Crappie, Bluegill,
White Catfish, Channel
Catfish, Steelhead and
Chinook Salmon

Stocks: None

Facilities: Boat Launch,
Boat Rentals, Marinas,
Gas, Bait & Tackle,
Restrooms and Fish
Cleaning Stations

Need Information?
Contact: Bass Fishing
Guide Randy Pringle
(209) 543-6260, Delta
Bait and Tackle
(916) 665-6588

The San Joaquin River is a thoroughfare for chinook salmon, stripers, sturgeon and steelhead as they migrate up the river to spawning areas each year. The river also harbors resident populations of catfish, bass and panfish. During some portion of the year anglers can find good action on more than a dozen species of fish.

The San Joaquin River has a lot of water. It's a large system that speaks volumes when it comes to the amount of territory fish have to roam. The key is knowing where to find each species and during what season.

Stripers are the most sought after fish in the system. While other species of bass can be found in marinas, on bends, in coves and off points, stripers still dominate the water especially during the migrating season. Traditionally, the influx of stripers begins in the fall and extends through spring. Fish range from one-to-three-pound schoolies to 40 pounders.

There are two types of tendencies stripers have in the Delta: ambushing and tracking down. While stripers track down bait in bays and sloughs, they stick to ambush points on the San Joaquin. The trick to becoming successful is knowing where to look for these ambush points, or feeding stations.

Stripers like to stay in the current and allow the bait to come to them. Here's a list of common feeding stations to look for: points, flats, bends in the river, sloughs or river mouths, marinas and rock walls. An important factor to consider is stripers always face the current when they feed.

Stripers in the San Joaquin are migratory fish. You can't expect to go out and catch the same group of fish in the same place Monday as you do on Wednesday. They are constantly moving through the system. The idea is to fish the above mentioned areas. Stay away from fishing slack tides. It's more productive to fish where there is water movement.

Dozens of techniques work. Bait anglers will toss minnows or anchovies, trollers work Rebels and Rapalas, tournament style bass anglers throw topwater baits and Diamond Shad's along rock walls and just about everyone jigs with Luhr Jensen half-ounce Crippled Herrings.

If you plan to make the trip, supplies are available in Stockton.

Also nearby is the rest of the Delta.

Directions: *There are dozens of access points to the San Joaquin River in the Delta region. Please consult a map for the best the suits your needs.*

OAK GROVE PARK POND

Rating: 4

Species: Rainbow Trout

Stocked with 3,200 pounds of rainbow trout.

Facilities: Restrooms, Picnic Areas and Paddleboat Rentals

Need Information? Contact: Lodi Parks and Recreation (209) 333-6742

Oak Grove Park Pond is a small, three-acre pond in an urban area that is well stocked with rainbow trout in the winter by the California Department of Fish and Game. As soon as the summer temperatures fizzle out and the water cools enough to allow for trout to live, the stocking truck backs in and unloads some 4,555 half-pound rainbow trout. The bite stays solid for Power Baiters through the spring. Keep in mind that this is the only stocked pond in the greater Stockton area.

Oak Grove Park is an excellent place for a birthday party. Aside from the fishing, there are plenty of activities for kids to enjoy, not to mention clean cut grass and plenty of trees to keep you from sweltering in the heat. There are also paddleboats available to offer as an alternative when the fishing is poor. There are camping facilities on the property, however, they are only available to church and youth groups.

If you plan to make the trip, supplies are available in Lodi. The park is only open for day-use. Call ahead for seasonal hours.

Also nearby is Lake Amador.

Directions: *From the junction of the 4 Freeway and Interstate 5 in Stockton, drive north on Interstate 5 for nine miles to Eight Mile Road. Exit east and drive a half-mile to Oak Grove Park on the right.*

Oak Grove Park Pond

HOG SLOUGH

Rating: 6

Species: Largemouth Bass, Smallmouth Bass, Crappie, Bluegill, Striped Bass and Channel Catfish

Stocks: None

Facilities: None

Hog Slough is one slough up on the right from Sycamore Slough and while both have many similarities, they also have many differences. Unlike Sycamore, Hog doesn't have many islands and has fewer tules. While it's true this gives bass less cover, it also gives them fewer places to hide. The lack of structure makes it easier for anglers to locate fish. Key in on fallen trees, points and pipes.

It's best to fish Hog during the top of the switch and bottom of the switch. Stay away from slack tide. Hog is a significant point in the South Fork of the Mokelumne River system. From Hog on up you'll find more smallmouth and fewer largemouth. Hog isn't a great smallmouth fishery in the slough itself, but it does pose a good bite for anglers fishing the mouth of the slough with plastics and crankbaits.

Fall is an excellent time to fish Hog. During the fall and early winter, you'll find largemouth bass and some stripers towards the back of the slough. The bass have migrated to this area to find warmer water and shad. Anglers flipping plastics towards the bank can expect to do well. The downfall with Hog for some anglers is there is no public access. You need a boat to cash in on the action.

Directions *or trip info for Mokelumne River (North Fork) also apply to Hog Slough.*

Fishing around structure is important in Hog Slough.

SYCAMORE SLOUGH

Rating: 6

Species: Largemouth Bass, Crappie, Bluegill, Striped Bass and Channel Catfish

Stocks: None

Facilities: None

Sycamore Slough is a good place for anglers looking to catch largemouth bass. The slough, a tributary to the South Fork of the Mokelumne River, has more islands to fish than other sloughs nearby. In the spring and early summer when weeds aren't as prevalent, you can effectively toss three-eighths or half-ounce white/chartreuse Persuader spinnerbaits along the banks which are more exposed.

Fishing the pipes is always productive. There are dozens of pipes in the slough that take water in and out of the slough and pump it into farmlands. These pipes provide cover and structure for bass, while at the same time pumping nutrients into the slough that bass feed on. If there are bass in Sycamore, rest assured they'll be near the pipes.

Fishing the pipes is relatively easy. Flip-shotting four-inch black and red and black and blue Mister Twister craws and six-inch Doc Water's Helix watermelon black flake worms is standard. Shad and crawdad-pattern crankbaits and three-eights to half-ounce Strike King Pro flipping jigs in brown, black and red or black and blue are best. Flip-shotting allows you to keep your bait in the strike zone longer.

Directions *and trip info Mokelumne River (North Fork) also apply to Sycamore Slough.*

Sycamore Slough

BEAVER SLOUGH

Rating: 6

Species: Smallmouth
Bass, Largemouth Bass,
Crappie, Bluegill,
Striped Bass and
Channel Catfish

Stocks: None

Facilities: None

Beaver is the shortest slough in the South Fork of the Mokelumne River Drainage. It also holds more smallmouth bass than the other sloughs, but doesn't offer a great largemouth fishery. Beaver's water is colder than Sycamore which isn't conducive to a largemouth's liking, but it does keep weeds from overtaking.

Beaver is different than other nearby sloughs. For some reason the farmers who own land here didn't cut down all the trees, as was done at Sycamore and Hog Slough. This can be important at high tide because many of the bass will take cover under the trees.

In the winter when tides rise the temperature of the top four feet of water fluctuates tremendously. The bass then move into deeper water where they can find a comfort zone. If bass can locate a steady temperature zone they are more prone to feed than if they were stuck in a slough with a rapidly changing temperature. So, if you find the deepest water, you'll find the most active fish.

A good thing about Beaver is it does have some public access. Many anglers spend the day fishing off the bridge on Blossom Road, which hovers directly over the slough. Although most counties prohibit anglers from fishing from a bridge because of the traffic hazard, there are no signs posted that anglers can't fish here. I'd check with authorities before fishing from the bridge just in case. Nonetheless, you'll find other anglers tossing bait all day.

Directions and trip info for Mokelumne River (North Fork) also apply to Beaver Slough.

Bullfrogs are common in Beaver Slough

Unfortunately, there isn't much shore access available at Beaver Slough.

MOKELUMNE RIVER (NORTH FORK)

Rating: 6

Species: Steelhead, Chinook Salmon, Smallmouth Bass, Largemouth Bass, Crappie, Bluegill, Striped Bass and Channel Catfish

Stocks: None

Facilities: None

Need Information? Contact: Bass Fishing Guide Randy Pringle (209) 543-6260, B & W Resort Marina (916) 977-6161

The North Fork of the Mokelumne River may only be a short distance from the South Fork, however it differs drastically. While the South Fork has a few sloughs on it, the North Fork has none. Because of this, the North Fork holds few largemouth bass, but has a good population of smallmouth. Largemouth tend to be closer to sloughs where warmer water can be found.

The North Fork also boasts more migratory fish, including stripers and Chinook salmon. Trollers bombard the river for stripers from fall through spring. It's best to troll broken back Rebels in pink, red, chrome and black or chrome and blue. Others cast half to three-quarter ounce Diamond Shad rattling baits or Hair Raisers towards boiling shad. For salmon, fish deeper holes where there is current. A spoon is best, but unfortunately many anglers snag the salmon rather than catch them.

During the winter the stripers are driven into the North Fork to follow shad. The formula is simple: if you find shad, you'll find stripers and other fish. During the winter and early spring water clarity can be horrible. When water is released into the Sacramento River system it floods the Delta with milky water and can hurt the bite for weeks. Keep in mind, these bass and stripers are used to seeing and feeding in clear water. They aren't from Mississippi or Arkansas where muddy canals are common. When there's low visibility, slow down your retrieve. It gives the fish a chance to react to it. Try and use something with a rattle. Sound is important.

If you plan to make the trip, supplies are available in Lodi. There is a boat launch fee.

Mokelumne River (North Fork)

Also nearby is the Mokelumne River (South Fork).

Directions: *From Sacramento, drive south on Interstate 5 (or drive north from Stockton) and take the Highway 12 exit 10.1 miles left to the B&W Launch area.*

MOKELUMNE RIVER (SOUTH FORK)

Rating: 6
Species: Steelhead, Chinook Salmon, Largemouth Bass, Crappie, Bluegill, Striped Bass and Channel Catfish
Stocks: None
Facilities: None

The South Fork of the Mokelumne River is an excellent choice for anglers looking to catch resident large and smallmouth bass and anadromous salmon and striped bass. Because there are sloughs on the system, you'll find largemouth at the mouth of Sycamore and Hog Slough and smallmouth at Beaver.

The key to catching bass is fishing areas that hold fish. In this main system, that includes points and rock walls. Also important is locating bait. If you find shad, bass will be close behind.

Several methods are effective, including plastics, crankbaits and jigs. You'll want to fish six-inch Doc Water's plastics on points and crankbaits on weed lines and rocky walls. During the cooler months the rock walls hold heat which draws bass to them. Pitching jigs along the shoreline is also an option.

The South Fork can be good for smallmouth above Hog Slough. Because the water is colder up here, the weeds and algae die off quicker. Smallies tend to average one-to-two pounds, but not much bigger. The South Fork also has stripers and salmon, however many anglers come for the bass. Stripers are residents and anadromous and can be caught in good numbers from fall through spring.

Unfortunately, there isn't much public access. In fact, without a boat there's only one place you can fish: at Westgate County Park, which doesn't provide much access.

Directions *and trip info for Mokelumne River (North Fork) also apply to Mokelumne River (South Fork).*

Mokelumne River (South Fork)

STEAMBOAT SLOUGH

Rating: 8

Species: Steelhead, Chinook Salmon, Sturgeon, Largemouth Bass, Spotted Bass, Striped, Bass, Smallmouth Bass, Channel Catfish, Crappie and Bluegill

Stocks: None

Facilities: Restrooms, Picnic Area and a Launch Ramp

Need Information? Contact: Fishing Guide Mark Lassagne (925) 676-3474

To many anglers, smallmouth bass fishing in the Delta is embraced about as much as the internet was in the early Nineties. Just as most folks didn't believe the internet would take off, few anglers think there are smallmouth bass in the Delta. Yet if you fish Steamboat Slough, you'll be convinced that the Delta is one of the better smallmouth fisheries in the state.

Steamboat is an open ended slough that dumps in the Sacramento River Deepwater Channel and the Sacramento River. It harbors all species of bass, but is prime territory for smallmouth. Steamboat is great for numbers and size. Anglers can expect to catch a variety of bass. You'll get lots of fish smaller than 12 inches, many fish in the 12-13 inch range and a few in the two-to-three-pound range.

Steamboat fishes much different than the rest of the Delta. It has many rocky areas, current and deep water. Action is tops from April through October. It's always important to fish rocky areas. Smallmouth are drawn to rocks because they harbor crawdads, which are found in the rocks. There's a big difference between these rocks and the ones you'd find in the lower Delta. Here, the rocks taper all the way to the bottom, rather than subsiding to weeds and then silt like you would find in many other areas of the Delta.

Paying attention to current is imperative. When there is little current, smallmouth head to deeper water and mill around. If there is no current, fish 10-15 feet deep. You'll find fish at these depths during an incoming tide. The incoming tide slows the water down as the two forces meet up. When the current is moving fast, smallmouth move towards the bank and to ambush points. If there's current, you'll want to fish bends, points and pipes. You'll have fast current on an outgoing tide.

Fishing crankbaits can be productive. It's easy to parallel the shoreline and cast cranks. The trick is knowing what size crankbait to use and at what time to use them. Luhr Jensen has a great line of cranks for Steamboat. Speed Traps are best from zero to six feet. Radar 10's are applicable in four-to-eight feet of water and quarter-ounce Hot Lips works best deeper than

Largemouth Bass

eight feet. Another factor is color. If there is six inches to one foot of visibility use Delta Craw. With one-to-1.5 feet, try Crystal Craw and with two or more feet, Olive River Craw and Green Craw are best.

In the warmer months, there can also be a great topwater bite. Try a chrome or chrome and black Spook, a chartreuse Persuader buzzbait or a 5/8 ounce Luhr Jensen Nip-I-Diadee in white or black. There can also be a great

Crankbaits

spinnerbait bite. I fished the river with pro angler Mark Lassagne, who throws a half-ounce Southern Shad Persuader Assassinator spinnerbait with a No. 2 khale Eagle Claw treble hook. Lassagne stresses that most bass will short strike your baits and without changing out the hooks, you'll miss most of the bites. You can also throw weightless baits such as Doc Waters Helix on pipes and structure.

If you plan to make the trip, supplies are available in Rio Vista. There is a day use fee.

Also nearby is the Sacramento River Deepwater Channel.

Directions: From Interstate 5 in Sacramento, drive south and exit west on Twin Cities Road. Drive four miles and turn left on Highway 160 (River Road). Continue 6.6 miles to Walker Landing Road and turn right. Drive three miles to Grand Island Road and turn left. Drive one-tenth of a mile to the right turnoff for Hogback Recreation Area.

Guide and pro angler Mark Lassagne is one of the best at catching smallmouth in Steamboat Slough.

193

DISAPPOINTMENT SLOUGH

Rating: 8

Species: Steelhead, Chinook Salmon, Largemouth Bass, Crappie, Bluegill, Channel Catfish, Sturgeon and Striped Bass

Stocks: None

Facilities: Boat Launch, Bait & Tackle, Houseboat Rentals, Restrooms

Need Information? Contact: King Island (209) 951-2188, Paradise Point Marina (209) 952-1000, Herman and Helen's (209) 951-4634, Fishing Guide Randy Pringle (209) 543-6260

Disappointment Slough rarely pumps disappointment into anglers who fish it for largemouth bass. In fact, many B.A.S.S. tournaments are won here. Disappointment is an opened ended slough with drive to access off Eight Mile Road. This tributary to the San Joaquin River began its' fame years ago when local bass clubs stocked Florida strain largemouth bass in this slough. The slough is great for bass for several reasons: it has a lot of deep water access for fish to escape to, great spawning areas, many protected areas where anglers can fish during the wind and harbors a lot of giant fish.

Spring is the best time to catch trophy bass. In spring, weightless baits, such as a Doc Waters Helix or a Strike King Zero can be effective. Using a weightless bait allows you to make casts that are less likely to spook fish. If you can find areas where vegetation is minimal, spinnerbaits and crankbaits will be effective.

Summer has a much different appeal to it. Due to the warmer water, weed growth is more evident than it is in most sloughs. Summer is prime time for topwater action. From June through September, you'll want to use Pop-R's and Spooks on calm days and a Persuader Double Buzz or a Luhr Jensen Nip-I-Diadee when there's a chop on the surface. Don't discount fishing yellow-headed blackbird Snag Proof frogs on mats.

If you plan to make the trip, supplies are available in Lodi and Stockton. There is also drive to access available.

Also nearby is New Hogan Reservoir.

Directions: *From Interstate 5 in Sacramento, drive south and exit Eight Mile Road. Drive west for roughly five miles to Atherton Road and King Island Resort.*

Disappointment Slough

WHITES SLOUGH

Rating: 8

Species: Steelhead,
Chinook Salmon,
Largemouth Bass,
Crappie, Bluegill,
Channel Catfish,
Sturgeon and Striped
Bass

Stocks: None

Facilities: Boat Launch,
Bait & Tackle

Whites Slough is a spitting image of Disappointment Slough. Located in the East Delta, Whites rests between 14 Mile Slough and Disappointment Slough and is a prime slot for largemouth bass. It can be fished the same way as Disappointment. The biggest draw for Whites is likely its' clarity. Because of its location and the little amount of fluctuation that occurs in relation to the rest of the Delta, Whites remains remarkably clear when other sloughs look like milk. It also harbors many trophy bass.

A result of its' high dikes and narrow sloughs, when the wind is howling many anglers head to Whites. Whites tends to be more protected than many other sloughs giving anglers a break from harsh conditions that plague more open areas.

Trip info for Disappointment Slough also applies to Whites Slough.

Whites Slough

Directions: *From Sacramento, drive south on Interstate 5 and exit west on Highway 12. After driving three miles, there are several roads that you can turn left on that take you to White's. Consult a map for more detailed information.*

Delta bass expert and guide Randy Pringe with a quality Delta largemouth taken on a crankbait.

Region 8 Sacramento Metro

Rancho Seco Park Lake
Elk Grove Park Lake
William Land Park Ponds
Southside Park Pond
American River
Arden Bar Pond
Lake Natoma
Folsom Lake
Howe Park Pond
Gibson Ranch Park Lake
Big M Fishery
Camp Far West Reservoir

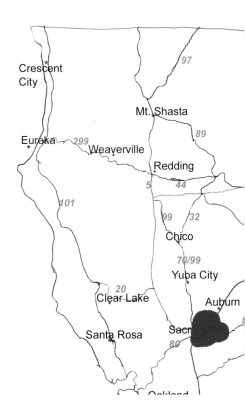

RANCHO SECO LAKE

Rating: 7

Species: Rainbow
Trout, Channel Catfish,
Crappie, Bluegill and
Largemouth Bass

Stocked with 6,500
pounds of rainbow
trout.

Facilities:
Campgrounds, Picnic
Areas, Boat Launch,
Fish Cleaning Station,
Restrooms, Swimming
Area, Paddle Boat and
Kayak Rentals, General
Store, Showers, Fishing
Piers and a Wildlife
Preserve

Need Information?
Contact: Sacramento
Municipal Utilities
District (916) 452-3211
Ex. 4408

Bass anglers have a false perception of Ranch Seco Park Lake. Thinking it's just another small park lake stocked with bite size trout in the winter and a few catfish in the summer, the hog-hunters ignore the lake. Ranch Seco has yet to earn status as a trophy bass water. However, as soon as anglers can overlook the fact that in most cases small park lakes haven't been able to produce trophy bass, the lake will become a respected fishery.

In the last several years, three bass weighing more than 17 pounds have been checked. The majority have been released. So why are these bass growing so big? The most logical explanation points to stable water levels. Fed by the South Folsom Canal, the lake is always kept full. Additionally, the lake has great spawning areas and good forage for bass. Planted trout and bluegill serve as growth pills. With no live bait permitted, a good number of the big bass are caught on plastics, particularly dark brown colors.

Rancho Seco isn't only for bass fishermen. The shallow lake is heavily stocked with rainbow trout. The California Department of Fish & Game stocks 9,665 half-pounders and the Sacramento Municipal Utilities District (SMUD) plants another 8,000 pounds of Donaldson trout, purchased from Lake Amador. The trout purchased from Amador range from two-to-eight pounds. There isn't a best spot to catch the rainbows. They roam the entire lake. Green Power Bait is the choice bait. Trollers can score trout working the area in front of the dam, along the shoreline or in the middle of the lake. No leadcore or downriggers are needed. The lake is only 47 feet at its deepest point.

Using red worms and small white jigs gives anglers limits of crappie and bluegill in the summer. The only species that seems to struggle are catfish. SMUD plants 1,700 pounds of cats every three-to-four years.

If you plan to make the trip, supplies are available in Galt. There is a day-use fee. Boat rentals, the general store, showers and the swimming beach are only open from May to September.

Also nearby are Lake Amador and Mokelumne River.

Directions: *From the junction of Highway 50 and 99 in Sacramento, drive south on Highway 99 for 20 miles to the Jackson exit (Highway 104). Drive east on Highway 104 for 12 miles to the signed turnoff for Ranch Seco Park Lake. Turn right and drive 1.4 miles to the lake.*

ELK GROVE PARK LAKE

Rating: 4

Species: Rainbow Trout and Channel Catfish

Stocked with 2,600 pounds of rainbow trout and 5,600 pounds of channel catfish.

Facilities: Restrooms, Picnic Areas, Swimming Pool, Soccer Fields, Baseball Diamonds, Snack Bar, Horseshoe Pits and Volleyball Courts

Need Information? Contact: Elk Grove Community Services (916) 685-3917, Sacramento County Parks and Recreation (916) 875-6961

Elk Grove Park Lake would definitely win the award for having the greenest water in California, if there were such a thing. During my last visit to the lake in May of 2001, the water was greener than the surrounding grass. It's really hard to believe that any fish survive in this, but they do. In actuality, the green tint is simply a dye that was put into the lake to kill off weeds. The water color is harmless to fish and humans. It's still really odd to see, though!

Located next to Elk Grove High School, Elk Grove Park Lake is a three-acre lake enclosed within the confines of the 125-acre Elk Grove Park. Fishing is not the main attraction. The park is most frequently the site for youth sports leagues, including soccer and softball. The lake is pretty though. It's surrounded by grassy shorelines and oak trees.

Elk Grove Park Lake is stocked with thousands of rainbow trout in the winter and spring and catfish in the summer and fall. Because of the pond's size, catching the planted fish can be easy. Your best bet is to use Power Bait. Most of the trout are half-pounders. As May approaches try night crawlers, chicken liver or cut mackerel to nab a few catfish in the evening.

If you plan to make the trip. supplies are available in Elk Grove.

Also nearby are Southside Park Pond, William Land Park Ponds, Lake Natoma, Arden Bar Pond and Folsom Lake.

Directions: From Sacramento at the junction of Highway's 50 and 99, drive south on Highway 99 for 11 miles to Elk Grove Blvd. Turn left, drive one-mile to Elk Grove-Florin Avenue and turn right. Drive eight-tenths of a mile to the park entrance on the right. Turn right and continue three-tenths of a mile to the lake on the left.

Elk Grove Park Lake

WILLIAM LAND PARK PONDS

Rating: 5

Species: Rainbow Trout, Channel Catfish and Largemouth Bass

Stocked with 2,600 pounds of rainbow trout and 5,600 pounds of channel catfish.

Facilities: Restrooms and a Picnic Area

Need Information? Contact: California Department of Fish and Game (916) 445-0411

Like nearby Elk Grove Park Lake, the first thing anglers notice about William Land Park Ponds is that the water is greener than the leaves on the trees that surround the ponds. Why is the water so green? Responding to a weed problem, the Sacramento Parks and Recreation Department pours die into the lake that kills the unwanted weeds. Fortunately, the die is harmless to fish and humans.

Located across from Sacramento City College and near a zoo and large urban park, William Land has two ponds, roughly two acres each.

Although only stocked with 200 pounds a week, the ponds are a consistent urban fishery for those who don't have the time to drive to the Sierras. The California Department of Fish & Game stocks rainbow trout in the winter and channel catfish in the summer. The only downfall is that most of the fish planted are caught shortly after being released into the lake. Regulars know the planting schedule, so they show up at the same time each week to meet the stocking truck, catch an easy limit and go home happy.

As for bait, nothing special is required. The day the one-pound rainbows are stocked tossing any spinner works. For anytime after, use Power Bait. The one-to-three-pound catfish take a little longer to hook and are best fooled with night crawlers or chicken liver.

If you plan to make the trip, supplies are available in Elk Grove.

Also nearby are Southside Park Pond, Arden Park Pond and Howe Park Pond.

William Land Park Ponds

Directions: *From Interstate 5 in downtown Sacramento, drive south and exit east on Sutterville Road. Drive a half-mile to Land Park Drive and turn left. Continue three-tenths of a mile to the lake on the right. There are two ponds in the park. The other can be reached by turning right on a street two-tenths of a mile past the first lake.*

SOUTHSIDE PARK POND

Rating: 4

Species: Rainbow Trout, Channel Catfish and Largemouth Bass

Stocked with 800 pounds of rainbow trout and 1,400 pounds of channel catfish.

Facilities: Restrooms, Picnic Area and a Playground

Need Information? Contact: California Department of Fish and Game (916) 445-0411

Southside Park is not a place you want to be caught after dark. While reading directions to reach the lake in the California Trout and Bass Fishing Guide, published by the California Department of Fish & Game, I scanned over the comments provided about the lake when I came across "Gang activity common at night." Since it was near dusk when I arrived I was a little worried. The two-acre pond that can be seen on your right if you are exiting Highway 50 north onto Interstate 5 put a scare into me. And when I arrived, a few dudes that didn't make me feel too comfortable starred me down, and before I decided to dip my line in the water in search of a catfish, I snapped a few pictures and drove off.

In downtown Sacramento, Southside Park Pond isn't the kind of place you'll want to bring youngsters for their first fishing experience. Jokingly, I call it "Shopping Cart Lake," as I must have seen three or four carts, along with soda and beer bottles scattered along the shoreline. Paper trash was everywhere. I'd be afraid to see what they would find if they drained the lake! The sad part is that Southside Pond is one of the deeper urban lakes in the region, and could be a much better fishery if it was treated with more respect.

Southside Park Pond

Despite the night "gang activity" and the sad use of the lake as a trashcan, the CA DFG plants fish weekly, with catfish from June through October and rainbow trout from November through April. Traditional methods work; Power Bait for the rainbows and night crawlers for the catfish.

If you plan to make the trip, supplies are available in the nearby community.

Also nearby are William Land Park Ponds, the Sacramento River, American River, Howe Park Pond and Arden Bar Pond.

Directions: *Driving west on Business 80 in Sacramento, take the 16th Street exit to W Street. Follow W Street west to 8th Street. The park is on the north side of the road.*

AMERICAN RIVER

Rating: 8

Species: Rainbow
Trout, Sturgeon,
Steelhead, Striped Bass,
American Shad,
Chinook Salmon,
Largemouth Bass,
Bluegill and Channel
Catfish

Stocks: None

Facilities: Boat
Launches, Restrooms
and Picnic Areas

Need Information?
Contact: Fisherman's
Warehouse (916) 362-
1200, Fishing Guide JD
Richey (916) 388-1956

Flowing from Nimbus Dam to the Sacramento River, the main stem of the American River is framed by runs of anadromous fish. While no trout plants take place, each season brings a fresh group of sea-run fish. One of the greatest attributes of the American is that it provides good access and good fishing in a heavily urbanized area. Throughout the year, anglers have the opportunity to chase steelhead, chinook salmon, striped bass and American shad in addition to resident rainbows, bass, bottom feeders and panfish.

The American can be a tough fishery to judge. Because releases from Folsom Lake vary week to week, it's tough to predict how the bite will be. Each species reacts differently to high and low water. One thing is for sure, flows never seem to be perfect. They are either too high or too low. Regardless, there are always ways to find success.

The fall run of salmon tends to draw the most anglers. At one time salmon fishing was promising as early as late June, but now fish are showing up later for some reason. Most salmon are in the river in October and November. The downfall to salmon fishing is that crowds can be overwhelming. Unfortunately, poaching is also common. Many anglers snag a few salmon before work and then come back again after work to do some more fishing. Double limits aren't legal and neither is snagging. Vertical jigging is legal, however, side jigging spoons and jigs are not permitted. Here's a basis rule to follow: if you catch a salmon anywhere other than in the mouth, it must be returned to the river.

While a few wild salmon are available, the American is primarily a hatchery reliant system. The California Department of Fish and Game places gates in the American just above the Nimbus Hatchery, forcing salmon to enter the hatchery rather than continuing upriver. Once the hatchery meets their quota though, the gates are removed and salmon are free to swim to Nimbus Dam. (This dam is the furthest they can swim.)

The wall below Nimbus Dam used to be a prime spot to fish, however after September 11, access is now limited here. A fence was installed to keep people

The fish ladder at Nimbus Hatchery

from getting too close to the dam. Nonetheless, anglers can still fish from shore and on the south side of the river. Whether bait fishing from shore, fly fishing or fishing out of a drift boat, all methods are effective.

A spawning king salmon just below the hatchery wier

From a boat, the best drift is from Sailor Bar to Sunrise. No boats are permitted from Nimbus Dam down to the American River Hatchery. Though drift boats allow anglers to fish in areas that aren't being overly harassed by bank anglers, they aren't completely necessary. From a drift boat, Flatfish and Quickfish with sardine wraps soaked in Pautzke Liquid Krill and fresh roe do best. Salmon average 12-18 pounds, although a 62.5-pound fish caught in October of 1998 proves there are bigger fish in the system.

Shoreline access is excellent. There are dozens of notable areas where salmon can be taken, but the best tend to be from the hatchery on downriver a few miles. From shore, tossing a No. 5 Mepps, soaking roe or using yarn or beads is best. Depending on your skill level, anglers should use 12-20 pound test. For the most part (depending on water levels), you'll want to use a quarter-to-one-ounce weight.

Preparing to spawn steelhead

Locating salmon isn't difficult. Look for deep holes with a little current. Salmon rest in these areas. You'll find salmon in the heads of the holes early and late in the day. Don't bother fishing slow water. Find water that funnels salmon into runs.

Steelhead are also a big part of the American's fishery. While there are many wild fish in the system, most are hatchery bred. Regardless, they provide an excellent urban fishery. Steelhead swim out of the Pacific Ocean, up the Delta and into the Sacramento River before the American. Just below the weir, downriver of the Hazel Avenue Bridge, is a fish ladder that many salmon and steelhead enter. The ladder takes them into the American River Hatchery where they are spawned. It's an interesting process.

An American River steelhead

Once they swim up the 100-yard long ladder, a crowder is used to force the fish towards the hatchery building where the egg taking operations

California Department of Fish and Game scientific aids send steelhead into a holding areas after they are spawned.

occur. Before the fish are brought in the building they are sedated so they can be handled without being harmed.

Steelhead are then elevated from the fish ladder into a room where the eggs are taken. Hatchery workers then handle the fish, some of which are returned to the river because they are not ready to spawn. Others are sent to holding pools where they'll be spawned later, and some are spawned immediately.

Eggs are removed from females. A male's sperm is taken to fertilize those eggs. Each female can produce upwards of 10,000 eggs. The hatchery likes to take as least a half-million eggs each year.

After the eggs are removed, hatchery workers pump the air out of the belly so it can again swim. The fish are then placed in a holding pond where they stay for 21 days before being returned to the river. Luckily, steelhead don't die after they spawn as salmon do.

Salmon eggs waiting to hatch

The eggs are then cared for until they hatch. Some are put in incubators and others in barrels. As they grow, steelhead are moved out of the building and into raceways. Before being released, their adipose fin is clipped so they can be identified when they return to the river after a two-to-three year stay in the Pacific Ocean. At four-to-a-pound, steelhead are driven to and released into the Sacramento River. At least 430,000 steelhead are reared and stocked annually at the American River Hatchery.

American River steelhead

While there is a small fall run, most steelhead come during the winter run, which begins in late December and goes into late February. The best place to catch steelhead is from the hatchery to Sailor Bar and from Sailor Bar to Rossmour Bar. Unlike salmon, you'll find most steelhead in riffles. Steelhead can be taken from a drift boat, on a fly rod or from shore on roe, Panther Martin spinners and spoons. Traditionally 1,500-3,000 steelhead come to the American on a good year. These fish run five-to-seven pounds with some to 15 pounds.

Striped bass trickle in during April. May and June are peak months, yet you can catch them throughout summer and fall. In September and October, a small run of stripers enter the river, yet since salmon are also present, few anglers pay attention to the stripers.

The striper run on the Feather and Sacramento River no doubt are much larger than the run that finds the American, however more big fish are taken from the American. Stripers bigger than 40 pounds are caught yearly, although the average fish runs eight-to-10 pounds. For stripers, use 30-pound braided line with a 20-pound fluorocarbon leader.

Stripers can be found from the mouth of the American to the hatchery. Nonetheless, because there is less current near the mouth, spots that you would likely find stripers aren't as obvious. It can be intimidating to fish this lower section. There are submerged trees and a lot of wood, plus the water can be hard to read. It's best to use a fish finder to locate deeper holes where many stripers will be. Any break or deep spot that is out of the ordinary harbors stripers. Try to fish breaks and where a tailout drops into a pool.

Stripers can be found in many areas, yet weed beds tend to harbor lots of fish. The weeds attract bugs, which draw in baitfish that stripers feed on. Deep holes with moderate current also hold fish. Early in the spring when juvenile steelhead are migrating out of the system, you'll even find stripers in riffles.

The most common methods are soaking live jumbo minnows and squawfish, fishing sardines off the bottom and tossing Lucky Craft Pointer Minnows and Smithwick Rattling Rogues. While bait seems to work best, you also have an early morning and late evening topwater bite on rainbow trout and silver Pencil Poppers and Super Spooks.

Stripers can be challenging to catch when American shad are in the system. Because the shad are a prime food source and they are so abundant, it's much tougher to get the stripers to feed on other baits.

When shad are in the system, they are easy to catch. Shad are a non-native species that most folks catch and release because they are so boney. Nevertheless, others love to prepare them in a smoker. The limit is 25 shad per day.

Shad move into the lower end of the river in late April. By early May, they'll have found their way to Goethe Park, and by the second week of May and shortly after, shad will occupy the whole river. Traditionally, the first half of June is prime time, but a few fish remain in the system until early July. Male American shad average two-to-three pounds, while females are closer to three-to-five. Four-to-six-pound test is recommended.

As a general rule, the last hour of the day is best. The shad get aggressive when the sun isn't striking the water. On the other hand, the bite can shut off fast too. For the most part, anglers jig fish. One-and-two-inch curly tail grubs and jigs on a 1/64 or 1/32 jig head with a small split shot to aid in castability and taking your bait down are best. Bobbers can be used if desired. Other anglers fish Dick Nite spoons.

Shad are easy to catch because they typically school up in massive numbers. Look for them in areas with moderate current, tailouts, flats and deeper holes. Tailouts can be especially good if you have decent water flow. Shad are lazy. Ideally, try and seek fast moving water that slows down into a holding area or pools up. Don't look for them in fast water, dead water or riffles.

If releases are low, the shad aren't apt to move upriver. They'll pool up in the lower river and wait for increased flows to make their journey upriver easier. Shad can be taken from boat or shore. It's easier to catch them from a boat because you can position yourself better. However, anglers fishing from Sunrise Bridge and those willing to wade in the river can catch limits without a boat.

If you plan to make the trip, supplies are available in several cities along the river. At some access points there is a day use fee. Check updated sportfishing regulations for bag limits, gear restrictions and closures. All anadromous fish that enter the American River are governed by specific regulations.

Also nearby are Folsom Lake, Arden Bar Pond and Lake Natoma.

Directions: *The American River can be reached off several exits from Interstate 5, Interstate 80 and Highway 50. Consult a map for the section of the river that best suits your needs.*

Tim Reiley (Left) and guide JD Richey with a pair of AmericanRiver shad caught in early June.

ARDEN BAR POND

Rating: 5

Species: Rainbow Trout, Channel Catfish, Bluegill and Largemouth Bass

Stocked with 4,000 pounds of rainbow trout.

Facilities: Restrooms, Picnic Areas, Hiking Trails and Fishing Docks

Need Information? Contact: Sacramento County Parks (916) 875-6672

Arden Bar Pond is one of the few urban park lakes in the Sacramento region that gives anglers a rural feeling. Located in the American River Parkway, Arden Bar is an 80-acre lake that borders the American River, but never makes direct contact with the river, so the salmon, shad, steelhead and striped bass that spawn up the American can't get into the lake.

Arden is a shallow lake that has some islands and is most popular to trout fishermen from December through March when the California Department of Fish & Game shows up twice a week to plant 5,970 rainbows. Float tubers who cast and retrieve spinners in the middle of the lake have the best action, although floating Power Bait off the fishing piers works well too. Pushing a pound, most of the trout caught are twice the size of the other urban lakes in the region.

As summer arrives, the trout bite quiets down and the spotlight turns to evening catfish fishing. There are also a sprinkle of bass and bluegill.

If you plan to make the trip supplies are available in the urban area near the lake. There is a day-use fee.

Also nearby are Southside Park Ponds, Lake Natoma and Folsom Lake.

Directions: *From Sacramento at the junction of Interstate 5 and Highway 50, drive east on Highway 50 for six miles to Watt Avenue. Turn left and drive 1.1 miles to Fair Oaks Blvd. Turn east and drive 2.5 miles to Arden Way. Turn southeast and continue seven-tenths of a mile to the entrance kiosk. Pay the day-use fee and continue 1.3 miles to the lake.*

Arden Bar Pond

LAKE NATOMA

Rating: 5

Species: Rainbow
Trout, White Catfish,
Red Ear Sunfish,
Crappie, Channel
Catfish, Bluegill,
Spotted Bass,
Smallmouth Bass and
Largemouth Bass

Stocked with 650
pounds of rainbow
trout.

Facilities: Boat Launch,
Picnic Areas,
Restrooms,
Campgrounds and RV
Hookups

Need Information?
Contact: Folsom Lake
State Recreation Area
(916) 988-0205

In January of 2000, Lake Natoma became known statewide when an angler broke the California record for a rainbow trout with a surprising 23-pound fish. Was this really a surprise? To anglers, yes. To the state's leading biologists, no. Here's why.

Anglers catch rates for trout at Natoma are on the small side; however, biologists know that huge trout reside in the 540-acre narrow and shallow body of water near Sacramento. Natoma is fed by water released from Folsom Lake. Natoma is used as an afterbay for Folsom. Like most afterbays, it serves as a smorgasbord for fish as threadfin shad and pond smelt get washed through the turbines.

Rather than swimming the entire lake and working their butts off for food, the smart rainbows swim upstream, wait for the food to be brought to them and forge all day. This is how these fish get huge. Common sense would send anglers to this area to fish. Unfortunately, this section of Natoma is closed to fishing. In essence, the fish are protected and allowed to surge to huge proportions from the Folsom Prison Line just upstream of Rainbow Bridge to the base of the Folsom Dam.

Because more than enough food is available, there is no reason for the lunkers to leave this area, and seldom do they. Occasionally, increased releases push the fish downstream into fishable waters and make these brutes vulnerable. However, this doesn't occur often enough. These fish can't be targeted. Most often they are caught on accident by inexperienced anglers looking to catch one of the 1,300 half-pound planted rainbows by the California Department of Fish and Game. Natoma has wonderful access for anglers.

Natoma's warm water fishery is just ok. There are bass, but they aren't heavily targeted, nor do they get huge. Springtime is best, especially for anglers who fish the warmer backwaters near the Highway 50 Bridge.

If you plan to make the trip, supplies are available in Citrus Heights and Folsom. There is a day-use and boat launch fee. There is a 5 mph speed limit. Gas-powered motors are prohibited between Willow Creek and Nimbus Dam, but are allowed upstream of Willow Creek.

Also nearby are Folsom Lake, Howe Park Pond and Mather Lake.

Directions: *From Sacramento, drive east on Highway 50 for 16 miles to the Hazel Avenue exit. Exit left and continue two miles to Madison Avenue. Turn right and drive 2.5 miles to the Negro Bar entrance.*

FOLSOM LAKE

Rating: 7

Species: Largemouth Bass, Smallmouth Bass, Spotted Bass, Crappie, Bluegill, Rainbow Trout, Brown Trout, Chinook Salmon, Channel Catfish and Carp

Stocked with 1,200 pounds of fingerling Chinook salmon, 200 pounds of sub-catchable rainbow trout and 14,000 pounds of rainbow trout.

Facilities: Campgrounds, Boat Launches, Picnic Areas, Restrooms, Boat Rentals, Gas, Bait & Tackle, Swimming Areas, RV Hookups, Marina, General Store and Snack Bar

Need Information? Contact: Folsom Lake State Recreation Area (916) 988-0205, Folsom Lake Marina (916) 933-1300, Fishermen's Warehouse (916) 362-1200, Bass Fishing Guide Lunker Larry Hemphill (530) 674-0276

When shown to a Southern Californian, Folsom Lake is a gigantic reservoir. On the other hand, Northern California residents consider the 11,450-acre reservoir a fairly small lake. Ironically, many folks who live near the reservoir refer to it as the "Dead Sea," a place where catches are few and far between and the thought of fish living in its' waters is giggled at.

Let's set the record straight: Folsom is a great bass fishery and offers a fair coldwater fishery and solid action on carp and catfish. It's a diverse fishery set in the heart of a major metropolitan area. Nonetheless, anglers must pick and choose how they approach Folsom. From Easter through Labor Day the lake is a virtual highway, swamped with wave runners, speed boats, luxury boats and finally, anglers. It's a busy place where fishing isn't the main attraction. However, when the weather still isn't warm enough for swimming, the fishing is great.

Folsom has a lot of history buried under millions of gallons of water. Remnants of the great California gold rush, the town of Mormon Island rests underwater in the main body. Several bridges, which used to cross the American River, are also submerged. Folsom rests downriver of the famous town of Coloma, where John Marshall discovered gold. However, much of the historic value disappeared when the lake's bottom was gutted of trees and filled. The gold site still remains several miles up the South Fork of the American River though.

Folsom Lake is a dammed portion of the South Fork and North Fork of the American River. Each arm is quite different, but make up most of the composition of the reservoir. Only a small portion of the lake is found in the main body of Folsom. Because of different altitude changes, you'll find a difference in terrain between the two forks.

The North Fork is comprised of big boulders, lots of flats, gravel tailings and pits. The South Fork is home to red mud, willows, steep bluff walls and has more feeder creeks coming in. Prior to the drought years in the Eighties, the lake had few trees below the waterline. Fortunately, many willows grew during the low water years and make for excellent fish structure.

Folsom is a good spotted bass lake and offers a legitimate chance at largemouth and smallmouth bass. The winter bite at Folsom is possibly the best bass bite in Nor Cal. From November through February, anglers can catch tons of spots fishing deep. When it gets cold, a lot of the big spots go shallow (10-20 feet in the winter). This is prime crankbait time. A medium to deep diving crankbait in shad pattern, or a medium to deep diving rip bait is best. Concentrate on the main lake points, rock piles and island tops. Shallow gravel piles in the North Fork shouldn't be overlooked.

Kent Brown and a Folsom spotted bass.

More than spotted bass fishing is possible in November, December and January. In fact, Folsom's most successful anglers use their camera to photograph the lake's structure this time of year. Folsom is drawn down in the winter months. The lake's structure is exposed and at the hands of anglers who want to examine it and come back to fish when the areas are submerged in the spring and summer.

Spotted bass move shallow when it's cold. A key to wintertime fishing is to slow down. Another is to know when to fish shallow. In winter, the majority of bass are living in 30-60 feet of water because that's where their food can be found. On the other hand, they do come shallow in the morning to feed on crawdads and baitfish. Oftentimes they are only shallow for one-to-two hours. Then they drop down deep.

If the fish aren't shallow, they'll be deep. Drop-shotting small Robo worms 30-60 feet deep is standard. The bass are in these depths because they are feeding on baitfish (shad & pond smelt).

Other anglers enjoy decent swimbait action in winter and early spring. Fish them near launch ramps where trout are planted, in creek inlets or areas where you'd find spawning trout.

From mid-February through March, bass are in pre-spawn mode (weather permitting). Bass raise with the lake and begin to feed as they look for warmer water while seeking out spawning grounds. The South Fork Arm is productive during this time. There's one way to guarantee success: run a spinnerbait past every submerged willow. In fact, you may get bit a lot. A

Guide Lunker Larry with a Folsom smallmouth.

half-or-three-quarter ounce white/chartreuse or chartreuse spinnerbait is best. Make sure to spend time in the Jack Shack and New York Creek areas.

If spinnerbaits aren't working, rip baits will. Try a Lucky Craft Stacee Pointer 78 or Ghost Minnow or a Smithwick Rattling Rogue in black and gold or black and silver. If bass aren't super aggressive, a rip bait stays in the strike zone longer than a spinnerbait, increasing your odds of getting bit. If neither works, head over to Salmon Falls Bridge and drop a live crawdad. Crawdads, minnows and night crawlers work any time of year.

April and May are the easiest time to catch bass. All three species of bass are in spawn mode, although the smallmouth tend to finish early on in the cycle. Some anglers choose to sight fish. Others drag a Carolina rigged lizard or a brush hog. A green pumpkin lizard fished near Beale's Point, Granite Bay or any of the main lake humps is a ticket to success. On the other hand, any cove or creekbed in the entire lake will hold fish. Don't discount the back of New York Creek. Regardless of time of year, the Peninsula produces great action. It offers lots of brush piles, island tops and deep water access. What more could you ask for!

Folsom Lake

Spring is when the water is warm, the fish are shallow and the most anglers are fishing. Ninety percent of the lake's bass population is 20 feet or shallower. They are aggressive, on spawning beds and can be taken with Doc Water's jigs and tubes.

June through September are dominated by water sport enthusiasts, but 5 mph zones give anglers calm water. Or, you can opt to fish mid-week evenings. Beginning in May, you'll want to throw topwater. Folsom is an excellent topwater lake. Fish the main lake early in the morning, then creep your way into the river arms by 10 a.m. to avoid the crowds. Fish island tops, long points, islands and flats with Pop-R's and Zara Spooks in baby bass and shad patterns. Otherwise, try drop-shotting a four-inch Robo worm in 15-25 feet. Shad patterns and Aaron's Magic are standard colors.

Not that anyone cares, but Folsom is one of the better carp lakes in the region. Anglers can find carp in creek channels in the spring. Unfortunately, that's their spawning time. They are more active from late spring through fall.

Catfish is a summertime gig. Fish the flats and coves in the early morning and you'll be successful.

Despite what many Nor Cal anglers think, Folsom is no small pond. The reservoir has five launch ramps (Folsom Point, Granite Bay, Rattlesnake Bar, Brown's Ravine and the Peninsula), lots of open water and a full service marina.

The California Department of Fish and Game utilizes the reservoir to give Sacramento area anglers a coldwater option by dumping more than 19,350 half-pound trout and 2,040 sub-catchable trout each year. Folsom isn't an excellent trout lake, but there are fish to be taken by anglers who keep an eye on where the trout are congregating. At different times of the year, the trout migrate into certain parts of the lake. Winter yields the most consistent action. Try running a Rebel Holograph Minnow in front of the dam or the dykes.

Recently, the CA DFG chose to add Chinook to the bag of coldwater species. More than 100,000 fingerlings are stocked annually.

If you plan to make the trip, supplies are available in Folsom, Granite Bay and Roseville. There is a day-use and boat launch fee.

Also nearby are Lake Natoma and American River.

Directions: *From Interstate 80 in Roseville, exit Douglas Blvd. east and follow it for roughly six miles to Auburn-Folsom Road. Continue one-mile to the Granite Bay entrance.*

Folsom Lake

HOWE PARK POND

Rating: 4

Species: Rainbow Trout, Channel Catfish, Bluegill and Largemouth Bass

Stocked with rainbow trout in the winter.

Facilities: Restrooms, Picnic Areas and Playground

Need Information? Contact: Fishermen's Warehouse (916) 362-1200

If I were a trout, the lake I would least want to be stocked into is Howe Park Pond. Smaller than one-acre, the urban pond in Howe Community Park averages roughly two feet deep and becomes immersed in weeds and algae by April. The weeds get so thick by summer the fish get stuck in small pockets of open water. The lake is smaller than the size of one NBA court. Catching fish is easy, though.

While being put in Howe is bad for the fish, it's good for fishermen. In the winter when the weeds aren't thick anglers do well casting small Panther Martins or Roostertails. The clear water allows anglers to see the fish and cast right towards them. Power Bait and marshmallows do the trick too. The California Department of Fish & Game stocks rainbow trout in the winter.

Although there are only a few largemouth bass and bluegill in the lake, make sure you use a weedless lure. From June through September channel catfish are planted, giving local residents something to look forward to in the evenings.

If you plan to make the trip, supplies are available off El Camino Avenue near the lake.

Also nearby are Southside Park Pond, William Land Park Ponds, Arden Bar Pond and Gibson Ranch Pond.

Directions: *From Interstate 5 in downtown Sacramento, drive north and exit east on El Camino Avenue. Continue 5.4 miles to Bell Street and turn right. Drive three-tenths of a mile to the park on the right.*

Howe Park Pond

GIBSON RANCH POND

Rating: 5

Species: Rainbow
Trout, Channel Catfish,
Largemouth Bass,
Crappie, Bluegill and
Carp

Stocked with 2,600
pounds of rainbow trout
and 2,500 pounds of
channel catfish.

Facilities: General
Store, Campgrounds,
Picnic Areas,
Swimming Area and
Restrooms

Need Information?
Contact: Sacramento
County Parks and
Recreation
(916) 875-6336

Gibson Ranch Pond is a small farm pond located on a 325-acre working ranch. At eight acres, and less than 12 feet deep, the lake is run as a put-and-take fishery. The California Department of Fish & Game shows up once a week to stock 100 pounds of fish: catfish in the summer and rainbow trout in the winter. Because there is no place for fish to hide, most are caught shortly after a stock. The lake is so small you can cast across it.

Most trout fishermen use Power Bait and are often surprised when they hook a large carp instead of the normal half-pound rainbow. Casting silver Thomas Buoyants with red and black spots, white Phoebes and red and gold Super Dupers also works well.

Once temperatures warm in late April, trout plants are halted and catfish are stocked. Prior to the Nineties, the lake, which is surrounded by grassy lawns and filled by well water, was drained each year. Gibson hasn't been drained in more than a decade though, and with the CA DFG planting some cats to 10 pounds, there are some lunkers to be caught. Chicken and beef liver work best.

If you plan to make the trip, supplies are available in Elverta. There is a day-use fee. No float tubing or boats are permitted.

Also nearby are Sacramento River, American River and Howe Park Pond.

Directions: *From Sacramento, drive north on Interstate 5 to Highway 99. Drive north on Highway 99 to Elverta Road. Turn right and drive 7.2 miles to Park Road. Turn north and drive seven-tenths of a mile to the lake.*

Gibson Ranch Pond

BIG M FISHERY

Rating: 7

Species: Channel
Catfish, Largemouth
Bass and Rainbow
Trout

Stocked periodically
with rainbow trout in
the winter.

Facilities: Restrooms,
Bait & Tackle and a
Picnic Area

Need Information?
Contact: Big M Fishery
(916) 645-0802

Catfish fishing can't get much better than fishing in a catfish farm, and at Big M Fishery, just north of Sacramento, the dream of doing so becomes reality. Big M Fishery is one of the few working catfish farms in Nor Cal. While Big M sells to private ponds for farm stocking, it opens its rearing ponds to the public and averages about 3,000 anglers each year.

Closed from December through February, the farm dedicates one of its ponds to trout fishermen in March and April. Trout are trucked in from Mt. Lassen Trout Farm, however, only about 1,000 fish are released each season because once the water hits 68 degrees the ponds are drained and trout fishing ends for the year. Trout will cost you $3.95 per pound. Once the water becomes too warm for trout the catfish action heats up.

These ponds, located in agriculture area, were built in 1991. In addition to sport fishing and private vendors, the farm also caters to seafood restaurants. Big M is the lone catfish farm in an area made up of 80 percent rice farms. It encompasses 60 acres, 30 of which are used for rearing. All supplied by well water there are five ponds on the property, three of which are fishable.

There are two one-acre fingerling catfish and bass ponds, each with 12,000 fish in them. Also, three five-acre ponds used to raise fish have 10,000 fish in each. The rule to follow when raising catfish is to have no more than 2,000 fish per acre. Averaging two-to-three pounds, but weighing up to eight pounds, there are 1,000 catfish in the fishing pond. Another pond is set aside for catch & release bass fishing on one-to-three pound fish.

Recently, the farm has had a problem with pelicans. In May, pelicans migrate to Canada and stop off at Big M, consuming up to five fish per day. Unfortunately, about 200 landed on Big M's ponds in 2001 and took a toll on its' fishery.

If you plan to make the trip, supplies are available in Lincoln. No fishing license is required. There is a fishing fee. Fish are sold on a per pound basis.

Also nearby is Camp Far West Reservoir.

Directions: From the junction of the 99 Freeway and Interstate 5 in Sacramento, drive north on the 99 Freeway for 10 miles and exit Howsley Road. Turn right and drive 2.9 miles to Pleasant Grove Road. Turn left and drive 4.9 miles to Marcum Road. Continue 3.4 miles to a gravel road on the right and the sign for Big M Fishery. (In one mile from Marcum Road, at the Placer County sign, the road becomes Nicolaus.) Turn right at the sign for Big M Fishery and drive a half-mile to the fishery on the right.

CAMP FAR WEST RESERVOIR

Rating: 7

Species: Spotted Bass,
Smallmouth Bass,
Largemouth Bass,
Striped Bass, Crappie,
Bluegill and Channel
Catfish

Stocks: None

Facilities: General
Store, Boat Launch,
Campgrounds,
Restrooms and Picnic
Areas

Need Information?
Contact: Sportmart
(916) 782-3700

Camp Far West Reservoir is one of the best spring bass fisheries in Northern California, yet for some reason few anglers take advantage of it. The consensus I took leads me to believe that Camp Far West is ignored mostly because it lacks trophy fish, but also because once Memorial Day arrives the 2,000-acre reservoir is swamped by water-skiers and wakeboarders.

On the other hand, in spring, when action is best, the lake can be deserted. Camp Far West is a spotted bass fishery, but it hasn't always been this way. Prior to the introduction of spots, stripers, largemouth and smallmouth thrived. All are still available, but are widely outnumbered by spots. Targeting smallmouth and largemouth bass isn't an option. While you may catch one fishing for spots, it's almost impossible to set out looking for either species. Their population has been cut drastically by out-competing spotted bass.

The reservoir fishes best in the spring when water levels are high. By fall, the lake can be drawn down by more than 100 vertical feet. Nonetheless, local pro bass fishermen Kent Brown, who frequents the reservoir this time of year to cash in on a superb topwater bite, says spring can be fantastic. Topwater is effective from May through fall in the Bear River Arm and around the dam for anglers fishing Zara Spooks and Pop-R's. Dragging darterheads is effective, but don't discount drop-shotting at the mouth of either arm or around the submerged islands near the dam.

The CA DFG hasn't planted stripers in decades, yet they've managed to survive. The situation here is a lot like Santa Margarita and San Antonio Reservoirs on the Central Coast; biologists said the populations of stripers would die out because there wasn't enough incoming water for stripers to spawn, yet stripers remain. In this case, there must be enough water coming in the Bear River for stripers to spawn and keep their life cycle going.

The reservoir also offers a good evening and twilight catfish bite in the summer and fall. Target the backs of coves with mackerel.

If you plan to make the trip, supplies are available in Roseville. There is a day-use and boat launch fee.

Also nearby is Folsom Lake.

Directions: From Interstate 80 in Roseville, exit north on Highway 65 and drive 17.3 miles to Riosa Road. Turn right, drive one-tenth of a mile and turn left on Camp Far West Road. Continue seven miles to McCourtney Road. Turn right and drive nine-tenths of a mile to the left turnoff for the South Shore Recreation Area.

Region 9

Colusa/Glenn County/Solano/Yolo

Lagoon Valley Lake
Solano Lake
Putah Creek
Lake Berryessa
East Park Reservoir
Stony Creek (Middle Fork)
Letts Lake
Plaskett Meadows Reservoir
Stony Gorge Reservoir
Black Butte Lake

LAGOON VALLEY LAKE

Rating: 3

Species: Largemouth Bass, Yellow Perch, Channel Catfish and Bluegill

Stocks: None

Facilities: Boat Launch, Restrooms, Playground and Picnic Areas

Need Information? Contact: Sportmart (707) 451-6800

Located in Lagoon Valley Regional Park, Lagoon Valley Lake is a 106-acre lake that has been ignored by the fishing community for decades. Averaging just six feet, the lake is heading down the path of becoming a marshland unless funds are derived to dredge it. For example, in 1980, the lake averaged nine feet. In 2002, the number was cut to six. There have been talks by the City of Vacaville to restore the lake's fishery, but nothing has been set in stone.

Locals talk of a once thriving yellow perch and largemouth bass fishery, but none of that holds true today. The fishery isn't actively managed by the California Department of Fish and Game, which can be deceiving to anglers who see the fishing icon next to the sign for the regional park on Interstate 80.

The lake offers good access and a paved boat launch, although gas-powered boats aren't permitted. Sadly enough, the groundwork is here for a great fishery for Fairfield and Vacaville residents, unfortunately, the fish aren't. There are a few catfish, bass, perch and pan fish to go around, but nothing to brag about. Put this lake on the backburner for now, but know that with improved management it could quickly reappear on the list.

If you plan to make the trip, supplies are available in Vacaville. There is a day-use parking fee. No gas-powered motors are permitted.

Also nearby is Lake Solano and Putah Creek.

Directions: *From Interstate 80 in Vacaville, exit Pena Adobe Road and follow signs to the park.*

Lagoon Valley Lake

SOLANO LAKE

Rating: 5

Species: Rainbow Trout, Brown Trout, Largemouth Bass, Smallmouth Bass, Channel Catfish, White Catfish, Crappie and Bluegill

Stocked with 18,000 pounds of rainbow trout.

Facilities: Campgrounds, Restrooms, RV Hookups, Boat Rentals, Picnic Areas, Hot Showers and a Boat Launch

Need Information? Contact: Solano Lake Park (530) 795-2990

If you live in Winters, chances are you know all about Solano Lake. By definition, Solano Lake is a true lake, but most consider it a dammed portion of Putah Creek, which it is. Solano Lake is a long, narrow and shallow portion of Putah Creek that gets infested with weeds and can be challenging to fish.

While most hardcore anglers fish in Putah Creek, Solano is mostly fished by oldtimers or families who wait for the California Department of Fish and Game's stock truck. Each year Solano is planted with more than 33,000 half-pound rainbow trout, which do have the ability to holdover. Most of the trout are pan sized, but anglers dunking Power Bait or an inflated night crawler have a shot at rainbows up to a few pounds. Browns aren't planted, but it's possible that they'll swim down from Putah Creek.

This 25-acre lake also holds largemouth and smallmouth bass, which are likely escapees from Lake Berryessa. There are also channel catfish. The cats were planted years ago, and although not abundant, they are available to anglers who are willing to patiently soak bait.

If you plan to make the trip, supplies are available in Winters. No gas-powered boats are permitted.

Also nearby is Putah Creek and Lake Berryessa.

Directions: From the junction of Interstate 5 and 80 in Sacramento, take I-80 west for 30 miles to the 505 Freeway. Drive north on the 505 for 10.3 miles to the Highway 128 exit. Exit Highway 128 and turn left. Drive 5.2 miles to Pleasants Valley Road. Turn left, cross the bridge and turn into the day use area on either side of the road.

Solano Lake

PUTAH CREEK

Rating: 8

Species: Rainbow Trout and Brown Trout

Stocked with 2,000 pounds of brown trout and 8,000 pounds of rainbow trout.

Facilities: RV Hookups, Campgrounds, Picnic Areas and Restrooms

Need Information? Contact: Berryessa Sporting Goods (530) 795-1278

Special Note: In 2004, Putah Creek was closed to fishing when the New Zealand mud snail was found along its' banks. Check sportfishing regulations.

Putah Creek is an excellent tailwater fishery. Fed from cold water released out of Lake Berryessa, the creek stays cold and perfect for trout throughout the year. Putah is a two tier fishery. During the summer, the California Department of Fish and Game plants catchable rainbow trout to cater to recreational anglers. Then, from November 16 to the last Saturday in April, the fishery switches gears to a fly fishing only stream where anglers chase after rainbow and brown trout.

Unlike many others streams in this region, Putah is a special fishery. Stuffed full with trout, the summertime angling can be great for bait anglers and spin casters. During the spring and summer the CA DFG unloads some 4,400 brown trout and 15,800 rainbow trout into this creek that flows into Solano Lake. Unfortunately, flows are the highest in the spring and summer when irrigation needs downstream are met. Increased flows make for challenging angling conditions.

There is a lot of drive-to access for anglers. There are several designated fishing areas from the base of the dam to Solano Lake. Pretty much all the water holds trout, but the best spawning grounds are gravel beds located near the dam. December offers anglers at good chance at trophy fish, as larger rainbows and browns swim up from Lake Solano to spawn.

During the winter and early spring, all angling is catch and release. The shorelines are dominated by fly anglers. Many use sculpin imitations, but others fish with small nymphs under an indicator. The size of wild trout in this stretch is convincing. Many anglers catch 14-16 inch trout with some greater than 20 inches. It's a great fishery that is close to the Bay Area and Sacramento.

If you plan to make the trip, supplies are available in Winters. From November 16 to the last Saturday in April all fishing is catch and release. Only artificial flies with barbless hooks may be used.

Also nearby is Lake Berryessa.

Directions *for Solano Lake also apply to Putah Creek. Putah parallels Highway 128 from the lake to Berryessa dam.*

Putah Creek

LAKE BERRYESSA

Rating: 8

Species: Rainbow
Trout, Brook Trout,
Chinook Salmon,
Kokanee, Largemouth
Bass, Smallmouth Bass,
Channel Catfish,
Crappie, Bluegill and
Carp

Stocked with 690
pounds of fingerling
Chinook salmon, 250
pounds of fingerling
kokanee, 2,600 pounds
of brook trout and
55,500 pounds of
rainbow trout.

Facilities: Boat
Launches, Marinas,
Gas, Boat Rentals,
Houseboat Rentals, Fish
Cleaning Stations,
Lodging, Bait & Tackle,
General Store, Food,
RV Hookups,
Campgrounds,
Restrooms and
Picnic Areas

Need Information?
Contact: Berryessa
Sporting Goods (707)
795-1278, Lake
Berryessa Marina
Resort (707) 966-2161,
Spanish Flat Resort
(707) 966-7700,
Markley Cove Resort
(707) 966-2134,
Pleasure Cove Resort
(707) 966-2172,
Steele Park Resort
(707) 966-2123,
Rancho Monticello
Resort (707) 966-1611

Berryessa is a solid coldwater fishery that is showing signs of improvement. The California Department of Fish and Game treats the lake as a put-and-take fishery. However, recent efforts between the CA DFG and California Inland Fisheries Foundation have introduced kokanee, Chinook salmon and trophy size rainbows.

Rainbow trout have always been on tap. The CA DFG dumps more than 91,600 half-pound rainbows and 3,900 brooks annually. However, this has been a reason for controversy. The CA DFG is aware that many of the planted rainbows in Berryessa don't carry over to the following year. A percentage of the fish are caught right away by trollers and bank anglers, a small number of fish carry over and the rest can't figure out how to eat on their own and die.

These hatchery fish were able to grow on a pellet diet, but struggle in Berryessa because they don't have the instinct to feed on natural food. The planters that do have the instinct don't have mouths big enough to eat the food that's in the lake. Pond smelt, shad, minnows and aquatic insects make up most of the food base.

To help provide a trophy trout fishery and a larger population of holdovers, the CIFF began working with Markley Cove Marina on a pen raising program. The fish are provided by the CA DFG. By the end of the year, more than 1,000 16-20-inch fish are released into the lake. While the planters struggle with the inability to transition from pellet food to natural food, the pen raisers don't have this problem. Living in the pens, these fish are forced to not only eat pellets, but natural food that swims into the cages.

Berryessa is a year-round trout fishery, but a premier trout fishery in the spring when plants take place. During the winter and spring you'll find bows on top, then down to 25 feet by Memorial Day and between 40-70 feet through the summer and early fall. While the entire lake can hold trout, the north end is rather shallow and harbors fewer fish. The southeast end is best. The water is much deeper and colder. The most consistent areas to troll are Skier's Cove, the mouth of The Narrows, The Wires, The Narrows, the mouth of Markley Cove and the dam. Try a Sep's pearl Pro Secret, a green Pro

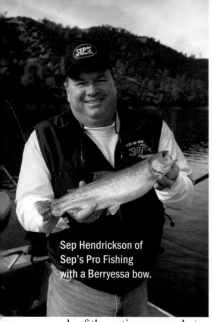

Sep Hendrickson of Sep's Pro Fishing with a Berryessa bow.

Scented grub or a red Pro Trolling fly.

For drive-to trout access, your best bet is between the dam and Markley Cove. This area offers shoreline access to good trout fishing zones. Pleasure Cove also has some access.

In 2001, more than 48,000 kokanee were introduced to Berryessa. The idea was stirred up by tackle manufacturers Sep and Marilyn Hendrickson of Sep's Pro Fishing and the project has since been deemed successful. The first fully mature fish were caught in summer of 2004. The next step for the CIFF is to attempt to make the lake a trophy kokanee lake rather than a lake that has good numbers of fish. To do so, the CA DFG will likely cut the number of kokanee being planted.

Kokanee can be taken year-round. However, much of the action occurs between June and September. In May, expect kokanee to be in 15-40 feet, before moving into 48-52 degree water in June and then into 70-80 feet by July. In August, look for fish down 90-110 feet. Stick to fishing within sight of Montecello Dam. Try running a Sep's Kokanee Kandy with a size 1-4/0 hammered watermelon dodger or run any bright colored lure behind a rainbow pattern dodger.

Berryessa isn't one of the state's premier bass fisheries, but it's definitely not a water that should be overlooked. Berryessa's suffers from a lack of trophy bass. Don't get me wrong, there are big bass available. On the other hand, the frequency they are caught isn't convincing. Each spring a few bass in the teens are taken. Otherwise, you can expect a one-to-two-pound average.

The great aspect of the reservoir is that it's a well-balanced fishery. Spotted, largemouth and smallmouth bass coexist well. A day on the water will yield a mixed bag of all species. Maybe the most important factor of the fishery is the stability of water levels.

Many Nor Cal bass waters suffer from extreme fluctuation. At Berryessa, almost every spawn is successful because water levels remain stable. It also has structure to support all species of bass. Berryessa can be broken down into three separate lakes: The Narrows, the main body and the creek arms.

There are two major creek arms: Putah and Pope Creek. Each can be excellent fisheries. Both have standing timber, coves and your standard creek channels. These sections support resident fish and springtime spawners.

Marilyn Hendrickson of Sep's Pro Fishing nailed this Berryessa bow on a Sep's Pro grub.

During the spring, The Narrows can kick out great action. The Narrows hold the highest concentrations of spotted bass. In the spring, fish jigs and worms in 15 feet of water or less. Your best bet may be fishing Senkos around fallen timber.

The main body fishes a bit different. The spring rip bait bite is exceptional for anglers fishing Lucky Craft Stacee 90s in clown or ghost minnow, Bomber Long A's and half-ounce Smithwick Rattling Rogues in black and silver with an orange belly. Target points and flats.

Many anglers overlook the crankbait bite. Medium diving cranks, like an Excalibur Fat Free Shad in the fingerling series, Bomber 6A and 7A's and Rebel Wee R's are top producers. Fish them anywhere there isn't grass and stick to using crawdad patterns. There's a big population of crawdads .

You don't want to be caught on Berryessa from Memorial to Labor Day. If you can, choose another water. The amount of boat traffic is so horrendous that they almost need traffic signals to keep boating accidents from happening. Winter on the other hand, is a ghost town. Fortunately, fishing is good for anglers shaking worms or fishing Doc Waters jigs or Hula grubs in deep water.

If you plan to make the trip, supplies are available in Winters and Napa. In some areas there are day-use launching fees.

Also nearby is Putah Creek, Solano Creek and Lake Hennessey.

Directions: *From the junction of Interstate 80 and 505 in Vacaville, drive north on Highway 505 to the exit for Highway 128 in Winters. Exit and follow the highway to the reservoir.*

Gary Dobyns, the all-time leading money winner in the West, fished Berryessa for the first time in more than five years to prove quality largemouth and smallmouth bass are still available here.

EAST PARK RESERVOIR

Rating: 6

Species: Largemouth Bass, Crappie, Bluegill and Channel Catfish

Stocks: None

Facilities: Picnic Areas, Outhouses and Primitive Campgrounds

Need Information?
Contact: Bureau of Reclamation
(530) 968-5274

East Park Reservoir has no entrance, day-use or camping fee, nor does it offer any services and its' visitors seems to love it. The fishery itself is recognized as a warm water lake. However, because fishing isn't as good, it takes a backseat to Oroville, Black Butte and Stony Gorge.

East Park is a good bass fishery. Unfortunately, the dirt road to enter the lake and the dirt launch ramp spook off many bass anglers who don't want their pretty boats getting dirty. Unfortunately, they miss out. There is huge bass available and little pressure. In the Seventies and Eighties the lake consistently kicked out bass to 15 pounds. Sadly, a ton of those fish were hung on the wall, taking a good portion of great genes out of the lake. Fish submerged humps, islands and rocky shorelines. There are many of each.

Nonetheless, word is the fishery is on the rebound. Hopefully, this time anglers will release some of the big fish. Stuck between 30 miles of narrow, windy roads to the flat, shallow waters, this lake also yields a good crappie bite in the spring and cats throughout the summer and fall.

If you plan to make the trip, supplies are available in Stonyford. The boat ramp is dirt, but solid and suitable for bass boats.

Also nearby are Stony Creek (Middle Fork) and Black Butte Reservoir.

Directions: From Interstate 5 in Maxwell, take the Maxwell Road exit west for 23 miles to Lodoga. Turn right on Lodoga/Stonyford Road and drive 7.5 miles to Stonyford. Turn right on East Park Road (it may not be signed) and drive 2.7 miles to the lake.

East Park Reservoir

STONY CREEK (MIDDLE FORK)

Rating: 6
Species: Rainbow Trout
Stocks: None
Facilities: Campgrounds
Need Information? Contact: Mendocino National Forest (530) 934-3316

The Middle Fork of Stony Creek is proof that Colusa County does have a wilderness setting to counteract with a mostly flat, dry contour. This cold running stream on the east slope of the coastal range begins in the Snow Mountain Wilderness and runs through the Mendocino National Forest, harboring thousands of small, wild trout eager to take dry flies, nymphs and small spinners.

Stony Creek is a wild trout stream governed by special regulations. Its' lower stretches are easily accessible to anglers, most of whom are fly fishermen looking to fish a small, yet productive stream on the west side of the Upper San Joaquin Valley. Red Bridge is a good starting point for anglers. It rests upstream from where the South and Middle Forks of Stony meet. Anglers should concentrate on the Middle Fork as it often has more water than the South and North Fork, which also enter a short distance downstream.

While the hillsides are dry through the summer (so dry they appear to be ready to explode in flames) trout still bite. This stream is best fished with roll casts. Unfortunately, there isn't a lot of room to cast. Anglers are forced to compete with overgrown banks and usually lose out. While you won't catch many fish greater than 10 inches, there are smaller dinks ready to yank your line.

If you plan to make the trip, supplies are available in Stonyford. Check sport fishing regulations. From the last Saturday in April through November 15, only artificial lures with barbless hooks may be used. There is a two-fish limit. From November 16 to the Friday proceeding the last Saturday in April, only artificial lures with barbless hooks may be used. All fishing is catch and release during this period.

Also nearby are East Park Reservoir and Letts Lake.

Directions: From Interstate 5 in Maxwell, take the Maxwell Road exit west for 23 miles to Lodoga. Turn right on Lodoga/Stonyford Road and drive 7.5 miles to Stonyford. Turn left on Market Street in Stonyford and drive three-tenths of a mile to Fouts Springs Road. Turn left and drive eight miles to the junction on the right. Turn right on Forest Service Road 18N01 and drive two miles to the bridge crossing over the creek.

Stony Creek (Middle Fork)

LETTS LAKE

Rating: 5

Species: Largemouth
Bass and Rainbow
Trout

Stocked with 2,000
pounds of rainbow
trout.

Facilities: Picnic Areas,
Restrooms,
Campgrounds and a
Fishing Pier

Need Information?
Contact: Mendocino
National Forest
(530) 934-3316

Letts Lake is a small reservoir on the east slope of the Mendocino National Forest where anglers can pitch a tent and catch pan size trout. Letts Lake has gone through its' ups and downs in the last few decades, but the fishery may have finally stabilized.

The lake was built in the Fifties and was planted with trout prior to the illegal introduction of golden shiners. The shiners took over the lake, destroying the water quality and the fishery. The California Department of Fish and Game poisoned Letts in 1965, 1976 and 1978 unsuccessfully, before trying a biological control, namely bass, catfish and bluegill. The warm water fish ate most of the shiners and cured the problem.

However, more issues surfaced and where tackled in 2003, when the 33-acre lake resting at 4,500 feet was drained to remove unwanted silt and weeds. With 1.4 miles of shoreline, an average depth of six feet and a maximum depth of 18 feet, the lake naturally refilled in the winter of 2004 and is fishing as good as ever. The CA DFG dumps roughly 4,000 bows in a year.

Surrounded by pines, Letts has great shoreline and wheelchair access and can be fished by float tubers and car top boats. No outboard motors are permitted. It's a great place to chuck bait from shore or pitch spinners. Count on catching mostly half-pound bows.

If you plan to make the trip, supplies are available in Stonyford. In winter and spring call ahead for road conditions. Some of the road to the lake is dirt or gravel and may not be suitable for small vehicles.

Also nearby are East Park Reservoir and Stony Creek (Middle Fork).

Directions: From Interstate 5 in Maxwell, take the Maxwell Road exit west for 23 miles to Lodoga. Turn right on Lodoga/Stonyford Road and drive 7.5 miles to Stonyford. Turn left on Market Street in Stonyford and drive three-tenths of a mile to Fouts Springs Road. Turn left and drive eight miles to the junction on the right. Continue straight and drive 5.8 miles to a split in the road. Stay left and drive 1.3 miles to another split. Stay left and drive three-tenths of a mile to the lake.

Letts Lake in the summer of 2003

PLASKETT MEADOWS RESERVOIR

Rating: 6

Species: Rainbow Trout, Bluegill and Largemouth Bass

Stocked with 800 pounds of rainbow trout.

Facilities: Restrooms, Picnic Area, Fishing Piers and Campgrounds

Need Information? Contact: Mendocino National Forest (530) 934-3316

Rather than beating around the bush with all the details, know this first: anglers who want to fish Plaskett Meadows Reservoirs are going to have to endure a long, slow drive to get there. The small pond-size impoundment is more than 54 miles from Interstate 5 and more than half of those miles are on winding roads, not to mention 10 miles on dirt.

What you need to decide is whether the drive is worth it? At 4,500 feet, Plaskett Meadows Reservoir is a small, pretty lake in a remote section of the Mendocino National Forest. It doesn't receive a heck of a lot of fishing pressure, yet is stocked with 1,600 rainbow trout each year. Catch rates tend to be high as the trout are pretty much corralled into a small confinement and restricted to swimming in circles looking for food.

That food is usually Power Bait or any spinner or spoon. Anglers can find good access and willing fish, especially in the spring when the California Department of Fish and Game begins their annual stocking program. The incentives aren't great, yet many visitors are happy to find a quiet campground within walking distance in this heavily pined lake.

While most anglers stick to fishing the upper lake, just downstream of the dam is a smaller, shallower lake which is home to hundreds of small bass. This lake doesn't hold many trout, only escapees from the upper lake, but has a stable population of small largemouth that speak kindly of any night crawler tossed their way.

If you plan to make the trip, supplies are available in Maxwell. In winter and early spring call ahead for road conditions. The road may be closed due to snow or muddy conditions.

Also nearby are Black Butte Reservoir and Stoney Gorge Reservoir.

Directions: *From Interstate 5 in Willows, exit Highway 162 and drive west for 19.8 miles to Road 306 (also signed for Highway 162.) Turn right and drive 3.6 miles to the left turnoff for Alder Springs (again signed for Highway 162). Turn left and drive 29.3 miles to the Plaskett Campground turnoff on the left. Turn left and drive seven-tenths of a mile to the day-use area. Tips: at 15.1 miles the road turns to dirt and at 24.7 miles you'll come to a three-way split. Take the left fork.*

Plaskett Meadows Reservoir

STONY GORGE RESERVOIR

Rating: 5

Species: Crappie, Catfish, Bluegill, Smallmouth Bass and Largemouth Bass

Stocks: None

Facilities: Boat Launch, Restrooms, Picnic Areas and Campgrounds

Need Information? Contact: Bureau of Reclamation (530) 275-1554

Stony Gorge Reservoir isn't one of Northern California's most popular bass fisheries. However, it is a fair, warm water fishery that doesn't get a heck of a lot of pressure like nearby Oroville. It also attracts a lot of campers. Not surprisingly, this is because the reservoir offers free camping and lakeside spots for RVs and tents, many with fire pits and picnic tables.

With 18 miles of shoreline and nearly 1,300 acres of water, this dammed portion of Stony Creek supports a good crappie and catfish population. Crappie are best in the spring and catfish make for great evening and night bites in the summer months and throughout the fall. Coves are best for catfish, as are natural baits soaked in Liquid Krill. Summer is so hot and dry that most anglers fish in the wee morning hours or at night.

Large and smallmouth bass are available in good numbers, yet not a lot of bass anglers fish the lake. This is most likely related to the lack of trophy fish and fishing info for Stonyford. Also note: there are no tackle shops near the reservoir. Springtime is best for both species of bass.

If you plan to make the trip, supplies are available in Willows and Elk Creek.

Also nearby are Black Butte Reservoir, Stony Creek and East Park Reservoir.

Directions: From Interstate 5 in Willows exit west on Highway 162 for 19.6 miles to the left turnoff for the lake. Turn left and drive 1.4 miles to the reservoir.

Stony Gorge Reservoir

BLACK BUTTE RESERVOIR

Rating: 6

Species: Largemouth
Bass

Stocks: None

Facilities:
Campgrounds, Picnic
Areas, Boat Launches,
Restrooms, Hiking
Trails, RV Hookups,
Fish Cleaning Station
and a Playground

Need Information?
Contact: Black Butte
Lake (530) 865-4781

At first sight Black Butte Reservoir left me confused. This was a big lake, only a half-hour from Chico, yet the place was deserted and on a summer weekday when other nearby reservoirs such as Oroville and Stoney Gorge were packed. With a second look I quickly found some answers.

Black Butte has lived through a drought of what I like to call irresponsibility by anglers who - for decades - have continually kept undersize fish and taken more than their limits. The poaching has nearly decimated the fishery. If not for recent efforts by park rangers and anglers to stop the harvesting of undersize crappie, bass, catfish and just about any fish that swims, the lake would be doomed.

The other hazard is wind. Traditionally, many boaters and anglers have been run off this lake by howling winds and don't take their chances on it happening again. The wind can make for dangerous boating conditions.

On the flip side, Black Butte is still a decent warmwater fishery without the possibility of a coldwater aspect. No trout exist and will most likely never be planted. Located in the rolling hills of the Upper Sacramento Valley, if this reservoir wasn't so close to Oroville, it would likely get more respect as a fishery. With Oroville so close, few anglers see a reason to fish Black Butte.

At full pool, Black Butte is 4,460 acres, offers 41 miles of shoreline and is seven miles long. It is, however, drawn down considerably in the fall. The reservoir was constructed primarily for flood control by the US Army Corps of

Mark Lassagne with a traditional size Black Butte bass. 229

Engineers. The lake is relatively shallow. There's a deep channel in front of the dam, but it's not deeper than 80 feet even at full pool. The lake averages only 26 feet.

Black Butte isn't totally destroyed as many anglers guess. The reservoir does harbor several species of warmwater fish including bass, catfish and panfish. Several years ago the reservoir was chalked up as one of the top crappie fisheries in the state. While crappie are still on the plate, the stardom comes in cycles, which naturally arrive every three, or so, years. It's best to fish in the spring during the spawn. At that time, crappie to 17 inches aren't uncommon. Try tossing white or brown tube baits and marabou jigs in the Burris Creek Area and the old marina.

Next to crappie, catfish may be the best thing at Black Butte. In summer and early fall, cats are most active at night and can be caught on any of the flats. It's uncommon to catch cats up to 15 pounds with some larger. All night fishing is permitted which allows catfish anglers to be more successful. The west end and Grizzly Flat area is most productive.

Bass fishing is best in the spring. Concentrate on fallen logs and flooded willow trees. During the warmer months, anglers will have to fish deep. The lake poses a good reaction bite early in the morning and late in the evening. During the daytime and in the afternoons, you'll have to key in on submerged structure. Fish jigs and soft plastics. Bass are most prevalent in the willows south of the Orland Buttes area.

If you plan to make the trip, supplies are available in Orland. There is a day use and boat launch fee.

Also nearby are Stoney Gorge Reservoir and East Park Reservoir.

Directions: *From Interstate 5 in Orland, take the Black Butte exit and drive 11 miles to a split in the road. Stay right and drive one-half mile to Buckhorn Road. Turn left to the lake.*

Black Butte Reservoir

Region  Trinity County

10

Ruth Lake
Ewing Gulch Reservoir
Union Hill Pond
Lewiston Reservoir
Trinity River (Lewiston to Douglas City)
Trinity River (Douglas City to Junction City)
Trinity River (Junction City to Helena)
Rush Creek
Trinity Lake
Trinity River (Stuarts Fork)
Swift Creek
Carrville Trout Pond
Coffee Creek Trout Pond
Coffee Creek
Trinity River (Upper)
Rush Creek Lakes
Canyon Creek (Upper)
Canyon Creek Lake (Lower)
Canyon Creek Lake (Upper)

RUTH LAKE

Rating: 7

Species: Crappie,
Bluegill, Channel
Catfish, Largemouth
Bass, Smallmouth Bass
and Rainbow Trout

Stocked with 13,050
pounds of rainbow trout
and 1,400 pounds of
sub-catchable trout.

Facilities:
Campgrounds,
Restrooms, Boat
Launch, General Store,
Bait and Tackle and
Boat Rentals

Need Information?
Contact: Trinity
National Forest
(530) 628-5227

As a bass reservoir, Ruth Lake's time was short lived. Sometime in the early Seventies the California Department of Fish and Game planted smallmouth bass, which took well in reservoir. However, unknown sportsmen introduced largemouth bass in the Eighties, which screwed up the system. After a quick boom in the bass fishery, an even bigger bust occurred. Small bass dominated the fishery. In an effort to clean up the mess, the CA DFG implemented a 15-inch minimum size limit on bass. This was expected to drive the average size of the fish up.

In 2000, the CA DFG revisited the lake to see how the limits were working. Expecting to find mostly 12-15 inch fish, they were shocked to run into bass that averaged nine-to-10 inches. The locals weren't happy either, as there were unable to catch legal size fish. They instead began working with the CA DFG to implement a slot limit. Some bass were going to have to be removed from the system in order to allow the fishery to rebound. Electrofishing efforts found that 12-inch bass were five years old. In 2002, a 12-inch minimum, five fish limit was then introduced.

The problem is that Ruth's bass don't have much to eat. The number of bluegill and crappie are minimal. The forage is stocked trout and small juvenile fish, resources the fish have outgrown. At the time the new regulations were put in place, roughly 25-35 percent of the bass were over a 12 inch minimum. There was a need to allow anglers to take fish out, basically because there wasn't enough food to support the fishery.

These small bass were competing for resources and weren't

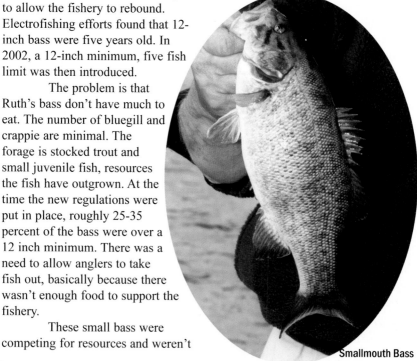

Smallmouth Bass

growing. Ideally, CA DFG biologist Larry Hanson hopes to introduce a forage fish (pond smelt) as bass food. If this happens, plan on catching quality bass at Ruth in a few years. For targeting bass, think of Ruth as two lakes. Near the dam is the deep end, which harbors mostly smallmouth. The shallow end is where the Mad River enters. Largemouth find better habitat here.

Ruth may be a marginal bass lake, but it's an excellent trout fishery. The CA DFG dumps more than 21,175 half-pound trout and 15,000 sub-catchables into the 1,178 acre reservoir each year. At 2,655 feet in the Six Rivers National Forest, the Mad River brings an influx of cool water in the normally stable reservoir. The planted fish join 14-15 inch carryovers, in addition to the wild fish that reproduce naturally in this seven-mile long reservoir. Trout spawn in the Mad River and many of the lake's other tributaries.

Ruth is the closest lake for residents of Eureka, Fortuna and Arcata and is mainly fished by locals. Historically, kokanee were planted, but with no interest, the fishery is all about rainbow trout now. The reservoir was built in 1962.

If you plan to make the trip, supplies are available in Fortuna.

Also nearby is the Van Duzen River.

Directions: *From the junction of Highway 36 east and Highway 101 in Fortuna, drive east on Highway 36 for 48 miles to the turnoff for Mad River Road on the right. Turn right and drive 6.7 miles to the dam or 8.7 miles to the right turnoff for the marina.*

Ruth Lake

EWING GULCH RESERVOIR

Rating: 7

Species: Largemouth Bass, Bluegill, Red Ear Sunfish, Brown Bullhead and Rainbow Trout

Stocked with 2,500 pounds of rainbow trout.

Facilities: Picnic Areas and Restrooms

Need Information? Contact: Trinity National Forest (530) 628-5227

The town of Hayfork isn't frequented by out-of-towners. Nonetheless, the folks in this small rural town would probably like to keep it that way. Hayfork is easy to picture: it's a town where everything is named Hayfork, whether it be Hayfork Feed, Hayfork Market, etc. It's the kind of town where people are born and live there until they die.

Surrounded by the Trinity National Forest, Hayfork is a pretty place that is packed with deer who act like dogs. The deer walk through front yards, lie down on lawns and pick through delicate gardens. Hayfork is also a place where everyone knows everyone and an out-of-towner sticks out like a Red Sox fan in Yankee Stadium. Especially when someone sees you turn on Brady Road.

See, Brady Road is the route taken to 40-acre Ewing Gulch Reservoir, the town's prized fishery, a place I might say is perfect for locals. What keeps the reservoir off the radar of folks from other cities and towns is that it doesn't harbor many trophy fish. It's better described as a put-and-take pond where shoreline fishing is the rule. Trout can be caught year-round, but since the shorelines are relatively shallow, you'll need to fish off the dam or find a point to locate deeper water. The California Department of Fish and Game dumps some 4,125 half-pound trout each year.

Ewing Gulch Reservoir

Ewing Gulch also bass. In the spring when the bass are close to the shoreline, it's not uncommon to catch and release more than 30 bass per day. They won't be trophies though. Most will run one-to-two pounds. However, there is that exception to the rule: the one bass that has sucked down stocked trout and bluegill his whole life and is much larger than the others.

If you plan to make the trip, supplies are available in Hayfork.

Also nearby are Hayfork Creek and the Trinity River.

Directions: From the junction of Highway 299 and Interstate 5 in Redding, drive west on Highway 299 for roughly 39.5 miles to the Hayfork turnoff. Turn left on Highway 3 and drive 23.1 miles to the right turnoff for Brady Road. Turn right and drive seven-tenths of a mile to Ewing Road. Turn right and drive four-tenths of a mile to the lake.

UNION HILL POND

Rating: 4

Species: Largemouth
Bass, Bluegill and
Brown Bullhead

Stocks: None

Facilities: None

Need Information?
Contact: Bureau of
Land Management
(530) 224-2100

The good old boys from the backwoods of Mississippi and Alabama feel right at home at Union Hill Pond. Union Hill Pond isn't your typical Trinity County fishery equipped with good shoreline access and lots of planted trout. Union Hill Pond is the opposite. It's a pond sporting shorelines so heavily overgrown that you'd need a world-class machete to reach the water in most places.

Union Hill is bassy though. While fished by few anglers each year, the ones who know what they are doing can find battles with bass up to 10 pounds. Be prepared though. The lake is lined with trees, weeds and tules. In most places the cover is so thick you'd need 20-pound test to win.

Without a car top boat, like a Sea Eagle Paddle Ski, you are wasting your time. Don't bother dragging a boat and trailer. There is a makeshift boat launch fit for car tops, but nothing larger. Motors will be clogged with weeds before you even turn them on. It's best to bring a long pole or paddle to glide yourself around the pond.

Come prepared to fish weeds and thick structure, because that's what you will be up against. From late spring through early summer, there can be an excellent frog bite. Others choose to shake weightless baits on weed beds. There are bass, but they aren't easy to catch. These fish are smart and use cover to their advantage. You have to outsmart them. The second you set the hook be sure to keep their head up and the fish out of the weeds. Otherwise, you'll be in trouble.

If you plan to make the trip, supplies are available in Douglas City. The road to the reservoir may be closed due to poor road conditions. Call ahead.

Also nearby is the Trinity River.

Directions: *From the junction of Highway 299 and Interstate 5 in Redding, drive west for roughly 39.5 miles to the Douglas City turnoff. Reset your odometer and drive 1.4 miles to the right turnoff for Union Hill Road. Turn right and drive 1.2 miles to a spilt in the road. Turn right and drive six-tenths of a mile to the lake.*

Union Hill Pond

LEWISTON RESERVOIR

Rating: 8

Species: Rainbow Trout, Brook Trout, Brown Trout Chinook Salmon and Kokanee

Stocked with 10,335 pounds of rainbow trout.

Facilities: Bait & Tackle, Boat Launch, Boat Rentals, Fishing Piers, Campgrounds, Picnic Areas and Restrooms

Need Information? Contact: Pine Cove Marina (530) 778-3770

Lewiston Reservoir is a classic tail water fishery. Benefiting from direct flows of year-round cold water from Trinity Lake, Lewiston is one of Nor Cal's better trout fisheries. The reservoir has a promising number of quality carryover rainbow trout that were stocked the first year at one-half pound and have since grown to two-to-four pounds after roughly one year.

What's allowing them to grow so rapidly? Several factors, including lots of insect productivity on the north end as well as many young kokanee being blown into Lewiston from Trinity. These fish are growing pills for trout. Locals consider freshwater shrimp to be a food source, but the California Department of Fish and Game has no documentation to verify this 100 percent.

Each year, the CA DFG drops more than 17,013 rainbows in the lake, in addition to 100 brood fish between three and five pounds. In recent years, Pine Cove Marina has helped pump big fish in the reservoir. The marina has four cages used for pen rearing trout. One load of fish is supplied by the CA DFG. Those fish are released at three-to-five pounds. However, three other loads purchased from Mt. Lassen Trout Farms are released between five and 10 pounds. Roughly 1,500 fish are raised annually.

Lewiston can be described as a reservoir with many characteristics. From the dam to roughly a quarter-mile above the marina, the reservoir is basically a moving river channel. This section is shallow, with the deepest spot being six-to-eight feet; however, this area can be navigated in a boat. Next, you'll find a big, broad flat near the marina and a deeper old river channel near the dam. On a positive note, the cool water allows anglers to fish the same areas year-round.

Despite what you may read about its' brown trout fishery, Lewiston is primarily a rainbow trout fishery. There are a few browns, but they aren't planted and haven't been since 1996 when 8,400 catchable fish were released. Brooks were planted off and on from 1969-1997 and steelhead from 1977-79.

At 1,900 feet in the Shasta-Trinity National Forest, this 610-acre reservoir is best fished from a vessel. There are good shoreline options and fishing piers but anglers with boats do best. There is no bank access on the side of the lake opposite of Trinity Dam Blvd. The quickest way to grab a limit is to start at the buoy line near the inlet and boondoggle. Shoreline anglers should have no problems catching fish either.

If you plan to make the trip, supplies are available in Lewiston. There is a 10 mph speed limit.

Also nearby is the Trinity River, Rush Creek and Trinity Lake.

Directions: *From Interstate 5 in Redding, exit west on Highway 299 and drive 31 miles to the right turnoff for Trinity Dam Blvd. Turn right and drive nine miles to the lake.*

TRINITY RIVER (LEWISTON TO DOUGLAS CITY)

Rating: 7

Species: Steelhead, Brown Trout and Chinook Salmon

Stocks: None

Facilities: Lodging, Gas, Restaurant, Boat Launches, Restrooms, Campgrounds and RV Hookups

Need Information? Contact: Fishing Guide Tim King (530) 623-3438, Trinity Fly Shop (530) 623-6757

The less water a river has the easier it is to fish. Smaller water tends to produce greater catch rates in many cases because you have more concentrated fish and fewer holding areas. From the Highway 299 Bridge in Douglas City upriver to Lewiston Dam, the Trinity River is much smaller than it is in its' lower stretches. While this section is enjoyed by bait dunkers and drift boaters, the water is primarily fished by fly anglers.

The shining attribute of this upper reach is that it's often fishable, even when other areas are blown out. The difficulty lies in not spooking the fish. The small river technicalities can be challenging to overcome. Basically, the river is so narrow that in some places if you are fishing from a drift boat, you are constantly cruising over fish.

Anadromous fish are found in this section during their respective seasons, but also they tend to be fewer in numbers compared to other areas of the Trinity. The explanation is relatively simple. There are only four places where steelhead and salmon go in this section: some spawn in the main river, others head up Rush and Grass Valley Creeks to spawn and the rest head into the Lewiston Fish Hatchery (which is federally funded and not in danger of losing funding). Most salmon and steelhead have veered off into lower tributaries before reaching this portion of the river.

From a drift boat running plugs is effective, especially using size 40 and 50 pink or black and silver Hot Shots. Bait is productive from shore or a boat. Steelhead season lasts roughly from November through March. Springers

A Trinity River steelhead

tend to find their way into the region in July. Then you'll have a fall run, which comes in late August and remains in the system through October.

There are four great drifts. Here's a list: roughly six miles long, Lewiston to the Bucktail Fishing Access; roughly six miles, from Bucktail to Steel Bridge; roughly 3.5 miles, from Steel Bridge to Indian Creek and finally from Indian Creek to Steiner Flat, a four-mile drift. The only downfall to the final drift is that on its' bottom end you'll have to face Weaver Creek, which tends to pump lots of mud into the system after a good rain.

Trinity River steelhead

If you plan to make the trip, supplies are available in Douglas City. Check sport fishing regulations for updated bag limits, gear restrictions and closures.

Also nearby are Rush Creek, Lewiston Reservoir and Trinity Lake.

Directions: *From the junction of Interstate 5 and Highway 299 in Redding, drive west on Highway 299 for 34.2 miles to Lewiston Road. Turn right and continue to Lewiston where access can be found in several locations. Access can also be found off Steelhead Bridge Road and in Douglas City.*

Guide Tim King with an average Trinity River steelhead.

TRINITY RIVER (DOUGLAS CITY TO JUNCTION CITY)

Rating: 8

Species: Rainbow Trout, Brown Trout, Chinook Salmon and Steelhead

Stocks: None

Facilities: A Boat Launch

Need Information? Contact: Trinity River Outfitters (530) 623-6376

The Trinity River between Douglas City and Junction City is set aside for anglers with drift boats and canoes. This eight-mile section of the Trinity runs through a canyon that offers little public access to anyone other than land owners. There is fishing access in Douglas and Junction City, but not in the heart of the section. Anglers with their own craft can legally drift the run by putting in at Dutton Creek River Access in Douglas City and taking out at Evans Bar near the weir in Junction City. There are also logging roads that run alongside the west side of the river near Junction City. Oftentimes, water releases dictate how fishing will be. Standard summer releases are 450 cfs.

Much of the land bordering this drift rests on private grounds. You'll have to book a guide or have your own drift boat and means of a shuttle service to fish it. The shuttle, unfortunately, isn't convenient.

The river is framed by runs of steelhead and salmon. There are few resident rainbows in this section. Sea-run browns inhabit the river, but aren't caught often and can't be targeted. The river is closed to fishing from April 1 to the fourth Saturday in May.

Salmon arrive in late May and early June. These springers trickle in through early August when they are joined by the fall Chinook run that lasts through November.

The Trinity isn't known for enormous salmon. In fact, most of your fish will run between 10-15 pounds. However, the intimate setting is hard to beat. This section of the river is scenic and cuts through a narrow canyon with steep cliffs in a heavily forested area with gin clear water. The river has a rocky bottom with gravel and sandy areas.

The Trinity, unlike the Sacramento and other systems, isn't a deep river system, 20 feet is a deep hole! In this eight-mile section there aren't many quality salmon holding areas. You'll find fish schooled up in seven, or so, consistent spots, which unveil below.

The put-in can be found at Dutton Creek River Access, which is operated by the Bureau of Land Management. This is where Dutton Creek dumps into the Trinity.

The first hole downriver is known as Cathedral Hole. This 12-foot deep hole is a big horseshoe. The water runs fast on both sides of the rocks that rest at the top of the hole. In this case, the water has dug out a deep spot in the middle. The hole is roughly 20 yards long and 10 yards wide.

Local names are all the river offers. The next hole is Wayne's World, creatively named after the dude who owns the property. He's the only year

Traditional steelhead baits

round resident on the right side of the river in this section and keeps close eye on this 25-foot deep, 40-yard long hole.

Next is Stove Pipe Hole, hence its' name, is located next to an old stove pipe. If you miss the pipe, the rock outcroppings should give the hole away. It's small, even by Trinity standards, yet holds fish.

Shortly downstream, the Big Hole can contain upwards of 250 fish. It's a slow hole that sees an immense amount of pressure, but can be difficult to fish due to slow water.

Three-miles from the Dutton put-in is the Hornet's Nest, marked at one time by a large hornets nest, that no longer hangs. The 40 yard long hole holds quality fish. It can be approached by tossing roe where the fast current meets glassy water.

The Camp Hole is an easy one to spot. Once fishing season starts, you'll known the hole because there's a tree atop the hole that can resemble a Christmas Tree, not literally, but figuratively because this tree is covered with bait, lures and fishing line, not traditional ornaments. On the other hand, the hole is small. Many anglers float right past it. Even less dramatic is the Secret Hole, where the river forms a backwards "s" pattern.

Next is the Cabin Hole, a long, slow moving hole that can be tough to approach for newcomers and experienced anglers alike because the water moves so slow. The Marijuana Hole follows, but has lost its' popularity since it became heavily silted. Locals hint that the drug used to be and is probably still is grown around this area.

Creatively named, 6.5 miles in the "Last Hole on the Left," is a long, slow moving run roughly six-to-eight feet deep. To find fish, cast on the west side of the river. You'll have to cast under the trees and let it drift downriver. When salmon fishing, concentrate on deep holes.

As for gear, a seven-and-a-half-foot light to medium action rod is ideal. Under normal conditions a half-to-three-quarter ounce weight is best, with a 10-pound, 30-inch leader and a No. 1 barbless hook.

The river can be approached with roe, Kwikfish and FlatFish. Due to low flows, the use of a Jet Diver is necessary. When using roe, cast upriver and allow to the bait to bounce along the bottom while waiting for a delicate bite. Typically, the fish won't hammer your bait, rather pick at it.

The Trinity also has a rare strain of sea-run brown trout. Typically, they are caught by anglers fishing for salmon and steelhead, mostly in the winter on flies. You'll find them in deep holes in the summer and in three-to-six feet of water chasing flies in the winter. They average two-to-five pounds and are rare.

Fall means less crowds, cooler temperatures and better fishing. In early September, steelhead trickle in and come in greater numbers as Halloween and Thanksgiving arrive. During the early part of the run, steelhead average four-to-six pounds. That number increases slightly as the season progresses. Some fish greater than 10 pounds are caught annually. For steelies look for three-to-five-foot deep holes with a little chop on the water.

There is also a summer run of steelhead that enter the river in May and continue through September overlapping with the winter run. Catching the steelies is a different game than the salmon. Smaller pieces of roe, Glo Bugs soaked in Pautzke Liquid Krill, golden stone flies in size 10 and 12, a No. 2 Blue Fox, Panther Martin or Mepps spinner, mini or half night crawlers or backtrolling Hot Shots and Wee Warts is best.

If you plan to make the trip, supplies are available in Douglas City and Junction City. Check sport fishing regulations for updated bag limits, gear restrictions and closures.

Also nearby are Trinity Lake and Lewiston Lake.

Directions: From the junction of Highway 299 and Interstate 5 in Redding, drive west for 39.5 miles to the Douglas City turnoff. Turn left to river access. Or, continue on Highway 299 for roughly 52 miles Junction City.

The best access to the Trinity River surely comes with a drift boat. (Above) Guide Tim King's boat

TRINITY RIVER (JUNCTION CITY TO HELENA)

Rating: 7

Species: Chinook Salmon, Steelhead and Brown Trout

Stocks: None

Facilities: Boat Launches and a General Store

Need Information? Contact: Fishing Guide Tim King (530) 623-3438

Anglers can float dozens of quality drifts on the Trinity River as a whole. However, when it comes to its' wintertime fishery, there are few drifts that can beat the run from Junction City to Helena. Roughly eight miles long, this stretch of water is great for steelhead fishing. The water doesn't get blown out as quickly as the lower river and isn't as small as the river near Lewiston. Basically, it tends to be ideal, or fishable, when much of the river is too high or muddy to fish.

Junction City to Helena is a pretty stretch of water. Although there are a few homes along the bank, this water tends to remain fairly quiet and free of heavy boat traffic. The drift begins in Douglas City and terminates where the North Fork enters on the right side of the river. Locals refer to this spot as Baghdad.

During the winter months you find some half-pounders, but mostly adult steelhead, which are primarily fished with Luhr Jensen Hot Shots and roe. The tricky thing is knowing when to use a Puff Ball. When the system gets low and clear, it's best to fish without one. However, if it's running normal, or high, you'll want to use a Puff Ball. Don't worry; this water is easy to read. It shouldn't be tough distinguishing between where to run plugs or when to toss roe. Steelhead can be found in this section from late October through March.

From late spring through fall you'll find Chinook salmon. It's easy to find the salmon holes. They are much deeper than the rest of the river. First you'll have springers running through in June, and then a fall run of fish. These fish run from 12 to 25 pounds on average and take roe and plugs.

If you plan to make the trip, supplies are available in Weaverville. A salmon punch card is necessary to fish for salmon on the Trinity River. Check sport fishing regulations for updated daily bag limits.

Also nearby are Canyon Creek, Trinity Lake and Lewiston Lake.

Directions: *From the junction of Interstate 5 and Highway 299 west in Redding, drive west on Highway 299 for roughly 52 miles to Junction City. Access is available from here to the Helena turnoff.*

Guide Tim King and a Trinity steelhead.

RUSH CREEK

Rating: 3

Species: Rainbow Trout and Brook Trout

Stocks: None

Facilities: Campgrounds and Restrooms

Need Information?
Contact: Shasta-Trinity National Forest
(530) 623-2121

Rush Creek is one of the Trinity National Forest's nicest, small streams. It doesn't offer great fishing, but it does make for great streamside camping in a quiet, friendly atmosphere. Rush Creek runs well in the spring and early summer, but can possibly dry up in poor rain years by fall. Fortunately, the latter scenario isn't likely.

Rush Creek isn't planted with trout by the California Department of Fish and Game. A tributary to the Trinity River, trout plants could possibly interfere with native salmon and steelhead runs, so they aren't bothered with. Rush doesn't have a lot of trout, yet it does have small rainbows and brooks in its riffles and pools. The population tends to fluctuate depending on water levels. If there has been good rainfall in recent years, expect good things. During drought conditions the fish may not fair as well. Even under great conditions don't expect anything over 10 inches. Most of your fish will be in the six-to-eight-inch class.

My suggestion would be to cast the smallest Panther Martin you can find into small pools or pluck Pautzke salmon eggs. There is plenty of roadside water available along Rush Creek Road and upstream of the Highway 3 Bridge.

If you plan to make the trip, supplies are available in Weaverville. Rush Creek is closed to fishing from November 16 to the last Saturday in April.

Also nearby are Rush Creek Lakes, Trinity Lake and Trinity River.

Directions: From the junction of Interstate 5 and Highway 299 in Redding, exit west towards Weaverville on Highway 299. Drive 45.6 miles to the Trinity Lake/Highway 3 turnoff. Turn right and drive roughly nine miles to the left turnoff for Rush Creek Campground.

Tuck your food away! Racoons are commonly seen around Rush Creek at night.

TRINITY LAKE

Rating: 10

Species: Largemouth Bass, Smallmouth Bass, Bullhead, Channel Catfish, Crappie, Bluegill, Chinook Salmon, Rainbow Trout, Brown Trout and Kokanee

Stocked with 2,300 pounds of fingerling brown trout and 3,290 pounds of rainbow trout.

Facilities: Restrooms, Marinas, Bait &Tackle, Campgrounds, RV Hookups, Lodging, Boat Launches, Boat Rentals, Houseboat Rentals, Restaurant, General Store, Gas, Fish Cleaning Stations and Showers

Trinity Lake isn't your average California reservoir. It only took me one trip with fishing guide John Gray to realize that. Gray moved from Maine to Trinity Lake so he could be close to some of the best bass fishing in the West. Gray's move improved his quality of life. He discovered Trinity Lake offers the chance of seeing bald eagles diving down to catch trout, otters playing near the boat dock, osprey soaring from nest to nest following anglers hoping they'll release a injured fish they could eat for dinner, deer sipping water on the shoreline and enough fresh air and tall pines to make anglers feel like they are hundreds of miles from civilization.

Situated in a secluded portion of the Shasta-Trinity National Forest, Trinity Lake rests under the shadow of the Trinity Alps Wilderness. The nearest city is Weaverville, some 20 minutes away. Weaverville provides all the amenities that a major city does, but gives off a much different feeling. Lifestyles, and the quality of life, are different here than in most California cities. People are extremely laid back, friendly and are on their own time clock. There is no sense of urgency.

Trinity is one of California's last unknown gems. It's a phenomenal fishery that is actively managed by the California Department of Fish & Game. Its grandeur stems from not just the relaxed setting, but also for the quality of fish. With more than 16,000 acres, there's a ton of room for fish to grow. That space has allowed Trinity's trout and bass to become some of the largest and most prosperous in the state, yet, still few anglers venture here.

The most logical reason is simple. Trinity isn't a short jaunt from anywhere in California. Redding is the closest city and at least an hour and a half drive. Sacramento puts you at almost four hours, the Bay Area five and Los Angeles, say 10 hours to be safe. Plus, the last 50 miles are on windy, high gradient mountain roads. It's no easy trip, but more than worth it.

Trinity is enjoyed by all sorts of recreationists. Fortunately for anglers, usually water skiers and boaters stay in the middle and southern portions. The lake is also a popular houseboating destination. Trinity can be split into

Editor's Note: Because of the large number of contacts for Trinity Lake, we've listed all info numbers below in an easy to use format:

Fishing Guides: Bass Fishing Guide John Gray (530) 623-4352, Trout Fishing Guide Vince Holson (530) 623-1693

Resorts and Campground Info: Trinity National Forest (530) 623-2121,Estrellita Marina (800) 747-2215, Trinity Alps Marina (800) 824-0083, Trinity Lake Marina (800) 892-2279, Wyntoon Resort (800) 715-3337

three sections: the south end is found below Captain's Point and includes the dam, the midsection is comprised of The Narrows and the north end is everything above Trinity Center Marina.

Trinity poses one of the best and most underutilized fisheries in California, probably on the entire West Coast. The state record smallmouth bass was taken here in 1976. That 9.1-pound fish could be topped soon. It's no secret larger smallies are available. Additionally, the lake is one of only two lakes in California with a pure strain of Northern largemouth bass. They too, get huge. A 14.1-pound largemouth stands as the biggest fish to date. We'll talk about the big trout later on though, and chinook salmon.

Guide John Gray and a Trinity smallie

Trinity's bass get huge for several reasons. First off, there is an enormous population of stunted kokanee. The kokanee might not grow longer than eight inches, yet they are as abundant as shad are in most reservoirs. Forage also includes rainbow trout and crawdads. In addition, several large tributaries bring an influx of cold water and nutrients. There's no shortage of food.

Trinity's bass also benefit from a tremendous amount of structure. The north end is found near the town of Trinity Center and is famous for its' tailings. Prior to the construction of the dam, this now submerged section was dredged and mined for gold. The quarries now make excellent bass habitat and are frequented by bass anglers.

Trinity can kick out consistent numbers of quality fish. The great thing about Trinity is that you never know what you are going to catch. Expect a mix of small and largemouth. Trinity is likely your best shot at catching a smallmouth greater than five pounds in California, but its' clear water can be hard to fish. Anything heavier than six-pound test will decrease catch rates.

One thing about Trinity's bass is that they don't follow the same rules as do the bass in many other California reservoirs. Weather plays a huge part in fishing. Trinity can experience heavy snow, hail, wind, sleet and sun one day and be 70 degrees the next. Keeping a close tab on the bass is a must. Conditions change daily except in the summer when weather patterns stabilize.

Springtime fishing can be difficult to predict. One day you'll find bass preparing to spawn and then a sudden cold snap will send them into 50 feet of water. It's best to utilize a guide like Gray, who always keeps tab of the bass. Trinity's bass don't spawn all at once. Smallmouth will spawn on full moons in April if temperatures are warm enough. Largemouth spawn in May or June. However, all this can change drastically depending on weather patterns and runoff.

Bald eagle

Spring is the best time when it comes to pure numbers of fish. When the water level is high at Trinity, you'll find many areas that hold bass. The north end couldn't fish better. Tossing Gitzets near brush, submerged trees, in creek channels, around the tailings, on points and flats will put fish in the boat. These areas harbor fish year-round: the cove at Trinity Center Marina, the Swift Creek Channel, the Ballpark, the tailings, Squirrel Flats, the East Fork and main lake points. Don't discount fishing Senkos around willows.

June through September isn't the ideal time to fish. Anglers can still catch bass, but the size tends to fall drastically. Post spawn is when the big fish escape to deep water. Most likely, you'll find the bigger bass 50 feet down, just above the thermocline. Smaller bass can be found in shallow water flats from five to 15 feet. Slow rolled spinnerbaits and darter head jigs work best.

Summer and early fall is marked by a good topwater bite. Fishing any flat or creek channel with a Zara Super Spook or a Pop-R is a sure way to put fish in the boat. The next transition occurs in late fall when bass move back to the shallows to feed and bulk up for the winter. Offshore submerged tailing piles are also good.

From January through March, a slow retrieve is required to target bass. At times, snow can be found along the shorelines. Nonetheless, it doesn't seem to put a damper on the fishing. Drop-shotting, split-shotting and dragging darter heads are popular methods. The winter rip bait bite can be excellent, but you'll have to employ a slow retrieve. Try casting a Smithwick Rattling Rogue. Let it sit for 10-15 seconds before retrieving.

Fish the rock piles on the north end. On the south end, the Covington Mill Arm and Chicken Flat are good areas. Try not to ignore fishing stumps in the Buckeye Arm. Expect the bass to be in 10-25 feet of water. On warmer days, the bass will move even shallower to feed. February is the best time to land a big fish.

There are several methods besides Gitzets that are effective. Casting

Guide John Gray and a Trinity largemouth

Bald Eagle

Zoom baby brush hogs or a four-inch Pro Worm in Pro Gold red flake and fishing crankbaits, such as a white quarter-ounce Luhr Jensen Speed Trap are also productive.

Trinity's coldwater fishery has needed unprecedented help to get where it is today. The DFG had their hands full when they looked to mend the unhealthy fishery. Trinity's dam filled in 1961, the same year kokanee were introduced. Additional plants took place in 1963 and 1965. Kokanee quickly became established as a self-sustaining population. Kokanee unfortunately overpopulated their resources and stunted without establishing the sport fishery they were introduced for. Kokanee are abundant, but some of the smallest in the West. There is no food source for them, so the population is stunted. A nine-inch kokanee is huge.

At the time, the DFG planted more than 200,000 fingerling rainbow trout annually, but their return to creel was minimal. Studies showed a mere 1-18 percent of the trout were being harvested. Even worse, a full grown kokanee was six-to-eight inches. The CA DFG acted fast to cure the problem.

They opted to exploit the kokanee population by bringing in a predator that would eat kokanee, thus reducing their numbers, which would hopefully drive the average size of the kokanee up. The program began in 1997, when 25,000 Chinook were planted, followed by 20,000 in 1998. Every year following, except for 2000, 25,000 chinook have been planted. Chinook have essentially replaced the allotment of rainbow trout since 1997.

It's still unsure if the plan has been effective. On the other hand, chinook are growing to adult sizes and are abundant, yet few anglers are targeting them most likely because they are unaware of how to approach the species. Chinook are found in the same areas as trout and are caught with similar methods.

The CA DFG sent in another vehicle to aid the chinook in reducing the number of kokanee. In spring of 2001, sub-catchable browns were stocked. The CA DFG wanted to find out if the browns would eat more kokanee than chinook. Browns are stocked at only 4.5 inches, but they are growing to 11 inches within two years. Browns can eat kokanee at 15 inches. Roughly 50,000 browns are planted each year.

There are still rainbows in Trinity. The lake is planted with 6,000 half-pound trout a year. There is a

California Department of Fish and Game scientific aid Brandy Norton and a Trinity Lake smallmouth.

self-sustaining population of wild trout. In addition, trout which are planted into the Trinity River (above the lake) and in Stuarts Fork of the Trinity River also migrate into the lake, because both waters are sterile and provide little forage.

Besides small gamefish and baitfish, there is little food in Trinity. The lake is too cold and sterile to support plankton or shad. Because the lake drains into the Trinity River which harbors endangered species (coupled with the fact that Trinity Dam has no fish screen on it), the CA DFG has had a difficult time approving the introduction of baitfish. Word has it that minnows would survive and provide a good food source for all the lake's species, but that plan may be just a plan forever.

While there is little talk about Trinity's coldwater fishery, there is an excellent population of wild rainbows that spawn in the Upper Trinity River, Swift Creek, the East Fork of the Trinity River and Stuarts Fork of the Trinity River. Locating these trout is easy, but catching them requires non-traditional methods.

Locals troll the inlets from January through April to intercept spawning fish, namely rainbows in this case. For some reason, the bigger trout show up early, but catching them isn't always a treat. Below freezing temperatures can force many anglers off the water long before bites arrive. The spawn tapers off by mid-April.

Trolling in river channels is a bit different trolling than most California anglers are used to. Plan on trolling from where the river enters the lake for roughly one-mile. It's best if you are able to locate the old river channel and follow it. The Upper Trinity sees the most spawners. Here, you'll start in 40 feet of water and end up in four

Guide Vince Holson and a Trinity Lake rainbow caught in late winter.

feet by the time you reach the river itself. It's best to be 12-22 feet below the surface, which can obviously change when you reach shallower water. In the winter, you'll have to check your lines often. There's a lot of debris in the water. There's no need for downriggers. Trolling upriver, it's best to run 1.4-2.2 mph, a little faster when you are headed downriver. An orange broken-back Rebel is best. Nonetheless, any gold lure works as well. Rainbows average three pounds, yet fish to eight pounds are common. If you are looking to cash in on smaller planted trout, try the Stuarts Fork Arm in the spring.

A Trinity racoon

Many anglers would like to see lake trout introduced, however, because of drainage reasons and the fact that it would only provide a new fishery for anglers with downriggers, it may never happen. The CA DFG has however, admitted that lake trout would do well here.

Pacific lamprey, an anadromous fish native to the system, is also found in Trinity. The lamprey are a form of an ancestral stock that was trapped when the dam was built. The lamprey might try to feed on small trout; however, they provide forage for bass. Bass eat juvenile stages of lamprey.

If you plan to make the trip, supplies are available in Weaverville.

Also nearby are Rush Creek, Rush Creek Lakes and Carville Pond.

Directions: *From Highway 3 in Weaverville, drive north to the lake. There are several access sites along the way.*

Trinity Lake is lush with bald eagles. This one was on its' way to grabbing a fish.

Trinity River (Stuarts Fork)

Rating: 7

Species: Rainbow
Trout, Kokanee,
Chinook Salmon and
Brown Trout

Stocked with 800
pounds of rainbow
trout.

Facilities:
Campgrounds, Lodging,
Restrooms, General
Store and a Restaurant

Need Information?
Contact: Trinity Alps
Resort (530) 286-2205

The drive-to section of the Stuarts Fork of the Trinity River serves anglers several purposes. Namely, it's a put-and-take fishery for locals and vacationers and maintains a stable population of wild browns and rainbows, while during different seasons harboring spawning rainbows, browns, kokanee and Chinook salmon from Trinity Lake. Running between Trinity Lake and the Trinity Alps Wilderness, it's an easy 15-minute drive from Weaverville to the rocky banks.

In the fall, kokanee and browns spawn. In the spring, rainbows and, at times, you'll see Chinook in the river as well. Oftentimes, these fish are of trophy size. This is the "unknown fishery". Most anglers arrive for the planters, which are scheduled to arrive weekly or bi-monthly depending on usage.

There are several access points to accommodate you. The first is at the Highway 3 Bridge. Anglers who wish to fish the shorelines at Trinity Alps Resort may do so if they park off the side of the road outside of the resort's property and walk in. The California Department of Fish and Game plants fish on the resort's property.

Trinity River (Stuarts Fork)

In fact, the best hole on the river is arguably at the bridge visible on the left as you enter the resort. This bridge precedes a monster hole geared with rope swings off the bridge, a sandy beach and schools of planted half-pound rainbow trout. Sometimes the fish can be difficult to catch because of swimmers, but if you beat them to the beach in the morning, you'll do fine.

Further upriver, Bridge Campground offers good access and willing fish. The river parallels the road the entire way to the campground, yet steep banks make for difficult access. This medium size river is similar in size and comparison to the Stanislaus River near Sonora Pass. It has long runs, deep holes, riffles and pockets and can be approached with Power Bait, night crawlers, spinners, spoons and flies.

Trip info for Swift Creek also applies to Trinity River (Stuarts Fork).

Directions: *From the junction of Interstate 5 and Highway 299 in Redding, drive west on Highway 299 for 45.8 miles to the Trinity Lake/Highway 3 turnoff. Turn right and drive 12.8 miles to the turnoff for Trinity Alps Resort on the left. (It's just after crossing the bridge over the river.) Continue 1.2 miles to the resort or 3.4 miles to the end of the road at Bridge Campground.*

SWIFT CREEK

Rating: 5

Species: Chinook
Salmon, Kokanee,
Rainbow Trout and
Brown Trout

Stocks: None

Facilities:
Campgrounds and
Restrooms

Need Information?
Contact: Trinity
National Forest
(530) 623-2121

Come during the right time of year and Swift Creek will leave a sweet taste in your mouth; arrive when runs of fish aren't occurring and you'll never want to return. I last fished the creek in late July when I met a father and his three kids who were told by a teller at a nearby resort that Swift Creek was the place to catch big fish, much bigger than planters. The man held his arms apart, spreading each at least six inches past his shoulders, showing me that he was going to catch humongous salmon. He was obviously misguided.

Swift Creek isn't a place for families. It's a seldom fished destination where hardcore anglers can pounce through rugged terrain for a chance at small wild rainbow, brown and brook trout, and spawning kokanee and chinook. Swift is a vital organ to Trinity Lake. Many of the fish stocked by the California Department of Fish and Game in the lake spawn in the fall, winter or spring in Swift Creek. This is when anglers should approach the stream, not during the hot, summer tourist season. (You can't always fish during the spawning season though. Check sportfishing regulations.)

Access to the creek isn't great, yet attainable. Closer to the headwaters you can make your way to the creek at the Swift Creek Trail Parking Area, via a steep decline at Preacher Meadow Campground and at the Highway 3 bridge crossing.

If you plan to make the trip, supplies are available in Weaverville. Swift Creek is closed to fishing from November 16 to the last Saturday in April.

Also nearby are Trinity Lake, Trinity River (Stuarts Fork), Coffee Creek and Carrville Dredge Pond.

Directions: *From the junction of Interstate 5 and Highway 299 in Redding, drive west on Highway 299 for 45.8 miles to the Trinity Lake/Highway 3 turnoff. Turn right and drive 26.7 miles to the Preacher Meadow turnoff on the left and continue to the campground. Or, drive 28.4 miles to a pullout on the left side of the road, just after crossing a bridge over the creek.*

Swift Creek

251

CARRVILLE DREDGE POND

Rating: 6

Species: Rainbow Trout, Largemouth Bass and Bluegill

Stocked with 3,170 pounds of rainbow trout.

Facilities: None

Need Information? Contact: Trinity National Forest (530) 623-2121

Carrville Dredge Pond isn't an ideal destination to bring a fly rod and fish for wild trout. However, for young children banking on spending a few hours fishing with dad, prospects are excellent. Heavy trout plants, easy access and willing fish make for a quality angling experience. Steep shorelines allow anglers to make short casts to deep water, and at only three acres, the trout are always concentrated. Expecting to put fish in the skillet after a few hours is a realistic goal.

On the north end of Trinity Lake, roughly five miles north of Trinity Center, the dredge pond can be seen from Highway 3 and offers easy roadside access in rocky terrain. Fortunately, you can drive to the bank and fish. The pond is managed as a successful put-and-take fishery and is planted regularly by the California Department of Fish and Game (nearly 6,000 are planted annually). The best time to fish is after April or May, depending on when the trophy fish are planted for the annual kids fishing derby. The fish are never all caught during the derby and are much larger than the CA DFG trout.

If you plan to make the trip, supplies are available in Weaverville.

Also nearby is Trinity Lake, Trinity River (Upper) and Coffee Creek.

Directions: *From the junction of Interstate 5 and Highway 299 in Redding, drive west on Highway 299 for 45.8 miles to the Trinity Lake/Highway 3 turnoff. Turn right and drive 33.5 miles to an unsigned dirt road on the left. Turn left and continue a quarter-mile to the lake.*

Carrville Dredge Pond

COFFEE CREEK TROUT POND

Rating: 3

Species: Rainbow Trout

Stocked with rainbow trout as needed.

Facilities: A Picnic Area

Need Information?
Contact: Trinity County
Chamber of Commerce
(530) 623-6101

California has many trout ponds where parents can take their children and be guaranteed to catch a fish. Of course, there is a price involved but, it's the memory that counts. Unfortunately, at Coffee Creek Trout Pond nothing is guaranteed. The trout pond, located across from the Forest Service office in the small community of Coffee Creek, isn't your usual pay to catch operation.

At Coffee, fishing can be quite difficult at times. I visited in July and watched a mother, father and son fish for at least a half-hour without getting bit or seeing a trout. Management plants trout, but a lack of interest from tourists restricts them from bolstering the population to make it easier to catch fish. Also, unlike most trout farms, at Coffee Creek Trout Pond you can't even see the fish. Stained water puts a damper on the youngsters' success. On a positive note, prices are far cheaper than many trout ponds; $3.50 each or three for $10.

If you plan to make the trip, supplies are available in Trinity Center. Call ahead for hours. This is a seasonal operation and can close at any time.

Also nearby are Coffee Creek, Kickapoo Falls, Trinity River (Upper), Carrville Pond and Trinity Lake.

Directions: *From the junction of Interstate 5 and Highway 299 in Redding, drive west on Highway 299 for 45.8 miles to the Trinity Lake/Highway 3 turnoff. Turn right and drive 35.8 miles to the left turnoff for Coffee Creek Road. Turn left and drive seven-tenths of a mile to the trout pond on the left.*

Coffee Creek Trout Pond

COFFEE CREEK

Rating: 4

Species: Rainbow Trout

Stocked with

Facilities: None

Need Information?
Contact: Trinity
National Forest
(530) 623-2121

Leave Coffee Creek to the few locals who reside year-round in this small town north of Trinity Lake. Coffee does harbor pan size rainbows and some brown trout, however the stream isn't typically kind to beginning anglers. Due to challenging fast water and only a few pools, many anglers get skunked fishing Coffee. Anglers who know how to cast small spinners and work night crawlers in quick riffles will find mostly half-pound planters and the occasional larger fish.

The California Department of Fish and Game plants 1,762 rainbows each season. For best results, fish from the Coffee Creek Bridge downstream for roughly one-quarter mile. Nevertheless, only a few holes in this section actually receive fish. The hole can be found by locating small trails along the steep hillside that runs from Highway 3 down to the rocky creekbed. (There are paths in between the brush.) Follow the established routes directly to the creek and you'll stumble on trout.

If you plan to make the trip, supplies are available in Weaverville. Coffee Creek is closed to fishing from November 16 to the last Saturday in April.

Also nearby are Kickapoo Falls, Trinity River (Upper) and Carrville Dredge Pond.

Directions: *From the junction of Interstate 5 and Highway 299 in Redding, drive west on Highway 299 for 45.8 miles to the Trinity Lake/Highway 3 turnoff. Turn right and drive 35.7 miles to the Coffee Creek Bridge or 35.8 to the left turnoff for Coffee Creek Road.*

Coffee Creek

TRINITY RIVER (UPPER)

Rating: 6

Species: Rainbow Trout and Brown Trout

Stocked with 2,950 pounds of rainbow trout.

Facilities: None

Need Information?
Contact: Trinity National Forest
(530) 623-2121

The Trinity River above Trinity Lake isn't a blue ribbon trout stream. In fact, hardcore anglers don't bother fishing it at all. It's remote, has a low gradient and is mostly fished by campers, not day users and locals. Also, keep in mind this section of the Trinity is situated above Trinity Lake, therefore it doesn't have anadromous salmon and steelhead runs as do the more well known sections of the river.

What is available are spawning kokanee, chinook salmon, rainbows and browns. The Trinity River is the chosen spot for most coldwater fish that have been planted into Trinity Lake. Ironically, each year more larger fish are caught out of Trinity River than the lake. The most popular section locals fish is where the river meets the lake. Here, browns and rainbows to eight pounds are common.

The California Department of Fish and Game plants 5,290 trout, but unfortunately not many quality ones. The river is planted frequently in the summer, yet with the trout being smaller than 12 inches, many anglers drive right by. For the angler interested in fooling a limit of trout, stop by any of the campgrounds, day-use areas or pullouts alongside Highway 3 and you'll be in business. As long as you bring a jar of Orange Deluxe and Yellow Deluxe Pautzke salmon eggs, luck should be on your side.

If you plan to make the trip, supplies are available in Weaverville. The Trinity River (Upper) is closed to fishing from November 16 to the last Saturday in April.

Also nearby are Coffee Creek, Carrville Dredge Pond and Trinity Lake.

Directions: From the junction of Interstate 5 and Highway 299 in Redding, drive west on Highway 299 for 45.8 miles to the Trinity Lake/Highway 3 turnoff. Turn right and drive 36.5 miles to the Trinity River crossing. The river can be access from here upriver for several miles.

Trinity River (Upper)

RUSH CREEK LAKES

Rating: 3

Species: Brook Trout and Rainbow Trout

Stocks: None

Facilities: None

Need Information?
Contact: Trinity
National Forest
(530) 623-2121

My first experience in the Trinity Alps nearly scared me away for good. I expected the Alps to be as advertised; one of the last remaining great wilderness areas in California, filled with crisp air, teeming with trout and panoramic vistas. When we arrived at the empty trailhead, Big Todd McLean and I were anxious to tame another California wilderness zone.

We filled our camelbacks, stuffed a few granola bars and containers of dehydrated food in a pack, laced up our boots and set off. We passed the initial trailhead sign later to discover that would be one of only two signs we saw all day.

The first 20 minutes was on a well maintained trail that suddenly broke through the canopy of pines and oaks to an abandoned dirt road. Ok, what do we do now? There were no signs or trail markers. Nada. This shouldn't be too bad, I thought. Big Todd (BT) and I weren't weekend warriors, rather experienced cross country hikers and backpackers, so to ensure we acknowledged this part of the trail when we returned, we made a large arrow in the road with sticks to point us in the right direction when we came back.

We chose to walk uphill. After no more than 20 yards, a faint trail appeared through thick shrubs on the left. How anyone was suppose to know this was a trail, I have no idea. In my travels, I've been on many crappy trails so I knew what to look for. Kicking and fighting through overgrowth, we plowed through it and wound up on some switchbacks.

Still, we had yet to see a sign since the trailhead. Not yet bothered, we pushed forward. Trucking up a few switchbacks, we finally passed a beaten up sign acknowledging our passage in the Trinity Alps Wilderness. An hour, or more, had slipped by.

We knew now we were at least walking the right direction. The climb, however, never ended. After the switchbacks we were greeted by a steady climb along a steep ridge. The route was carved in the dirt mountainside. Unfortunately, the tree trimmers must not have been contracted to maintain this route. The shrubs and manzanita growing along the ridge were obviously doing well. So well, that they were inhibiting our ability to continue on our way to Rush Creek Lakes.

The loose dirt and rocks wouldn't have been able to hold our weight had we climbed up and around the shrubs. It would be like taking one step forward and two steps back. Maneuvering around the left side of the foliage wasn't an option either as a steep mountainside prohibited that idea. We had two options: deal with it or turn back.

Battling through at least one-half mile of pointy, prickly, rough and damaging brush, in shorts I might add, we fought through. We figured the worst was over. For a while it was. The route required only a few encounters with bushes over the next mile. Most of it was flat, maybe a little uphill, yet heavily shaded. By now, snow capped, jagged peaks appear in the distance to the north as well as a few gnarly looking pinnacles on the left. (By the way, you will reach those by the time the first portion of the hike ends.)

Having traveled roughly two-and-a-half hours or more, we quickly learned the hard part was still ahead. Roughly five miles and a 1,800 foot elevation gain had passed on a doable trail. The rest is downright tough, not to mention there is no water for at least another hour.

From here the mostly dirt trail turns to rock, loose dirt and gets steeper. It's also tougher to navigate (and there's no water). Be sure to watch your first several steps as small deep trails stray away from the main route, which need to be avoided. The trail will loop around to climb up a short ridge. After the first small peak, the mile-and-a-half ascend will be a climb of more than 1,000 feet, three more peaks to conquer and another battle with overhanging brush and manzanita. Be sure to wear pants.

From here, instead of scooting along the ridge straight to the trio of lakes, you are led downhill on a steep decent of nearly 700 feet over the next mile to a small stream.

By this time our patience were being tested. The dream hike we were suppose to be on had unfolded into a rude awakening packed in a long, boring climb, with no water, cut up legs, exhausting inclines and what I found to be two of the largest blisters I'd ever produced. Again, we had a choice. Continue on what the map showed to be a 30-minute scramble to the lakes or turn back due to exhaustion. BT wasn't sure what to do, but for me the near bleeding blisters weren't going to get in the way of seeing these seldom visited lakes. BT wasn't enthused, but he agreed to push forward.

The obstacles intensified. When we reached the bottom of the decline, a small stream tempted us to refill our water. However, I was preoccupied with locating the trail, which had disappeared. Consulting my map I knew where the lakes were, yet cross country travel at this point would have drained more energy from us. That wasn't an option. We bushwhacked through greenery taller than me and crossed the stream. Luckily, the trail emerged. Fewer than 100 yards further, the path bent to the right and for the first time, the Rush Creek Drainage could be seen an heard.

Our second wind kicked in instantly. Unfortunately, it only lasted a few minutes. The route again vanished. This time success seemed

Big Todd attemps to push his way through an overgrown trail near Rush Creek Lakes.

257

Rush Creek Lake

all but inevitable. BT was more than six feet tall and the thick manzanita was taller than he. Way taller. It also owned the trail. We could tell where the path meandered, but getting through was another story.

These shrubs and trees weren't tules, tall grass or weeds where the mere step of a foot would create a path. BT tried jumping on the trees to pave the way, but even his 220-plus pound build didn't get them to budge. BT was determined to turn around. Already scarred, neither of us was up for anymore struggles. On the other hand, we had come this far. And, with the lake's outlet in sight, I wasn't about to turn around.

Most likely cursing, bleeding and having a youthful blast all at the same time, BT and I fought, scrapped and punched our way through at least a football field's length of un- pruned, unwanted and aggravating foliage that had forged its way across the path. When the manzanita ended, the route quickly turned to granite. Carefully stacked rocks created a weaving route across Rush Creek to the first of Rush Creek Lakes.

Speechless couldn't describe us better. Nearly four hours of hiking, hundreds of deep scratches, bloody cuts, fatigue, dehydration and several blisters later, we had arrived at a shallow lake roughly half the size of a high school swimming pool. The lake was, however, set in gorgeous plethora of wildflowers teeming in a lush green meadow.

There wasn't another human within at least seven miles. BT's first cast changed our attitude. Seconds after the Panther Martin spurred a series of rings as it plopped into the still lake, a brook trout responded. As did another. And another. A limit could have been attained in five casts. We chose to catch and release. The colors on the brookies were exuberant and vivid. Their size, unfortunately, didn't crack the seven-inch mark.

To reach the second lake, a short cross country scramble is necessary. It's simple, but requires hiking up a steep granite grade and one stream crossing. The second lake is small as well, but can be more difficult to fish. The outlet area is extremely shallow, nonetheless does harbor fish. The deterrent is marshy shorelines. The best section is where Rush Creek Lake Falls empties into the lake. Brookies congregate here. You'll have to cross Rush Creek to reach this section. Again, anything you want to toss will catch fish.

Reaching the third and final lake is a chore. A steep rock-hop is required on rugged terrain. There is no established trail. This lake, at 6,938 feet and one-third of a mile from lake number two, has the largest trout. Rainbows, brooks and great scenery are on tap in this intimate granite setting. Smile, you now have an eight-mile trip back with some 3,100 feet to walk down. Allow at least four hours for the trip and pack extra water. Remember, none is available on the trail.

A Rush Creek Lake trout

The day after we completed the hike I cordially walked into the Forest Service office in Weaverville and asked them why they don't maintain the route to the lakes. The woman at the counter said she was positive that the trail is cleared every three years. That seemed far fetched considering the trees growing in the middle of the route were six inches thick. She was correct in saying it's a very low use area. Therefore, it gets attention after other more popular trails. Her estimate was that no more than 50 hikers visit the lakes each year. Sounds like a place to be alone to me.

If you plan to make the trip, supplies are available in Weaverville. Call the Forest Service before setting foot on the trail. Snow can remain on the path through June. Some years the lakes can be frozen into early July.

Also nearby is Trinity Lake, Stuarts Fork of the Trinity River, Swift Creek and Rush Creek.

Directions: From the junction of Interstate 5 and Highway 299 in Redding, exit west towards Weaverville on Highway 299 and drive 45.6 miles to the Trinity Lake/Highway 3 turnoff. Turn right and drive 9.6 miles to the left turnoff for the Rush Creek Lakes Trail. Turn left and drive 2.4 miles to the trailhead on the left.

Rush Creek Lake No. 1

CANYON CREEK (UPPER)

Rating: 4
Species: Rainbow Trout and Brook Trout
Stocks: None
Facilities: None

Very few rivers and streams in the backcountry are planted with trout. In fact, most streams don't need to be planted at all because the trout populate the streams on their own as they move into them from connecting lakes to spawn and search for food. Upper Canyon Creek, however, is different.

Set between Lower Canyon Creek Falls and Upper Canyon Creek Falls, there isn't a way for trout to enter, as this section is blocked by waterfalls from above and below. Additionally, there is no fishing below the falls, as this section is closed off to protect salmon and steelhead spawning grounds. Overall, this leaves a small section for trout to grow in, which essentially could even be split further by the presence of two more waterfalls which sit as roadblocks for migrating trout. So, in order to maintain recreation and to give backpackers a source of food, the California Department of Fish and Game decided to plant trout in this heavily visited upper section of the creek. Canyon Creek was last planted in the late Nineties, however, its still harbors brook and rainbow trout.

In order to determine whether there were any carryover fish from the last plant in the 90's, the CA DFG returned a year later to survey their survival rates. Before planting the trout they had clipped off the adipose fin of each fish so that later identification would be easier. During that survey, the CA DFG found that those fish were in fact still in the system and had grown.

While the CA DFG believes that brooks can positively reproduce in the stream, it is still questionable if rainbows can. Nonetheless, both exist here. I saw juvenile and adult fish which is a sign that spawning is occurring. Most trout in this section run six-to-seven inches, but larger do exist. I caught a few in the 12-in class the last time I visited.

Fish can be found in several sections: from the top of Lower Canyon Creek Falls to the base of Middle Canyon Creek Falls, and then from Middle Canyon Creek Falls to Upper Canyon Creek Falls. Look for fish in the small pools and the slow moving runs in between. When fishing this section beware, there are many smaller waterfalls that can be mistaken for the larger ones. A good map is helpful. Fishing this section of the stream is best with small Panther Martins and nymphs fished under an indicator.

To reach Upper Canyon Creek, park at the Canyon Creek Trailhead and take the Canyon Creek Trail towards Canyon Creek and Boulder Lakes. You'll follow Bear Creek before crossing it at four-tenths of a mile and then heading towards Canyon Creek. Then the path follows, yet stays above Canyon Creek for roughly 3.25 miles to the top of Lower Canyon Creek Falls. Access is available from this point to Lower Canyon Creek Lake. The route parallels the stream.

Directions *and trip info for Canyon Lake (Upper) also applies to Canyon Creek.*

CANYON CREEK LAKE (LOWER)

Rating: 4

Species: Rainbow Trout and Brook Trout

Stocked with 12 pounds of rainbow trout.

Facilities: None

The Canyon Creek Lakes are two of the most publicized backcountry lakes on the West Coast. Located inside the Trinity Alps Wilderness, this pristine area has been exploited by nearly every major hiking and backpacking magazine in the country. With the exposure came crowds. On any given day there could be enough people up here to make it seem like there's a road around the corner.

Nonetheless, the lakes still provide a woodsy feeling. Fishing Lower Canyon Creek Lake differs from the upper lake even though they are only a few hundred feet apart. The lower lake sees much more use. Many backpackers hike to the lower lake and stop, never making it to the upper lake. This is probably because there are better camping spots on the lower lake. Also, pack mules can't make it past the lower lake. Therefore, it's the destination of large parties.

At 5,600 feet, Lower Canyon Creek Lake has rainbow and brook trout. The fishing is better in the upper lake, but chances are the lower lake won't disappoint you. Lower Canyon Creek is planted some years with fingerling rainbow and brook trout. More than 3,000 fingerling rainbows were planted in 2003. While it's uncertain if the rainbows spawn, the brooks certainly do. Pan size rainbows and brooks are common for anglers tossing Panther Martins, Thomas Buoyants or Cripplures. Look for the steep drop-offs and you'll always find fish.

Reaching Canyon Creek Lake is a short jaunt from Upper Canyon Creek. From the creek simply head upstream along the path to the lake. You'll pass several waterfalls and a few great fishing holes on the way.

Directions and trip info for Canyon Lake (Upper) also applies to Lower Canyon Creek Lake.

Canyon Creek Lake (Lower)

CANYON CREEK LAKE (UPPER)

Rating: 4
Species: Rainbow Trout and Brook Trout
Stocked with 22 pounds of fingerling rainbow trout.
Facilities: None
Need Information? Contact: Trinity National Forest (530) 623-2121

Upper Canyon Creek Lake is managed much differently than its' lower counterpart. This lake is a diverse fishery. It's been more than a decade since browns were planted, yet they still co-exist with the rainbows and brooks. Amazingly, the last time the California Department of Fish and Game gillnetted the lake they found a six-pound brown, proof that trophy fish are available. Brooks and browns naturally reproduce in the small, unnamed stream that enters the lake.

At 5,659 feet in the Trinity Alps Wilderness, the CA DFG manages the lake as a put-and-grow rainbow trout fishery. In 2003, 5,500 fingerling rainbows were stocked. Nonetheless, rainbows, brooks and browns make up the mixed bag. There are some trophy fish to be caught, however, most fish run eight inches. The browns are by far the largest fish in the system. The entire fishery can be approached the same. Since half of the lake is bordered by steep cliffs and large, loose boulders, I'd simply toss spinners, spoons or fly and bubble combos from shore. The entire shoreline holds fish. Because it receives less fishing pressure, the fishing is better at the upper lake.

To reach the upper lake from the lower lake there is a faint path you can follow, but it's likely you'll have to make your own. The path extends from the route that leads to Lower Canyon Creek Lake. Look for trail makers and you'll be fine. However, be sure to have a good map in hand just in case. The trail is not marked.

If you plan to make the trip, supplies are available in Junction City. A wilderness permit is required for overnight travel into the Trinity Alps Wilderness. Canyon Creek (Upper) is closed to fishing from November 16 to the last Saturday in May. The trail may not be snow free until sometime in July. Call the Forest Service for updated conditions.

Also nearby is the Trinity River.

Directions: *From the junction of Highway 299 and Interstate 5 in Redding, drive west on Highway 299 for 53.7 miles to the Canyon Creek Trailhead turnoff in Junction City. Turn right and drive 11 miles to the Canyon Creek Trailhead.*

262 David Savage with a typical Upper Canyon Creek Lake brown trout.

Region

11

Siskiyou County

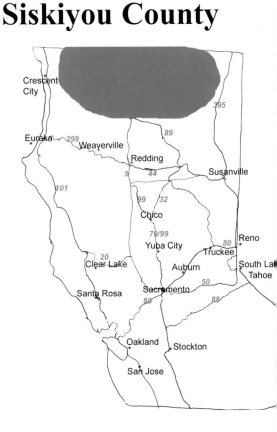

CASTLE LAKE

Rating: 6

Species: Rainbow
Trout and Brook
Trout

Stocked with 2,515
pounds of rainbow
trout, 60 pounds of
fingerling rainbow
trout and 700 pounds
of brook trout.

Facilities: Vault
Toilets

Need Information?
Contact: The Tackle
Shop (530) 841-1901

When you reach Castle Lake there will be no doubt in your mind that it is one of the prettiest drive-to lakes in California. There is no cement or rock-built dam or services of any kind. At 5,400 feet in the Shasta National Forest, you are in the wilderness. Snow capped peaks and four waterfalls which tumble into the lake in the spring make for picturesque conditions. Kodak quality reflections are heart warming year-round.

Castle Lake is a tourist attraction for both sightseers and anglers. However, primitive campsites, vault toilets and a small parking area do their best at keeping crowds away. Even when crowds form, the smell of fresh air, pines, cascading water and crying scrub jays coupled with the fact that no gas powered boats are permitted keep the experience a quality one.

Castle Lake was formed by a glacier. Known as a cirque lake, the granite, steep rock side is 110 feet deep and the shallow side, which is close to the road, is only three to 15 feet deep. The lake is a natural lake and has a silt

deposited natural dam towards the middle. When the glacier melted, the debris left behind formed the dam.

Castle Lake isn't always a great fishing lake though. Many anglers fish on the shallow flats rather than the deeper sections where more trout are found. The lake is heavily planted by the California Department of Fish and Game. The CA DFG plants 15,000 fingerling rainbow trout, 23 trophy rainbows, and 4,500 half-pound bows, in addition to 700 pound-size brooks. There is a self sustaining population of brooks as well.

Most of the best fishing occurs during ice fishing months. However, the road isn't always plowed. Most of the time the roads are clear, but it may take a week or so for crews to clear the road before the lake becomes accessible. Ice fishing typically occurs from January through April, but that can change depending on the year. When ice fishing,

Castle Lake Falls

be sure to fish the deeper portion, rather than the shallow flats.

During the spring, fishing can be good for anglers will to work at it. There are four seasonal waterfalls that spill into the lake and attract planted trout. However, none are accessible by foot, unless you are a billy goat. You'll need a canoe, row boat or float tube to get in on the action. In spring, plan on catching 10-14 inch holdover rainbows. Cast a small spoon or spinner towards the inlets or float a night crawler off a bobber and you should do well on this 47-acre lake.

By summer, the water tends to warm and trout move deeper, hence getting further away from shoreline anglers. To do well, walk to the backside of the lake and locate deeper water. It's best to fish in the early morning or late evening when you can spot fish on the surface rather than trying to predict where they are going to be.

If you plan to make the trip, supplies are available in Mt. Shasta. In winter and spring call the Forest Service for road conditions. The road may be closed or chains may be required.

Also nearby are Lake Siskiyou, South Fork of the Sacramento River, Wagon Creek and Cold Creek.

Directions: *From the junction of Highway 299 east and Interstate 5 in Redding, drive north on I-5 for 56.5 miles to the Mt. Shasta exit. Turn left (drive over the freeway) and continue one-half mile to a stop sign. Turn left on North Old Stage Road and drive two-tenths of a mile to a split in the road. Veer right on WA Barr Road and drive 2.2 miles to the left turnoff for Castle Lake. Turn left and drive seven miles to the lake.*

Castle Lake

LAKE SISKIYOU

Rating: 8

Species: Smallmouth Bass, Largemouth Bass, Black Crappie, Brown Bullhead, Channel Catfish, Rainbow Trout, Brown Trout and Brook Trout

Stocked with 2,415 pounds of fingerling brook trout, 400 pounds of fingerling brown trout, 350 pounds of fingerling Eagle Lake Trout, 2,570 pounds of fingerling rainbow trout, 6,225 pounds of brook trout, 9,574 pounds of rainbow trout and 500 pounds of brood stock brown trout.

Facilities: Campgrounds, Picnic Areas, Restrooms, Fishing Docks, Fish Cleaning Station, Hot Showers, Laundry Facilities, Snack Bar, Horseshoe Pits, Boat Launch, RV Hookups, General Store, Boat Rentals and a Swimming Beach

Need Information? Contact: Lake Siskiyou Camp-Resort (888) 926-2618, The Tackle Shop (530) 841-1901

Lake Siskiyou is one of Northern California's great family destinations. The facilities are excellent, the hospitality is warm, the lake is clear and clean and the scenery is gorgeous. The fishing isn't too bad either. Actually, Siskiyou is a perfect place for a beginning or hardcore angler. It has both a cold and warm water fishery and is kept stocked full with trout to keep anglers happy year-round. The view of Mt. Shasta is breathtaking and can be downright overwhelming at times. Plus, a 10 mph speed limit keeps the lake quiet and enjoyable.

At 3,200 feet in the Shasta National Forest, Siskiyou stays relatively full and gets heavy use from out-of-towners in the summer and from locals year-round. When the fishing isn't great, many anglers are more than content with the view of Mt. Shasta which looms overhead. Lake Siskiyou is hard to beat.

The lake doesn't freeze over, yet it gets cold and wintry enough from December through March to keep most anglers away. Those who dress warm and come prepared for wet weather are rewarded with good brown trout fishing, but high catch rates can be had all year.

At only 430 acres, Siskiyou is planted with an enormous amount of trout. Partly because it is so close to the Mt. Shasta Fish Hatchery, the lake is planted often with both fingerling and catchable trout. While there is no baitfish to munch on, Siskiyou's trout gorge on small invertebrates like bugs and zooplankton. The catchables also grub on fingerling trout. There are plenty of those to go around! On average, more than 56,000 fingerling brook trout, nearly 5,000 fingerling brown trout, 100,000 fingerling Eagle Lake trout and 2630,000 fingerling rainbow trout are planted.

Siskiyou is also a put-and-take fishery. The California Department of Fish and Game makes it a habit to stock often. While tons of half-pound fish get planted, you don't always catch a lot of dinks. The average trout range from one-to-three pounds.

Each year 7,851pound-size brooks and 14,661 half-pound rainbow trout are planted. Wait, there's more. Wild fish are also common. Brook and brown trout commonly spawn in the tributaries in the fall. Rainbows use the tributaries in the spring. In addition, trout planted in Cold and Wagon Creeks and the South and North Forks of the Sacramento River often swim downstream into the lake where there is more food.

The lake has the potential to produce trophy size fish. Expect to catch 70 percent rainbows and 30 percent browns. At times, depending on the area you are fishing, brooks are caught too. The brooks tend to stay near the South Fork of the Sacramento River inlet.

Shoreline access is excellent. Anglers who soak Power Bait or night crawlers from any of these areas should do well: near the boat launch, at Box Canyon Dam, the shoreline on both sides of the swim beach, near where Wagon Creek enters the lake and across from the boat launch where green meadow like flats are found. The reason why shoreline fishing is hot is because all around the lake (except for where the South Fork of the Sacramento River and the area south of the green meadows) there is a fairly steep drop-off where the trout spend most of their lives feeding.

Trolling can yield exceptional catch rates. For rainbows and browns, work the cove where Castle Lake Creek and Scott Camp Creek enter the lake. This is one of two large coves on the lake and is well protected from the north wind that cuts through Siskiyou frequently.

The cove on the other side of the dam where Wagon Creek enters is also an excellent place to troll. You don't have to troll deep in Siskiyou. I like to run two

A Siskiyou brown

toplines, one with a red and gold Thomas Buoyant and the other with a red and black Sep's Trolling fly behind a red and black Sep's Pro dodger. Then, on two downriggers or leadcore line, try a brown trout patterned Needlefish and a silver Kastmaster. Have one set down 16 feet and the other 22 feet. The best action is found in the spring. If you want to catch primarily rainbows, troll about 30 yards offshore of the meadows or in front of the swim beach.

Recently, bass have started to show more in the reservoir. The rumor is that a flood that swept thousands of pounds of debris into the lake in the mid-Nineties blessed the bass with structure to spawn and a place to hide from predators. Fish and Game sees the situation a bit different though. In 1997-98 there was, in fact, a flood that dumped heaps of sediment into the lake, but little structure was added. This was just a natural event. Some anglers think the flood placed hundreds of pieces of wood into the lake, yet the CA DFG says cobble, mud and silt are now more abundant, not wood. In reality fewer than two percent of the habitat is classified as bass structure.

Siskiyou is a cold water reservoir which harbors predominately smallmouth and is comprised of mostly small fish. A 15 incher would be huge and you'll have to put in a lot of hours to land one of those fish. Bass are common in the slot and below it. The slot limit was put into effect in 1993 and may never be lifted. There is a lot of forage for the bass, however, the cold water and competition with hundreds of thousands of trout keep them from getting huge.

If there's one issue that needs to be dealt with at Siskiyou it's carp. A farm pond (that is a tributary to Cold Creek) which dumps into Siskiyou, illegally contained carp. They were planted into the pond in the mid-to-late Eighties and were believed to have been washed into Siskiyou during the 1998 flood. Carp were first discovered in Siskiyou in May of 2002 and have since frightened the CA DFG. The worry is that the carp may sneak out and populate the Upper Sacramento River, a wild trout river. Thus far, only a few adult carp has been seen. The carp are not known to be reproducing; however, the CA DFG is compiling a plan to eradicate carp as a precaution.

If you plan to make the trip, supplies are available in Mt. Shasta. There is a day use fee for boat launching and for persons entering the lake via the west shore at Lake Siskiyou Resort. Lake Siskiyou Camp-Resort is open from April through Labor Day.

Also nearby are Castle Lake and the South Fork of the Sacramento River.

Directions: *From the junction of Highway 299 east and Interstate 5 in Redding, drive north on I-5 for 56.5 miles to the Mt. Shasta exit. Turn left (drive over the freeway) and continue one-half mile to a stop sign. Turn left on North Old Stage Road and drive two-tenths of a mile to a split in the road. Veer right on WA Barr Road and continue to the lake.*

The view of Lake Shasta from Lake Siskiyou can be breathtaking on clear days.

WAGON CREEK

Rating: 5

Species: Brook Trout,
Rainbow Trout and
Brown Trout

Stocked with 495
pounds of rainbow
trout.

Facilities: None

Need Information?
Contact: The Tackle
Shop (530) 841-1901

Wagon Creek's location can pose a danger to anglers at times, as it is not the safest place to fish. I first fished the creek on a weekday in June and was nearly run off the road several times by cars speeding past. Most people driving down North Shore Road don't realize that this area contains fishermen, as those driving by are usually focused on getting to Lake Siskiyou and don't have Wagon in mind. North Shore Road parallels Wagon Creek, but also takes visitors to the free access side of the lake. Mostly locals come here, because most out-of-towners aren't aware of access on this side of the lake. That is why people drive so ferocious. The locals think they own the road and no one else should use it.

Moving on though, the California Department of Fish and Game does plant rainbows or browns during the fishing season, yet fishing can be tough from the opener through June because of increased runoff. Most fish that are planted prior to the 4th of July end up being washed into Lake Siskiyou.

Wagon Creek is planted with 920 trout from where the stream crosses under the road down to the lake, a distance of less than a half-mile. The best fishing is found where Wagon spills into Siskiyou. Not only do you have fresh planted fish, but holdovers that were stocked in previous years, swim out of the lake as they prepare to spawn in Wagon, or at least attempt to. A chance at rainbows, brooks or browns is possible for anglers soaking Power Bait, tossing small Panther Martins or throwing Kastmasters.

If you plan to make the trip, supplies are available in Mt. Shasta. Wagon Creek is closed to fishing from November 16 to the last Saturday in April.

Also nearby are Cold Creek and Castle Lake.

Directions: *From the junction of Highway 299 east and Interstate 5 in Redding drive north on I-5 for 56.5 miles to the Mt. Shasta exit. Turn left (drive over the freeway) and continue one-half mile to a stop sign. Turn left on North Old Stage Road and drive two-tenths of a mile to a split in the road. Veer right on WA Barr Road and drive eight-tenths of a mile to the right turnoff for North Shore Road. Turn right and drive three-tenths of a mile to where the creek crosses under the road.*

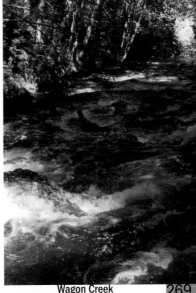

Wagon Creek

COLD CREEK

Rating: 3

Species: Rainbow Trout
and Brown Trout

Stocked with 480
pounds of rainbow
trout.

Facilities: None

Need Information?
Contact: The Tackle
Shop (530) 841-1901

Cold Creek's fishery has some good to it and some bad. Fortunately, at 3,200 feet near the city of Mt. Shasta, the creek is close enough to the Mt. Shasta Fish Hatchery that you could throw a rock and hit it. This means that despite poor access and low flows, the California Department of Fish and Game still plants.

While the plants are minimal they do serve a purpose, which in this case is to give local kids something to do after homework and chores are done. From the opener through September, the creek is planted with 879 rainbow trout, which join a small population of resident browns.

Cold Creek runs alongside the road before crossing underneath it and emptying into Lake Siskiyou a short distance downstream. To have the best chance at catching a few planters, fish the culvert with Balls O' Fire salmon eggs or Power Bait. The culvert is easy to spot. It can be found where the road splits, exactly two-tenths of a mile from the hatchery.

Keep an eye out for no trespassing signs. While some of the creek is open to the public other sections run through private land. Be sure to wear pants when fishing here. Shorelines are overgrown with willows and blackberries, and steep banks can make for difficult access.

If you plan to make the trip, supplies are available in Mt. Shasta. Cold Creek is closed to fishing from November 16 to the last Saturday in April.

Also nearby are Wagon Creek and Lake Siskiyou.

Directions: *From the junction of Highway 299 east and Interstate 5 in Redding, drive north on Interstate 5 for 56.5 miles to the Mt. Shasta exit. Turn left (drive over the freeway) and continue one-half mile to a stop sign. Turn left on Old Stage Road and drive two-tenths of a mile to a split in the road. Veer right on WA Barr Road. The creek flows on the left side of the road.*

Cold Creek

SOUTH FORK SACRAMENTO RIVER

Rating: 5

Species: Rainbow Trout

Stocked with 1,750 pounds of rainbow trout.

Facilities: Restrooms

Need Information? Contact: The Tackle Shop (530) 841-1901

The South Fork of the Sacramento River is similar to only a few rivers in California. While many rivers go through several seasonal stages depending on snowmelt and rain runoff, few see such drastic changes as the South Fork. In spring and early summer, the river is almost pure whitewater from its' headwaters at Gumboot Lake downstream roughly seven miles, where it crosses under Forest Service Road 24. During this period the river is almost completely unfishable.

However, come fall, the South Fork may be so low that it nearly dries up. What used to be whitewater now looks like a seasonal tiny stream. Somehow many of the 3,255 half-pound rainbow trout that the California Department of Fish and Game plants do make it through the flood like spring conditions. Many others get washed downstream into Lake Siskiyou.

When it comes to being successful your best bet is to wait until the river slows, when flows are less treacherous. Pautzke salmon eggs, Power Bait and grasshoppers are excellent baits to drop into small pools and holes. Fish where the river crosses under Road 24 and at places where it looks as if the CA DFG would have an easy path down to the river. The South Fork is planted from where the river first crosses under Road 24 to a bridge that can be seen crossing the river on the left of the road.

If you plan to make the trip, supplies are available in Mt. Shasta. The road to the South Fork of the Sacramento River is closed due to snow in winter and spring. Call ahead for updated road conditions. No motors are permitted.

Also nearby are Gumboot Lake, Mumbo Lake and Lake Siskiyou.

Directions: *From the junction of Highway 299 east and Interstate 5 in Redding, drive north on Interstate 5 for 56.5 miles to the Mt. Shasta exit. Turn left (drive over the freeway) and continue one-half mile to a stop sign. Turn left on North Old Stage Road and drive two-tenths of a mile to a split in the road. Veer right on WA Barr Road, continue around Lake Siskiyou to the river. The river parallels the road for several miles.*

South Fork Sacramento River

GUMBOOT LAKE

Rating: 5

Species: Rainbow Trout

Stocked with 1,480
pounds of rainbow
trout.

Facilities: Restrooms

Need Information?
Contact: Shasta-Trinity
National Forest
(530) 926-4511

Gumboot is a lake you have to time right to be successful. The trick is calling the Mt. Shasta Ranger Station to find out when the road to Gumboot opens. This event can range from mid-May to early July, depending on how much snow pack there is. As soon as the road clears, the California Department of Fish and Game rushes to Gumboot and unloads a few buckets of rainbow trout. Plants will continue weekly for a few weeks until the water becomes too warm for the trout.

In fact, when I last fished the lake in June of 2003 I had to pull a CA DFG stocking truck out of the snow and mud. It got stuck trying to provide anglers with a good fishing experience. The lake isn't stocked in the summer, however, the CA DFG brings plants back as the water cools. Nearly 2,567 rainbows are planted annually.

At roughly 6,000 feet in the Shasta-Trinity National Forest, Gumboot marks the headwaters of the South Fork of the Sacramento River. Only seven acres, the entire shoreline can be fished in less than an hour. Most anglers do best in float tubes, yet shore anglers tossing spinners and soaking bait experience good success rates in the spring and fall.

Shafdog Publications attempting to pull Fish and Game's stocking truck out of the snow at Gumboot

If you plan to make the trip, supplies are available in Mt. Shasta. The road to Gumboot is closed due to snow in winter and spring. Call ahead for updated road conditions. No motors are permitted.

Also nearby are the Mumbo Lake and Lake Siskiyou.

Directions: *From the junction of Highway 299 east and Interstate 5 in Redding, drive north on Interstate 5 for 56.5 miles to the Mt. Shasta exit. Turn left (drive over the freeway) and continue one-half mile to a stop sign. Turn left on North Old Stage Road and drive two-tenths of a mile to a split in the road. Veer right on WA Barr Road and drive roughly 16 miles to the left turnoff for Gumboot Lake.*

KANGAROO LAKE

Rating: 6

Species: Rainbow Trout

Stocked with 20 pounds
of fingerling rainbow
trout and 2,745 pounds
of rainbow trout.

Facilities: Picnic Areas,
Campgrounds and
Restrooms

Need Information?
Contact: Klamath
National Forest
(530) 468-5351

Most high mountain drive-to lakes are extremely easy to catch fish at. However, Kangaroo seems to be the oddball. At 21 acres, you'd think nabbing stocked trout would be a synch. Yet without a float tube or car top boat, action can and will most likely be slow. The problem isn't a lack of fish. The California Department of Fish and Game plants more than 4,589 half-pound trout and 5,000 fingerling rainbows each year, yet a lack of access where the fish are most available sends many anglers home sad.

Kangaroo can be looked at as one lake with two sections: the shallow and deep part of the lake. There's excellent access to the shallow portion. On the other hand, the deep portion (which holds most of the fish) can only be reached with some sort of watercraft. There is no launch ramp and no motors are permitted. Don't get me wrong, anglers can catch wandering fish in the shallows from shore. Unfortunately, the majority of the fish are found in deeper water.

At 6,050 feet in the Klamath National Forest, Kangaroo's rainbows tend to hang out on the side opposite the wheelchair accessible path. This side has no path and is too steep to navigate. At 110 feet deep, it's also the side that harbors most of the trout. If you can paddle over to the deeper water, expect to do well fly fishing with small gnat or black fly patterns. Casting red Cripplures and Kastmasters will also do the trick. In spring when runoff is high, casting near the inlet can be productive.

If you plan to make the trip, supplies are available in Callahan and Weed. The road to Kangaroo is closed in the winter and spring. Typically it opens sometime in mid-June. Call the Forest Service for updated road conditions.

Also nearby is Lily Pad Lake.

Directions: *From Interstate 5 in Weed, drive north for roughly three miles to the Edgewood/Gazelle exit. Exit, turn left and then turn right on Old Stage Road. Continue approximately seven miles Gazelle/Callahan Road and turn left. Drive 15.9 miles to Rail Creek Road and turn left. Continue roughly seven miles to the lake.*

Kangaroo Lake

LILY PAD LAKE

Rating: 4

Species: Rainbow Trout

Stocked with 595 pounds of rainbow trout.

Facilities: None

Lily Pad Lake's trout are hurt substantially by its depth. At a mere nine feet deep, the lake doesn't stay cool enough year-round to support trout. Lily Pad can be an excellent trout fishery from ice out through June. Unfortunately, action slows dramatically by July.

The California Department of Fish and Game plants only 943 half-pound rainbows each year, far less than the number needed to supply all the anglers who fish it. Lily Pad Lake is located on the road to Kangaroo and gets hit hard by anglers as soon as the road opens. Oftentimes, anglers drive their cars as far as they can in the spring. When snow gets too thick to continue, they park and walk the rest of the way to try and cash in on fish that haven't eaten in several months. The lake typically thaws in early June, but can do so before or after depending on how harsh the winter was.

At 1.5 acres, when fish are planted action is hot. Power Bait fished from shore or tossing spoons and spinners can yield a quick limit of bows if the bite is on. By fall, Lily Pad is pretty much depleted of its' trout population and most anglers head up to Kangaroo.

Trip info for Kangaroo Lake also applies to Lily Pad Lake.

Directions: *From Interstate 5 in Weed, drive north for roughly three miles to the Edgewood/Gazelle exit. Exit west and then turn north on Old Stage Road. Continue approximately seven miles Gazelle/Callahan Road and turn left. Drive 15.9 miles to Rail Creek Road and turn left. Continue 6.5 miles to the lake.*

Lily Pad Lake

SCOTT RIVER

The Scott River is one of California's last remaining waters that don't get pounded daily. Unfortunately, there are good reasons for this: all fishing is catch and release, there are no full-time fishing guides, few services exist, there's intermittent public access and only barbless hooks and flies can be used.

On the other hand, this makes for an adventure for many anglers who want to try their luck on a system not well known.

The Scott is a bank angler's paradise. The river is useless to drift boaters. At one time, access was available on the upper stretch in the Scott River Valley, but it's all private property now. The only way to fish is

on foot. The section downriver of Scott River Valley isn't conducive to boats anyway. It's more like a boulder field. It's impossible to carefully drift.

Salmon do enter the river in the fall to spawn, but by the time they reach the Scott they are torn up from their long journey. Almost no one fishes the river for salmon, especially since you can't keep fish. Steelhead, on the other hand, are in excellent shape.

The Scott doesn't have long riffles or deep holes. Oftentimes, you'll find steelhead in little cascades, holes and falls. They'll mill around, and then push upriver to spawn. Being a major tributary to the Klamath, the Scott gets a good run of steelies, most of which average two-to-five pounds. Keep in mind that all salmon and steelhead are wild. There is no hatchery on this system.

The first steelhead push into the system in October. However, the biggest part of the run doesn't occur until after the first major rainfall. Rain is another stumbling block. The

Scott Drainage has an erosion problem. When it rains the river muddies pretty bad. It can take up to a week to clear after a major storm.

Here are the best opportunities for river access: Johnson's Bar River Access, Sugar Pine River Access (hike in only), Townsend Gulch River Access, Gold Flat (hike-in only), Tompkins Creek River Access, Scott River Lodge, Bridge Flat Campground, Canyon Creek River Access and Campground, Indian Scotty Campground and Jones Beach Picnic Area. Roughly a quarter-mile upriver of Jones Beach, anglers are forced to content with private land as the river leaves the Klamath National Forest.

Other access is available through mining camps and off four-wheel drive roads, but they can get pretty nasty in the winter. Most anglers do fine utilizing the listed access points. Steelhead can be taken on the fly or spinners. However, most anglers choose to fly fish. Wet flies are the norm. Allow them to sink deep and slow. Dry flies are useless in the winter. Tie on a size four or five woolly bugger, silver hilton or egg sucking leech.

If you plan to make the trip, supplies are available in Yreka. The Scott River is closed to fishing from March 1 to the fourth Saturday in May. All fishing is catch and release only. Only barbless hooks and flies may be used.

Also nearby is the Middle Klamath River.

Directions: *From Interstate 5 in Yreka drive north, or from Medford, drive south and take the Central Yreka exit. Turn west, drive one-tenth of a mile and take a right on Highway 263. Follow Highway 263 alongside the Shasta River to the junction with Highway 96. Turn left and drive 31.2 miles to Scott River Road. Turn left. Access is available at several access points along the highway.*

Although they aren't targeted, salmon do spawn in the Scott River.

KELLY LAKE

Rating: 5

Species: Rainbow Trout

Stocked with 1,012 pounds of rainbow trout.

Facilities: Restrooms and a Picnic Area

Need Information? Contact: Klamath National Forest (530) 493-2243

Kelly Lake isn't a prime fishery, but the fact that any trout exist is the work of genius. Situated in a heavily forested area of the Siskiyou Wilderness, Kelly rests at 3,500 feet in the Klamath Mountains, but while it may appear to be a drive-to lake on your map, it's not. A quarter-mile walk on a flat, well graded path is required to reach the 15-acre pond.

There are no native fish, but the California Department of Fish and Game decided to add some into the mix by placing trout into wheel barrels and pushing them to the lake. (This is done annually.) The idea has worked well and provides Happy Camp and Southern Oregon residents with a quiet place to catch small trout in the spring and summer months.

It's a 15-20 minute drive on a dirt road from Indian Creek Road to Kelly Lake, but the crisp mountain air and 1,900 half-pound (or smaller) rainbows are incentive to make the drive. The lake can freeze in the winter, but ice fishing isn't an option for most. Snow commonly closes the road. The lake has a path which circles the lake. It's best to fish with medium size spoons or bait. Krocodiles, Cripplures and other spoons work well.

If you plan to make the trip, supplies are available in Happy Camp. In winter and spring, call ahead for road conditions. The road may be closed due to inclement weather.

Also nearby is the Middle Klamath River.

Directions: *From Happy Camp on Highway 96, drive north for 7.3 miles on Indian Creek Road. Turn left on South Fork Road and drive one-half mile to a gravel quarry on the right. Turn right at the unsigned road and drive 7.1 miles to USFS Road 18N30. Turn left and drive 1.9 miles to 18N34. Turn left and drive seven-tenths of a mile to the parking area for Kelly Lake near the restrooms.*

Kelly Lake

KLAMATH RIVER (MIDDLE)

Rating: 8

Species: Rainbow Trout, Steelhead and Chinook Salmon

Stocks: None

Facilities: Gas, Restaurant, General Store, Campgrounds, Lodging, RV Hookups, Picnic Areas, Primitive Boat Launches and Restrooms

Need Information? Contact: Wally Johnson's Seiad Valley Guide Service (530) 496-3291, Klamath National Forest (530) 493-2243

Happy Camp isn't a traveler's paradise. It may look like a decent size city on the map, but it's not. There's no Radisson, Chilis or drive-thru Walgreens. Nonetheless, this rustic town offers enough amenities to keeps its' visitors fed and warm. Happy Camp is a destination for travelers who want to escape city life.

It's also a place with a rich tradition. Happy Camp was once a gold rush town. Then, it became a logging town. Now, the struggling economy relies on fishing and seasonal rafting.

Because of its' length, the amount of tributaries it has and the success of Iron Gate Hatchery, the middle Klamath has more salmon and steelhead than many other Northern California rivers. And, there's no pressure.

Action hasn't always been banner-like though. From roughly 1988-98, fishing was horrendous. Drought, over harvesting in the ocean and other factors led to a rapid decline. However, new regulations in the ocean and wetter years have allowed the fishery to rebound.

Yet there are still few anglers to be found.

Part of it may have to do with the economy. For decades, Happy Camp prospered from logging. Local mills were designed for big timber. Recently, big timber was becoming more difficult to find. Environmental concerns with the spotted owl and other endangered species hurt logging operations. Cooperating with regulations, loggers weren't allowed to cut down trees within three miles of any spotted owl. This put a strain on which timber the loggers could take and a hurt on the local economy. Logs not only generated sales for the limber companies, but some money went back into the county. Local schools were the greatest beneficiary. Now they suffer from lesser funds.

By 1990, it's safe to say the mill was gone. Shortly after, a huge migration of people out of the area was evident. With mill operations gone, jobs were tougher to find. Many anglers who loved to fish were forced to relocate in search of jobs. Local veteran fishing guide Wally Johnson put it best. "When the mill died, Happy Camp died," he said.

For some, Happy Camp still generates a living. The biggest employer is the Forest Service. The Klamath National Forest has an office in town. Others rely on the service industry: hotels, food and camping.

Located along Highway 96, this section of the Middle Klamath River is still foreign to many California anglers. Nonetheless, more than 75 miles of river water from Interstate 5 to below Happy Camp makes for great angling opportunities.

Situated in the Klamath Mountains, this section of the Klamath

National Forest is blessed with oaks, cedars, firs, pines, alders, maples, locust, willows, dogwoods and others. It's a beautiful area with good fishing.

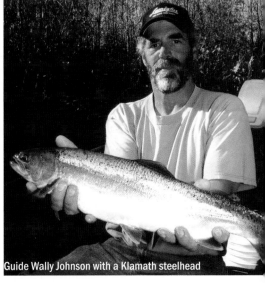
Guide Wally Johnson with a Klamath steelhead

This wild and scenic river can be fished with barbless hooks only. Unlike other coastal waters, it's not a gin clear system. Salmon are the first to arrive. From mid-September to late October, you'll find salmon averaging 15-20 pounds, with some 30-40 pounders. You don't get huge fish in the system.

Steelhead arrive in September and remain in the system through March. While they average three-to-six pounds, it's not uncommon to catch larger. And, you'll catch dozens of half-pounders as well. Anglers with drift boats are impressed. There are several great drifts to fish.

The first drift stretches from Horse Creek to Hamburg. There is no paved ramp, but a doable put in at Brown Bear River Access and a take out of Sarah Totten Campground. Fit with nice holes and spawning tributaries, this seven-mile run heads by the mouth of the Scott River, a haven for salmon and steelhead.

Push on and you'll find the section from Rocky Point to Portuguese Creek, a five-mile stretch of good water. Running through Seiad Valley, here you'll want to fish deep runs and riffles.

China Point to Happy Camp is my favorite run. In the 10 miles you scoot, it's common to see more bears and Bigfoot than anglers. This section isn't a roadside option. There are only three access points, two of which are the put in and take out. The other is Gordon's Ferry Road. The run flows through a canyon where you'll rarely see homes or other humans.

The section just below Happy Camp isn't an area for boats. In fact, this is the summer whitewater section. However, further downstream anglers can put in at Wind Gate Bar and float to Ferry Point for a six-mile run.

If you don't have a drift boat, it's no big deal. Shore options are promising. One of the best locations is from the mouth of the Scott to Tom

Martin Creek. Remember though, the mouth is closed year-round within 500 feet of the confluence. You can fish off the rocks at the mouth of Tom Martin Creek. You'll find most of your steelhead in the riffles and tailouts.

In this section all tributaries to the Klamath are closed except for the Scott. Upriver, near the Highway 263 Bridge, is another quality hole. There's a big pullout roughly a quarter-mile downriver from the bridge where anglers can find good shore fishing. On the other hand, there are some crowds to deal with because you are fairly close to Yreka. Salmon back up in this area because they are staging to head up the Shasta River. Steelhead are always close behind.

In Happy Camp many anglers set up shop at the mouth of Indian Creek. Indian itself harbors a good run of wild steelhead, but is closed to fishing. The mouth of the creek, though, is open.

The Middle Klamath tends to handle normal rainfall well. If it comes down hard though, it can take up to a week to clear. The culprit is the Scott River. The Scott tends to muddy and pump colored water into the Klamath. If you fish above the confluence, you should be ok.

Techniques are standard for both species. For steelhead, running Luhr Jensen Hot Shots in silver and gold, silver and copper, copper or reddish copper is best. Panther Martin spinners

An average Klamath River steelhead

take their share of fish after salmon spawn has ended. During the spawn, plugs and roe are the way to go.

Fly fishing is popular. While a dry fly is useless during the steelhead season, nymphing is productive. Try a bead head assassin, green or olive bead head woolly bugger or silver hiltons with a dap of Liquid Krill on them.

In the fall, fish riffles before switching over to deep, slow holes when the cold of winter arrives. Salmon are taken on Kwikfish and roe.

If you plan to make the trip, supplies are available in Happy Camp and Yreka. Check fishing regulations. Daily bag limits change annually for the system. All hooks and flies must be barbless.

Also nearby are Kelly Lake and the Scott River.

Directions: From Interstate 5 in Yreka drive north, or from Medford, drive south and exit west on Highway 96. The road parallels the river for the entire stretch.

The Klamath River near Happy Camp during the fall.

KLAMATH RIVER (UPPER)

Rating: 8

Species: Rainbow Trout, Chinook Salmon, Silver Salmon and Steelhead

Stocked with 18,974 pounds of fingerling Chinook salmon and 10,097 pounds of yearling steelhead.

Facilities: RV Hookups, Campgrounds, Restrooms, Restaurant, Gas, Bait and Tackle, Fish Hatchery Viewing Area, General Store and a Boat Launch,

Need Information?
Contact: The Tackle Shop (530) 841-1901, Wally Johnson of Seiad Valley Guide Service (530) 496-3291, Fishing Guide Scott Caldwell (530) 905-0758

Special Note: *In 2004, budget cuts tempted the California Department of Fish and Game to cut the yearling Chinook program at Iron Gate Hatchery. Prior to 1981, salmon were released as smolts, rather than yearlings, which are much older and have a greater survival rate. From 1962-81, an average of 4,799 salmon returned to the hatchery under the smolt program. From 1982-2003, that number increased to 16,357 as fish were released at yearling size. If the yearling program is removed, the salmon fishery on the Klamath River will suffer tremendously.*

The Upper Klamath River is a fishery that lives and dies by the success of its' hatchery system. In this case, the Iron Gate Fish Hatchery spawns Chinook salmon, silver salmon and steelhead each year to ensure quality fishing for years to come. Other than the mouth near Klamath Glen, this is the most heavily fished section of the Klamath.

This stems from two good reasons: lots of fish and good access. The Upper Klamath offers easy access between Interstate 5 near Hornbrook and Iron Gate Reservoir. This section is heavily fished from drift boat and shore.

Salmon are the main attraction. Salmon file in as early as August, but the bulk of the run correlates with deer season. From late September through October, 10-30 pound salmon stuff the river. If you are looking for edible fish, try casting a line before October 15. By then, most salmon will be pretty nasty looking and their meat soft.

Salmon can be attained by shoreline anglers and drift boaters. From a drift boat, there is one possibility. A put in is found near Iron Gate Hatchery and a take out at Klamath On Bridge. This seven-mile drift can easily take a day. From shore, the frontage road out of Hornbrook offers good access, as does the rest area near I-5. Most salmon are taken on Kwikfish and roe soaked in Pautzke Liquid Krill.

Wintertime poses the best steelhead fishing, but many anglers are scared off by the cold. Daytime temperatures average 15-50 degrees. Snow is common, as is wind. Techniques are widely varied. Steelhead can be taken on size six and eight sculpin imitations, bead head glimmer stones, prince nymphs, woolly buggers and egg sucking leeches. For non-fly fishermen (which there are a ton of in this stretch), an array of baits work: Corky and a night crawler, side drifting or back bouncing roe, Spin-N-Glos, Glo Bugs and size 30, 40 or

50 Luhr Jensen Hot Shots in black, silver or gold.

Local fishing guide Scott Caldwell has some unorthodox methods to catching steelies. He drifts CD-5 brown trout Rapalas and Rebel Crawdads. Actually, the Wee and Tiny Craw in Texas red and ditch brown are deadly. His reasoning: when the salmon are done spawning and roe is gone, the steelhead key in on crawdads as their main food source. Steelhead average two-to-five pounds with a few peaking over 10 each year.

For many anglers, the best time to fish this section of the Klamath isn't when the salmon and steelhead are in the river, rather during the annual salmon fly hatch. While it varies a few weeks from year to year, the hatch takes place sometime between mid-May and the 4th of July. When the water warms to 70 degrees or above for five or more days, the hatch blossoms and lasts for three to four weeks. Action can be insane with fish taken on every cast. Try a size eight or 10 salmon fly or a No. 8 stimulator. Any small dry fly can work. Blue or brown dunns, No. 6 black bead head woolly buggers or for nymph fishing, a size 14 or 16 hair's ear or any small stonefly nymph works well. Use a four-or-five-weight rod with floating line and a 6x tippet.

Fishing can be tremendous, yet frustrating at the same time. During this time the Iron Gate Fish Hatchery releases more than 1.7 million fingerling Chinook salmon and 141,000 yearling steelhead. These fish often get in the way of catching larger fish. The question is, are these steelhead or rainbow trout you are catching? Basically, they are steelhead who forgot to swim to the ocean. Most residents average 12-16 inches, but you'll find some up to five pounds.

Spinners also take fish. Toss a small Mepps or Panther Martin. A black body with red spots or gold body with red spots is best. Silver or copper Hot Shots are on tap for those who choose to run plugs.

If you plan to make the trip, supplies are available in Yreka. Only barbless hooks may be used. Check sportfishing regulations. Daily bag limits and quotas change annually. The Upper Klamath is closed to fishing from Iron Gate Dam on downriver for 3,500 feet. The boundary is marked by a cable over the river.

Also nearby are Iron Gate Reservoir, Copco Reservoir and Shasta River.

Directions: *From Yreka, drive north on Interstate 5 to the Hornbrook exit. The river can be accessed both upriver and downriver from this point.*

Guide Scott Caldwell used a Rebel crawdad to trick this Klamath River steelhead.

SHASTA RIVER

Rating: 6

Species: Rainbow Trout, Steelhead and Chinook Salmon

Stocks: None

Facilities: None

Need Information? Contact: The Tackle Shop (530) 841-1901

The Shasta River is not a name that sounds familiar to most anglers. You rarely hear it talked about, almost never see it publicized and if you aren't shown where to access the river by a local, you may never weave your way through private property to find fishable water. In fact, many residents do their part to make sure that you aren't successful in locating access.

Locating the river isn't a problem. However, bogus "no trespassing signs" usually throw people off track. After dinner at a restaurant in Yreka, I hung out with a trio of CHP officers and told them I'd been unable to fish the river because of no trespassing signs. Ironically, those signs were a fraud. Residents, I was told by the officers, put them up to deter anglers from fishing the river. They told me they would be down in the morning to remove the signs, and I was to drive on through and call them if I had any problems. They said they've heard these complaints before. The roads that were being blocked were county maintained roads, therefore open to the public.

The Shasta River is one of the region's overlooked waters. While no plants are made, the Shasta harbors a population of wild rainbow trout. The Shasta River receives little to no pressure. Trout are available, but getting to them can require bushwhacking in many places. A pair of full body waders is a must. The Shasta fishes best in the spring, usually around Memorial Day when the salmon fly hatch comes off. Spring also poses several caddis hatches. Unfortunately, spin casters have a difficult time on the river. When fishing the Shasta, look for seams and fish under overhanging trees.

A typical rainbow is going to run eight-to-12 inches. Some are larger, just not common. By the time summer arrives, the river gradually begins to warm and shrink in size as runoff becomes less available. The sweltering heat also brings out rattlers. Time to head to the Klamath.

If you plan to make the trip, supplies are available in Yreka. The Shasta River is closed to fishing from March 1 to the fourth Saturday in May and from October 1 to November 15. All fishing is catch and release. The river is closed during the bulk of salmon and steelhead season.

Also nearby are Iron Gate Reservoir and Copco Reservoir.

Directions: *From the Highway 3 west and Interstate 5 junction in Yreka, drive north on Interstate 5 for 12 miles to the Highway 96 exit. Exit the freeway, turn left, drive under the freeway and over the Klamath River before coming to a T intersection. Turn left and drive 2.3 miles to a split in the road. Veer left on Highway 263 and drive seven-tenths of a mile to Hudson Road on the right. (The road is just after the bridge.) Turn right. The road passes by several houses and then parallels the river.*

GREENHORN RESERVOIR

Rating: 5

Species: Rainbow Trout, Largemouth Bass, Brown Bullhead and Bluegill

Stocked with 7,006 pounds of rainbow trout.

Facilities: Restrooms, Picnic Area and a Playground

Need Information? Contact: The Tackle Shop (530) 841-1901

Greenhorn Reservoir gets no attention from out-of-town anglers. In fact, other than a few kids who fish after class on weekdays, the reservoir sees little fishing pressure. On the other hand, the reservoir is the most heavily stocked rainbow trout water in the Shasta Valley. Each year the California Department of Fish and Game unloads more than 12,153 half-pound rainbows into this 23-acre reservoir just outside the city of Yreka. Seems like way too many trout to me.

Why are so many fish planted if so few anglers are catching them? Good question. Action doesn't reflect the number of trout planted. When it comes to trout, catching fish can be tough after spring when temperatures increase, forcing the rainbows to search for cooler water and becoming less active. The best time to fish here is late winter and early spring when Power Baiters and anglers tossing spinners nab limits of fish from the shore.

Other than trout, a resident population of largemouth attracts a few visitors in the warmer months, yet with Trout, Bass, Iron Gate and Copco so close, most anglers don't want to waste time at Greenhorn. Sounds fair enough to me. Leave this place to the local kids.

If you plan to make the trip, supplies are available in Yreka.

Also nearby is the Shasta River.

Directions: *From Interstate 5 in Yreka, take the Highway 3 exit signed for Callahan/Weaverville and turn right on South Main Street. Drive six-tenths of a mile to Greenhorn Road. Turn left and drive seven-tenths of a mile to the left turnoff for the reservoir.*

Greenhorn Reservoir

TROUT LAKE

Rating: 8

Species: Rainbow Trout, Bluegill and Largemouth Bass

Stocked with 1,500 pounds of rainbow trout.

Facilities: Launch Ramp, Fishing Pier and Restrooms

Need Information? Contact: The Tackle Shop (530) 841-1901

Trout Lake is a mirror image of Bass Lake, also located in the Shasta Valley Wildlife Refuge. However, Trout Lake's fish are typically larger and because the lake is a bit deeper, the weeds don't arrive as early as they do in Bass Lake.

Even with heavy pressure Trout Lake stands tall. Because only artificial lures can be used, there's a much better survival rate. Fish tend to live longer, thus allowing them to grow larger. Largemouth tend to average 10-14 inches, although, fish to five pounds are common. If you have a boat you'll be able to cover more water and target submerged trees and tule lines that you can't properly approach from shore.

Shoreline fishing is more conducive at Trout than Bass Lake. While trout aren't typically caught from shore, bass can be easily attained. Dark colors are the rule. A watermelon green Senko with black flake or a four-inch black Senko with red flake will land fish all day. In the spring and early summer, it's common to see bass near the surface aiming at eating blue dragonflies. The main food source is bluegill, however, an abundance of bugs and flies keep the bass well fed.

Trout are also on the menu. The California Department of Fish and Game plants 2,700 half-pound Eagle Lake trout each year. Those fish often come out at two-to-five pounds. Only two trout may be kept per day. For trout troll black woolly buggers, leach patterns or salmon flies on a sinking fly line. Power Bait is not allowed. Bait dunkers should plan on fishing somewhere else.

If you plan to make the trip, supplies are available in Yreka. Only one bass, 22 inches or greater may be taken each day. Trout Lake is only open to fishing on Wednesdays, Saturdays and Sundays between April 1 and September 30.

Also nearby are Greenhorn Reservoir, Shasta River and the Klamath River.

Directions: *In Yreka, take the Highway 3 east exit and drive 6.3 miles to the town of Montague and the end of Highway 3. Highway 3 turns in Ball Mountain/Little Shasta Road. Continue for eight-tenths of a mile to a turnoff on the right for the Shasta Valley Wildlife Area. Turn right and drive 2.2 miles to a split in the road. Turn left and continue 1.1 miles to the lake.*

Trout Lake

BASS LAKE

Rating: 7

Species: Rainbow
Trout, Bluegill, Channel
Catfish and Largemouth
Bass

Stocked with 2,975
pounds of rainbow
trout.

Facilities: Launch
Ramp, A Fishing Pier
and Restrooms

Need Information?
Contact: The Tackle
Shop (530) 841-1901

Wildlife areas are some of the most overlooked fisheries in the country. Therefore, it's no surprise the Shasta Valley Wildlife Area is one of California's unseen bass fisheries. A short drive from Yreka and only about a half-hour south of the Oregon border, Bass Lake, has acre-for-acre some of the best bass action in California, yet it's rarely publicized or fished by anyone other than a few locals. I believe the lake is ignored by most bassers because of its lack of trophy size fish.

Size aside though, it's difficult to find another lake where you can catch a bass on nearly every cast. At just 85 acres it's not difficult to locate the fish. The bite is best in May and June, but does last through the summer. The key is fishing in the tules. Anglers who toss three-or-four-inch plastics in any dark color can expect to land 25-50 fish if they fish their way around the lake. The trick is casting as close to the weeds as possible. If your worm lands three feet from the tules, recast. The bass aren't going to come out and get it.

Additionally, Bass Lake is a great place to tune up your skills and increase confidence. To be successful, you really need a boat. No gas-powered motors are permitted and there's only limited shoreline access which can keep shore anglers from doing well. A fishing pier and some bank access exist, but it's not located in prime areas. From shore you are better off targeting bluegill. The lake is chock full of hand-size bluegill that can be caught by the hundreds.

Trout are also part of the mixed bag in Bass Lake, as the California Department of Fish and Game scatters 5,070 half-pound rainbows. By mid-June weeds typically cover the lake, even though trout can still be caught by anglers dangling night crawlers in the middle of the lake. Get your bait near the bottom and you'll have a good chance. Surprisingly, there are some bows that reach up to four pounds. However by June the water is too warm to allow shore anglers a shot at trout.

The fishing at Bass Lake is definitely enhanced by the wildlife. It's not uncommon to see deer, river otters and orange headed blackbirds dangling from the tules. This place is truly a wildlife area.

If you plan to make the trip, supplies are available in Yreka. Bass Lake is closed to fishing from October 1 to January 31.

Also nearby are Trout Lake and the Shasta River.

Directions: From the entrance to the Shasta Valley Wildlife Area drive 2.2 miles to a split in the road. Turn right and continue one-tenth of a mile to the lake.

IRON GATE RESERVOIR

Rating: 10

Species: Rainbow
Trout, Largemouth
Bass, Smallmouth Bass,
Channel Catfish,
Bluegill, Crappie,
Green Sunfish and
Perch

Stocks: None

Facilities: Boat Launch,
Campgrounds,
Restrooms, Fishing
Piers and Picnic Areas

Need Information?
Contact: The Tackle
Shop (530) 841-1901

Hands down, Iron Gate Reservoir is the best yellow perch fishery in California, maybe the best in the West. As New York is known as the Big Apple, Iron Gate is known as the perch capitol of California. Excellent perch fishing is an understatement. You can realistically land 50-100 perch, per angler, per day. No joke. The difference between Iron Gate and nearby Copco Reservoir is that at Iron Gate, you won't be tossing fish into a cooler by yourself. There'll be dozens of other anglers doing the same! Plus, the camping here is free.

This is perch country. Located a few miles south of the Oregon border, the dam at Iron Gate is operated by the Pacific Power Company. The 1,000 acre reservoir is seven miles long and open to fishing year-round.

If you are considering introducing a child or a friend to fishing, this is the place to come. No prior experience is necessary to catch fish.While the perch aren't huge, they are a blast to catch. And, you are pretty much guaranteed fish. If you are going to eat them, the California Department of Fish and Game encourages anglers to keep as many as you can clean. While catch and release is encouraged in many instances, this isn't one of them. The perch population needs to be thinned. If more anglers remove perch, it will drive the size of the perch up. Fewer perch means less competition for food, quicker growth rates and more meat on their bones. Everyone wins. You couldn't put a dent in the perch population if you took 100 perch a day, everyday of the year! Perch average five to 10 inches.

Dozens of boats hit the water in search of fish fillets to serve at a family barbeque. They aren't disappointed. Fish cleaning stations stage assembly lines to make the cleaning process smoother and quicker. Perch sticks are a commodity in this northern most portion of the state (which refers to itself as the Jefferson State). The concept is simple: break off from California and create our own state with our Southern Oregon neighbors. It'll never happen, though. Their water is too valuable.

Locating perch is easy. Concentrate on weed lines, which won't be difficult to find. The entire lake has them. Fortunately, perch aren't picky. Bait fishing can be fantastic, yet costly. If you use a full worm, plan on

Panfish are abundant at Iron Gate Reservoir

287

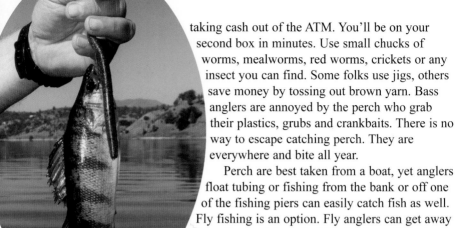

Iron Gate is one of the best perch fisheries in the West.

taking cash out of the ATM. You'll be on your second box in minutes. Use small chucks of worms, mealworms, red worms, crickets or any insect you can find. Some folks use jigs, others save money by tossing out brown yarn. Bass anglers are annoyed by the perch who grab their plastics, grubs and crankbaits. There is no way to escape catching perch. They are everywhere and bite all year.

Perch are best taken from a boat, yet anglers float tubing or fishing from the bank or off one of the fishing piers can easily catch fish as well. Fly fishing is an option. Fly anglers can get away with a four weight rod with a 6x tippet. Your basic size 10 woolly bugger or leach pattern will do.

Iron Gate isn't just an amazing perch fishery. Other species prosper as well. Pan fish action is excellent. Half-pound to pound-and-a-half size crappie, bluegill and green sunfish are common. For pan fish use at least half of a night crawler fished two feet below a bobber.

Bass are on tap, but are not the most desirable species. Bass can be found two places: outside or inside the weed line. Depending on the water level, this changes daily. Don't overlook rock piles and fallen trees. Towards where the Klamath River enters, there are steep cliffs that hold some decent smallmouth.

Trout are available but rarely targeted. If you are going to fish for trout, work the east side where the Klamath comes in. These fish can average one-to-three-pounds and are ancestors of steelhead that were trapped when the dam was constructed in 1962. No plants are made.

If you plan to make the trip, supplies are available in Hornbrook.

Also nearby are Copco Reservoir, Upper Klamath River and Trout Lake.

Directions: *From Interstate 5 in Yreka, drive north for 15.2 miles to the Hornbrook exit. Exit east and drive nine miles to the reservoir.*

Bald Eagles reside at Iron Gate Reservoir

COPCO RESERVOIR

Rating: 6

Species: Rainbow Trout, Largemouth Bass, Smallmouth Bass, Channel Catfish, Bluegill, Crappie and Perch

Stocks: None

Facilities: Boat Launch, Boat Rentals, Campgrounds, Restrooms, Bait & Tackle and a General Store

Need Information? Contact: The Tackle Shop (530) 841-1901

Copco Reservoir is almost an exact replica of Iron Gate Reservoir. The reservoir is a dammed portion of the Upper Klamath River and is infested with yellow perch, yet also has bundles of bass, catfish and trout that keep anglers busy. The difference between Iron Gate and Copco is that Copco receives few visitors, whereas Iron Gate gets packed.

Tucked away in a sparsely populated section of Siskiyou County close to the Oregon border and east of Interstate 5, Copco is a terrific perch fishery. It's realistic to catch more than 100 perch per person and not see another angler. Unfortunately, those fish will average five to 10 inches, but they are fun to catch on two-pound test. A small jig, worms or yarn is all you need.

Trout can grow upwards of five pounds in Copco. They aren't planted, rather descendants of the Upper Klamath. For trout, trolling is best. Many anglers troll small spinners and spoons near the bridge on the east side. Casting from shore can also be effective.

The bass fishery is pretty much untapped. Largemouth and some smallmouth are available and average roughly one-to-three pounds. They can be taken on plastics near any of the rocky banks.

A Yellow Perch   Copco Reservoir

If you plan to make the trip, supplies are available at the Copco Store.

Also nearby are Iron Gate Reservoir and the Upper Klamath River.

Directions: From Interstate 5 in Yreka, drive north for 15.2 miles to the Hornbrook exit. Exit east and drive 2.9 miles to a split in the road. Turn right, cross over the Klamath River and drive 3.2 miles to the left turnoff for Copco Reservoir. Turn left and continue 13 miles to the lake.

INDIAN TOM LAKE

Rating: 3

Species: Cutthroat Trout

Stocked with 2,500 pounds of sub-catchable cutthroat trout.

Facilities: None

Need Information?
Contact: Klamath National Forest
(530) 398-4391

Indian Tom Lake is even a mystery to the California Department of Fish and Game. Shown as a large marsh on a map, Indian has been planted by the CA DFG with fingerling trout for more than a half century. In 2003, the size of planted fish increased from fingerling to sub-catchable. However in 2003, when the CA DFG's wild trout crew went in to survey Indian Tom to see if their allotted fish were surviving or perhaps becoming bird food their results were discouraging.

Even with their electrofishing boat, the CA DFG didn't see a single cutthroat trout in Indian Tom. In fact, they only shocked a half dozen fish, none of which were gamefish. No cuts were seen at all. A local DFG warden told biologists that he personally has seen a few anglers with cutthroat, yet few people fish the lake. Soon, if DFG snorkeling efforts don't discover fish, the 25,000 fingerling cutthroat will be taken off the allotment.

There is a possibility that some cutthroats are surviving, but, don't be surprised if none are found. Indian Tom is located roughly a half-mile south of the Oregon border, just north of the town of Dorris on Highway 97. The lake is shallow and warms quickly. To catch any fish at all you'll need a small car top boat or a float tube to allow you to reach deeper water. Find the deepest hole you can and if you don't get any nibbles, don't feel so bad. At least we know someone got fed. Tip your hat to the birds!

If you plan to make the trip, supplies are available in Dorris.

Also nearby are Orr Lake, Juanita Lake and the Klamath National Wildlife Area.

Directions: *From Weed, drive north on Highway 97 for 52 miles to the turnoff for Highway 119. Turn right, drive two-tenths of a mile and turn right on Indian Tom Road. Drive one-tenth of a mile to the lake on the left.*

Indian Tom Lake

Rating: 1

Species: None

Stocks: None

Facilities: None

Need Information?
Contact: Klamath
National Wildlife
Refuge (530) 667-2231

The Klamath Wildlife Area has the potential to an be excellent bass fishing water. However, there's one huge problem: no fishing is allowed in the wildlife area. Ironically, hunting is permitted during selected periods, yet anglers aren't given the opportunity to utilize the water. The wildlife area is comprised of several lakes including Lower Klamath, Sheepey and Tule Lake, none of which are open to fishing.

A few locals boasted to me (off the record) about poaching on the wildlife refuge because they, "knew the rangers and no one ever enforces the laws there anyway." It's not worth the risk guys. While some largemouth bass and bullhead can be found, their numbers are small. You have a better chance at seeing more than 100 species of birds in a given day than catching a single fish anyway. Leave this shallow, warm water to the birds. After all, they need a place to fish too.

If you are an avid bird watcher, prime time here is in the winter when the largest concentrations of bald eagles in the Lower 48 show up.

If you plan to make the trip, supplies are available in Tule Lake and Dorris.

Also nearby is Indian Tom Lake.

Directions: *From 97 in Weed, drive towards Klamath Falls for 52 miles to the right turnoff for Highway 119. Turn right and drive 3.4 miles to Sheepey Lake or six miles to Lower Klamath Lake.*

Tule Lake

LITTLE MEDICINE LAKE

Rating: 5

Species: Rainbow Trout and Brook Trout

Stocked with 350 pounds of brook trout.

Facilities: Picnic Area, Fishing Piers and Restrooms

Need Information? Contact: Modoc National Forest (530) 233-5811

Seasonally, Little Medicine Lake can be an excellent fishery for small planted trout. Your window to do well is limited to a few weeks in late June or early July. As soon as the road to Medicine and Little Medicine opens, the California Department of Fish and Game plants the lake once or twice in the first few weeks of the season (560 brooks in all).

When plants occur at this 3.5-acre pond size lake, catch rates are high. Unfortunately, fishing tends to lag more and more each day after the plants take place. Every so often the CA DFG will surprise anglers again in the fall with another load of fish; however, this doesn't happen every year. Keep an eye on the newspaper. If you see Little Medicine listed on the stocking list you'll catch trout. If not, don't bother fishing it after Labor Day weekend. It will be slim pickings. When fish are available, any bait works. This isn't a tough place to catch fish.

Other anglers fish Little Medicine after winds blow them off larger Medicine Lake. Drive to fishing access is favorable for all anglers. A trail loops around the lake and two fishing piers are available for public use. This spot in the Modoc National Forest is blessed with pan size brook and rainbow trout. It's the kind of place where you can cast from a float tube and admire a deer chewing grass in the meadow. That is, until someone takes their dog for a walk and sends the deer darting to safety.

Trip info for Medicine Lake also applies to Little Medicine Lake.

Directions: *From the stop sign at the entrance to Medicine Lake, stay right and drive 1.4 miles to the parking area on the right for Little Medicine Lake.*

Little Medicine Lake

MEDICINE LAKE

Rating: 8

Species: Brown Trout,
Rainbow Trout and
Brook Trout

Stocked with 16,000
pounds of brook trout
and 9,000 pounds of
rainbow trout.

Facilities:
Campgrounds, Boat
Launch, Swimming
Beach, Picnic Area,
Fishing Piers and
Restrooms

Need Information?
Contact: Modoc
National Forest
(530) 233-5811

Medicine Lake is one of California's least known, yet best fisheries for anglers looking to catch pan size trout from shore or boat. The downfall is this lake isn't a short jaunt from anywhere in Northern California, unless you are one of the few residents who live in one of the small towns on the western edge of the Modoc Plateau.

The 440-acre lake, located at 6,700 feet in the Modoc National Forest, is stuffed with willing rainbows and brooks, while supporting a number of wild browns. Surprisingly, few anglers have fished along its' pristine, pretty and quite shorelines. Medicine Lake isn't difficult to find, just a long drive from any of Nor Cal's major cities.

Fishing is a partial reason to come. There are a load of other touristy activities to take part in. Fewer than a one-half hour drive is the Burnt Lava Flow, Lava Beds National Monument, The Ice Caves and other volcanic remnants that litter the landscape. Medicine Lake itself rests in a basin formally active as a volcano.

Medicine Lake isn't a trophy producing lake, rather a relaxing put-and-take fishery. While record setting catches shouldn't be expected, they are possible. Medicine doesn't receive much fishing pressure, but the California Department of Fish and Game is merciful with their fish plants. More than 37,000 rainbows and brooks between one-half and three-quarters of a pound are stocked annually.

Todd McLean in the Ice Caves, located
a few miles from Medicine Lake.

The typical trout ranges between 10-14 inches. Don't be surprised, however, to land a fish from 14-18 inches. Some fish in the 18-22 inch class are landed weekly, but that's not a common occurrence, more a matter of being in the right place at the right time.

Each year it's a mystery when the road to the lake will open. The lake can only be fished four to five months of the year. Nestled between Mt. Shasta and the Modoc Plateau in the Modoc National Forest, the roads aren't heavily traveled and don't necessarily open when temperatures warm in the Central

Valley. It may be 105 degrees in Sacramento, but unfortunately, the paved road to Medicine could still have six feet of snow on it.

Don't bother coming before June and stay away after mid-November. Fallen trees, snow drifts, ice and other hazards cause the Forest Service serious headaches in the spring when they attempt to open the road between

Magnificant views of Mt. Shasta are common on the drive to Medicine.

Memorial Day and Fourth of July, depending on how bad the winter was. The road also closes between Halloween and Thanksgiving. It's subject to closure after the first major snow. No roads to the lake are maintained in the winter. A snowmobile is the only way in.

During the fair months, fishing is excellent for anglers. Fathers and sons with Snoopy Poles, hardcore trollers, bait dunkers, fly fishermen and spin casters all have a place here.

While you won't see it in writing, all indications point to Medicine being managed as a fishing lake. A 10 mph speed limit from 10 a.m. to 5 p.m. is enforced by daily patrols from a sheriff's boat, as well as the 5 mph limit within 200 feet of the shore. Water-skiing is permitted, but only during the middle of the day and afternoon, luckily when anglers aren't typically on the water.

Most anglers troll. Trolling couldn't be more simplistic. Cruising the shorelines with a worm behind a dodger is the easiest way to land fish. The lake is as deep as 150 feet, but only averages 22 feet deep. For anglers who aren't keen on dragging a set flashers, try a gold Flatfish, Kastmasters, Hum-Dingers, Needlefish, Dick Nite spoons or a Wedding Ring. To be realistic, it doesn't matter what you pull as long as you target the right sections of the lake. Fortunately, that happens to be anywhere. While Medicine's trout school up, there are always some scattered over the lake. Troll the middle of the lake with figure eights and cruise the shoreline for increased success.

From shore, there are several areas that are productive. The most consistent tends to be fishing from the rocks near the swim beach, although the launch ramp area can be hot for a few days after a stocking. A small Panther Martin is all you need to catch fish near the ramp.

Few have been known to move in on the opportunity, but fly anglers can expect to do equally well. woolly buggers and leeches, size 10 damsel nymphs, prince nymphs, hairs ears or midge pupas fished underneath a Corky and an indicator are an assortment of offerings that you can be successful with.

One deterrent can be wind. Almost daily, at one point or another the wind will blow. Whether morning, mid-day or afternoon, plan for either a slight breeze, steady 15-25 mph winds or gusts. On a positive note, the winds tend to lay down each day.

If the winds are howling, you can avoid the swells by shore fishing Little Medicine Lake. Resting less than a quarter-mile away, Little Medicine is also planted with rainbows and brooks and can be hot for bait dunkers and spin casters in the spring, and again in the fall if the CA DFG plants a second load of fish. This small pond is best for teaching children how to fish.

When the wind is absent at Medicine, many more experienced anglers take the opportunity to jig. It's best to correlate your jigging depth with a fish finder, but it's not absolutely necessary. To stay on the safe side, jig between 25-50 feet. One of the best spots is near the red buoy by the swim beach.

If you plan to make the trip, supplies are available in Dorris and Mt. Shasta. In spring call ahead for road conditions. The road may be closed between November and June in some years.

Also nearby are Little Medicine Lake, Bullseye Lake and the Ice Caves.

Directions: From the junction of Interstate 5 and Highway 299 east in Redding, drive north on Interstate 5 for 54.5 miles to the Highway 89 turnoff. Exit east on the Highway 89 and drive 25.6 miles to the left turnoff for Harris Springs Road. Turn left, drive 4.3 miles and turn right at the sign for Medicine Lake (Road 49). Continue for 25.8 miles to a sign on the left for Medicine Lake. Turn left and drive three-tenths of a mile to a stop sign. Stay left to the lake.

Medicine Lake

BLANCHE LAKE

Rating: 1

Species: None

Stocks: None

Facilities: None

Need Information?
Contact: Modoc
National Forest
(530) 667-2246

Deer hunters know Blanche Lake. On the other hand, anglers don't know and don't care where Blanche is, unless, however, the campground is full at nearby Bullseye Lake. Blanche is a small pond set in the Modoc National Forest that is well known by deer hunters who camp here in the fall on their annual deer hunts. The lake offers primitive camping and no services.

Oftentimes, I'll run into anglers fishing Blanche, unaware that the lake is fishless. Hunters swear by jumping fish in the evenings, however, this lake hasn't been planted by the California Department of Fish and Game in at least the last few decades. Maybe the "fish" are simply being mistaken for pollywags! There are tens of thousands of them which are known to splash around the shorelines in the evening.

Blanche is a shallow, clear, small pond that is best utilized as a free camping option, mostly for overflow campers from Bullseye. Plus, it's close to the Ice Caves, so dress warm.

If you plan to make the trip, supplies are available in Dorris and Mt. Shasta. In spring call ahead for road conditions. The road may be closed between November and June in some years.

Also nearby are Medicine Lake, Little Medicine Lake, Bullseye Lake and the Ice Caves.

Directions: *From the junction of Interstate 5 and Highway 299 east in Redding, drive north for 54.5 miles and exit Highway 89 east. Drive 25.6 miles to Harris Springs Road and turn left. Drive 4.3 miles and turn right at the sign for Medicine Lake (Road 49). Continue 23.8 miles to the right turnoff for Bullseye Lake. Turn right and eight-tenths of a mile to the right turnoff for Blanche Lake.*

Blanche Lake

BULLSEYE LAKE

Rating: 4

Species: Rainbow Trout and Brook Trout

Stocked with 250 pounds of brook trout and 400 pounds of rainbow trout.

Facilities: None

Need Information? Contact: Modoc National Forest (530) 667-2246

Bullseye Lake is the kind of place you see on a map and figure that if you can find it, you'll have it to yourself. Then you show up only to find a full campground. Bullseye may be secluded, but it's no secret, at least not to Southern Oregon and Modoc County residents.

Surrounded by pines, you'll get a woodsy feeling at Bullseye, but may not catch fish without a float tube. For the most part, the shorelines are shallow, and other than cool mornings and evenings that bring trout into the shallows, your chance of catching fish from shore is slim. Deep water is important.

Fishing from a float tube or canoe any time of day can yield trout. The best time to fish is in the late spring when the road first opens, however, fish will remain in the system year-round. There is no inlet or outlet so they are stuck here. The California Department of Fish and Game arrives in early spring to plant one load of rainbows or brookies. Try casting a silver Kastmaster or stripping in a black woolly bugger.

Trip info for Medicine Lake also apply to Bullseye Lake.

Directions: *From the junction of Interstate 5 and Highway 299 east in Redding, drive north for 54.5 miles and exit Highway 89 east. Drive 25.6 miles to Harris Springs Road and turn left. Drive 4.3 miles and turn right at the sign for Medicine Lake (Road 49). Continue 23.8 miles to the right turnoff for Bullseye Lake. Turn right and drive one-mile to the right turnoff for Bullseye Lake. Turn right and drive three-tenths of a mile to the lake.*

Bullseye Lake

BEAR CREEK (LOWER)

Rating: 5

Species: Rainbow Trout
and Brown Trout

Stocked with 500
pounds of rainbow
trout.

Facilities: None

Need Information?
Contact: Vaughn's
Sporting Goods
(530) 335-2381

Lower Bear Creek is a small, remote trout stream situated off Highway 89 between McCloud and Burney State Park that doesn't get heavily fished. It's a late spring/early summer destination, but is often snowed in for the opener and suffers from extreme heat and low flows by late August.

Unlike the upper section, this lower section of Bear Creek has a nearly flat gradient and offers pools and runs, rather than riffle like water. The water is clear and it's likely you'll be able to see the fish you are casting too. The stream only offers day-use fishing. No facilities of any kind can be found.

Lower Bear Creek relies on the California Department of Fish and Game to replenish stocks of rainbow trout through planting. While lures can work they can also be hard to fish under low water conditions. This section of Bear Creek is shallow and unless you fish it in the spring and early summer you'll want to leave the hardware at home and stick to casting flies and drifting bait. Other than a handful of wild fish, you'll mostly be going after 10-inch, and smaller, planted rainbows. A scattering of browns also exist. In all, 887 small bows are planted each spring.

To increase catch rates, fish as close to the bridge as possible. The CA DFG can get lazy planting this stream and usually dumps a few buckets right near the bridge. Downstream of the bridge you'll run into private property.

Trip info for Bear Creek (Upper) also applies to Bear Creek (Lower).

Directions: *From Interstate 5 in Redding, drive north for 54.5 miles to the Highway 89 east exit just past Dunsmuir. Follow Highway 89 for 33.8 miles to the left turnoff for Pondosa. Turn left and drive nine-tenths of a mile to the bridge and creek. It's just after the stream crossing on the left.*

Lower Bear Creek

BEAR CREEK (UPPER)

Rating: 5

Species: Rainbow Trout and Brown Trout

Stocked with 500 pounds of rainbow trout.

Facilities: None

Need Information? Contact: Vaughn's Sporting Goods (530) 335-2381

Wider than a brook, but a bit smaller than a creek, the spring-fed upper section of Bear Creek is a perfect late spring and summer destination for trout anglers who like to fish bait. Upper Bear Creek flows under Highway 89 near McCloud.

While this stream may not be blessed with thousands of hatchery fish, it is a nice alternative to other crowded, better known streams in the region. Other than a few weekend warriors who read about the fish plants in the Redding Record Searchlight, few anglers fish here. The incentive is a total of 912 half-pound rainbows the California Department of Fish and Game plants annually.

Opportunity to nail eight-10-inch planted bows is solid between spring and early summer though. Fish will remain in the system year-round, yet with the planters being such easy pickings they won't be as thick in August when fish plants cease. The stream is best fished with Orange Deluxe Pautzke salmon eggs, although fly anglers dropping ants and midges into small holes will also be successful.

To make for easy access, a dirt road follows along the east side of the stream allowing anglers to drive to less fished sections of the creek. If no one is already there, try fishing the hole just before the bridge. It always seems to harbor trout.

If you plan to make the trip, supplies are available in McCloud and Burney. Bear Creek is closed to fishing from November 16 to the last Saturday in April. In the spring, call ahead for road conditions. Snow can keep the access road to the creek closed through June.

Also nearby are Mt. Shasta, McCloud River and Burney State Park.

Directions: From Interstate 5 in Redding, drive north for 54.5 miles to the Highway 89 east exit just past Dunsmuir. Follow Highway 89 for 32.4 miles to the unsigned right turnoff. Turn right on the dirt road to the creek.

Upper Bear Creek

Mc Cloud River (Lakin Dam)

Rating: 8

Species: Rainbow Trout and Brook Trout

Stocked with 1,215 pounds of brook trout.

Facilities: Fishing Pier (Wheelchair Accessible), Restrooms and a Picnic Area

Need Information? Contact: Shasta National Forest (530) 926-4511

Upriver of a chain of waterfalls, the McCloud River has a small diversion dam in the town of Mc Cloud that was once used as its' water supply. That portion of the river is known as Lakin Dam. Framed by a meadow, and characterized by slow moving water, Lakin Dam is a nice place to relax, fish and avoid crowds.

Sometimes experiments work out. When the California Department of Fish and Game decided to do a little testing at Lakin Dam, they hit the formula right on. The CA DFG opted to begin planting brook trout, rather than rainbows. Brooks, unlike rainbows, aren't susceptible to most diseases and they are less likely to breed with red band, rainbows, browns and other trout species. The brooks are now planted annually and have thus far done quite well. Roughly 1,805 brooks are stocked each spring.

Sadly though, many of the brooks don't holdover during winter because of cold weather and a limited food supply. Luckily, many are caught by anglers before such conditions set in. The brooks tend to put on several inches by fall from their initial plant when they started at 12-14 inches. Oftentimes anglers catch 18-20 inch brooks before winter sets in!

Studies have shown the brooks stay between Lakin Dam and one-half mile upriver. Your best bet is to stand on the dam and cast towards the small island or under overhanging brush. Any small spinner will do the trick or toss an inflated night crawler off the bottom. There is a nice fishing pier that offers wheelchair access.

McCloud River (Lakin Dam)

If you plan to make the trip, supplies are available in McCloud. The McCloud River is closed to fishing from November 16 to the last Saturday in April.

Also nearby are Upper, Middle and Lower McCloud Falls.

Directions: *From the junction of Interstate 5 and Highway 299 east in Redding, drive north for 54.5 miles to the Highway 89 exit. Exit and drive roughly 14.5 miles to the right turnoff for Camp Fowlers Road. Turn right and follow signs to Lakin Dam.*

BOLES CREEK

Rating: 4

Species: Rainbow Trout

Stocks: None

Facilities: Restrooms and Picnic Areas

Need Information? Contact: The Tackle Shop (530) 841-1901

Boles Creek is located in Weed, Ca. Weed is an interesting name for a town. Oftentimes, teenagers get a laugh out of seeing the sign off I-5 for the town. Weed is one of the major refueling, lodging and eating areas for motorists commuting between Redding and Medford, Oregon. For the most part, much of the local economy is fueled by commuters using the town as a rest sto. From sun up to sun down, the town is littered with out-of-towners.

Surprisingly, only the locals fish Boles Creek. Flowing parallel to the main drag and under Highway 97, Boles Creek is a small stream that is stocked with half-pound rainbow trout by the California Department of Fish and Game several times during the fishing season. The creek is planted in the residential area above the Highway 97 bridge and in the rest area downstream from the bridge. (Note: in recent years the CA DFG hasn't planted the creek. There is no word on when plants will resume.)

Because of overgrown banks and the contour of the stream, anglers are restricted to fishing bait. The creek is too small for spinners. Look for small pockets of water and areas where the creek makes a mild turn for the best action. You'll find fish right outside the current. A single salmon egg hook fished with a red worm or Yellow Jacket Pautzke salmon eggs get the job done.

If you plan to make the trip, supplies are available in Weed. Boles Creek is closed to fishing from November 16 to the last Saturday in April.

Also nearby are Lake Shastina, Mt. Shasta and the Sacramento River.

Directions: *From the junction of Highway 299 east and Interstate 5 in Redding, drive north on Interstate 5 for 64.8 miles to the Highway 97 exit in Weed signed for Klamath Falls. Exit, turn right and drive three-tenths of a mile to the right turnoff for Highway 97. Turn right, drive over the freeway and make the first left after the bridge on an unsigned road signed for the CDF Station. The stream is on the left near the restrooms.*

Boles Creek

LAKE SHASTINA

Rating: 7

Species: Rainbow
Trout, Largemouth
Bass, Bluegill, Crappie
and Channel Catfish

Stocked with 2,100
pounds of rainbow
trout.

Facilities: Boat Launch,
Campgrounds and
Restrooms

Need Information?
Contact: The Tackle
Shop (530) 841-1901

Lake Shastina is best described as a boom and bust bass fishery. And, when it's booming it can be one of the best bass fisheries north of Lake Oroville. Unfortunately, Shastina can be a bust often.

Shastina is situated in cattle country. Fishing isn't tops on the menu. The lake was created to provide a year-round water source for ranchers and farmers. Sadly, the farmers could care less about the bass. While the reservoir fills in the spring, it can be drawn down to less than 20 percent of capacity by summer.

By the time summer begins in some years, the 1,850 acres look more like a narrow river channel with a small pool near the dam. When the lake is full, it's a different story. Shastina has the ingredients to hold huge trout and bass. "Just add water," says Larry Hanson, the man responsible for the management of the lake for the California Department of Fish and Game.

Hanson is speaking of Shastina's excellent nutrient base that is always present.Water is the variable. Shastina is set in a region where runoff flows over an area that is extremely rich. When runoff is high, the incoming water flushes so many nutrients into the lake that the productivity goes through the roof. The drainage rests on landscape that is utilized by cattle. Therefore, there's three inches of cow droppings throughout the drainage. Here's what happens:

Manure only supplies some of the food. In 1959, the CA DFG opted to introduce Japanese pond smelt into Shastina, which was also called Dwinnell Reservoir at one time. The smelt were imported from Japan and introduced to six waters: Dodge Reservoir in Modoc County, the Freshwater Lagoon on the North Coast, Spaulding Lake on Interstate 80 near Truckee, Jenkinson Lake near Placerville off Highway 50, Big Bear Lake in Southern California and Shastina. The smelt provide an astonishing food base in high water years, which again brings us to the theme here.

When there are high water levels for a few years in a row, both trout and bass thrive. The manure and pond smelt drive the fishery. When it's low, the bass get small and their numbers decrease. For example, in the early Nineties after several years of drought, the CA DFG found than most of the bass were six-to-eight inches. However, from 2000-03 when the lake was held at sufficient levels, bass averaged 13-18 inches. Largemouth averaged two-to-three pounds and fish to six pounds weren't unheard of. If this reservoir was full all the time, it would be one of the top trophy bass fisheries in Northern California. The nutrient loading is always available.

If you are coming for trout, you better arrive in the winter or spring when there is water available. Shastina is primarily a put-and-take fishery, however, when flows are sufficient rainbows and browns spawn in the Little Shasta River, which is the lake's main tributary. Also, trout holdover when there's more than just a small pool of water available.

Most of the fish you'll catch will be half-pound rainbows. The CA DFG unloads nearly 2,730 rainbows each year, in addition to 300 brood fish rainbows in the three-to-six-pound class. At times, browns and brooks are planted.

Trout are often caught trolling or bait fishing from a boat. Shoreline access isn't conducive to cold water fishing. Trollers work several areas of this relatively shallow lake. In spring, trout congregate near the inlet. However, night crawlers floated off the bottom and Power Bait outdo trollers because snags pose a big problem in this shallow area that is fewer than 10 feet deep.

If you are going to troll, use something light on your downriggers and keep it several feet off the bottom. Weed growth is extensive. Many anglers troll for hours without ever knowing their Needlefish is covered in moss and grass. In the spring I like to run four rods and fish in these areas: near the dam, around the islands and from the inlet to the dam on the west side of the lake.

Once you get a quarter-mile from the inlet, begin trolling towards the dam. Try a red and gold Thomas Buoyant and a red and black Sep's Trolling Fly behind a Sep's Pro Dodger on the top and drop two Needlefish on the downriggers. Set one at 11 and the other at 19 feet. A red and gold and all red Needlefish work best.

At 2,791 feet, Shastina also offers a mouth watering view of Mt. Shasta, yet that view can be harassed by daily winds which tend to kick up mid-morning. The winds can pose dangerous conditions for small boats.

If you plan to make the trip, supplies are available in Weed. In some rare instances, Lake Shastina may freeze over in cold winters. Call ahead for updated conditions. After June the lake may be too low to launch boats.

Also nearby are Little Shasta River and Lake Siskiyou.

Directions: *From Interstate 5 in Weed, exit Highway 97 and drive north for 4.6 miles to Ordway Road. Turn left and drive 1.7 miles to Jackson Ranch Road. Turn left and drive nine-tenths of a mile to Dwinnell Way. Turn right and continue 1.8 miles to the boat launch.*

Lake Shastina

ANTELOPE CREEK

Rating: 5

Species: Rainbow Trout and Brown Trout

Stocked with 295

Facilities: None

Need Information? Contact: Klamath National Forest (530) 398-4391

The town of Tennant was once a thriving logging town. During the Fifties, when the logging industry was thriving, a population of 800 people lived here. Presently though, logging operations have slowed and the economy has died in this small, remote town in the Klamath National Forest. Tennant is a quiet community with one historical marker in town acknowledging what once existed. Unfortunately, there's not much more to see.

Antelope Creek makes up for the lack of excitement. Flowing through town, the creek is a marginal stocked fishery in the spring and summer. While oftentimes difficult to fish in the early spring because of high runoff, summer provides good prospects for 586 half-pound planted rainbow trout. The stream is stocked in two places, both of which are located where the creek flows under the road. The first is just before town, and the latter is in town. Spinners, small spoons and bait all work here. Come the same week as the stocking truck, and you'll be in business!

If you plan to make the trip, supplies are available in Weed. Antelope Creek is closed to fishing from November 16 to the last Saturday in April.

Also nearby are Orr Lake and Butte Creek.

Directions: From the junction of Highway 299 east and Interstate 5 in Redding drive north on Interstate 5 for 64.8 miles to the Highway 97 exit in Weed signed for Klamath Falls. Exit, turn right and drive three-tenths of a mile to the right turnoff for Highway 97. Turn right, and drive 26.9 miles to the turnoff on the right for Bray. Turn right on the Bray-Tennant turnoff and drive five miles to a split in the road. Stay right and continue 6.6 miles to the stream.

Antelope Creek

BUTTE CREEK

Rating: 5

Species: Rainbow Trout
and Brook Trout

Stocked with 835
pounds of rainbow
trout.

Facilities: None

Need Information?
Contact: Klamath
National Forest
(530) 398-4391

There are two reasons visitors come to Butte Creek: fish and free camping. On the north side of Mt. Shasta, located off Highway 97 approximately 30 minutes from Interstate 5 in Weed, Butte Creek offers two miles of prime camping space for primitive campers and decent fishing. While no facilities are available several excellent campsites right along the river are. (Make sure you phone the Forest Service to verify this. Word has it that this area may be closed to campers soon because of private property issues.)

To save you the drive to Weed for a burger while you are camping, the California Department of Fish and Game plants rainbow trout (1,573 in all) from the spring through summer. (This may stop soon because of private property issues.) In the spring you'll have to locate pools or fish behind boulders to find trout. Swift water keeps the fish holding in selected areas. As summer arrives and levels subside the creek, which is heavily shaded by pines, Butte becomes easier to fish. Spinners, spoons, bait and fly fishing will work.

If you plan to make the trip, supplies are available in Weed. Butte Creek is closed to fishing from November 16 to the last Saturday in April. There are a lot of rattlesnakes in this area. Beware.

Also nearby are Orr Lake and Antelope Creek.

Directions: From the junction of Highway 299 east and Interstate 5 in Redding, drive north on Interstate 5 for 64.8 miles to the Highway 97 exit in Weed signed for Klamath Falls. Exit, turn right and drive three-tenths of a mile to the right turnoff for Highway 97. Turn right, and drive 26.9 miles to the turnoff on the right for Bray. Turn right on the Bray-Tennant turnoff and drive five 2.9 miles to Deer Mountain Road. Turn right and drive one-half mile to the stream which parallels the road.

Butte Creek

LITTLE SHASTA RIVER

Rating: 5

Species: Rainbow Trout

Stocked with 125
pounds of rainbow
trout.

Facilities: Restrooms,
Picnic Areas and
Campgrounds

Need Information?
Contact: Klamath
National Forest
(530) 842-6131

In this dry section of the Klamath National Forest east of Interstate 5, the Little Shasta River is a rare gem. Situated in a heavily wooded section of the forest, these headwaters meander through delicate meadows that harbor small rainbow trout.

The California Department of Fish and Game plants a mere 256 half-pound rainbow trout into this river, which looks more like a small brook. The plants begin as soon as the road can be cleared of snow and downed trees. (This usually occurs in early June.) Depending on water conditions, trout may be stocked up until mid summer. By late summer, flows become low, the water warms and deer season opens which takes the spotlight off fishing.

Fishing is simple. Anglers should concentrate on pitching Pautzke Balls O' Fire salmon eggs and flies. The creek is too small for the use of spinners. Look for areas with bends and overhanging banks. Typically you can see the trout in this gin clear, cold water. In the spring, a dry fly is an excellent choice. Concentrate your angling in Martin Daily Campground.

If you plan to make the trip, supplies are available in Weed. In spring call for updated road conditions. The road may be closed. The Little Shasta River is closed from November 16 to the last Saturday in April.

Also nearby is Juanita Lake and Orr Lake.

Directions: *From Weed, drive east on Highway 97 for roughly 27 miles to the left turnoff for USFS Road 46N10. Turn left and follow signs 12 miles to Martin Dairy Campground.*

Little Shasta River

ORR LAKE

Rating: 8

Species: Rainbow
Trout, Brown Trout,
Bluegill, Largemouth
Bass and Channel
Catfish

Stocked with 1,650
pounds of rainbow
trout.

Facilities: Vault Toilets
and Campgrounds

Need Information?
Contact: Klamath
National Forest
(530) 398-4391

I hadn't been at Orr Lake more than five minutes when a man came up from behind me, tapped my shoulder and said, "Son, here you walk in the middle of the road. Folks don't take a step around here without looking first. This is rattlesnake country."

This man wasn't kidding.

"I killed 20 just last week. There are huge fish in here, but I can't get anyone from Tule Lake to come fish it with me because of all the damn rattlers," he said. The man had been camping for 13 days. This was his last. The 14 day limit was about to expire. Fortunately, he had time to share his memories, experiences and knowledge with me before he left. This man, who was wearing a pair of full body waders had been coming to the lake for 50 years.

"This is a place all us locals and those who don't want to be bothered come. We aren't afraid of the snakes, but we don't move without looking," he said. "This is the kind of place us locals wouldn't mind dying at. The fishing is good. You don't have them damn teenagers who blast their radios and party like you do at Juanita Lake and it's pretty. Some guys come here when they know their time is coming and they just die in their campers."

Whoa I wasn't looking for stories about people coming to a lake to die. It must be a pretty good lake to warrant something like that. Let's check out the fishing.

Orr Lake is one of the top bass lakes in Northern California. However, few anglers fish it, mostly because it is far from any major city (even further and more remote than Trinity). Black flies, mosquitoes, boas, garter and king snakes also make up the list of deterrents. Another reason could be because of its' size. Orr is a mere 55 acres and looks no bigger than a large pond. Some come to admire the daylong mirror-like reflections of Mt. Shasta, others to view eagles, mallards and pelicans. For some reason, anglers are in the minority. They wouldn't be if they knew how good the fishing was.

Orr has a staggering number of largemouth that don't seem to be effected by anglers keeping fish or low water levels. The lake has a good population of chubs which the bass feed on. At no deeper than 10 feet, the fish are easy to spot, yet they aren't always easy to catch. First, since the lake is so shallow and the water is so clear, the fish can see you as you can see them. Plus, many anglers show up with six-to-eight-pound test and they end up breaking the fish off in the weeds. Locals use 20-pound test. Oftentimes, they still have to break off fish.

With the exception of early spring, Orr is very weedy. Weeds smother the shoreline and lily pads glob the body of the lake. There will, however, be a few open lanes for boats in the middle. This lake goes through four seasons. It freezes in the winter, has open water in the spring and by June, weeds own the lake. Fall again presents a time with more open water.

Bass fishing is always good if you use the right technique. For the best action, arrive in May and June when some of the big bass are close to shore. Baby brush hogs and lizards are the choice bait with some spinnerbaits also pulling bass. The lake has many seven-to-nine-inch bass, another group of 13-18 inch fish and a number of six-to-12-pound fish. Catch and release has kept this lake on the upswing. Locals know what they have and what it takes to keep it. They discourage keeping bass.

Trout, on the other hand, are up for grabs. They are both resident and planted. Anglers who see the most success match the hatch. A big food source for trout is hellgrammites, which can be found in the weeds along the bank. Successful anglers put on a pair of waders and walk the shoreline with a bucket grabbing as many hellgrammites as they can. Trout fishing is tough from the shore between June and October. To do well, you'll need to find a deeper hole towards the middle of the lake. Most of the catches are rainbows. The California Department of Fish and Game stocks 3,135 rainbows each year.

Stories of huge browns used to circulate here. However in recent years, they've been few and far between. Browns are still available and lunkers do exist just not in the numbers they used to.

If you plan to make the trip, supplies are available in Weed. Orr Lake has a slot limit. No bass between 12 and 15 inches may be taken. Call the Forest Service for updated motor restrictions.

Also nearby is Butte Creek.

Directions: *From Interstate 5 in Weed, exit Highway 97 and drive north for 27.8 miles to Bray-Tennant Road. Turn right and drive five miles to a split in the road. Turn left and drive 2.2 miles to the left turnoff for Orr Mountain Lookout. You'll cross the railroad tracks. Then, drive three-tenths of a mile and turn left on a dirt road. Continue 1.5 miles to the lake.*

Orr Lake

JUANITA LAKE

Rating: 6

Species: Rainbow
Trout, Brown Trout,
Channel Catfish,
Bluegill and
Largemouth Bass

Stocked with 1,800
pounds of rainbow
trout.

Facilities: Restrooms
and Picnic Areas

Need Information?
Contact: Klamath
National Forest
(530) 398-4391

Juanita Lake is one of the few lakes in California that has two dams which are used to retain water. Dams were constructed on both sides of a small meadow to flood the plain and create Juanita. In the good ole' days (as the locals refer to them), Juanita used to be an excellent fishery that provided free primitive camping.

Since the Forest Service constructed developed campsites, more and more people are visiting Juanita and consequently the fishing is going downhill. Weekends and holidays can especially get crowded. Oftentimes, finding a quiet spot to wet a line or read a book is a lot to ask for. The good facilities have drawn in more tourists and youngsters who blare music into the waning hours of the night.

Juanita is still a good fishing lake, just not as great as it used to be. At 5,100 feet in the Klamath National Forest, near the Meiss Lake Wildlife Area, this 55-acre lake is loaded with small bass and planted with 3,510 rainbow trout by the California Department of Fish and Game. A bonus about Juanita is that it caters to disabled anglers. There is a wheelchair accessible path that goes around the lake.

This pretty lake holds a large population of small bass. Most are six-to-eight inches, however, a six pounder proves larger fish are available. Fishing a night crawler along the weed line can yield dozens of bass per day. Night anglers are known to do well on catfish from the dock. The weed line gets thick in the summer and can make shoreline fishing difficult at times.

The big attractors are trout. The CA DFG keeps the lake well stocked. Boat and bank anglers have no trouble cashing in on the action. Trollers do well dragging light weight spoons and bank anglers see success with Kastmasters. Anywhere around the lake (and especially across from the launch ramp where the two inlets are) anglers can expect to catch trout.

If you plan to make the trip, supplies are available in Dorris and Weed. In winter, call ahead for road conditions. Juanita Lake can freeze over in the winter. No gas-powered boats are permitted.

Also nearby are the Little Shasta River, Orr Lake and Antelope Creek.

Directions: *From the junction of Highway 299 east and Interstate 5 in Redding, drive north on Interstate 5 for 64.8 miles to the Highway 97 exit in Weed signed for Klamath Falls. Exit, turn right and drive three-tenths of a mile to the right turnoff for Highway 97. Turn right, and drive 38.7 miles to Meiss Lake Road. Turn left and drive 6.3 miles to a split in the road. Veer left and drive 3.1 miles to the lake.*

Clear Creek
Brandy Creek
Whiskeytown Reservoir
Keswick Reservoir
Sacramento River (Redding)
Lake Shasta
Sacramento River (Upper)
McCloud Reservoir
Iron Canyon Reservoir
Lake Britton
Pit River (Section 1)
Fall River (Fall River Mills)
Fall River Lake
Fall River
Big Lake
Ja-She Creek
Horr Pond
Little Tule River
Tule River
Hat Creek
Crystal Lake
Baum Lake
Cassel Forebay
Hat Creek (Upper)
Lost Creek
Plum Canyon Reservoir
North Battle Creek Reservoir
Mc Cumber Reservoir
Grace Lake
Nora Lake
Keswick Canal
Darrah Creek Pond
South Cow Creek
Old Cow Creek

Clover Creek
Kilarc Reservoir
Little Cow Creek
Hatchet Creek
Pit River (Section 7)
Pit River (Section 5)
Pit River (Section 4)
Pit River (Section 3)
Rock Creek (Shasta)
Clark Creek (Lower)
Burney Creek (Middle)
Burney Creek (Upper)

Region

12

Shasta County

CLEAR CREEK

Rating: 4

Species: Rainbow Trout

Stocked with 900
pounds of rainbow
trout.

Facilities: Restrooms,
Playground and a
Picnic Area

Need Information?
Contact: Shasta
National Forest
(530) 246-5112

On the way to fishing the planted section of Clear Creek, anglers get a glimpse of what it's like to live in the country. French Gulch is a small rural town where everyone knows everyone and deer know where they can't be shot. In the fall, you'll see hunters drive through town watching huge bucks hanging out in front yards and on the side of the road. A retired woman watches from her porch to make sure her "pet" deer are safe.

The same goes with the fishing. While the California Department of Fish and Game plants the creek for public use, few anglers other than locals, get in on the action. Clear Creek is a major tributary to Whiskeytown Reservoir and much of the access through the town is located on private property. On the other hand, portions of this stocked section run though French Gulch on public land. Your options are limited to fishing at the bridge on Cline Gulch Road or at French Gulch Park. Nearly 1,425 rainbows are planted each year.

Clear Creek is a fairly small stream. However, action can be found in spring and summer when 1,160 half-pound, and better, rainbows are planted. The stream can be too small for spinners in some places and too overgrown for fly fishing. Salmon eggs and dough baits are standard.

If you plan to make the trip, supplies are available in Old Shasta. Clear Creek is closed to fishing from November 16 to the last Saturday in April.

Also nearby is Whiskeytown Reservoir.

Clear Creek

Directions: From Redding at the junction of Highway 299 and Interstate 5, drive west on Highway 299 for roughly 17.4 miles to the French Gulch turnoff on the right. Turn right and drive 3.7 miles to French Gulch Park.

BRANDY CREEK

Rating: 6

Species: Kokanee, Rainbow Trout and Brown Trout

Stocked with 400 pounds of rainbow trout.

Facilities: Campgrounds, Picnic Areas and Restrooms

Need Information? Contact: Shasta-Whiskeytown National Recreation Area (530) 242-3400

Whiskeytown Lake is one of Northern California's most used recreation lakes. It's safe to say that the Brandy Creek Recreation Area is one of the most heavily visited spots. To Redding area residents, Brandy Creek is as close to the Pacific Ocean as it gets. Many locals come here to lie on the sandy beach, get tan, have a picnic and go for a swim. On the other hand, others come to fish.

The California Department of Fish and Game stocks the creek with roughly 630 rainbow trout each spring. Some of the fish are stocked at the launch ramp however; bucket loads are also tossed where Brandy Creek crosses under the road and throughout Brandy Creek Picnic Area. (The beach can be found where the creek dumps into the reservoir.)

While crowds are common at the beach, things tend to be quieter along the creek. Many anglers cast bait at the rainbow trout, but at times in the summer it can be challenging for anglers to catch fish when teenagers are swimming in the creek. If you show up in the morning or evening, chances are no one will be in the water. This is a great stream to use Pautzke Balls O' Fire salmon eggs. Some of the pools are large enough for the use of Panther Martins spinners also. The stream which is 10-20 feet wide is also home to a few browns and spawning kokanee each fall, but the bulk of the fishing pressure focuses on rainbows.

If you plan to make the trip, supplies are available in Redding. There is a day-use fee. Brandy Creek is closed to fishing from November 16 to the last Saturday in April.

Also nearby is Whiskeytown Lake.

Directions: *From Interstate 5 in Redding, exit west on Highway 299 and drive approximately 15 miles to the Whiskeytown Lake Visitor Center. Turn left and continue four miles to Brandy Creek Campground.*

Brandy Creek

WHISKEYTOWN RESERVOIR

Rating: 8

Species: Kokanee, King Salmon, Rainbow Trout, Brown Trout, Brook Trout, Smallmouth Bass, Largemouth Bass, Spotted Bass, Channel Catfish, Crappie and Bluegill

Stocked with 23,436 pounds of brook trout, 156 pounds of fingerling kokanee and 765 pounds of sub-catchable Chinook.

Facilities: Restrooms, Fishing Piers, Boat Launch, Picnic Areas, Marinas, Campgrounds, Swimming Areas and RV Hookups

Need Information? Contact: Fishing Guide Gary Mirales (530) 275-2278, Whiskeytown Visitor Center (530) 246-1225, Whiskeytown Park Headquarters (530) 242-3400, Oak Bottom Marina (530) 359-2269

Whiskeytown Reservoir and Lake Shasta are alike in many ways. Both are heavily visited by Redding area residents. They also offer warm and cold water fisheries, have good facilities and multiple recreational opportunities. There is one major difference between the two: while Shasta is known and bombarded by tourists from all over California, Whiskeytown is more reserved for locals. For some reason, out-of-towners leave this place alone.

Whiskeytown is basically a holding pool for water going from Trinity Lake to the Central Valley Project and the Sacramento River. The lake always has a consistent water source and is maintained for recreational use. From May through October, the lake is kept near full pool. In addition, all personal watercraft has been banned, which makes life easier on anglers. Operated by the National Park Service, the lake is kept clean and offers excellent facilities.

Created in 1963, Whiskeytown encompasses 3,200 acres and 36 miles of shoreline. Located within the Shasta-Whiskeytown National Recreation Area, Whiskeytown has blossomed into a great fishing lake over the last decade. Staying relatively cool year-round, the surface temperature doesn't get much warmer than the low seventies. Thus, the lake is highly conducive to trout.

Recently, the lake has taken on a heap of kokanee anglers. Kokanee has always been a hit, however, in the last few years anglers began to cash in on the fishery. Kokanee reproduce naturally in Whiskeytown. In the fall, Brandy, Clear and Whiskey Creek turn bright red as spawning kokanee move upstream out of the lake to spawn.

Surprisingly, Whiskeytown has some of the largest kokanee in the state. A 20-inch fish is average in some years, while the size drops to 18 inches on the bottom rotation of a three-year cycle. The big fish stem from a stocking of Colorado raised kokanee that were introduced in 1965.

Kokanee thrive because they are not as crowded as in many other kokanee waters. When there is sufficient water in tributaries, kokanee spawn successfully. Kokanee are also washed in from Trinity Lake via the Carr Tunnel. The year after an unsuccessful spawn occurs, the CA DFG will plant 50,000 kokanee to maintain an adequate fishery. Other years the CA DFG may only release 25,000.

Gary Mirales, inventor of the Cripplure, with a 17-inch Whiskeytown kokanee.

From January through March, look for kokanee at the Oak Bottom Marina, Whiskey Bridge and scattered all over the lake in the top 30 feet of water. In April and May, target 15-30 feet of water as kokanee still cruise the lake looking to beef up on plankton. When the thermocline forms in June, expect the kokanee to hold in 40-60 feet. With a thermocline in place kokanee stick to cruising in 40-80 feet in July and August. By late August, kokanee begin to school up. Look for schools to form near the Whiskey Creek Bridge on Highway 299, around Buoy 7 and near The Curtain. Kokanee station themselves in these areas before migrating to creek inlets in October and November to spawn.

Rainbows used to be the big hit at Whiskeytown. Unfortunately, a problem with copepods forced the DFG to stop planting them for a few years in attempt to rid the lake of the problem. Anchor Worm, or lernia, have been a problem for decades. In order to reduce that population while still maintaining a good quality fishery, the DFG switched over to planting brook trout. The decision stemmed from the fact that brooks are not only immune to the worm, but they eat them as well. Between 2001 and 2003, nearly 32,000 brook trout were planted each year. No rainbows have been planted since 2000, however some still spawn in Whiskeytown tributaries, so there are some nice holdover rainbows to be had. Browns are rare.

Chinook Salmon are currently rising in popularity. Chinook were first introduced in the early Nineties. With forage such as sunfish, kokanee, small bass and trout, the DFG thought the fishery had excellent potential. Thus to experiment, the chinook were introduced in small numbers to reduce the risk of damaging other species since the reservoir was already an exceptional kokanee fishery and a solid put-and-take trout fishery. Between the mid-1990's and 2001, three plants of roughly 100-400 Chinook took place. Fortunately Chinook adapted well.

The DFG has begun to plant 5,000 yearling Chinook into the lake to provide a future trophy Chinook fishery. Fish are expected to grow as large as 20 inches. Typically, chinook are caught by anglers fishing for the kokanee, but note that the salmon characteristically run a little deeper. Target the main channel and under Whiskey Creek Bridge. In the spring, run your lures between depths of 20-100 feet, and in the summer, depths of 70-150 feet. Chinook average three pounds.

Whiskeytown is also home to one of Northern California's most quality trophy bass fisheries, but let me assure you and reiterate that you are coming to quality, not quantity. There are many large spots and largemouth bass, but the downside is that their numbers aren't convincing. Spots are the dominant fish, comprising roughly 60 percent of the population (largemouth hold the other 40 percent). Currently, an 8.5-pound spot is the largest bass to date. More enticing, however, the DFG officials are hinting that the next state record may soon be caught here.

On the flipside, Whiskeytown's bass are widely ignored because they are so difficult to catch. Extremely clear and cold water makes for challenging conditions. The bass here don't grow as fast as bass in warmer reservoirs. The water at Whiskeytown stays cold year round and keeps bass in a sluggish mood for longer periods of time than nearby Shasta, for example. Nevertheless, a large salmonid base provides plenty of food to eat.

You have to use light line and be patient to get in on the action. Many anglers wait for a storm to hit, and then fish, because muddy water reduces the clarity, making bass less wary. For largemouth in particular, which run up to six pounds, your best bet is to try and target fish suspended on structure during the winter.

If you plan to make the trip, supplies are available in Redding. There is a day use and boat launch fee.

Also nearby are Brandy Creek Falls, Clear Creek and Keswick Reservoir.

Directions: *From the junction of Interstate 5 and Highway 299 west in Redding, drive west on Highway 299 for roughly 10 miles to the lake.*

Gary Mirales shows off a Whiskeytown rainbow that ate a Hum-Dinger.

KESWICK RESERVOIR

Rating: 8

Species: Rainbow
Trout, Chinook Salmon,
Largemouth Bass,
Spotted Bass, Crappie,
Bluegill, White Catfish
and Channel Catfish

Stocks: None

Facilities: Restrooms
and a Boat Launch

Need Information?
Contact: Bureau of
Reclamation
(530) 225-5661

There are many tail water fisheries in California that are popular to trout anglers. These waters tend to be some of the best coldwater fisheries in the state. Keswick Reservoir is one of the least popular tail water fisheries, but is also one of the best. Why do few anglers care to fish Keswick? It's hard to tell, but several reasons can be factored in. For starters, the Sacramento River gets all the publicity, no trout plants occur and most folks think the reservoir is closed to fishing.

Located only a few miles from downtown Redding, Keswick Reservoir is fed by water from Lake Shasta and Whiskeytown Reservoir. There is always cold, moving water coming into the long, narrow reservoir. The reservoir has incredible productivity. The food that enters the reservoir is conducive to excellent growth rates. The California Department of Fish and Game seldom plants the reservoir with fish. However, many trout are washed through the dam and make a living feeding on insects and chewed up fish being rushed in from Lake Shasta.

Surprisingly, even with no fish plants there's a great population of rainbows. It's likely these fish derived from Shasta and Whiskeytown fish. Large is an understatement. In Keswick, a 14-inch fish is classified as a dink. Rainbows average 18-26 inches with fish pushing 30 inches a possibility.

Angling is by far better from a boat than shore. Shoreline access isn't great as steep or overgrown banks make fishing tough. With a boat you're in the game. Head towards where the water is coming into the reservoir and plan on back trolling Hot Shots or other plugs. The bigger trout soak in these areas waiting for food to be pushed in the reservoir.

If you plan to make the trip, supplies are available in Redding.

Also nearby is Clear Creek and Whiskeytown Reservoir.

Directions: From Redding, drive west on Highway 299 to Iron Mountain Road and turn right. Drive 3.8 miles to the right turnoff for the Keswick Reservoir Day-Use Area. (It's poorly signed.) Continue three-tenths of a mile to the lake.

Keswick Reservoir

SACRAMENTO RIVER (REDDING)

Rating: 10

Species: Chinook Salmon, Steelhead and Rainbow Trout

Stocks: None

Facilities: Boat Launches, Restrooms, Lodging, Gas, Food, Bait and Tackle and Picnic Areas

Need Information? Contact: Greg Squires of Access to Angling Guide Service (800) 551-3984, California Department of Fish and Game (530) 225-2300

During certain times of the year there are a few spots in California where anglers can realistically expect to hook 100 trout per day. Of course, the right technique, angler skill level and knowledge of the fishery is required, but on the Sacramento River near Redding trout can be caught on nearly every cast in the fall.

The Sacramento River harbors one of the best wild trout populations in California. While the lower Sacramento River system doesn't have the structure to support large populations of trout because of warmer and more turbulent water, sections upriver of the Chico area are ideal for them. The best section is from Bend Bridge to Deschutes Bridge. Even though upriver of Deschutes Bridge is closed to salmon fishing to protect spawning grounds, anglers are permitted to target trout on a catch and release basis.

You'll also find trout in staggering numbers per mile upriver of the Cottonwood and Anderson areas. While the number of trout is promising, you'll find that the size of fish is slightly decreasing. Here's why: More fish equals less food, which then means slower growth rates and overall smaller fish. The only cure for this problem would be to remove some trout from the system, but catch and release is standard here.

This section of the Sac is heavily promoted and fished by all types of anglers. Quality fish can be caught and

A Sacramento River wild rainbow trout

released by anglers using any method. Traditionally, trout tend to average 12-16 inches, but it's not uncommon to catch fish to six pounds.

Anglers can catch fish all year, however, nothing beats the fall bite. When salmon are on their redds, the trout are on the feed. Trout position themselves on or just downstream of the redds to pick up all loose salmon eggs. Using roe, Pautzke salmon eggs and Glo Bugs during this period can cause hook-ups on every cast. Salmon spawn from late summer through fall and into winter, so trout will be readily available.

Anglers can also take fish running plugs. A Luhr Jensen Hot Shot, size 35 or a K-5 Kwikfish is best. Spinners also work, but aren't as productive when the trout are keyed in on eggs. For best results, use six-pound test on your main line, a four-pound, four-foot leader and a No. 6 hook. Your weight depends on the current, which varies by season. During late summer and fall, ignore long runs. Instead, concentrate on riffles and where you see salmon spawning.

Being successful in this portion of the Sacramento has a great deal to do with water flows. Traditionally, flows are around 6,500 cfs from October to late November when fishing is best. However, the first major rain can boost the flows to 12,000-20,000 cfs. You can still catch fish from 10-15,000 cfs, but it becomes more difficult. The river can get as high as 50,000 cfs. When this occurs, the trout will lay in pockets until the levels recede. Winter is plagued by fluctuation.

In the spring, anglers do best with a mini night crawler threaded on a No. 6 bait hook. March and April you'll find trout in riffles, at the mouths of feeder streams and in deeper holes. May and June bring increased flows to cater to farmers downriver, but fish can still be caught. Bank access can be found between Knighton Road and downtown Redding. It's not imperative you fish from a boat, but it can help.

On the Sac, there's a difference fishing in a drift boat and a jet boat. Fly anglers are adamant about being pure and protecting the salmon, yet they strap on their waders, hop out of the drift boat and walk across the redds, killing more than 200-300 eggs per step. Other times they'll drop their anchor in the redds and destroy thousands of eggs. In a jet boat, you can fish alongside the redd and protect it from harm. Overall, fly fishermen tend not to get along with spin and bait fishermen on the Sac. Think about this next time there's a confrontation on the river. Just like there are different religions, there are different ways to catch fish and all legal methods should be respected.

Many anglers aren't aware of the steelhead run on the Sac. In late fall and winter, the Sac gets a decent run of steelhead which average three-to-six pounds. In fact, there's a hatchery run of steelhead that goes up Battle Creek. Anglers often catch them and think they are trout. You can't really target them, but you'll catch them while fishing for trout.

If you plan to make the trip, supplies are available in Redding. Check sportfishing regulations for updated bag limits and gear restrictions.

Also nearby are Whiskeytown Reservoir and Lake Shasta.

Directions: *This section of the Sacramento River can be reached directly of Interstate 5 from Anderson north to Redding. Consult a map for specific fishing sites.*

Guide Greg Squires shows off a quality Sac River rainbow taken in the fall out of a jet boat.

LAKE SHASTA

Lake Shasta is one of the West Coast's most popular reservoirs. The reservoir is well-known by nearly every boater and angler in California. Whether you come to fish, water-ski, swim, houseboat or just relax, Lake Shasta rarely disappoints. During the summer there can be more traffic on the lake than there is on Interstate 5, which crosses over the reservoir.

Lake Shasta is the largest manmade reservoir in California. With more than 370 miles of shoreline, the lake has secret coves for everyone to call their own. It's one of the most popular houseboat destinations in the nation. This houseboating Mecca appeals to several sets of groups including couples, anglers, families and wild college kids.

If you can afford it, definitely spend a week houseboating on Shasta. Imagine tying to the shoreline in a flat cove, fit with hundreds of pines and a small waterfall, yet still large enough to canoe, kayak or swim, all this while barbequing hamburgers and hot dogs and keeping an eye on your fishing rod which is offering a night crawler to any fish that will take it. As the sun sets, you can relax in the spa on top of the houseboat, admiring shooting stars overhead. Morning is greeted with deer, bald eagles, osprey and other critters framed in the stellar view of snow capped Mt. Shasta.

For those who don't want to spend a fortune on a vacation, there are more than 30 developed campgrounds, RV Parks and boat-in campsites.

Editor's Note: Because of the large number of contacts for Lake Shasta, we've listed all info numbers below in an easy to use format:

Fishing Info: California Department of Fish and Game (530) 225-2300, Trout Fishing Guide Gary Mirales of Shasta Tackle Company (530) 275-2278, Phil's Propellers (530) 275-4939, The Fishen Hole (530) 275-4123

General Tourism Info: Shasta Lake Information Center (530) 275-1589, Shasta Caverns (800) 795-2283, Redding Convention and Visitor Bureau (800) 874-7562, Shasta Cascade Tourism (530) 365-7500

Campgrounds and Marinas: Shasta Marina Resort (800) 959-3359, Lakeshore Marina (530) 238-2301, Antler's Resort (800) 238-3924, Jones Valley Resort (800) 223-7950, Sugarloaf Resort (800) 223-7950, Lakeview Resort (800) 223-7950, Packers Bay Marina (800) 331-3137, Holiday Harbor Marina (800) 776-2628, Silverthorn Resort (530) 332-3044, Bridge Bay Resort (800) 752-9669, Digger Bay (800) 752-9669, Salt Creek RV Park (800) 954-1824, Shasta Lake RV Resort (800) 3SHASTA

Enclosed by the Shasta National Forest, this is a truly unique place. Whether it be swimming, boating, fishing or relaxing, Shasta caters to everyone.

The lake is also well known for drastic drawdowns. During drought years, the actual lake may be 100 vertical feet down from its full pool mark. Construction for Lake Shasta began in 1935 and took more than 10 years to complete. The lake was filled in 1948. Shasta has the ability to store more than 4,550,000 acre-feet of water comprising roughly 30,000 acres. The lake was constructed to capture water from three major rivers: the Pit, Sacramento and McCloud. The lake also benefits from another five major creeks and 85 smaller drainages that bring water and food into the lake.

Marshall and Jessica Haraden show off bullfrog they caught during their summe houseboat adventure at Lake Shasta.

Shasta is also one of the most prolific fisheries in the state. Shasta is a two-tier fishery. Combining a cold and warm water fishery, the lake offers anglers more than 15 species of catchable fish. The lake is augmented with plants of trout and salmon and relies on a widely successful natural reproduction of warmwater species.

Shasta is an excellent rainbow trout fishery. An abundance of shad, plankton and food flushed in from hundreds of feeder streams keep Shasta's trout well-fed. The lake is not only planted with tens of thousands of catchable trout, but trout reproduce naturally in dozens of named and unnamed rivers and streams that are tributaries in the lake.

The California Department of Fish and Game plants some 78,500 rainbow trout. Anglers rarely catch rainbows under three-quarters of a pound. Most trout average a tad more than one pound. Nonetheless, rainbows to five pounds are caught on a regular basis. Expect your average rainbow to run 17 inches or 1.5 pounds. Several strains of rainbows can be found in Shasta: Pit River, Shasta, Coleman, Eagle Lake and Warm Springs are all present. Using the lake as their ocean, most of these fish follow migratory patterns. They grow in the lake itself and spawn in one of the many tributaries. Working Shasta for rainbow trout can be intimidating because the lake is so large. Nonetheless, by following simple instructions and fishing the right depth, success can be easily achieved. Trout can

320 Mule deer are a sure sight during a houseboat trip to Lake Shasta.

be found all over Shasta, yet fishing in these areas will increase your catch rates: Dry Creek, Squaw Arm, McCloud Arm, Pit River Arm, the Sacramento Arm, Shasta Dam and under the I-5 Bridge.

In the early winter, adult shad come up towards the surface, spurring a trout feeding frenzy. This is when you'll find trout feeding heavily on shad. The rainbows do so to beef up for the winter months when food is scarcer. Rainbows push the shad into shallow water where they are easier to ambush. If you find boiling shad, you'll find trout.

In January and February, the water cools drastically and the shad migrate into deeper areas. The rainbows are least active during this time of year because food is not as available as it is during the warmer months. Some say that Shasta's trout go into a semi- hibernation mode. During this time of year, target areas with flat bottoms in 20 feet of water. Jones Valley Cove and Ski Island are good prospects.

A Shasta brown trout

In March and April, fishing can either be excellent or horrible. You still have some nasty storms moving through the region which can shut the bite off really fast. On the other hand, a few days of sun and warm weather will spark a fantastic bite. In the early spring, fish near feeder streams. Trout station themselves in these areas to cash in on food entering the lake. During heavy runoff, the lake can muddy up quickly. No big deal. The trout still bite. Fish areas where the muddy water gives way to clearer water. Options include Hirtz Bay on the McCloud River Arm, Monday Flat on the Upper Squaw Arm and the Upper Sacramento Arm past Antlers Resort. There is excellent insect production in these creek inlet areas.

In the spring, the plankton bite on the Pit River can be phenomenal. Plankton thrives when the water reaches 60 degrees. Red and gold Cripplelures work well this time of year. Troll shorelines anywhere on the lake. In early spring when the water is in the forties, trout are relatively inactive. As the water reaches the fifties, trout begin to feed more actively. When the lake's temperature reaches the upper fifties, expect the trout to move to the surface and feed heavily.

Unfortunately, trolling can be a pain the spring. So much debris gets flushed down the lake's inlets that trees, sticks and weeds are commonly found on your lures. You'll have to check your bait

Christian Perez used a Thunderstick gizzard shad to hook this Shasta bow in March.

often to do well. Lazy anglers can troll around for hours not catching a thing before they realize their bait is covered in grass.

May can be the best trout month in Shasta. Shad are in the shallows and being actively chased by trout which are feeding heavily in the top 15 feet of water. In June, action can slow until the lake's thermocline forms and the shad hatch begins. Trout are sluggish as they struggle to find a comfort zone. You'll often find the bows on the surface in the morning and then down more than 150 feet in the middle of the day.

Ironically, in July when most people are jumping off houseboats, water-skiing and swimming, trout fishing is exceptional. First, you have the shad hatch, plus an established thermocline. Basically, what the thermocline does is ensure that the trout will be concentrated at one specific depth. At Shasta, that depth is most likely from 60-100 feet. This pattern tends to hold true through September.

Unfortunately, boaters can give anglers a headache on the main body of the lake. To avoid conflict and aggravation, fish in 5 mph zones. Most notably, Dry Creek, Waters Gulch and the Pit River Arm will get you away from speeders. In the early morning, trolling under the I-5 Bridge and around Ski Island are other options.

Several methods hold true in the summer. Using a downrigger or lots of leadcore line a Sling Blade and Hum Dinger combo will do the trick. Blue, silver, purple and white are your best bets.

When the temperatures begin to cool in early October, fishing lags for a few weeks as the lake "turns over". When this occurs, the shad come back to the surface and the fish again struggle to find a comfort zone. Once the lake stabilizes, the surface bite on trout is good. Any shad imitation lures will get the job done. Try a Storm Thunderstick Gizzard Shad, Rapala Shad Rap or a black and white Hum Dinger. Stick to fishing from the surface on down 15 feet. It's

Lake Shasta

not uncommon this time of year to catch 25-30 fish a day. This pattern holds consistent until winter weather sets in.

Wild brown trout are available; however, their numbers are minimal compared to the rainbows. Most often, browns are caught on accident by anglers trolling for rainbows. Springtime poses the best chance to hook into a brown, especially for anglers pulling rainbow trout patterned Rebels during low light hours. The McCloud River Arm is an excellent choice because it provides sufficient spawning grounds. Other notable spots are Campbell Creek, Hirst Bay and Kamloop Cove all on the McCloud Arm and Marshmallow Point and Elmore's Bay on the Sacramento River Arm. Browns tend to average four-to-five pounds

Shasta Tackle Company owner Gary Mirales with a Shasta salmon.

with some reaching the eight pound range. Each year a few browns greater than 10 pounds will also be caught. Browns have established a self-sustaining population in the lake. No supplemental fish plants are necessary.

Unfortunately, shoreline fishing isn't great. There are some areas to cash in on the trout from shore. Fishing from a boat is far more productive. There is a road that parallels the upper section of the McCloud Arm that provides some access, as well as fishing near Shasta Dam, Jones Valley Cove, Mariners Cove and on the north side of the I-5 Bridge. Fishing with a minnow and a bobber or soaking floating baits is your best bet from shore.

Chinook salmon are also a big hit. Ranging from a half-pound to 10 pounds, many anglers target the salmon which are most often caught by trollers. Mooching used to be popular fishing near the dam, yet with anglers required to fish at least 1,000 feet from the dam, that method is no longer productive.

Rarely do the salmon reach 10 pounds. On a good year, you'll be lucky to land one over six pounds. Salmon were introduced in the Seventies. The size of the fish often is a direct correlation to how many fish the CA DFG plants each year. When the CA DFG plants only 10,000 fish, expect those fish to grow larger than when they plant 20,000 salmon.

The salmon can be found all over the lake. However, most are picked up in the main channel. April and May tend to be the best months to catch salmon. They are most aggressive in the spring. In April, fish for them in 20-150 feet of water. By May and

Blake Lezak with a Shasta bow caught trolling. 323

into June, most salmon can be found in 70-120 feet of water. In March and April, the salmon often drift between 20-150 feet looking for a comfort zone. On the other hand, the bigger salmon are typically caught in deep water. Dry Creek, Waters Gulch, Packers Bay, Shasta Dam and the main channel hold the most salmon.

Dan and Blake Lezak caught this Shasta bass trolling.

Bait fishing with frozen shad or anchovies can be productive. Most anglers, however, troll. For the bigger fish, drag Rebels, three-inch J-Plugs, or any shad imitation lure. To catch more fish, but most likely smaller fish, a Sling Blade and a KOKE-A-NUT are local favorites. At one time kokanee, coho and browns were also planted.

Shasta is also one of Nor Cal's better bass lakes. The lake harbors smallmouth, largemouth and spotted bass. Shasta was a good smallmouth lake, however, when spotted bass were introduced in 1980-81, they took over. Traditionally, spotted bass compete with smallmouth. The original 700 spots have now grown to cover roughly 95 percent of the bass population.

Largemouth bass are still available, but not abundant. Your best bet is to sight fish for them in the spring when they are spawning. Otherwise, you are playing a numbers game that you'll likely lose.

Bass fishing can be frustrating for anglers and world class for others. Shasta has an explosive spotted bass population. However, they are also schooling fish. Oftentimes, if you catch one small spot you'll catch dozens. Many anglers make the mistake of throwing small plastics in flats and close to shore. You may need to fish submerged or offshore structure to find larger fish. While the average spot tends to be around legal size, there are much larger fish in the system.

Trolling is an unorthodox, yet excellent way to tie into bass. Personally, I've had 20 fish days trolling with Storms, Excels and Needlefish while working the shorelines for trout. Most of the time you'll catch larger bass trolling.

From December through February, the worm and jig bite is good. Yamamoto Hula grubs and Robo worms fished off points that have access to deep water and in creek channels can yield quality bass. From February through April, it's not uncommon to catch 20-pound five-fish limits of spotted bass.

March and April can be an excellent time to catch bass for anglers using rip baits, spinnerbaits, worms and jigs. In fact, you can't fish Shasta wrong this time of year. There's so many fish in shallow water and since most of them are spotted bass, they are extremely aggressive. Try fishing the main lake and the Sacramento River Arm. In reality though, you'll locate fish anywhere in 0-25 feet.

Summer is marked by an excellent topwater bite in the morning and worm bite the rest of the day. As long as you have shadows on the water, you'll be able to attain a topwater bite.

Nick Haraden fished at night from a houseboat for this cat.

Shasta's catfish sneak through under the scope. The lake has a tremendous population of catfish, but they aren't as heavily targeted as many of the other species. Cats spawn in the summer in the Pit River and Squaw Creek Arms. Recent efforts by Jones Valley Resort, Sugarloaf Resort and Lakeview Marina have helped boost the catfish population. In 2003, they each raised 750 from six inches to three pounds and released them in mid-November of 2003.

Catfish are a nighttime fishery at Shasta. During the summer and fall, you can fish in any cove or flat in the Pit or Squaw Arm. Toss out a night crawler to catch cats to 15 pounds. This is a favorite pastime for houseboaters. Also, key in on launch ramps and marinas in those areas. The catfish are drawn in by baitfish, which are brought in by the light.

Sturgeon are also part of the mixed bag, but only targeted by a selected few anglers. It's no secret that the sturgeon were trapped in the Sacramento River when Shasta Dam was built. However, the CA DFG isn't sure if sturgeon are spawning in the reservoir. They don't have the man power or funds to do studies. The Pit River Arm is known for sturgeon, however, they can be found scattered all over the lake.

If you plan to make the trip, supplies are available in Redding and at the lake. Many of the launch ramps have day-use fees.

Also nearby are the Upper Sacramento River, Whiskeytown Reservoir and Sacramento River (Redding).

Directions: *From Interstate 5 in Redding, drive north for 9.8 miles to the Bridge Bay exit, or drive 14.3 miles to the Packer's Bay/Shasta Caverns exit, 17.4 miles to the Salt Creek Road exit or 21.5 miles to Lakehead. There are dozens of other access points including Jones Valley, Shasta Dam Road, the Pit River Bridge and many more. Consult a Forest Service map for more detailed directions.*

UPPER SACRAMENTO RIVER

Rating: 8

Species: Rainbow Trout and Brown Trout

Stocked with 13,878 pounds of rainbow trout.

Facilities: Bait & Tackle, Lodging, Campgrounds, Picnic Area, Restaurants and Restrooms

Need Information? Contact: The Tackle Shop (530) 841-1901, Ted Fay Fly Shop (530) 235-2969, Siskiyou County Visitors Bureau (530) 926-3850

The Upper Sacramento River has long been known as one of the better wild trout fisheries in California, but the river has had to contend with several hardships through the years that have caused major fluctuations in trout populations. Fortunately, Mother Nature has always fought back.

The worst hardship the river suffered was in July of 1991 when a car from a freight train derailed on the tracks that parallel the river, spilling an estimated 19,000 gallons of chemicals into the Upper Sac. According to the California Department of Fish and Game, 200,000 trout perished along with most aquatic life in a 35-mile stretch of river. The aquatic composition of the river was destroyed from where the spill occurred near the Cantara Loop to Lake Shasta. Prior to reopening in 1994, the river was closed to fishing for several years.

As the river was close to returning to normal, tragedy struck again, this time in the form of floods. In 1997 and 1998, the Upper Sac saw ravishing water levels that killed off nearly 50 percent of the trout population. Fortunately, conditions have been favorable since and the population seems to have full recovered.

The Upper Sac fishes well year-round. Amazingly though, even during the summer months when temperatures top 100 degrees daily, action can be good. The key is knowing where to find trout. Traditionally from June through early October trout can be found in heavy whitewater, because it's most oxygenated. The summer months aren't necessarily the best time to fish the river, but it is when the most pressure occurs because many folks are vacationing.

While many anglers think the river is reserved for only fly anglers, that's definitely not the case. The river can be split into three sections: the upper, middle and lower. The upper stems from the base of Lake Siskiyou to the Scarlett Way Bridge. This section offers catch and release only. Anglers must use artificial lures with barbless hooks. From Scarlett Way Bridge (near Dunsmuir) to Sweetbriar County Bridge (near the town of Castella) there is a five-fish limit and no gear restrictions. This section is planted with more than 25,000 half-pound rainbow trout

326 (Left) Fly fishing the Upper Sac in summer

each year by the CA DFG. Trout are planted from Dunsmuir City Park to Soda Springs. (You can even use night crawlers and salmon eggs in this section.) The lower section runs from Sweetbriar County Bridge to Lake Shasta. Here there's a two-fish limit and only artificial lures with barbless hooks can be used. The river offers approximately 35 miles of accessible water.

When fishing any section of the Sac in the warmer months, anglers should plan on nymphing. The key is too keep your line short, use droppers and concentrate on runs, pools and pocket water. This is where the majority of trout will hold.

While the Upper Sac is considered a top-notch wild trout fishery, it's not a trophy fishery. There are some huge browns that swim up from Lake Shasta and a few wild trout in

Barbless flies and spinners are commonly used on the Upper Sac.

the 14-18 inch range, but the majority of trout run nine inches or so. You'll be disappointed if you plan to catch several trout better than 12 inches. Even with a guide, it's not going to happen at the present time. If you are looking to catch larger fish, stick to the lower section of the river. This area is much deeper and larger than the upper section and is able to harbor larger trout.

Fishing the Sac during the winter months is still in the early stages. The river was just opened year-round in 2004. Spring can be dictated by runoff. Some years, minimal runoff can make the river easy to fish. Others high runoff can make fishing difficult.

If you plan to make the trip, supplies are available in Dunsmuir, Mt. Shasta and several other smaller cities along the river and Interstate 5. Check updated sportfishing regulations for bag limits, gear restrictions and closures. Call local fishing tackle shops to inquire about fly hatches and effective patterns for the time you are fishing the Upper Sac.

Also nearby are Lake Siskiyou, Lake Shasta and Castle Crags State Park.

Directions: From Redding, drive north on Interstate 5 for roughly 25 miles. From this point and for the next 30 miles there are several roadside access points and frontage roads that parallel the river.

Prolific hatches are common on the Sac

Mc Cloud Reservoir

Rating: 7

Species: Rainbow Trout and Brown Trout

Stocked with 10,800 rainbow trout.

Facilities: Restrooms, Campgrounds and a Boat Launch

Need Information? Contact: The Tackle Shop (530) 841-1901

Mc Cloud Reservoir can be one of Northern California's secret gems or an angler's biggest nightmare. Many anglers think of Mc Cloud as their covert spot to catch browns. Other anglers curse their recollection of getting skunked. Depending on the time of year, Mc Cloud can be easy to fish or only fished with a pair of downriggers or leadcore line.

I look at the reservoir as having two main aspects: wild fish and planters. Telling the difference between the two is almost as easy as taking out the trash. The wild fish are impressive. They are well colored, full tailed and offer exhausting battles on light line. The planters, on the other hand, are easily caught, yet typically are only a half-pound or less, have dull colors and half tails.

At 2,650 feet in the Shasta National Forest, 520-acre Mc Cloud is a dammed portion of the Mc Cloud River. Operated by PG&E, the land above the high water mark is owned by the Hearst Corporation. (The same folks that own Hearst Castle and many other landmarks). The Forest Service has rights below the high water mark.

Fishing can be excellent. And, if you are an experienced angler it should be excellent, as long as you know the tricks. Starting with the wild fish, rainbows and browns are abundant. Most likely, however, you'll need to employ more than basic standard techniques to catch them. Know-hows catch quality browns on a daily basis. Browns tend to average one-to-three pounds. Browns and bows use Star City Creek and the Mc Cloud River to reproduce and do most of their feeding on smaller fish and mayflies.

For anglers who get lucky, the Mc Cloud Redband trout is still available. Most likely you'll catch a hybrid rainbow/redband, but the vibrant colors are remarkable. It's sort of a mix between a coastal rainbow and a native redband trout. At one time, Dolly Varden were found in the basin. Unfortunately, none have been recorded since 1975.

Most often, wild browns are caught in deep water. Sometimes, when either the weather is bad or when the browns are staging to spawn in the fall, they can be caught in the top 15 feet of water.

During winter and spring, troll from 20-50 feet deep. There are plenty of areas to troll and all

A McCloud Reservoir rainbow

need to be approached differently.

The most common area to troll is from the Mc Cloud River inlet to the cove where the boat launch is. This is the narrowest part of the lake and used as a highway by the browns to roam between the inlets where they spawn and sections where they feed. Trolling upriver from the boat launch is easy for the first portion of your troll. Depending on how high the lake is, the water is 20-100 feet deep. Work a green Krocodile, black and white Needlefish or a set of Rebels.

As you move upriver, things get more difficult. About 200 yards before reaching a green bridge, the water gets shallow. In this extremely clear lake, which poses a problem. For example, if you are using downriggers, you'll be able to see your downrigger ball and the bottom. Fish are spooked easily. There are lots of browns in this section, yet they are wary of artificial baits and line heavier than six-pound test. Retire downriggers and opt for a more stealthy method, like toplining with a medium to deep diving lure.

For anglers with more skill, dragging the bottom can be an efficient way to catch more browns. Nearly all coves harbor browns, but you have to work hard for them and be willing to lose gear. Locate 20-50 feet of water, either around the island, in Battle, Panther or Star City Creek Cove, and run your lures just off the bottom. At times, it's helpful to drag your downrigger on the bottom to stir up the dirt. Try and imitate a bait fish swimming through the sand. Unfortunately, snags can make that move dangerous.

Wild rainbows spend their time in two sections: in 20-35 feet of water looking for food in the main channel and near one of the lake's main tributaries. Trolling silver Kastmasters, a white Sep's Pro grub behind a silver Sep's Pro sidekick, a red and gold Super Duper or a red and gold Krocodile gets the job done.

The planters are easy to catch and good prospects for beginner anglers. You can troll anywhere and catch them in the spring and fall. Work the top five to 15 feet of water with a red and gold Thomas Buoyant. My favorite spots are Battle Creek Cove, Star City Creek Cove, where Lick and Quail Gulch Creek spill into the lake and finally at Tarantula Gulch. Expect planters to range from one-third to one-half pound.

While shoreline access isn't great due to private property and steep banks, there is opportunity for bank fishermen. The California Department of Fish and Game plants more than 18,450 rainbow trout at Tarantula Gulch each year.

If you catch a limit of planters and it's between November 17 and the last Saturday in April, take a drive upriver to where the Mc Cloud dumps in. This section of the river is closed to fishing during the

A McCloud Reservoir brown

above mentioned time. However, it's a golden opportunity to look into the water with a pair of polarized glasses and see hundreds of 12-16 inch wild rainbows swimming in and out of the fallen trees, rock walls and tree stumps.

If you plan to make the trip, supplies are available in Dunsmuir and Mt. Shasta. In the winter, call ahead for road conditions. The road may be inaccessible due to snow. During the winter the lake is drawn down drastically. The boat launch may be on dry land. Call ahead for launching conditions.

Also nearby are Mc Cloud Falls (Upper, Middle, Lower) the Mc Cloud River and Lower Mc Cloud River.

Directions: *From Interstate 5 in Redding, drive north for 54.5 miles to the Highway 89 east exit just past Dunsmuir. Follow Highway 89 for 9.6 miles to Squaw Valley Road in the town of Mc Cloud. Turn right and continue nine miles to an unsigned paved road on the left. Turn left to the boat launch.*

Uncle Ron Shaffer with a Mc Cloud River rainbow taken on a Sep's Pro grub.

IRON CANYON RESERVOIR

Rating: 7

Species: Rainbow Trout and Brown Trout

Stocked with 5,000 pounds of rainbow trout.

Facilities: Boat Launch, Campgrounds and Restrooms

Need Information? Contact: Shasta National Forest (530) 246-5112, Vaughn's Sporting Goods (530) 335-2381

When is the best time to fish Iron Canyon Reservoir? Depends on who you talk to. While many anglers choose to arrive in the summer when water levels are stable, others would rather arrive in the winter when larger fish tend to show.

Iron Canyon offers a two-tier fishery where wild brown trout show in the winter and planters are caught in the summer. Trout can be caught all year. However, if you are looking for the larger, 14-19 inch browns, you'll experience more success if you arrive December through February. Tossing olive and brown Woolly Buggers near any of the inlets can produce quality browns. Wintertime is quite different than summer at Iron Canyon. The 510-acre reservoir (when full) rests at 2,700 feet near the town of Big Bend and bobs up and down like a yo-yo. PG&E lowers and raises it based on their current needs. Oftentimes winter brings low water, yet good fishing.

In summer, on the other hand, Iron Canyon is usually kept near full pool. Arrive any earlier than June and the launch ramp may be on dry land! Since Iron Canyon is fed by several smaller creeks (Iron Canyon, Blue Jay, McGill, Deadlum, Cedar Salt Log, Little Gap, Gap and a 12-foot wide pipe carrying water from McCloud Reservoir), a lot of water/food gets pumped in, which is enjoyed by the 38,000 fingerling rainbows and another 7,450 half-pound fish.

Shoreline bait dunkers see some success in the warmer months, though productivity can be limited in the summer as trout seek cooler water. Iron Canyon is shaped like your left hand, with a thumb and four fingers. Trolling any one of them will yield limits of bows from 20-55 feet with a red Cripplure or Hum-Dinger. Nevertheless, anglers who take a chance at loosing gear can nab browns as well. Iron Canyon's bottom is complete with stumps which the browns hide behind. If you can drag the bottom with just about any lure, you'll see success. Unfortunately, you'll also lose lures and possibly a downrigger cable and ball.

If you plan to make the trip, supplies are available in Burney and Redding.

Also nearby are Hatchet Creek and Montgomery Creek Falls.

Directions: From the junction of Interstate 5 and Highway 299 east in Redding, drive east on Highway 299 and drive 34.1 miles to Big Bend Road. Turn left and drive roughly 23 miles to the reservoir.

LAKE BRITTON

Rating: 8

Species: Brook Trout, Rainbow Trout, Brown Trout, Channel Catfish, Bluegill, Crappie, Smallmouth Bass, Largemouth Bass and Carp

Stocked with 2,575 pounds of fingerling brook trout, 1,875 pounds of fingerling rainbow trout and 3,550 pounds of sub-catchable rainbow trout.

Facilities: Boat Launch, Restrooms, Campgrounds, Picnic Areas, Boat Rentals, General Store, Bait & Tackle, Showers and a Café

Need Information? Contact: Vaughn's Sporting Goods (530) 335-2381 Burney-McArthur State Park (530) 335-2777

Lake Britton is a place where you don't have to be a Bassmaster to be successful catching warmwater fish. Located partly in Burney McArthur State Park and in the Shasta National Forest, Britton sees relatively heavy use in the summer from boaters and anglers. However, there are enough coves to keep anglers shielded from power-boats. Britton combines a good smallmouth bass fishery with a traditionally good crappie bite and a sleeper coldwater fishery.

Lake Britton hasn't always been a great smallmouth lake. In fact, in the good ole' days largemouth bass were the dominate species. Largemouth were planted in 1925 and did well for the first decade, or so, before becoming just a mediocre fishery. Sometime in the mid-Seventies, California Department of Fish and Game biologists believe that the Intermountain Bass Club illegally planted smallmouth bass from Lake Almanor into Britton. Once the CA DFG learned of this they knew they couldn't remove the bass from the lake, therefore, they opted to aid the population by planting more than 100 adult bass to help out the gene pool.

While largemouth bass are available, they are rare. However, if you are fortunate enough to nab one, you'll be smiling: they average three-to-eight pounds. When the CA DFG electrofishes the lake, a mere five-percent of their sample is largemouth. Smallies, on the other hand, are abundant. Good rock structure and deepwater habitat make for a great fit.

There are piles of smaller bass, fortunately hogs are present too. The key is to fish them when they are up. This occurs in March and early April. Sounds odd that the fish would spawn so early in a lake that is higher than 3,000 feet, yet it's true. Britton's bass spawn before Shasta's most years. By May, the bigger smallies will be deep again.

The population of smallies is in no danger. The fish are blessed with an excellent food source consisting of pike minnows, hard heads, sculpin,

Britton smallmouth bass

tule perch, bluegill and crappie. There are no shad or minnows.

Most bassers fish Britton in the spring with plastics and crankbaits. Finding steep cliffs, points and rocky structure won't be an issue. After the bass spawn, anglers fishing crankbaits and night crawlers struggle to catch bass greater than 12 inches. Oftentimes, anglers fishing for crappie hook into smallies.

As with most lakes, Britton's crappie fishery fluctuates between good and fair. Yet, good seems to come more often than not. Crappie are usually pan size. However, fish to a few pounds are common every few years. Crappie can be caught from a boat in any cove where you find fallen trees or brush piles. For the larger fish, you'll have to fish deeper structure. Try a red worm, a piece of a night crawler or crappie jig. Some boat launches also have fishing docks where shoreline anglers can catch crappie.

Britton is also a sleeper trout lake. While the lake isn't planted with any catchable size trout by the CA DFG, it does receive hundreds of thousands of fingerling and sub-catchable trout each year. The Crystal Springs Hatchery uses Britton as a "dump lake" where excess fish are released. In 2003, 67,208 fingerling brook trout and more than 100,000 subs and fingerling rainbows were planted. Some become fish food, others become big trout. Few anglers target trout at this PG&E reservoir held up by Pit 3 Dam, however, trout are here.

While many trout can be caught in the thermocline, others waste no time looking for fresh water. The Hat and Burney Creek inlets and the Pit River inlet are excellent holding grounds for trout. The lake harbors brooks, rainbows and browns. They aren't taken often, yet huge browns are available. In 2001, a ranger at Britton discovered a carcass of a brown than measured 39 inches. Enough said.

To find success with coldwater fish, don't venture far from the inlets. Bait, hardware and trolling are effective.

If you plan to make the trip, supplies are available in Burney. There is a day-use and boat launch fee for anglers entering through the state park.

Also nearby are Burney Falls, Rock Creek Falls, Baum Lake and Pit River Section 4 & 5.

Directions: *From the junction of Highway 299 and Interstate 5 in Redding, drive east on Highway 299 for 53.7 miles to the junction with Highway 89. Turn left and drive 10 miles to the lake.*

Scott Wiessner with a Britton crappie.

Pit River (Section 1)

Rating: 8

Species: Rainbow Trout and Brown Trout

Stocks: None

Facilities: Campgrounds and Restrooms

Need Information? Contact: Vaughn's Sporting Goods (530) 335-2381, Fishing Guide Matt Hawkins (530) 336-7286

Overlooked? A Secret? Poor Access? Seldom Fished? All of these are true when you talk about Section 1 of the Pit River. As the Pit leaves Fall River Valley and heads toward Burney to be fed through hydroelectric power plants, anglers can find the least fished section of the main stem of the Pit, and also some of the best fishing.

No plants occur in the Pit River system, however, that's not to say there aren't trout available. In fact, the opposite is true. This section of the Pit River offers excellent action on rainbows that show in two classes: the prominent nine-to-14-inch fish and larger 16-24 inch trout. Catching 20-30 fish per outing, per angler, isn't uncommon. However, reaching those fish can be a chore. A real chore.

There are several problems with fishing Section 1. All stem from poor access. There's only one way to fish this portion with ease and be successful at the same time: with a drift boat. Sounds easy? Where do you put in and take out? That's part of the problem. There is no official launch ramp. In fact, there are only three spots where a boat could be launched. The first is at the BLM campground near Pit River Lodge where a ledge that boaters with a four-wheel drive vehicle could manage to drop a boat in. The next is at the Pit River Bridge on Highway 299 and the third is on the upper end of Lake Britton.

Finding a place to launch is only half the battle. Navigating through the Pit is another story. While most of the river is easily manageable, there are a few areas where Class III rapids can pose a problem to anglers. I was hooked up with Matt Hawkins (the only guide I am aware of who drifted the river). His boat is proof of the danger. Several rough scratches and large dents prove the risk, not to mention our trip where he was forced to jump out of the boat in dangerous whitewater and pull us to the next run.

Another issue? Once you reach Lake Britton you have to paddle a mile or so to the unofficial take out, which can be reached via dirt roads from Highway 299. It would be possible to bring a trolling motor, but you'd need to have the space for it. One strong enough to get you where you need to go could cost several hundred bucks. Your best bet? Hire a guide, like Hawkins, to do the paddling while you admire wildlife and untouched scenery. Hawkins takes on the

334 Scott Wiessner caught and released this small rainbow trout on the Pit.

Pit River rainbow

Squawfish

danger because he opts to catch only trophy fish. His dedication to fishing Pit 1 exclusively has paid off. Through the years, Hawkins has learned that most trout are only found in whitewater (riffles and roiling water). Only squawfish are found in the slow moving areas. The reason: chemicals from farms in Fall River Valley are washed into the Pit and dissolve oxygen in the water. Trout are forced to remain in places where more oxygen can be found.

The Pit is also fished differently than many other rivers in the region. The river doesn't have a good dry fly hatch; yet fishing the surface can be productive at times. Hawkins experiences success fishing exclusively with streamers. He sends large Woolly Buggers and leeches to the bottom and slowly retrieves them. Fishing smaller runs with a nymph and an indicator is also productive. If you are a spin caster, a yellow Panther Martin with a silver blade is best. If you can't get a hold of any of those, just make sure to use something with a silver blade. For the bait caster, night crawlers also produce.

The best fishing can be found in the fall when larger rainbows are the prominent catch. It's not uncommon to land several bows in the 18-24 inch class per outing from late August through the fishing season. Spring and summer can be excellent, however, you'll be looking at mostly smaller fish.

Fishing Pit 1 without a boat can be tough. Most anglers are aware that the Pit is extremely difficult to wade through and nearly impossible without a wading staff. While access roads do parallel the Pit, oftentimes they don't travel close to it. You'll need to work hard to reach the bank. This includes walking through tall, dead grass, brush and then scrambling down steep hillsides. There are two areas where drive-to access can be found: the Pit River Bridge on Highway 299 and the BLM campground.

If you plan to make the trip, supplies are available in Burney. The Pit River is closed to fishing from November 16 to the last Saturday in April.

Also nearby are Hat Creek, Lake Britton, Burney Falls, Fall River and Pit River Falls.

Directions: *From the junction of Highway 299 and Interstate 5 in Redding, drive east on Highway 299 for 58.1 miles to the Pit River Bridge.*

Guide Matt Hawkins specializes in catching trophy rainbows on the Pit.

FALL RIVER (FALL RIVER MILLS)

Rating: 6

Species: Rainbow Trout, Brown Trout, Largemouth Bass and Channel Catfish

Stocks: None

Facilities: None

Need Information? Contact: Shasta Angler Tackle Shop (530) 336-6600

There's a big difference between the Fall River above Fall River Lake and the Fall River Mills section which reaches from the base of the lake to the confluence with the Pit River. While this section does experience the same hex hatch as the upper portion of the river, the fishing isn't as great. This lower section, which stretches only a few miles, isn't as clear and pretty as the upper stretch and also holds bass, catfish and other species that come out of Fall River Lake.

Fall River in the town of Fall River Mills doesn't display the same great growing conditions and water clarity as the section of water above the lake. This stretch is hurt by warmer water than the upper river and subsequently holds fewer trout. Fortunately, the river is conducive to bait fishing, spin cast and fly fishing. The trout bite is best in the spring and late fall. Blazing hot summertime temperatures can put a damper on fishing, yet anglers in the know can catch fish here throughout the open season. Ironically, bass can be taken on the surface in the evenings on Pop-R's.

If you plan to make the trip, supplies are available in Fall River Mills. The Fall River is closed to fishing from November 16 to the last Saturday in April. There is scattered access along this lower stretch of the river from Fall River Lake to the Pit River.

Directions: From the junction of Highway 299 and Interstate 5 in Redding, drive east on Highway 299 for 64.8 miles to the bridge over the river.

Fall River in the town of Fall River Mills

FALL RIVER LAKE

Rating: 5

Species: Rainbow Trout, Channel Catfish, Largemouth Bass and Crappie

Stocks: None

Facilities: Restrooms and a Boat Launch

Need Information? Contact: Shasta Angler Tackle Shop (530) 336-6600

Large trout, yet poor fishing access is what most anglers think of when questioned about Fall River Lake. In actuality, those anglers are referring to Fall River. Fall River Lake, on the other hand, is a dammed portion of the Fall River used successfully by PG&E as a holding pool to later be transferred to the Pit River to produce hydroelectric power. Fall River Lake is quite opposite of Fall River, as it doesn't have large trout, but does have good access.

Fall River Lake is primarily a warm water fishery with largemouth bass, crappie and catfish, the latter providing the most action. If bass is your desire, come in the spring and toss night crawlers from shore. There are several dirt boat launch areas that enable boaters to fish areas difficult to reach from the shoreline. During the warmer months, catfish action can be hot when using cut mackerel and anchovies to con the fish into feeding.

Overall, Fall River Lake provides a nice recreational getaway for the locals of the Fall River Valley. While the lake is considered a local hangout, you don't have to be a local to enjoy it. It's simply that out-of-towners sparsely frequent it. Locals water-ski in the warmer months, but pretty much stay away in the winter.

If you plan to make the trip, supplies are available in Fall River Mills.

Also nearby are the Pit River, Fall River, Pit River Falls and Hat Creek.

Directions: *From the junction of Highway 299 and Interstate 5 in Redding, drive east on Highway 299 for 64.6 miles to an unsigned road on the left just before the Fall River Bridge. Turn left and drive one-half mile to the lake.*

Fall River Lake

FALL RIVER

Rating: 10

Species: Rainbow Trout and Brown Trout

Stocks: None

Facilities: Lodging and a Launch Ramp

Need Information?
Contact: Steve Marugg of Finwing Guide Service (530) 336-6423, Vaughn's Sporting Goods (530) 335-2381, Shasta Angler Tackle Shop (530) 336-6600

The Fall River definitely has found a niche that allows it to rise above nearly all other wild trout waters in California. The neat thing about the river is that the water is so clear and moves at such a slow speed that you can see the fish you are trying to catch. Not just a few fish, rather thousands as you cruise upriver. We aren't talking about dinks. While small trout can be seen, rainbows in the 14-24 inch class are the majority.

What's even more amazing is that unlike Hat Creek where banks can be lined with anglers and where public access makes for legendary crowds, because the Fall River offers only limited access, crowds tend to be light except for a few highly regarded holes.

The serenity adds to the experience of landing big fish. I laid my fly rod down to watch two bucks hanging out in the grass along the riverbed. They didn't budge when we cruised alongside of them to snap a picture. Neither did the dozen, or so, muskrats we witnessed carrying supplies back to their nests. More than 100 species of birds can be seen on any given day, as well as views of Mt. Shasta, the tip of Mt. Lassen, Burney Peak, Soldier Mountain and the scenic ranches on both sides of the river. Even better, you don't see empty beer cans, Taco Bell wrappers, diapers or any other trash along the bank. Private property keeps that stuff under a trash can lid.

Excellent water and forage pave the way for above average trout. A mixed bag of rainbows can be expected. While you see lots of eight-to-12-inch fish, the majority of your catch will be in the 14-20 inch class, with an occasional 20 plus inch fish. Each year, some trout to 10 pounds are landed. The known record is 17 pounds.

The Fall River is spring fed, except for Bear Creek which is the only major tributary that is comprised of runoff. The other sources are Spring Creek, Rainbow Spring and Thousand Springs. Trout from the Fall River spawn either in Bear Creek, which is located on the upper river, or Squaw Creek, which is a up the Tule River.

Fall River spells great opportunity, but has one major downfall: access. The river offers

Jean Rodgers of Burney with a Fall River bow

poor access unless you own property alongside it. There are only a few ways to fish the river and they all are in a boat, canoe or kayak. On the flip side, private property keeps the river from being over-fished. The easiest access can be found at Island Bridge where Cal Trout owns a small parcel of land. Boats may be launched, however, no gas powered motors can be launched from this point. Gas powered motors are allowed on the

Deer along the Fall River

river. There is a 5 mph speed limit upriver of the confluence of the Tule River. Other public access can be found behind the town of McArthur at Rat Ranch. All other access is via Bed and Breakfasts, lodges and private rental houses.

The river can be split into three sections. The lower river can be spotted from Fall River Mills upriver to the Tule River confluence. The middle section is between the confluence and Island Bridge and the upper stretch extends from Island Bridge to the headwaters at Rainbow Spring. Most anglers care about one section of the river and that's it: from Spring Creek Bridge to Whipple Bridge. This famous stretch of water is referred to as Zug Bug Alley and harbors more fish than any other stretch.

The lower river varies widely from the middle and upper stretches. Downriver from the confluence, the water temperature is often 10 degrees warmer and much less clearer. This section doesn't see as prolific hatches either, except for the hex hatch. There are also fewer pods of fish, however, still some hogs are available. Big rainbows live under cut banks in this section and gorge on minnows and crawdads to grow fast. Most anglers spinner fish or bait fish in this section. There are no gear restrictions. Some anglers even troll flies.

The middle section is not quite as clear as the upper section, nor does it harbor as many fish, but it receives less fishing pressure, which is cause for opportunity. The same bugs live in this section, but for some reason the bite isn't as consistent. Perhaps because there isn't as much grass as you see in the

Hex bugs

upper stretch. It's more of a weed that isn't as conducive to insect hatches.

The upper section harbors browns, yet few anglers pay attention. Browns, on the other hand, can be found near the headwaters and spawning grounds feeding on juvenile rainbows. The best water is found from Spring Creek on down two miles. Upriver of this section, the weed beds thin out and there isn't as much bug life or fish. You'll find more of a sandy bottom upriver of Spring Creek, which means less bugs and little food. On the contrary, upriver near Spinner Fall Resort action can be excellent in the spring and early summer when the spinner fly hatch occurs.

Fall River rainbow

While most anglers fish the river with an indicator and a nymph (which is basically bobber fishing) there are several ways to vary your approach and be successful.

For starters, you'll want to use a five-weight rod and most likely a 10-12 foot leader with a 6x tippet. The water is crystal clear and moves slow, which allows the rainbows lots of time to look at your fly and make a decision if they'll take it or not. The fish aren't necessarily easily spooked, rather leader shy. Stay light and you'll be ok. Also, stick to making downriver casts. It's best to motor upriver until you spot a couple of fish working the surface. Then, motor above those fish and allow your line to drift back over them. The fish won't take upriver casts because they can see your fly line and the leader.

Every day, barring a heavy downpour or gusty winds, you can expect some sort of hatch to occur. Hatches typically occur between 10 a.m. and 2 p.m. Typically, a sunny afternoon is plagued by either a brisk breeze or winds that knock out potential hatches. The best bite in the summer happens on drizzly, cloudy or overcast days when it almost looks like popcorn is hatching all over the water because the bug life is so active.

On a normal day, dry flies and nymphing works. Early in the hatch it can be productive to use an emerger or a dunn. Mohagany and para dunns are excellent. When you hook a fish, be sure to raise your rod tip high. If not, the trout will head down into the weeds and you'll be forced to break it off.

Precise casting is important on the Fall River. The further you can cast, the better chance you'll be successful. If there is no surface action it's a good idea to cast roughly 45 degrees across the current and let your fly swing down until it has completely swung around. Then, you can start the slow retrieve. It's best to use a No. 2 or 3 sinking line with either a small nymph on 6x or a small leach or Woolly Bugger on 4 or 5x.

This method imitates a swimming nymph moving above the weed bed. Typically, before a hatch there's a lot of activity below the surface. Popular nymphs are size 16 and 18 pheasant tails, zug bugs, hair'seEar, black AP and a olive mayfly nymph.

The most prolific hatch of the year is known as the hex. The Hexegenia is an insect that burrows itself in the mud and

The clarity of the Fall River is excellent.

A typical Hex bug in comparison to a quarter.

hatches at sunset. The hex is a short hatch. It lasts weeks rather than months. Traditionally, the hatch begins either the last week of May or the first week of June. It apparently starts near the town of Fall River Mills and works upriver as water temperatures warm. Some years the hatch won't begin until June and continues through mid-July. Concentrate on fishing the hex hatch from the upper end of Fall River Lake to Island Bridge. The hatch occurs at night, roughly 30 minutes after sunset.

Interestingly enough, the hex bug has smartened up over the years. To increase chances of survival, the hatch avoids evening because so many of the bugs get picked off by blackbirds patiently waiting on a fence post. Nighttime is dangerous because bats pick them off. Therefore, the hatch is strongest 30 minutes after sundown. Then, the trout are the biggest predators.

Anglers set up facing the sun and begin using nymph hex patterns after 7 p.m. Facing the sun allows for the last rays of light to aid you in seeing your fly. The hatch begins in town and as time progresses it moves upriver, yet doesn't extend beyond Island Bridge. When the hatch is coming off it can't be mistaken. There are so many bugs you'll have trouble spotting your own fly.

You don't need a fly rod to fish the hex. A spinning rod rigged with eight-pound test, a six-pound leader and a fly and bubble combo setup is applicable. To cash in on the action and have a good shot at a five-or-six-pound bow, cast hex imitation flies upriver or where you see the hatch occurring and let her drift.

If you plan to make the trip, supplies are available in Fall River Mills. Fall River is closed to fishing from November 16 to the last Saturday in April. Above the Fall River's confluence with the Tule River there is a two-fish limit and each fish must be 14 inches or smaller to take. General fishing regulations apply to the water below the confluence.

Also nearby is Fall River Lake.

Directions: From the junction of Highway 299 and Interstate 5 in Redding, drive east on Highway 299 for roughly 65 miles to Fall River Mills. Turn left on Road A-20, drive five miles to a split in the road and veer right. Drive three-tenths of a mile to McArthur Road and turn north. Drive 1.2 miles to Island Road and turn north. Continue one mile to the access site.

Fall River

BIG LAKE

To have a good chance at trout at Big Lake, you'll need a boat, some time, patience, light tackle and a trolling motor, and chances are you may still not be successful. Big Lake isn't planted by the California Department of Fish and Game. All of its fish are wild, easily spooked and only a few stragglers tend to be found near the springs at the back of the lake. Trout aren't abundant here, yet are available and some grow as large as eight pounds. You don't tend to find a lot of dinks and if you don't fish in the back near the springs, chances are you won't find any trout at all.

Big Lake is a big lake (for the Fall River Valley); unfortunately, it is extremely shallow and warms quickly, except for the back of the lake near the springs. Located in Ahjumawi Lava Springs State Park, Big Lake's clarity suffers from an overwhelming algae bloom most of the year. Most anglers don't bother fishing because of visibility and poor access. No foot traffic is available. You have to boat to the lake. This can be done two ways: by boating up the Fall River to the Tule River or by launching at Rat Ranch on the Tule and heading upriver.

If you don't fish the springs most of the rest of the lake isn't worth a damn. There are some largemouth bass here, but the entire shoreline basically is the same levy-like topography and offers little to no structure for bass to relate to. You'll have to work hard for the bass unless you get lucky and fall upon a pod of fish. Some anglers try and bass fish in the winter, however, the occasional thin sheet of ice on the surface scares most anglers off.

If you plan to make the trip, supplies are available in McArthur. The lake is governed by special regulations. Only two trout may be kept per day.

Also nearby are Tule River, Little Tule River, Fall River and Horr Pond.

Directions: *From the junction of Highway 299 and Interstate 5 in Redding, drive east on Highway 299 for 68.7 to Main St. in McArthur. Turn left and drive 3.7 miles to Rat Ranch Access.*

Guide Steve Marugg with a Big Lake bow.

JA-SHE CREEK

Rating: 10

Species: Rainbow Trout, Brown Trout and Largemouth Bass

Stocks: None

Facilities: Restrooms

Formally known as Squaw Creek, Ja-She Creek is a portion of Ahjumawi State Park and offers some of the best fishing in the West. In fact, few places in California can compete with the quality of rainbows available at Ja-She. Wild rainbows between one and 10 pounds rule this place. Rarely do you see any dinks. Unfortunately, you have to work hard to be successful. There isn't an abundance of trout available, yet the rewards of quality fish are worth the effort.

Ja-She Creek is the location of one of the largest springs in North America. The water comes from Tule Lake, more than 50 miles away. It travels through lava tubes and emerges at Ahjumawi. The serenity of Ja-She is much different than you'd find anywhere else in California. On a clear day, it's like being in the Caribbean. The color of the water is mesmerizing.

Fishing Ja-She can be challenging. From mid-June through early September, the entire Ja-She Arm is covered in algae, making sight fishing impossible. Your alternative is to arrive from fall through spring when waters are so clear you could place a watch on the bottom and read the time without squinting. Ja-She is one of the most beautiful places in the United States. Imagine fishing in a freshwater coral reef. Two-to-eight feet deep, this spring fed creek is gin clear, relatively angler free and teeming with monster rainbows.

What's the catch then? How come everyone doesn't fish here? No drive to access is available. You need a boat to reach the state park and Ja-She Creek. Also, this is a delicate fishery. No fish plants take place. All fish are wild, self-sustaining and must be caught and released if you plan on allowing the fishery to continue for future generations.

Jack Marugg caught and released this whopper rainbow at Ja-She Creek during the month of June. 343

Ja-She Creek

While you won't have a problem spotting these mosters, if you don't have a trolling motor and cruise softly you might find difficulty catching them. The trout are extremely skittish. The water is so clear they can spot you coming more than 100 feet away. You best be a good caster!

You won't have a problem locating areas to fish. Seek areas where fish are rising or simply rely on sight fishing. Try not to discount the backwater located near the actual springs. Some hiking is required; however, many of the larger fish stay in this calm water. Above and below the footbridge is also an excellent spot. In fact, this is the only portion of Ja-She that actually looks like a creek and has flowing water. The rest is like a large, still pond. Nymphing with an indicator can be productive. Personally, my five-pound bow came on a Yo-Zuri Crystal Minnow.

For the most part, there are no real insect hatches. Dry fly action is slow. Fly anglers should fish with streamers, brown leeches, any minnow pattern or a size eight or 10 Woolly Bugger. Unfortunately, the majority of anglers bait fish. This can be detrimental to the trout if they swallow the hook. Instead of bait, try a yellow and silver Panther Martin.

To reach Ja-She Creek you have two options: launch into the Fall River at the Cal Trout access or into the Tule River at Rat Ranch and motor up to the creek. There are no plans for road access in the near future.

Directions and trip info for Big Lake also apply to Ja-She Creek.   **Ja-She Creek**

HORR POND

Rating: 2

Species: Rainbow Trout and Largemouth Bass

Stocks: None

Facilities: None

Horr Pond isn't a great fishery; however, it does have the ingredients to be a decent bass fishery. Back in the days when Henry Horr and his father were involved the pond was a dike. The 40-acre dike has since become a widening in the Big Lake area. With no maintenance the dike was destroyed and most likely won't be repaired.

Now part of the Ahjumawi State Park, the pond, which by definition is no longer a pond because it isn't enclosed, is a poor fishery. Larry Hanson, a fisheries biologist for the California Department of Fish and Game, made it a point to study the fishery a few years back. He found an abundance of food for bass (hardheads, bluegill, squawfish), but he didn't see many bass after a few days electrofishing. He ran into a few small largemouth bass, but that's it. The CA DFG has received reliable reports of bass greater than 10 pounds coming from the Big Lake area, but it's rare.

As for the future of Horr Pond, there are some bass, rainbows and small bluegill, but not enough to warrant anglers to fish it. Basically, they wander in Horr on their swim between the Tule River and Big Lake. You have to have a boat to fish the pond. There is no shoreline access.

Directions *and trip info for Big Lake also apply to Horr Pond.*

Horr Pond

LITTLE TULE RIVER

Rating: 5

Species: Rainbow Trout, Brown Trout and Largemouth Bass

Stocks: None

Facilities: None

Many anglers believe that fishing in the Fall River Valley is pure and that all trout are wild. We don't know that for sure, however. In the Forties, Fifties and into the early Sixties the California Department of Fish and Game and many residents stocked every water you could drive a hatchery truck to. What strains of these fish survived is another issue. The Fall River Valley is plagued by a natural parasite known as ceratomyxa which kills many strains of rainbow trout. In fact, the Pit River strain is the only bow known to overcome the terminal illness. While ceratomyxa doesn't bother brooks or browns, it kills all strains of trout other than the Pit River rainbows when water warms above 54 degrees. It's highly unlikely that any stocked trout other than Pit River rainbows inhabit the Little Tule River.

The Little Tule River is seldom fished, yet harbors some rainbows and a sprinkling of browns and bass. The most consistent spots are where Eastman Lake dumps into the Little Tule and where the Little Tule meets the main stem of the Tule. The fact of the matter is that there are so many consistent trout producing spots in the region that anglers don't need to mess with this place. If you have the time to experiment, try trolling a black or olive Woolly Bugger or soaking a night crawler. Otherwise, plan on covering a ton of ground before landing your first fish.

Directions *and trip info for Big Lake also apply to the Little Tule River.*

Little Tule River

TULE RIVER

Rating: 5

Species: Rainbow
Trout, Brown Trout and
Largemouth Bass

Stocks: None

Facilities: Launch
Ramp and Restrooms

Need Information?
Contact: Vaughn's
Sporting Goods
(530) 335-2381

Prior to 1911 much of Northern California didn't have a problem with muskrats. That was soon to change though. In 1911, a farmer began to raise the rats for harvest at his ranch along the Tule River. The operation was successful until later that same year when a flood swept through, damaging the ranch and washing the muskrats into the wild. Soon, they could be found in the Fall River, Pit River system and eventually in the Sacramento Valley. We can credit Rat Ranch for some of the muskrat problem we have in California.

On the upside, that ranch provides anglers with the opportunity to fish the Tule River and other areas in the Fall River Valley. Rat Ranch is situated on the shoreline of the Tule. Unfortunately, the Tule doesn't offer the same exceptional fishing as nearby Fall River and Ja-She Creek. However, opportunity remains.

Trout use the Tule as a highway to swim between the Fall River and the waters of Ahjumawi State Park, where some of them spawn. Unfortunately, the Tule doesn't get the same world class hatches that the Fall River does. There are weeds in the river, yet not the weed beds that promote great bug life, which is a great thing for trout. Only once in a while the famed Hex hatch spreads into the Tule drainage.

Primarily rainbows inhabit the river. Most often they are caught in three areas: where the Tule spills into the Fall River, the confluence with the Little Tule and at the river's headwaters near Big Lake. Many anglers see the most success bait fishing with minnows or night crawlers. Trolling can also be productive. Be careful to use a lure that doesn't sink much. The river is shallow. If you have a fly rod troll Woolly Buggers.

Tule River

If you plan to make the trip, supplies are available in McArthur.

Also nearby are Fall River Lake, Horr Pond and Big Lake.

Directions: *and trip info for Big Lake also apply to the Tule River.*

HAT CREEK (WILD TROUT SECTION)

Rating: 6

Species: Rainbow Trout and Brown Trout

Stocks: None

Facilities: Picnic Area and Restrooms

Need Information? Contact: Fishing Guide Matt Hawkins (530) 336-7286, Vaughn's Sporting Goods (530) 335-2381, Clearwater House (530) 335-5500

Keeping up with the times is important. Unfortunately, it's not always the best way to go. More than a decade ago, Hat Creek was known as one of the better wild trout fisheries in the West. In fact, anglers from across the country flocked to this spring fed Shasta County stream during the Seventies and Eighties to experience some of the most fantastic wild rainbow and brown trout fishing in country.

Sad enough, those days are a thing of the past. While there are still bows and browns to be caught, the trout are much smaller than they once were. Overall angler satisfaction is flirting with all-time lows. Despite what you read in many old books and magazines, Hat Creek is no longer one of California's premier wild trout streams.

Some folks go as far as to blame themselves. Much of the habitat in the stream has been altered due to extensive wading. If you have 10,000 anglers walking on spawning beds each year, it is going to affect the area. Many of the fly fishermen who wish to protect and preserve this fishery forever are the ones ruining it. (They will surely tell you otherwise though.)

Several obstacles have helped remove Hat Creek's popularity in recent decades. Those include: vegetation boom and bust, muskrats, sediment buildup, cycles and possibly over fishing.

Mike Dean of the California Department of Fish and Game's Wild Trout Program attributes some of the decline of the fishery to a boom and bust, per say, of the stream's vegetation. A lack of funds in Dean's budget hasn't allowed him to study the issue as extensively as he would like though. However, we do know that Hat Creek is no longer supporting the banner shoreline and stream vegetation that it did during the hay day. While some years we'll see reminisce of the superb vegetation, it doesn't remain long.

It can be best described as sporadic. Some years, or months, the vegetation is great. Others, it's horrible. The vegetation plays a vital role in the flow of Hat Creek and the creek's ability to retain water. However, it also provides fish habitat and structure, while giving that same shelter to bugs and insects. If the vegetation doesn't grow, the food chain loses. You'll have less structure for fish, which makes them more susceptible to eagles and other prey. Not to mention growth rates decline rapidly.

The muskrat problem for Hat Creek doesn't look like it's going away. Muskrats are not native to the drainage, rather descendants of escapees from the now famous Rat Ranch near McArthur. These critters burrow into the bank. Then, the bank collapses and they dig and new hole and burrow again. It can be cancerous for the shoreline.

Historically, cows also destroyed the banks when they drank water. However, that problem was cured years back. The muskrats, on the other hand, can't simply be fenced off. They are too expensive to trap and it's not economical to put a bounty on. Muskrat pelts go for just a buck and traditional trapping methods have been outlawed in California, making it not worth the money to pursue these critters.

Something will need to be done in regards to bank restoration soon though. Many of Hat's islands are beginning to disappear. And, the creek is widening and becoming shallower. Not a good sign for the once world class fishery. A few groups have set plans to restore the banks. However, the cost simply isn't feasible at this time.

Sediment buildup in Hat is another issue that the CA DFG hopes will go away in time. In the mid-Eighties the creek was flooded with tons of sediment, which not only filled in some spawning areas, but deep holes. The sediment has gradually moved down the system and towards Lake Britton, but it may take several years to leave Hat Creek altogether.

If some of these issues are solved, Hat may again return to the table as one of California's premier wild trout streams. Part of the recent decline came with age. Every system goes through a cycle. Big fish die and the young may take several years to grow to trophy sizes. Unfortunately, the CA DFG fears that many of the streams best genetic fish are leaving the system. How is this possible?

Hat Ceek rainbow

In 1968 the CA DFG, in cooperation with other agencies, built a weir on Hat Creek to stop the migration of unwanted fish into the system. Let's talk a little history to understand this process better. Prior to the construction of Lake Britton in 1925, Lower Hat Creek was an excellent trout fishery. However when Britton was constructed, the fishery began to decline. By the late Fifties and early Sixties, it was a horrible trout fishery.

It was estimated that more than 90 percent of the biomass of fish in the system were hardheads, suckers and pike minnows. Trout were the minority. The non trout species were swimming up from Britton and inhabiting Hat Creek, therefore taking a majority of the food source and simply out-competing the trout.

Then the CA DFG opted to step in and built the barrier in 1968. They electrofished the entire stretch of Hat above the barrier and removed all the fish. The trout were kept in a safe haven while the stream was chemically treated. After ensuring the treatment went well, the wild trout were put back into the stream where they were the only game fish at the time. The unwanted fish could no longer swim up from Lake Britton. The fishery again began to shine.

While the barrier has worked magic, it also offers a one-way ticket out of dodge. Another issue with Hat is that there isn't a great deal of spawning grounds. Much of the spawning areas are located near the barrier. Conversely, there isn't enough of it to supply all the trout. Some of the larger trout see fish already occupying the spawning grounds and see the barrier as opportunity. They think that if they swim to the other side of the barrier, they'll find better and less crowded conditions. That's true, but once they leave they can't return. The CA DFG is researching methods to fix this problem. But, the money it would take to complete it is an unlikely fix.

Hat is facing a tough battle, but not everyone thinks Hat Creek's time to star is over. The fishery has showed signs of a comeback, yet has been inconsistent since the late Eighties. Nonetheless, there are still trout to be caught. Most of the trout are rainbows. Many of them are fewer than six inches, but a fair numbers of six-to-12 inch trout and some larger reside. There are still browns. The few available are exceptionally large.

Beginning as early as May, fly hatches go off and action can be great. However, many argue these hatches only last 30 minutes and if you aren't out during that time, you miss out.

If you plan to make the trip, supplies are available in Burney. Hat Creek is closed to fishing from November 16 to the last Saturday in April.

Also nearby are Baum Lake, Pit River and Crystal Lake.

Directions: *From the junction of Highway 299 and Interstate 5 in Redding, drive east on Highway 299 for 53.7 miles to the junction with Highway 89. Continue on Highway 299 for 3.7 miles to the left turnoff for Hat Creek Park.*

Guide Matt Hawkins with an average size Hat Creek rainbow trout.

CRYSTAL LAKE

Rating: 5

Species: Rainbow Trout

Stocks: None

Facilities: None

Need Information?
Contact: Vaughn's
Sporting Goods
(530) 335-2381

Crystal Lake is the kind of place that alters the normalcy of nature. Historically, rainbow trout are spring spawners. However, studies prove that many of Crystal's bows spawn in late fall and winter. November through January yields several pairs of spawning rainbows near the lake's outlet at Baum Lake. Spawning is successful at Crystal. In fact, without spawning there wouldn't be any trout left. The California Department of Fish and Game doesn't plant the lake and hasn't in more than 50 years. However, water from Crystal runs directly in the CA DFG settling ponds, therefore a few escapees from the hatchery possibility make it into the lake each year.

Crystal harbors a self sustaining population of rainbows, which many anglers give the credit to PG&E for their existence. Following some type of mitigation, PG&E placed spawning gravel in the lake in the Sixties.

Overall though, Crystal isn't a great fishery. Solely fed by springs, the lake has no inlet and unfortunately, the water is gin clear. Because of the high visibility the fish are extremely spooky and tough to reach. The shoreline is composed of tules and marshy in other places. Poor access plays a part in low catch rates. A float tube helps.

For best results, target the south side of the lake. Walk to the shoreline, look for a rocky point, and then look for a white bottom. This signifies springs. Springs tend to hold most of the trout. Most anglers don't do well because they lack patience. If you can spare a few hours - letting a night crawler sit - chances are you'll pick off a wandering trout. Making a few casts and moving on won't cut it.

If you plan to make the trip, supplies are available in Burney. The Crystal Lake outlet stream is closed to fishing from November 16 and the last Saturday in April.

Also nearby are Cassel Forebay, Baum Lake, Hat Creek and Pit River (Section 1).

Crystal Lake

Directions: From the junction of Highway 299 and Interstate 5 in Redding drive east on Highway 299 for 55.8 miles to Cassel Road. Turn right and drive 2.0 miles to Baum Lake Road. Turn left and drive 1.1 miles to the left turnoff for Baum Lake Fishing Access. Park and walk to Crystal Lake. Access can also be found on Cassel Road.

BAUM LAKE

Rating: 9

Species: Rainbow Trout, Brown Trout and Brook Trout

Stocked with 565 pounds of fingerling brown trout, 11,450 pounds of brown trout and 15,070 pounds of rainbow trout.

Facilities: Restrooms and Campgrounds

Need Information? Contact: Vaughn's Sporting Goods (530) 335-2381

Baum Lake is one of Northern California's top trout lakes, that is widely underutilized. This lake doesn't yield your typical bite-size California Department of Fish and Game trout and has the potential to produce several trout to 15 pounds. Surprisingly, most of the trout grow large in Baum rather than in a hatchery.

Runner up only to Whiskeytown Reservoir, Lake Shasta and Upper Hat Creek, Baum is the fourth most heavily planted water in Shasta County. Acre-for-acre, Baum is stuffed with many more fish than the other waters. Each season the California Department of Fish and Game plants 16,350 browns, 176,280 fingerling browns and more than 19,565 three-quarter pound rainbow trout. In addition, more than 324 brood stock Pit River strain rainbows between two-and-eight pounds are also planted. Here's a secret between you and I: because the lake is located within fish throwing distance of the Crystal Lake Hatchery, Baum gets plants of "bonus fish" each year as well. In 2002, 1,360 three-quarter pound brook trout were planted. No brooks were planted in 2003.

(Left to Right) Albino, brook and rainbow trout from the Crystal Lake Hatchery

Best of all, those planted fish grow fast. Wintertime Baum-goers are known to catch several 10 plus pound hogs every few weeks. The food base for the planters is incredible. To see for yourself, head to the lake and pick up a handful of grass or dunk your hands into a pile of moss. Then, get a bowl that your mom would use to make a salad and put all the bugs, insects and critters you could find in that handful into the bowl. Without much effort, you'd be able to fill the bowl up. Yet there's still more feed. Scuds, baitfish and crawdads are also available, not to mention the night crawlers, salmon eggs and globs of

Power Bait anglers lose along the shoreline each year.

The key to being successful is arriving when the big boys will be feeding. Unfortunately, Baum fishes best when the least people are fishing: the winter. For obvious reasons many city slickers avoid fishing Baum when the air is cold. However, that's when conditions are right for lunkers to be caught. In the winter, there are fewer weeds and less food available. Thus, the larger fish are more opt to bite a lure or take down a fly.

Woolly Buggers and size 20-24 midges in black and white and gray and black work great in the winter, as do standard spinners and spoons. Most of the traffic arrives during the summer when the hard core wild trout anglers are off fishing the Fall River, Hat Creek and the Pit River. Limits are still easily attainable, however, monster fish aren't typically landed. The downfall to summer fish is that weeds tend to take over the lake and can make fishing in some places difficult.

Blue winged olives are the hot ticket from March through May. By June, pale morning dunns have come into the mix. Floating night crawlers and standard Power Baits are also big producers.

In the summer, concentrate on fishing where Hat Creek enters into Baum Lake, which in reality is a dammed portion of the creek. This area is excellent, especially for anglers fishing Power Bait or salmon eggs under the bridge or where the water comes out of the Powerhouse. The inlet from Crystal Lake, the pipe where waters spills into the lake from the hatchery and the entire pipe system that feeds Baum are other good options. A boat allows you to reach more and deeper water, yet it's not completely necessary. No gas-powered motors are permitted.

If you plan to make the trip, supplies are available in Burney.

Also nearby are Crystal Lake, Cassel Forebay, Hat Creek and the Pit River.

Directions: From the junction of Highway 299 and Interstate 5 in Redding drive west on Highway 299 for 55.8 miles to Cassel Road. Turn right and drive 2.0 miles to Baum Lake Road. Turn left and drive 1.1 miles to the left turnoff for Baum Lake Fishing Access or continue two-tenths of a mile to the powerhouse.

Baum Lake

CASSEL FOREBAY

Rating: 6

Species: Rainbow
Trout, Brown Trout and
Brook Trout

Stocked with 4,019
pounds of brook trout
and 9,200 pounds of
rainbow trout.

Facilities: Restrooms
and Campgrounds

Need Information?
Contact: Vaughn's
Sporting Goods
(530) 335-2381

In reality, Cassel Forebay is a dammed portion of Hat Creek. The creek is dammed to send water via a flume to the Hat Creek Powerhouse. Putting the explanation of how PG&E does this aside, know one thing: there are always fish to be caught in Cassel. While they may not be huge, they are plentiful and easily attainable to anglers willing to make a few casts.

Each year the California Department of Fish and Game plants more than 18,397 trout in the Forebay: 13,400 are rainbows and 5,920 are brooks. Most of the fish are pound-size planters, which is not a bad size for stocked fish. However, some hogs do exist and are often caught by anglers sight fishing with polarized glasses on the post office side of the bridge. The CA DFG also plants 97 trophy brooks. This cement lined flume (which looks like the California Aqueduct) flows relatively fast and is best approached with crickets, night crawlers, Rebel Minnows and Panther Martin spinners.

There are also some wild fish. Typically, the wild fish show early and late in the season. Rainbows and browns to 18 inches are common to anglers tossing spinners and fly anglers fishing caddis in the evening.

If you plan to make the trip, supplies are available in Burney. Cassel Forebay is closed to fishing from November 16 to the last Saturday in April.

Also nearby are Baum Lake, Crystal Lake and the Pit River.

Directions: From the junction of Highway 299 and Interstate 5 in Redding, drive east on Highway 299 for 55.8 miles to Cassel Road. Turn right and drive 3.6 miles to a bridge over Hat Creek.

Cassel Forebay

HAT CREEK (UPPER)

Rating: 7

Species: Brook Trout, Brown Trout and Rainbow Trout

Stocked with 13,040 pounds of brook trout and 16,650 pounds of rainbow trout.

Facilities: Restrooms, Picnic Areas, Campgrounds, RV Hookups, General Store, Bait & Tackle, Lodging, Restaurants, Showers and a Visitor Center

Need Information? Contact: Lassen National Forest (530) 336-5521, Hat Creek Resort (530) 335-7121

Many people often have a false perception of Hat Creek. Contrary to popular belief, Hat Creek isn't just a wild trout stream set aside for fly fishermen. Upper Hat Creek, which runs along and crosses under Highway 44 and 89 several times, is just the opposite. This section is reserved for anyone who wants to fish. Bait casters, fly anglers, spin fishermen and others are all welcome.

Upper Hat Creek is one of the most heavily fished and planted creeks in California. Each year, the California Department of Fish and Game dumps more than 20,080 brook trout and 28,840 rainbow trout into an eight-mile section of the stream. The creek gets hit so hard that from opener through mid-November the CA DFG stocks it twice a week. Hat also harbors a wild population of rainbows, brooks and browns. Plus, the CA DFG plants 97 three-to-eight-pound brooks.

Upper Hat is the ideal spot for a family camping trip. Hundreds of picnic areas and campgrounds line the river. There are also motels, cabins for rent, RV Parks, gift shops and the occasional restaurant. You can grab all the amenities you need or obtain that woodsy feeling. The choice is yours.

While loaded with trout, Upper Hat isn't necessarily the easiest creek to fish. The spring fed creek maintains high volume year-round. It rarely fluctuates. Also, it's composed of mostly rocky, riffle-like pools. Basically, it's fast moving water and unless you know how to properly approach it, don't expect to do well.

The key is fishing the transition zones where fast water meets slow water, dropping bait behind large boulders and drifting bait under overhanging banks. The CA DFG plants the same places each week. Here's a low down on where to go and what to look for at each spot.

Heading east on Highway 44 out of Redding, the first section of the creek that is planted is at Twin Bridges. This area can be tough to fish because of fast, shallow water. You'll find mostly riffles and fewer trout in this area than downstream. Primitive camping is popular along the creek.

Next stop is Big Pine Camp where flooded trees and campsites are abundant. Fish behind stumps in the campground area. A few downed pines have become submerged residents and established fish holding pools. Drop Pautzke salmon eggs behind the logs and you should do well.

Moving on, Big Springs is one of Hat's major water sources. This roadside spring can be seen bubbling up from under the road. Fortunately, you'll be able to spot any fish in this gin clear water. If you can't see the trout, plan on lowering baits under weeds and other plant life. From where the springs pour into Hat Creek, head 30 yards downstream, to find a large trash can size boulder in the creek where trout hide behind. The rest of the area is fast moving water. Your only chance is to fish the banks on the highway side of the creek. What I'd do is use a small Rebel crawdad.

Hat Creek Resort is located on private property, yet it does allow anglers to fish on its grounds. Noticing this act of kindness the CA DFG makes biweekly plants at the resort to accommodate the visitors. Fish both sides of the creek and the highway.

If you are a day user don't bother fishing at Hat Creek Campground. While trout are always present fishing pressure is high. Campers should fish the inside of the weed lines or in them if you are a good caster.

One of the most popular and heavily fished areas is the Old Station Day Use Area. It's not uncommon for hundreds of anglers to fish this section daily. Also, wheelchair access is available. Pay attention to fishing the bends. Fish the areas where the bend corrects itself (the tail end of it). There is a 200 yard section of good, fishable water.

Subway Cave Campground provides lots of low gradient water, but is predominately a campers only spot. A short distance downstream is an unsigned dirt road with a bridge that crosses over the creek. There are a few larger pools in this high desert like area.

Rocky Point Campground is one of the best spots on Upper Hat. Finally! Pools that are easily fishable. The campground is situated in a heavily wooded area that is kept cool by a canopy of trees. This is a hit and move section. There are pools every 10 feet and some good over hanging banks. A bridge was recently built to allow you to fish both sides of the creek. While Rocky Point has a much higher gradient than the Subway Cave area its still easy to catch fish.

Bridge Day Use and Campground offers a lot of user friendly and fishable water. There's a great pool above and below the bridge and several pools downstream of the bridge that provide holding areas for trout. Toss salmon eggs and Power Bait or drift a night crawler or cricket.

The last place to target is Honn Campground. Honn is not located on Hat Creek. It's a canal that holds water that is diverted off Hat Creek and then back to Hat Creek. Offering wheelchair access this small creek has slow moving water that is easy to fish with bait. It's too small to fish lures.

If you plan to make the trip, supplies are available in Burney and Old Station. Hat Creek is closed to fishing from November 16 to the last Saturday in April.

Also nearby are Plum Canyon Reservoir, Subway Cave, Ice Caves, Lassen National Park and the wild trout section of Hat Creek.

Directions: *From the junction of Interstate 5 and Highway 44 in Redding drive east on Highway 44 for 55 miles. For the next several miles the highway parallels the creek.*

Hat Creek

LOST CREEK

Rating: 5

Species: Rainbow Trout

Stocks: None

Facilities: None

Need Information?
Contact: Vaughn's
Sporting Goods
(530) 335-2381

Lost Creek is one of the smallest and least fished waters in the greater Burney area. The reasons are understandable: the stream is small, offers limited access, holds small fish, isn't planted by the California Department of Fish and Game and has no facilities. Due to the above mentioned reasons few anglers fish it, which is why others specifically plan a trip to this relatively unknown stream that is a tributary to Hat Creek. Situated in the Lassen National Forest, Lost Creek is a small to medium size trout stream that poses a chance at catching small, but wild rainbow trout. Most trout average five-to-seven inches, with the occasional 10 inch fish.

Lost Creek is best fished with a fly rod. A two-weight rod with a 6x tippet works best. Because the streambed is overwhelmed with trees and brush, wading is the best way to go. Dry flies can also be productive. Caddis, adams and pale morning dunns are best.

Look for shadows, overhanging trees and small pockets of water to fish. Some anglers fish nymphs, however, the shallow water can make it difficult. If you opt to, try a caddis nymph, pheasant tail or prince nymph in size 18. A size 1/64 Panther Martin or a No. 1 Mepps will also work.

A wild rainbow from Lost Creek

The best access is available from the small forebay on upstream to the Wilderness Unlimited Boundary.

If you plan to make the trip, supplies are available in Burney. Lost Creek is closed to fishing from November 16 to the last Saturday in April.

Also nearby are Hat Creek, Manzanita Lake and Lassen National Park.

Directions: *From the junction of Interstate 5 and Highway 299 in Redding, drive east on Highway 299 for 53.7 miles to the junction with Highway 89. Turn right on Highway 89 and continue to Wilcox Road. Turn left and continue to the creek.*

PLUM CANYON RESERVOIR

Rating: 5

Species: Largemouth Bass

Stocks: None

Facilities: None

Need Information?
Contact: Vaughn's Sporting Goods
(530) 335-3226

Sometimes locals take fish planting matters into their own hands. At a place like Plum Canyon Reservoir, these practices do no harm to the fishery. At 4,698 feet in the Lassen National Forest, Plum Canyon Reservoir is a small pond on the Hat Creek Rim that is filled most years by Plum Creek. When water levels are sufficient, a few locals catch bass at local lakes and transport them into Plum to create their own private fishery void of tourists.

Most of the time they are successful, except for the odd year when the reservoir goes dry. Plum Canyon is a place where you can bring a kid to catch as many bass as you desire. Unfortunately, those bass aren't going to bend your rod. The reservoir is stuffed with six-to-eight-inch bass that will chomp on a mini night crawler or an olive Pistol Pete.

If you plan to make the trip, supplies are available in Old Station. The road to the reservoir is closed during the winter and early spring.

Also nearby are the Subway Cave, Hat Creek and Lassen National Park.

Directions: *From Interstate 5 driving north in Redding, exit Highway 44 east. When you leave the off ramp and are on the highway, reset your odometer and drive 59.8 miles to the Highway 44/89 junction in Old Station. Staying on Highway 44, turn right and drive 2.7 miles to the left turnoff for the Hat Creek Rim Scenic Viewing Area. Turn teft, drive 50 yards and make a quick right on Forest Service Road 34N34. Continue 1.7 miles to the reservoir on the right.*

A Plum Canyon Reservoir largemouth

NORTH BATTLE CREEK RESERVOIR

Rating: 5

Species: Rainbow Trout and Brown Trout

Stocked with 3,800 pounds of rainbow trout.

Facilities: Restrooms and Campgrounds

Need Information? Contact: Lassen National Forest (530) 336-5521

The North Fork of Battle Creek Reservoir can be a sleeper fishery for trout. Each year the California Department of Fish and Game plants roughly 5,720 rainbow trout into this 80-acre reservoir that rests at 5,900 feet in the Lassen National Forest, a few miles away from Hat Creek and Lassen National Park. North Battle Creek Reservoir is similar to nearby Mc Cumber Reservoir. It is planted each year with three-quarter pound rainbow trout and has self-sustaining populations of wild browns.

The difference is that North Battle Creek Reservoir gets fewer fishermen, which is astonishing considering the number of trout that are stocked. It's obvious that many fish holdover, although the CA DFG has reported fish kills due to poor water quality. While trollers may land some trout greater than two pounds, most of your creel will be in the three-quarter to one-and-a-half-pound class.

Trollers see the best action, but you may have trouble launching a big boat. The dirt road in can be rough. Unfortunately, the boat launch itself isn't paved, but it's good enough for boats 15 feet and smaller. Trolling night crawlers and flashers, small trolling flies or small spoons are sure bets for trout.

North Battle Creek Reservoir

Fly anglers hit the lake in the spring and fall when trout are commonly rising. There's plenty of shoreline access available.

If you plan to make the trip, supplies are available in Old Station. From fall through early summer call the Forest Service for updated conditions. The road may be closed due to downed trees and snow.

Also nearby is McCumber Reservoir, Hat Creek (Upper) and Lassen National Park.

Directions: *From Lassen National Park, drive east on Highway 44 to the left turnoff for North Battle Creek Reservoir. Follows the road signs to the lake.*

MCCUMBER RESERVOIR

Rating: 6

Species: Rainbow Trout and Brown Trout

Stocked with 3,200 pounds of rainbow trout.

Facilities: Campgrounds and Restrooms

Need Information?
Contact: Lassen National Forest
(530) 336-5521

McCumber Reservoir could be an excellent trout lake, however, because the lake stratifies so hard, trout are faced with poor water quality in the summer. Despite the problem, the California Department of Fish and Game plants more than 5,720 half-pound, or better, rainbows in the 85-acre reservoir. Fishing is better in late fall and winter when the surviving trout increase their activity levels as cooler water prevails.

Anglers who use an electric trolling motor to drag Needlefish, a night crawler behind a flasher or dodger or a red Cripplure can expect to do well on rainbows and the occasional brown. For browns, fish a Woolly Bugger near the stumps towards the back of the lake in fall and winter.

No gas-powered motors are permitted on McCumber. It tends to remain a quiet lake where bait, fly and spin fishermen take part in catching the planters and resident browns. The lake is set in a heavily forested area off Highway 44 near Lassen National Park. It can be tough to reach in the winter when snow falls. A dirt road is necessary to reach the lake, however, it's a lot easier to reach than North Battle Creek Reservoir.

If you plan to make the trip, supplies are available in Shingletown. In winter, call ahead for road conditions. The road may be closed due to snow.

Also nearby are Manzanita Lake, Bailey Creek and Hat Creek (Upper).

Directions: From the junction of Interstate 5 and Highway 44 east in Redding, drive east on Highway 44 for 36.8 miles to Lake Mc Cumber Road. Turn left and drive 1.8 miles to the lake.

McCumber Reservoir

GRACE LAKE

Rating: 7

Species: Rainbow
Trout and Brook Trout

Stocked with 21,500
pounds of rainbow
trout and 800 pounds
of brook trout.

Facilities: Picnic Area
and Restrooms

Need Information?
Contact: California
Department of Fish
and Game
(530) 225-2300

While many lakes and streams off the Highway 44 corridor between Susanville and Redding are widely overlooked by anglers, Grace Lake is one of the few waters that isn't. Grace is a favorite day-use spot to thousands of anglers in Northern California and it's no secret why. At only five acres, Grace is a small pond maintained and operated by PG&E that is overloaded with trout. Anglers enjoy easy access and steady action all year. Less than a 30-minute drive from Redding, anglers can almost be assured of catching fish.

The California Department of Fish and Game plants 1,520 half-pound brook trout, 34,500 half-pound rainbow trout and 60 two-to-four-pound rainbows from spring through fall at this reservoir near Shingletown. Weekly plants ensure solid action for bait anglers, spin casters and fly fishermen.

Most anglers set up shop on the dam and fish Power Bait, inflated night crawlers or a fly and bubble combo, yet, anglers with a fly rod can see excellent action on mid-day mayfly hatches in the spring and early summer.

If you plan to make the trip, supplies are available in Shingletown.

Also nearby are Nora Lake and Keswick Canal.

Directions: From Interstate 5 driving north in Redding, exit Highway 44 east. When you leave the off ramp and are on the highway, reset your odometer and drive 26.6 miles to Wilson Ranch Road. Turn right and drive nine-tenths of a mile to an unsigned dirt road on the left. Turn left and continue seven-tenths of a mile to Grace Lake on the left.

Grace Lake

NORA LAKE

Rating: 5

Species: Rainbow Trout

Stocked with 1,900 pounds of rainbow trout.

Facilities: Restrooms, Picnic Areas and a Fishing Pier

Nora Lake is Grace Lake's smaller neighbor that gets little fishing pressure and a relatively small allotment of trout, yet offers good access and a solid shot at catching planters. Nora is a 3.5-acre lake used by PG&E, who allows anglers day-use access. A few minutes from Shingletown, Nora is located in the foothills only a short drive from Lassen National Park. Most of its' anglers tend to be day-users from local communities, rather than travelers from Redding.

Nora can be fished with either a spinner or bait. If you opt to fish with bait its' best to fish off the piers rather than the shallow section you'll see when you first drive in. Also, access can be difficult on the roadside of the lake where tules cover much of the shore. Looking to toss a spinner? Head over to the inlet where Keswick Canal pumps in. Here, you can toss small spoons or spinners into the fast moving current. Make sure to use a slow retrieve. The slow return allows the lure to flutter in the water and reach greater depths than a fast retrieve that keeps the bait right on the surface. The California Department of Fish and Game plants 3,080 rainbows each year. This is a spot where drifting an Orange Deluxe Balls O'Fire egg is a smart choice.

Nora Lake

Trip info for Grace Lake also applies to Nora Lake.

Directions: *From Interstate 5 going north in Redding, exit Highway 44 east. When you leave the off ramp and are on the highway, reset your odometer and drive 26.6 miles to Wilson Ranch Road. Turn right and drive nine-tenths of a mile to an unsigned dirt road on the left. Turn left and continue seven-tenths of a mile to Grace Lake on the left. Continue three-tenths of a mile past Grace to Nora Lake.*

KESWICK CANAL

Rating: 4

Species: Rainbow Trout

Stocked with 700 pounds of rainbow trout.

Facilities: Restrooms and a Picnic Area

Location is the key to being successful at Keswick Canal. For many anglers, fishing the canal is not good because they tend to target areas that aren't productive. There's one way to figure out if you are fishing the right place: if you can see Nora Lake, chances are you aren't going to have a banner day. Where Keswick runs into Nora and for roughly 100 yards upstream, Keswick flows fast and can be difficult to fish for beginners and anglers who aren't familiar with fishing fast flowing water. If you are going to target this type of water here, make sure to use bait and concentrate on undercut banks with Rebel crawdads.

To ensure more success, drive past Nora on the road that parallels the canal. The California Department of Fish and Game scatters trout from Nora for roughly one-mile upstream. As you get further upstream from the lake, the canal moves slower and slower. One of the best places is where a small stream dumps into the canal and at spots where the canal bends. In this section small spinners and bait will get the job done. Keswick is planted with

Keswick Canal

roughly 1,085 rainbows each year and it receives little pressure. Find the right hole and you'll be successful.

Trip info for Grace Lake also applies to Keswick Canal.

Directions: *From Interstate 5 driving north in Redding, exit Highway 44 east. When you leave the off ramp and are on the highway, reset your odometer and drive 26.6 miles to Wilson Ranch Road. Turn right and drive nine-tenths of a mile to an unsigned dirt road on the left. Turn left and continue seven-tenths of a mile to Grace Lake on the left. Continue three-tenths of a mile past Grace to Nora Lake. Keswick Canal feeds into Nora Lake.*

DARRAH CREEK POND

Rating: 2

Species: Rainbow Trout

Stocks: None

Facilities: Restrooms

Need Information?
Contact: California
Department of Fish and
Game (530) 474-3141

Anglers can blame themselves for the lack of fish at Darrah Creek Pond. This pond, located just outside the grounds of the Darrah Springs Fish Hatchery, used to be planted with thousands of trout each year. It was a favorite spot for anglers who wanted to catch an easy limit of trout.

However in 2001, the California Department of Fish and Game got tired of picking up trash left behind by anglers at the pond (which is a mere three-tenths of an acre) and decided to no longer plant fish. Many anglers still fish for trout, but they don't see much action. Other than a few escapees from the fish hatchery there are no trout to speak of in the pond.

If there are any trout you won't have a problem seeing them. The pond is clear, no deeper than three feet and smaller than many backyard swimming pools. If anglers can learn to be responsible and begin cleaning up after themselves, the allotment may soon return. When, and if it does, plan on casting just about anything into the water to catch a quick limit. Until then, you'll have to come to the hatchery to look at the rearing ponds. Leave the rods at home.

If you plan to make the trip, supplies are available in Palo Cedro.

Also nearby are Digger Creek, Digger Creek Ranch and Antelope Creek (North Fork).

Directions: *From Interstate 5 driving north in Redding, exit Highway 44 east. When you leave the off ramp and are on the highway, reset your odometer and drive 20.4 miles to Black Butte Road. Turn right, drive 3.4 miles and veer left at a split in the road. Drive 3.5 miles and turn right at the sign for the Darrah Springs Hatchery. Continue one-mile and veer right at a split in the road. Then, make a quick left, drive three-tenths of a mile and veer right. Drive one-tenth of a mile to the pond.*

Darrah Creek Pond

SOUTH COW CREEK

Rating: 6

Species: Rainbow Trout

Stocked with 200 pounds of rainbow trout.

Facilities: None

Need Information? Contact: California Department of Fish and Game (530) 225-2300

There's a huge different between Little Cow Creek located off Highway 299 and South Cow Creek, which flows under Ponderosa Road between Whitmore and Shingletown. While Little Cow Creek is too warm for trout by June and may turn to a mere trickle by summer, South Cow Creek is suitable for trout year-round. If you show up in June and wade through the water without waders, you probably won't make it longer than five minutes without scurrying out. This water is cold, but fish love it.

Unfortunately, the California Department of Fish and Game only plants the stream with 230 pound-class rainbows each year, far less than are needed to supply the anglers who fish here. South Cow Creek has excellent fishing access, deep pools, nice pockets, rifles and even a few runs. This stream deserves thousands of fish each year, as it can support them.

If you plan to make the trip, supplies are available in Shingletown. South Cow Creek is closed to fishing from November 16 to the last Saturday in April.

Also nearby are Keswick Canal, Grace Lake, Nora Lake and Mc Cumber Reservoir.

Directions: From Interstate 5 driving north in Redding, exit Highway 44 east. When you leave the off ramp and are on the highway, reset your odometer and drive 23.5 miles to Ponderosa Way. Turn left and drive 1.5 miles to a split in the road. Veer left, drive one-half mile and turn left going back onto Ponderosa Way. Continue 8.1 miles to a bridge over the creek.

South Cow Creek

OLD COW CREEK

Rating: 4

Species: Rainbow Trout

Stocked with 150 pounds of rainbow trout.

Facilities: None

Need Information?
Contact: California
Department of Fish and
Game (530) 225-2200

Each year the California Department of Fish and Game plants 255 rainbow trout into Old Cow Creek. The plants or plant, depending on how many fish are stocked at one time, usually takes place in the summer when only a few anglers come up here to fish. Mostly the folks who live in the region see the truck and head down to the creek to attempt to nab a few trout in the fast flowing water.

Now that you know how many fish are planted, do you still want to fish Old Cow Creek? My guess is that most of you will say no, and that's probably a good idea. Old Cow Creek doesn't see enough fish to handle much fishing pressure. Also, poor access can limit an anglers' effectiveness. If you must take a stab at these pound-size bows, try dipping Pautzke salmon eggs behind boulders, in small pockets or any small pool you can locate.

If you plan to make the trip, supplies are available in Whitmore. Old Cow Creek is closed to fishing from November 16 to the last Saturday in April.

Also nearby are Kilarc Reservoir, South Cow Creek and Clover Creek.

Directions: From Interstate 5 driving north in Redding, exit Highway 44 east. When you leave the off ramp and are on the highway, reset your odometer and drive 23.5 miles to Ponderosa Way. Turn left and drive 1.5 miles to a split in the road. Veer left, drive one-half mile and turn left going back onto Ponderosa Way. Continue 11.4 miles to Whitmore Road and turn right. Drive one-half mile to Fern Road and turn left. Continue 3.9 miles to the bridge north of the powerhouse.

Old Cow Creek

CLOVER CREEK

Rating: 5

Species: Rainbow Trout

Stocked with 150 pounds of rainbow trout.

Facilities: None

Need Information? Contact: Shasta National Forest (530) 246-5112

Sometimes you just want to head down to the stream and fish exactly where you know fish will be. This is possible each time you visit Clover Creek. The California Department of Fish and Game only plants one-tenth of a mile of Clover Creek, which most of the time translates into one pool. It's not hard to miss.

Standing on the road, if you look downstream, the pool below the culvert is a dandy, ideal for stocked trout. It's big enough to sustain all the trout and possesses enough incoming volume to keep the water well oxygenated. Fishing is typically good as long as plants occur and kids aren't swimming in the water. Each season the CA DFG plants roughly 167 trout, not enough to raise your eyebrows, yet enough to supply the few anglers that fish Clover. (No trout were planted in 2003. The stocking numbers used here are from 2002.)

This is your typical put-and-take Power Bait, Pautzke salmon eggs and spinner stream. Arrive within a few weeks of the last fish stocking and you'll do just fine. Remember, fish below the culvert.

If you plan to make the trip, supplies are available in Whitmore. Clover Creek is closed to fishing from November 16 to the last Saturday in April.

Also nearby are Old Cow Creek, Kilarc Reservoir and South Cow Creek.

Directions: *From Interstate 5 driving north in Redding, exit Highway 44 east. When you leave the off ramp and are on the highway reset your odometer and drive 23.5 miles to Ponderosa Way. Turn left and drive 1.5 miles to a split in the road. Veer left, drive one-half mile and turn left going back onto Ponderosa Way. Continue 11.4 miles to Whitmore Road and turn right. Drive one-half mile to Fern Road and turn left. Continue 7.5 miles to Oak Run to Fern Road. Turn right and drive 1.2 miles to the creek.*

Clover Creek

KILARC RESERVOIR

Rating: 5

Species: Rainbow Trout

Stocked with 4,000 pounds of rainbow trout.

Facilities: Restrooms and a Picnic Area

Need Information? Contact: California Department of Fish and Game (530) 225-2300

Some places are so far out of the way that few anglers spend the time to fish them. Kilarc Reservoir is one of those places. At 4.5 acres, Kilarc is a small holding pool that PG&E uses most of the year. The California Department of Fish and Game takes advantage of the generally consistent water levels and cool temperatures by planting trout each summer.

Kilarc is a good jaunt from Redding, and with so many other fishing options closer and more diverse, few day-users come here. In fact, other than a few Whitmore locals you can typically find plenty of open shoreline. Heavy plants keep catch rates high for anglers tossing spoons, dunking night crawlers or using Power Bait. Each summer the CA DFG unloads 5,710 trout, some of which run between three-and-six pounds.

If you ever fished Kilarc when the water is down, you've witnessed what great structure this lake offers. You have several options: the incoming flow of water has cut a steep channel in the lake that holds hungry trout, as well as the dam and tules.

If you plan to make the trip, supplies are available in Whitmore.

Also nearby are South Cow Creek, Old Cow Creek and Clover Creek.

Directions: *From Interstate 5 driving north in Redding, exit Highway 44 east. When you leave the off ramp and are on the highway, reset your odometer and drive 23.5 miles to Ponderosa Way. Turn left and drive 1.5 miles to a split in the road. Veer left, drive one-half mile and turn left going back onto Ponderosa Way. Continue 11.4 miles to Whitmore Road and turn right. Drive one-half mile to Fern Road and turn left. Continue 2.3 miles to Kilarc Reservoir Road and turn right. Drive 3.4 miles on the dirt road to the reservoir.*

Kilarc Reservoir

LITTLE COW CREEK

Rating: 4
Species: Rainbow Trout
Stocked with 450 pounds of rainbow trout.
Facilities: None
Need Information? Contact: Vaughn's Sporting Goods (530) 335-2381

To say that Little Cow Creek is a marginal put-and-take is an overstatement. Little Cow Creek is a poor put-and-take fishery because of several factors that include little public access, small numbers of fish planted, inadequate summer water temperatures and volume. Little Cow Creek is one of the easiest streams for Redding residents to reach; however, it's only planted with 832 rainbow trout per season.

Little Cow Creek parallels Highway 299 west of Round Mountain and east of Redding. However, only small parcels of land are open to the public. The California Department of Fish and Game wisely plants only a few fish. Fortunately, the rainbows tend to be near a pound, much larger than the average trout planted in many other local waters. The trick is arriving when the stocking truck does.

Springtime is the only chance you have. From the opener until roughly late May plants take place every week while water temperatures and volume are sufficient for trout. This is a Power Bait/salmon egg stream. Your best bet is to look for pullouts alongside the highway. Walk down the paths on the steep bank, make a few casts and if you don't see any fish, move on. Driving east from Redding, the best pullouts are located at 18.1, 18.3, 18.5, 18.7 and 19.6 miles. All are located on the right side of the Highway.

Little Cow Creek

If you plan to make the trip, supplies are available in Redding. Little Cow Creek is closed to fishing from November 16 to the last Saturday in April.

Also nearby are Hatchet Creek Falls, Montgomery Creek Falls and Hatchet Creek.

Directions: *From the junction of Interstate 5 and Highway 299 in Redding, drive east on Highway 299 for 16.5 miles to where the highway parallels the creek.*

HATCHET CREEK

Rating: 5

Species: Rainbow Trout

Stocked with 1,100 pounds of rainbow trout.

Facilities: None

Need Information? Contact: Vaughn's Sporting Goods (530) 335-2381

There are many streams in the mountains east of Redding that get pounded day after day by day-users, campers and locals. These streams need to be stocked bi-weekly, weekly or every other week to maintain adequate populations of catchable trout. However, there are a few streams that are frequently planted that don't get bombarded by thousands of anglers. Roughly 10 miles west of the tourist trap of Burney, Hatchet Creek is planted often, yet fished only sporadically. Nearly 1,900 trout are planted annually.

The section of the creek located off Moose Camp Road is less than a half-mile from Highway 299, but for some reason, is seldom fished. Most likely it's because it isn't heavily publicized and doesn't offer any facilities or nearby campgrounds. Action can be found both up and downstream of the bridge. The best section of water is upstream of the rock wall, where Goat Creek spills into Hatchet. This pool most always holds fish. Don't, however, discount fishing under the bridge. On blazing summer days, the trout hide under the bridge where the sun isn't beating down on the water. You can get away with fishing small spinners, yet the stream is better designed for Power Bait and Pautzke salmon eggs.

Hatchet Creek

If you plan to make the trip, supplies are available in Burney. Hatchet Creek is closed to fishing from November 16 to the last Saturday in April.

Also nearby are Hatchet Creek Falls, Montgomery Creek Falls and Burney Creek (Upper).

Directions: *From the junction of Interstate 5 and Highway 299 in Redding, drive east on Highway 299 for 37.4 miles to Moose Camp Road and turn right. Continue four-tenths of a mile to the bridge and creek.*

PIT RIVER (SECTION 7)

Rating: 7

Species: Rainbow Trout, Brown Trout, Channel Catfish, Largemouth Bass, Smallmouth Bass, Spotted Bass, Sturgeon, Crappie, Bluegill and Squawfish

Stocks: None

Facilities: None

Pit River Section 7 can be better described as the headwaters of the Pit River Arm of Shasta Lake. Depending on when you arrive, angling opportunities can differ drastically. If Lake Shasta is at full pool, or within 10 feet of topping off, this area will in fact look like a lake. However if draw downs have begun, you'll be fortunate to find a long dyke between the Pit River Bridge near Potem Creek and Pit 7 Dam.

When available, this dam (at Fenders Flat) provides access for anglers to cash in on a mixed bag of warm and cold water fish. Bait fishing is the easiest way to hook up. Anglers set up chairs on the dam and toss out night crawlers or crickets downriver.

Pit 7

Targeting a specific species can be difficult. Bass, trout, pan fish and catfish are commonly found in this area. They position themselves to enjoy food being brought in via the Pit River. Toss out a line and wait for a nibble. Many anglers catch 16-18 inch browns in this area as they look to spawn. Some anglers launch boats below the dam and fish the steep hillsides for bass, but you don't necessarily need a boat to do well.

Trip info for Pit River (Section 4) also applies to Pit River (Section 7).

Directions: *From the junction of Interstate 5 and Highway 299 east in Redding, drive east on Highway 299 for 29.6 miles to Fenders Ferry Road. Turn left and drive 8.1 miles to a split in the road. Veer right and drive a half mile to a split in the road. Veer left and continue a half-mile to the river.*

PIT RIVER (SECTION 5)

Rating: 7

Species: Squawfish, Smallmouth Bass, Rainbow Trout and Brown Trout

Stocks: None

Facilities: None

There are several things you'll notice about fishing Pit 5 as opposed to Pit 3 and 4. While Pit 3 and 4 are heavily wooded, have overgrown banks and difficult wading, Pit 5 offers a different scene. The water is gin clear and the banks are mostly open and composed of loose softball size rocks. In addition, the river itself tends to have less pocket water; riffles, pools and runs are more like it. Pit 5 also receives more pressure from non-anglers. Weekends can be swamped by swimmers and teenagers partying along the riverbed.

Nonetheless, fishing is pretty good. Most rainbows average 12-16 inches, however, fish to five pounds aren't uncommon. Unfortunately, what oftentimes appears to be a big bow will enter your net as a huge squawfish. When it comes to catching trout, the trick is to be willing to lose gear. As with other sections of the Pit, it's imperative that you fish the bottom to do well. Use caution though, the bottom is comprised of fields of boulders making snags frequent.

Look for seams, riffles and the upper portion of pools. Don't pay much attention to slow moving water or runs. A yellow Panther Martin with red spots and a silver blade can be extremely effective if fished along the edges of seams. A plus is that access is better at Section 5 and crowds tend to be lighter and less snobbish when it comes to fishing with bait and spinners. In fact, fly anglers are a minority. Pit 5 begins at the Pit 4 Powerhouse and runs to the Pit 6 Dam.

Trip info for Pit River (Section 4) also applies to Pit River (Section 5).

Directions: *From the junction of Highway 299 and Interstate 5 in Redding, drive west on Highway 299 for 53.7 miles to the junction with Highway 89. Turn left onto Highway 89 and drive 4.1 miles to Clark Creek Road. Turn left and drive 3.7 miles to Five Corners. Take the left fork and continue roughly 15 miles Pit 5 Lake. Pit 5 runs from here on down the road for several miles. It can also be accessed via a 13.2 miles drive on Big Bend Road from Highway 299. Turn left on Pit 5 Road and drive four miles to the river. Hagen Flat Road also provides access.*

Jean Rodgers caught this Pit River bow on a

PIT RIVER (SECTION 4)

Rating: 7

Species: Squawfish, Smallmouth Bass, Rainbow Trout and Brown Trout

Stocks: None

Facilities: None

Need Information?
Contact: Vaughn's
Sporting Goods
(530) 335-2381

It's funny how anglers are always breaking the law to try and catch more fish. This is evident at Pit 4 Reservoir, where some anglers make a habit out of fishing from float tubes and car top boats so they have better access to trout and bass. Pit 4 Reservoir is a dammed portion of the Pit River, found just downriver of the Pit 3 Powerhouse and the famed wild trout section. The reservoir harbors rainbow trout and smallmouth bass, but can be tough to fish from shore.

Your best bet to it fish where the water is released from the powerhouse. Fortunately, there is drive-to access. Fish stack up here to cash in on incoming food that was chopped up in the turbines. Try dunking a night crawler or tossing a quarter-ounce Kastmaster in this area. Pit 4 Reservoir is roughly 3.5 miles long.

Below the reservoir is the stretch known as Pit 4. This stretch is nearly identical to Pit 3, however, it has no angling restrictions. That means anglers can fish with bait. In fact, night crawlers are an excellent way to nab 12-16 inch rainbows. Plunk crawlers in pockets and holes. Spinners can work well in larger pools, but just like Pit 3, you'll need to get your bait on the bottom. Don't mess with fishing slow moving water and long runs unless you are looking to catch squawfish. Trout tend to harbor in riffle-like water in this river.

This section of the Pit suffers from poor access. There are some access points that bring you close to the river, yet other places it's more than a 400-foot near vertical drop from the road down to the water. To best inquire about access point invest in a good map or consult with the locals who know these areas well. The hard to reach areas are seldom fished, however can offer excellent fishing.

If you plan to make the trip, supplies are available in Burney. The Pit River is closed to fishing from November 16 to the last Saturday in April.

Also nearby are Iron Canyon Reservoir, Pit Section 3 and 5.

Directions: From the junction of Highway 299 and Interstate 5 in Redding, drive west on Highway 299 for 53.7 miles to the junction with Highway 89. Turn left onto Highway 89 and drive 4.1 miles to Clark Creek Road. Turn left and drive 3.7 miles to Five Corners. Take the left fork and continue 5.5 miles Pit 4 Lake. Pit IV runs from here on down the road for roughly 10 miles.

Pit 4

PIT RIVER (PIT 3)

Rating: 8

Species: Squawfish, Rainbow Trout and Brown Trout

Stocks: None

Facilities: None

The Pit River can be chopped, sliced and diced into several sections. In fact, each of these sections fish differently, offer drastic changes in water temperature, fish species, size and quantity. The Pit has so much to offer that many anglers would be content with learning how to fish the Pit exclusively for several years.

While the entire main stem of the Pit River is framed by wild fish, only one section is designated as a wild trout water: Pit 3. Located directly below Lake Britton Dam, this section of the Pit is popular with fly fishermen. Stretching roughly 5.5 miles, this water is governed by special regulations. There is a two-fish, 18-inch minimum size limit from the base of Britton's dam to the Pit 3 Powerhouse. Most of the river consists of pocket water. While resident browns exist, 12-15 inch rainbows are the dominant species.

A Pit River bow

Spinners work great, however, many fly fishermen will look at you in disgust if they see you tossing Panther Martins. Let 'em. As long as you abide by regulations and clamp all barbs down on your hooks, you are in compliance with the law and fully legal. This water belongs to everyone, not just anglers who've spent half their paycheck to fish here with a guide.

If you own a fly rod, you really don't need to hire a guide. Knowing where to fish is half the battle. Be forewarned that wading this section of the Pit can be a chore. A wading staff is necessary as is extreme caution with each step. This river is slippery and dangerous. Access to this portion of the river is doable, yet not convenient or easy. You have to work to fish it. Brush, trees, blackberry bushes, spider webs and other nuisances are a problem. You need waders to fish the river. Access is available by walking down several flights of stairs at the dam or via short walks from the road that parallels the river. None of the access is easy.

High stick nymphing with indicators is popular. Fishing surface flies isn't a big hit. Fly fishermen should target faster, swifter pocket water and make sure to get their offerings down. Many anglers fish with droppers to be able to figure out where the fish are feeding. This can be a good idea, especially in summer. Spin casters have the option of targeting pools, runs and holes, as well as those areas you'd opt to send a fly through.

Whereas casting spinners allows you to cover more water, if you add a split shot 12 inches above your silver bladed Panther Martin with a yellow body, your lure will go down deeper and stay in the strike zone longer. High stick nymphing can be tough because getting the right drift to escort your nymph down to the fish can be a chore. To be more effective, pay close attention to presenting your fly in the strike zone.

There are several hatches to key in on each year. While caddis come off throughout the season, many anglers arrive from mid-May until mid-June to fish the salmon fly hatch. Late in the day in September and October, plan on an excellent October caddis hatch.

Nymphing with size six and eight dark stonefly nymphs and black rubber legs, size 16 prince nymphs and copper johns are your best bets, but don't discount bead headed pheasant tails and caddis pupa in cream and green.

When it comes to fishing the surface, salmon flies are key in May and June. Elk hair caddis in size 16 are typical on summer evenings. Falls marks the time for October cadis. Try a size six or eight orange stimulator.

Trip info for Pit River (Section 4) also applies to Pit River (Section 3).

Directions: *From the junction of Highway 299 and Interstate 5 in Redding, drive west on Highway 299 for 53.7 miles to the junction with Highway 89. Turn left onto Highway 89 and drive 4.1 miles to Clark Creek Road. Turn left and drive 3.7 miles to Five Corners. Take the left fork and continue to the river access. (The river can also be reached via a stairway on the dam.)*

Author Chris Shaffer caught this Pit River bow on a Panther Martin in June on Pit 3.

ROCK CREEK

Rating: 5

Species: Rainbow Trout

Stocked with 500
pounds of rainbow
trout.

Facilities: None

Need Information?
Contact: Vaughn's
Sporting Goods
(530) 335-2381

When it comes to planting trout, the California Department of Fish and Game tends to stock in places where the fish are going to be easily accessible to anglers and still convenient for CA DFG employees. At Rock Creek, a tributary to the Pit River, the easiest place to plant rainbow trout is downstream of the culvert. The fish truck drivers simply drive onto the culvert, dip a few nets full of fish and toss them into the pool.

This pool isn't just any pool, rather a place where tons of fish can hang. It's large, well oxygenated and easily fishable. Each spring, roughly 925 rainbows are planted. Most of those fish are taken the week they are tossed in. Yellow Jacket Balls O' Fire salmon eggs, white mini jigs and Panther Martins are favorite fish teasers.

Rock Creek is easily accessible to anglers up and downstream of the culvert, although fishing is more productive in the pool below the culvert. Less than a half-mile downstream is the Pacific Crest Trail and Rock Creek Falls, a 70-foot waterfall that can be dazzling in the spring. The creek is closed to fishing downstream of the falls to protect spawning trout that swim out of the Pit River into Rock Creek.

If you plan to make the trip, supplies are available in Burney. Rock Creek is closed to fishing from November 16 to the last Saturday in April.

Also nearby are Clark Creek (Lower), Rock Creek Falls, Lake Britton, Burney Falls and Burney Creek (Lower).

Directions: From the junction of Highway 299 and Interstate 5 in Redding, drive east on Highway 299 for 53.7 miles to the junction with Highway 89. Turn left onto Highway 89 and drive 4.1 miles to Clark Creek Road. Turn left and drive 3.7 miles to Five Corners. Take the second road from the left (signed as Forest Service Road 37) and drive 2.6 miles to the creek.

Rock Creek

CLARK CREEK (LOWER)

Rating: 4
Species: Rainbow Trout
Stocked with 200 pounds of rainbow trout.
Facilities: None
Need Information? Contact: Vaughn's Sporting Goods (530) 335-2381

Clark Creek Lodge is a specialty plant. The California Department of Fish and Game shows up each spring to plant 370 rainbows. These rainbows are enjoyed almost exclusively by anglers fishing at the lodge. The creek is planted in a section that extends only three-tenths of a mile. When you arrive it will be apparent exactly where that stretch is: both above and below the bridge.

The places trout can be found are evident. Above the bridge there are a few small pools that hold trout, and a well oxygenated pool directly below the bridge. This is a salmon egg/Power Bait stream, and one that you should only fish in the spring when plants are made. Most years Clark Creek is only planted in May and early June. Come any later and you'll be the only one casting along the bank. The trout will have already been caught.

If you plan to make the trip, supplies are available in Burney. Clark Creek (Lower) is closed to fishing from November 16 to the last Saturday in April.

Also nearby are Rock Creek, Rock Creek Falls, Lake Britton, Burney Falls and Burney Creek (Lower).

Directions: From the junction of Highway 299 and Interstate 5 in Redding, drive east on Highway 299 for 53.7 miles to the junction with Highway 89. Turn left onto Highway 89 and drive 4.1 miles to Clark Creek Road. Turn left and drive 3.7 miles to Five Corners. Continue straight and drive 1.2 miles to the creek.

Clark Creek (Lower)

BURNEY CREEK (MIDDLE)

Rating: 5

Species: Rainbow Trout and Brook Trout

Stocked with 2,200 pounds of rainbow trout.

Facilities: Lodging, Gas, Food, General Store, Bait & Tackle, Restrooms and a Picnic Area

Need Information? Contact: Vaughn's Sporting Goods (530) 335-2381

The middle section of Burney Creek is split into two subsections: the part of the creek that locals fish and the part tourist fish. Tourists fish where Burney Creek crosses under Highway 299 in town. The California Department of Fish and Game plants the creek here at least monthly during the summer. Anglers lodging in town oftentimes make the quick trip after dinner to nab a few trout.

The bulk of the 3,910 fish the CA DFG plants in the middle section take place in the residential district of the town of Burney. Plants occur at several bridges off the main drag in town, including Park Street, Jackrabbit Flat and Tamarack Road. While a few out-of-towners do fish this section, it's basically reserved for locals. Since the stream here runs through a lot of private property, only the local kids have the go ahead to fish their way through the private land. This gives children a safe and close place to catch a few trout after doing their homework.

For the most part, the middle section of Burney is fished with Balls O' Fire salmon eggs and night crawlers. Look for trout to be bunched up in small pools, under overhanging brush, in pockets and riffles. Rainbows and the occasional brook from one-half pound to a pound are common.

If you plan to make the trip, supplies are available in Burney. Burney Creek is closed to fishing from November 16 to the last Saturday in April.

Also nearby are Burney Creek (Upper), Pit River, Hat Creek and Baum Lake.

Directions: *From the junction of Interstate 5 and Highway 299 in Redding, drive east on Highway 299 for 48.6 miles to where Burney Creek crosses under the highway.*

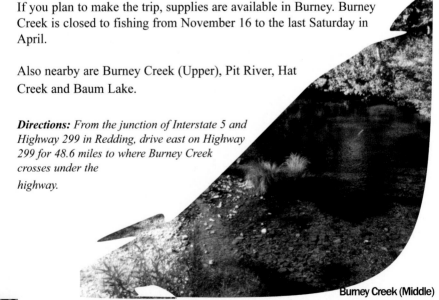

Burney Creek (Middle)

BURNEY CREEK (UPPER)

Rating: 6
Species: Rainbow Trout, Brown Trout and Brook Trout
Stocked with 2,200 pounds of rainbow trout and 1,200 pounds of brook trout.
Facilities: None
Need Information? Contact: Vaughn's Sporting Goods (530) 335-2381

Sometimes when fishing, the outdoor experience and the time spent with friends is often more special than the water itself, or how many fish you catch. Steve Vaughn, owner of Vaughn's Sporting Goods in Burney for more than 45 years, was my personal tour guide for the upper section of Burney Creek. To say Vaughn knows this high mountain stream like the back of his hand is an understatement. Vaughn knows when each road was built, where each trout lies, what to toss into each pool and the ins and outs of every logging road in the region. What I'm trying to get at is the upper section of Burney Creek is treasured by locals. Being that this stream is roughly 10 miles from the town of Burney, most anglers share special memories of the creek, so Upper Burney isn't a place for tourists to come, camp, litter and destroy the vegetation.

In this neck of the woods the creek is one of the prettiest you'll come by. It's heavily forested, has lots of riffles, pools and some small runs, and its' own population of small wild rainbow, brown and brook trout in addition to the 1,560 brook trout and 3,790 rainbows the California Department of Fish and Game plants annually. Plants occur weekly in the summer. The shorelines of this tumbling stream are heavily vegetated by pines, wildflowers and other foliage, and it's not uncommon to see osprey overhead while inhaling the crisp, clean air. As for the fishing, pop Power Bait, Pautzke salmon eggs or tiny ant patterns into a hole and you're in business as long as the fish truck has been by recently. If not, it will be slim pickings.

If you plan to make the trip, supplies are available in Burney. Burney Creek (Upper) is closed to fishing from November 16 to the last Saturday in April. Also nearby are Burney Creek (Middle) and Hatchet Creek.

Directions: *From the junction of Highway 299 and Interstate 5 in Redding, drive east on Highway 299 for 46.7 miles to Tamarack Road on the right. Turn right and drive 5.8 miles to an unsigned dirt road on the right. Turn right and drive 2.9 miles to the stream.*

Burney Creek (Upper)

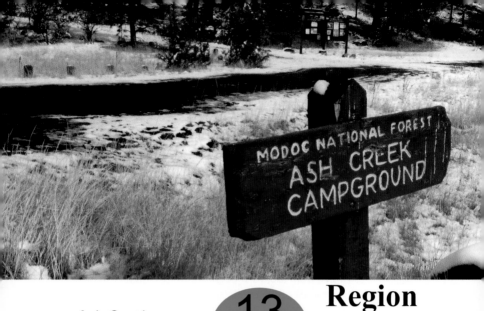

Region

13

Alturas Area

Ash Creek
Rush Creek
Duncan Reservoir
Reservoir F
Reservoir C
Big Sage Reservoir
Cave Lake
Lily Lake
Annie Reservoir
Fee Reservoir
Surprise Valley Hot Springs
Stough Reservoir
Dorris Reservoir
Pine Creek Reservoir
Ballard Reservoir
Bayley Reservoir
Delta Reservoir
West Valley Reservoir
Pit River (South Fork)
Clear Lake
Mill Creek
Blue Lake

ASH CREEK

Rating: 7

Species: Brown Trout and Rainbow Trout

Stocked with 1,100 pounds of rainbow trout.

Facilities: Campgrounds and Restrooms

Need Information? Contact: Lassen National Forest (530) 336-5521

Ash Creek is a quiet alternative to Hat Creek and other heavily-fished streams in the Lassen National Forest. At 4,200 feet, near the town of Adin, this stream doesn't receive that same fishing pressure that others located closer to Redding do. Ash is near Modoc County and receives a smidgen of the percentage of anglers that most planted streams see.

While some areas of Ash Creek are known for fly fishing wild browns, most anglers come for the planted trout. Each spring and summer Ash is planted by the California Department of Fish and Game with more than 2,035 half-pound rainbows, giving campers and day-users something to look forward to.

All plants take place at Ash Creek Campground. Fortunately, this area is conducive to all sorts of fishing, including fly fishing, spin casting and bait fishing. Anglers looking to bait fish have no problem finding small pockets to drop salmon eggs into. There are also runs deep enough to retrieve small size 1/64 Panther Martins and other water perfect for drifting a dry fly across in the late spring and summer.

The scenery found at the campground is a far cry from the flat wetlands located nearby at the popular bird watching Ash Creek Wildlife Area. This meadow is lined with pines and spruced up with star-filled nights.

If you plan to make the trip, supplies are available in Adin. Ash Creek is closed to fishing from November 16 to the last Saturday in April.

Also nearby is Rush Creek, Fall River and Ballard Reservoir.

Directions: *From the junction of Highway 299 and Interstate 5 in Redding drive east on Highway 299 for 98.5 miles to the town of Adin. In Adin, turn right on Ash Valley Road, which is signed as "Madeline 32" and drive 7.5 miles to the left turnoff for Ash Creek Campground. (In one mile the road turns to dirt.) Turn left on Road 22 and drive one-half mile to the creek.*

RUSH CREEK

Rating: 4

Species: Brown Trout, Rainbow Trout and Redband Trout

Stocks: None

Facilities: Campgrounds and Restrooms

Need Information? Contact: Modoc National Forest (530) 233-5811

Rush Creek has fallen victim to budget cuts and protection for the Modoc sucker. Rush Creek was planted with rainbows and browns by the California Department of Fish and Game. However, a lack of funds for the plants and fear that those fish would eat the endangered sucker prompted the CA DFG to remove Rush Creek from the allotment sheet.

There is hope, however. There are plans to move the Modoc sucker to the threatened species list and eventually delist its' status completely. This would allow the CA DFG to resume fish plants. Nonetheless, there are still some trout in the system. Redband are native to the drainage and browns, rainbows and Redband have adapted to the system and reproduce on their own.

Rush Creek is a fairly small stream, but can take on size in spring runoff. The stream is situated in a heavily forested section of the Modoc National Forest and is far enough from cities that it doesn't get pounded. It's best to fish Pautzke salmon eggs or drift a mini night crawler in small pockets. I'd try running a small Kwikfish into a run or two. Don't expect any whoppers though. This system isn't known for big fish.

If you plan to make the trip, supplies are available in Adin and Canby. Rush Creek is closed to fishing from November 16 to the last Saturday in April.

Also nearby is Ash Creek.

Directions: *From the junction of Interstate 5 and Highway 299 in Redding, drive east on Highway 299 for 106 miles to the right turnoff for Rush Creek Campground. Turn right on Road 107 and drive one-tenth of a mile to Road 40N05. Turn left and drive one-half mile to Lower Rush Creek Campground.*

Rush Creek

DUNCAN RESERVOIR

Rating: 5

Species: Rainbow Trout

Stocked with 1,000
pounds of rainbow
trout.

Facilities: Restrooms

Need Information?
Contact: Modoc
National Forest
(530) 233-5811

The California Department of Fish and Game fights many uphill battles in Modoc County. Not only do they face low water levels, they have to deal with locals who think they are biologists. Many ranchers and farmers who live in this region take it upon themselves to illegally stock lakes. While these folks think they are creating excellent fisheries for themselves, they usually create hundreds of thousands of dollars of problems for the CA DFG.

Duncan Reservoir is a perfect example of a Modoc National Forest water that has been destroyed by locals. For some reason, a small group of locals have made a habit of planting brown and yellow bullhead into Duncan. These fish do extremely well, but make it nearly impossible for any other species to prosper.

The CA DFG has tried to develop a quality fishery several times, but the illegal and unauthorized introduction of fish has blocked these efforts. Still, the CA DFG has battled back. The reservoir was chemically treated in 1983-84 and then pumped dry in 2002 to rid the lake of yellow bullhead in an attempt to reestablish a trout fishery. If the locals let it be, Duncan's trout will flourish.

Duncan Reservoir

However for now; a lack of funds is keeping the CA DFG from bringing bass and other species into the system. At the present time, Duncan is all about trout. Each season the CA DFG dumps 2,000 half-pound rainbows into the 353-acre reservoir. Those fish grow rapidly and can be greater than one-or-two pounds within a year of entering the system. Catching them can be a blast on dough baits and inflated night crawlers.

Trip info for Big Sage Reservoir also apply to Duncan Reservoir.

Directions: From the junction of Highway 395 and 299 in Alturas, drive west on Highway 299 to Highway 139. Turn right and drive 6.9 miles to Loveless Road. Turn right, cross the railroad tracks and drive two-tenths of a mile to a right turnoff to Duncan Reservoir. Turn right and drive 1.3 miles to a split in the road. Veer left and drive 1.1 miles to the reservoir.

RESERVOIR F

Rating: 5

Species: Rainbow Trout, Brown Trout, Largemouth Bass and Brown Bullhead

Stocked with 1,000 pounds of brown trout, 20 pounds of fingerling rainbow trout and 2,000 pounds of rainbow trout.

Facilities: Restrooms, Boat Launch and Primitive Campgrounds

Start your rain dance. If there is good water conditions for consecutive years, Reservoir F can be an excellent fishery. If water levels are low, wipe it off your list of places to fish. Reservoir F has excellent growing conditions for trout. In fact, if you have favorable conditions for three consecutive years you'll find some of the fattest Eagle Lake trout in the state.

Each year, Reservoir F, located at 5,000 feet in the Modoc National Forest, is planted with 3,200 three-to the pound browns, 4,000 half-pound rainbows and 10,000 fingerling Eagle Lake trout. When water is available, growth rates are stunning. Seeing trout to eight pounds isn't out of the ordinary.

Trout fishing hasn't always been good though. The reservoir was chemically treated in the early Nineties to remove tui chubs. However, they and bullhead have found their way back into the lake. Fortunately, as long as the population doesn't get out of hand, both will provide a good food source for the trout.

While trolling does work, 640-acre Reservoir F is a shallow lake so you'll need to drag something that isn't going to sink much; a Sep's Pro Dodger with a night crawler, Needlefish, Dick Nite or small Hum-Dinger will work magic. Casting bait from shore is also productive.

Trip info for Big Sage Reservoir also applies to Reservoir F.

Directions: *From the junction of Highway 395 and 299 in Alturas, drive west on Highway 299 to Highway 139. Turn right and drive 6.9 miles to Loveless Road. Turn right, cross the railroad tracks and drive 4.5 miles to a split in the road. Veer right on Road 43N36 and drive 2.6 miles to another split. Stay right and drive 3.4 miles to the reservoir.*

Reservoir F

RESERVOIR C

Rating: 6

Species: Crappie,
Brown Bullhead,
Brown Trout, Channel
Catfish, Rainbow Trout
and Largemouth Bass

Stocked with 1,500
pounds of rainbow
trout.

Facilities: Boat Launch,
Restrooms and
Primitive Campsites

Reservoir C is almost a replica of Reservoir F. However, C can provide excellent trout fishing and also offers a warmwater fishery. The trout co-exist with largemouth bass and crappie. The bass fishery is untapped. Few anglers fish for the bass, yet they and crappie are available. If water levels have been good for consecutive years, it won't be hard to find bass in the five-pound range. Nonetheless, fishing can be poor during low water years.

Trout fishing can be superb. The California Department of Fish and Game dumps some 3,000 rainbows into the system each year. These trout grow rapidly, especially with tui chubs that drive the system. Chubs serve as growing pills for the trout, which can reach double digits if water levels remain stable for three or more years.

At 4,900 feet in the Modoc National Forest, this 160-acre reservoir can be fished from shore or boat. Bait fishing from a boat can be good, but don't limit yourself to it. Trolling lightweight spoons and fly fishing with Woolly Buggers is equally productive. Anglers soaking bait from the shore can also find consistent action.

Trip info for Big Sage Reservoir also applies to Reservoir C.

Directions: *From Alturas at the junction of Highway 299 and 395, drive west on Highway 395 for 3.5 miles to Crowder Flat Road (Road 74). Turn right, drive 9.6 miles and turn left at the sign for Reservoir C. Drive 5.8 miles to the right turnoff for the reservoir. Turn right and drive seven-tenths of a mile to the reservoir.*

Reservoir C

BIG SAGE RESERVOIR

Rating: 4

Species: Crappie, Channel Catfish and Largemouth Bass

Stocks: None

Facilities: Boat Launch, Restrooms and Primitive Campsites

Need Information? Contact: Modoc National Forest (530) 233-5811

It's called boom or bust. The irrigation reservoirs on the Modoc Plateau live and die with rapid swings of productivity. Without long explanations of how the scenario pans out know this: the reservoirs of the Alturas region can be some of the best fisheries in the West. Only one ingredient is necessary, water. If any of the reservoirs in this area hold good water for two or more years in a row, fishing can be top notch.

Big Sage Reservoir is one of those irrigation reservoirs that follow the boom or bust cycle. Because of grazing practices in its drainage, the reservoir is loaded with nutrients and minerals. Just add water and you have productivity rates that go through the roof. Consistent water levels for consecutive years can grow bass upwards of four pounds and trout larger than seven. If you have three or more good water years the fish can be huge.

Big Sage Reservoir has been devastated by low water in recent years. The dam was constructed in 1921 and holds more than 5,270 acres. Sadly though, the reservoir can be sucked down to less than five acres. After all, in this neck of the woods it's all about irrigation, not fishing.

The California Department of Fish and Game has made an effort to create a viable warmwater fishery here. However, low water levels have been devastating to it. In the early Nineties, 10,000 fingerling channel catfish were introduced. Some of those fish are now well over 20 pounds, but many of them are no longer in the system. The CA DFG transferred many of those fish to other waters during low water years.

There was also a quality largemouth bass and pan fish aspect, but much of that has disappeared with the low water levels. The water got so low that in June of 2001 the CA DFG rescued 150 crappie and 150 largemouth bass and transported them to Janes Reservoir. Again, if there are a few consecutive good water years plan on fishing Big Sage otherwise put it on the backburner.

If you plan to make the trip, supplies are available in Alturas. During winter and spring, the road to the reservoir may be closed due to snow. Call the Forest Service for updated conditions.

Also nearby are Reservoir F and C.

Directions: From Alturas at the junction of Highway 299 and 395, drive west on Highway 299 for a few miles to Crowder Flat Road (Road 74). Turn right and drive six miles to Forest Service Road 180. Turn right and drive 3.4 miles to a split. Stay left and drive four-tenths of a mile to the boat launch and campground.

CAVE LAKE

Rating: 6

Species: Brook Trout
and Rainbow Trout

Stocked with two
pounds of fingerling
rainbow trout.

Facilities: Picnic Area,
Restrooms and
Campgrounds

Need Information?
Contact: Modoc
National Forest
(530) 233-5811

Cave Lake is a small pond in the Modoc National Forest that is managed strictly as a put-and-take fishery. The lake is a tiny dab of water that harbors roughly 1,000 fingerling rainbows each summer.

Situated a short distance south of the Oregon border, Cave is a great place for families to camp for the weekend. Primitive campsites make for a true wilderness feeling. This high mountain lake rests in a heavily wooded area and tends to yield pan size trout throughout the open season.

Cave isn't a destination for hardcore anglers, rather for families with children and weekend fishermen looking to hook a few stocked trout. The lake is best fished with bait on a sliding sinker rig or a red and gold Krocodile casted from shore. Float tubes are an option.

Located in the Warner Mountains, Cave Lake's accessibility isn't always what anglers would like. The road to the lake is covered in thick snow from November through June in most years. Ice fishermen have a good shot if they can find a snowmobile, but otherwise this is a summer and early fall fishery.

If you plan to make the trip, supplies are available in Lakeview, Oregon and Alturas. From fall through early summer call ahead for road conditions. The road may be closed due to snow.

Also nearby are Lily Lake, Annie Reservoir and Fee Reservoir.

Directions: *From the junction of Highway 299 and Highway 395 in Alturas, drive north on Highway 395 for 37.4 miles to County Road 2. Turn right and drive 6.4 miles to the Cave Lake turnoff. Turn left and drive three-tenths of a mile to the lake.*

Cave Lake can freeze as early as Halloween and may not thaw until the 4th of July

LILY LAKE

Rating: 7

Species: Brook Trout and Rainbow Trout

Stocked with 500 pounds of brook trout and 500 pounds of rainbow trout.

Facilities: Picnic Area, Restrooms and Campgrounds

Need Information? Contact: Modoc National Forest (530) 233-5811

Lily Lake is the epitome of the Warner Mountains. The Warner's are known by many folks as the last frontier in California, a place where families can count on open campsites, unpublicized tourist attractions and good fishing. Located near the Oregon border, Lily Lake is as advertised, full of lily pads. These pads freeze under the ice in the winter and emerge in the summer when the lake thaws.

Unfortunately, unless you have snowmobiles, don't bother thinking about fishing Lily lake from Halloween to roughly the Fourth of July. It takes a long time for the snow to melt in this desolate country. If you have the means of transportation, ice fishing can be good and you'll have the place to yourself.

Lily is nestled in a heavy forested section of the Modoc National Forest. At roughly 6,000 feet, trout do well. A combination of brookies and bows are planted. Each year, some 750 brooks and 900 rainbows are planted, keeping action steady for bank anglers tossing bait and lures. Float tubers are permitted. At 2.5 acres, Lily is too small for boaters.

Float tubers traditionally do best. The first 10 yards from the shoreline is shallow, forcing many of the trout to congregate near the middle of the lake. It's best to use something you'll be able to heave at least 20 yards.

Lily is an excellent destination for Southern Oregon and Modoc County residents looking for a day trip where they can fish, take nice strolls around the lake through breathtaking scenery and have a picnic along the shore. It's truly a gorgeous setting.

If you plan to make the trip, supplies are available in Lakeside and Alturas. In winter and spring, the road is impassible due to snow. Call the Forest Service for updated conditions.

Also nearby are Cave Lake, Goose Lake, Annie Lake and Fee Reservoir.

Directions: *From the junction of Highway 299 and Highway 395 in Alturas, drive north for 37.4 miles to County Road 2. Turn right and drive six miles to the Lily Lake Picnic Area turnoff the on left. Turn left and drive three-tenths of a mile to the lake.*

Lily Lake

ANNIE RESERVOIR

Rating: 4

Species: Rainbow Trout

Stocked with eight pounds of fingerling rainbow trout and 1,000 pounds of rainbow trout.

Facilities: None

Need Information?
Contact: Bureau of Land Management
(530) 279-6101

The Surprise Valley in northeast California isn't one of California's most sought after tourist destinations. In fact, other than a few tractors, trucks carrying hay and Ford F-250's dragging trailers, you may not run into much else around here. Fort Bidwell is such a small community that there are more goats, cows and horses than people.

Annie Reservoir is located just north of town and it's not always the most comforting destination for anglers. Annie is another Modoc County irrigation reservoir. It's located in a small basin tucked outside thousands of acres of farmland. Getting to it reminds me of a ride through Iowa. You'll pass tractors plowing fields, livestock and ranches that appear to be in the middle of nowhere. So you'll probably feel like an out-of-towner right away! Some even feel like they are trespassing. The reservoir is open to the public though.

Fishing isn't always exceptional, but most of the time it's fair. When the reservoir has water, action can be good and growth rates are promising, but some years the reservoir dries up. The lake is managed as a put-and-grow and a put-and-take fishery. Each year some 4,000 fingerling rainbow trout and 2,000 half-pound Eagle lake trout are stocked, making for a good springtime bite for anglers dunking bait off the rocks on the east shore. Spinners can be good when the water is clear. However, even the slightest rain can muddy up the water.

Annie Reservoir

If you plan to make the trip, supplies are available in Cedarville. The lake may freeze in the winter.

Also nearby are Fee Reservoir, Cave Lake and Lily Lake.

Directions: *From the junction of Road 2 and 1 in Fort Bidwell drive north for two-tenths of a mile to split in the road. Stay left and drive 1.9 miles to a turnoff on the left. Turn left and drive 2.5 miles on Road 4 (its not signed) to the lake.*

FEE RESERVOIR

Rating: 8

Species: Rainbow Trout
and Cutthroat Trout

Stocked 1,250 pounds
of rainbow trout.

Facilities:
Campgrounds and
Restrooms

Need Information?
Contact: Modoc
National Forest
(530) 233-5811

Fee's rating is subject to water. Unfortunately when I showed up with a rod and reel in the fall of 2003, the 500-acre reservoir was dry. I was appalled. Not native to Modoc County, I wasn't accustom to seeing large reservoirs go dry. The shock escalated as I drove out to the middle of the reservoir where normally 25 feet of water would stand. The structure I was out to study was nowhere to be found. It was evident Fee is a flat reservoir with little habitat for fish. The only conducive habitat I could find were two creek channels near the dam. Otherwise, it's mostly gentle, flat land. We stumbled upon a few bald eagles, a herd of pronghorn and dozens of hawks. No fish though.

Nonetheless, when there is water in Fee Reservoir it can be one of the state's better fisheries. Fee's growth rates benefit from resting downstream of farmland, which means minerals and nutrients are constantly flowing into the reservoir which helps the fish grow like crazy. What we have to remember though, is that Fee is an irrigation reservoir, meaning for the most part farmers control the water. If they need it or want it, they take it. That's what it's for. On the other hand, if the water level is not depleted for consecutive years and the trout carryover, you can expect to find huge fish.

Bald Eagles are common at Fee

Native to this range, the California Department of Fish and Game plants Lahonton cutthroat, which with good water easily reach five-to-seven pounds. Unfortunately, recent glitches in the budget have not allowed the California Department of Fish and Game to raise cutthroat and they are not being stocked at the present time. Hopefully, that will be reversed shortly. When water and fish are available, 5,000 sub-catchable cutthroat and 2,500 pounds of half-pound Eagle lake trout are planted, providing a good fishery for trollers and shoreline anglers.

If you plan to troll, use a lightweight spoon

Pronghorn frequent the shoreline at Fee.

Sad, but true. Fee Reservoir dried up completely in October of 2003.

like a Needlefish or Dick Nite spoon or drag a Sep's Pro Flasher with a night crawler. Don't use a lure that is going to sink fast. Sadly, when the water doesn't flow the fish die and become food for coyotes, mountain lions, hawks and eagles. When water is present, the fish are food for people.

If you plan to make the trip, supplies are available in Cedarville. The road to the lake isn't maintained in the winter. Call for updated road conditions. Fee Reservoir can freeze in the winter.

Also nearby are Annie Reservoir, Surprise Valley Hot Springs Resort, Cave Lake and Lily Lake.

Directions: From the junction of Road 2 and 1 in Fort Bidwell drive north for two-tenths of a mile to a split in the road. Stay left and drive 1.9 miles to a turnoff on the left. Ignore it. Instead, turn right on Road 6 and drive six miles to the lake.

A small cove at Fee Reservoir prior to it drying up in October of 2003.

SURPRISE VALLEY HOT SPRINGS PONDS

Rating: 5

Species: Largemouth Bass, Bluegill and Channel Catfish

Stocks: None

Facilities: Lodging, Restrooms and Soaking

Need Information? Contact: Surprise Valley Hot Springs (877) 9276-420

Surprise Valley Hot Springs is not a getaway for the adventurer, rather for couples and families looking for a relaxing, soothing vacation. This quiet resort in the Surprise Valley is located a few minutes outside of Cedarville is known for its' day spa amenities. However, fishing ponds were added to their list of activities.

The ponds aren't the world's greatest fisheries, but they are a place where you are almost guaranteed to catch bass and bluegill. The fish, bass and bluegill that were relocated several years ago from nearby reservoirs, have adapted well to these waters. Unfortunately the ponds are shallow and can get weedy. Luckily, the fish always seem to cooperate. In fact, they are so easy to catch you'll feel like a "Bassmaster" overnight. There's more bluegill than bass, but a few bass greater than two pounds make things exciting.

The ponds were constructed as holding tanks for water pumped out of the artesian wells. The water is first used by guests who take advantage of the private hot tub outside their hotel room. Then, the water is pumped into the ponds. Despite below freezing temperatures, the ponds don't freeze.

If you plan to make the trip, supplies are available in Cedarville. There is a fishing fee.

Also nearby are Stough Reservoir and Fee Reservoir.

A bluegill

Directions: From the junction of County Road 1 and Highway 299 in Cedarville, drive east on Highway 299 for 4.2 miles to the right turnoff for Surprise Valley Hot Springs. Turn right and drive eight-tenths of a mile to the ponds.

Chris Cocoles with a largemouth caught on a spinner at Surprise Valley Hot Springs.

Water from natural hot springs is pumped into spas behind the rooms at Surprise Valley Hot Springs

STOUGH RESERVOIR

Rating: 5

Species: Rainbow Trout

Stocked with 500 pounds of rainbow trout.

Facilities: Restrooms and Campgrounds

Need Information? Contact: Modoc National Forest (530) 233-5811

When you get home cooking in Modoc County, you get what you pay for. In fact, you get more than you pay for. I learned quickly with my first two sittings in Cedarville's own Country Hearth and the Cedarville Café and Saloon. The food was good and they give you enough to feed their livestock. If you can finish the plate you are well above the curve.

The fish don't always have the same appetite at Stough Reservoir. However, if they are hungry they'll be easy pickings. Stough Reservoir is a relatively new addition to the California Department of Fish and Game's allotment list. In fact, recent cutbacks nearly put it on the chopping block. Fortunately, the small reservoir will still receive fish, rather in just scaled-back numbers. Less than 900 half-pound trout will be planted.

Stough is a small pond located near Cedar Pass Ski Area. The lake typically freezes by Halloween, but doesn't provide good ice fishing prospects. The best time to fish is during late spring and early summer when a fresh load was stocked. Come any later and its' likely those fish will be

Stough Reservoir

gone. Stough is more of a kid's pond than a reservoir. You can cast a spoon across the lake with no problem, and Power Bait takes fish at ease. This heavily shaded area is also a nice overnight camping destination in the Modoc National Forest.

If you plan to make the trip, supplies are available in Cedarville. In winter, the road to Stough may be impassible due to snow. Call for updated road conditions.

Also nearby is Dorris Reservoir.

Directions: *From the junction of Highway 299 and 395 in Alturas, drive north on Highway 395 for 5.4 miles to the Cedarville turnoff. Turn right and drive 11.5 miles to the left turnoff for Stough Reservoir. Continue eight-tenths of a mile to the lake.*

DORRIS RESERVOIR

Rating: 4

Species: Largemouth Bass and Rainbow Trout

Stocked with 1,750 pounds of rainbow trout.

Facilities: Boat Launches

Need Information? Contact: Modoc National Wildlife Area (530) 233-3572

Dorris Reservoir is so close to the town of Alturas you might as well include it as part of the town. Most local anglers don't pay much attention to the lake though, as Dorris isn't a great fishing lake. In fact, up until a few years ago Dorris' bass were starved of habitat. If you fished the lake you'd find several bass on each piece of submerged structure, but no bass anywhere else. Unfortunately, there was very little structure so bass didn't fare well and the few bass available were small. In recent years, stumps and portions of juniper trees were installed to help the bass in the future. Results of that project will soon be evident.

Dorris is a quality springtime trout fishery. Each spring the California Department of Fish and Game plants more than 4,000 half-pound rainbows that can be picked off by trolling and shoreline bait dunkers. Trout fishing dies off as the water warms in summer. Dorris rests inside the boundary of the Modoc National Wildlife Refuge and is closed to fishing during specific waterfowl migrations.

If you plan to make the trip, supplies are available in Alturas. The reservoir is closed to fishing from mid-October through mid-January to protect migratory waterfowl. The reservoir is open to boating from April 1 through September 30.

Also nearby is Pine Creek Reservoir.

Largemouth are available at Dorris Reservoir

Directions: *From the junction of Highway 395 and Highway 299 in Alturas, drive south for nine-tenths of a mile on Highway 395 to Road 56. Turn left and drive 4.2 miles to the right turnoff for the reservoir. Turn right to the lake.*

PINE CREEK RESERVOIR

Rating: 5

Species: Rainbow Trout

Stocked with 1,300 pounds of rainbow trout.

Facilities: None

Need Information?
Contact: The Belligerent Duck
(530) 233-4696

If you haven't visited Modoc County before, you will quickly learn that the locals rule the land. Despite what you may hear from tourist groups, the locals either want you around or cannot wait for you to leave. The ranchers and the farmers, I'm told, would love to keep all visitors away. Those in the service industry beg to keep anglers, campers and hikers in town as long as possible as their livelihood depends on it.

Located at 5,000 feet in the hills above Alturas, Pine Creek Reservoir is small and shallow. Overall you won't find many out-of-towners at this 19-acre spring hotspot, since the locals work so hard to keep it their secret.

When the California Department of Fish and Game plants trout in the spring and summer, action is fabulous. Roughly 2,600 half-pound bows are dumped in each year. Anglers tossing spinners and soaking bait in this high desert terrain can nab quick limits. Fishing is best through July and then action begins to slow. By mid-summer many of the fish have been picked off and no more plants are on the to-do list. By fall, there are few fish leftover.

If you plan to make the trip, supplies are available in Alturas. In winter check road conditions. The road may be impassable due to snow.

Also nearby is Dorris Reservoir.

Directions: *From the junction of Highway 299 and 395 in Alturas, drive south on Highway 395 for one mile to County Road 56. Turn left and drive six-tenths of a mile to County Road 115. Turn right and drive 2.5 miles to County Road 59. Turn east on Road 59B and drive seven-tenths of a mile. Turn left and drive 2.2 miles to a T intersection. Turn right on Road 57 and continue 3.1 miles to the reservoir.*

Pine Creek Reservoir

BALLARD RESERVOIR

Rating: 5

Species: Rainbow Trout

Stocked with 1,600
pounds of rainbow
trout.

Facilities: None

Need Information?
Contact: Bureau of
Land Management
(530) 279-6101

Ballard Reservoir is one of the rare Modoc County waters that doesn't typically dry up. While it is used for agricultural purposes, it's often spared from complete drawdown and maintains its load of 2,880 half-pound Eagle lake trout. Ballard isn't a huge reservoir, but can take on some size in the spring when runoff is retained. The sad thing is if you arrive in the fall you'll stumble on what appears to be a completely different reservoir.

Fishing is best in late spring and late fall, just before the snow falls or while there's snow on the ground. The reservoir is best fished from shore, where in the fall you'll notice that the springtime water line is some 25-50 vertical feet above you. Nonetheless, fish can carry over. If you have a few good rain years in a row, it's not uncommon to catch five-to-six-pound trout.

Not all the trout get this big though. Many folks soak night crawlers and dough bait to catch half-pound to one-pound trout. Tossing spinners and spoons or using fly and bubble combos is also productive. The key is knowing where to fish. The flat side of the reservoir is fairly shallow, while across the reservoir you'll find a rocky shoreline with submerged trees. If you don't see fish surfacing near the flats, it's a good idea to fish off the rocks. There will always be fish in this area.

If you plan to make the trip, supplies are available in Canby. In winter and spring call for road conditions. The road may be impassible due to rain and or snow. Ballard commonly freezes over in the winter.

Also nearby is Rush Creek, Ash Creek and Duncan Reservoir.

Ballard Reservoir

Directions: *From the junction of Interstate 5 and Highway 299 in Redding drive west on Highway 299 for 119.6 miles to the right turnoff for Road 54 in Canby. Turn right and drive nine-tenths of a mile to Road 175. Drive seven-tenths of a mile on Road 175 to a fork in the road. Stay left and drive two miles to another split. Again, stay left and drive eight-tenths of a mile to another split. Veer left and drive eight-tenths of a mile to the unmarked left turnoff for Ballard Reservoir. Turn left to the lake.*

BAYLEY RESERVOIR

Rating: 3

Species: Rainbow Trout

Stocked with 28 pounds of fingerling rainbow trout and 1,300 pounds of rainbow trout.

Facilities: None

Condition factors are important when it comes to growth rates of trout. Unfortunately, conditions aren't good at Bayley Reservoir where wind frequently shoots through the canyon churning up and muddying the water. For trout this isn't a good thing. Trout have difficulty feeding by sight in Bayley. Due to the turbid water, many trout have to rely on smell to feed, which can reduce their intake and growth rates.

Coupled with low water levels, Bayley is a tough reservoir to manage. Traditionally, Bayley is a good fishery a few times each decade. Basically, if you have a few good water years in a row you'll find some trout big enough to fill a cooler. The California Department of Fish and Game plants roughly 2,290 half-pound, and smaller, rainbows and 14,000 fingerlings in Bayley. Sadly, at times, they die. Bayley can go dry in poor rain years.

When Bayley is full it, can be a good fishery. A gravel boat launch is an option for anglers with small boats. I wouldn't drag in anything over 15 feet. The road isn't great. If you can get a boat in the water use a lightweight spoon, like a Needlefish or Dick Nite. These spoons will keep you off the bottom. Dunking inflated night crawlers from shore is another option.

Bayley Reservoir

On a side note, in the past Bayley has been the center of controversy. Bayley was chemically treated in 1988-89 to remove unwanted bullhead and chubs that were destroying the trout fishery.

Trip info for Delta Reservoir also applies to Bayley Reservoir.

Directions: *From the junction of Highway 395 and 299 in Alturas, drive south on Highway 395 for nine-tenths of a mile to Carlos Avenue. Turn right and drive six-tenths of a mile to the California Pines turnoff. Turn left and drive 1.1 miles to a split in the road. Turn left on Road 60 and drive 6.6 miles to County Road 62. Turn right and drive 6.8 miles to a split. Veer left and drive 3.8 miles to the reservoir.*

DELTA RESERVOIR

Rating: 5

Species: Rainbow Trout and Brown Trout

Stocked with 500 pounds of brown trout, 250 pounds of rainbow trout and 20 pounds of fingerling rainbow trout.

Facilities: None

Need Information? Contact: Bureau of Land Management (530) 233-4666

Most years it takes an above average rainfall in Modoc County to fill Delta Reservoir. Some years Delta has no hope at all. Delta is an overflow reservoir utilized by excess water routed into Delta from Bayley Reservoir. When water is plentiful, Delta can be a substantially large reservoir, yet when I last visited in November of 2003, it looked more like a pelican sanctuary. The water line was 100 yards from its' high mark and thousands of pelicans floated on the shallow, weedy water. Thankfully, this isn't always the case.

Water means good things for Delta Reservoir. The California Department of Fish and Game plans for the high water years by dumping in 10,000 fingerling rainbow trout, 1,500 catchable brown trout and 325 rainbows. When the water is low, they may die and go to waste. However, when water is plentiful they grow like weeds. Delta benefits from much needed nutrients flowing into the lake from farms. It's not uncommon to find trout in the three-to-five-pound range if there has been a few continuous years of good water.

Delta Reservoir

Delta is a rough ride from nearby Bayley. If fact, the ruts in the roads are so severe the CA DFG stocking truck has difficulty planting the lake some years. There is no boat launch. Anglers are limited to shoreline angling and small car-top boats. Standard angling techniques that work in any California trout reservoir are equally effective.

If you plan to make the trip, supplies are available in Alturas. In winter and spring call for updated road conditions. The road to the lake may be impassible.

Also nearby is Bayley Reservoir.

Directions: *From the junction of Highway 395 and 299 in Alturas, drive south on Highway 395 for nine-tenths of a mile to Carlos Avenue. Turn right and drive six-tenths of a mile to the California Pines turnoff. Turn left and drive 1.1 miles to a split in the road. Turn left on Road 60 and drive 6.6 miles to County Road 62. Turn right and drive 6.8 miles to a split. Veer left and drive 4.9 miles to the reservoir.*

WEST VALLEY RESERVOIR

Rating: 5

Species: Largemouth
Bass, Crappie, Channel
Catfish, Sacramento
Perch and Rainbow
Trout

Stocked with 2,500
pounds of rainbow
trout.

Facilities:
Campgrounds,
Restrooms and a Boat
Launch

Need Information?
Contact: Bureau of
Land Management
(530) 233-4666

At 970 acres, West Valley Reservoir is a good size body of water for Modoc County. However it has its downfalls, particularly low water and water-skiers. Since West Valley is the only reservoir from Reno to Susanville that allows waterskiing, it gets mobbed by skiers and personal watercraft in the summer and fall. In turn, this chaos makes for horrible fishing conditions.

Each year the irrigation reservoir is yanked down making for harsh winter conditions. Oftentimes, you'll find winterkill on trout. Plus, the reservoir muddies with high winds or rain (which come often) making it hard for fish to see and feed. The low productivity hurts growth rates in this turbid system.

Nonetheless, there are fish available. While some 5,000 trout are planted, they aren't the mainstay. Most folks fish the summer and fall for crappie, channel catfish and Sacramento perch.

If you plan to make the trip, supplies are available in Alturas. The lake may freeze over in winter.

Also nearby are the Pit River (South Fork), Clear Lake, Mill Creek and Blue Lake.

Directions: From the junction of Highway 299 and 395 in Alturas drive south on Highway 395 to Jess Valley Road in Likely. Turn left and drive 2.1 miles to the right turnoff for West Valley Reservoir. Drive 4.1 miles to a split in the road. Veer left and drive three-tenths of a mile to the reservoir.

West Valley Reservoir

PIT RIVER (SOUTH FORK)

Rating: 5

Species: Rainbow Trout, Brown Trout and Redband Trout

Stocked with 700 pounds of rainbow trout.

Facilities: None

Need Information? Contact: Bureau of Land Management (530) 233-4666

The South Fork of the Pit River offers the best drive-to stream fishing opportunity in Modoc County. This is partially because it's the only river or stream in the region that receives consistent plants of fish. The California Department of Fish and Game dumps more than 1,220 half-pound rainbows into the system annually. With the pressure it receives the allotment is enough to satisfy anglers. In fact, there are wild rainbows, a few browns and native Redband trout also in the system.

The river is planted over a three-mile stretch in the Modoc National Forest. This roadside water is filled with lots of riffles and pocket water, not a lot of deep holes and long runs. It is, therefore, conducive to fly fishermen, bait casters and spin casters. The lower section is best fished with Pautzke salmon eggs or night crawlers, while the upper stretch has more flat, open areas better fit for drifting a dry fly.

Rainbows average one-half to three-quarters of a pound, yet the native Redband are closer to a half-pound. Angling is best in the spring and fall. During the summer it gets hot and puts a lot of stress on the fish.

If you plan to make the trip, supplies are available in Alturas. The Pit River (South Fork) is closed to fishing from November 16 to the last Saturday in April.

Also nearby are Clear Lake, Mill Creek, West Valley Reservoir, Mill Creek Falls and Blue Lake.

Directions: *From the junction of Highway 299 and 395 in Alturas, drive south on Highway 395 to Jess Valley Road in Likely. Turn left and drive 5.6 miles to the first crossing of the Pit River. Access is available from here upriver through the canyon.*

Pit River (South Fork)

CLEAR LAKE

Rating: 6

Species: Rainbow
Trout, Brown Trout,
Brook Trout and
Redband Trout

Stocks: None

Facilities: None

Need Information?
Contact: Modoc
National Forest
(530) 233-5811

The South Warner Wilderness is considered one of California's last remaining untouched wilderness areas. While it's true that the region isn't bombarded with as many hikers and anglers as other forests in the state that are closer to major cities, the South Warner has been explored and it's no secret that Clear Lake is one of the better fisheries in its' boundaries.

Although it may appear to be a drive-to lake on a map, actually it takes a short hike to reach Clear Lake. The hike begins in Mill Creek Falls Campgrounds and ascends for a bit more than a quarter-mile on the Poison Creek Trail to the lake. Clear Lake doesn't have the productivity to be a great trout lake. Poor condition factors don't provide the best growing situation for trout. However, trout can use its' tributary (Mill Creek) to spawn.

Clear Lake isn't planted with trout. Nonetheless, at one time before the wilderness area was created, it was. Fortunately, many of those trout have reproduced naturally. There are rainbows, Redband, brooks and browns, including some quality browns up to a few pounds.

Unfortunately, the lake isn't a great shoreline fishery. While it's common to see trout rising you can't always reach them. The shoreline has a gradual slope. You need to use a heavy spoon or large spinner to reach good water. A fly and bubble combo or Pistol Pete works well. It's best to fish from a float tube.

The road to Mill Creek Falls Campground isn't maintained during the winter. But it is plowed to Mill Creek Lodge, which is fewer than a mile from the campground. Many anglers hike the road in the winter and ice fish. The best action can be had in the winter when anglers can fish the deeper water. Try soaking a night crawler or jigging a Crippled Herring.

Directions *and trip info for Mill Creek also applies to Clear Lake.*

Clear Lake in October of 2003

MILL CREEK

Rating: 7

Species: Brown Trout and Redband Trout

Stocks: None

Facilities: None

Need Information? Contact: Modoc National Forest (530) 233-5811

When compared to the South Fork of the Pit River, Mill Creek isn't a big creek. It's better described as a small, high mountain stream. However, Mill Creek's productivity for trout parallels any other stream on the Modoc Plateau. Mill Creek has a good food base, excellent spawning areas and great water quality, which is evident in the condition trout that live in the system are in.

While there are trout in Mill Creek below Mill Creek Falls, the best fishing can be found in the South Warner Wilderness, just below and above the Clear Lake. These sections hold good numbers of Redband and brown trout. In fact, the fishing is better than in the lake itself.

Traditionally, you won't find enormous trout. On the other hand, browns to three pounds aren't uncommon. Fall and spring are good times to fish from Clear Lake upstream. The outlet is another prime spot. You'll find larger pools than you would upstream of the lake. Fly fishing and spin casting are productive, but remember this isn't a large system. You'll need to downsize your Panther Martins.

Chris "Pescado" Cocoles caught this Mill Creek brown in October

If you plan to make the trip, supplies are available in Alturas. Mill Creek is closed to fishing from November 16 to the last Saturday in April. The road to the trailhead is impassable due to wintry conditions.

Also nearby is Mill Creek Falls, Blue Lake and the Pit River (South Fork).

Directions: *From the junction of Highway 299 and 395 in Alturas, drive south on Highway 395 to Jess Valley Road (County Road 64) in Likely. Turn left and drive 9.2 miles to a split in the road. Veer left and drive 1.9 miles to the trailhead in Mill Creek Campground.*

BLUE LAKE

Rating: 8

Species: Brown Trout, Rainbow Trout and Brook Trout

Stocked with 1,000 pounds of brook trout and 3,900 pounds of rainbow trout.

Facilities: Picnic Area, Fishing Pier, Boat Launch, Campgrounds and Restrooms

Need Information? Contact: Modoc National Forest (530) 233-5811

At one time, Blue Lake rivaled any other lake in the state when it came to producing quality brown trout. However, that was back in the Seventies and Eighties. Blue was a staple for big browns back then. It was common to see browns between 10-20 pounds. In fact, the California Department of Fish and Game has file photos of browns well above 20 pounds, and many anglers still believe there are few monster browns left in Blue Lake.

At 6,000 feet in the Modoc National Forest, this Lassen County water is 163 acres and one of the most popular trout lakes in the region. Therefore it's heavily fished and most anglers don't practice catch and release. Most of the genes of big browns are hanging on the wall of a Brown Bagger's home. At one time browns were consistently planted. However, plants of browns are now augmented to place more fish in the system every few years. They aren't part of the yearly allotments.

Fortunately, anglers can find five-to-seven-pound browns spawning in Parson Creek in the fall; proof some quality fish do remain. Browns are a self-sustaining entity. Please don't fish for them during the spawning period. If you want a shot at a big brown, you'll likely have to fish the shelf with a rainbow pattern Rebel minnow. There's an obvious drop-off where browns lurk.

Blue is much different that other waters in this region. Its' waters are clear rather than murky. The lake is managed more as a recreational fishery instead of a trophy fishery though. The CA DFG pumps 6,660 rainbows and 1,900 brooks into the lake each year. Action can be found by trollers dragging silver, gold and bikini Needlefish along the shelf, down the middle of the lake or along the shoreline. Others are content with sitting next to the launch ramp and tossing spinners.

Blue is also used as a dump lake. It often receives fish that are destined for others waters that don't have enough capacity or good enough water quality to maintain the fish. You never know what you'll catch out here.

Blue Lake hasn't always been a banner operation for the CA DFG as they've had issues with unwanted fish in the past. The lake was chemically treaded to kill chubs and bullhead in the early Eighties. While many fish were killed others still remain. Those that the browns don't eat are a problem still.

If you plan to make the trip, supplies are available in Alturas. Blue Lake can freeze in the winter. The road may also be closed due to snow. Call the Forest Service for updated road conditions.

Also nearby are Pit River (South Fork), Mill Creek, Mill Creek Falls and Clear Lake.

Directions: From the junction of Highway 299 and 395 in Alturas, drive south on Highway 395 to Jess Valley Road (County Road 64) in Likely. Turn left and drive 9.2 miles to a split in the road. Veer right and drive 6.5 miles to a split in the road. Turn right on Road 39N30 and drive eight-tenths of a mile to a final split. Veer right and drive three-tenths of a mile to the lake.

Blue Lake

Region
14

Lassen National Park
Caribou Wilderness

Manzanita Lake
Reflection Lake
Summit Lake
Bench Lake
King Creek
Cold Boiling Lake
Boiling Springs Lake
Emerald Lake
Helen Lake
Butte Lake
Cowboy Lake
Jewel Lake
Elanor Lake
Black Lake
North Divide Lake
Gem Lake

MANZANITA LAKE

Rating: 8

Species: Rainbow Trout and Brown Trout

Stocks: None

Facilities: Campgrounds, Restrooms and Picnic Areas

Need Information? Contact: Lassen National Park (530) 595-4444

In the late Eighties, when my age stood tall in single digits, I was introduced to Manzanita Lake. Uncle Ron Shaffer (my dad's brother) took me for a stroll around Manzanita Lake's shoreline; He was going to teach me how to fish. We had no live bait, all lures, and waited patiently as a family-friend caught fish next to us. I stuck close to Uncle Ron thinking our luck would change. It didn't.

Our pal walked right by us with a huge smirk on his face as he put a juicy night crawler on his hook. Did I mention that bait is illegal at Manzanita? He knew he was breaking the law, though it sure didn't seem to faze him. Only a few minutes passed before he caught a trout. Again, we were still waiting patiently.

Luckily, our pal stuck his foot in his mouth as he walked through the campgrounds boasting his prized catch. Accidentally, he told an undercover park ranger of his catch, and instead of enjoying that meaty rainbow for supper he was slapped with a hefty fine and the trout was confiscated. Karma, I guess.

Compared with my boyhood memories, Manzanita's fishery has changed drastically. For the most part, fishing in Lassen National Park is poor. There are a few lakes that have maintained excellent populations of trout in spite of absent fish plants though. The park's best fishery, Manzanita is governed by special regulations to protect the fish. Only artificial lures with barbless hooks may be used, and you are prohibited to fish within 150 feet of the lake's inlet.

Manzanita Lake has quality rainbow and brown trout. In September of 2001, the California Department of Fish and Game did a survey and found 75 percent of the fish to be browns, 25 percent rainbows. A decade ago the results were flip flopped: 80 percent were rainbows and 20 percent browns. It's uncommon to catch a fish smaller than 14 inches. To do well, fly fishing is recommended. Your focus should be imitating baitfish with olive or brown

A Manzanita rainbow

Woolly Buggers and damsel flies. Ant patterns are also effective. Other anglers fish Panther Martins from float tubes and canoes.

For starters, fish the northeast side of the lake near in inlets in the early morning until the sun hits the water. (Remember, you must stay 150 feet from the inlet.) Size six or eight Woolly Bugger or other nymphs like damsel flies or baetis nymphs are productive. In June and July, return to the same area between 10 a.m. and 2 p.m. to cash in on the callebaitis hatch.

July brings success with midge patterns. Stick to a No. 20. For browns, target the shallower bays on the north and south side near the outlet. Ant patterns work well near the willows along Highway 89. These willows harbor thousands of ants that climb the trees and fall into the lake.

If you plan to make the trip, supplies are available in Old Station. There is a fee to enter the park. No live bait can be used. Only single barbless hooks may be used. The lake is governed by catch and release only.

Also nearby are Hat Creek, Reflection Lake and Lily Pond.

Directions: *From the junction of Interstate 5 and Highway 44 east in Redding, drive east on Highway 44 for 46.9 miles to the Lassen National Park turnoff on the right. Turn right and drive seven-tenths of a mile to Manzanita Lake on the right.*

Jean Rodgers shows a Manzanita rainbow taken on a nymph in June of 2003.

REFLECTION LAKE

Rating: 3

Species: Brook Trout

Stocks: None

Facilities: Boat Launch, Campgrounds, Restrooms and Picnic Areas

Need Information? Contact: Lassen Volcanic National Park (530) 595-4444

Too bad baitfish are too small to catch, because Reflection Lake in Lassen Volcanic National Park has become overloaded with them. Reflection was a good brook trout fishery. However, with no plants taken place since 1984, there are few left. Some anglers catch rates are so poor they strongly believe there are no fish at all.

The baitfish, shiners in this case, have taken over. The shiners were placed in the lake by anglers using them for bait. According to the California Department of Fish and Game, baitfish are in danger of hurting Manzanita Lake's fishery. The shiners have begun to sneak out of Reflection via Reflection Creek and entered Manzanita. Most anglers think shiners are a good thing for Manzanita's browns to feed on. They are partly correct. However, the shiners eat juvenile trout, which could be detrimental to Manzanita's wild trout population.

The CA DFG wanted to drain Reflection a few years ago to remove the non-native shiners. Unfortunately, they couldn't get cooperation from the National Park Service. There is a possibility it may happen in the future though.

If you plan to make the trip, supplies are available in Old Station.

Also nearby are Hat Creek and Manzanita Lake.

Directions: *From the junction of Interstate 5 and Highway 44 east in Redding, drive east on Highway 44 for 46.9 miles to the Lassen National Park turnoff on the right. Turn right and drive 1.1 miles to Reflection Lake on the left.*

The Subway Caves are a big attraction near Reflection Lake.

Summit Lake

Rating: 3

Species: Rainbow Trout

Stocks: None

Facilities:
Campgrounds and
Restrooms

Are there any fish in Lassen National Park's Summit Lake? Old timers will say yes, but many anglers who have fished in the last decade will likely tell you no. It's no secret Summit used to be a good fishery. The lake was planted with rainbow trout from the California Department of Fish and Game from 1928-85. Plants were stopped because the fish were non-native to the park. With the shallow lake being a roadside water along Highway 89, the stocked fish were easily available to anglers and especially to those who staying at Summit Lake's North and South Campgrounds, only rock throwing distance from the lake.

Harvesting and a lack of good spawning grounds have prompted many anglers to believe there are no longer fish present. However, anglers' eyes are opened a few times each summer when some lucky angler catches a rainbow trout. Here are some possibilities for Summit retaining trout: the rainbows could possibly leave Summit via its outlet stream, Summit Creek and then spawn in the creek. Or a few curious fish swam upstream Summit Creek from Kings Creek a distance of two miles. One thing is for sure, if fish are present they are few in numbers. Best bet is to use the lake as a swimming hole, not a fishing hole.

Trip info for Bench Lake also applies to Summit Lake.

Directions: *From the junction of Interstate 5 and Highway 44 east in Redding drive east on Highway 44 for 46.9 miles to the Lassen National Park turnoff on the right. Turn right and drive 12.9 miles to Summit Lake on the left.*

A fawn in Lassen National Park   Lassen National Park's Cinder Cone

BENCH LAKE

Rating: 1

Species: None

Stocks: None

Facilities: None

Need Information?
Contact: Lassen
National Park
(530) 595-4444

Scanning over the stocking records for Lassen National Park I found no evidence of fish plants in Bench Lake. This could be for several reasons. The most likely reasons are that the lake is too shallow to support year-round populations of fish and that Bench is a good candidate for winterkill. Nonetheless, there are no fish in Bench Lake now. Just to make sure, I personally dove in with a mask and snorkel and swam every inch of the lake.

At one time, however, trout did inhabit the lake. They weren't planted, but after hearing stories from the old timers, how the fish got here was revealed. In the Thirties and Forties many anglers caught fish in Kings Creek and transported to them to Bench Lake.

Those practices are long gone and from now and most likely through eternity there will no longer be fish in Bench Lake. Lassen National Park has begun managing the waters in the park as they were in their former state, before humans brought fish in. Therefore, the lake will no longer hold fish. The park won't allow it to happen.

On a positive note, Bench Lake is situated in the mix of several top notch tourist spots. A short walk away is Kings Creek Falls, Cold Boiling Lake, Devil's Kitchen and the beautiful lush meadows of the park. Bench Lake is a great side trip, a place to wade in water that is much warmer than Kings Creek and an ever better place for a picnic.

To reach Bench Lake follow the signs to Kings Creek Falls. Just before the falls, take the right turnoff to Bench Lake.

If you plan to make the trip, supplies are available in Mineral. There is a day-use fee to enter Lassen National Park. Highway 89 may be closed through July some years. Call for updated road conditions.

Also nearby is Devil's Kitchen, Mt. Lassen and Reflection Lake.

Directions: *From I-5 in Redding, turn east on Highway 44 and drive 46 miles to the park entrance. Continue on Highway 89 for 17 miles to the trailhead on the left side of the road at mile post 32.*

KINGS CREEK

Rating: 3
Species: Rainbow Trout
Stocks: None
Facilities: Campgrounds and Restrooms

When it comes to stream fishing, Lassen Volcanic National Park doesn't produce large fish. In fact, few anglers catch any fish at all while fishing the park's streams. Lassen's streams and lake's receive no plants and haven't been planted with any fish since 1985. There are a few fish in the park's streams, but definitely not enough to warrant you to make a trip to fish 'em.

Kings Creek is roughly 11 miles long and empties into Warner Creek. With it's origin on the backside of Mt. Lassen, a few hundreds yards from Lake Helen, Kings Creek sure is pretty as it meanders mostly through lush meadows frequented by herds of deer. Unfortunately, unless you are a pro the fish tend not to cooperate. King's small wild rainbow trout are witty. It takes that extra effort to catch them, like crawling to the streambed on your belly so the fish can't see you, and keeping your human scent off your bait. It may not sound difficult, but even the slightest sign of a human sends these skittish fish scattering for cover. Try applying some Pautzke Liquid Krill.

The best way to visit the creek is to not fish it at all and concentrate on its best trait, Kings Creek Falls. The waterfall is impressive and is an easy and splendid three-mile hike from Road Marker 22 along Highway 89. Along with the breathtaking view of the waterfalls, the trail shines through with dozens of vibrant wildflowers and close encounters with deer.

Directions *and trip info for Bench Lake also apply to Kings Creek.*

COLD BOILING LAKE

Rating: 1

Species: None

Stocks: None

Facilities: None

Are there fish in Cold Boiling Lake? That's one question that isn't easy to answer. One thing is for sure, Cold Boiling Lake has never been planted. However, there is a path the fish could take to get there. It's a long one, but fish have been known to participate in far more strenuous activities. Cold Boiling has no inlet stream, but the lake is fed by numerous springs stemming far below earth's surface. Anglers have reported seeing fish here and trout have been known to be able to spawn in lakes with springs, so trout could reside here.

If there are trout in the lake, their path would be a long one. Beginning at the North Fork of the Feather River, the fish would have to swim up the South Arm of Rice Creek to the North Arm of Rice Creek and into Crumbaugh Lake. From Crumbaugh they could possibly swim into Cold Boiling Lake. Bottom line, the chances are slim that you'll catch fish. On the other hand, come for the intriguing scene of watching cold water bubble up from beneath the soil. It's the same concept of a hot spring, yet the water is cold.

To reach Cold Boiling Lake, begin at the trailhead for Kings Creek Falls. From Kings Creek Campground the path descends for a half mile to a trail junction. Stay left and continue a tad more than one-tenth of a mile to the turnoff for Cold Boiling Lake. The lake is within rock throwing distance from the junction.

Directions *and trip info for Bench Lake also apply to Cold Boiling Lake.*

Cold Boiling Lake

BOILING SPRINGS LAKE

Rating: 1

Species: None

Stocks: None

Facilities: None

Need Information?
Contact: Lassen
National Park
(530) 595-4444

The second you find yourself fishing Boiling Springs Lake stop what you are doing, find a pay phone and please give me a call. Boiling Springs has no fish, and hopefully, you wont need me to tell you that. When you first see the lake, noticing steam rolling across the surface and milky water so thick your visibility is zero, it should be apparent there are no fish here. In a seldom-visited area of Lassen National Park, Boiling Springs Lake has never held fish due to extreme geothermal conditions.

With the help of underground steam vents, Boiling Springs remains at a constant 125 degrees year-round. The water is so hot contact would cause an instant burn. There is no reason to bring along a fishing pole, however a trip to this wondrous lake is a must for anyone in the region. Just remember to steer clear of the shore. Be safe and keep your distance.

Here's how to get there. It's a 2.8 roundtrip mile walk from the day use parking area. The trail is well signed and easy to follow.

If you plan to make the trip, supplies are available in Mineral. The road to the lake closes in the winter.

Also nearby are Warner Creek, Terminal Geyser and Devils Kitchen.

Directions: *From Interstate 5 in Red Bluff, take the Highway 99/36 exit and drive east for 2.2 miles to the junction of Highway 99/36. Turn left on Highway 36 and drive 67.7 miles and turn left on Feather River Road. Drive seven-tenths of a mile and veer left. At approximately six miles, turn right at the Drakesbad turnoff and continue 1.1 miles to Warner Creek Campground. Follow signs from here to Lassen National Park and the day use parking area.*

Boiling Springs Lake

EMERALD LAKE

Rating: 1

Species: Rainbow Trout

Stocks: None

Facilities: None

Each lake in California that has been closed to fishing has its' own unique story as to why fishing is no longer permitted. Most stem from private property issues, to protect spawning or dangerous winter or water conditions. However, the reason for closing Emerald Lake in Lassen National Park makes me chuckle. Fishing was closed to the general public because the National Park Service (NPS) thought it was the only way they could stop anglers from planting fish into the roadside water near Lassen Volcano.

Between 1928 and 1965, Emerald was stocked yearly with rainbow trout. When the plants stopped, anglers illegally took it upon themselves to stock the lake. The lake was deemed ecologically dead in a recent California Department of Fish and Game study, thus rainbows don't reproduce here. Therefore, the only way for anglers to catch fish is to plant them on their own. The last survey the NPS conducted showed one fish in the lake and that fish was found dead on the bottom. There is talk of reopening the lake to fishing, but with no fish present (unless another angler has made a new plant) and the NPS prohibiting future stocks the plan to reopen the lake is worthless. Don't waste your time. Climb Mt. Lassen instead. You have the same chance at catching a fish!

Trip info for Bench Lake also applies to Emerald Lake.

Directions: *From Interstate 5 in Redding, turn east on Highway 44 and drive 46 miles to the park entrance. Continue on Highway 89 for 15 miles to the lake on the left.*

HELEN LAKE

Rating: 1

Species: None

Stocks: None

Facilities: None

From 1928-35, Helen Lake was a top destination for anglers who visited Lassen National Park. The scenic lake bordering Highway 89 was planted with either brook or rainbow trout throughout that period, but unfortunately hasn't been planted since. Nevertheless, Helen will most likely never hold fish again. The National Park Service (NPS) has taken a strong position to return all waters in the park back to their original state. That means how they were before there were fish planting trucks. Unfortunately, Helen never had a native population of fish.

Regardless, Helen Lake isn't barren on fish because stocking no longer takes place. According to the (NPS), the lake has been deemed too poisonous for fish, therefore the fish never made it too long here anyway. Geothermal activity from Mt. Lassen seeps gases into the lake. As for now, Helen is a great destination for a quick pit stop for snapping a few pictures or to change drivers, but that's about it. Keep the rods tucked away in the back of your car.

Trip info for Bench Lake also applies to Helen Lake.

Directions: *From Interstate 5 in Redding turn east on Highway 44 and drive 46 miles to the park entrance. Continue on Highway 89 for roughly 15 miles to the lake on the left.*

Helen Lake

BUTTE LAKE

Rating: 3

Species: Rainbow Trout

Stocks: None

Facilities: Restrooms, Campgrounds and a Ranger Station

Need Information? Contact: Lassen Volcanic National Park (530) 595-4444

While more than 60 lakes and streams in Lassen National Park were stocked with trout at one time, according to National Park Service, Butte Lake was never stocked with fish. Nonetheless, plants in the park have been non-existent for more than two decades, yet ironically trout remain in Butte Lake.

In fact, even if there were native trout present in Butte, the lava flows that occurred from the 1908 eruption of Mt. Lassen would have heated the water too much for fish to sustain life. Miraculously, Mother Nature has figured a way for trout to make a life in Butte. Most likely the fish swam up Butte Creek from below the lake. The California Department of Fish and Game must have stocked it at one time. While there is no scientific data I came across to prove the trout are spawning and reproducing in Butte Lake, fingerling and adult fish visible in the lake backup the theory that successful spawning is occurring somehow.

Still, Butte isn't a great fishery. Most anglers can spend a week fishing it and not catch a fish. While fish are present, catches are rare. The trout population is small. One of the few ways to be successful is to get lucky walking the shorelines tossing a Kastmaster or Little Cleo out to the middle and retrieving slowly. The outlet and inlet areas are best.

Butte Lake is located on what most visitors refer to as the backside of the park and receives few visitors. The main focus at Butte is for hikers who opt to climb the Cinder Cone. Personally, I think this hike is one of the best California has to offer. The route winds through a burnt lava flow before taking you up a former volcano and drops you to walk down into the cone. The route also gives you classic views of The Painted Dunes. Come for the hiking, rather than the fishing.

If you plan to make the trip, supplies are available in Old Station. In winter and early spring call ahead for road conditions. The road doesn't typically open until sometime in June.

Also nearby are Hat Creek, Juniper Lake and Plum Canyon Reservoir.

Directions: *From Interstate 5 going north in Redding, exit Highway 44 east. When you leave the off-ramp and are on the highway, reset your odometer and drive 59.8 miles to the Highway 44/89 junction in Old Station. Staying on Highway 44, turn right and drive 10.8 miles 44 to the right turnoff for Butte Lake. Turn right, drive 6.5 miles and turn right at the trailhead sign for Painted Dunes and Cinder Cone.*

COWBOY LAKE

Rating: 1

Species: None

Stocks: None

Facilities: None

Cowboy Lake offers superb morning displays of magnificent mirror-like reflections for hikers, yet can't provide the same incentives anglers seek. Cowboy is barren of fish and no plants are in the works to stock the small lake in the Caribou Wilderness. Due to its' shallow depth, Cowboy is a solid candidate for winterkill. For this reason, the California Department of Fish and Game has refrained from trying to introduce fish into it.

There is in the spring, however, a chance for fish to cruise up from Caribou Lake during the short spurt when Cowboy's outlet has water, yet the ordeal is highly unlikely. Caribou is home to brooks and rainbows and since brooks are traditionally fall spawners, the only chance you may have are rainbows headed up Cowboy's outlet. Unfortunately, this is a hypothesis and no scientific data or angling records prove that Cowboy has any population of trout. Don't bother wetting a line here.

To reach Cowboy, begin at the trailhead near the restrooms at Caribou Lake. The path parallels Caribou, while staying relatively level before crossing into the wilderness area and passing three small, fishless ponds. Then, a route signed for Haywood Meadow breaks off to the left and heads to Gem Lake. Stay right and walk only a few minutes to the lake which will be on the left side of the path. Total time in route: 10-15 minutes.

If you plan to make the trip, supplies are available in Susanville. In winter and spring call the Forest Service for updated road conditions. The road may be impassable due to mud and snow.

Also nearby are Silver Lake and the Upper Susan River.

Directions: *From the junction of Highway 395 and 44 in Susanville, take Highway 44 west to the junction with Highway 36. Stay on Highway 44 and drive 18.4 miles to Road A21. Turn left on Road A21 and drive 4.4 miles to an unsigned road on the right. (This is known as Silver Lake Road. There's a stop sign.) Turn right and continue 5.1 miles to a split in the road. Veer right and drive one-half mile to another split. Veer right and continue three-tenths of a mile to a dirt road on the left. Take the left and continue two-tenths of a mile to the lake.*

Cowboy Lake

JEWEL LAKE

Rating: 4	
Species: Rainbow Trout	
Stocks: None	
Facilities: None	

The walk to Jewel Lake may be one of the best beginning backpacking options in California. In fact, I was shocked to find three-to-five-year olds on the path as a mom pushed a three-wheel stroller alongside. The mostly flat, easy route makes for great family outings.

Jewel's fishery isn't awing, rather available. Trout are present, not exactly in convincing numbers though. Small fingerlings were abundant along the shore when I last visited. For anything worth casting a line to and slapping on a skillet, you'll need to find deeper water, which means casting off a point. Don't bother fishing where the trail first meets the lake; rather wait until the trail loops around the backside. Your best bet is waiting until the late evening or early morning when trout are rising and it's easy to spot them.

From Cowboy it's a fairly steady, yet easy climb up the ridge towards Jewel before the path levels out in a thick, wooded forest. After a few short minutes, you'll be at the lake.

Directions *and trip info for Cowboy Lake also apply to Jewel Lake.*

Jewel Lake

Cinder Cone

ELANOR LAKE

Rating: 3

Species: None

Stocks: None

Facilities: None

While typical backcountry waters are known for their charm and elegance, Elanor Lake looks shallow, fishless and unappealing. Elanor isn't one of the Caribou Wilderness' better fishing lakes. The trailside of the lake is worthless to an angler as shallow, silted water and downed trees make for poor habitat and tough fishing.

To locate any fish you'll need to walk to deeper water found on the opposite side of the lake. It's best to wait until the evening when surface action occurs to experience any success. During the summer, extreme dryness and heat can make Elanor a very tough place to catch fish. Any way you approach it, Elanor isn't a premier backcountry lake and can be easy to miss if you aren't looking carefully for it.

From Jewel Lake, pay close attention to the first body of water you see on the right side of the path. While there is a sign nailed to a tree on the lake's shoreline, it's not easy to see from the path. Rest assured this is the shallow, fishless end of Elanor. Make your own path around the shoreline to the deeper sections of the lake.

Directions and trip info for Cowboy Lake also apply to Elanor.

Elanor Lake

BLACK LAKE

Rating: 4

Species: None

Stocks: None

Facilities: None

Set in a fairly flat meadow, Black Lake is a quiet, pretty lake in the Caribou Wilderness that doesn't get heavily fished. It's a short hike, but with Gem and Jewel closer, many anglers don't find it necessary to fish here. If you want to wet a line make sure to tie on something that you can heave a good distance.

The shorelines are shallow and most of the time you'll need to find deep water to be successful. Black offers a decent trout fishery; however many anglers who make small 10-foot casts never see any action. Black's immediate shoreline is a lot like a meadow, being very shallow and gently sloped. To do best you'll need a float tube or some means to reach deeper water consistently. A large spoon or spinner will work if you have a reel than can make long distance casts. If you have the energy to drag in a float tube, try slowly striping in a small Woolly Bugger.

Getting to Black Lake from Jewel Lake is pretty easy. Leaving Jewel, you'll embark on a short climb over another small ridge before leveling out and coming to a junction. Veering away from signs pointing to Cone Lake, stay left on the flat path to Black.

Directions *and trip info for Cowboy Lake also apply to Black Lake.*

Black Lake

NORTH DIVIDE LAKE

Rating: 1

Species: None

Stocks: None

Facilities: None

Unfortunately, North Divide Lake doesn't have much to attract anyone other than a few overnight backpackers looking for flat ground. The lake is shallow, void of fish and although it's warm enough to swim in the summer months a heavily silted bottom can take away from the enjoyment. Regrettably, unless you have wings and are seeking flat, calm water to land on, you aren't going to be impressed.

North Divide is a small lake in the Caribou Wilderness that is overlooked by dozens of other more visited waters that harbor trout. What's best about North Divide is the camping opportunities. There are several areas along the shoreline that are flat and heavily shaded, making for excellent overnight options for backpackers looking to make day trips to dozens of other lakes in the drainage.

From the turnoff to Gem Lake, stay on the main route heading away from Gem and towards North Divide, which is roughly a 15-25 minute hike away.

Directions *and trip info for Cowboy Lake also apply to North Divide Lake.*

North Divide Lake

GEM LAKE

Rating: 3

Species: Rainbow Trout

Stocked with two
pounds of fingerling
rainbow trout.

Facilities: None

Gem Lake is one of those lakes that look like it's teaming with fish, yet fishing isn't great. When a few buddies and I fished it, there was nothing to prove that it deserved much, if any, attention. Gem is set in its' own little basin and is seldom fished, and while it may seem like those would be ideal conditions to catch a limit, it's not that way at Gem.

Ideally, all you would need to do is walk out on one of the fallen trees and cast towards deeper water. The shallow flats along the shore aren't traditionally productive. Gem is a clear lake. If there were fish in the shallows, you wouldn't have a problem seeing them, especially if you had polarized glasses. We, however, saw none. Only the middle of the lake, roughly 20-30 yards out from the shoreline, is deep water and may hold fish that could evade the naked eye.

Gem is planted by the California Department of Fish and Game from the air. In 2003, 2,000 fingerling rainbow trout were planted. Sadly, I can't comment on the size of the fish because when I last visited it was over 100 degrees and no fish were surfacing or biting, nor could any be seen in the clear water. Are there any adult trout in the lake? Good question. I can't be sure.

Neither could the CA DFG when I inquired with them.

To reach Gem: from the junction just before Cowboy Lake, take the left fork signed for Haywood Meadow. In roughly five minutes you'll pass by a fishless, unnamed lake and head up a few switchbacks before leveling out on the route in a heavily wooded forest. Shortly you'll come to a dry lake. If you look at the rocks and trees that line the lake, you'll be able to see the water line that once was the high water mark. Soon after the dry lake, keep an eye out on the right for a small trail spur that breaks off to the right. Take the right fork and follow it for 100 yards uphill before dropping down to the lake.

Directions *and trip info for Cowboy Lake also apply to Gem Lake.*

Gem Lake

Graeagle Pond
Feather River (Middle Fork)
Jamison Creek
Eureka Lake
Grass Lake
Wades Lake
Jamison Lake
Rock Lake
Little Last Chance Creek
Frenchman Reservoir
Lake Davis
Spanish Creek
Crystal Lake
Snake Lake
Smith Lake
Silver Lake
Bucks Lake
Little Bucks Lake
Grizzly Forebay
Three Lakes
Round Valley Reservoir
Feather River (North Fork, Belden)
Little Grass Valley Reservoir
Sly Creek Reservoir

15

Region

Quincy
Graeagle

GRAEAGLE POND

Rating: 5

Species: Rainbow Trout

Stocked with 800 pounds of rainbow trout.

Facilities: General Store, Gas, Restaurant, Paddle Boat Rentals, Swimming Beach and Bait & Tackle

Need Information? Contact: Graeagle Store (530) 836-2519

Each year, the California Department of Fish and Game plants half-pound rainbow trout into Graeagle Pond. Wait a minute though, it's not the 1,240 CA DFG fish that draw anglers to fish here. In exchange for the use of water, Graeagle Land and Water Company also stocks fish into the pond. These are quality fish, some which push eight pounds, and are planted once a year for a kid's fish derby. Most of those fish get caught fast. On the other hand, some do survive year-round. There are always fish to be caught.

Unfortunately, summertime brings thousands of visitors to Graeagle, and most of them make a pit stop at the pond. At 7,200 feet in the Mohawk Valley and just a few feet from the banks of the Middle Fork of the Feather River, this two-acre pond is warm enough for swimming during the water months. Water is diverted off Gray Eagle Creek to ensure the pond stays full.

If you are going to fish, I suggest you get here early. By 10 a.m. this place is crawling with sun tan lotion, beach towels and swim suits for the remainder of the day. Graeagle gets bombarded by kids, teenagers and adults. It's a local hangout that every tourist knows about. Anglers should fish near where the water is being pumped into the lake. Just about any method works as long as you aren't competing with the swimmers.

If you plan to make the trip, supplies are available in Graeagle. Fishing is permitted year-round. At times in the winter, ice partially covers the lake.

Also nearby are the Gold Lakes Basin and Plumas-Eureka State Park.

Directions: *From the junction of Highway 70 and 89 south in Blairsden, drive south on Highway 89 for 1.4 miles and turn left into the Graeagle Pond parking area.*

Graeagle Pond

FEATHER RIVER (MIDDLE FORK, GRAEAGLE)

Rating: 4

Species: Rainbow Trout, Brown Trout and Mountain Whitefish

Stocked with 2,800 pounds of rainbow trout.

Facilities: None

Need Information? Contact: Plumas National Forest (530) 283-2050

The Middle Fork of the Feather River, which flows near the town of Graeagle, doesn't offer the same great fishing that can be found in many other portions of the Feather. This section of the Middle Fork isn't located in a narrow gorge, or along a winding canyon road with cold and tumbling water, deep holes, riffles, pools and long runs. No sir, this part of the Feather is a definite letdown.

There are several factors that characterize this fishery: slow moving water, easy to read water, trash fish, and only handful of planted fish. Generally, the river doesn't support sufficient wild populations of trout.

In an effort to give local kids and tourists a place to nab a few trout, the California Department of Fish and Game plants more than 5,250 rainbow trout each spring and summer. Concentrate on the area near where the river crosses under Highway 89. Make a few casts and if you don't get any takers, move on.

The river can be ok for planted fish in the early season. Unfortunately, by June the water warms, slows and fishing takes a hit on the nose. Honestly, when this happens don't bother coming. The water is christened with a film of foam and the smell of urine. It can be that bad.

During the summer, squawfish take over the show. Its quiet comical because many anglers think they are huge browns and waste a whole day fishing for them. The

The Middle Fork of the Feather River

squawfish can reach upwards of seven pounds and are known to take a night crawler or two, but they sure aren't browns!

If you plan to make the trip, supplies are available in Graeagle. The Middle Fork of the Feather River is closed to fishing from November 16 to the last Saturday in April.

Also nearby are Plumas-Eureka State Park and the Gold Lakes Basin.

Directions: *From the junction of Highway 70 and 89 south just north of Graeagle, drive south on Highway 89 for a half-mile to a bridge that crosses over the river.*

JAMISON CREEK

Rating: 5

Species: Brook Trout

Stocked with 500 pounds of rainbow trout.

Facilities: Campgrounds, Restrooms and a Visitor Center

Need Information? Contact: Plumas Eureka State Park (530) 836-2380

Jamison Creek is a mountain stream almost exclusively fished by campers staying in Plumas Eureka State Park. The creek flows through the state park and more importantly, it cuts right through the campground. The creek is planted by the California Department of Fish and Game with 1,000 rainbow trout from late April through 4th of July weekend. With high fishing pressure in the park, you'd expect most of the rainbows to be caught within a few weeks. Surprisingly, a large number of stocked trout live through winter. How? There are tons of large boulders in the streambed for the trout to hide under.

The creek used to be in excellent shape. It had deep pools, great structure and good spawning grounds. However, high water during the El Nino of 1998 silted many of those holes. The population of wild rainbow and browns has slowly declined since.

Shaded with pines, the stream is easy to fish. Some use Power Bait, others use size 1/32 Panther Martins in the deeper holes. One thing is for sure: don't expect to catch anything over a pound.

If you plan to make the trip, supplies are available in Graeagle. In winter, call ahead for updated road conditions. Chains may be required. Jamison Creek is closed to fishing from November 16 to the last Saturday in April.

Also nearby are Renee Falls, Solano Falls and Eureka Lake.

Jamison Creek

Directions: *From the junction of Highway 70 and 89 in Blairsden, drive south on Highway 89 for one mile to Road A14 and turn right. Continue 1.1 miles to a split in the road. Stay left. Drive 1.7 miles to another split and again stay left. Continue 5.2 miles to another fork. Turn left and drive 1.1 miles to a final spilt. Turn left into the campground and the creek.*

EUREKA LAKE

Rating: 4

Species: Brook Trout

Stocks: None

Facilities: Restrooms

Need Information?
Contact: Plumas
Eureka State Park
(530) 836-2380

What looks on a map like an easy drive on a dirt road to Eureka Lake, in reality is a rough neck-jarring experience. This puppy isn't for most folks. The 1.3 mile stretch from where the road turns to dirt takes about 15 minutes and will likely leave your neck sore for a few days. Does the fishing warrant the drive? Let's decide.

There are some brook trout in Eureka Lake, however, fishing has never been the icon of Plumas Eureka State Park. For the most part, these fish are difficult to catch. The shorelines are shallow and tree stumps make for tons of snags. Anglers with float tubes or canoes have a much better chance at catching fish. Try an inflated night crawler. While the fishing is a bit below average, the scenery is great as 7,447-foot Eureka Peak looms overhead.

If you plan to make the trip, supplies are available in Graeagle. The road to Eureka closes in the winter. Call ahead for updated conditions.

Also nearby are Jamison Creek and Little Jamison Falls.

Directions: *From the junction of Highway 70 and 89 north of Graeagle, drive south on Highway 89 for one mile to Road A14 and turn right. Continue 1.1 miles to a split in the road. Stay left. Drive 1.7 miles to another split and again stay left. Continue 5.2 miles to another fork. Stay right and drive 1.4 miles. The road turns to dirt. Continue 1.3 miles to the lake.*

Eureka Lake

GRASS LAKE

Rating: 4
Species: Rainbow Trout and Brook Trout
Stocks: None
Facilities: None
Need Information? Contact: Plumas Eureka State Park (530) 836-2380

In reality, Grass Lake is a widening of Little Jamison Creek. But, to those with a float tube it's a place where anglers have a good shot at catching rainbow and brook trout. The lake is extremely shallow and while there are a few spots shoreline anglers can get in on the action the opportunity is minimal. If you can get to the middle of Grass near one of one the dead tree stumps, your chances increase. One downfall is the fish aren't big. A 10 incher would earn bragging rights. Fly fishing out of float tubes is best.

Grass Lake is an easy backcountry lake to reach. The trail begins in Plumas Eureka State Park near Jamison Mine. The route wastes no time climbing and does so consistently over the first three-quarters of a mile before coming to a junction. This is where the bulk of the 585-foot elevation gain occurs. The left fork peters off to Smith Lake. Stay right following signs towards Grass Lake. Shortly, you'll cross into the Plumas National Forest, then, pass a sign for Jamison Falls on the right. After taking a quick peek of the waterfall, push forward. The route levels out and comes to Grass Lake three-tenths of a mile past the falls.

If you plan to make the trip, supplies are available in Graeagle. The road to Grass Lake closes in the winter. Call ahead for updated conditions.

Also nearby are Wades Lake, Rock Lake and Jamison Lake.

Directions: *From the junction of Highway 70 and 89 in Blairsden, drive south on Highway 89 for one mile to Road A14 and turn right. Continue 1.1 miles to a split in the road. Stay left. Drive 1.7 miles to another split and again stay left. Continue 4.7 miles to a turnoff on the left for Jamison Mine and Grass Lake Trail. Turn left and drive 1.3 miles to the trailhead.*

Grass Lake

WADES LAKE

Rating: 4

Species: Rainbow
Trout and Brook
Trout

Stocks: None

Wades is the least fished lake in the Jamison Creek Drainage. It holds brooks and a few rainbows, nevertheless most anglers figure they can catch the same size and quantity of fish at Grass Lake and don't make the trip. What Wades Lake does offer is an exceptional backpacking option. Crowds are light and the fishing pressure is non-existent.

The lake rests at 6,549 feet in the Plumas National Forest. Wades is three miles from the trailhead. The downfall is that a 1,300-foot elevation gain awaits you. Action is best at Wades when the wind is blowing, yet it can make for difficult casting. Typically, the wind comes from the west, blowing the bait to the east shore. Trout stack up in this area looking to capitalize on the concentration of food. Fly anglers do best when the wind is down on midges. There's an excellent summer midge hatch.

To reach Wades from Grass Lake, follow the path towards Wades Lake. The route is lined with vivid wildflowers as it parallels and gives you exceptional views of Grass Lake. As you reach the end of the lake, the path cuts through a heavily forested area before crossing Jamison Creek at three-quarters of a mile from

Wades Lake

where the trail first reached Grass' east shore. Continue two-tenths of a mile to a junction. Take the right fork signed for Wades Lake and continue eight-tenths of a mile to the lake. The section of the trip is a butt kicker, but the 550-foot gain is eased by great views of Grass Lake.

Directions *and trip info for Grass Lake also apply to Wades Lake.*

JAMISON LAKE

Rating: 5

Species: Brook Trout

Stocks: None

Facilities: None

In 1982, Plumas Eureka State Park ranger Mike Krause was sitting in his office when a man carrying a gunny sac walked in and asked him if he could identify a fish he had in the sac that he caught at Jamison Lake. Surprised by the size of the trout, Krause was stunned. The man had an eight-pound brown, the largest fish on record from any of lake in the Jamison Creek Drainage. Most likely, none of us will ever catch a fish of that size at Jamison. On the other hand, eight-to-nine-inch brook trout are common in this backcountry lake.

Three key areas hold fish. The best is the inlets. Near the back of the lake there are two streams that form the headwaters of Little Jamison Creek. Brookies stack up here, but due to an overwhelming number of fallen trees and tree stumps, snags are difficult to avoid. It's better to float an inflated night crawler than to cast spinners. Other hotspots include the point on the north shore near the dam and the channel between that point and the dam. This dam is a five-foot tall stone built to increase water storage.

At 6,275 feet in the Plumas National Forest, fishing Jamison can be a bit difficult. The shoreline is rugged, not flat and not easy to traverse. If you aren't in good shape, it might be too much on your knees after the 2.5-mile hike in. Personally, I found it more productive to fish Little Jamison Creek below the dam where pan size brookies are abundant.

To reach Jamison from the trail junction past Grass Lake, take the left fork and continue six-tenths of a mile as the route gradually ascends and crosses over Wade Lake's outlet stream. When you come to a junction, stay left, walking away from Wades Lake. It's a quarter-mile to Jamison.

Directions *and trip info for Grass Lake also apply to Jamison Lake.*

Jamison Lake

ROCK LAKE

Rating: 5
Species: Brook Trout
Stocks: None
Facilities: None

Rock Lake is one of those lakes where you come to fish, but by the time your line hits the water it's been an hour. At 6,300 feet in the Plumas National Forest, the scenery here is unforgettable, so spectacular many anglers don't end up fishing. The water is sparkling clear. Its' gem allure is addicting. The view of the Little Jamison Creek Drainage and Graeagle from the east side of the lake is inspiring. You may never want to go home.

As for the fishing, if you don't arrive in the early morning or late evening to fish the surface bite, expect action to be sluggish. During the day the brooks head for deep water and without a medium size spoon you'll have difficulty reaching the depths. Rock is a deep backcountry lake with steep drop-offs. Daytime fishing is most productive for anglers using bait. Power Bait rigged with a sliding sinker is your best bet. In the evening, try casting a midge pattern or a dry fly.

From Jamison Lake, Rock Lake is a mere two-tenths of a mile. From Jamison's dam, cross over Little Jamison Creek and continue on the path as it brings you to Rock Lake.

***Directions** and trip info for Grass Lake also apply to Rock Lake.*

Rock Lake

LITTLE LAST CHANCE CREEK

Rating: 5

Species: Rainbow Trout
and Brown Trout

Stocked with two
pounds of fingerling
brown trout.

Facilities:
Campgrounds and
Restrooms

Need Information?
Contact: Wiggins
Trading Post
(530) 993-4683

Little Last Chance Creek isn't one of the premier stream fishing destinations in the Sierra Valley. In fact, fishing is just fair here. This small tailwater fishery is blessed by releases from Frenchman Reservoir and maintains enough volume to support trout year-round. Records show the fishery has been managed by the California Department of Fish and Game since 1951, however, the species and sizes of planted fish has changed many times.

Almost annually (except during the eighties) the CA DFG planted either rainbow or brown trout. Early on, the fishery was managed as a put-and-take and was planted with catchable size trout. However, only sub-catchable and fingerling trout have been planted since 1996. Rainbows or browns are planted every year.

Public access is limited in this section of the creek. The best area to fish is from the campground up to the base of the dam. It's possible for anglers to drift bait and Pautzke salmon eggs, however, because it's such a small water, casting lures can be a challenge. Fly anglers do well if they can effectively roll cast.

Don't expect to catch lunkers. This fishery is dominated by mostly six-to-nine-inch fish, yet some greater than 10 inches are caught. In 1989, the CA DFG electrofished a one-mile section of the creek downstream from the dam and found estimates of up to 2,400 fish per mile. However, only 800 fish per mile were greater than catchable size.

If you plan to make the trip, supplies are available in Portola. Little Last Chance Creek is closed to fishing from November 16 to the last Saturday in April.

Also nearby are Frenchman Reservoir and Lake Davis.

Directions: *From the junction of Highway 395 and 70 north of Reno, drive west on Highway 70 for 5.6 miles to Frenchman Road. Turn right and drive 5.6 miles to the creek. Access is available from this point to the dam.*

Little Last Chance Creek

FRENCHMAN RESERVOIR

Rating: 7

Species: Rainbow Trout
and Brown Trout

Stocked with 600
pounds of fingerling
rainbow trout and
11,300 pounds of sub-
catchable rainbow trout.

Facilities: Boat Launch,
Restrooms and a
Campground

Need Information?
Contact: Wiggins
Trading Post
(530) 993-4683

Frenchman Reservoir was one of the most talked about fisheries in the West. Unfortunately, it wasn't because it was an excellent fishery. Frenchman, prior to the illegal introduction of northern pike sometime in the mid-Eighties, was a staple for put-and-grow fisheries in California. However, the pike rapidly reproduced and put a serious damper on the trout population. Barring a long explanation, the California Department of Fish and Game chemically treated Frenchman in spring of 1991. There have been no pike reported since. Here's what transpired.

Pike were officially recognized in Frenchman in August of 1988. Prior to the pike, Frenchman boasted an excellent put-and-grow fishery. During the summer, the CA DFG planted three-inch fingerling rainbow trout. Those trout reached eight-to-nine inches by the fall and 10-12 inches by spring. The establishment of pike decreased those levels drastically. This was reminiscent of what happened when golden shiners took over the lake in the Seventies. Keep in mind, Frenchman Reservoir was also treated in 1975 to remove golden shiners.

The CA DFG states that pike weren't the sole reason for the poor trout angling, but they played a big part. The chemical treatment was based on the fact that if pike were to slip through the dam or slide over the spillway during high water levels, they could possibly swim down Little Last Chance Creek, into the canals in the Sierra Valley and to the Middle Fork of the Feather River. By getting this far, it's likely the pike could make it to Lake Oroville and ultimately in the Central Valley where they would upset anadromous runs of native fish.

Treating the lake was expected to prevent the migration of fish to the Central Valley and to improve the rainbow trout fishery by creating a healthier environment, paving the way for more rapid growing conditions for trout.

The decision to chemically treat the lake was well thought out. There were several plans on the table prior to the lake being chemically treated. They are as follows: no project; leaving everything how it is and letting nature take its' course; combination management which basically would allow the pike to coexist with other species, while taking measures to ensure pike don't escape the system; chemicallying treat the reservoir, while reducing the size of the reservoir: which would save the CA DFG money by allowing them to treat a smaller portion of the lake; draining the lake would have worked, but the possibility of pike being flushed into the Feather River system during the draining process was too great; blasting as a successful method of removal, however, it was expected that five percent of the pike would survive; trapping and netting, but unfortunately this method is very costly and is ineffective. There were several other methods, including a partial draining of the reservoir during pike spawning season, summer treatment and a fall treatment.

The CA DFG chose to treat the reservoir during the spring. After deeming the operation a success, Frenchman was restocked with 25,000 pounds of catchable rainbow trout, 100,000 fingering rainbows and 150,000 sub-catchable bows. Today, it's again fishing the way it did prior to the introduction of the pike. Each year Frenchman is planted with 150,000 fingerling Eagle Lake trout and 80,390 sub-catchables.

Frenchman's trout are enjoyed by shore anglers and trollers. During the spring and early summer, trout can be found scattered across the lake and at the mouths of all inlets. Most anglers are content with bait fishing near the dam, but fishing any point or cove with bait can be productive. Trollers, on the other hand, get by with flasher and night crawler combos and small spoons like a Needlefish or Dick Nite spoon.

When full, Frenchman offers 21 miles of shoreline, 1,470 acres and depths to 110 feet. On the other hand, the lake is drawn down in the winter. Wintertime is dominated by ice fishing. Frenchman freezes enough to permit ice fishing, which is best near the dam, unless you have a snowmobile and can reach other popular areas.

If you plan to make the trip, supplies are available in Chilcoot. Check ice conditions before venturing out on the ice in winter.

Also nearby are Lake Davis and Little Last Chance Creek.

Directions: *From Reno, drive north on Interstate 395 to the junction with Highway 70. Take Highway 70 west for 5.6 miles to Frenchman Road. Turn right and drive eight miles to the lake.*

Frenchman Reservoir

LAKE DAVIS

Rating: 6

Species: Rainbow
Trout, Brown Trout,
Northern Pike,
Pumpkinseed, Sunfish
and Brown Bullhead

Stocked with 17,000
pounds of rainbow
trout.

Facilities: Lodging,
Restrooms, Picnic
Areas, Boat Launches,
Campgrounds, General
Store, Fish Cleaning
Station, RV Hookups
and Bait and Tackle

Need Information?
Contact: Dollard's
Market (530) 832-5251,
Gold Rush Sporting
Goods (530) 832-5724,
Lake Davis
Resort/Grizzly Store
(530) 832-1060

Lake Davis isn't your average California rainbow trout fishery. While it's probably the most well known trout water in the state, its' fame stems from controversy. Lake Davis became nationally known in the late Nineties when major newspapers, magazines and networks such as the LA and New York Times, Sports Illustrated and CNN exposed the reservoir's issues with illegally introduced northern pike. These pike viciously took over and ate nearly all of the trout, devastating the local economy (which relies heavily on recreation) and putting Lake Davis in the national spotlight.

In 1997, the lake was treated with rotenone. No one knows if the treatment itself was unsuccessful or if new pike were dumped into Lake Davis. However, in a manner similar to how ants show up in your yard after spraying a week earlier, these hardy pike returned. For more than a decade Lake Davis has been in turmoil. The rainbow trout fishery that used to rival any other is again slipping and keeping the pike is check is sucking money out of the California Department of Fish and Game. The community is in desperate need of a fix.

After the lake, that boasts 32 miles of shoreline, was chemically treated and pike were again found, the CA DFG and a local steering committee came up with a plan to help reduce the pike and rid them from the 4,000-acre lake that rests at 5,775 feet in the Plumas National Forest. The plan was intended to suppress, contain and remove the pike population via several methods. Those methods included the use of nets, barriers, electrofishing, explosives and entrapment. Tributary barriers were constructed, spawning areas were blocked off to prohibit pike from attempting to reproduce, pike food was reduced and predator species were stocked in hopes of achieving their goal.

Pike prey on rainbow trout, and by not stocking fingerling rainbows, it's possible to reduce the amount of food. By stocking brown trout, there would be a species present that would eat juvenile pike and help reduce their numbers. The CA DFG would also encourage pike fishing by anglers to help remove pike. Drag, encircling, fyke and tap nets and electrofishing would also aid in the reduction of pike. Could all this really work? Or, would poison again be necessary? Regrettably, pike managed to establish themselves again.

The question many of us ask is why go through all this trouble to remove pike? Who cares right? Let the pike stay. In many areas of the country, pike are a sought after gamefish. Why not let California have a great pike fishery? The equation isn't that simple. It was known that in 1994, pike were illegally introduced into Lake Davis. They were likely brought from outside California or Frenchman Reservoir. The CA DFG is terrified of the pike because they are worried they will make there way out of the reservoir and into downstream waters.

Lake Davis is located in Plumas County, roughly an hour north of Reno on Big Grizzly Creek. Big Grizzly Creek is a tributary to the Middle Fork of the Feather River, which flows into Lake Oroville and ultimately the Feather River, Sacramento River, Delta system and Bay Area. If pike were to escape Lake Davis, which they have already in the past, it could be detrimental to downstream fisheries. While the possibility is extreme, pike could endanger steelhead and salmon populations downriver, as well as other species. Pike can escape via humans conducting illegal fish transportations, when a major storm forces high releases from the dam or when the dam overflows.

Another other issue, which may be more important to some, is the toll pike have taken on the local economy. Lake Davis used to be one of the best rainbow trout fisheries in the state. Anglers from California and Nevada fished and kept the city of Portola alive. With trout fishing hurting, the economy has felt the punch too. The CA DFG is trying to restore hope, but it's not that easy.

Unfortunately with pike in town, trout fishing may again lag until major action is taken. It's estimated that a pike can eat from one-third to one-half of their body weight, which makes a traditional stocked trout dinner. Removing adult pike is a tough task. Pike can deposit 9,000 eggs per pound and prior to the chemical treatment of the lake in 1997, they had nearly abolished all trout under 17 inches in the lake.

Pike were again found in Davis in May of 1999 after more than one million trout were stocked to replenish the fishery. To this day, pike seem to do best in Mosquito Slough, where a 27-inch fish was taken in 1999. Pike don't have a problem growing in Davis, or any lake. Studies show they can grow

Lake Davis

roughly two pounds or more a year.

Trout don't have much of a chance against the pike. Lake Davis averages less than 20 feet deep and with 30 percent of it covered by vegetation, there are few areas for trout to hide and escape pike. Trout and pike can coexist in waters that are deep where trout can relocate into deep water and avoid being eaten. This contour isn't available at Davis.

So what now? The battle with eradicating pike has cost the CA DFG more than $5 million. The options available are dewatering, blasting, water fluctuation, chemical treatments or no action at all. Regardless of what path is taken, it won't be a quick fix. Red tape and politics force a two year environmental review; therefore it won't be until at least the fall of 2006 before action is taken and that's if everything goes smoothly. In reality, 2007 is more realistic. For now, the pike will continue to multiply and eat trout.

There have been proposals to turn Davis into a trophy pike lake, but in addition to the fear of losing fish downstream, the plan likely wouldn't pan out. Pike would do well in the short term, but Davis' food chain isn't conducive to pike. Pike would rapidly eat up their forage, including trout, minnows and panfish, and likely would become stunted. Research shows that pike need a food source of at least 10 inches to grow to trophy sizes. Without trophy fish, the CA DFG presumed anglers wouldn't fish for the pike.

Ok, how about we just drain Lake Davis and start again? Not so easy. Davis isn't a typical reservoir where you can open the gates and let water out. Releasing water wouldn't be an issue, but there are several depressions that would remain and be able to support fish life. That water could be pumped out, yet stopping Freeman, Big Grizzly and Cow Creek (Davis' three year round tributaries) would be nearly impossible. And, it could be challenging to remove pike possibly in those waters as well. If just a few pike were overlooked, it would defeat the purpose of draining the lake.

It's come to the point where something drastic needs to be done. The CA DFG has now eradicated more than 51,000 pike since they were rediscovered in 1999, and while they may be slowing the growth of the population, they are definitely not getting rid of them. The only hope left is draining the lake completely or using a chemical like rotenone.

When pike are removed, Lake Davis will return to a great trout lake. In fact, the fishery isn't too shabby now. Despite a 38-inch, 16-pound pike that was taken in spring of 2003, many of the pike in Davis are juvenile fish and unable to eat trout. The CA DFG is still planting roughly 35,000 half-pound rainbows each year, joining holdovers from years past.

Lake Davis is an excellent trout grower. Because of its' shallow water, aquatic life is abundant which promotes a tremendous amount of snails and midge and damsel larva. Davis is a rich lake with impressive growth rates. While pike will continue to inhabit the lake, trout will also be stocked and will provide a fair to good fishery. Regardless of the pike, growth rates are still great. A half-pound trout planted in June can grow to 1.5 pounds by late September. It's not uncommon to catch rainbows up to five pounds.

Ironically when recreational use is highest (during the summer) fishing is the poorest. Because Davis is a shallow fishery, the water gets warm trout become sluggish. The few anglers who can find the narrow thermocline tend to catch fish. Fall, on the other hand, can be great.

Once cooler nights prevail and water temperatures fall, trout go into feeding mode. They waste no time moving shallow, which puts almost any presentation from shore in the strike zone. Try to get your bait in six-to-eight feet of water. You can't go wrong in Mallard Cove and along the north tip. Trolling can also be excellent. In the fall, trout can be found in the top five feet of water. Trolling any Needlefish or Krocodile on the northwest end will bring in fish.

Lake Davis is one of California's traditional ice-fishing destinations, but planning a trip in advance can be tough. Historically, the lake freezes in late January, although it can happen as early as November and may last through March. Davis often thaws and freezes several times a year.

Through the ice, Mallard Cove and fishing in front of the dam are options unless you have access to snowmobiles, whereas then Mosquito Slough is a good spot. Try fishing the point where Freeman Creek and Mosquito Slough meet. When fishing through the ice it's ideal to locate water that is 10 feet or less and fish roughly a foot off the bottom. Dough baits and night crawlers are best.

Davis is an excellent springtime fishery. Trout move close to shore to spawn. This is when fishing tends to be excellent near the mouth of tributaries. Shoreline fishing is always fair to good at Fairview, Eagle Point, Camp 5, Honker Cove and Grasshopper Flat Campground. A glob of rainbow Power Bait set on a sliding sinker rig is the most consistent method.

Fly fishing is popular in spring and fall when the famed damsel hatch takes place. Normally this occurs on west side between May 15 and June 15. Anglers can find success from shore or boat as trout creep into two-to-four feet of water to follow the damsels in. Some fly and a bubble combos work, but olive, gold and brown damsel nymphs are best.

Fall is a fantastic time to employ flies. In fall, snails become the primary food source for trout. This is when cinnamon Woolly buggers, pheasant tails, prince nymphs, scuds and blood midges fished under an indicator three-to-four feet below the surface in the Freeman Arm, Cow Creek or Mosquito Slough are best.

If you plan to make the trip, supplies are available in Portola. In winter and spring, call ahead for water conditions. The lake may be frozen.

Also nearby is Frenchman Reservoir.

Directions: *From Reno, drive north on Highway 395 to the left turnoff for Highway 70. Turn left and continue to Portola. Turn right on Davis Road and continue seven miles to the dam.*

SPANISH CREEK

Rating: 5

Species: Rainbow Trout and Brown Trout

Stocked with 1,000 pounds of rainbow trout.

Facilities: Restrooms and a Playground

Need Information? Contact: Plumas County Visitor Bureau (530) 326-2247

Almost nobody fishes Spanish Creek except for a few locals. If you do the math, the lack of visitors combined with more than 1,780 rainbow trout planted by the California Department of Fish and Game spells a recipe for success. The stream flows right through town, where visitors eat and sleep, yet for some reason, few cash in on the trout plants. More airplanes take off from the Quincy Airport (which is spitting distance from the stream) than there are rainbow trout caught each day.

The fish are planted from Highway 89 down through the park. Unfortunately, the creek isn't a great place for beginners. There are few pools. Most of the water comes in the form of riffles. Your best bet is finding pockets of water behind small boulders or drifting bait underneath the overhanging brush found along the banks. Don't expect to catch any rainbows over a pound. However, there are a few resident browns that can push a few pounds.

If you plan to make the trip, supplies are available in Quincy.

Also nearby are Indian Falls, Round Valley Reservoir and Bucks Lake.

Directions: *From Highway 89 in Quincy turn east at Gansner Park sign. You'll have to look carefully for the sign because there is no sign on the road.*

In addition to planted rainbows, wild bows, like the one shown above, are available in Spanish.

CRYSTAL LAKE

Rating: 6

Species: Brown Trout

Stocks: None

Facilities: None

Need Information?
Contact: Plumas
National Forest
(530) 283-0555

Crystal Lake is one of California's true hidden gems. People come for the brown trout, but by the time they get to the lake half of the day is gone because anglers are overwhelmed by the stunning vistas seen from above the lake at Mt. Hough. There is a Forest Service fire lookout tower near the lake where memorable panoramas of Mt. Lassen, Lake Almanor, Taylorsville, Quincy and the Tahoe National Forest can be taken in. If you are polite, most likely you be allowed to snap a few pictures from the top of the tower.

Most people make the choice not to visit Crystal. Because the road to the lake and lookout tower is dirt, it scares many anglers off. While the road does require fairly slow driving, it's well graded and offers a smooth ride for a mountain dirt road.

Crystal Lake is more beautiful than the stellar vistas from the tower. The lake is set in a crater and like Crater Lake in Crater Lake National Park in Oregon; it has no year-round inlet or outlet. It offers some of the more magnificent, stunning emerald blue waters in the country. Yes, it is that good.

As far as the fishery itself, this small lake holds only brown trout. It also doesn't get over fished. There are browns available, but clear, deep water protects them from anglers. There's a small shelf that drops off quick and gets extremely deep. Most anglers are shore anglers and can't properly drop their bait off this shelf. Float tubers do best. If you bring a boat make sure it's small.

However, during the fall when the browns are in the shallows and in the spring just after ice out, you can find the browns cruising the shoreline for food. This is the only time they are susceptible to anglers. For several years before the turn of the century, Crystal Lake wasn't stocked due to the possibility of mountain yellow legged frogs being at the lake, yet many of the browns still manage to survive. There is still a population of browns in the lake, but it's not as good as it used to be. Plants of fingerling browns may resume.

If you plan to make the trip, supplies are available in Quincy. In winter and spring call ahead for road conditions. The road may be closed due to snow.

Also nearby are Spanish Creek, Indian Falls, Silver Lake and Bucks Lake.

Directions: From downtown Quincy, drive north on Quincy Junction Road for 2.7 miles and turn left on Mt. Hough Road. Continue 2.5 miles (in 1.6 miles the road splits, stay left) to a four-way intersection. Continue straight on Road 403 for 1.7 miles to another split. Stay right and drive three-tenths of a mile to another split. Stay left on Road 403 and drive 2.9 miles to another split. Again stay left on Road 403 and drive 2.5 miles to another split. Stay left and continue to the lake. (If you choose to go straight you'll reach the lookout tower in four-tenths of a mile.)

SNAKE LAKE

Rating: 2

Species: Brown
Bullhead and Channel
Catfish

Stocks: None

Facilities:
Campgrounds

Need Information?
Contact: Plumas
National Forest
(530) 283-2050

Snake Lake was named properly. Marshy, weedy, muddy and covered in lily pads this large pond looks like a place snakes would certainly live. (At least that's what I got from watching the Discovery Channel!) Unfortunately, many locals use Snake's shoreline as a dump. It's not uncommon to see old microwaves, printers, typewriters, clothes, ovens, fridges, carpet, wood or just about anything else found around the house.

While Snake has some size to it, only about 10 percent is open water. The rest is covered with lily pads. I didn't see anyone fishing for fish. On the other hand, I saw two locals with fly rods who were casting near the lily pads to try and catch bullfrogs.

The main feature of Snake that attracts anglers is the free camping. Many travelers who want to save money end up here. While the fishing isn't good, there are plenty of frogs to go around. There are a few bass and thousands of small bullhead. Try a night crawler.

If you plan to make the trip, supplies are available in Quincy.

Also nearby are Smith Lake, Bucks Lake and Silver Lake.

Directions: *From the junction of I-80 and Highway 89 in Truckee, exit north on Highway 89 and drive 23.6 miles to the junction with Highway 49. Turn left on Highway 49/89 and continue five miles to where Highway 89 and 49 split. Stay right and continue 18.3 miles to the junction of Highway 70/89. Turn left on Highway 70/89 and continue 23.6 miles to Bucks Lake Road. Turn left on Bucks Lake Road, then make a quick right and drive 5.4 miles to a sign on the right for Snake Lake. Turn right and continue 2.5 miles to the lake.*

Snake Lake

SMITH LAKE

Rating: 3

Species: Catfish

Stocks: None

Facilities: None

Need Information?
Contact: Plumas
County Visitor Bureau
(800) 326-2247

If you are looking for solitude, Smith Lake is your place. On the other hand, if its solitude and good fishing you're seeking, its time to look elsewhere. Smith Lake is a small, shallow lake in the Plumas National Forest that is more likely to yield frogs than fish. While locals swear by catching bullhead, there isn't much more action for the angler to find.

Like its neighbor Snake Lake, Smith is a almost entirely covered in lily pads through most of the warmer months and in no way is it a desired angling destination. No fish plants take place, and with no inlet or outlet there is no way for fish to come in via another system. It's said the pond was stocked with bullhead catfish by locals. For those of you aware of what bullhead can do you'll also know that catching them isn't a chore. On the other hand, catching four-to-eight-inch fish with a night crawler isn't ideal for most anglers.

If you plan to make the trip, supplies are available in Quincy.

Also nearby is Snake Lake, Silver Lake and Bucks Lake.

Directions: *From the junction of I-80 and Highway 89 in Truckee, exit north on Highway 89 and drive 23.6 miles to the junction with Highway 49. Turn left on Highway 49/89 and continue five miles to where Highway 89 and 49 split. Stay right and continue 18.3 miles to the junction of Highway 70/89. Turn left on Highway 70/89 and continue 23.6 miles to Bucks Lake Road. Turn left on Bucks Lake Road, then make a quick right and drive 5.4 miles to a sign on the right for Snake Lake. Turn right and drive 1.6 miles to Road 25N20 on the left. Turn left, drive 1.4 miles to Road 47 and veer right. Drive eight-tenths of a mile and veer right on Road 25N82 and continue three-tenths of a mile to the lake.*

Smith Lake

SILVER LAKE

Rating: 5

Species: Brook Trout

Stocks: None

Facilities:
Campgrounds

Need Information?
Contact: Plumas
National Forest
(530) 863-2575

Silver Lake is one of the best float tube/canoe lakes in the Plumas National Forest. Reached via six miles of a well-graded dirt road, the lake provides somewhat of a woodsy feeling, while still being close enough to civilization to allow for a short and easy afternoon trip. By civilization I'm referring to the small mountain town of Quincy, not a populace city.

The California Department of Fish and Game isn't currently planting any fish. Fortunately, there are brook trout to be caught. At times, the evening bite can provide good shoreline action. When targeting the evening bite, try to fish off points or wait till dusk when fish surface and cash in on the most recent fly hatch.

At 5,790 feet in the Plumas National Forest, Silver Lake is pretty and peaceful. No gas-powered motors are permitted. Nonetheless, there is no launch ramp anyhow. This quiet lake is reserved for anglers who try to avoid crowds. Unfortunately, as people realize how easy this lake is to reach, the fishing, along with woodsy atmosphere, will suffer.

Silver Lake

If you plan to make the trip, supplies are available in Quincy. Call ahead for updated road conditions. The road to the lake may not be snow-free until sometime in late June. There is no paved launched ramp. Only car top boats are recommended.

Also nearby are Bucks Lake, Grizzly Forebay and Lower Bucks Lake.

Directions: From the junction of I-80 and Highway 89 in Truckee, exit north on Highway 89 and drive 23.6 miles to the junction with Highway 49. Turn left on Highway 49/89 and continue five miles to where Highway 89 and 49 split. Stay right and continue 18.3 miles to the junction of Highway 70/89. Turn left on Highway 70/89 and continue 23.6 miles to Bucks Lake Road. Turn left on Bucks Lake Road, then make a quick right and drive 8.7 miles to the turnoff for Silver Lake on the right. Turn right and drive 6.3 miles to the lake.

BUCKS LAKE

Rating: 7

Species: Rainbow
Trout, Brown Trout,
Brook Trout, Lake
Trout and Kokanee

Stocked with 10,400
pounds of brook trout,
1,100 pounds of brown
trout, 6,350 pounds of
rainbow trout and 15
pounds of fingerling
brook trout.

Facilities: Lodging,
Gas, General Store,
Picnic Areas, Boat
Rentals, Boat Launch,
RV Hookups,
Campgrounds, Picnic
Areas, Bait & Tackle
and Restrooms

Need Information?
Contact: Bucks Lake
Marina and Cabin
Rentals (530-283-
4243), Big Daddy's
Guide Service
(530) 283-4103

Buck's Lake is one of California's best family vacation lakes. Let's not forget it's also a great fishery. I didn't learn what a great secret it really was until shortly after I wrote an article about the lake for Fishing and Hunting News in the summer of 2002. I interviewed fishing guide Bryan Roccucci and printed comments by him talking about how great the lake was. When the article hit the newsstands Roccucci couldn't walk through town without being battered by the locals. "This place is ours," one yelled. "Don't go telling everyone about our secret."

The word is out. However, there are many different theories on how good Bucks is. Before I first visited this lake near Quincy I was misled by local tackle shop owners. They tried to coerced me into believing Bucks was one of the state's best trophy lake trout lakes. I later discovered the shop had too many J-Plugs on the shelves and needed to move inventory. Here's the truth from an unbiased source. Bucks is a wonderful lake for planted fish and a great kokanee lake, not a trophy lake. There are trophy browns and lake trout. However, if you arrive convinced you are going to catch one, you'll surely be disappointed.

Bucks is an ideal water to introduce kids to fishing. The 1,827-acre lake in the Plumas National Forest glimmers with rainbow, brown and brook trout, kokanee and lake trout; many of which are stocked by the tens of thousands. Plus, if the fishing is slow, which it rarely is, the scenery will keep those youngsters from getting droopy. Pines decorate the shorelines, not to mention osprey and eagles swooping down to nab trout sneaking their way towards the surface to get a eye level look at beautiful women tanning on the rocks. Like I said, there's something for everyone!

A self-sustaining kokanee population tops the list as the lake's biggest attractor. Kokanee plants no longer take place, but natural spawning occurs. Years ago, the California Department of Fish and Game dammed Bucks Creek to stop the kokanee run, but the dam broke free and kokanee continue to prosper. While the kokanee aren't huge by any means, fighting them on light tackle is a blast. Unfortunately, fish greater than 13 inches are rare. Easy limits, on the other hand, are a synch. That is, if you use the right tackle at the right depths and speeds.

Proper hardware is essential. Four ultra light rods, all with different

Guide Bryan Roccucci with a pair of Bucks koks

combos, is the quickest way to a limit. Combo No. 1 is equipped with a Sep's Pro Dodger or Pro Sidekick Dodger in watermelon or neon chartreuse and then a doubled up Kokanee Kandy, one with half chartreuse and half flame and the trailer with all flame. Combo No. 2 is set up with an Uncle Larry's pink tiger spinner. No. 3 has a Mepps Bantam Syclops #00 with a Wedding Ring. No. 4 uses a Spin-N-Glow with a single red bead and a small dodger with a Tru-Trun size 2 hook trailing. (Of course, about anything else will do.)

In late summer there are several areas that harbor kokanee, although they do tend to school up near Bucks Lake Marina. The rocks across from Bucks Lake Marina, from the dam to Sandy Point and from Rainbow Point to Mill Creek are also good spots to work. They key is to locate 55 degree water. If you have a pair of Canon downriggers, set them sporadically from 35 to 55 feet. Don't forget to tip your hooks with corn, white works best. Attaching Sep's Downrigger Flashers in copper or silver should increase your catch rates.

Perhaps the biggest plus here is there's no need to practice catch and release. This is a put-and-take fishery. The fish are planted to be caught and cooked. Keeping the kokanee not only puts a meal on the table, but helps create a bigger fish by thinning out the already over abundant population.

For anglers who don't have downriggers or leadcore, trolling for the mix of 30,590 rainbow, brook and brown trout that are planted annually by the CA DFG can be a blast. The plants have scattered all over the lake, yet these spots are the biggest producers: the Bucks Creek Arm and the mouths of Mill, Right Hand, Left Hand and Haskins Creek. Trolling isn't mandatory. Shoreline anglers positioned near the inlets do well soaking Power Bait or night crawlers. If you plan to troll stay close to the shore at first light and work your way into deeper water as the sun strikes the lake. Toplining is best in the spring and fall; however, you'll need to drop your offerings down 20-40 feet in the summer when surface temperatures can reach 78 degrees. White Sep's Pro Secrets and silver Kastmasters are local favorites.

Don't come expecting to hook a giant. While there are a few trophy fish around, a lack of abundant food source keeps the average fish at pan size. Browns in the half-pound class are abundant. A few larger fish are nailed each year. Dating back to 1976, the lake record stands 16.1 pounds. Most browns are taken near the Mill Creek Cove area. They love to reside near the stumps on the bottom in this area.

Unfortunately, a few locals have outrageously exaggerated the success of the lake trout fishery. Bucks doesn't compare to California's real lake trout lakes such as Donner and Tahoe. Gibberish scattered around town points the false perception of a world-class lake trout fishery having to do with making money and trying to lure in anglers. Don't get me wrong, there are lake trout in this 110-foot deep lake. Yet, the average size is one to two pounds, not the eight pound average that is commonly reported. Huge lake trout are caught each year, but they are scarce and typically caught right after ice out. Summer isn't the ideal time frame. According to Bucks Lake Marina, the lake record caught in 1998 is 27.5 pounds, but by the time you reach tackle shops in town that fish could weigh 32 pounds!

Concentrate on jigging during the summertime bite. If you can locate the fish on a depth finder, three-and-four-pound fish can be common jigging in 50-100 feet of water near the dam and in front of the marina. Black and white and rainbow patterned Mepps Light Syclops jigs, size 3, are a local favorite. Trolling is best right after ice out. Try surface running size 11 Rapalas in black and silver to resemble kokanee and be sure to stay within the bottom five feet of the lake. Jigging is best in the summer.

An average Bucks Lake brookie

If you plan to make the trip, supplies are available at the lake. The road to Bucks closes in late-November and doesn't reopen until mid-May. Call ahead for updated conditions.

Also nearby are Lower Bucks Lake and Grizzly Forebay.

Directions: *From the junction of I-80 and Highway 89 in Truckee, exit north on Highway 89 and drive 23.6 miles to the junction with Highway 49. Turn left on Highway 49/89 and continue five miles to where Highway 89 and 49 split. Stay right and continue 18.3 miles to the junction of Highway 70/89. Turn left on Highway 70/89 and continue 23.6 miles to Bucks Lake Road. Turn left on Bucks Lake Road, then make a quick right and drive 9.3 miles to a split in the road. Cars stay right and continue 7.1 miles to the lake. For RV's, stay left and drive nine miles to the lake.*

LITTLE BUCKS LAKE

Rating: 4

Species: Kokanee, Rainbow Trout, Brown Trout, Brook Trout and Lake Trout

Stocks: None

Facilities: Campgrounds

Keep an eye on this lake in the future. If all go as planned, the California Department of Fish and Game will mostly likely begin planting Little Bucks Lake with trout. For now, no plants are on tap. However, a move to stop planting Hamilton Branch Creek and defer those fish to Little Bucks Lake could also be in place shortly.

For now, at 5,026 feet in the Plumas National Forest, Little Bucks Lake isn't a great place to fish. No fish are planted, yet trout are present. There are no fish screens on Bucks Lake. When water is released, some fish get sucked with it and taken to Little Bucks. The most abundant fish are browns. Nonetheless, rainbows, brooks, kokanee and lake trout are found. The water in Little Bucks stays cool enough for trout year-round. Few anglers fish this water because of the lack of fish. However, almost every year some lucky angler soaking a night crawler from shore will catch a good size brown. Little Bucks is also a popular camping area which offers lots of elbow room for anglers.

The lake is basically used as a holding pool by PG&E. The best area is the culvert near the dam where water enters Little Bucks from Three Lakes. The inlet can also provide decent action to anglers fishing night crawlers off the bottom or tossing Little Cleos.

Trip info for Buck Lake also applies to Little Bucks Lake.

Directions: *From the junction of I-80 and Highway 89 in Truckee, exit north on Highway 89 and drive 23.6 miles to the junction with Highway 49. Turn left on Highway 49/89 and continue five miles to where Highway 89 and 49 split. Stay right and continue 18.3 miles to the junction of Highway 70/89. Turn left on Highway 70/89 and continue 23.6 miles to Bucks Lake Road. Turn left on Bucks Lake Road, then make a quick right and drive 9.3 miles to a split in the road. Cars stay right and continue 7.7 miles to a T intersection. Turn right on Route 20 and drive 1.2 miles. Turn right on Road 33. Continue three miles to a split in the road. Veer left to the lake.*

Little Bucks Lake

GRIZZLY FOREBAY

Rating: 3
Species: Rainbow Trout and Brown Trout
Stocks: None
Facilities: Campgrounds
Need Information? Contact: Plumas National Forest (530) 283-0555

Grizzly Forebay can humble anglers without warning. The California Department of Fish and Game doesn't plant the Forebay with fish, nor are they many wild fish that inhabit the water. However, Grizzly benefits from water that is released from Lower Bucks Lake and of course, the smaller fish that enter from Grizzly Creek. The opportunity for browns, bows, brooks and lake trout to get sucked out of Bucks Lake into Lower Bucks and then out of Lower Bucks and into Grizzly Forebay, is possible. However, not as many fish end up in Grizzly as many anglers would like.

Grizzly primarily holds brown trout. Anglers who don't know the few holes in the lake will likely go home unhappy. There also can be a tremendous amount of weed growth in the lake by July. On a positive note, even during crowded summer weekends there are often open campsites at Grizzly. Most anglers get lucky here. It's traditionally not experience that does them well. The guy who dunks a night crawler is more likely to hook a brown than a finesse angler casting a fly. Sometimes it just works that way.

Trip info for Little Bucks Lake also applies to Grizzly Forebay.

Directions: From the junction of Interstate 80 and Highway 89 in Truckee, exit north on Highway 89 and drive 23.6 miles to the junction with Highway 49. Turn left on Highway 49/89 and continue five miles to where Highway 89 and 49 split. Stay right and continue 18.3 miles to the junction of Highway 70/89. Turn left on Highway 70/89 and continue 23.6 miles to Bucks Lake Road. Turn left on Bucks Lake Road, then make a quick right and drive 9.3 miles to a split in the road. For cars, stay right and continue 7.7 miles to a T intersection. Turn right on Route 20, drive 2.4 miles and turn right on Road 32 (Signed as 24N36). Drive 7.6 miles on the paved road (many dirt roads veer off, stay on the main road) to a T intersection. Veer left onto Road 9 and drive 1.8 miles to the signed turnoff for Grizzly Forebay. Turn left and drive 1.1 miles to the lake.

Grizzly Forebay

THREE LAKES

Rating: 6

Species: Rainbow Trout
and Brown Trout

Stocks: None

Facilities:
Campgrounds

Need Information?
Contact: Plumas
National Forest
(530) 534-6500

Three Lakes can be deceiving. Oftentimes, anglers who arrive prior to August have no problem finding two lakes. However, locating all three is impossible. When Three Lakes are full or near full pool there are only two lakes. When draw downs begin, however, the narrow channel between the lower lakes dries up and you'll see all three.

Three Lakes sees little fishing pressure. If you ever try to drive here, you'll know why right away. The road to the lakes is one most anglers should avoid. It's narrow, wide enough for one car and has steep cliffs on one side. The first part of the road is manageable with a 15 mph speed limit. Unfortunately, the last section can make drivers jittery because of steep cliffs and a rough road.

A fire that destroyed Feather River Canyon also cleared the trees from the mountainside along the route to Three Lakes. There is nothing between your car and the steep, sure-death drop down to the river. Drive slow, be courteous and safe and you'll be ok. The drive should take about an hour. Hopefully, no one will be driving the other direction. There are only a few turnarounds.

Three Lakes is one of the few in California where you can drive into a wilderness area with a car top boat on your car and catch a limit of trout. Located in the Bucks Lake Wilderness, the lakes used to harbor brook trout. Now however, the California Department of Fish and Game only stocks fingerling rainbow and brown trout. Shore fishing can be productive, yet trolling tends to yield the most fish.

When trolling, stay as slow as you can. If you have a trolling motor, work the slowest two speeds. It doesn't matter what lures you troll as long as they are lightweight. A large Kastmaster or Cripplure won't work here because they are too heavy. Three Lakes are shallow. You'll need a Needlefish or Super Duper. A night crawler and flasher combo can be deadly. Keep an eye out for snags. There are a ton. For best results, only let out about 30 yards of line. Surprisingly, there are many 14-16 inch trout and few anglers catching them.

For shore anglers, there are plenty of options. The easiest and best area to fish is the dam. Casting night crawlers or Power Bait produces fish, but most fish are caught near the rocks toward the back of the lake.

To reach the backside of Three Lakes, park in the only parking area there is and locate the trailhead sign. You can't miss it. The route passes the sign and heads into the Bucks Lake Wilderness, while paralleling the lower lake's shoreline before coming to a junction. A half-mile trek to the left takes you to the Pacific Crest Trail. Stay right and within five minutes you'll arrive at the middle lake and brush-free shoreline access. For the upper lake, continue another five minutes on the path. When the lake is full, much of the path will be flooded, forcing you to get your feet wet. Before you consider a trip to Three Lakes, keep in mind there are only three campsites and they tend to fill fast.

If you plan to make the trip, supplies are available at Bucks Lake. Call ahead for updated road conditions. The road to the lake may not be snow free until sometime in late June. There is no paved launched ramp. Only car top boats are recommended. A high clearance vehicle is ideal.

Also nearby are Bucks Lake, Grizzly Forebay and Lower Bucks Lake.

Directions: *From the junction of I-80 and Highway 89 in Truckee, exit north on Highway 89 and drive 23.6 miles to the junction with Highway 49. Turn left on Highway 49/89 and continue five miles to where Highway 89 and 49 split. Stay right and continue 18.3 miles to the junction of Highway 70/89. Turn left on Highway 70/89 and continue 23.6 miles to Bucks Lake Road. Turn left on Bucks Lake Road, then make a quick right and drive 9.3 miles to a split in the road. Cars stay right and continue 7.7 miles to a T intersection. Turn right on Route 20 and drive 1.2 miles. Turn right on Road 33. Continue three miles to a split in the road. Stay left and drive 5.4 miles to a split in the road. Veer right and drive 5.4 miles on a rough dirt road to the lake.*

Three Lakes

ROUND VALLEY RESERVOIR

Rating: 6

Species: Largemouth
Bass, Channel Catfish,
Bluegill, Brown
Bullhead and Crappie

Stocks: None

Facilities: Restrooms,
Campgrounds, Picnic
Areas and Boat Rentals

Need Information?
Contact: Indian Valley
Chamber of Commerce
(530) 284-6633

Round Valley Reservoir is one of the most productive non-trout fisheries in the Sierra. As a matter of fact, you can almost guarantee you'll catch fish here. Round Valley Reservoir is the kind of place where father and son can show up, toss a night crawler and a bobber out and expect to catch fish even on a bad day. It takes no skill. The reservoir is a great place to introduce children to fishing. During the late spring and through summer, kids can see bass and bluegill from the shoreline.

The reason why few anglers visit Round Valley is due to the lack of trophy fish. Most of the bass are under three pounds. Bluegill rarely grow larger than pan size. For the most part, bass and bluegill are caught within 20 yards of the shoreline. Your best bet is bobber fishing. Have your kids sit on the dam and toss out pieces of night crawlers set roughly 12-24 inches below a bobber.

Located in the mountains above Greenfield between Lake Almanor and Quincy, Round Valley Reservoir's bluegill weigh less than a half-pound. For bass, use a full night crawler and fish near lily pads. Some larger bass are also caught, but you'll need to walk to the backside of the lake and fish near the stumps to have a shot at the larger fish. At one time, Round Valley held the state record for largemouth bass. However, that was before many of the big bass producing reservoirs in Southern California were built.

Located at 4,466 feet, the reservoir provides the city of Greenfield with water. Most anglers who fish in the evening do best on bullhead. The lake's catfish population has yet to establish itself, although the resort has been planting cats over the last few years.

Round Valley Reservoir

If you plan to make the trip, supplies are available in Greenville. In winter, call ahead for updated conditions. The lake may be iced over. On some maps, the lake may be known as Bidwell Lake.

Also nearby are Indian Falls, Indian Creek and Spanish Creek.

Directions: *From the 99 Freeway in Oroville, exit east on Highway 70 and drive 67 miles to the junction with Highway 89. Turn right on Highway 70/89 and continue to the town of Greenfield. In Greenfield, turn right on Hideaway Road and drive one-mile to Round Valley Road. Turn left and continue 2.2 miles to the lake.*

FEATHER RIVER (NORTH FORK, BELDEN)

Rating: 6

Species: Rainbow Trout and Brown Trout

Stocked with 5,500 pounds of rainbow trout.

Facilities: General Store, Campgrounds and Restrooms

Need Information? Contact: Plumas National Forest (530) 534-6500

Stocked along a 2.7-mile stretch of mostly fast moving water, the North Fork of the Feather River near Belden is a classic put-and-take water. Indeed there are small wild rainbow and brown trout too. However, planters widely outnumber wild fish. The river is stocked with more than 10,840 half-pound rainbow trout by the California Department of Fish and Game. Overall though, fishing pressure is low.

The river holds the most fish from Highway 70 up to Queen Lily Bridge. Unfortunately, much of the outdoorsy feeling is overshadowed by towering power lines overhead. For the most part, this stretch of the Feather River flows swiftly and tends to be 20-40 feet wide. Water is first released out of Lake Almanor and then from Belden Forebay before it arrives at the section you'll be fishing. Oftentimes, you'll see more people tubing down the river than fishing it. If you are going to fish, Queen Lily, North Fork and Gansner Bar Campgrounds are your best bets.

Beyond the campgrounds, shoreline access can be tough. Much of the land is overgrown. Also, keep in mind that fish don't like to stay in the middle of the current. They rest just outside of it where they can conserve energy. Ironically, I saw most anglers casting in the current. If you do that, plan on getting skunked. Stick to targeting areas where the water slows.

If you plan to make the trip, supplies are available in Oroville and Quincy. The Feather River (North Fork, Belden) is closed to fishing from November 16 to the last Saturday in April.

Also nearby is Butt Valley Reservoir.

Directions: *From the junction of Highway 89 and 70 in Indian Falls, drive west on Highway 70 for 16.6 miles to Caribou Road. Turn right. The road parallels the river.*

The North Fork of the Feather River near Belden

LITTLE GRASS VALLEY RESERVOIR

Rating: 5

Species: Rainbow Trout, Kokanee, Brown Trout

Stocked with 7,000 pounds of rainbow trout and 209 pounds of fingerling kokanee.

Facilities: Campgrounds, Picnic Areas, Restrooms, Swimming Areas and Boat Launches

Need Information? Contact: Plumas National Forest (530) 283-0555

Little Grass Valley Reservoir is one of California's most underutilized kokanee fisheries. Why? Let's assume several reasons: it offers some of the smallest kokanee in the state, isn't near any major cities, it's a long drive on a curvy mountain road to its' banks and is rarely publicized.

There are fish, but Little Grass Valley can be best described as a family lake. There are great camping facilities, decent fishing and rustic wooded surroundings. It also has some private cabins along the shoreline. Little Grass Valley Reservoir isn't so little. At 1,400 acres, it has 16 miles of pined shoreline and is best fished by trollers. Rainbow trout are the easiest fish to catch, yet kokanee garnish most of the attention.

Little Grass Valley is heavily planted. The California Department of Fish and Game stocks 13,230 half-pound rainbow trout in addition to 40,128 fingerling kokanee. Kokanee average 10-14 inches. Don't expect to catch any big boys. A 15 incher would be noteworthy. The finest kokanee can be found in the Black Rock area and caught on Sep's Kokanee Kandy in flame and pearl.

The rainbows don't get big either. The lake used to have a stable population of big browns. However, a group of locals who knew how to catch them raped the lake by not practicing catch and release. Some browns still reside, but unfortunately, the numbers of them are way down.

If you plan to make the trip, supplies are available in La Porte.

Also nearby are Nelson Creek, Collins Lake and Sly Creek Reservoir.

Rainbows are common in Little Grass Valley Reservoir

Directions: From the junction of Highway 20 and 70 in Marysville, take Highway 20 east for 12 miles to County Road E-21/Browns Valley turnoff. Turn north and drive 20 miles to La Porte Road. Turn east, drive through Brownsville and continue on E-21 for approximately 25 miles to La Porte. Continue through La Porte and drive 3.5 miles to Little Grass Valley Road and turn left. Follow signs to either the east or west shore.

SLY CREEK RESERVOIR

Rating: 4

Species: Rainbow Trout
and Brown Trout

Stocks: None

Facilities: Boat Launch,
Restrooms and
Campgrounds

Need Information?
Contact: Plumas
National Forest
(530) 534-6500

Sly Creek Reservoir is one of the unfortunate stories of Northern California reservoirs. In the last half-decade its' fishery has declined tremendously due to a lack of management. The California Department of Fish and Game couldn't fill an opening for the Butte County fisheries biologist for several years. The job was filled a few times; however, turnover hurt the fishery. During that time, the allotment for trout was dropped and the lake has gone downhill ever since.

The reservoir isn't being actively managed by the CA DFG. Part of the problem is that the reservoir gets sucked dry nearly every year. The reservoir is fed by water from Lost Creek. However, water isn't kept in the reservoir long enough to maintain an acceptable cold water fishery.

Personally, I call this place Dry Creek Reservoir. Owned by the Oroville-Wyandotte Irrigation District, I arrived in mid-July only to find the water was more than a half-mile down from the launch ramp. And, this isn't a huge reservoir. At just 562 acres, the draw downs are devastating to the fishery. However, there are some fish left. At 3,531 feet in the Plumas National Forest, wild fish do enter the reservoir via Lost Creek. Nonetheless, the numbers of fish don't warrant a fishing trip, especially with so many other great waters nearby.

If you plan to make the trip, supplies are available in Strawberry Valley.

Also nearby are Lost Creek Reservoir, Little Grass Valley Reservoir and Bullards Bar Reservoir.

Directions: *From Oroville take Highway 162 east for roughly 23 miles to La Porte Road. Turn left and continue to the left turnoff for Sly Creek Reservoir.*

Sly Creek Reservoir suffers from low water levels. This was in June of 2002.

Region
16

Highway 36
Corridor Eagle Lake

DIGGER CREEK

Rating: 4

Species: Rainbow Trout

Stocked with 300
pounds of rainbow
trout.

Facilities: None

Need Information?
Contact: Lassen
National Forest
(530) 258-2141

Digger Creek is a California Department of Fish and Game planting truck's nightmare. Along Digger, there is tons of private land, little public land and only some of the private land is signed. Several locals told me they don't bother to fish the stream - which is right down the street from their house - because of all the private land, poison oak and rattlesnakes that can be found along Digger's banks.

Even though the banks are way overgrown and public land can be tough to find, the CA DFG manages to plant 460 rainbow trout each spring. The stocking occurs where Ponderosa Way crosses over the creek, near the town of Manton. So yah, there are plenty other small streams to target nearby. Don't waste your time worrying about private property. Go somewhere else. If you still want to try and fish it, plan to arrive in the spring and early summer.

If you plan to make the trip, supplies are available in Manton.

Also nearby are Digger Creek Ranch, Antelope Creek (South Fork) and Battle Creek (South Fork).

Directions: *From Interstate 5 in Red Bluff, take the Highway 99/36 exit and drive east for 2.2 miles to the junction of Highway 99/36. Turn left on Highway 36 and drive 11.5 miles to the town of Dale's Station and turn left on County Road A-6. Drive 15.7 miles to Forward Road in Manton. Veer right and drive 3.9 miles to Ponderosa Way. Turn left and continue 1.9 miles to the bridge and stream.*

Digger Creek

DIGGER CREEK RANCH

Rating: 6

Species: Rainbow Trout
and Brown Trout

Stocked periodically as
fish are needed.

Facilities: Lodging and
Restrooms

Need Information?
Contact: Digger Creek
Ranch (530) 242-6744

Digger Creek Ranch sure isn't for everybody. However, if you are a rich doctor, lawyer or anyone with a lot of money this spot might be a place to call home. The ranch caters to the wealthy and offers them a sheltered, but quality fishing experience. Digger Creek Ranch has three ponds which are planted each year with oversize rainbow and brown trout that were raised by the American Trout and Salmon Company or Donnelson Trout. Some California Fish and Game fish are also present, but they wash in with Digger Creek.

For a lofty fee you can fish these catch and release only ponds, as the ranch is opened to the public. Fly-fishing is preferred. No bait fishing is allowed. The ranch encompasses more than 1,600 acres and two miles of stream which is connected to the three, eight and one acre ponds. According to the ranch caretaker (who escorted me on the property) there are more than 1,000 trout in the upper pond and 3,000 in the lower pond. However, that number seems more than bloated to me. It think it belongs somewhere between 100 and 300.

If you plan to make the trip, supplies are available in Manton. The ranch is open year-round. There is a fee and reservations must be made in advance.

Also nearby are Digger Creek and Antelope Creek.

Directions: From Interstate 5 in Red Bluff, take the Highway 99/36 exit and drive east for 2.2 miles to the junction of Highway 99/36. Turn left on Highway 36 and drive 11.5 miles to the town of Dale's Station and turn left on County Road A-6. Drive 15.7 miles to Forward Road in Manton. Veer right and drive 3.9 miles to Ponderosa Way. Turn left and continue to the ranch.

Digger Ranch caretaker Jeff Coleman with a Digger bow.

DEER CREEK

Rating: 8

Species: Rainbow Trout

Stocked with 23,354
pounds of rainbow
trout.

Facilities:
Campgrounds and
Restrooms

Need Information?
Contact: Lassen
National Forest
(530) 258-2141

Deer Creek is one of the best trout streams in the Lassen National Forest. For the residents of Chico and vacationers staying in and around Lassen National Park and along the Highway 36 corridor, there's no better place to go to catch a limit. This section of Deer Creek upstream of Deer Creek Falls is reserved for catching and keeping. Another section of the creek is designated for catch and release only fishing and has been set aside for fly-fishermen.

Fortunately, Deer Creek is a medium size trout stream that can handle hoards of fishing pressure. At roughly 4,000 feet in the Lassen National Forest, Deer Creek caters to all anglers. The creek has it all: long pools, deep holes, swift water, slow water, eddies, riffles, you name it. Plus, it has both wild and planted trout. Deer Creek is one of the most heavily planted streams in the Sierra. With the California Department of Fish and Game stocking more than 34,988 half-pound trout, it's surely the most heavily planted stream in Tehama County.

If you plan to catch and keep, or use Power Bait or anything besides a barbless fly or a lure with a single barbless hook you'll have to fish above Deer Creek Falls. No big deal. There are plenty of great areas to fish. Just make sure you fish above Upper Deer Creek Falls. The creek below the falls is governed by special restrictions. If you can't find Deer Creek Falls, look 1.5 miles upstream of Potato Patch Campground. There is an eight-mile stretch of water upstream of Upper Deer Creek Falls where fish are planted. Ranging from 3,600 feet near the falls to 4,800 feet closer to Highway 36, Deer Creek is heavily shaded by a vast canopy.

Many of the best spots are visible from the road. If you are coming from Highway 36 start working the creek just below Deer Creek Meadows. Look for spots where day-use areas are easily accessed from Highway 32 and fish in and around Alder, Elam, and Alder Creek Campgrounds. However, planted trout and a mix of wild fish are scattered throughout the eight-mile stretch of water. Fishing sections of Deer where tributaries enter are also a good idea. Try the area where Gurnsey, Alder, Elam, Swamp Creek and Round Valley Creek, Forked and Cub Creek enter. Any good topo map will show these locations.

Time of year can dictate your success. Deer Creek can be difficult to fish in the spring when runoff is at its' peak. Fish slower pockets and deeper holes through June. Then, once July comes around and the creek retreats a bit, you'll have a chance to broaden your horizons and fish any portion of the creek.

Techniques can vary. Some anglers fish the deeper holes and longer runs with small Mepps or Panther Martin spinners. Others do well dropping a night crawler to the bottom of a deep hole or working Power Bait or salmon eggs behind large boulders and beneath overhanging brush and undercut banks.

If you plan to make the trip, supplies are available in Chester and Chico. Deer Creek is closed to fishing from November 16 to the last Saturday in April.

Also nearby is Butte Creek.

Directions: From Interstate 5 in Red Bluff, take the Highway 99/36 exit and drive east for 2.2 miles to the junction of Highway 99/36. Turn left on Highway 36 and drive 56.8 miles to the Highway 32 turnoff. Turn right and continue one-mile to the first roadside access. Fish from here downstream.

DEER CREEK (WILD TROUT SECTION)

Rating: 7

Species: Rainbow Trout and Brown Trout

Stocks: None

Facilities: Restrooms and Campgrounds

Need Information? Contact: Chico Fly Shop (530) 345-9983

Deer Creek can be sliced into two sections: the home of bait anglers upstream of Potato Patch Campground and the wild trout section downstream of the Potato Patch, primarily reserved for fly anglers. Only artificial lures with barbless hooks can be used in the downstream section.

The downstream section isn't for everyone. While wild trout are abundant, so is poison oak and rattlesnakes. Keep your eyes open, watch where you step and you'll hopefully be safe. The key is to beware.

Deer Creek last went through a healthy cycle in 1997 when a flood swept through and killed off many large trout. Fortunately, the creek has since recovered beautifully. Mostly small bows inhabited the stream in the late Nineties, however, larger fish are now available. Deer is primarily a rainbow trout fishery. A few browns are caught, but not often. Rainbows average 12-15 inches, yet some to 18 inches can be found. The creek is best fished with a three-to-four-weight rod and a 5x tippet.

From the opener through the first few weeks in May, anglers should key in on the salmon fly hatch. When the salmon fly hatch expires, switch over to size 12 gray mayflies. Stimulators, elk hair caddis, pear drake mayflies or a parachute adam mayfly work best. Caddis between size 12 and 16 and stimulators from size four to 14 are prime choices.

Deer Creek Falls

If you plan to make the trip, supplies are available in Chico. Deer Creek is closed to fishing from November 16 to the last Saturday in April. Deer Creek is catch and release only from 250 feet below Upper Deer Creek Falls downstream for 31 miles to the US Geological Survey gauging station cable crossing at the mouth of Deer Creek Canyon. Only artificial lures with barbless hooks may be used.

Also nearby are Deer Creek Falls, Butte Creek, Forks of Butte Creek and Old Mine Falls.

Directions: *From the junction of the 99 Freeway and Highway 32 in Chico, drive east on Highway 32 for 41 miles to Potato Patch Campground.*

ANTELOPE CREEK (NORTH FORK)

Rating: 5

Species: Rainbow Trout

Stocks: None

Facilities: None

Need Information?
Contact: Lassen
National Forest
(530) 258-2141

Sometimes you need to travel the wrong path before you find the right one. That was the case in my travels to the North Fork of Antelope Creek. Instructions given by the California Department of Fish and Game tell anglers to follow Ponderosa Way to the creek. Following Ponderosa will get you to Antelope Creek, but probably not without a few more scratches on your car and a slow, rough ride. The first five miles of the 12.6-mile drive to the creek is rough and overgrown. The second portion of the drive won't scratch up your car, but plan on driving 10 mph or less.

On the other hand, there is a much quicker way to reach the creek. Following the directions below drive past Ponderosa Way to Little Olant Mill Road and turn right. Continue to Plum Road and turn right again. Drive to Ponderosa Road and turn left. Follow Ponderosa to the stream. While the route the DFG tells you to take can take more than an hour to reach this way takes fewer than 20 minutes.

Antelope Creek is a great trout stream in the Lassen National Forest. However, because of its lack of services and poor road conditions, few anglers come. In the spring, the CA DFG used to truck in rainbow trout every other week, but the stocking has been suspended. No word on when it will resume. On the upside, the creek is easy to find and the fish are concentrated. The fish are planted from where the creek crosses the road on upstream for three-tenths of a mile.

If you plan to make the trip, supplies are available in Dale's Station. Antelope Creek (North Fork) is closed to fishing from November 16 to the last Saturday in April.

The North Fork of Antelope Creek

Also nearby are Battle Creek (South Fork), Deer Creek and Digger Creek.

Directions: *From Interstate 5 in Red Bluff take the Highway 99/36 exit and drive east for 2.2 miles to the junction of Highway 99/36. Turn left on Highway 36 and drive 30 miles to Ponderosa Way. Turn right and drive 12.6 miles to the creek, which crosses over the road. (See the write-up for the other route to the creek.)*

BATTLE CREEK (SOUTH FORK)

Rating: 6

Species: Rainbow Trout

Stocked with 11,300 pounds of rainbow trout.

Facilities: Campgrounds and Restrooms

Need Information? Contact: Lassen National Forest (530) 258-2141

The South Fork of Battle Creek is the first medium size trout stream you'll come to driving east along Highway 36 from Red Bluff. The others are small streams that receive minimal plants of fish. Battle Creek itself isn't huge, but it is much larger and gets planted with more fish than its' neighbors Digger Creek and the North Fork of Antelope Creek. The South Fork is loaded with more than 17,080 half-pound rainbow trout each year and all those fish are stuffed into a half-mile section of the stream. The South Fork's sufficient volume allows it to be planted from spring through fall.

This section of Battle Creek is the type of place where you can pitch a tent in Battle Creek Campground and walk down to the water to catch your dinner. The best fishing is found in the campground and below the bridge. There is no public fishing access at

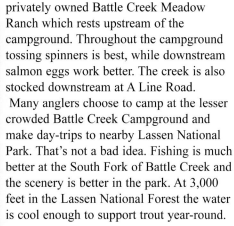

privately owned Battle Creek Meadow Ranch which rests upstream of the campground. Throughout the campground tossing spinners is best, while downstream salmon eggs work better. The creek is also stocked downstream at A Line Road.

Many anglers choose to camp at the lesser crowded Battle Creek Campground and make day-trips to nearby Lassen National Park. That's not a bad idea. Fishing is much better at the South Fork of Battle Creek and the scenery is better in the park. At 3,000 feet in the Lassen National Forest the water is cool enough to support trout year-round.

If you plan to make the trip, supplies are available in Mineral. The South Fork of Battle Creek is closed to fishing from November 16 to the last Saturday in April.

The South Fork of Battle Creek

Also nearby are Bluff Falls, Gurnsey Creek, Antelope Creek (North Fork) and Deer Creek.

Directions: *From Interstate 5 in Red Bluff, take the Highway 99/36 exit and drive east for 2.2 miles to the junction of Highway 99/36. Turn left on Highway 36 and drive 39.7 miles to Battle Creek Campground on the right.*

GURNSEY CREEK

Rating: 4

Species: Rainbow Trout
and Brook Trout

Stocked with 200
pounds of rainbow
trout.

Facilities:
Campgrounds and
Restrooms

Need Information?
Contact: Lassen
National Forest
(530) 258-2141

Situated between Lassen National Park and Chester, Gurnsey Creek is just enough out of the way from those heavily visited touristy areas to remain peaceful. Yet, the fishing is fair, even at its' peak time. At nearly 5,000 feet, Gurnsey Creek is a small stream in the Lassen National Forest that suffers from low water levels as mid-summer arrives. While few reach nine inches, there are many five-to-eight-inch wild rainbow and brook trout in the stream, but it's the planters most folks fish for.

Prior to August, the five-to-15-foot wide and shallow creek offers a planted fishery for both fly and bait fishermen. The creek is to shallow for the use of spinners. It's a great place to fish Pautzke salmon eggs. The California Department of Fish and Game manages to plant some 375 half-pound fish. Fortunately, the creek has a lot of open space along its' banks so fly fishing can be productive. Power Bait works well too.

The creek is best fished near Gurnsey Campground. Stick to fishing as close the camp as you can. The CA DFG only plants a three-tenth of a mile stretch of the creek. The stockers stay near the campground to make fishing access easy for campers.

If you plan to make the trip, supplies are available in Chester. Gurnsey Creek is closed to fishing from November 16 to the last Saturday in April.

Also nearby are Bluff Falls, Lake Almanor and Deer Creek.

Directions: From Interstate 5 in Red Bluff, take the Highway 99/36 exit and drive east for 2.2 miles to the junction of Highway 99/36. Turn left on Highway 36 and drive 54.5 miles to Gurnsey Campground

Gurnsey Creek

BUTT VALLEY RESERVOIR

Rating: 7
Species: Rainbow Trout and Brown Trout
Stocks: None
Facilities: Campgrounds, Picnic Areas, Boat Launch and Restrooms
Need Information? Contact: Plumas National Forest (530) 283-2050

Butt Valley Reservoir is a get away from it all lake. It's tucked in the woods, a short drive from Lake Almanor, and offers camping for folks looking for a quiet setting alongside a shallow lake harboring rainbow and brown trout. The 1,600 acre reservoir at 4,144 feet in the Plumas National Forest is popular with Upper Sacramento Valley residents.

Butt Valley isn't a premier fishery for shore anglers. It's known as a premier brown trout fishery among locals. While some try and keep the secret to success hush-hush, the word has been out for decades; the bite is only worth a damn when water is being pumped into Butt Valley from Lake Almanor. This is when some gamefish, pond smelt and other baitfish get washed through the turbines prior to entering Butt Valley. The ground up fish gets the attention of Butt Valley's big browns and rainbows as they move towards the inlet for easy meals. These fish get big sucking down all this food. Many anglers take advantage of the vulnerable fish.

The big browns and bows are less wary when the pumphouse is in operation. They aren't as concerned with anglers as they'd normally be. So much food is coming in that eating is their main focus. Anglers fishing from boats near the inlet have a good shot at quality trout. In fact, rainbows and browns upward of 10 pounds have been caught and can be quite common for folks in the know.

Your best bet is to fly fish with baitfish imitations, jig with white Gitzets on a lead head jig or any pond smelt imitation. Cast towards the incoming water, allow it to sink to the bottom and then bounce it off the bottom during your retrieve. It's also productive to drift night crawlers and to cast large trout and pond smelt imitations such as Bomber Long As.

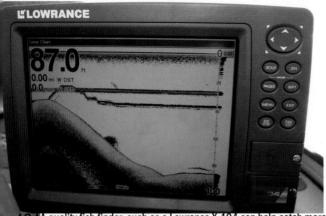

Directions: From Interstate 5 in Red Bluff take the Highway 99/36 exit and drive east for 2.2 miles to the junction of Highway 99/36. Turn left on Highway 36 and continue to the junction with Highway 89 south. Turn right and continue to the right turnoff for Butt Valley Road. Turn right and continue roughly three miles to the lake.

464 A quality fish finder, such as a Lowrance X-104 can help catch more fish.

FEATHER RIVER (NORTH FORK, ALMANOR)

Rating: 7

Species: Rainbow Trout and Brown Trout

Stocked with 7,450 pounds of rainbow trout.

Facilities: Campgrounds and Restrooms

Need Information? Contact: Lassen National Forest (530) 258-2141

When most people think of the Feather River, salmon, steelhead and crowds come to mind. That's certainly the case when it comes to the main stem, but crowds and the North Fork of the Feather River definitely don't belong in the same sentence. A few miles from Chester, the North Fork is one of the finest trout streams in the Plumas County.

At roughly 4,600 feet in the Lassen National Forest, this river isn't your typical small mountain stream. A tributary to Lake Almanor, the North Fork is wide, deep in some spots and flows with swiftness at times and with elegance at others. It offers a combination of high desert scenery with a mix of pines.

The North Fork is also a great stretch of water that holds masses of trout. Each year the California Department of Fish and Game plants more than 10,755 half- pound trout in the river. The North Fork is also planted with more than 16 trout in the three-to-four-pound class. This is a classic put-and-take river, but there also wild rainbows and browns that inhabit the waters.

This stretch of water isn't always friendly to anglers, however. As it can maintain a great deal of force, the river poses a challenge for many anglers, especially during the springtime when runoff peaks. Due to such conditions, plan on not tossing spinners until late summer and fall. Try drifting Power Bait and Pautzke salmon eggs behind rocks in the early season as well. The best access can be found in High Bridge Campground and along Collins Pine Road, which parallels the river.

Fortunately for those not interested in battling the currents, there is a great deal of public access along the North Fork's banks. More than a six-mile stretch of the river offers drive-to access. The lower stretch of the river is situated in the town of Chester. You could grab a pizza and be back out on the river in a matter of minutes!

If you plan to make the trip, supplies are available in Chester. The North Fork of the Feather River is closed to fishing from November 16 to the last Saturday in April.

Also nearby are Clear Creek Pond, Hamilton Branch Creek and Lake Almanor.

Directions: From Interstate 5 in Red Bluff, take the Highway 99/36 exit and drive east for 2.2 miles to the junction of Highway 99/36. Turn left on Highway 36 and drive 67.7 miles to Feather River Road. Turn left, drive seven-tenths of a mile and veer left. From here and for the next six miles the road parallels the river.

WARNER CREEK

Rating: 5

Species: Rainbow Trout and Brown Trout

Stocked with 1,200 pounds of rainbow trout.

Facilities: Campgrounds and Restrooms

Need Information? Contact: Lassen National Forest (530) 258-2141

Warner Creek is the smaller, much easier fished option to the North Fork of the Feather River. While the river flows high and fast, Warner stays mildly mellow and is more user-friendly. Which of the waters you choose is a personal preference. The fish stocked in both waters are the same size. In fact, they come from the same fish planting truck.

Most of the fishing pressure at Warner Creek stems from overflow campers at Warner Creek Campground. Many of these campers are forced to stay in the campground when all sites are full in nearby Lassen National Park. Warner's headwaters are located in the Lassen National Forest (just outside of the park) where Hot Springs and King Creek meet. This year-round stream maintains enough cool water throughout the summer to allow trout to inhabit the stream through all seasons. During the spring and early summer the California Department of Fish and Game plants more than 1,720 half-pound rainbow trout to replenish those that were caught in the previous year.

Most successful anglers fish eggs. The stream is shallow and it can be difficult to toss lures. Warner Creek has a rocky base and at roughly 4,600 feet, fishermen who target the stream's small pools do best.

If you plan to make the trip, supplies are available in Chester. Warner Creek is closed to fishing from November 16 to the last Saturday in April.

Also nearby are Lake Almanor, Hot Springs Creek Falls and Devils Kitchen.

Warner Creek

Directions: *From Interstate 5 in Red Bluff take the Highway 99/36 exit and drive east for 2.2 miles to the junction of Highway 99/36. Turn left on Highway 36, drive 67.7 miles and turn left on Feather River Road. Drive seven-tenths of a mile and veer left. At approximately six miles turn right at the Drakesbad turnoff and continue 1.1 miles to Warner Creek Campground.*

LAKE ALMANOR

Rating: 9

Species: Chinook
Salmon, Rainbow
Trout, Brown Trout,
Smallmouth Bass,
Largemouth Bass,
Channel Catfish,
Yellow Bullhead,
Bluegill

Stocked with 20,000
pounds of brown trout,
20,950 pounds of rain-
bow trout, 655 pounds
of fingerling rainbow
trout, 2,950 pounds of
sub-catchable rainbow
trout and 176 pounds of
fingerling chinook
salmon.

Facilities: Marinas,
Gas, Lodging, Bait &
Tackle, Boat Launches,
Picnic Areas,
Campgrounds,
Restrooms, RV
Hookups, Restaurants,
Showers, General Store
and Boat Rentals

Need Information?
Contact: Sports Nut
(530) 258-3327,
Ayoob's (530) 258-
2611, Lassen View
Resort (530) 596-3437,
Lake Almanor Chamber
of Commerce (800)
350-4838, Lassen
National Forest
(530) 258-2141

Lake Almanor is one of Northern California's largest and most diverse fisheries. This high mountain lake is 13 miles long, six miles wide and provides anglers what many other premier trophy lakes can't: quantity and quality. The lake shows off a mix of wild and stocked browns and rainbows in addition to chinook salmon. Almanor identifies the meaning of diversification and is set near the community of Chester, offering anglers full amenities.

Each year the California Department of Fish and Game stocks roughly 60,000 three-to-the-pound browns, 40,000 half-pound Eagle Lake trout, 15,000 fingerling rainbow trout, 36,000 sub-catchable trout and more than 100,000 fingerling chinook salmon. The CA DFG has also entered into an agreement with the Lake Almanor Fishing Association. The CA DFG provides 50,000 fingerling trout at four-to-five inches, cages and feed, while the association rears them in Almanor until late May when the trout reach 12-14 inches and are released.

Almanor also provides the chance to catch wild rainbows and browns. In addition to stockers, the lake has thousands of naturally spawned trout. Trout utilize the North Fork Feather River near Chester, Hamilton Branch Creek near Clear Creek, Bailey Creek on west shore and several unnamed creeks on the east and west shore for spawning grounds. Chinook do attempt to spawn, but aren't often successful.

The large stocking base is more than necessary. Almanor is over fished in the spring and summer months. The absence of stocking would pave the way for a depleted fishery. Despite 28,000 acres of water, each section of the lake gets pounded on a daily basis. What's incredible is that there's enough food to go around.

Food is most plentiful on the west shore where the North Fork of the Feather River comes in. This area is home to dozens of insect hatches each year, including the hex and midge hatch, likely two of the most prolific hatches that take place. The west shore is in a sense a grocery store for trout. Trout inhabit this area from late October through May. They abandon it during the warmer months. This area is fairly shallow, mostly five to 20 feet and warms quickly.

The biggest driver of Almanor's trout population is pond smelt. Pond smelt reproduce naturally and serve as growing pills for the salmon and trout. Without pond smelt, Almanor's fish would be in trouble.

There are nearly a dozen waters in California where inland chinook are planted. On the other hand, none are as successful as Almanor. Each year, 100,000 fingerling chinook are planted, except for 2003 when the entire load of chinook were lost in a flood at the Silverado Fish Hatchery. In 2004, 176,000 fingerling chinook were planted.

Chinook live four-to-five years in Almanor and grow up to eight pounds. Historically fish reached close to 12 pounds, but those days are long gone. The population boomed the first few years after chinook were introduced, but has since settled into a range where the common fish runs two-to-five pounds. There's too much competition for food for the chinook population to explode like it once did.

Christopher Crawley with a quality bow.

Chinook are usually found a bit deeper than rainbows and browns. While they can be located anywhere on the lake, it's likely that you'll only find them on the west shore between October and May. Otherwise the 60 foot depths of Big Springs and 90 feet near the dam are more likely to harbor them. There are several ways to catch chinook. However, it's hard to beat soaking anchovies saturated with Pautzke Liquid Krill or jigging white or pearl spoons over springs in the summer. Simple trolling Rebel or Bomber pond smelt imitations or a half-ounce Krocodile spoon works magic.

At one time kokanee were available. However, when pond smelt were introduced in 1973, kokanee felt the hurt. Kokanee and pond smelt are plankton feeders. The pond smelt out competed the kokanee which rapidly become stunted. When adult kokanee began to reach just nine inches the CA DFG opted to quick stocking kokanee. There are no plans for kokanee to be planted in the future.

Rainbows are readily available. Toplining from fall through spring is ideal. Some anglers use a Sep's Pro Dodger and a night crawler or Needlefish. Others employ spoons such as a glow Cripplure, Thomas Buoyant or a Kastmaster smeared with Gel Krill.

The great thing about rainbows here is that you likely won't catch dinks. Bows under a pound are uncommon. In the summer when water temperatures warm, many anglers bait fish with salmon eggs, worms and crickets on top of springs. Jigging with a Crippled Herring or Megabait Live Jig will also do the trick.

Browns are abundant in Almanor. Some big browns over 10 pounds are taken each year, but two-to-five pounders are more realistic. The best time to fish the browns is in June or July when they come to the surface each evening to fill up on hex bugs. This famous hatch is when the browns are most vulnerable.

Nevertheless, browns can be taken year round. In the summer, browns seek places with cooler water just like the rainbows and salmon do. You'll have to troll with downriggers or leadcore or baitfish from a boat to catch them. Troll stickbaits. Rebel Holographic Minnows and Mother of Pearl Bomber Long A's will do the trick. If you have a quality fish finder, it's a good idea to try and place your bait within a few feet of the tree stumps on the bottom.

Winter is a great time to take browns close to the surface. Toplining the west shore is ideal. Weather can be tricky to predict though. During the winter the lake is like a sheet of glass unless a storm is passing through. When this happens you won't want to be anywhere near the lake. The worst time for wind is summer when the wind comes up daily by noon.

Almanor doubles as an excellent bass fishery. On the other hand, this fishery acts different than others in Nor Cal. Almanor offers a chance at trophy fish, but most are much smaller. Smallmouth and largemouth are available. Nonetheless, you'll be shocked to catch anything other than smallmouth.

The smallmouth fishery is awesome, one of the better in the state. Ted Pilgrim of the Almanor Bass Association landed a lake record eight pounder in September of 2002, but a catch like that is rare. Most are in the one-to-three pound class. Keep in mind though, Pilgrim's fish was released and should be in state record class. Smallies make a living eating crawdads and pond smelt.

March, April, May and first part in June offer the most consistent action to anglers fishing reaction baits. The smallies become active once water temperatures creep into the forties. Action slows in summer when water temperatures rise, but picks up again in September and October. In the fall, fish slow with crawdad or minnow imitation in eight to 20 feet. Regardless of the season, anglers can catch fish dragging a worm off points.

Prior to the Sixties, Almanor had an established largemouth population. However, before they opted to raise the lake level by 45 feet, they gutted most of the trees and other structure. The lake's

A Lowrance 104 fish finder can make finding trout and salmon easier at Lake Almanor when trolling or jigging.

469

surface capacity was increased, structure was lost and the largemouth population was devastated.

The Lake Almanor Bass Association has taken a stand to aid largemouth and reestablish habitat, but it's been an uphill battle thus far. No plans are in the works to stock more largemouth. Instead, they are focusing on adding Christmas trees each year to create spawning structure. For now, there is a small population of 10-14 inch largemouth and a smaller group of four-to-five-pound fish.

If you plan to make the trip, supplies are available in Chester. Call ahead for updated conditions. At times during the winter snow and ice may close access to the lake.

Also nearby is Hamilton Branch Creek, Butt Valley Reservoir, North Fork of the Feather River and Lassen National Park.

Directions: From Interstate 5 in Red Bluff, take the Highway 99/36 exit and drive east for 2.2 miles to the junction of Highway 99/36. Turn left on Highway 36 and continue to the junction with Highway 89 south. From here, either continue on Highway 36 towards access near Chester or turn right for the dam.

Alan Jaquias with a quality rainbow trout like one you'd expect to catch at Lake Almanor.

HAMILTON BRANCH CREEK

Rating: 8

Species: Rainbow Trout
and Chinook Salmon

Stocked with 1,700
pounds of rainbow
trout.

Facilities: None

Need Information?
Contact: Lassen
National Forest
(530) 258-2141

Hamilton Branch Creek does gets planted with trout by the California Department of Fish and Game. Nonetheless, it's the trout (and Chinook salmon) that swim up from Lake Almanor into the creek that make fishing so good. During summer, the CA DFG plants roughly 2,200 half-pound rainbow trout. Those fish are joined by larger trout that have swam up from Almanor.

Hamilton Branch Creek is one of the shortest streams in the state. The creek flows out of Mountain Meadows Reservoir and into Lake Almanor. By mid July the upper stretch of the stream can be poor for bait fishermen and spin casters because of low flows and lots of aquatic growth. On the other hand, the lower stretch remains good through summer. From the bridge down to the diversion dam, the creek holds a ton of fish. Planted, wild and Almanor fish are present.

Many anglers quit coming in July because the plant and algae growth in the creek can be so severe. Anglers who don't mind catching weed fish every dozen or so casts do well. The greenery in the river promotes insect growth, which in turn provides more feed for the fish. Fish swim up Hamilton Branch from Almanor because they are seeking cooler water.

Trout and salmon feed on pond smelt in Almanor and get drawn to the Hamilton Branch inlet in the summer and fall because of the cold water the creek pumps into Almanor. Some trout and salmon also swim up the stream to spawn. Hamilton Branch is a spring creek and extremely rich. As it has the potential to be a trophy trout stream, the CA DFG is looking into managing the stream differently soon.

The CA DFG may soon take the entire of allotment of fish from Hamilton Branch and transfer them over to Little Bucks Lake. Plants aren't necessarily needed at Hamilton Branch because of the wild fish and Almanor spawners. Keep in mind, there is a fish ladder located near Red Bridge. Legally, you can't fish within 100 yards of a fish ladder. Unfortunately, there are no regulations posted.

If you plan to make the trip, supplies are available in Clear Creek. Hamilton Branch Creek is closed to fishing from November 16 to the last Saturday in April.

Also nearby are Clear Creek Pond and Goodrich Creek.

Directions: *From Interstate 5 in Red Bluff, take the Highway 99/36 exit and drive east for 2.2 miles to the junction of Highway 99/36. Turn left on Highway 36 and drive 78.1 miles to Highway 147. Turn right, drive six-tenths of a mile and turn west on Highway 147. Continue 1.4 miles and turn left on a dirt road. Cross the railroad tracks and continue two-tenths of a mile to a split in the road. The stream is just past the split.*

CLEAR CREEK POND

Rating: 4

Species: Rainbow Trout

Stocked with 700 pounds of rainbow trout.

Facilities: Restrooms, Lodging, Gas, Restaurant, General Store and a Playground

Need Information? Contact: Lassen National Forest (530) 258-2141

Clear? Like glass. Shallow? Even more so. The water doesn't get deeper than two feet and you can see right through it. In spite of the depth, Clear Creek Pond is stocked with trout, especially on holiday weekends. Actually, locals know where it gets planted because both the osprey and kids show up to fish. Locals refer to it as "The Kids Pond". In this small pond located in Clear Creek Park the trout are easy to catch and the pond is equally intriguing. Bubbles surface all over the lake hinting at springs and nutrient rich water.

Clear Creek is planted by the California Department of Fish and Game with some 1,345 rainbow trout. However, being a tributary to Hamilton Branch Creek and having many fish use the fish ladder to leave Hamilton Branch and enter Clear Creek Pond, there are also wild trout and those that have swam up from Almanor. Some spawning also occurs. Oftentimes, fish raised by students at Feather River Junior College are released into the pond.

If you are going to fish the pond successfully, plan on using bait and keep movement to a minimal. Because the water is so clear and shallow the trout can easily see you coming. The kids who fish mostly use Power Bait. Lures can be difficult to keep off the bottom.

Clear Creek Pond

If you plan to make the trip, supplies are available in Clear Creek. Clear Creek Pond is closed to fishing from November 16 to the last Saturday in April.

Also nearby are Hamilton Branch Creek and Lake Almanor.

Directions: From Interstate 5 in Red Bluff, take the Highway 99/36 exit and drive east for 2.2 miles to the junction of Highway 99/36. Turn left on Highway 36 and drive 78.1 miles to Highway 147. Turn right, drive six-tenths of a mile and turn right on Highway 147. Continue four-tenths of a mile to the pond on the right.

GOODRICH CREEK

Rating: 3

Species: Rainbow Trout

Stocks: None

Facilities: None

Need Information?
Contact: Lassen
National Forest
(530) 258-2141

Some of us have been fortunate enough to fish Goodrich Creek at its' best. Unfortunately, the creek may never be worth fishing for most anglers again. Located near Lake Almanor and a tributary to Mountain Meadows Reservoir, Goodrich is no longer planted with rainbow trout by the California Department of Fish and Game. The creek used to be planted three times in the spring, but a discrepancy over private property and little to no public access prompted the CA DFG to wash their hands of all association with the creek.

At nearly 5,100 feet in the Lassen National Forest, few anglers fish this stream anymore. Word has it that some quality fish do live in the stream, especially in the meadows downstream in Highway 36. However, confusion on where anglers are allowed to fish keeps most anglers off the property. Call the Forest Service before you arrive to check on where public access can be found. The stream isn't marked well. Goodrich Creek is an extremely small stream located in open meadows near where it crosses Highway 36. Most of the creek is shallower than two feet and narrower than four.

If you plan to make the trip, supplies are available in Westwood. Goodrich Creek is closed to fishing from November 16 to the last Saturday in April.

Also nearby are Lake Almanor, Eagle Lake and Mountain Meadows Reservoir.

Directions: *From Interstate 5 in Red Bluff, take the Highway 99/36 exit and drive east for 2.2 miles to the junction of Highway 99/36. Turn left on Highway 36 and continue approximately 85 miles to Goodrich Creek.*

Hamilton Branch Creek (Pictured Above) is a more viable option than Goodrich Creek.

473

SUSAN RIVER (LOWER)

Rating: 4

Species: Rainbow Trout

Stocked with 800
pounds of rainbow
trout.

Facilities: None

Need Information?
Contact: The
Belligerent Duck
(530) 233-4696

Unfortunately by late June, you may find more teenagers, shopping carts and big orange construction cones in the Lower Susan River than fish. For local youngsters, summer vacations are spent here. They ride their bikes to the river, leave them on the side of the road and spend the rest of the day swimming and leaping off the rocks into this murky water. The day I visited, kids were throwing shopping carts off the bridge. So don't expect serenity.

To have a chance at catching fish you'll have to arrive in the spring when the California Department of Fish and Game plants 1,600 half-pound rainbow trout. Action is never great, but at a fishery located in the middle of town, you can't expect too much. This is an urban stream enhanced by seasonal fish plants. For best results, use Power Bait. It's a good idea to add some sort of scent, such as Pautzke Liquid Krill. The water is so dirty and murky, the fish can smell better than they can see.

Susan River (Lower)

If you plan to make the trip, supplies are available in Susanville. The Susan River (Lower) is closed to fishing from November 16 to the last Saturday in April.

Also nearby is Eagle Lake.

Directions: *From the junction of Highway 395 and Highway 36 in Susanville, take Highway 36 west. Continue to South Weatherlow Street and turn left. Drive two-tenths of a mile to the river.*

EAGLE LAKE

Rating: 10

Species: Rainbow Trout

Stocked with 129,900
pounds of rainbow trout.

Facilities: Campgrounds,
RV Hookups, Picnic
Areas, Lodging,
Restrooms, Boat
Launches, Gas,
Restaurants, Bait &
Tackle, Boat Rentals,
General Store, Showers
and Fish Cleaning
Stations

Need Information?
Contact: Lassen National
Forest (530) 257-2151,
Bureau of Land
Management (530) 257-
0456, Eagle Lake Marina
(530) 825-3454

Eagle is one of our most sought after fisheries. It has a "big fish" feel to it. Boasting 100 miles of shoreline and 28,000 acres, Eagle is the second largest natural lake in California, has no outlet or year round inlet and is a great wildlife viewing area. Bald eagles and osprey frequent the lake and attract bird watchers from all over Northern California.

Eagle Lake is one of the Golden State's premier trout lakes. Many consider it one of the best trout fisheries in the West. Eagle Lake is one of the few places in California where the average angler can catch two-to-four-pound trout in a wild and free environment. Unlike many of the state's pay-to-fish lakes, Eagle's trout do most of their growing in the lake, rather than in fish pens. Since 1996, the California Inland Fisheries Foundation has worked closely with the California Department of Fish and Game to provide monitory assistance and volunteers to aid the CA DFG in egg taking and structural enhancement projects.

Eagle isn't your typical lake. Eagle is an alkaline lake, which brings its share of problems. Alkaline waters are tough on fish's gills. When Ph levels increase, trout become stressed and have trouble processing oxygen through their gills. What exactly is alkalinity? For non-scientists here's an easy way to understand. Alkalinity is a measure of the amount of chemical makeup of soils that have a high level of alkaline. Alkaline is concentrated in many of the lakes on and near the Modoc Plateau. High alkalinity in Eagle Lake is related to high water temperatures and low dissolved oxygen. Cattle grazing alters the natural runoff and carries unwanted waste products into the lake, which can help fish grow faster than normal, but can effect water quality. Fortunately, Eagle Lake trout (ELT) have adapted to the high alkalinity.

Eagle Lake trout are native to the Modoc Plateau. Most likely a unique subspecies of rainbows, the ELT were first described in Eagle Lake in CA DFG documents. Eagle was formally a portion of Lake Lahonton. Lahonton covered the entire Modoc Plateau and stretched as far as Utah at one time. It was a huge inland sea with high alkalinity. When the water receded it gave way to several smaller high alkaline lakes, including Eagle.

Eagle hasn't always been only a trophy trout lake though. Over the years the CA DFG has attempted to introduce more than 16 different species into the lake, including kokanee, brown bullhead and largemouth bass in the Twenties. Luckily, none of those fish did well. Otherwise, the ELT wouldn't flourish as flawlessly as they do today.

There are several food sources available for them: tui chub, speckled dace, Lahonton red side minnows, leeches, insects and freshwater shrimp make up the bulk of the ELT's diet. Growth rates are tremendous. Their first year in Eagle Lake the ELT averaged one-half to three-quarters of a pound, before growing to 2.5 to three pounds the second year. By the third year they'd already grown to four pounds. If the ELT can survive without getting caught, by their fourth year the fish will weigh more than four pounds. Few lakes in the West have such a prolific growth rate.

Eagle is a put-and-grow fishery. Each year 203,650 pounds of half-pound ELT are planted. Some natural reproduction occurs, however, it's minimal. Water doesn't exist in Eagle's tributaries long enough for eggs to hatch. Pine Creek is Eagle's largest tributary and it only flows into the lake two months of the year. Most tributaries are pitiful and offer little runoff. Much of the natural runoff is diverted to cattle farms.

Big Todd McLean with a Eagle Lake trout

To protect the fish and reduce the number of fish taken from the lake, the typical five fish bag limit has been reduced to two fish. At Eagle, the season has also been cut short, which could be a good thing. It's too cold here in the winter anyway. Eagle is closed to fishing from January 1 to Memorial Weekend. The closure was implemented for a few reasons, the first being to protect spawning. The ELT are spring spawners, however, the fish begin to fill with eggs in December. During this time the fish aren't in a good condition for human consumption anyway. Their flesh turns dark instead of pink. Secondly, the lack of fishing pressure allows for better growth rates and due to winter freeze many anglers don't use the resource in the winter. Year-round the marinas are closed to fishing to protect big trout that move in to feed on minnows that congregate in these areas.

Eagle Lake is a trophy trout fishery. A one-pound trout, which would be cherished anywhere else in California, is ignored here. Fish average two-to-three pounds, but it takes a four-to-six-pound fish to get any attention. The lake record is a 10.5-pound fish.

Blake Lezak with an Eagle Lake trout

The fishing can be phenomenal. That is, if you know what you are doing. Trolling is simple. The topography stays flat and there aren't a lot of snags, which keeps trolling fairly simple. However, the fish are picky when it comes to colors and sizes. During the summer months we ran dozens of different Rapalas and couldn't catch fish. However, smaller Needlefish and Sep's Pro Secrets trolled at the same depths did the job.

In June, trout transition from the north to the south end. Fish congregate near several areas in the summer. Most fish dart to the deeper, cooler water along the south shore. Eagle's Nest and Springs 1, 2 and 3 are prime areas. At 93 feet deep, White Trees, the deepest part of the lake, is found in this area as well. Fish hold in these areas because the springs cool the water, keep it oxygenated and attract baitfish. Yes, the fish do sit right on the springs.

During summer, troll anywhere from .5 to 1.5 mph in 40-60 feet of water. The bite is solid from 50-300 yards offshore. In the early mornings, start trolling in 30-45 feet of water. As soon at the sun hits the water, move into 45-60 feet. A common mistake by anglers is top-lining in the summer. Anglers see trout feeding on the surface and so they move their lines to the top. What is actually happening is the trout are down some 30-50 feet and then shoot up to the surface to snatch a bug and then head back to cooler water. So keep your lines down for best results. These depths are a good rule of thumb, but keep in mind any weather change can prompt the fish to relocate.

To prove this theory, we trolled toplines in July for three straight days without a bite. White Needlefish and silver Needlefish with red tips are excellent lures. In the spring and summer, red or pink are big producers. They imitate the spawning Lahonton red side minnows.

Eagle's fish are like cattle. They scour the lake hunting baitfish and are successful. When the bite is on, Eagle Lake gets swamped with anglers. We encountered 35 boats in a 200 yard stretch of water. And that was a weekday!

Biologist Paul Chappell shows off an Eagle Lake trout taken on a Sep's Pro grub.

Trolling can get tough because of all the traffic. Many anglers choose to bait fish near shore. Anchored in 30-50 feet of water, anglers do well with inflated night crawlers and Power Bait. Shore angling is good at The Circus, along breakwaters and at Rocky Point.

Some sections of the lake have sandy bottom and shorelines lined with thick tules. This makes for great still fishing from a float tube or boat. This is the best area on the lake to float night crawlers. The number one used bait on the lake is an inflated night crawler.

Another area fish congregate is near Pelican Point and from Shrimp Island to Wildcat Point. Work the shoreline, but try to keep your boat in 14 feet of water. For best results, send your lures down seven feet. With a map, any of these spots are easy to find.

In September, once the early morning chill casts itself on the lake, the trout begin to relocate to the north end to look for food. During fall, the biggest fish are caught in October and December as they gorge on bait looking to beef up for the winter. White out can hit the lake in October through December though. Getting on the water this time of year isn't always easy. Use the white Pro Grub or any other minnow imitation in the fall. Frog patterned lures and black and brown are other top fall colors.

Like every lake, Eagle has its' obstacles. Particularly when a low pressure system moves in, winds whip up from the southwest and the lake can look like an ocean within minutes. The south wind doesn't necessarily hurt the fishing, but the bite does shut down when the wind comes from the north.

Anglers ducking below the wind-shield and lying on the floor of their boats to avoid the cold winds is common. If winds get nasty, get off the lake in a hurry.

Eagle isn't just for anglers. In January and February, bald eagles move into the area. In 2002, 169 were spotted. There is also an ecological preserve on the west side of the lake set aside for osprey.

If you plan to make the trip, supplies are available in Spaulding. Eagle Lake is closed to fishing from January 1 to Memorial Day weekend.

Also nearby is the Susan River.

Directions: From Susanville on Highway 36, drive west to the right turnoff for County Road A-1. Turn right and drive 18 miles to the lake.

Author Chris Shaffer with an Eagle Lake trout

Blake Lezak (Left) and Big Todd McLean show off a quality Eagle Lake bow taken on a Needlefish.

PINE CREEK

Rating: 5

Species: Brook Trout
and Rainbow Trout

Stocked with 500
pounds of rainbow
trout.

Facilities:
Campgrounds and
Restrooms

Need Information?
Contact: Lassen
National Forest
(530) 257-4188

Pine Creek has come under controversy in recent years. Not well known, Pine Creek is an important aspect to Eagle Lake. The only major tributary to Eagle, Pine Creek (during high water years) is the only viable spawning habitat for the Eagle Lake trout (ELT). The eggs are collected by the California Department of Fish and Game and volunteers from the California Inland Fisheries Foundation to rear ELT. Unfortunately, Pine may only flow two months of the year, so the window to collect eggs is short. Issues with Pine also revolve around brook trout. The CA DFG is terrified that the brooks that thrive in Pine will migrate into Eagle, taking away some of the food source of the flourishing ELT. The brooks could also interbreed with the ELT and destroy the pure bred population.

How did the brooks get into Pine in the first place? Well, that was actually the CA DFG's fault. The CA DFG planted brooks into Pine in 1949 and then from 1950-75. Quickly adapting to the water, they became self-sustaining. The CA DFG is trying to eliminate them though, in hopes of establishing permanent, protected spawning grounds for the ELT. When you fish don't feel obligated to release the brooks.

Here's what the goal is: the CA DFG is trying to establish spawning grounds in Pine Creek (for ELT) and eliminate the brookies. Right now, the brookies are out-competing the ELT. Pine Creek is an important nursery for ELT.

Today, Pine is a great brook trout fishery. The brooks can grow as large as 15 inches, with the average size closer to eight-to-10 inches. Clear, cold, clean water makes for excellent conditions. Several angling opportunities arise. Some areas are best targeted with a fly rod, while others provide dynamite catch rates with Power Bait and night crawlers. In the larger pools, small spinners work.

There are several roadside access points upstream of Highway 44, making for easy access to this five-foot wide stream in the Lassen National Forest. The best is at Bogart Flat by the rest area and along Forest Service Road 10.

If you plan to make the trip, supplies are available in Old Station. From Highway 44 downstream to Eagle Lake, Pine Creek is closed to fishing. The CA DFG is getting this section ready for the introduction of Eagle Lake trout. Pine Creek is closed to fishing from Nov. 16 to the last Saturday in April.

Also nearby are Crater Lake, McCoy Flat Reservoir and Caribou Lake.

Directions: *From Interstate 5 in Red Bluff, exit Highway 36 and drive approximately 105 miles east on Highway 36 to the junction with Highway 44. Turn left on Highway 44 and drive 21.1 miles to a road on the left signed for Bogart Campground. Turn left and continue 1.6 miles to a dirt road on the right. Turn right and drive a half-mile to the campground and stream.*

MC COY FLAT RESERVOIR

Rating: 5

Species: Brown Trout,
Brook Trout and
Rainbow Trout

Stocked 2,000 pounds
of brook trout and
1,000 pounds of
rainbow trout.

Facilities: None

Need Information?
Contact: Lassen
National Forest
(530) 257-4188

Mc Coy Flat Reservoir looks like a puddle of water set aside for cows and birds. There are hundreds of rocks lining the shoreline, yet none seem to go unclaimed by bird droppings. Looks can be deceiving though. Mc Coy Reservoir is one of the most productive lakes in Northern California. When water is available, the fish thrive.

Unfortunately, water isn't always present. Mc Coy Flat is an irrigation reservoir. The Honey Lake Irrigation District can suck it dry if they want. They did just that in 2001. Due to pre-1914 water rights, the lake is allowed to be completely drained. But, when there's enough water to plant fish, the California Department of Fish and Game rushes to the reservoir and tosses them in. In good water years, 3,700 half-pound brook trout and 1,800 half-pound Eagle Lake rainbow trout are stocked.

If water levels remain high for back-to-back years, the fish grow like crazy. At full pool, the 1,800-acre reservoir at 5,500 feet in the Lassen National Forest can look deep, but is actually shallow. It's not uncommon for trout to reach three pounds after being in the lake two years. An abundance of invertebrates keep the fish growing fast.

Fishing can be a bit tough at times. Low water and limited oxygen can keep the trout on the bottom and out of feeding mode. When the lake is full, however, fishing stays good. Spin casting, bait fishing with night crawlers and fly fishing can yield fabulous catch rates.

If you plan to make the trip, supplies are available in Susanville.

Also nearby are Pine Creek, Crater Lake and Silver Lake.

Directions: *From Interstate 5 in Red Bluff, exit Highway 36 and drive approximately 105 miles east on Highway 36 to the junction with Highway 44. Turn left on Highway 44 and drive 10.4 miles to the turnoff for Mc Coy Flat Reservoir on the left. Turn left and drive one mile to a split in the road. Veer right and drive one-tenth of a mile to the lake.*

Mc Coy Flat Reservoir

SUSAN RIVER (UPPER)

Rating: 5

Species: Rainbow Trout, Brown Trout and Brook Trout

Stocked with 500 pounds of rainbow trout and 1,000 pounds of sub-catchable fingerling cutthroat trout.

Facilities: None

The Susan River is a cold water fishery maintained entirely by hatchery plants. Some years brown, rainbow and brook trout are planted. The river (which is more of a stream) flourishes when water is available in the spring. However, by late-June flows diminish and fish plants cease. By mid-July the river looks like a pathetic stream. Even the most gracious get disappointed!

The Susan River isn't a premier trout water. It's a marginal stream, enhanced by 900 half-pound rainbow trout and 6,000 sub-catchable cutthroat trout. There are wild brook, rainbow and some brown trout in the system, but a lack of water keeps their populations from flourishing. Most anglers stick to using salmon eggs. The planted fish tend to stack up in pools and can be easy to catch. The best areas to fish are where the river crosses under the road.

Trip info for Silver Lake also applies to Susan River (Upper).

Directions: *From the junction of Highway 395 and 44 in Susanville, take Highway 44 west to the junction with Highway 36. Stay on Highway 44 and drive 18.4 miles to Road A21. Turn left on Road A21 and drive 4.4 miles to an unsigned road on the right. (This is known as Silver Lake Road. There's a stop sign.) Turn right. The river runs alongside the road.*

The Upper Susan River can get low after June.

SILVER LAKE

Rating: 7

Species: Rainbow
Trout, Brown Trout and
Brook Trout

Stocked with 4,000
pounds of rainbow trout
and 600 pounds of
brown trout.

Facilities: Restrooms,
Picnic Area,
Campgrounds and a
Boat Launch

Need Information?
Contact: Lassen
National Forest
(530) 258-2141

Like every lake, Silver Lake has its' good and bad qualities. Here's the good: because Silver is part of the Susan River Drainage and not the Pine Creek Drainage, (as it's neighbor Caribou Lake is) brook trout are planted, as well as thousands of rainbow trout and a sprinkling of browns. Shoreline access is good and there is a boat launch to allow for power boats. Now here's the bad: water-skiing is permitted, which on this 112-acre lake can easily disrupt fishing. The lake is too small to cater to anglers and power boaters at the same time.

When boaters aren't pushing up large wakes, the fishing can be good. One downfall to Silver's fishery is that there isn't a great deal of feed. Growth rates aren't as promising as other nearby lakes. Fishing is definitely better with a boat. For shore anglers, there are several private cabins on the shoreline so private property becomes an issue. From a boat you don't have to worry about these issues.

Brook trout aren't planted annually, however they are available and often hang out near the outlet. Rainbows are the lakes dominant fish. The California Department of Fish and Game plants 7,000 half-pound Eagle Lake trout each year. Most of the bows average three-quarters of a pound. While browns aren't abundant, they are available and are often taken from the steep shoreline opposite Silver Bowl Campground. There are a few browns in the three-to-four-pound range, but they are seldom caught. Rainbows are the name of the game at Silver Lake.

Trolling is your best bet. Keep your speed down and lures small. At 6,000 feet in the Lassen National Forest and surrounded by pines, big Rapalas don't work well. Downsize with Hum-Dingers and Needlefish. Bank anglers do best with Power Bait.

If you plan to make the trip, supplies are available in Susanville. In winter and spring call the Forest Service for updated road conditions. The road may be impassable due to mud and snow.

Also nearby are Caribou Lake and the Upper Susan River.

Directions: From the junction of Highway 395 and 44 in Susanville, take Highway 44 west to the junction with Highway 36. Stay on Highway 44 and drive 18.4 miles to Road A21. Turn left on Road A21 and drive 4.4 miles to an unsigned road on the right. (This is known as Silver Lake Road. There's a stop sign.) Turn right and continue 5.1 miles to a split in the road. Veer right and drive one-half mile to another split. Veer left and continue two-tenths of a mile to the lake.

CARIBOU LAKE

Rating: 7

Species: Rainbow Trout and Brook Trout

Stocked with 2,050 pounds of rainbow trout.

Facilities: Restrooms

Need Information?
Contact: Lassen
National Forest
(530) 258-2141

Almost no one outside the city of Susanville has heard of Caribou Lake, and because of its' close proximity to rich fisheries (loaded with trophy size fish) such as Lake Almanor and Eagle Lake, most anglers wouldn't give a hoot even if the lake was in their backyard.

On the other hand, anglers who enjoy solitude and non-stop action on one-to-two-pound Eagle Lake trout couldn't have asked for a better destination. Only a short drive on a dirt road from Highway 44, Caribou borders the Caribou Wilderness and is a good place for shoreline and boat anglers to have a chance at limits of trout.

While the California Department of Fish and Game has opted to halt stocks of brook trout, rainbows are planted annually. Each summer some 3,690 bows are stocked. Brooks are no longer planted because Caribou is part of the Pine Creek Drainage. The CA DFG is attempting to rid the creek of brooks to help develop ELT spawning grounds.

The best way to cash in on the action on this 90-acre lake at 6,000 feet in the Lassen National Forest is with a boat. Car top boats and canoes equipped with electric trolling motors will do the trick. Try to maintain a slow speed. Anything less than 1.3 mph is fine. When the wind picks up you can turn your motor off and fish the drift. For best results troll a Sep's neon blue Pro dodger in front of a firetiger Needlefish. Silver Super Dupers are a local favorite. As you might have guessed, small lightweight lures work best here.

For shore anglers, there's two miles of shoreline to cover. The dam area is a big producer on night crawlers and white Power Bait. Tossing spinners can be useful in the evenings, but action for spin fishermen is slow during the day. Try using white mini jigs about two feet under a bobber in the morning for pan size brookies.

If you plan to make the trip, supplies are available in Susanville. In winter and spring call the Forest Service for updated road conditions. The road may be impassable due to mud and snow.

Also nearby are Silver Lake and the Upper Susan River.

Directions: *From the junction of Highway 395 and 44 in Susanville, take Highway 44 west to the junction with Highway 36. Stay on Highway 44 and drive 18.4 miles to Road A21. Turn left on Road A21 and drive 4.4 miles to an unsigned road on the right. (This is known as Silver Lake Road. There's a stop sign.) Turn right and continue 5.1 miles to a split in the road. Veer right and drive one-half mile to another split. Veer right and continue three-tenths of a mile to a dirt road on the left. Take the left and continue two-tenths of a mile to the lake.*

Frank Timmons displays a rainbow trout he caught trolling at Caribou Lake.

SHOTOVERIN LAKE

Rating: 4

Species: Rainbow Trout and Brook Trout

Stocked with 1,000 pounds of rainbow trout and four pounds of fingerling brook trout.

Facilities: None

Need Information?
Contact: Lassen National Forest
(530) 258-2141

Shotoverin Lake is plagued by fish die-offs. Winter freezes unfortunately kill many of the fish planted each spring and summer. However, Shotoverin is a put-and-take lake, not a put-and-grow lake. Catchable size fish are planted. While a die off diminishes holdover fish, new fish are trucked in each summer. There are always fish to be caught.

At 6,524 feet in the Lassen National Forest, Shotoverin is a small, shallow lake surrounded by pines. Primitive campsites can be found along the lake and Eagle Lake trout in the lake. The California Department of Fish and Game spills more than 1,800 in each summer. An additional 1,000 fingerling brook trout are also planted. Fishing is fair. Sliding sinker methods with rainbow Power Bait and silver Phoebes tossed from shore take the bulk of the fish.

Trip info for Silver Lake also applies to Shotoverin Lake.

Directions: *From the junction of Highway 395 and 44 in Susanville, take Highway 44 west to the junction with Highway 36. Stay on Highway 44 and drive 18.4 miles to Road A21. Turn left on Road A21 and drive 4.4 miles to an unsigned road on the right. (This is known as Silver Lake Road. There's a stop sign.) Turn right onto the dirt road and continue 5.1 miles to a split in the road. Veer right, drive one-tenth of a mile and veer left. Drive another one-tenth of a mile and veer left again. Continue 1.4 miles to the lake on the right.*

Shotoverin Lake

CRATER LAKE

Rating: 6

Species: Brook Trout
and Rainbow Trout

Stocked with 3,500
pounds of rainbow trout
and 32 pounds of
fingerling rainbow
trout.

Facilities: Boat Launch,
Campgrounds and
Restrooms

Need Information?
Contact: Lassen
National Forest
(530) 257-4188

Whoa…slow down. Don't get so excited. Let's make sure we are all on the same page here. Crater Lake is in California. This isn't Oregon's Crater Lake, the National Park visited by hundreds of thousands of people each year from all over the world. Lassen County's Crater Lake doesn't get that many visitors, especially no one from outside of Northern California. Crater Lake is a small, hidden, brook trout filled water in the Lassen National Forest. At 7,420 feet, this 25-acre lake doesn't have the capacity to cater to hundreds of anglers. Because of its size and the lack of room available in the small basin it rests in, Crater remains a kind of scenic, high mountain, relaxing spot.

The fishing is always fair to good. Each year the California Department of Fish and Game plants some 8,000 fingerling rainbow trout and 6,000 half-pound Eagle Lake rainbows. This put-and-take and put-and-grow lake often kicks out rainbows and brookies to three pounds. Brookies were planted prior to 2003. Most fish are taken on inflated night crawlers and Power Bait.

Crater does in fact rest in a crater and freezes over in the winter. The road to the lake is not maintained. A snowmobile is required to reach it in the winter. In summer both shoreline and boat anglers enjoy action. There is a boat launch however, no motorized boats are permitted.

If you plan to make the trip, supplies are available in Old Station. The road to the lake is not maintained in the winter and may be inaccessible due to snow. Call the Forest Service for updated conditions.

Crater Lake

Also nearby are Pine Creek, Mc Coy Flat Reservoir and Eagle Lake.

Directions: *From Interstate 5 in Red Bluff, exit Highway 36 and drive approximately 105 miles east on Highway 36 to the junction with Highway 44. Turn left on Highway 44 and drive 22.9 miles to the turnoff for Crater Lake (Road 32N08). Turn right on Road 32N08 and drive eight-tenths of a mile to a split in the road. Veer right and drive 1.1 miles to another split, Veer left and drive five miles to the lake.*

Region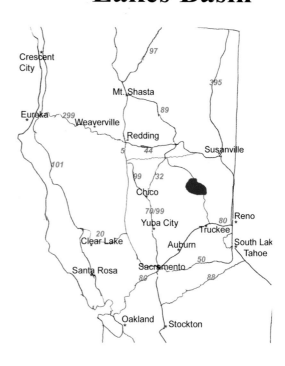

17

Lakes Basin

PACKER LAKE

Rating: 6

Species: Rainbow Trout and Brook Trout

Stocked with 600 pounds of rainbow trout and 2,000 pounds of brook trout.

Facilities: Picnic Area, Restrooms and Lodging

Need Information? Contact: Packer Lake Lodge (530) 862-1221

For the angler who wants to avoid loud, annoying and fume-filled exhausts from boats, Packer Lake is one of your few drive to options in the Lakes Basin. With all gas-powered motors outlawed, the soothing sounds of osprey chirping and ducks quacking are all you'll hear. With the exception of a canoe or float tube, don't expect to see any watercraft. The lake is mostly used as a swimming hole, but the California Department of Fish and Game keeps fishing fair with plants of rainbow and brook trout from spring through summer. Fish totals peak at roughly 4,500 half-pound fish each year.

Unfortunately, landing trophy fish is out of the question. There are some pound-size holdovers caught weekly, however, bigger fish like the lake record nine-pound brown landed in May of 1981 are a rarity. This small, 12-acre lake is tucked into a basin overshadowed by looming jagged ridges and kept cool by pines. Roughly 25 feet deep, the best area to fish is directly in front of Packer Lake Lodge, with the area in front of the large rock being the top producer. However, don't count out the dam. Because the shorelines are weedy and shallow, tossing lures isn't an angler's top choice, but it can be productive. Use rainbow Power Bait for better results.

Trip info for Gold Lake also applies to Packer Lake.

Directions: *From the junction of I-80 and Highway 89 in Truckee, exit north on Highway 89 and drive 23.6 miles to the junction with Highway 49. Turn left on Highway 49/89 and continue five miles to where Highway 89 and 49 split. Following the left fork, stay on Highway 49 and continue 36.6 miles to Lakes Basin Road. Turn right and continue 1.4 miles to Sardine/Packer Lake Road on the left. Turn left and drive three-tenths of mile to a split in the road. Veer right on Road 93 and drive 2.7 miles to the Packer Lake turnoff. Veer right on Forest Service Road 621-06. Continue one-tenth of a mile to the lake.*

Packer Lake

TAMARACK LAKES

<table>
<tr><td>

Rating: 4

Species: Brook Trout

Stocks: None

Facilities: None

</td></tr>
</table>

Tamarack Lakes can be approached two ways. The drive-to option is only available to those with four-wheel drive vehicles. I made it halfway with my four-wheel drive Ford Excursion, and probably could have made it to the lake, but I grew cautious and parked before walking the last half mile. Walking isn't such a bad thing. From the trailhead it's 1.1 miles to the lake and all the hiking is done on a dirt road. You don't have to worry about brushing up against bushes or confusing trail junctions.

Lately, visitors haven't been coming to the Tamaracks for the fishing. There are brook trout in both lakes, however, with the absence of trout plants since 2000 there aren't an abundance of fish left. And, the fish tend to be on the small side, so an eight incher is a trophy. The best way to approach the lakes, which are set at 6,754 feet (Upper Tamarack) in the Tahoe National Forest is as a half day hike from Packer Lake. It's not necessary to set aside an entire trip. On the other hand, the scenery might keep you here longer than you might expect. The snow tipped, jagged and towering Sierra Buttes, combined with pockets of wildflowers make this trip always worthwhile.

Trip info for Gold Lake also applies to Tamarack Lakes.

Directions: *From the junction of I-80 and Highway 89 in Truckee, exit north on Highway 89 and drive 23.6 miles to the junction with Highway 49. Turn left on Highway 49/89 and continue five miles to where Highway 89 and 49 split. Following the left fork, stay on Highway 49 and continue 36.6 miles to Lakes Basin Road. Turn right and continue 1.4 miles to Sardine/Packer Lake Road on the left. Turn left and drive three-tenths of mile to a split in the road. Veer right on Road 93 and drive 2.7 miles to a split in the road. Stay left and if you have a four-wheel drive vehicle continue 1.1 miles to the lake. Otherwise, drive one-tenth of a mile to a pullout on the right. Park and walk.*

Tamarack Lake

490

SAND POND

Rating: 2
Species: Rainbow Trout and Brook Trout
Stocks: None
Facilities: Picnic Area and Restrooms

Sand Pond isn't a natural pond. It was created as a result of old mining operations. According to the Tahoe National Forest, gold ore was extracted from the Young America Gold Mine in the early 1900's. Waste material resulting from the crushing of gold ore was deposited downstream of the mine. When the waste was removed, it formed the depression now know as Sand Pond.

Sand Pond is the most popular swimming hole in the Lakes Basin Recreation Area of the Tahoe National Forest. Water released from Sardine Lake's dam feeds the pond and keeps 1000's of swimmers, sunbathers and anglers happy all summer long. In contrast, the fishing is never better than poor. A few wanderers have snuck their way into the pond, but these fish are extremely difficult to catch.

If you want any shot, arrive before the swimmers do. The pond gets bombarded by tourists and campers staying at Sardine Lake Lodge and nearby campgrounds. The water is clear and comfortable in the summer, up to 10 feet deep and has shallow, sandy shorelines ideal for youngsters.

I think of Sand Pond as a giant freshwater aquarium. Bring along a mask and snorkel and you'll know why. A few rainbow and brook trout reside, as well as bluegill, largemouth bass, pollywogs, bullfrogs and minnows. Towards the middle of the pond the bottom is lined with extensive plant life. It's a rare opportunity to see fish in their environment without having to use diving gear.

Trip info for Gold Lake also applies to Sand Pond.

Sand Pond

Directions: *From the junction of I-80 and Highway 89 in Truckee exit north on Highway 89 and drive 23.6 miles to the junction with Highway 49. Turn left on Highway 49/89 and continue five miles to where Highway 89 and 49 split. Following the left fork, stay on Highway 49 and continue 36.6 miles to Lakes Basin Road. Turn right and continue 1.4 miles to Sardine/Packer Lake Road on the left. Turn left and drive three-tenths of a mile to a split in the road. Veer left and continue four-tenths of a mile to the lake.*

SARDINE LAKE (UPPER)

<table>
<tr><td>Rating: 5</td></tr>
<tr><td>Species: Rainbow Trout, Brown Trout and Brook Trout</td></tr>
<tr><td>Stocks: None</td></tr>
<tr><td>Facilities: None</td></tr>
<tr><td>Need Information? Contact: Sardine Lake Lodge (530) 862-1196</td></tr>
</table>

Upper Sardine Lake can be one of the best or worst places you'll ever fish. It all depends on whether or not you can get a boat in. Easier said than done, I might add. While Upper Sardine is only a half-mile from the paved road at Lower Sardine, the road quickly changes to dirt and rock. Without a four-wheel drive vehicle you aren't going to make it. Additionally, this road was made for one way traffic and not for trailers. On the other hand, anglers who get a boat on the water are rewarded with staggering catch rates. Hint: bring a canoe or car top boat with an electric trolling motor.

Because of its remote location few anglers fish Upper Sardine. Most years the California Department of Fish and Game treats this lake as a put-and-grow fishery. These fish grow beautifully. Each year, upwards of 25,000 fingerling rainbow trout are stocked. Most of the shoreline access inhibits bank fishing. For boat anglers there's a shelf in the middle of the lake that is an important landmark. Once you locate it don't worry about finding the hot lures to troll. These fish are rarely targeted and will hit just about anything.

Surprisingly, the fish grow pretty fast in this high mountain lake at 5,995 feet in the Tahoe National Forest, surrounded by towering jagged snow-capped peaks. Average length tends to be in the 10-12 inch class, but larger fish are common. The majority of fish are rainbows; however, brooks are abundant near the inlet. Browns are often caught by trollers. Bank anglers can do well too, but you need to be willing to rock hop a bit. There is no trail around the lake. The shorelines are rugged, but good bank fishing can be had off points and in coves in the evenings.

Don't arrive hoping to catch trophy fish. It is ok, however, to plan on being awed. The surroundings are breathtaking. If you have an adventurous side Sardine Lake offers more than just fishing. For the rugged hiker, walk to the back of the lake and locate the Sardine Creek inlet. There's a small waterfall that drops into the lake. Keep chugging up the creek and you'll arrive at Young America Lake, the only water in the region to hold golden trout.

Trip info for Gold Lake also applies to Sardine Lake (Upper).

Directions: *From Lower Sardine Lake: If you have a four-wheel drive vehicle continue a half-mile to the lake. Otherwise park and walk the road.*

492

Upper Sardine Lake

SARDINE LAKE (LOWER)

Rating: 7

Species: Rainbow Trout and Brook Trout

Stocked with 8,000 pounds of brook trout.

Facilities: Boat Launch, Restaurant and Lodging

Need Information? Contact: Sardine Lake Lodge (530) 862-1196

If you were to look over the California Department of Fish and Game's fish planting records for the Lakes Basin (which is split between Sierra and Plumas Counties) one question would come to mind, "Why is little Lower Sardine Lake planted with many more fish than the bigger lakes in the region?"

I posed that discrepancy to some of the local resort owners. Ironically, they all had the same answer as to why. Unanimously, all agreed that the owners of Sardine Lake Lodge aren't afraid to speak up for themselves.

Sardine Lake Lodge has put a tremendous amount of pressure on the CA DFG to stock fish. Luckily, their persistence has paid off. Nearly 11,400 fish are planted into this 38-acre lake each summer and fall. What boggles me the most is Sardine is seven percent the size of nearby Gold Lake and oftentimes much less fished, yet Gold is only planted with 8,000 trout (3,400 less than Sardine). The folks over at Sardine Lake Lodge have definitely worked their butts off to get more fish for their clients. They've done a good job, that's for sure.

Fishing Sardine with a boat is a sure way to catch limits. A dirt launch ramp and little room to turn around, keep larger boats off the water though. Trolling is red hot! It's especially good for those of you who can handle fishing with four-pound test. The troll is simple. Start from the launch and either troll the shorelines, down the middle of the lake, or zigzag across it. Basically, go anywhere you want! Use small lures; Needlefish, Thomas Buoyants, Cripplures. Heck it doesn't matter, just troll slow.

Shore anglers find the best access near the dam, where the typical bait dunker methods work like a charm. The Sardine Creek inlet near the back of the lake is also a big producer, but it's a walk. Most anglers don't bother.

Trip info for Gold Lake also applies to Sardine Lake (Lower).

Directions: From the junction of I-80 and Highway 89 in Truckee, exit north on Highway 89 and drive 23.6 miles to the junction with Highway 49. Turn left on Highway 49/89 and continue five miles to where Highway 89 and 49 split. Following the left fork, stay on Highway 49 and continue 36.6 miles to Lakes Basin Road. Turn right and continue 1.4 miles to Sardine/Packer Lake Road on the left. Turn left and drive three-tenths of a mile to a split in the road. Veer left and continue six-tenths of a mile to the lake.

Lower Sardine Lake

SALMON LAKE (UPPER)

Rating: 7

Species: Rainbow Trout and Brook Trout

Stocked with 4,000 pounds of brook trout.

Facilities: Boat Launch, Restrooms and Lodging

Need Information? Contact: Salmon Lake Lodge (530) 757-1825

In the Lakes Basin achieving that Adirondack feeling is all possible. At Upper Salmon Lake expectations aren't let down. At 6,500 feet in the Plumas National Forest, Upper Salmon Lake has the amenities and natural surroundings to create a memorable family outing. Ducks, including their newborns, cruise the lake's rugged shorelines, osprey hover overhead scanning the water for a meal and jagged peaks lurk overhead, while the water taxi shuttles visitors from the boat launch across to Salmon Lake Lodge. The scenery is splendid.

As for the fishing, the lake is heavily planted. The CA DFG pumps 5,900 brook trout into the 41-acre lake each year. It's full with fish for tourists to have a blast. The only downside is there are no trophy fish. Yet, there are hundreds of holdovers that reach the one-pound class. Fishing will be fantastic from a boat if you can troll slow, 0.5 to 1.2 mph. Troll anything with flashers or dodgers. A Sep's watermelon dodger with a Needlefish is the way to go. For the best results use a lure with silver or red.

You can put anything behind your boat and catch fish as long as you keep the speed down. A valuable tip, there are a few places where you'll be in deep water and without warning you'll see a house size boulder getting ready to snag your lines or take a chunk out of your boat. After one trip around the lake you'll know where they are. Just keep an eye out.

While this lake is perfect for trollers in a small boats and canoes; bank fishing and float tubing can also be epic, especially in the evenings when the surface action is superb. The lake is small enough that fishing anywhere around the shoreline with Power Bait, inflated night crawlers or tossing lures will produce fish. The best shoreline rig is a fly-and-bubble combo in the evening when the fish are rising. The rocks adjacent to the boat launch are easily accessible and not only provide good fishing, but stellar views.

Trip info for Gold Lake also applies to Salmon Lake (Upper).

Directions: *From the junction of Interstate 80 and Highway 89 in Truckee exit north on Highway 89 and drive 23.6 miles to the junction with Highway 49. Turn left on Highway 49/89 and continue five miles to where Highway 89 and 49 split. Following the left fork, stay on Highway 49 and continue 36.6 miles to Lakes Basin Road. Turn right and continue 4.1 miles to Salmon Lake Road on the left. Turn left and drive 1.1 miles to the lake.*

Salmon Lake Lodge

SALMON LAKE (LOWER)

<table>
<tr><td>

Rating: 4

Species: Rainbow Trout and Brook Trout

Stocks: None

Facilities: None

Need Information?
Contact: Plumas
National Forest
(530) 836-2575

</td></tr>
</table>

A few years back, Lower Salmon Lake was a typical roadside water where anglers drove to the shoreline, unloaded their gear and began fishing. Things have changed. The dirt access road to Lower Salmon is no longer open to vehicular traffic. The closure is an effort by the Forest Service to provide a "non-motorized recreation experience." Don't worry though, the walk on the wide, well graded dirt road is easy doable. It's a half-mile long with a 161-foot loss in elevation.

The fishing at Lower Salmon isn't anything like Upper Salmon. The crowds are light and fishing is poor. On occasion the California Department of Fish and Game does plant fingerling rainbow and brook trout into the lake. However, those fish don't show well in creels. It's thought that many of the fish dart up or downstream into Salmon Creek.

The lake is heavily silted and provides poor access for anglers. From shore can be tough. Those with float tubes have the best shot at landing brook and rainbow trout. For best results, fish the late evening with a fly and bubble combo or small spinner near the inlet.

Trip info for Gold Lake also applies to Salmon Lake (Lower).

Directions: *From the junction of Interstate 80 and Highway 89 in Truckee exit north on Highway 89 and drive 23.6 miles to the junction with Highway 49. Turn left on Highway 49/89 and continue five miles to where Highway 89 and 49 split. Following the left fork, stay on Highway 49 and continue 36.6 miles to Lakes Basin Road. Turn right and continue 4.1 miles to Salmon Lake Road on the left. Turn left and drive six-tenths of a mile to an unsigned turnoff on the left. Park at the locked gate.*

Lower Salmon Lake

SNAG LAKE

Rating: 2

Species: Brown Bullhead

Stocks: None

Facilities: Vault Toilets

When it comes to fishing, Snag Lake is self explanatory. You have a much better chance of getting snagged than catching a fish at this roadside water in the Lakes Basin Recreation Area of the Tahoe National Forest. Except for a few elusive and clever trout, this lake, which once flourished as one of the best trout lakes in the region, is barren of gamefish.

In a gill net survey taken by the California Department of Fish and Game in 2000, five brook trout, five rainbow trout, two bullhead, 10 golden shiners and two Lahonton red sides were found. With heavy fishing pressure, those fish are now gone. I assure you that's the truth. Big Todd McLean and I snorkeled the lake and found only one dead bullhead. No trout.

Snag has no inlet or outlet and reproduction is non-existent. Because the endangered mountain yellow legged frog was found in the area in 2000, the CA DFG opted to cease all trout plants to this popular pond-size lake that averages five feet deep, managing to hit nine feet in its' deepest section. The lake is lined with pines, and while catching rainbow or brook trout is out of the question, there are a few brown bullhead which can be caught with a piece of a night crawler.

Trip info for Gold Lake also applies to Snag Lake.

Directions: *From the junction of I-80 and Highway 89 in Truckee, exit north on Highway 89 and drive 23.6 miles to the junction with Highway 49. Turn left on Highway 49/89 and continue five miles to where Highway 89 and 49 split. Following the left fork, stay on Highway 49 and continue 36.6 miles to Lakes Basin Road. Turn right and continue 5.4 miles to a dirt parking area on the left that accesses Snag Lake.*

Snag Lake

HAVEN LAKE

Rating: 3
Species: None
Stocks: None
Facilities: Vault Toilets

At 6,673 feet in the Lakes Basin, Haven Lake's future is two faced. The unfortunate has happened: the California Department of Fish and Game found the endangered mountain yellow legged frog at Haven. On the other hand, studies conducted by the CA DFG show that the frogs aren't reproducing at the lake. Nonetheless, a mere two adult frogs were found in 2001, forcing the CA DFG to halt plants.

Prior to 2000, a combination of rainbow and brook trout were planted each summer and fall. Unfortunately, with heavy fishing pressure and no known reproduction, the lake is pretty much barren of fish except for a few stragglers that somehow evaded anglers. The last gill net attempt took place in 2001 and yielded just nine brookies. Big Todd McLean and I snorkeled the lake in June of 2002 and failed to see any fish. We did, however, learn that the lake's maximum depth is four feet and its' floor is smothered by a blanket of silt nearly a foot thick.

With increase pressure from local businesses and complains from anglers, there is a slight possibility of fish plants returning to this lake. Nonetheless, that decision won't be made for a few years. For now, stay away. The fish are gone.

Trip info for Gold Lake also applies to Haven Lake.

Directions: *From the junction of I-80 and Highway 89 in Truckee, exit north on Highway 89 and drive 23.6 miles to the junction with Highway 49. Turn left on Highway 49/89 and continue five miles to where Highway 89 and 49 split. Following the left fork, stay on Highway 49 and continue 36.6 miles to Lakes Basin Road. Turn right and continue 5.7 miles to a dirt parking area on the left for Haven Lake.*

Haven Lake

GOOSE LAKE

Rating: 1
Species: None
Stocks: None
Facilities: Vault Toilets

Goose Lake's prime has passed. Formerly known as a great roadside water for anglers to drop by and nab quick and easy limits of rainbow and brook trout, Goose has turned into a small lake where sightseers come to watch deer sip water, listen to birds chirp and enjoy gorgeous reflections on summer afternoons.

A roadside water in the Lakes Basin Recreation Area of the Plumas National Forest, Goose Lake is no longer that angler's paradise it used to be. Prior to 2000, rainbows and brooks were planted into Goose. When a California Department of Fish and Game survey team found the endangered mountain yellow legged frog, trout plants were halted and most likely won't return soon. As for the fish that were planted, they are pretty much gone. Fish cannot reproduce here and to further prove that theory, only one rainbow trout was netted during a gill netting operation that took place in the summer of 2001.

Our angling attempts were also unsuccessful. We did see some juvenile fish, which later were identified as golden shiners. While the fishing is basically non-existent, there are other recreational opportunities to be found, mainly canoeing and swimming. Because of its' size (this place is no lake, a pond would better describe it) and depth (12 feet is maximum depth, most of the lake averages four to five feet) the water warms fast and is comfortable for swimmers by late June in most years. There are a few dozen fallen trees around the shoreline and two small islands as well. As for now, leave your rods in the trunk and keep your swimming trunks handy when coming to Goose. Check back on the fishing in a decade. Maybe the frogs will have relocated.

Trip info for Gold Lake also applies to Goose Lake.

Directions: *From the junction of I-80 and Highway 89 in Truckee, exit north on Highway 89 and drive 23.6 miles to the junction with Highway 49. Turn left on Highway 49/89 and continue five miles to where Highway 89 and 49 split. Following the left fork, stay on Highway 49 and continue 36.6 miles to Lakes Basin Road. Turn right and continue 5.9 or 6.1 miles to parking lots on the left that access Goose Lake.*

Goose Lake

SQUAW LAKE

Rating: 2

Species: Brook Trout

Stocks: None

Facilities: None

Squaw Lake is the perfect destination for a beginning backpacking trip except for one thing: the lake which used to be loaded with brook trout now holds none. An absence of fish plants since the turn of the century has left Squaw's anglers glum. A study conducted in summer of 2001 yielded five brook trout. I showed up with a mask and snorkel in summer of 2002 and failed to spot any fish.

The California Department of Fish and Game chose to stop air plants of fingerling brook and rainbow trout while a study was conducted to determine whether the endangered mountain yellow legged frog was present at the lake. Fortunately for anglers, it wasn't. If all goes as planned, fish will again be stocked when the CA DFG issues a new management plan for the region. Once the deal is struck, give the lake a few years to hold pan-size fish. The fish are planted as fingerlings and take a few years to grow to catchable sizes.

For now, try swimming. The lake is a good 20 feet deep and extremely clear. Here's how to get there. From the four-wheel drive staging area, walk a half-mile on the wide, dirt road. After crossing a small stream, look to the left and locate the sign for Squaw Lake. Following the sign, break left and continue a quarter-mile to the lake. If you have a four-wheel drive jeep, this whole journey can be reached without ever having to lace up your boots.

Directions and trip info for Gold Lake also apply to Squaw Lake. Once you get to Gold Lake turn left and drive a half-mile to a split in the road. Continue straight for one-tenth of a mile to the staging area. You can either park and walk to the lake or continue if you have a four-wheel drive vehicle.

Squaw Lake

LITTLE GOLD LAKE

Rating: 3

Species: Brook Trout

Stocks: None

Facilities: None

At the present time Little Gold Lake is in pitiful shape. This once excellent brook trout fishery has suffered from a lack of plants by the California Department of Fish and Game. As we speak, a new management plan is being written up and things may change here.

The issue, as with every other lake in the drainage, has to do with frogs. The endangered mountain yellow-legged frog was found in the basin and plants were halted. Upon further review, the CA DFG found no frogs at Little Gold. A senior biologist told me he's pushing for the reintroduction of brook and rainbow trout into Little Gold. Approval is needed, however, and could take a few years.

From personal experience, I saw tens of thousands of fingerling fish in a mask and snorkel survey Big Todd McLean and I conducted in the summer of 2002. What was unclear is if those fish were brook trout, minnows, golden shiners or Lahonton red sides. One thing is for sure. There are few, if any, of catchable size.

When the CA DFG gill netted the lake in 2001, 33 brook trout ranging from eight-to-nine inches and golden shiners were taken. Take this piece of advice; don't bother fishing Little Gold until at least 2007. While there is a possibility of restocking fish, the approval takes time. If and when they are approved, it will take the fish two years to grow to catchable sizes.

To reach Little Gold from the staging area near Gold Lake, walk or drive if you have a high clearance four-wheel drive vehicle, 1.75 miles to the turnoff for Little Gold Lake. Turn left and continue a quarter-mile to the extremely shallow lake at 6,430 feet in the Plumas National Forest.

Directions *and trip info for Squaw Lake also apply to Little Gold Lake.*

Little Gold Lake

SUMMIT LAKE

Rating: 1
Species: None
Stocks: None
Facilities: None

After reading this, if you still end up with a rod in hand on the way to Summit Lake you need to have your head examined! Summit Lake is barren of fish. Talking about it hits a tender spot in my memory. I was convinced by a con artist in our campsite that there were fish in Summit Lake and that I should include it in my book. Let's just say that when I returned from my seven-mile roundtrip hike that day, the prankster couldn't stop laughing. He knew there weren't any fish, but he didn't want me and my "posse" catching all his lake trout in Gold Lake so he sent me up to Summit Lake to catch what he always caught, nothing!

Tucked just inside the boundary of the Tahoe National Forest, little Summit Lake rests near the border of the Plumas National Forest. It has no fish, nor any plans for them in the future. Why? It's too shallow, has no spawning grounds and is a great candidate for winter kill. What Summit is, is a frequent stop for off road vehicles and their operators who make a habit of drinking and eating lunch along the shoreline. That's about it. The only advantage I can think of for ending up here is the breathtaking view of Gold Lake you'll see on the way back.

To reach Summit from the staging area near Gold Lake, continue on the rocky road, which will shortly turn to dirt, for one mile to the signed turnoff for Squaw Lake. Ignore it and continue two miles to a signed trail spur that breaks off to the left for Little Gold Lake. Don't take it. Keep walking on the path as it winds around Gold Lake before coming to a junction. To avoid private property and stay on track for Summit Lake, break left and begin walking uphill. The path splits one final time. Take the left fork and continue to the top of the ridge and Summit Lake. It's 3.5 miles from the staging area.

Directions *and trip info for Squaw Lake also apply to Summit Lake.*

Summit Lake

501

GOLD LAKE

Rating: 6

Species: Lake Trout,
Rainbow Trout, Brown
Trout and Brook Trout

Stocked with 53 pounds
of fingerling lake trout
and 5,000 pounds of
rainbow trout.

Facilities:
Campgrounds, Lodging,
Picnic Area, Restrooms
and a Boat Launch

Need Information?
Contact: Plumas
National Forest (530)
863-2575, Gold Lake
Lodge (530) 836-2350,
Gold Lake Beach
Resort (530) 836-2491

Gold is a gorgeous lake with breathtaking reflections and air so crisp and clean many anglers almost forget about the fishing. The mirror images are world class and will make you lose fish by not paying attention to your lines. If you haven't figured it out yet, Gold Lake is a masterpiece of high mountain scenery coupled with great camping and ok fishing. Unlike many destinations in California, Gold is a natural lake fed by runoff and underwater springs. It fills each year and doesn't suffer from draw downs.

There are few better destinations in Northern California for a weeklong family camping trip than Gold. The diverse facilities offer something for every type of outdoorsperson. There are pay campsites with picnic tables, fire pits and restrooms, primitive sites with only Andy Gumps and sites near the back of the lake that can only be reached with a four-wheel drive vehicle. Some sites have lakefront views, others are shaded by tall pines.

Situated in the Lakes Basin at 6,400 feet in the Plumas National Forest and half split between Sierra and Plumas Counties, this 510-acre lake freezes over in the winter and is loved by water-skiers and anglers in the summer. There is no speed limit on the lake. However, winds tend to keep the lake from filling with water sport lovers. This is a fishing lake. Water-skiers and jet skiers are often welcomed by campers hiding in the bushes with water balloon and potato launchers. They don't like sport recreation boats up here.

Gold Lake gets a "10" for it overall family experience and natural surroundings. Unfortunately, because the fishing has taken a nose dive in the last decade, it only gets a "6." And, that's being kind. For decades, Gold was known as the seldom fished, quiet, serene northern alternative to crowded big

lake trout waters like Donner and Tahoe. However, the fishery has slumped in recent years. Take this with a grain of salt. Gold has an abundance of lake trout, but those once common lunkers have gradually begun to disappear.

Jim Reed, owner of Gold Lake Beach

Gold Lake

Blake Lezak and a Gold Lake lake trout.

Resort and lifetime Gold angler put it best. "They just aren't here anymore. Things are definitely not the same. You really have to put the time in. It's an hourly thing here. If you fish for two hours you can expect to catch one two pound fish. If you fish for five hours you can expect to catch a five pound fish. People don't stay here anymore. They come and go because the fishery bites." Reed remembers the years when anglers would foolishly follow his 2,500 gallon water tank from Downieville to Gold Lake because they thought he was hauling fish. Now they don't even bother to make the drive to the lake. It's a sad saga to those who grew up here. Hopefully, a new fisheries management plan will solve it.

With a jug full of patience, the right technique and perfect execution, there are plenty of lake trout to be caught. The lake record is a 22-pound fish caught in the mid-Nineties. Gold's lake trout are out of the ordinary. No matter what local published maps tell you, they only hold consistently in two places: a deep hole adjacent to the launch ramp and on a shelf near the back of the lake. The shelf near the back of the lake is located just off a clearly visible, exposed granite rock on the south side. The hole near the boat launch ranges from 60-87 feet and can be reached by driving adjacent to the launch towards the opposite side of the lake. Both spots can be productive if approached correctly. A fish finder is imperative. Gold's lake trout are constantly on the move. You'll find them on the west end one day and won't be able to locate them the next. Also, a depth finder enables you to eyeball suspended lake trout. While we saw few lake trout suspended, we did locate hundreds hugging the bottom.

Fortunately, much of Gold's bottom is silted with thick mud, so dragging your lures along the bottom isn't a dangerous approach towards losing expensive hardware. After a few days of unsuccessful angling, we found that without scraping the depths with our lures, the lake trout weren't interested in biting. Here's the secret. You need to pinpoint the right depth. Gold's lake trout tend to stay in water from 60-85 feet deep. Fish any shallower and don't plan

Glen Allison (Left) and David Harvey show off a limit of Gold Lake lake trout caught jigging.

Chris Shaffer (Left) and Todd McLean brave the cold to conduct research at Gold Lake in late spring.

on catching anything. Also, our typical Rebels and J-Plugs were laughed at by these lake trout. They craved smaller baits like Needlefish; a yellow and red one was our bread and butter. A green Quickfish is a local favorite. Once you locate the shelf remember this, troll point to point and you should do ok. The most successful anglers only target the big fish in low light and miserable conditions. In 2003, nearly 10,000 fingerling lake trout were planted.

The most productive method is jigging. Use light line though. We used 10-pound test and hammered the fish. When using our typical 20-pound test to jig, the fish didn't even look at it. Four-ounce blue or white Crippled Herring or Megabait jigs worked great. Sounds like a great lake trout fishery right? Here's the downside. Gold's lake trout don't break the size barrier. One-to-two- pound fish are the norm, but the numbers were astonishing. We caught 17 in an hour one day, then eight in a half day trip the following morning! While the size can be disappointing, the numbers are intriguing. This lake sure is loaded with lake trout. I wonder if an over abundance of lake trout is paving the way for a smaller fish. Lake trout better than four pounds seemed to be caught as often as snow falls in the summer at Gold.

On a positive note there is a stable food source, mostly minnows and some crawdads. Big Todd and I mask and snorkeled the lake to locate what the food sources were, and were shocked at the astonishing amount of dead crawdads we saw. I'm talking hundreds, not to mention that the live ones were covered in leeches. The dead crawdads could be blamed on a small oil spill that was never reported. The Forest Service constructed a new boat launch in late-October of 2001. The locals will tell you that when the Forest Service was pouring concrete, thick oil slicks developed near the launch area, not to mention completely silting up the cove and ruining all fish habitat. I don't have an official comment on why the crawdads were dying though. The oil problem is just a hypothesis with no recorded data to back it up, rather chatter from folks who know Gold best.

Consider this: when planning to fish Gold, create your itinerary around the weather patterns. Each day winds tend to kick up gradually around 9 a.m. and gust in the afternoons. Then, the water becomes navigable again roughly an hour before dusk. The wind blows west to east all summer and east to west in the fall and winter. Windsurfing used to be popular, but that all stopped a few years ago when a competition was cancelled because they didn't have the proper permits to hold the event. The windsurfers never came back which made the anglers happy.

Gold also used to be known as a trophy brown trout lake, but as you can guess, not enough catch and release and overfishing has depleted the lake of the fish. At the current state browns are rare, yet at one time more than a decade ago, 10-pound browns were caught on a monthly basis. Now they aren't targeted.

Gold Lake lake trout

The rainbow trout fishing has also slid off the deep end. Rarely are rainbows caught from shore or by boat. As you might have guessed, yes, rainbow trout fishing was also good in the old days. The California Department of Fish and Game used to plant brook trout each summer for bank and boat anglers without deep water trolling gear to be able to catch fish, but in a sense the 8,375 brookies that were planted in 2002 have dove into a black hole. No one seems to be catching them. Reed and I had polled more than 25 boats that week, most of who failed to catch a fish. The bite has really slowed, so much that Reed said he's beginning to lose customers. In 2003, 10,000 half-pound rainbows were stocked.

If you plan to make the trip, supplies are available in Graeagle. The road to Gold Lake typically closes in December and doesn't reopen until the second week of June. The lake freezes as early as late-November and thaws by mid-May. The only way in is with a snowmobile.

Also nearby are Little Gold Lake, Summit Lake and Squaw Lake.

Directions: From the junction of I-80 and Highway 89 in Truckee, exit north on Highway 89 and drive 23.6 miles to the junction with Highway 49. Turn left on Highway 49/89 and continue five miles to where Highway 89 and 49 split. Following the left fork, stay on Highway 49 and continue 36.6 miles to Lakes Basin Road. Turn right and continue 6.5 miles to the turnoff for Gold Lake on the left. Turn left and drive a half-mile to a split in the road. Veer right and continue two-tenths of a mile to the lake.

Gold Lake

ROUND LAKE

Rating: 5

Species: Brook Trout

Stocks: None

Facilities: None

Most of the backcountry waters near the Lakes Basin offer horrible fishing, but there are a few good spots to add to your family vacation. Near Gold Lake, in the Plumas National Forest, Round Lake, has a stable population of brook trout, but they can be difficult to catch in its' crystal clear water. Round is surrounded by oftentimes year-round jagged snow capped peaks and lots of history. In the old days there was a mine at Round. The reminisce is still visible along Round's shore.

There are two prime areas to target, the best being the drop-offs on the south end and also at the outlet area. The bookies use the outlet as a transition zone. They wander from the creek (where they look for food) back into the lake's deep water to avoid predators. When fishing the drop-offs, a heavier lure is necessary.

Round Lake is extremely deep for a backcountry water. The fish tend to stay down, except during the late evenings. Your best bet is tossing medium size Kastmasters, Cripplures and Thomas Buoyants. Let them sink for a good 20 seconds before retrieving. When you move to the outlet you'll have to downsize. The water is shallow and there's a lot of vegetation to get snagged on. But, that plant life is home to many insects, which attracts trout. The smallest Panther Martin you can find is best.

To reach Round, begin at the trailhead for Round Lake, near Gold Lake Lodge. The trail is easy to follow and well signed. The route begins on a dirt path and slowly gains elevation for the first quarter-mile before coming to a junction. Ignoring signs for Bear and Long Lakes, stay left and continue under the cover of trees for about a mile to a small pond. Don't bother to get your rod out; there are no fish in it.

Take a swig of water and keep walking as the path gets steeper. The dirt path transitions into softball size rocks. Within a half-mile you'll come to a trail junction. Just before the junction, look over your right shoulder for breathtaking views of Bear and Little Bear Lake. At the junction look to the right and you'll be able to see Round. Take the right fork and you'll be able to fish it. If you stay left the path meets up with the PCT.

Trip info for Gold Lake also applies to Round Lake.

Directions: *From the junction of Interstate 80 and Highway 89 in Truckee, exit north on Highway 89 and drive 23.6 miles to the junction with Highway 49. Turn left on Highway 49/89 and continue five miles to where Highway 89 and 49 split. Following the left fork, stay on Highway 49 and continue 36.6 miles to Lakes Basin Road. Turn right and continue eight miles to the turnoff on the left for Gold Lake Lodge. Turn left and drive one-tenth of a mile to the trailhead for Round Lake.*

SILVER LAKE

Rating: 4
Species: Brook Trout
Stocks: None
Facilities: None

At Silver Lake, time of day and weather plays a huge part in an angler's success rate. Plan it right and you'll have a blast. Come at the wrong time and you'll think the lake is barren of fish. I assure you, brook trout are present. Not abundant, but available. The brooks are active in the early morning, late evening and when cloud cover is present. During times when sunlight penetrates the lake, fishing is poor because the brooks relocate into deep water. The lake is more than 30 feet deep. You need a heavy spoon to target brooks during the day. Rather than wasting your time at midday, stick to fishing the rises during low light conditions. At 6,670 feet in the Plumas National Forest, fly & bubble combos and medium size spinners work best for brookies that are mostly pan-size.

Reaching Silver Lake from Round Lake is simple. Walk across Round's outlet stream and continue on the path around Round's shoreline for roughly 30 yards. Shortly after, you'll see a small pond on the left. Sorry, it has no fish. Keep moving. In another two-tenths of a mile Silver Lake appears on the left. Like Round, Silver is a deep, clear lake with a stunning snow capped backdrop most of the year.

Directions *and trip info for Round Lake also apply to Silver Lake.*

Round Lake

LITTLE BEAR LAKE

Rating: 2

Species: Brook Trout

Stocks: None

Facilities: None

Jim Reed cherishes the time he spent backcountry fishing in the Lakes Basin. As a child and a group leader for the local Boy Scout troop, Reed raised his children and many others in the outdoors. No matter what lake they fished, the kids had a blast as they caught and released dozens of fish. Reed, now the owner of Gold Lake Beach Resort, is losing business. Not just from lifelong customers, but family members who have chosen to take vacations elsewhere. The problem: fishing backcountry lakes in the Gold Lakes Basin has been horrendous. Few anglers are having success. And, no, the fish aren't getting smarter. They are simply gone. No fish plants, little fishing pressure and poor spawning grounds have spelled doom.

As for Little Bear Lake itself, I had no luck. Not one chaser, nor did I see a fish. The most exciting thing I saw was a garter snake. Heck that's the only creature I spotted moving in the water. The lake is shallow and clear so you'd be able to see fish if they were around. In a gill netting survey conducted by the California Department of Fish and Game in summer of 2001, a pitiful two rainbow trout and one speckled dace was found. Those fish are no longer in the lake.

If there were fish to be caught they'd be found in three places: the inlet from Round Lake, the inlet from Cub Lake or the outlet area which feeds Big Bear Lake. To reach Little Bear Lake, at 6,480 feet in the Plumas National Forest, walk 200 yards past Big Bear Lake to Little Bear Lake on the left.

Directions *and trip info for Round Lake also apply to Little Bear Lake.*

Little Bear Lake

BIG BEAR LAKE

Rating: 3

Species: Brook Trout, Rainbow Trout and Brown Trout

Stocks: None

Facilities: None

Big Bear Lake is the most popular hike-to destination in the Lakes Basin. The hike is easily doable for those of all ages, and offers exceptional panoramas that are taken advantage of by professional photographers, day hikers, families and anglers. Anglers are fortunate the backdrop is scenic. It gives them something to admire while they are getting skunked.

Plants at Big Bear were halted at the turn of the century when it was thought that the lake harbored the endangered mountain yellow-legged frog. California Department of Fish and Game surveys found no frogs, so you would think stocking could resume quickly. That hasn't been the case. The lake has suffered dearly. Each fall and spring a few browns in the three-to-five-pound range are taken, but that's about it. Poor spawning grounds and heavily silted areas have hurt the reproduction of fish. With heavy fishing pressure this lake at 6,485 feet in the Plumas National Forest, is nearly barren of fish. The last CA DFG survey conducted in 2001 produced just one rainbow and brook trout.

To reach Big Bear, start at the Round Lake Trailhead and walk a quarter-mile to a split in the trail. Veering away from Round Lake, take the right fork signed for Bear Lake. Continue a half-mile to a pond on the right. This isn't Big Bear. Push on another 20 yards and Big Bear is on the left. You can't miss its steep drop-offs and deep water.

Directions *and trip info for Round Lake also apply to Big Bear Lake.*

Big Bear Lake

CUB LAKE

Rating: 1
Species: None
Stocks: None
Facilities: None

Cub Lake is proof that in the Lakes Basin it doesn't take long for a lake to become barren of fish. Since the turn of the century, an absence of fish plants by the California Department of Fish and Game in the backcountry has left many waters barren of fish. Decent fishing pressure, coupled with no spawning grounds or fish plants, has left Cub sadly a dead lake.

At 6,575 feet in the Plumas National Forest, it's no secret the brookies are gone. The lake is so shallow and clear you'd be able to see them without a doubt. Because of its' shallowness, Cub is a solid candidate for winterkill. This lake could possibly freeze solid, which is one of the reasons plants aren't taking place at this time.

The other reason for plant halts is the never ending nuisance of the mountain yellow legged frog. Perhaps there is hope for Cub. A recent CA DFG survey found no frogs present at Cub. Stocking could resume soon, but for now add this to the ever quickly growing list of lakes in the region that go on the backburner. To reach Cub from Little Bear, follow the path 100-yards upstream to the lake on the right.

Directions *and trip info for Round Lake also apply to Cub Lake.*

Cub Lake

LONG LAKE

Rating: 6
Species: Brook Trout
Stocks: None
Facilities: None

At last, frogs are not an issue. Even if they were, there is nothing anyone could do to remove all the fish from Long Lake. With three miles of shoreline, this is an abnormal backcountry water. Long is so large and deep that the fish couldn't be removed without draining the lake. Additionally, Long is the only backcountry lake in the area with a great population of trout. Rainbows, browns and brooks do well here. Rainbows are the lake's dominant species. They tend to average 8-14 inches.

Long isn't a hit and run backcountry water. You'll need to spend some time here. Because of its' size and depth, Long is a difficult backcountry water to fish. There is so much water to cover that it's smart to plan to spend the entire day. The best way to fish Long is with a boat or float tube. Unless you have an inflatable, there's only one way to get a boat on the water, renting one. Boats with trolling motors are available to those staying at Elwell Lake Lodge. Hardcore anglers have been known to book a night at the lodge to gain use of the boats.

Long Lake

Aside from Gold Lake, Long is the largest lake in the Lake's Basin, but while it is only reached via a short hike, some of its backcountry allure is lost at first site of its' dam. Few folks expect to see a dam in the backcountry. Shoreline fishing can be challenging. Long is equipped with steep shores dappled by pines. It's not easy to fish from shore.

While brook trout stack up near the Mud Lake inlet, trolling is the best way to catch rainbows and browns. It doesn't matter what spoon or plug you use. These fish are rarely targeted. The lack of fishing pressure keeps them eager to attack hardware. Troll anywhere along the shorelines. Long's fish are always searching for food. A boat allows you to find them quicker. Shore angling is fair. An inflated night crawler is your best bet. Toss it out as far as you can and wait.

To reach Long from Cub Lake head uphill, walking away from the Bear Lakes to a trail junction. The left fork heads to Silver Lake, the right to Long. Veer right and continue to the lake.

Directions *and trip info for Round Lake also apply to Long Lake.*

GRASSY LAKE

Rating: 5

Species: Rainbow Trout and Brook Trout

Stocks: None

Facilities: None

Grassy Lake isn't a place for non bug lovers to visit in the summer months. Set in the Plumas National Forest, as its' name implies, Grassy is a shallow, grassy natural lake. Grassy isn't planted by the California Department of Fish and Game, yet still maintains a population of small brook and rainbow trout. It also bodes well with mosquitoes I might add. Being shallow and marshy, skeeters can be overwhelming in the evening. Bring along bug spray or you'll be sorry!

In terms of fishing Grassy, stealth is required to be successful. Even the slightest movement through the shoreline can send the pan-size trout darting for safety. Spin casters only find minimal success. Fly fishermen fare best here. Dry fly fishing in the spring and summer is excellent, but it's likely you won't catch much over eight inches.

The evening bite can be epic. Since the lake is too shallow and weedy for spin casting, fly anglers traditionally have this place to themselves. By the time summer rolls around, most folks don't fish Grassy because of the mosquitoes. No big deal. There are many other hot spots to fish in the Lake's Basin.

Grassy can be reached via a short walk. From the dirt parking area designated for the Grassy Lake Trail, cross the bridge over the creek and continue roughly 100 yards to the lake. The best fishing is found near the lake's outlet.

Trip info for Gold Lake also applies to Grassy Lake.

Directions: *From the junction of I-80 and Highway 89 in Truckee, exit north on Highway 89 and drive 23.6 miles to the junction with Highway 49. Turn left on Highway 49/89 and continue five miles to where Highway 89 and 49 split. Following the left fork, stay on Highway 49 and continue 36.6 miles to Lakes Basin Road. Turn right and continue nine miles to the turnoff on the left for Lakes Basin Camp. Continue four-tenths of a mile, veer right and drive two-tenths of a mile (through the campground) to the trailhead parking for the Grassy Lake Trail.*

Grassy Lake

LILY LAKE

Rating: 3

Species: Brook Trout

Stocks: None

Facilities: None

Over the last decade the small, hike-to lakes in the Lakes Basin have been sadly left off fishery management plans by the California Department of Fish and Game. The lack of planning has left many waters, that once thrived as healthy fisheries, now barren of fish. That's the case at Lily Lake.

Lily Lake is a small pond that can be seen by driving exactly 10 miles on Lakes Basin Road from Highway 49 to a large paved pullout on the left, and is reached via a short hike from the road. However, anglers don't have a reason to fish this pond anymore. At one time, anglers reported good fishing on brook trout. Times have changed. This lake is gorgeous, but fishless! No inlet or outlet for spawning and heavy fishing pressure has taken its' toll on this fishery.

Photography, on the other hand, still flourishes. An extremely forested setting, coupled with daily heart throbbing reflections and families of mallards, bode for great snap shots. Leave this still and weedy pond to those with cameras, not fishing poles. To reach this pond at 5,900 feet in the Lakes Basin Recreation Area of the Plumas National Forest, pick up the signed route on Lakes Basin Road and follow it through the wooden forest for a tad less than two-tenths of a mile to the lake. A trail circumferences the lake.

Trip info for Gold Lake also applies to Lily Lake.

Directions: *From the junction of I-80 and Highway 89 in Truckee, exit north on Highway 89 and drive 23.6 miles to the junction with Highway 49. Turn left on Highway 49/89 and continue five miles to where Highway 89 and 49 split. Following the left fork, stay on Highway 49 and continue 36.6 miles to Lakes Basin Road. Turn right and ontinue 10.1 miles to a dirt parking area on the left and the signed trailhead for Lily Lake.*

Region Yuba River Drainage

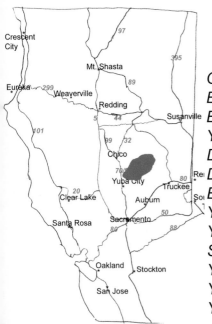

Collins Lake
Bullards Bar Reservoir
Englebright Reservoir
Yuba River (South Fork, Bridgeport)
Dry Creek (Lower)
Dry Creek (Upper)
Ellis Lake
Yuba River (North Fork, Planted Section)
Yuba River (North Fork, Downieville)
Sierra Pines Pond
Yuba River (North Fork, Sierra City)
Yuba River (South Fork, Nevada City)
Yuba River (South Fork, Washington)

COLLINS LAKE

Rating: 7

Species: Rainbow
Trout, Brown Trout,
Largemouth Bass,
Spotted Bass, Channel
Catfish, Bluegill and
Crappie

Stocked with 25,000
pounds of rainbow trout
and 2,100 pounds of
brown trout.

Facilities: Restrooms,
Boat Launch, Bait and
Tackle, RV Hookups,
Swimming Area,
General Store, Showers,
Picnic Area and
Campgrounds

Need Information?
Contact: Collins Lake
(530) 692-1602

In the foothills of the Sierras, Collins is a super managed 1,600-acre lake, with the California Department of Fish and Game and Collins Lake Resort entered into co-op fish stocking agreements. In addition to heavy plants, extensive habitat work by volunteers has allowed the lake to become a quality warm and cold water fishery.

Rainbow trout are the main course at Collins. Heavily stocked and even more profoundly fished for, the bows pay the bills for Collins Lake Resort. On the other hand, you help pay some of the resort bills when you come through the gate. Anglers are charged an entrance and fishing fee.

Is the fee worth it? You decide. The resort funds the planting of 30,000 rainbow trout, many one-to-two pounders and the rest trophy size. The fish come from three hatcheries: American Trout and Salmon Farm, Mt. Lassen Trout Farms and Kemoo.

The cold water fishery flourishes from mid-February through May and then requires deepwater trolling techniques to tackle trout as they scatter for deeper, cooler water. In winter and spring, topline Rebels and Megabaits. In early June, switch over to a Sep's Colorado Large flasher in front of a night crawler and then to a Needlefish in the summer. The trick is to locate 32 feet. That's where the thermocline is and also where the fish are! Bank anglers do best with night crawlers and Power Bait.

Collins is again regaining its brown trout fishery. The California Department of Fish and Game stocked browns in the Seventies. The lake maintained a stable population of browns through the Eighties, but the population dwindled and nearly collapsed after a new lake record nine-pound brown was caught in 1990. In the latter Nineties, the CA DFG again began to plant browns with mostly fingerling fish and the population has begun to reestablish itself. In 2001, the CA DFG dumped more than 6,000 browns at one-third of a pound each. The bows average 14-16 inches, however, a lake record 13.1-pound fish keeps anglers searching for the lunker.

Rainbows are the dominate target, yet Collins' warm water fish are worth looking at. The smallmouth bass that flourished in the Seventies and Eighties were suppressed by the largemouth bass that were introduced in the late Eighties. Largemouth bass and spotted bass have adapted well to the lake. A consistent food supply of crawdads, minnows, threadfin shad and trout have allowed the bass to grow quickly.

The lake record 15.4-pound largemouth caught in 1998 and the 9.8-pound spot prove big fish reside here. Extensive fish habitat work, including a 400-foot long, five foot high brush pile have given the bass and feeder fish good structure to spawn. Unfortunately, beginning in June and ending in October, draw-downs occur here too. The 140-foot deep lake drops approximately 35 vertical feet each year.

The bass population should benefit even more by an introduction of 12,000 bass, crappie and bluegill in 2003. The bass were Florida and Alabama strain largemouth and averaged roughly a pound and a half. Nearly 25 percent of the stock was bass. In January of 2004, another 8,750 Florida bass and bluegill were planted.

Those without deepwater trolling gear should concentrate on the self-sustaining catfish population in the warmer months. Cats up to 25 pounds are caught. However, most anglers get into fish in the two-to-four-pound class. Work the backs of coves in mid and late summer. In spring, stick to muddy areas where water is pouring in.

If you plan to make the trip, supplies are available at the lake. There is a day-use and fishing fee.

Also nearby is Bullards Bar Reservoir.

Directions: *From Sacramento, drive north on Interstate 5 to the junction with Highway 99. Drive north on Highway 99 to the Highway 70 turnoff. Exit Highway 70 and continue to Marysville. In Marysville, exit east on Highway 20. Continue 12 miles to the Marysville Rd (Rd E-21) turnoff. Turn left and drive 10 miles to the right turnoff for the lake.*

Collins Lake

BULLARDS BAR RESERVOIR

Rating: 6

Species: Rainbow Trout, Brown Trout, Channel Catfish, Kokanee, Largemouth Bass, Smallmouth Bass, Spotted Bass, Bluegill, Red Ear Sunfish and Crappie

Stocked with 2,000 pounds of fingerling rainbow trout and 252 pounds of fingerling kokanee.

Facilities: Campgrounds, General Store, Bait and Tackle, Gas, Restrooms, Boat Launch and Houseboat Rentals

Need Information? Contact: Emerald Cove Resort and Marina (530) 692-3200

There are two things that come to mind when we talk about Bullards Bar Reservoir. The first is that if you don't have a boat, don't bother fishing Bullards Bar. The second is it's one of the easiest places to catch kokanee.

Bullards Bar Reservoir is referred to as a catch-all lake. Basically, the CA DFG plants as many kokanee as it takes to make the fish easy to catch. This is a great beginner lake for kokanee anglers. Here, size matters. And, unfortunately, you'll be disappointed. Most average 11-13 inches.

Kokanee are the prized fish. They aren't huge and are dependant on fish plants. Kokanee reproduce naturally, but again the population is augmented to ensure great fishing. Nearly 50,000 kokanee are planted each year.

Bullards Bar Reservoir isn't a good shore fishing lake. The reservoir is primarily a boat fishery because of poor bank access. Unfortunately, fishing for the planted rainbows can be a drag. There is a stable population of rainbow and brown trout, however, the return to creel isn't convincing. The lake is simply too big and the fish have tons of habitat to hide in. The CA DFG dumps nearly 50,000 fingerling rainbow trout into the 4,800-acre lake each year.

There is however an opportunity to aim at the lake's wild browns. Most often they are found in the spring in the North Fork of the Yuba River arm. Fishing for browns can be good on the upper end of the lake. Browns and rainbows spawn in the New York Arm. Browns feed heavily on the lake's minnow population and don't have a problem getting chubby.

Smallmouth bass can come on strong in the spring when they are found on points. Surprisingly, you'll catch some fish up to three pounds. The warm water fishery goes unnoticed.

Spotted bass were introduced in the mid to late Seventies and have widely out-competed the largemouth bass which suffer greatly from poor structure. The reservoir is steep which doesn't usually bode well for largemouth.

If you plan to make the trip, supplies are available in Marysville.

Also nearby are Collins Lake and Englebright Reservoir.

Directions: *From Marysville, take Highway 20 east for roughly 12 miles to Marysville Road (County Road E21). Turn left and drive roughly 12 miles to Old Marysville Road. Turn right and drive 14 miles to the dam.*

ENGLEBRIGHT RESERVOIR

Rating: 6

Species: Rainbow Trout, Brown Trout, Largemouth Bass, Smallmouth Bass, Kokanee, Channel Catfish and Sunfish

Stocked with 9,000 pounds of rainbow trout.

Facilities: Marina, Gas, Boat Launch, Bait and Tackle, General Store, Boat Rentals, Restrooms

Need Information? Contact: US Army Corps of Engineers (530) 639-2342, Skippers Cove Marina (530) 639-2272

Englebright Reservoir is a dammed portion of the Yuba River that has been managed as a two-tier fishery by the California Department of Fish and Game. The CA DFG has attempted to establish a largemouth bass fishery to go along with seasonal trout plants in this long, narrow reservoir. At 815 acres, Englebright is a fairly deep system and is best tackled by anglers with boats since there isn't a great deal of shoreline access. Located at 815 feet, Englebright is situated downriver of Bullards Bar Reservoir and framed by rolling hills decorated with oaks and some pines.

Englebright is a fair to good fishery for trollers. Each year, the CA DFG plants more than 17,000 half-pound rainbows which tend to cruise the lake's 24 miles of shoreline. At nearly nine miles long, trolling can be fairly easy. Tie on a Needlefish, Sep's Pro Dodger in front of a night crawler or a Cripplure and you're in business.

The most unique aspect of the reservoir is that only boat-in camping is offered. This gives anglers that distinctive California wilderness experience where you can camp and not hear generators and cars creeping through the campsite at 3 a.m. This lake also offers houseboating and decent bass fishing for anglers fishing steep, rocky points for smallmouth and coves for largemouth. Catfish angling is fair during the warmer months.

If you plan to make the trip, supplies are available in Smartville.

Also nearby is Bullards Bar Reservoir.

Directions: *From the junction of Highway 20 and 70 in Marysville, drive east on Highway 20 for roughly 20 miles to Mooney Flat Road. Turn left and drive three miles to the reservoir.*

Englebright Reservoir

YUBA RIVER (SOUTH FORK, BRIDGEPORT)

Rating: 5

Species: Rainbow Trout and Brown Trout

Stocks: None

Facilities: Restrooms and Picnic Areas

Need Information? Contact: Bridgeport Ranger Station (530) 432-2546

The South Fork of the Yuba River used to receive seasonal plants of rainbow trout by the California Department of Fish and Game. However, budget cuts put an end to those stocks. Nowadays a few trout are planted by the Parks and Recreation for a derby, but they aren't enough for the fishery to withstand heavy pressure.

On the other hand, the South Fork of the Yuba River at Bridgeport has some quality seasonal trout. In the winter and spring, larger rainbows and browns migrate upriver out of Englebright Reservoir to the bridge at Bridgeport. If you are coming to catch limits of trout you might want to head elsewhere. However, a few quality fish are landed each year by anglers drifting night crawlers or tossing spinners.

While there isn't that many trout as a whole in this section of the Yuba, there are enough to prompt anglers from Marysville to bombard the river on weekends. In the summer, expect fishing to take a backseat to swimmers and tubers. This section of the Yuba is located in Bridgeport State Park where the famous covered bridge is found and it gets a heck of a lot more attention than the trout!

If you plan to make the trip, supplies are available in Marysville.

Also nearby are Bullards Bar Reservoir and Englebright Reservoir.

Directions: From the junction of Highway 70 and 20 near Ellis Lake in Marysville, drive southeast on Highway 20 for 25 miles to Pleasant Valley Road. Turn left and drive 7.9 miles to Bridgeport State Park.

Yuba River (South Fork, Bridgeport)

DRY CREEK (LOWER)

Rating: 3

Species: Steelhead,
King Salmon and
Striped Bass

Stocks: None

Facilities: Restrooms

Need Information?
Contact: California
Department of Fish and
Game (916) 445-3400

There is an upper and lower section of Dry Creek and its' no secret where the break between the two is. Dry Creek Falls is a huge and powerful freefall that inhibits fish from continuing upstream on Dry Creek. Because of the presence of anadromous fish, no trout plants occur in the lower section and they never will. Above the falls, the upper section is loaded with wild rainbows.

Below the waterfall, Dry Creek can turn into an interesting fishery. While the runs are scarce, anadromous fish such as stripers, salmon and steelhead have been noted spawn in the creek. In fact, once the spawns were verified by the California Department of Fish and Game, a fish ladder was built in Beale Air Force Base (which the creek flows through) to aid the fish in their quest upstream. The ladder is found on a 15-acre artificial lake with a 15-foot high dam that the Air Force's pilots use to train for battle. The ladder was constructed in the early Nineties.

Don't take this the wrong way, but your chance of catching anadromous fish isn't great. The runs are small and the fish are scattered at best. On the other hand, largemouth bass, bluegill, red ear sunfish and channel catfish also inhabit the creek. All can be caught on an inflated night crawler. During the early mornings in the summer, rolling white spinnerbaits can yield small bass. Otherwise, use some sort of stink bait for the small cats.

If you plan to make the trip, supplies are available in Marysville.

Also nearby is Dry Creek Falls.

Directions: *From the junction of Highway 70 and 20 in Marysville, drive east on Highway 20 for roughly 19.5 miles to Smartsville Road. Turn right and drive five miles to Waldo Road and veer left on the gravel road. Continue on Waldo Road for 1.9 miles to Spenceville Road. Turn left and drive 2.4 miles to the end of the road.*

This waterfall can be found at Lower Dry Creek.

DRY CREEK (UPPER)

Rating: 5

Species: Rainbow Trout

Stocks: None

Facilities: Restrooms

The upper section of Dry Creek is much different than its' lower counterpart; it produces action on wild rainbow trout. As a matter of fact, Dry Creek is one of the better wild trout streams in the region. Dry Creek isn't designated as a wild trout stream by the California Department of Fish and Game, but it only harbors wild fish. No stocks take place. Why not? Simple. The CA DFG is concerned that if they plant rainbow trout above Dry Creek Falls, where the upper section begins, there is a possibility that a few of those fish could get washed over the waterfall and breed with the wild steelhead that have been noted to spawn up the creek. Steelhead can't surmount the large waterfall. Not a chance!

The upper section of Dry Creek isn't for everyone. No drive-to access is permitted. Realistically, a bike is the best way to reach this section. Otherwise, you'll face a 2.7 mile uphill walk. Located in the Spenceville Wildlife Area, the upper stretch of Dry Creek offers mostly pan size trout. However, fish to 15-inches have been caught. The creek is a medium size stream, wide enough for tossing spinners. With deep holes and long runs it's also conducive to fly fishing.

For those of you who aren't into fishing, there's plenty more to do here. Wildlife is the main focus. The walk to Dry Creek Falls is a pleasurable trip along Dry Creek, on what begins as a dirt road and turns into a single track trail. You can walk or bike to the falls. The upper section can be found directly above the falls.

Directions *and trip info for Dry Creek Lower also apply to Dry Creek (Upper).*

Dry Creek Falls is the boundary between the upper and lower sections of the creek.

ELLIS LAKE

Rating: 5

Species: Rainbow
Trout, Channel Catfish,
Bluegill, Largemouth
Bass and Carp

Stocked with —
pounds of rainbow
trout.

Facilities: Restrooms,
Picnic Area,
Playground, Paddle
Boat Rentals and a
Recreation Center

Need Information?
Contact: Johnson's
Bait and Tackle
(530) 674-1912

Ellis Lake is a small eight-acre urban reservoir in Marysville. Shaded by trees and surrounded by lawns, coupled with a recreational path that follows the perimeter, Ellis Lake can be a nice spot to take the family for an afternoon. Additionally, Ellis is stocked with rainbow trout from December to June by the California Department of Fish and Game.

During the stocking season when rainbows are planted fishing is fair, yet never great. Shore fishing is best, particularly for those drowning Power Bait or night crawlers about 20 yards from the shore. Don't expect to catch any lunkers. Rarely are fish larger than one pound caught.

The largest fish in the lake are carp. There are hundreds of carp in the five-to-10-pound range. If the carp are in an aggressive mode they will hit small spinners, but your best shot at catching one is using corn, dough or bread. The trick is to bring along a loaf of bread, break off some small pieces and throw them into the water where you see the carp. Do it just like you are feeding ducks. Then when they think you are feeding them, put a piece of bread on a hook. Make sure you loosen your drag. These carp are good fighters. If you don't play them carefully, they'll break your line.

There are a lot of bluegill as well, but many anglers don't fish for them because rarely do they grow larger than palm size.

If you plan to make the trip, supplies are available in Marysville.

Also nearby are Dry Creek Falls, Englebright Reservoir and Collins Lake.

Directions: From Sacramento, drive north on Highway 99 to Highway 70. Take Highway 70 north to Marysville. The lake is located in Marysville on Highway 70 at the junction with Highway 20.

Ellis Lake

YUBA RIVER (NORTH FORK, PLANTED SECTION)

Rating: 6

Species: Rainbow Trout, Brown Trout and Mountain Whitefish

Stocked with 3,500 pounds of rainbow trout.

Facilities: Campgrounds, Picnic Areas and Restrooms

Need Information? Contact: Indian Valley Outpost (530) 289-3630

If gold panning, camping, swimming or fishing tickles you the right way, the North Fork of the Yuba River is the place for you. This free flowing river is best accessed from Downieville downstream to the Yuba River Crossing and offers enough pools, riffles and long runs for every angler to enjoy their own fishing hole. In addition to wild trout, the California Department of Fish and Game plants more than 6,500 rainbow trout from late April through August.

No matter what your niche is, you can expect to do well if you hit the right spots. The river is planted from Fiddle Creek down to Jim Crow Creek. Most of the planted fish tend to harbor in deep holes and large pools close to where they were planted. The CA DFG plants the fish at any easy access point they can find. Campgrounds, picnic areas and pullouts near the river are the best spots to target.

The river is an excellent choice for a family camping trip. You can camp right near the water and the kids can fish, swim and pan for gold without moving the car. While this section of the North Fork is heavily targeted by gold panners, it doesn't disrupt the fishing. At 2,000-3,000 feet in the Tahoe National Forest, the river is set in a dry, yet forested area. Fly fishermen do extremely well, yet most fly anglers are found upstream in the wild trout area. Try using a dab of pink Predator and you'll catch fish all day. Additionally, this roadside water that flows along Highway 49 is also popular with tubers.

If you plan to make the trip, supplies are available in Downieville. The North Fork of the Yuba River is closed from November 16 to the last Saturday in April.

Also nearby are Fiddle Creek Falls, Bullards Bar Reservoir and the Downie River.

Directions: *From Nevada City, drive north on Highway 49 for approximately 32 miles to the Yuba River Crossing. The road parallels the river from here to Downieville.*

The North Fork of the Yuba River 523

Yuba River (North Fork, Downieville)

Rating: 5

Species: Rainbow Trout, Brown Trout and Mountain Whitefish

Stocked with 3,500 pounds of rainbow trout.

Facilities: Food, Lodging, Gas, General Store and Restrooms

Need Information? Contact: Tahoe National Forest (530) 288-3231

It's hard to tell which activity is more popular here: fishing, swimming or watching the fish. The North Fork of the Yuba River in the town of Downieville is no doubt a popular place. It's enjoyed not only by anglers, but a handful of tourists and locals as well. Some fish the river in town for trout stocked by the California Department of Fish and Game, others stand on the Courthouse Bridge and watch trout and big squawfish swimming down in the clear water.

Just two hours from Reno and Sacramento, this former mining town gets pounded by visitors from both sides of the Sierra. Oftentimes, many of the tourists remain in the shops or eat at one of the many mom-and-pop restaurants along the highway. There are no chain stores, which makes you feel as if you've traveled further than you actually have!

The fishing, however, doesn't get too much attention. During spring and summer the CA DFG does dumps a few buckets of fish every few weeks into the river, yet only some anglers take advantage. Instead, many fish either upstream around Sierra City or downstream closer to the Yuba River Crossing. If you head a bit upstream of the Courthouse Bridge, which can be found at the junction of Nevada Street and Main Street, you'll come into quality wild trout fishing, especially near where the Downie River spills into the North Fork. The river is stocked directly behind the pizza joint near the bridge. Grab a jar of Power Bait and stay out of the main current and you'll do just fine.

If you plan to make the trip, supplies are available in Downieville. The North Fork of the Yuba River is closed from November 15 to the last Saturday in April.

Also nearby are Loves Falls, Big Springs Falls, Fiddle Creek Falls and Sierra Pines Resort.

Directions: *From Nevada City, drive north on Highway 49 for approximately 45 miles to Downieville. Turn right on Nevada Street and continue to the river.*

(Right) Where the Downie and Yuba River meet in Downieville

SIERRA PINES POND

Rating: 4

Species: Rainbow Trout

Stocked yearly with rainbow trout as needed.

Facilities: Lodging and Food

Need Information?
Contact: Sierra Pines
(530) 862-1151

Sierra Pines Pond is a trout pond, a small concrete impoundment set aside for tourists with children. Kids won't be disappointed. They will catch fish. The rainbow trout that reside are descendents from a trout farm near Oroville.

Almost no one plans a trip to fish Sierra Pines Pond. Stumbling upon it, on the other hand, is common. The pond is open to the public daily from May through October. Many parents stop and choose to stick to the cheaper method, that is putting 25 cents in the machine to buy fish food and let their children feed the fish, rather than emptying their wallet to catch them.

As with all private trout ponds no fishing license is needed, yet by the end of your fishing excursion, the trout may cost more than a fishing license would. Fish are charged by the pound. Weighing anywhere from one-half pound to three pounds there is no limit. Remember; only catch what you can afford! These fish aren't cheap.

If you plan to make the trip, supplies are available in Sierra City and Downieville. The pond is opened from May through October. Prices vary year by year. No fishing license is required.

Also nearby is the Yuba River.

Trout are easy to spot at Sierra Pines.

Directions: *From the junction of the Downie River Bridge and Highway 49 in Downieville drive north for 12.3 miles to the Sierra Pines on the right.*

YUBA RIVER (NORTH FORK, SIERRA CITY)

Rating: 5

Species: Rainbow Trout and Brown Trout

Stocks: None

Facilities: Restrooms and Campgrounds

Need Information?
Contact: Tahoe National Forest (530) 288-3231

When you are referring to the North Fork of the Yuba River near Sierra City you are closing in on its' headwaters. This section of the Yuba maintains good flows year-round, yet its' volume is much less than is found downstream in Downieville.

No stocks take place below Sierra City. The section below is designated as a wild trout water. However, the California Department of Fish and Game plants a few bucketloads of fish at Harrington's Resort and again slightly upstream. Some trout are also planted in Bassetts at the Bassetts Bridge. One thing is certain no plants take place below Ladies Canyon Creek.

The North Fork of the Yuba River can be fished with bait, spinner or flies. The river is comprised of pools, riffles and a few runs. It's heavily forested and much cooler than the Downieville section.

If you plan to make the trip, supplies are available in Bassetts. The North Fork of the Yuba River at Sierra City is closed to fishing from November 16 to the last Saturday in April.

Also nearby are the Gold Lakes Basin, Downie River, Loves Falls and Big Springs Falls.

Directions: *From the junction of I-80 and Highway 89 in Truckee, exit north on Highway 89 and drive 23.6 miles to the junction with Highway 49. Turn left on Highway 49/89 and continue five miles to where Highway 89 and 49 split. Following the left fork, stay on Highway 49 and continue 30 miles. The river parallels the highway.*

The North Fork of the Yuba River near Sierra City

YUBA RIVER (SOUTH FORK, NEVADA CITY)

Rating: 7

Species: Rainbow Trout and Brown Trout

Stocks: None

Facilities: None

Need Information?
Contact: Tahoe National Forest (530) 265-4531

You can catch more than just trout at the South Fork of the Yuba River near Nevada City. Trout are common, however, even more available are glimpses of nude men and women. My buddy Big Todd McLean calls this place the "Nudeba River", rather than Yuba River. We came to view Yuba River Falls, located on a small tributary to the Yuba, and had trouble avoiding the bare bodies which can either spice up or ruin your angling experience. It all depends on what you see!

As for the actual fishing, trout are abundant. However, catching trout in the summer is reserved for anglers who arrive early in the morning, before the nudists make their way down. Anytime after 10 a.m. there are so many people (both nude and clothed) partying and swimming in the river that the fish cling to structure on the bottom.

While rainbow and brown trout are available here, no fish plants occur. In 1987, the California Department of Fish and Game cancelled all fish plants in response to budget cuts. Luckily, the wild trout have taken over the river and flourish. Fly fishing can be excellent if you walk enough up or downstream of the river crossing to avoid the crows. Anglers tossing Panther Martins and Roostertails can also get in on the action. Because the trout are wild, using bait is discouraged. (This place is more reserved for wild trout anglers.)

If you plan to make the trip, supplies are available in Nevada City. The South Fork of the Yuba River is closed to fishing from November 16 to the last Saturday in April.

Also nearby is Englebright Reservoir.

Directions: From the junction of Highway 20 and 49 in Nevada City, take the Highway 49 exit and drive three-tenths of a mile to North Bloomfield Road and turn right. Continue nearly a half-mile and veer right to stay on North Bloomfield Road. Drive seven miles to Edwards Crossing where you'll see the Yuba River.

Look Out! Nude women are a common occurance at the South Fork of the Yuba River near Nevada City.

YUBA RIVER (SOUTH FORK, WASHINGTON)

Rating: 7

Species: Rainbow Trout
and Brown Trout

Stocks: None

Facilities: None

The crowds who come to fish the South Fork of the Yuba River near the little town of Washington have changed drastically over the last few decades. Prior to the late Eighties, the river was heavily fished by bait fishermen who were concerned with catching mostly planted trout. However, trout plants were pulled in 1987 when severe budget crunches forced the California Department of Fish and Game to stop planting the rainbows. Stocking used to take place just outside of town where the road crosses over the river.

For many anglers, the stoppage of trout plants turned out to be a good thing. According to the CA DFG, studies have shown approximately 2,000-3,000 fish per mile along this section of the Yuba. Further downstream, warmer water makes for fewer trout.

Drive-to access is available however, you'll need to scramble upstream or downstream from the drive-to areas to find better fishing. Fly fishing, tossing spinners and using bait all work well. Your best bet is to fish deep holes and sections where tributaries feed into the Yuba. Locals and out-of-towners spend lots of time rafting, tubing and swimming in the river during the summer months, which puts a damper on the fishing.

Trip info for Yuba River (South Fork, Nevada City) also applies to Yuba River (South Fork, Washington).

Directions: *From the junction of Interstate 80 and Highway 20, take Highway 20 towards Nevada City for 14 miles to Washington Road. Turn right and continue 6.1 miles to a fork in the road. Veer right on Maybert Road and continue eight-tenths of a mile to Kelehair Picnic Area.*

The South Fork of the Yuba River near Washington

Region  19

Chico/Oroville/Paradise

Big Chico Creek
Horseshoe Lake
Paradise Lake
Feather River (West Branch)
Upper Miocene Canal
DeSabla Reservoir
Philbrook Lake
Butte Creek (Forest Ranch)
Butte Creek (Butte Meadows)
Feather River (Main Stem)
Thermalito Forebay
Thermalito Afterbay
Lake Oroville
Feather River (Middle Fork)
Sacramento River (Sacramento to Orland)
Sacramento River (Orland to Red Bluff)

BIG CHICO CREEK

Rating: 3

Stocks: None

Species: Rainbow
Trout, Chinook Salmon
and Steelhead

Facilities: None

Need Information?
Contact: Chico
Park Department
(530) 895-4972

Big Chico Creek is one of those places where some anglers discover how to be clever. Anglers who fish Big Chico Creek often twist the truth when they tell their girlfriends/wives what they are up to. "I'm going fishing," some say. "Yah, over at Bidwell Park." To Bidwell Park they go, but many don't necessarily go to fish.

While they carry a rod - just to be safe - it's the women many come for: college women, and many others who didn't bother to enroll in classes. Beautiful tanned women lining the river in bikinis and some completely nude. We aren't talking just a few either. Nearly a one-mile section of the river is lined with women, families, old men, and yes, a few anglers too. Some of the more popular areas are named: Alligator Bar, Salmon Hole and Bear Hole.

Swimming in Big Chico Creek

Bidwell Park is more than a traditional park. It was established in 1905 when Annie Bidwell donated nearly 2,500 acres of land to the city of Chico. In 1995, the Chico City Council used tax dollars to purchase more land, bringing the total acreage of the park to 3,670. Bidwell Park is the third largest municipal park in the US.

The California Department of Fish and Game doesn't plant any fish in Big Chico Creek. The decision not to plant makes sense. Wild steelhead, rainbow trout and salmon inhabit the creek and the CA DFG realizes that if they plant trout there's a possibility of the stocked fish breeding with the wild fish, thus destroying their pure genes.

Face it, people come here to swim, not fish. As you may have guessed Big Chico Creek is one of Chico's big party spots – and people here know how to party. Don't expect serenity anywhere along this section of the creek. Beer, radios, nude women and swimmers own the place.

Big Chico Creek offers some of the most inviting pools in the state. They are located in a small gorge, surrounded by volcanic rock. Many teenagers spend their summer days jumping off the rocks and drinking beers along the shoreline. Unfortunately, jumping and diving isn't safe. The water is murky and it's impossible to see submerged rocks. Stay safe and stick to swimming.

If you plan to make the trip, supplies are available in Chico. At times, the road to the popular swimming areas is closed. You may need to park and walk in. Check updated fishing regulations. In 2004, these regulations governed Big Chico Creek: from the mouth of Big Chico Creek to Bear Hole, located approximately one mile downstream from the upper end of Bidwell Park, only artificial lures with barbless hooks may be used from Oct. 16 through Feb. 15. No fish may be taken at this time. From June 16 through Oct. 15 there are no gear restrictions, however no fish may be taken. Moving upcreek, from the Bear Hole to the upper boundary of the Big Chico Creek Ecological Preserve, no fish may be taken from Nov. 15 to Feb. 15, and only artificial lures with barbless hooks may be used. Finally, from the upper end of the Big Chico Creek Ecological Preserve to Higgins Hole Falls, located about one-half mile upstream of Ponderosa Way, the creek is closed to fishing all year.

Also nearby are Horseshoe Lake and the Sacramento River.

Directions: *In Chico, take the 99 Freeway and exit Highway 32 east (towards Chester and Susanville). Drive 1.6 miles and turn left on Bruce Road. Continue 1.8 miles and turn right on Wildwood Avenue. Drive 3.6 miles to the Bear Hole parking area.*

Big Chico Creek

HORSESHOE LAKE

Rating: 3

Species: Channel Catfish, Largemouth Bass, Crappie and Bluegill

Stocked with 500 pounds of channel cats.

Facilities: Restrooms

Need Information? Contact: Sportsman's Den (530) 891-5238

"Yikes," I thought to myself. They don't really put fish in here? Do they? Ugh…There can't be fish in here. Horseshoe Lake looked like the place where they bring all the fish that have been bad and release them (like from Santa's naughty list). The water is low, warm, depleted of oxygen and milky.

I first interviewed a 14-year old boy who was smoking a cigarette and drinking a Budweiser. He told me he fishes a lot, but doesn't catch much. Next was a seven-year old who fished with a complete stranger after she wandered away from her parents, who were riding their bikes somewhere in the park. She caught her first bluegill while I was passing by. I stopped long enough to watch her ask the man to take the fish off the hook and drop it in her plastic Subway sandwich bag. She was going to find her dad and show it to him. It was a mere five inches. She said she'd put it back in the water later. Mind you, it was in a plastic bag that wasn't filled with water. Eating it was out of the question. She promised me she was going to put it back when she was done.

Then there was the Asian lady who I spend half the afternoon learning from. She had no license and told me that she comes every week and used leftovers from her kitchen to catch crawdads, which she uses for bait to catch one-to-two-pound catfish. So to answer your question, yes, this isn't a place where hardcore anglers fish. Locals rule here.

I pondered over where the fish that inhabited the lake were coming from. Horseshoe wasn't listed in the California Department of Fish and Game stocking records. Yet, there were lots of small catfish available. Turns out that local organizations plant catfish for kids here once a year.

Filled with thousands of small bluegill, few larger than the palm of you hand, Horseshoe Lake is home to bite-size fish. The catfish too, are small. I failed to check one in over a half-pound. Regulations prohibit anglers older than 14 to keep fish. So, many adults bring along their children, force them to sit by the rod and say the fish belong to them. Not my ideal way to spend an afternoon fishing. Nonetheless, bluegill and catfish are readily available.

Directions *and trip info for Big Chico Creek also apply to Horseshoe Lake. You'll see signs near Big Chico Creek for Horseshoe Lake.*

Horseshoe Lake

PARADISE RESERVOIR

Rating: 6

Species: Rainbow Trout, Brown Trout, Smallmouth Bass, Largemouth Bass, Bluegill and Catfish

Stocked with 5,000 pounds of rainbow trout.

Facilities: Picnic Area, Restrooms and a Boat Launch

Need Information? Contact: Paradise Irrigation District (530) 877-4971

Paradise Reservoir is a place fit to be fished by locals. To me, this reservoir is better suited for a birthday party set in a pretty, outdoor atmosphere, than for a fishing trip. The reservoir has a wonderful and scenic picnic area that overlooks the lake; it remains quiet and has that park atmosphere. Paradise reminds me a lot of Lake Shasta. Like Shasta, Paradise's shorelines are covered with memorable red brick colored mud on the shore.

Nonetheless, fishing can be good. Prospects for rainbow trout remain good year-round. At 2,543 feet, Paradise is located in a mountainous setting where pine trees surround the lake. Paradise is maintained as a successful put-and-take lake. Wild brown trout exist, and once in a blue moon someone will catch a lunker, as was the lake record, a 16-pound brown caught in 1987.

Most anglers hook into rainbows. The California Department of Fish and Game dumps more than 8,200 rainbows in the reservoir yearly. Most are caught by trollers dragging a Sep's Pro Flasher in front of or night crawler or any spoon.

Paradise surprises many anglers with its' bass fishery. While kept quiet the reservoir holds small and largemouth bass. The records may be impressive - 8.5-pound smallie and 15 plus pound largemouth are tops - however, the numbers of bass aren't so stunning. Also, much of the shoreline is closed to angling so it can be tough to fish. Not to mention, no gas-powered boats are permitted on this 244-acre reservoir with 7.5 miles of shoreline. Being the supplier for drinking water to the city of Paradise, no live bait is allowed. To create the reservoir, Little Butte Creek was dammed in 1956 and enlarged in 1976.

If you plan to make the trip, supplies are available in Paradise. No boats are permitted from November 16 to the last Saturday in April. No waterskiing is allowed, nor are gas-powered motors. There is a day-use and boat launch fee.

Also nearby are the West Branch of the Feather River and De Sabla Reservoir.

Directions: *From Highway 99 in Chico, take the Paradise/Park Ave. exit and follow signs to Paradise/Skyway. Drive east for 16.5 miles to the junction of Coutolenc and Skyway. Turn right on Coutolenc, drive 2.8 miles to Lucerita Road and turn left. Continue seven-tenths of a mile to the day-use parking area.*

Paradise Reservoir

FEATHER RIVER (WEST BRANCH)

Rating: 5

Species: Rainbow Trout
and Brown Trout

Stocks: None

Facilities: None

Need Information?
Contact: Paradise
Sporting Goods
(530) 877-5114

It's hard for anglers to do well fishing the West Branch of the Feather River. Dredgers, miners, swimmers, rapidly changing seasonal water levels and clear water hinders anglers at times.

The West Branch of the Feather River is a tributary to Lake Oroville. It can reach flood levels in the winter and spring, be prefect for fishing in the summer and then almost too low to fish in the fall. Seasons play a big part in the fishability of the river. So does human interaction. The river is one of the best places to swim, jump off rocks and mask and snorkel in California, and those in-the-know take advantage of it. Because the river is lined with a rock and sand bottom, the water is extremely clear. Visibility is exceptional. Personally, I spent a few days combing a four-mile section of the river with a mask to see what kind of fishery the West Branch offered.

Here's what I discovered. There is a solid amount of wild rainbow trout in the river and some browns. However, human distractions hurt the fishing. Additionally, nearly every deep hole is claimed by dredgers and miners. Avoiding them can keep anglers out of the better holes.

In many areas there isn't a lot of cover on the shorelines. The fish can definitely see you coming. Also, the crystal clear water requires you to use four-pound test to have any shot at being successful.

Low light hours yield the best catch rates. Also, keep one thing in mind: many trout that were planted into Oroville swim up the West Branch river arm in the summer and fall to find cooler water. However, those fish can't get above Head Dam.

West Branch Feather River

Therefore, concentrate your efforts below Head Dam. Nevertheless, many wild rainbow trout are found above the dam, though access can be tough to navigate.

Some Forest Service roads and trails lead to the river. However, much of the upper section is rugged and steep. The West Branch begins at Snag Lake and is fed by dozens of tributaries, which compensate for much of the West Branch's volume.

Unfortunately, sucker fish or mountain whitefish have taken over a lot of the river. I saw a few anglers salivating over what they though was a brown, but was a mountain whitefish in reality. At any rate, anything over a pound will most likely not be a trout. Trout average seven to 11 inches.

In this section of the West Branch, the best access can be found at the intersection of Skyway and Coutolenc Roads. From the parking area, take a right on Coutolenc Road and walk 25 or so feet to a locked gate on the right side of the road. Walk around the gate and follow the dirt access road as it winds down to the river. The one-mile walk is easy on the way in, but the 750-foot climb back out keeps many anglers from the riverbank.

At 1,550 feet in the Lassen National Forest, Head Dam and the river downstream offers an excellent late evening and early morning bite on bows. Because of the hike in, fishing pressure is typically low. Before casting, take in the scene on the far corner of the dam. If water is flowing over the dam, which is does in most years through early June, you'll be able to see small bows trying to jump over the dam. Without a fish ladder this isn't possible, though.

Fly-fishing works best in the evening. However, small Panther Martins work well too. Target areas where the flume is pumped back into the West Branch and where moving water meets up with the larger pools. Oftentimes, you'll find fish harboring under overlaying rocks during daylight hours. Many of the pools run more than 20 feet deep.

Direct access to the river can be tough. There is no trail that parallels the river itself. However, the Upper Miocene Canal parallels the river to Oroville. Along the way several trails break off the path descending to the river.

While the fishing isn't as good here, there is also a drive-to section of the West Branch. This can be found off Dean Road. Consult a local map for directions.

If you plan to make the trip, supplies are available in Paradise. The West Branch of the Feather River is closed to fishing from November 16 to the last Saturday in April.

Also nearby are Paradise Reservoir, Philbrook Lake and De Sabla Reservoir.

Directions: *From Highway 99 in Chico, take the Paradise/Park Ave. exit and follow signs to Paradise/Skyway. Drive east for 16.5 miles to the junction of Coutolenc and Skyway. Park in the dirt parking lot. Walk down the access road to the river.*

The West Branch of the Feather River near Paradise offers some of the best swimming holes in the West.

UPPER MIOCENE CANAL

Rating: 5

Species: Rainbow Trout and Brown Trout

Stocks: None

Facilities: None

While the West Branch of the Feather River is known for offering poor bank access, Upper Miocene Canal, which parallels the West Branch, has great access. Often used by mountain bikers, the Upper Miocene Canal also provides quality fishing. Nonetheless, only anglers practicing stealth like techniques do well. Rainbows make up 95 percent of the catch, averaging seven to 10 inches.

The rainbows and the few browns that exist are easily spooked. They are all wild fish that have been diverted out of the West Branch and into the canal at Head Dam, which is where the Upper Miocene begins. The trout constantly have to content with swift water that can be difficult to fish.

To overcome the current, look for bends in the flume where the trout can tuck themselves out of the current, reserve energy and wait for food to be brought to them. The flume is too swift for the use of most lures and a lack of open space can make fly fishing difficult. This place is for bait anglers. In many of the bends, overhanging brush has established itself along the bank. Drift a night crawler or cricket underneath the brush for best results. But, you can drift plugs like a FlatFish or grasshopper/cricket Rebel.

Directions *and trip info for Feather River (West Branch) also apply to Upper Miocene Canal.*

Miocene Canal   Bo Shaffer walks across the Upper Miocene Canal

DE SABLA RESERVOIR

Rating: 5

Species: Rainbow Trout and Brown Trout

Stocked with 5,000 pounds of rainbow trout.

Facilities: None

Need Information?
Contact: Paradise
Sporting Goods
(530) 877-5114

It's amazing what a group of cabins owned by PG&E employees can do. In the case of De Sabla Reservoir, where the above mentioned cabins were built, those PG&E workers somehow convinced the California Department of Fish and Game to fill their small, man-made lake with trout. And fill they do.

De Sabla is a mere six-percent of the size of nearby Paradise Reservoir. Nonetheless, De Sabla gets roughly 800 more trout, 9,700 to be exact. Paradise, however, does receive slightly larger trout. Fortunately, more than just PG&E cabin owners can benefit from the plants. The lake is opened to day-use for visitors.

Most anglers walk the dam area casting small spinners or soaking Power Bait from shore. No boats are permitted. At 2,700 feet, this 15-acre lake yields half-pound rainbow trout. Unfortunately, browns are only caught once or twice a year, likely by an angler soaking a night crawler. An added plus is, as opposed to Philbrook Lake, which is reached via a dirt road, getting to De Sabla is accomplished entirely on paved roads.

If you plan to make the trip, supplies are available in Paradise.

Also nearby are Paradise Lake, Philbrook Reservoir and Snag Lake.

Directions: *From Highway 99 in Chico, take the Paradise/Park Ave. exit and follow signs to Paradise/Skyway. Drive east for 16.5 miles to the junction of Coutolenc and Skyway. Continue 5.4 miles on Skyway to the reservoir on the left.*

De Sabla Reservoir

PHILBROOK LAKE

Rating: 5

Species: Smallmouth
Bass, Brown Trout and
Rainbow Trout

Stocked with 4,700
pounds of rainbow
trout.

Facilities: Restrooms,
Campgrounds and a
Boat Launch

Need Information?
Contact: Jones Resort
(530) 873-3879

Philbrook Lake is a marginal put-and-take fishery. The lake is planted with 20,000 sub-catchable trout by the California Department of Fish and Game each year and is able to maintain a stable population of wild browns. Philbrook acts like a reservoir. It reaches full pool in the spring only to see a huge batch of its water siphoned off and sent to Butte Creek by summer.

Philbrook is mobbed by residents from Chico, including water sport recreationists. Anglers should fish early and late. The time in between is destroyed by boaters. When the boaters aren't around, shore anglers do well. Walk up and down the shoreline near the boat launch and dam areas tossing size 1/16 silver Panther Martins and red and blue Thomas Buoyants. Most of the fish are pan size rainbows. However, a few big browns exist. They are caught by luck, not skill. One angler got lucky and landed a nine-pound brown in 2000.

If you plan to make the trip, supplies are available in Forest Ranch. In winter, call ahead for road conditions. Chains may be required.

Also nearby are DeSabla Reservoir and West Fork of the Feather River.

Directions: *From Highway 99 in Chico take the Paradise/Park Ave. exit and follow signs to Paradise/Skyway. Drive east for 16.5 miles to the junction of Coutolenc and Skyway. Continue 13.5 miles on Skyway to Sterling City. From Sterling City drive 12.2 miles to a split in the road. Stay right, drive two-tenths of a mile and veer right again. Drive 1.2 miles to another split. Again, stay right and continue 3.1 miles to another split. Stay right and drive three-tenths of a mile to the day-use area.*

A Philbrook Lake brown

BUTTE CREEK (FORKS OF THE BUTTE)

Rating: 6

Species: Rainbow Trout and Brown Trout

Stocks: None

Facilities: Primitive Campgrounds

Need Information? Contact: Bureau of Land Management (530) 224-2100

There's no doubt The Forks of the Butte is a place truly fit for the locals of Forest Ranch. While there are some BLM campgrounds along the river, only a few out-of-towners use them. Good news for the locals, this 15-25-foot wide section of Butte Creek is home to staggering numbers of wild rainbows and browns. Don't get too excited though. Most of them fail to reach nine inches. Nevertheless, a few pound-size fish are caught.

There are so many trout in this stretch of the creek that there is a major competition for food. That's why just about any lure, fly or bait you choose will work. Expect to catch 70 percent rainbows and 30 percent browns. They key is to either walk up or downstream of the bridge. The bridge was built in 1936 and is best known as "rope swing heaven" to local teenagers.

As you may have guessed, there is a lot of history here. Miners worked all along the steambed and remnants are visible on both sides of the creek. Dredging still occurs. The BLM has divvied the creek up into sections that are clearly marked on trees that line the river. These sections are reserved by dredgers months in advance.

Back to the fishing, anywhere up or down from the bridge holds trout. The bridge area is so frequented by swimmers that fishing is often poor. One of the best spots is roughly a quarter-mile downstream at the diversion dam and further downstream in the pool below Forks of the Butte Falls. Keep in mind, there are no planted fish in this stretch of Butte Creek. All the fish are wild. So leave them in the river where other anglers can enjoy them too. Fly fishing can be excellent, as is tossing a size 1/31 or 1/16 Panther Martin spinner as long as they are small. Live bait is strongly discouraged in order to keep the wild population of trout in tact.

If you plan to make the trip, supplies are available in Forest Ranch. During the winter and spring, Garland Road may be impassible without a high clearance and/or four-wheel drive vehicle. The road is a dirt road, much of which isn't grated.

Also nearby are Butte Creek (Butte Meadows), Forks of the Butte Falls and Horseshoe Lake.

Butte Creek brown trout

Directions: *From the 99 Freeway and Highway 32 in Chico, exit Highway 32 towards Chester and drive 18 miles to Garland Road. Turn right, drive 2.7 miles and stay left at a split in the road. Continue 1.8 miles to the bridge and creek.*

Butte Creek (Butte Meadows)

Rating: 6

Species: Rainbow Trout and Brown Trout

Stocked with 5,150 pounds of rainbow trout.

Facilities: Campgrounds, Restrooms, Restaurant and General Store

Need Information? Contact: Lassen National Forest (530) 258-2141

Butte Creek is separated into several sections. While some are catch and release only, others are completely closed to fishing and are governed by special regulations to protect wild runs of fish. The area of Butte Creek which flows through Butte Meadows is one of the few spots where you don't have to worry about when you can fish or what you can use for bait. This section was set aside for anglers who want to catch and keep fish, without having to agonize about catching and releasing anadromous fish. Fish populations are maintained by plants of rainbow trout by the California Department of Fish and Game.

The river is heavily fished by primarily day users from Chico. These anglers often do well on pan size trout, which are planted in campgrounds and at places where the creek crosses under the road. Nearly 7,500 rainbows are stocked each year. Here are the best areas to fish, all of which are located off Humboldt Road: five miles east of the turnoff from Highway 32 in Butte Meadows Campground, at 5.4 miles you can turn right on Skyway and continue to the bridge over Butte Creek, at 6.1 miles Humboldt Road crosses over Butte and at 8.8 miles the road again crosses over the creek. While these areas are the most heavily planted, stocked trout are scattered throughout the stream. Located in the Lassen National Forest, Butte Creek is a medium size trout stream and also maintains a population of wild rainbow and brown trout. The wild fish are, however, small.

Fortunately, Butte Creek is mostly drive-to access, so you don't have to work much for the fish. At times, depending on water flow, the creek can be difficult to fish. There aren't a ton of pools, so you'll do best with salmon eggs and Power Bait. Only a few pools are large enough for the use of spinners.

If you plan to make the trip, supplies are available in Butte Meadows.

Also nearby are Snag Lake and Philbrook Lake.

Directions: *From the junction of the 99 Freeway and Highway 32 in Chico, take Highway 32 northeast for 27.3 miles to the Butte Meadows exit (Humboldt Road). Turn right and drive five miles to Butte Meadows Campground.*

Butte Creek near Butte Meadows

FEATHER RIVER

Rating: 8

Species: Steelhead,
American Shad,
Chinook Salmon,
Sturgeon, Channel
Catfish, Spotted Bass,
Crappie, Bluegill, Carp
and Striped Bass

Stocks: None

Facilities: Lodging,
Boat Launches,
Restrooms, Primitive
Campsites and Bait &
Tackle

Need Information?
Contact: Fishing Guide
Kevin Brock (800) 995-
5543, Fishing Guide
Steve Huber (530) 623-
1918, McGrath's Bait &
Tackle (530) 533-8564,
Oroville Outdoors (530)
533-4990, Johnson's
Bait & Tackle (530)
674-1912, Kittle's
Outdoor Sports
(530) 458-4868

Being one of the Upper Sacramento Valley's three main urban river systems, the Feather River can strike a different pose to each angler who fishes it. Some witness serenity by taking long jet boat rides to find secluded areas, while others drift sections of the river or fish with fly rods. You'll see plunkers bait fishing from shore in old beat up, rusted chairs next to coolers of beer. Others fish the combat zones where hundreds of anglers fish shoulder to shoulder for a chance at hooking or snagging a salmon.

The Feather River offers something for every angler, yet is dependant on anadromous runs of striped bass, sturgeon, steelhead, American shad and salmon. These seasonal runs dictate what techniques anglers employ and which genre of anglers fish the river. Luckily, there's no down time on the Feather. There's always at least one species for anglers to target. Some runs are dependant on the Feather River Hatchery, others stem from wild fish.

The main stem of the Feather extends from the base of Lake Oroville to its' confluence with the Sacramento River near Live Oak. The water travels a distance of 67 miles and differs drastically as it moves downriver. The river is divided into two sections: the low flow and high flow. The low flow runs from roughly the Feather River Hatchery to the Thermalito Afterbay outlet. Much of this section is comprised of riffles, while the low flow section downriver of the Thermalito outlet offers riffles, runs, pocket water, frog water and deep holes.

One great aspect of the Feather is that it offers space for both boaters and bank anglers. No one is left out of the action. There is excellent drive-to access along many frontage and dirt roads near Oroville and also three launch ramps for boaters. The most common drift is from McGrath's to the Thermalito Afterbay, approximately a four-mile stretch. The other is from the Afterbay to Palm Avenue, another four-mile run and the final drift is from Palm to the Gridley launch ramp, some five miles downriver.

The Feather harbors wild and hatchery steelhead. However, hatchery fish make up most of the fishery. The Feather doesn't support a large population of wild fish. While anglers catch wild steelhead, many may not truly be wild. They could be descendants from the Feather River Hatchery that weren't clipped or the young of hatchery fish that spawned in the river, rather than at the hatchery.

Not all Feather River fish spawn in the hatchery, many do so in the main river. Keep in mind, in 1998, the Central Valley wild steelhead were placed on the threatened species list by the US Fish & Wildlife Service. The population appears to be rebounding slowly. Wild or hatchery fish, steelhead are readily available. Most average three-to-four pounds; however, fish to 10 pounds are caught often. While a spring run does occur, the winter run is more prevalent. It takes place from October through February.

Catching steelhead can be easily correlated to matching a food source. In the fall, steelhead key in on salmon eggs. You can throw all the spinners, flies and night crawlers you want, but nothing will be as effective as roe fished below salmon redds early in the steelhead run. When salmon are done spawning, steelhead move off the roe bite and focus on other baits. This is when running size 40 and 50 gold or silver Luhr Jensen Hot Shots is effective.

In fall and early winter, locating steelhead isn't difficult. Look for gravel beds and salmon redds. Concentrate on these areas: near the Feather River Hatchery, from the low flow to Gridley and at the Thermalito Afterbay outlet. Steelhead stack up at the outlet because they think they are suppose to head upstream here. Ignore the river downstream of Gridley and any frog water.

Winter is a good time to fish flies. Egg imitations fished with a size 12 or 14 olive nymph as a dropper and Glo Bugs are prime baits. A six-weight fly rod with a 5x tippet is recommended. Use a 12-foot leader. As spring approaches and the water slowly warms, steelhead are more apt to grab a mini night crawler or a black Panther Martin.

Anglers lined up for their shot at hooking a chinook salmon in the summer.

As steelhead action slows, anglers key in on striped bass. Stripers are in the Feather all year, but March through May is when the most fish are in the system. The Feather doesn't see as many stripers as the Sacramento River, but definitely has a bigger run than the American River. If you had to choose one area to fish for stripers, Verona would be the place. Verona is where the Feather meets the Sac and is a great holding area for stripers.

Anglers can find success sitting on the anchor with cut baits or live minnows. If you are going to fish cut baits, try soaking them in Pautzke Liquid Krill for up to two days prior to using them. Look for calm water and long runs. Stripers are ambush feeders. You'll find that if you fish the seam lines, you'll catch more fish. Most stripers caught are schoolies, but fish to 40 pounds are taken each year.

The Feather also offers an exceptional shad fishery. Every year in May and June, the Feather receives a consistent run of American shad. Fish can be caught throughout the system, but it's hard to find a better spot than underneath the power lines just below the Thermalito outlet. The best areas for the shad tend to be gravel corners with a soft current. Traditional jigs and Dick Nite spoons work great.

It's hard to judge the Feather when it comes to salmon. Unfortunately, the Feather can be downplayed by anglers who fish the Sacramento River for salmon. The Sacramento River surely sees a larger run than the Feather, but the Feather may be easier to fish for most anglers. When salmon are thick in the Feather the same can be said for the Sac. If most anglers had a choice, they'd fish the Sac over the Feather because there is more space and fish.

Not to knock the Feather, though. When there are lots of fish in the system, salmon are concentrated because there are fewer places on the Feather for salmon to hold than in most rivers. So why isn't the Feather a premier fishery? Namely crowds. Boat traffic can hinder the bite. The Feather can't support hoards of anglers the way the Sac can. Fishing midweek is best or you'll be forced to contend with spooked fish and too many anglers still fishing with anchors. This can make fishing tough as it's easy for anglers to get tangled in the lines.

Feather salmon run 10 to 15 pounds on average, but 30-pounders are quite common. Trophy fish are caught daily. Unlike the Sac, holding water on the Feather is more spread out. Consequently, there are fewer holes as well. For salmon, fishing holes is best. Try and fish upriver of the Highway 70 Bridge.

Some salmon can be found in riffles that have good current flow and seven-to-eight feet of water. Most anglers use Kwikfish; Lighted K-16 Xtremes in Banana and Prancer and a K-16 chrome with chartreuse bill or a chartreuse with a chartreuse bill are standard Feather River plugs. It's a good idea to apply drops of Pautzke Liquid Krill on your sardine wrap and Gel Krill on plugs.

Hands down, the Thermalito Afterbay outlet is the most crowded section of the Feather. Mostly shore anglers fish here, yet experienced jet boat operators have a chance at quick limits if you know how to maneuver your boat well. To be successful, try and keep your roe in the swirl. It's likely that 10-12 ounces of lead will be necessary to do so. Others use a Megabait or Crippled Herring jig.

Even for salmon, shoreline anglers have a chance at catching fish. From the bank, seek the upper ends of holes and the bottom of riffles. Side drifting roe and casting Mepps and Panther Martin spinners are your best bets. Many anglers choose to cast jigs and spoons, but unfortunately most fish caught with jigs here are snagged. Snagging is illegal.

The Feather is notorious for its' combat-like fishing at the Thermalito outlet. When salmon are in the river, it's not uncommon to find 100 anglers shoulder to shoulder on each side of the outlet casting beads and yarn at salmon. For the most part, the majority of these fish are snagged, not hooked in the mouth, but most folks don't abide by the rules and keep these fish regardless. The crowds can get rowdy here, especially on weekends where fights over fish and scuffles between boaters and shoreline anglers are common. This isn't a place to come for serenity, that's for sure.

If you plan to make the trip, supplies are available in Oroville, Live Oak, Gridley, Yuba City and other cities along the river. Check sportfishing regulations for updated gear restrictions, bag limits and closures.

Also nearby is Lake Oroville.

Directions: The Feather River can be access along dozens of freeways, highways and frontage roads from Verona to Oroville. Please consult a local map for detailed directions.

Guide Kevin Brock with an average Feather River steelhead.

LAKE OROVILLE

Rating: 9

Species: Red Eye Bass, Spotted Bass, Largemouth Bass, Smallmouth Bass, Crappie, Bluegill, Red Ear, White Catfish, Channel Catfish, Carp, Rainbow Trout, Brown Trout, Coho Salmon and Lake Trout

Stocked with Coho salmon some years by the California Department of Water Resources

Facilities: Houseboat Rentals, RV Hookups, Campgrounds, Fish Cleaning Stations, Restrooms, Boat Rentals, Launch Ramps, Bait & Tackle, Visitor Center, General Store, Picnic Areas and Gas

Need Information? Contact: Oroville Chamber of Commerce (530) 538-2542, Oroville Outdoors (530) 533-4990, McGrath's Bait & Tackle (530) 546-8425, Paradise Sporting Goods (530) 877-5114, Bidwell Marina (530) 589-3165, Lake Oroville Visitor Center (530) 538-2219

At 15,800 acres, Lake Oroville is the second largest reservoir in California. Boasting 167 miles of shoreline, Oroville is home to tens of thousands of fish and at 770 feet high, is the tallest earthen dam in the United States. The dam's crest is more than one-mile long.

Oroville is one of the easiest places to catch spotted bass in the West. However, fishing hasn't always been this easy. Prior to the early Eighties, Oroville was your typical Northern California reservoir that maintained largemouth and smallmouth bass. Now it's famous for being a spotted bass factory.

Oroville hasn't always been such a praised fishery. The California Department of Fish and Game opted to change the dynamics of Lake Oroville between 1982-84 when they stocked 200 spotted bass on two occasions. Within a few years, Oroville's spotted bass fishery exploded. Initially, Oroville offered anglers many quality spots to three pounds before the fishery began to balance out.

Depending on who you talk to, Oroville can be the best bass fishery in the country or a fishery that others can't stand fishing. Oroville is a straightforward reservoir to fish. Anglers are well aware that catching 100 fish a day in the spring is a common feat, but catching anything over two pounds is rare. This is the most disappointing part of the fishery. In fact, it's created a black cloud for many tournament anglers who avoid the lake because of its' lack of trophy size fish. Spots average 12-13 inches. If you catch anything over 2.5 pounds, you are doing well.

Some anglers look at this as a great thing. Where else can you go and catch 100 bass a day without struggling? Oroville is a great place for anglers to visit, tune up their bass fishing techniques or to simply have a blast catching dozens of fish. The average angler is thrilled with their experience at Oroville.

While the spots quickly boomed, the success of the largemouth and smallmouth bass deteriorated. Almost as fast as the spots took over, the small and largemouth lost ground. Now it's almost impossible to catch any bass other than spots. The lake is infested with them. It's estimated that 99 percent of the biomass of bass is spots.

Hope is on the way, though. From 2000-2004, the Chico Bass Club, DWR and the Black Bass Action Committee teamed up to stock more than 6,000 Florida strain largemouth. These fish range from fingerling size to four pounds. Most are 12-inches. The fish were planted in attempt to give anglers a chance at catching trophy bass. The idea is that the Florida's will take over the largemouth habitat and eventually make up five percent of the bass population.

Nonetheless, largemouth can be targeted by the determined angler who is up to the challenge of chasing after largemouth in a pool of spots. Here's a list of areas that will hold largemouth: Potter's Ravine, Canyon Creek, McCabe's Cove, Stringtown, Spring Valley, Dark Canyon and Railroad. These are spots that bass pro Gary Dobyns chooses to search for largemouth because they have standing trees and different structure than other areas. Smallmouth, on the other hand, are traditionally found in the North Fork of the Feather River Arm and are seldom targeted.

Oroville has four river arms in addition to the main body: the Middle Fork, North Fork, South Fork and the West Branch of the North Fork. Each arm has varying characteristics. The Middle Fork is steep, rocky and has the clearest water. The South Fork has more humps and a lot more sandstone. The North Fork has a lot of feeder streams, running water, coves and timber.

I spent the day on Oroville with local pros Dobyns and David Rush and asked them how they win tournaments year after year by weeding out the smaller fish and locating larger bass. Both agreed that spotted bass can be found in schools, often characterized by size. If you are catching small spots, you'll continue to catch small spots. Larger spots tend to be found together as well.

Nonetheless, Oroville is a place anglers can come and expect to get a lot of bites. Pros call it a fun fish lake. The easiest time of year to catch fish is in the spring when jerkbaits, spinnerbaits and worm fishing puts countless spots in your boat. You'll get fewer bites, but tend to catch larger bass on jerkbaits and spinnerbaits. If you simply want to catch tons of fish, try using a four-to-six-inch pink, oxblood or Aaron's Magic Robo worm. It's productive to pull up on any bank in the entire lake and catch fish.

Much of the year, bass fishing at Oroville is dictated by fishing at the depth pond smelt are found. Pond smelt is the main forage for bass in Oroville. Pond smelt is a small baitfish. It averages 1-1.5 inches and is mostly white.

During the winter and early spring, several techniques are productive. Many anglers jig fish. Dragging jigs from a few feet deep to 50 feet deep is effective. You'll find some fish on the bank and others in deep water. Carolina-rigging Yamamoto lizards and baby brush hogs are best. For quality bass, try running a rip bait or spinnerbait. Nevertheless, a medium or deep diving crankbait, such as the Bomber Fat Free Shad Fingerling Series are productive.

In February, anglers fish deep for bass. Many anglers fish 30-70 feet deep, but the 40-50-foot depths are more reliable for anglers Carolina-rigging, dragging a Hula grub and drop-shotting. Only a pro can effectively fish for bass deeper than 40 feet deep though. Others can fish a darterhead in 10-20 feet or work four-to-five-inch grubs.

Northern California Angler of the Year David Rush with an Oroville spotted bass.

Vince Harris shows off a three-pound Oroville spot he caught on a Robo worm.

Summer fishing is marked by topwater action. Anywhere on the lake in the morning or evening, a buzzbait, Zara Super Spook or Pop-R is effective. Boat traffic can be a definite issue. Fishing lowlight hours is imperative. Here's a trick courtesy of local fishing guru Steve Carson: when boat traffic is really bad, there will be in a noticeable mud line. Try throwing a plastic worm on the mud line and drag it into the clear water. You are bound to get bit!

Fall is the best time to catch huge numbers of bass. Traditionally, you'll have an all day topwater bite, in addition to a consistent worm bite.

It's important for Oroville bass anglers to know how to approach fluctuating water. The lake can fluctuate more than 100 vertical feet during the year. Ironically, Dobyns and Rush said they enjoy fishing the lake least when the reservoir is full. When the lake is full, there are far too many places for the fish to go. You can often lose contact with larger fish. As Rush would say, "The lower the water. The tighter the audience you are playing to."

Nevertheless, locating spotted bass is straightforward regardless of the time of year. Look between boulders and decomposed granite, off points and along drop-offs. At Oroville, the average angler can set out, look for a rocky point and have at least a half-successful day. Rush refers to Zoom Zipper grubs as spotted bass candy. Oxblood light, Mojave oxblood, Delta craw and Aaron's Magic are top colors. One traditional color that has always been good at Oroville is morning dawn.

Bait fishing can also be exceptional. Soaking crawdads and fishing minnows eight-to-12 feet below a bobber can yield good catch rates. It's best to have the minnow swimming two feet off the bottom.

Oroville is governed by a slot limit. Anglers can't keep bass between 12-15 inches. Originally, the slot was implemented to cut down an overwhelming number of small spots and red eye bass. The purpose was to give weekend anglers the ability to catch, eat and keep small bass, while removing red eye bass and a number of smaller fish out of the system.

While bluegill and red ear are only caught occasionally, for roughly one month each year there's a good crappie bite for anglers fishing small or medium live minnows on a No. 4 light wire hook in Dark Canyon or wherever submerged trees are found. Prime time is usually in May, but is based on water temperature. Ideally, the bite is best when the water is 62 degrees.

Oroville is a sleeper catfish lake. Mostly channels are found, yet a few white catfish are caught as well. Oroville has a lot of suitable underwater spawning structure, which paves the way for a good number of four-to-10 pound cats. Ironically, the best bite comes to houseboaters who throw a line out in a shallow cove at night during the summer months.

Oroville's coldwater fishery has been in limbo since the breakout of several diseases. Oroville has been plagued by four diseases: Infectious Hematopoietic Necrosis (IHN), Viral Hemorrhagic Septicemia (VHS), Infectious Pancreatic Necrosis (IPN) and Bacteria Kidney Disease (BKD). These diseases have caused the CA DFG to not plant some species of coldwater fish.

David Rush (Left) and Gary Dobyns show off a group of quality Oroville bass.

Rainbow trout were first planted in 1968, but have not been stocked since the late Eighties due to the above mentioned diseases. On the contrary, there are still rainbows in Oroville because all the stream and river inlets maintain populations of native Feather River Basin rainbow trout. These trout spend some time in the inlets and in the main body and are immune to the diseases. However, it's estimated that they make up only two-percent of the coldwater creel.

While none have been stocked since 2001, browns have been planted periodically since 1968. The DWR stopped planting them because their return to creel was very low. Nonetheless, big browns are available. In 2002, a 22-pound brown was taken from shore on a night crawler. Still few anglers fish for browns.

Other coldwater species have also been introduced. Kokanee salmon were first stocked in 1968, when 1.2 million fish were released. They continued to plant kokanee until 1977. Brook trout were planted in 1975. Lake trout were introduced in 1984-85 and king salmon from 1991 until the IHN outbreak in 2001.

The most recent coldwater fish to take part in Oroville's fishery has been coho salmon. Coho were planted from 1969-78, in 1987 and again in 2002, but the program has run into some turbulence. Coho are the only coldwater species that are more or less resistant to all the diseases in the lake and have developed a great sport fishery, but some parties are worried that the Coho may get washed over the dam and mix with anadromous species in the

Feather River.

Stocked at nine inches long in November, the Coho come from Domsea Brood Stock Company Inc. in Washington. These fish grow one-inch per month, yet only live one year. It's common to catch three-pound fish with some to five pounds. The CA DFG is positive Coho won't develop a self-sustaining population in Oroville or downstream in the Feather. The fish have been genetically altered to live only two years (one in the hatchery and one in the lake). The impressive thing about coho is they bite like crazy, aren't tough to catch and are good fighters.

Recently there has been resistance to stocking Coho. However as part of their re-licensing agreement, DWR is mandated to stock coldwater species, therefore either Coho or rainbows will likely be planted in the future. There's a plan in the works to rear Feather River rainbows found in the lake as well.

If you plan to make the trip, supplies are available in Oroville. At some launch ramps there may be a day use fee.

Also nearby are the Feather River and Thermalito Afterbay.

Directions: *From Highway 70 in Oroville, exit Oroville Dam Blvd. and drive five miles east to the dam. Drive across the dam to the launch ramp and parking area.*

Outdoor Writer Steve Carson with an Oroville coho

FEATHER RIVER (MIDDLE FORK)

Rating: 5

Species: Rainbow
Trout and Brown Trout

Stocks: None

Facilities: None

Need Information?
Contact: Oroville
Outdoors (530) 533-4990

The Middle Fork of the Feather River differs tremendously from the main stem. The Middle Fork empties into Lake Oroville, is remote and doesn't receive runs of anadromous fish. On the other hand, the Middle Fork does offer great seasonal fishing for rainbows and browns. Some browns and bows swim out of Lake Oroville to spawn. Others remain in the system year-round.

In the early Seventies, the Middle Fork was one of the first additions to California's Wild Trout Program. The river originates near Sierra Valley before dropping into a steep, remote and hard to reach canyon for 45 miles and terminates into Oroville. Because of its remote setting, few anglers spent time fishing the Middle Fork.

The Middle Fork is rumored to maintain a legitimate population of large browns. Dropping a Woolly Bugger or night crawler into one of the deep holes gives you at chance at these lunkers. Rainbows, on the other hand, are plentiful. Try fishing riffles and at the heads of pools with nymphs and small Panther Martins.

The trick to the Middle Fork is to time your trip right. Depending on snow runoff, the river may not be fishable until late July. When the river is running high, it's extremely difficult to fish. However, when flows recede, pools form, whitewater decreases and angling becomes more desirable. The downfall here is access. There are only a few spots in the canyon where anglers can reach the river. Each comes with a long drive on dirt road and a grueling hike. The river is best accessed at Milsap Bar and near Bald Rock via the Curtain Falls Trailhead.

If you plan to make the trip, supplies are available in Oroville. Check sportfishing regulations for updated bag limits and gear restrictions. The Middle Fork of the Feather River is closed to fishing from November 16 to the last Saturday in April. The hike to the Middle Fork is only for anglers in good physical condition.

Also nearby is Lake Oroville.

Directions: From the junction of Highway 70 and 162 in Oroville, exit Richvale/Oroville Dam Blvd. (162) and drive east for 1.8 miles to the Olive Highway (162) turnoff. Turn right and continue 13.8 miles. Without being signed, Highway 162 ends and becomes Oroville-Quincy Highway. Continue 3.8 miles to Bald Rock Road and turn right. Drive 4.8 miles and turn left on Zink Road. Continue 2.8 miles and turn right on Forest Service Road 21N51Y. Continue 2.6 miles and veer left on 21N71. Drive three-tenths of a mile to the trailhead on the left.

THERMALITO FOREBAY

Rating: 5

Species: Largemouth
Bass, Spotted Bass,
Bluegill, Channel
Catfish, Rainbow Trout
and Brook Trout

Stocked with 17,000
pounds of rainbow
trout.

Facilities: Picnic Area
and Restrooms

While trout fishing isn't particularly good at Lake Oroville, many Oroville and Chico residents spend their time trout fishing at Thermalito Forebay instead. Offering 11 miles of shoreline and 600 acres, the forebay can be found downstream of Lake Oroville and the diversion pool.

The forebay is comprised of very cold water. Dependant on releases from the bottom of Lake Oroville, the water temperatures are ideal for rainbow trout. While the California Department of Fish and Game plants brook trout once in a while, rainbows are the focus. Nearly 30,000 half-pound rainbows are planted each year. Plants take place weekly from February through September and monthly the rest of the year.

The reservoir is a classic day use trout fishery. Most folks set up on the shoreline and fish Power Bait. Within a week of a trout stocking, it can be effective to fish lures as well. Casting Krocodiles, Thomas Buoyants and Cripplures will definitely catch you fish. Nothing heavier than four-pound test is necessary.

The forebay is much smaller than the afterbay and isn't an ideal place for warmwater fish. There are bass, panfish and catfish available, unfortunately their numbers are small. Due to cold water, warmwater fish do much better in the afterbay.

Trip info for Thermalito Afterbay also applies to Thermalito Forebay.

Directions: *From Oroville on Highway 70, exit Grand Avenue and drive west for three miles to the right turnoff for the State Recreation Area.*

Spots like this one caught by Gary Dobyns are available in Thermalito Forebay.

THERMALITO AFTERBAY

Rating: 4

Species: Rainbow
Trout, Largemouth
Bass, Spotted Bass,
Channel Catfish,
Bluegill and Crappie

Stocks: None

Need Information?
Contact: Lake Oroville
Visitor Center
(530) 538-2219

Located downriver of Thermalito Forebay, the Thermalito Afterbay wasn't designed for anglers. It was, however, created for agricultural purposes, amongst other reasons. Barring a long explanation, the afterbay is a holding pool. The California Department of Water Resources designed the reservoir to store water and allow it to warm before it's sent out to nearby farms and ranches. The water coming out of Lake Oroville is extremely cold and needs to gain a few degrees before it's released into the fields to avoid the risk of shocking crops.

With 26 miles of shoreline and 4,300 acres, the afterbay is much larger than the forebay. Because the water is warmer, the California Department of Fish and Game doesn't plant trout, although some slip out of the forebay into the afterbay. The afterbay is more known for its' warmwater fishery. Unfortunately, it's also popular to boating and personal watercraft, so anglers have a lot of headaches to contend with.

The majority of the bass in the afterbay are largemouth, but be sure to know this isn't a great bass fishery. The best time to fish is when the water levels are raised and the tules are flooded. The lake fluctuates a lot. When the water is in the tules, the bass head in them for cover. Throw soft jerkbaits and spinnerbaits along the tule line or back in the tules. Most of the bass are one-to-three pounds.

If you plan to make the trip, supplies are available in Oroville.

Also nearby is the Feather River and Lake Oroville.

Directions: *From Highway 70 in Oroville, exit Oro Dam Road and drive west for 1.8 miles to Larkin Road. Turn left and drive 2.6 miles to the right turnoff for the Thermalito Afterbay.*

Alan Jaquias with a rainbow trout. Rainbows are more likely to be caught in Thermalito Forebay.

SACRAMENTO RIVER (SACRAMENTO TO CHICO)

Rating: 8

Species: Striped Bass, King Salmon, Steelhead, Sturgeon, American Shad, Channel Catfish, Brown Bullhead, Largemouth Bass, Crappie, Bluegill and Carp

Stocks: None

Facilities: Boat Launches, Restrooms, Bait & Tackle

Need Information? Contact: Johnson's Bait & Tackle (530) 674-1912, Kittles (530) 458-4868, Fishing Guide Greg Squires of Access to Angling Outfitters (800) 551-3984, Sportsmans Den (530) 891-5238

When it comes to fishing for stripers in a river system, the Sacramento River is hard to beat. Stripers run up the American, Feather, Yuba and many other tributaries north of the State Capitol, however, the numbers of fish are greatest in this section of the Sac, which stretches from roughly Chico on down to Verona, where the Feather spills into the Sac.

Striper fishing can be excellent. Stripers are much easier to catch than salmon and sturgeon that also move through this area. One downfall to striper fishing is that the window of opportunity can be short; April and May are pretty much it.

Unfortunately, this 45-mile section of river isn't packed with amenities. Much of the river is only accessible by boat. Boat access is limited. If you have a sensitive stomach, watch what you eat before you head out on the water. You aren't going to find floating SS Relief toilets or many riverside restrooms. Only a few places on this stretch have any facilities. Every five miles on the river you may find a boat launch with an Andy Gump, but dont expect much better than that.

Here's a list of your access points from Chico down to below Knights Landing: Scotty's Landing in Chico, Colusa Park, Bert's Steelhead Marina, Ward's Marina, Lovey's Landing, Tisdale Park, Knight's Landing and Verona, at the confluence of the Feather and Sacramento Rivers.

Fishing for stripers is best from Chico down to Knights Landing. This section is where most of the spawning occurs. Stripers begin to filter into this section of the Sac in late March. By the first of April, there are solid numbers of fish in the river. By tax day, striper season is in full swing. Males arrive first, with females showing up later. Stripers spawn every night, but big spawns occur on full moon nights.

Water temperature also plays a part in the run. Look for 58 degree temps as a sign fish will be active. Stripers spawn in 60-65 degree water. However, there is no consistency when it comes to striper habits. At times, when flows and temperatures aren't to their liking, stripers will swim downstream.

When it comes to size, you have to catch a lot of fish to get big fish, unless you get lucky.

A 25-pound striper

Then, you'll have some odd days where you'll catch only a few fish and they'll be huge. Stripers are schooling fish. Most average two-to-four pounds, although there is an impressive number of five-to-10-pound fish. There is also a fair number of 10-20 pound fish. Several 20+ pound fish are caught daily throughout the system.

Hands down, live minnows are the most common bait. You can still-fish them, drift them or vertical mooch them off the bottom. Minnows aren't a natural baitfish, however, they imitate steelhead and salmon smelt, which are coming down the Sacramento River when the striper run occurs.

When you still fish minnows, typically you anchor, release your line to the bottom and sit and wait for a bite. Some anglers use heavy line, but it's not necessary and takes a lot of thrill out of the fight. You'll have more fun with 10-pound test. Some guys like to use a No. 1 hook, but a No. 4 hook is better. Why? The smaller minnows can't swim for a long time with the weight of a No. 1, hook, so they end up sinking to the bottom rather than actively swimming. Only a jumbo minnow can handle a No. 1 hook. These are all secrets courtesy of Greg Squires of Access to Angling Outfitters.

Tony Abel with an average striper taken from the Sacramento River on anchovies.

Minnow selection is also important. The dirtier the water, the bigger the minnow you want to use. Though you should never go smaller than a large minnow, make sure to use jumbos when the water is high and muddy. A jumbo gets more sonic and creates more havoc. In clear water, jumbos don't fish as well. Switch over to using an extra large minnow.

The setup is fairly simple. Attach a swivel to the end of your line with a single bead head above it. Then put a five-ounce bullet weight jig or a half-ounce or three-eighths ounce, depending on the volume of water in the river. Then use a three foot leader with a No. 4 hook. Sometimes when the water is really high, you may need to bump up to a one-ounce weight.

Fishing with minnows takes work. If you let the minnow rest, they'll go right to the bottom and sit. For best results, try to gradually jig the minnow off the bottom. Then, the minnow will get aggravated and actively swim back to the bottom. This action stimulates bites. The more active the minnow, the more bites you'll get.

Drifting is best with an electric trolling motor. Gas motors spook fish. Gas motors send stripers into a scurry and away from your boat. Side drifting minnows is the most common method. Using the river's current to drift downriver, employ a trolling motor to keep your boat straight. First, let out enough line so your minnow is hanging out near the bottom. Then release about 10 more feet to get the minnow away from the boat. Keep an eye out for snags as you cruise downriver.

Try to find green water. Areas that have better than two feet, but less than six feet of visibility are best. You don't want the fish to see you!

Vertical mooching in deep swirls or places where you are marking fish on your fish finder also yields stripers. When you see jumping fish in calm water or when tons of boat traffic is pushing those fish into calm water, if the water is too slow to drift, than you should mooch. Here's how: let the minnows sink to the bottom and then gradually lift your rod tip to bring the minnow off the bottom. Lift roughly three feet and then let it fall again. When the water is high, oftentimes stripers will move into slack water to get out of the swift currents.

Striper fishing isn't always easy. Mother Nature can create havoc on the river in the spring. Powerful Pacific storms can swell and muddy the river, thus making it unfishable. There are a few basic rules that explain how fishing will be. When you have a falling barometer and rising water, the bite has a tendency to shut off. However, you can catch fish with a steady barometer and receding water. Most successful anglers wait for the river to crest before fishing. Oftentimes, the river doesn't crest until 10 hours after the storm passed because it can take a while for the runoff to come in from the tributaries. The river muddies up fast and can take two to three days to clear.

When the river is real muddy, live bait works well. Stripers use their sense of smell to feed when they can't necessarily see food. Pile worms, cut sardines, shad, Sacramento pike minnows and other baits work well because they put a scent in the water. To bait fish like this, you'll have to anchor and hope the fish come to you. Target 10-15 feet of water and fish near the bottom.

Dragging plugs can be effective in off-colored water conditions. However, you'll have to compete with snags and debris. Deep divers are the chosen bait, unfortunately pulling plugs can be expensive. Expect to lose hardware. To be effective, it's best to drag your lures right near the bottom. As far as how much line to let out, there is no real number. You need to let out just enough to reach the bottom. Trolling speed is dictated by the lure you are using. On average, 3 mph is a good number to follow. You can troll up and down river. Trolling can be more difficult when the water clears because stripers are easily spooked. Four- and six-inch Floating Rapalas and Luhr Jensen Power Dive Minnows are local favorites. White and red, blue back, chartreuse and silver and black are the best patterns. Don't discount broken back Rebels.

Some anglers chose to approach the stripers by casting plastics. Using a Carolina rig, cast towards the bank and then jig it back to the boat. It's best to cast downriver so your boat is catching up as you go. This method can be effective, but takes lots of work. Six-and-eight-inch black plastics with a chartreuse head seem to produce the most fish.

Tossing plugs and large trout imitations is another way to cash in on large stripers. Rather than trolling them, casting allows you to target specific areas you know hold fish, without risking getting snagged on underwater structure. Trout imitation lures do a sufficient job in imitating baby salmon and steelhead swimming downriver.

Salmon also run through this section of the river from July through October. However, catch rates can be better for anglers who fish upriver of Chico. Nonetheless, anglers drifting roe and running plugs can find exceptional days.

In the winter and spring, sturgeon are also on tap to anglers fishing deeper holes with cut baits and shrimps. Sturgeon fishing is a sit-and-wait game. It's a specialty gig, not a for sure deal.

If you plan to make the trip, supplies are available in several small towns along the river. There are dozens of access points. Consult a river map for specific details. This section of the Sacramento River is closed to salmon fishing from January 1 to July 15. From July 16 to December 31, two salmon can be taken.

Also nearby are the Feather River and the Yuba River.

Directions: *This section of the Sacramento River can be reached via many roads off of Interstate 5, Highway 99 and Highway 70. Consult a map for specific locations.*

558   A Sacramento River striper

SACRAMENTO RIVER (CHICO TO RED BLUFF)

Rating: 8

Species: Striped Bass, Chinook Salmon, Sturgeon, Steelhead, American Shad, Rainbow Trout, Largemouth Bass, Channel Catfish and Crappie

Stocks: None

Facilities: Boat Launches, Campgrounds, RV Hookups, Restrooms, Bait & Tackle, Lodging, Restaurants, Gas and General Store

Need Information? Contact: Fishing Guide Access to Angling Guide Service (800) 551-3984, Woodson Bridge State Recreation Area (530) 839-2112, Red Bluff Department of Parks and Recreation (530) 527-8177, Lake Red Bluff Recreation Area (530) 934-3316

Located between Chico and Red Bluff, this section of the Sacramento River is for specialized anglers to fish. This portion of the river, like many others, is framed by skilled anglers vying to catch anadromous fish. It's not the kind of place where you show up with a Snoopy pole and a gift basket of hooks and sinkers you got from grandma for Christmas. Most of the fishing is done by anglers fishing with guides or skilled anglers who have specialized gear to key in on natural spawning and hatchery bred fish. It's not easy to catch fish here.

The Sacramento River offers an excellent lowland wilderness area, marked by rolling hills and grasslands rather than cool air and pine trees like you'd find at the Trinity River. Located in the Upper Sacramento Valley, otters, minks, raccoons, possums, bald eagles, osprey, deer, bobcats, wild boars, turkeys, ducks, mountain lions and turtles are commonly seen in the early morning and late evening along the sandy and dirt banks. However, most anglers aren't concerned with the wildlife. That is, unless you are talking about fish.

The California Department of Fish and Game doesn't truck loads of planters into the river. In fact, they don't stock anything. Fishing depends on the most recent run of fish that enter the river naturally. During the year the river is blessed with runs of American shad, Chinook salmon, steelhead, striped bass and some sturgeon.

Salmon season is the biggest run and the most popular to anglers. Anglers prepare for the opener on July 16 and fish through December 31 each year. A winter, spring, fall and summer run embarks on the Sac each year. To protect the fish, no salmon may be taken during the winter run, though.

The one downfall to this section of the Sac is that there is little public access. To find success, you'll need a boat. The only river access from shore is found at boat launches, mainly in Red Bluff, Los Molinos, at Woodson Bridge, in Hamilton City and at Scotty's. There is some access at the Red Bluff Diversion Dam and where the river crosses under the highway, but that's it.

Fresh salmon roe

Guide Greg Squires (Left) and Brett Ross with a Sac salmon taken on a Kwikfish

The fall run is the largest. The average return of salmon is comprised of roughly 250,000 fish in the Sacramento River system, but that number can vary drastically from year to year. The fall run starts to show in late-July and lasts through January. Traditionally, the major part of the fall run has passed through the system by October 15. For this run, the average size is between 15-20 pounds, but 30s are not uncommon. Anything under 10 is considered a jack salmon. If you get one over 40, consider that fish special! The big fish have still yet to arrive.

The largest of the fish tend to arrive in late fall and early winter. The early part of the winter run can be fished, but the season closes during the latter part of the run. A small number of salmon migrate up the river in late November when rain begins to fall. This time poses the chance to hook into the bigger salmon.

Fortunately, the Sacramento River is never too clear that it affects your fishing approach. Dragging plugs and bait fishing are the most common methods employed on this section of the Sacramento. Fishing Kwikfish is imperative. A silver body with a chartreuse bill is standard. However, whites and some blacks work, too. In fast water, use a size K-14. Size 16 is best is slow water. Overall though, under most conditions, a K-15 is the best size to use in the system. Keep in mind, though, you do need a sufficient current to fish with these plugs.

Using bait is applicable in all conditions. Bait is best in deep, slow moving water, which will most likely be found in holes. One of the keys to successfully using roe is adding your own christened scent. Some anglers use crawdad flavor, others shrimp or herring. The newest craze to hit the market is soaking roe in Pautzke Liquid Krill.

There are several ways to fish roe. Boondoggling, a method where anglers cast upstream and drag the bait through the hole, works well, as does back bouncing. In this section of the Sac, depending on the current you'll want to use a four-to-eight-ounce weight. Lower your line to the bottom and carefully feel the weight tapping the bottom. The roe floats above the weight. One of the biggest mistakes anglers make is letting their weight sit on the bottom. This can promote snagging.

Vertical mooching is also popular. This method requires anglers to drift over areas with little to no current, while holding still or swirling in a hole and gently moving your roe up and down. Vertically lifting off the edge of the boat, let your weight sink to the bottom and then practice two-to-three-foot lifts. Keep your raises subtle. Remember, snagging fish is illegal.

Salmon tend to stay in the bigger holes to rest before continuing upstream. Most likely, the fish will harbor in the holes during the day and move most during low-light hours. Salmon fishing can get tricky in late fall. Along with cooler temperatures, heavy rains can swell and dirty the river. The Sac is not only fed by water from Lake Shasta, but dozens of small and large tributaries that commonly carry mud, rocks and other debris into the river.

I fished most of this section of the Sac with Greg Squires of Access to Angling Outfitters. Squires is no doubt one of the river's top guides, if not one

Anna and Marshall Haraden show off salmon caught with Greg Squires on the Sac

of the best anglers in the state. For salmon, Squires uses a medium weight rod, filled with 200 yards of braided line and a four-foot leader of 20-pound test. He uses red Gamakatsu hooks and ball weight sinkers. Ball weight sinkers put less friction on the line and require less weight to keep in touch with the bottom.

Squires has extensively studied the life of a salmon. His tips are priceless. Present bait so it is floating naturally down the river, he says. Keep in mind, many researchers believe that the salmon aren't feeding when you catch them in fresh water. You catch them as a result of their maternal instinct. They aren't eating the egg, rather smashing it or picking it up and spitting it. It's a natural reaction for salmon to pick up the egg. They've been accustomed to eating them during their young life. In this case, many believe they are picking up the egg, wanting to place it back in the dirt.

Recall the life of a salmon. Salmon leave the Pacific and venture up the Sac with one thing in mind; spawning. At the point when the salmon reach freshwater, they start their dying cycle. To prepare for this, they fatten up before entering the river. Once they reach freshwater, salmon lose their sense of hunger and rely on body fat for food. That's why most guides tell you that you have to stimulate a bite.

Nick Haraden with a pikeminnow

Stripers can also be found in the spring, but the best section lies downriver below the Chico area, though stripers stray all the way to the diversion dam. If you are adamant about striper fishing, locate backwaters, flats and areas when the current flows slower than it does in the main river channel. Stripers are looking for warmer water and can be caught on cut baits; shad and anchovies work best.

Largemouth bass are also available; however, almost no one targets them. If you have the urge to be a pioneer, start in the backwaters with plastics and crawdads. The backwaters are much warmer than the main river and maintain a consistent populations of bass. This is where you'll find panfish and catfish as well.

If you plan to make the trip, supplies are available in Red Bluff, Corning and Los Molinos. There are specific regulations set for all anadromous species. For updated bag limits, closures and gear restrictions, please consult sportfishing regulations.

Also nearby is the Feather River.

Directions: *From Sacramento, drive north on Interstate 5 to the Corning, Los Molinos or Red Bluff exit where access to the river is available. Consult a map for the location you plan to fish.*

Region 20

Truckee Area & Tahoe Basin

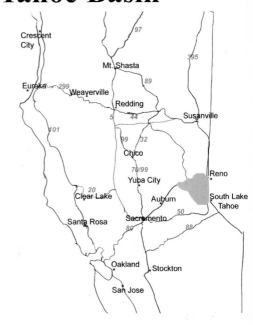

ECHO LAKES

Rating: 6

Species: Rainbow
Trout, Brown Trout,
Brook Trout and
Cutthroat Trout

Stocked with 3,800
pounds of rainbow
trout, 10 pounds of
fingerling cutthroat
trout and 13 pounds of
fingerling rainbow
trout.

Facilities: Restrooms,
Boat Launch, Boat
Rentals, General Store,
Food, Lodging, Bait &
Tackle and a Picnic
Area

Need Information?
Contact: Echo Lakes
Chalet 530-659-7207

Echo Lakes serve three purposes; their natural beauty creates a tourist trap, it's used as staging point for travel into the Desolation Wilderness and is a great place for anglers to cash in on a fishery well-stocked with trout. At 7,400 feet in the El Dorado National Forest, Upper and Lower Echo Lakes are in fact one body of water (when the lake is full) connected by a shallow, narrow channel.

Each summer, tens of thousands of tourists visit these scenic high country lakes set in a forested granite setting. Using boats to reach their cabins along the shore, another few hundred people call the lake home each summer. On top of that, thousands of hikers take advantage of a ferry service that taxis backpackers and hikers from the boat launch on the lower lake to the far end of the upper lake, allowing them to bypass a 2.5-mile section of the Pacific Crest Trail that parallels the shoreline and continues on to the Desolation Wilderness.

The anglers, well they are somewhere in the middle.

Rainbow trout are abundant here. The California Department of Fish and Game dumps 8,060 half-pound trout and 10,000-fingerling cutthroat into the lower lake and 10,000 fingerling rainbow trout into the upper lake. The rainbows do well. Nonetheless, the cutts have their share of problems competing for food and water space and rarely show in angler's creels. There are resident browns, but if you count on catching one you'll be let down. In the future, the CA DGF plans to switch the lakes entirely to cutthroat fisheries.

Connecting with the rainbow trout is your best option and one that doesn't require much skill. Trolling is the most consistent method. Working both

The roads to Echo aren't normally plowed, but if you have the means to get to the lake, ice fishing can be great.

shorelines on the lower lake is an option with small silver Kastmasters, white Phoebes and just about any Needlefish. The best spot however, is a shelf in the back of the lower lake. The trout congregate on the deeper side of the shelf. Trolling and bait fishing with night crawlers works great. For shoreline anglers, try casting small spinners or rainbow color Power Bait off the dam and anywhere on the upper lake. Several islands, submerged trees and rocks make trolling the upper lake difficult.

Coyotes are common at Echo Lake

If you plan to make the trip, supplies are available at the lake. There is a boat launch and taxi fee. No 2-stroke motors are permitted. Only 4-stroke or direct fuel-injected outboards are allowed. Due to snowfall and closed roads, Echo is inaccessible from late fall through mid-spring. Call ahead for updated conditions. There is limited parking at the lake. A lack of open space near the boat launch and in the parking area can make boat launching tough. Use caution when launching and parking your boat.

Also nearby are Lake Tahoe, American River (Silver Fork) and American River (South Fork, Riverton).

Directions: From the junction of Highway's 50 and 89 in South Lake Tahoe, drive south on Highway's 50/89 for 4.7 miles to Meyers. In Meyers, stay on Highway 50 west for approximately five miles to the turnoff for Echo Lakes. Turn right and follow signs to the lake.

Upper Echo Lake

ANGORA LAKES

Rating: 4

Species: Brook Trout and Cutthroat Trout

Stocked with 10 pounds of cutthroat trout.

Facilities: Lodging and Restrooms

Need Information? Contact: Angora Lakes Resort (530) 541-2092, El Dorado National Forest (530) 543-2600

Angora Lakes are two small lakes in El Dorado National Forest, located on the border of the Desolation Wilderness. Situated in the same general area as Fallen Leaf Lake, there is a road that leads to Angora's shoreline, yet you can't drive all the way to the lakes. The private road is maintained by Angora Lakes Resort (that operates a group of lakeside cabins) and only residents have a key to the locked gate. Angora is a popular summer family destination, but not a great fishery.

In the past, both Angora's were chemically treated to remove undesirable species of fish (bullhead and chubs). Unfortunately, the treatment wasn't successful as there are still bullhead and chubs present. In spite of fish plants from the California Department of Fish and Game, Angora isn't a great fishery.

Prior to the turn of the century, the Angora's were managed as a brook trout fishery and had some rainbows (3,000 fingerling brooks were last planted in 2003). However, focus has since switched to Lahonton cutthroats. No more brookies or rainbows will be planted. Brooks, nonetheless, can spawn in the lake and will maintain a self-sustaining population.

It's best to fish in the spring and early summer. By the time late summer and fall arrive, hundreds of anglers have fished the lakes and the trout are less active. There are two lakes and one pond that are each reached by a short walk on a dirt road, which is suitable for folks of all ages and fitness levels. It's a short jaunt that should take no more than five to 10 minutes. While both lakes have cabins built on them, they are open to the public. Casting spinners and fly-and-bubble combos are your best bet.

If you plan to make the trip, supplies are available in South Lake Tahoe. In winter and spring call ahead for road conditions. The road will likely be closed due to snow.

Also nearby is Fallen Leaf Lake.

Directions: *From the junction of Highway 80 and 50 in South Lake Tahoe drive northwest on Highway 89 for 3.1 miles to Fallen Leaf Road and turn left. Drive 1.9 miles to Tahoe Mountain Road and turn left. Drive four-tenths of a mile to Road 1214 and turn right. Continue 2.9 miles to the parking area for Angora Lakes.*

Lower Angora Lake

LILY LAKE

Rating: 3

Species: Brook Trout and Brown Trout

Stocks: None

Facilities: Restrooms

Lily Lake isn't your typical small lake in the mountains above the Tahoe Basin. While most lakes in this area are known to be in granite country, Lily is a flat and shallow pond that has been enlarged by beaver dams. Lily rests in the Tahoe National Forest, rather than the Desolation Wilderness, which is less than one-mile away. The lake is more of a shallow meadow on Glen Alpine Creek. It's set in a pretty area, but gets mobbed by visitors hiking into the Desolation Wilderness and day-users looking to attain a nice view after a short drive in the backwoods. So much for serenity! Even on a weekday, expect the parking lot to be full between Memorial Day and Halloween.

As for the fishing, Lily isn't a great lake. Because it's a drive-to destination, the lake gets hit pretty hard, thus making the trout wary. Each year, however, browns to five pounds are taken. Unfortunately, their population isn't great. You are more likely to catch brook trout, which are small, yet available. Try using a fly and bubble combo with either a Woolly Bugger or Pistol Pete. From Fallen Leaf Lake Marina, you'll find signs that point you to Lily Lake. You can walk or drive, but parking may be tough to find.

Directions *and trip info for Fallen Leaf Lake also apply to Lily Lake.*

Lily Lake

Rating: 7

Species: Rainbow Trout, Cutthroat Trout, Kokanee Salmon, Brown Trout, Lake Trout, Brook Trout and Rainbow Trout

Stocked with 228 pounds of fingerling kokanee.

Facilities: Boat Launch, Boat Rentals, Restaurant, General Store and Restrooms

Need Information? Contact: Tahoe National Forest (530) 543-2600, Fallen Lake Marina (530) 544-0787, Fallen Leaf Landing Store (530) 541-4671

Fallen Leaf Lake is one of those lakes classified as a sleeper fishery. While rich with several species of fish, due to factors that unfortunately, aren't related to technique, it's not always easy to catch them. Fallen Leaf is a big lake. A large water – called a miniature Lake Tahoe by some - and up to 425 feet deep, the lake has lots of acreage to learn. Not to mention shelves that would love to snatch one of your downrigger balls, if not the whole downrigger. The lake's structure is intense, steep, unpredictable and downright nasty in some places.

Yet, even more challenging can be getting a boat on the water. You'd better have some trailer maneuvering skills. At best this road is a one-laner, and at times, less. And, there are few pullouts. The first two miles on Fallen Leaf Road are easily doable; however, the last 2.5 are risky. Lots of vehicular traffic uses this road. Oftentimes someone is going to have to back up to allow for passing. If you have a boat, hope it's not you. There are steep drop-offs on the right, slopes hillsides on the left and few pullouts. We dragged in a 17-footer, but it took time, patience and an extremely carefully driver.

Is it worth it to drag a boat in? I'd say yes. There are more issues to contend with though, mainly a limited amount of parking. Spaces alone are scarce. Those for a boat and trailer are nearly non-existent. On a positive note, the launch ramp is always in good shape. You don't have to worry about low water conditions. At the wishes of waterfront homeowners (and successful lobbying), it's been decided behind closed doors that water flows on Taylor Creek (the lake's outlet stream and Tahoe's inlet) suffer rather than drawing the lake down to keep Taylor in good shape. The memorandum keeps water at homeowners' docks throughout the summer, but upsets trout in Taylor Creek.

On to the fishing. Formed by glaciers and bordering the Desolation Wilderness, Fallen Leaf is nearly an identical fishery to Tahoe. Tucked out of sight from the Tahoe hype, Fallen Leaf's pine covered shorelines typically don't get crowded. It has the same food sources, i.e., Lahontan redside minnows, tui chubs and Tahoe suckers and the same species of fish as Tahoe: browns, bows, brookies, lake trout (with the exception of the newly re-introduced Lahontan cutthroats). At three miles long and one mile wide, Fallen Leaf is chock full of fish, and that includes some lunkers, although the overall number of fish are on the small side. Fallen Leaf is about numbers, not size.

Fallen Leaf's most sought after fish are the lake trout. While the lake record stands better than 25 pounds, the number of lunkers that come out each year is small compared to Tahoe. Several fish bigger than 10 pounds are landed; however the frequency is low. The majority of lake trout tend to be in the one-to-three-pound class and are caught trolling or drifting minnows. While the concept isn't backed by scientific data many anglers blame too many lake trout in the system for the small fish.

Drifting minnows off the bottom near the Glen Alpine Creek inlet and on the west shore between the Stanford Camp and private residences is a consistent method to catch big lake trout. If you have trouble trapping minnows (you can't bring them in from other lakes), the jigging bite can also be productive. White or silver Crippled Herring spoons are the best colors, just making sure to stay in 50-120 feet of water.

There's plenty of room for trolling. Most lake trout are concentrated on the west shore, especially on shelves. We found the bulk of the fish staying put in 50-135 feet, and conned them into hitting a Storm Thunderstick Gizzard Shad and just about any large Rapala or Rebel.

Rainbows and browns tend to occupy the space just above the lake trout on up to the surface. In the spring and fall toplining can be good early in the morning, with larger browns being caught by anglers who have outriggers working the inlets and close to shore. In the summer, troll the dam area or down the middle of the lake for large browns. To be honest, you'll need to put a lot of time in to catch one. Neither bows nor browns are planted. Both are self-sustaining populations, along with the brooks that can be found in all of the inlets. They stay out of the main body of water to avoid being eaten by the lake trout and browns.

The kokanee haven't hit the big show yet. The easiest way to cash in on them is by trolling down the middle of the lake with Cannon downriggers set in 35-70 feet of water with a small red Krocodile or Needlefish. In 2001, a three-pound kok was weighed in at the Sportsman in South Lake Tahoe, but you'll be disappointed if you plan to catch fish that size.

Fallen Leaf's fishery could see drastic changes in the near future. The drawing board illustrates a trophy cutthroat lake, but the plan may be far fetched. The introduction of the cutts has begun, but they get eaten as fast as they are put in. In 2003, 134,292 fingerling cutts were stocked.

Another thing,

Mike Nielsen (Left) and Blake Lezak show a pair of Fallen Leaf lake trout taken on jigs in 100-120 feet of water.

the roads to the lake aren't plowed in the winter. Fishing is permitted year round, but the only way in is with a snowmobile or snowshoes. Keep in mind, a lot of the shoreline is taken up by private residences. Let me add, fantastic Adirondack looking homes. We saw a guy sitting on his dock in an old, wooden hot tub soaking a night crawler. Doesn't get much better than that!

The residents make an effort to keep a lid on the fishing reports. They don't want tourists and other anglers around. Luckily for them, the road doesn't have the capacity to allow for an influx of anglers, so maintaining their private retreat is entirely possible in a sense. You want to tackle the fishery from shore? Public access can be found near the Glen Alpine Creek inlet, Cathedral Boat Dock, near the dam and at points along the west shore.

If you plan to make the trip, supplies are available in South Lake Tahoe. The roads to the lake are typically closed from December to March. There is a boat launch fee. For motors over 25hpr, there's a stiff $25 fee. That'll keep people out!

Also nearby are Glen Alpine Creek Falls, Sawmill Pond and Lake Tahoe.

__Directions__: From the junction of Highway 80 and 50 in South Lake Tahoe, drive northwest on Highway 89 for 3.1 miles to Fallen Leaf Road and turn left. Drive two miles to a split in the road and veer right. Continue 2.5 miles to the marina.

Fallen Leaf Lake with Lake Tahoe in the backdrop.

SAWMILL POND

Rating: 6

Species: Rainbow Trout
and Channel Catfish

Stocked with 500
pounds of rainbow
trout.

Facilities: Restrooms
and a Picnic Area

Need Information?
Contact: The Sportsman
(530) 542-3474

Chances are, if you are in high school you're too old to be fishing Sawmill Pond. The pond, located at 6,250 feet, less than two miles from Lake Tahoe and the city of South Lake Tahoe, is run as a Jr. Fishing Preserve. Only anglers 14 and younger are allowed to fish here. Normally frozen over from January through March, the one-acre pond is stocked three times a year with rainbow trout. The El Dorado County Fish & Game Commission stocks twice a year, and the California Department of Fish & Game stocks once, a bonus plant of 1,060 rainbow trout on free fishing day in June.

Parents are permitted to assist their children in learning how to fish. However, they aren't allowed to reel fish in or make any casts. Sawmill is meant for children to be creative and learn by trail and error. If the youths can cast, chances are they will catch fish. The lake is replenished throughout the summer to allow children to enjoy their fishing experience.

Tossing Kastmasters, Thomas Buoyants and Super Dupers into the shallow lake located alongside Lake Tahoe Blvd. produces good catch rates. Power Bait is the most common bait.

If you plan to make the trip supplies are available in South Lake Tahoe.

Also nearby are Fallen Leaf Lake, Lake Tahoe and Tahoe Trout Farm.

Directions: *From South Lake Tahoe at the junction of Highway's 89 and 50 turn south on Lake Tahoe Blvd and continue 2.5 miles to the lake on the left.*

Sawmill Pond

TAHOE TROUT FARM

Rating: 5

Species: Rainbow Trout

Stocked with fish as
needed.

Facilities: Bait &
Tackle, Fish Cleaning
Stations and Restrooms

Need Information?
Contact: Tahoe Trout
Farm (530) 541-1491

It's no secret that Lake Tahoe is one of the best brown trout, rainbow trout and lake trout fisheries in the West. However, if you aren't an experienced trout angler be forewarned, these fish aren't easy to catch. Realistically, most anglers get skunked the first few times before they learn how to fish the lake.

On the other hand, on the South Shore of Tahoe, sure catch rates can be had at South Lake Fish Farm. Unfortunately, most anglers won't fish the fish farm because they consider it cheating. Here, not catching fish is impossible because the trout are trucked in and dumped into two sand box size fishing ponds. One plus is that no fishing license is required. On the contrary, the pristine wilderness feeling can't be attained while trying to sneak in to get a good spot around the pond.

Catching fish is about as tough as finding food in a grocery store. My first trip to the pond proved to be a memorable experience. Unaware of single barbless hooks on the end of our lines, my buddy Blake Lezak and I hooked 10 rainbows, only to lose each of them. We got scolded by the woman in charge before switching to reliable Panther Martins and proceeding to catch more than a dozen fish, which brings me to the reason it's so easy to catch trout. There is a fishing fee and a charge per length fee for each fish caught. The fish aren't fed. (They are always starving.) In my case, it cost Lezak more than $115. Yikes!

The larger pond holds smaller fish, while the smaller pond holds lunker trout. You won't see many hardcore anglers, however, it's a great place for tourists to bring kids to catch their first fish, and second, third, or however many you are willing to pay for.

If you plan to make the trip, supplies are available in South Lake Tahoe. A fishing fee is charged. The ponds are closed to fishing from Labor Day to Memorial Day.

Also nearby are Lake Tahoe and Sawmill Pond.

Directions: *From the junction of Highway 89 and 50 in South Lake Tahoe take Highway 50 north to Blue Lake Road. Turn right and continue to the trout farm.*

These dozen trout cost more than $100 at Tahoe Trout Farm.

TAYLOR CREEK

Rating: 3

Species: Kokanee, Rainbow Trout, Brook Trout and Brown Trout

Stocks: None

Facilities: Visitor Center and Restrooms

Need Information? Contact: Lake Tahoe Basin Management Unit (530) 543-2600

Taylor Creek is a better place for learning about fish than it is for fishing. Taylor flows out of Fallen Leaf Lake into Lake Tahoe and is famous for its' fall run of kokanee. It's estimated that up to 15,000 kokanee can file into the creek at one time. The creek is an excellent place for anglers and children to witness the rituals of how a kokanee spawns. There's an underwater viewing area and a path that parallels the stream. It gives visitors a close up view of thousands of spawning fish. More kokanee spawn in Taylor Creek than anywhere else in the state. In fact, the California Department of Fish and Game utilizes the kokanee here to generate eggs for kokanee plants in California.

Taylor isn't a great place to fish. For starters, the creek is closed to fishing for nine months out of the year. It's only opened during the summer when the rainbows and browns aren't traditionally in it. This closure is a good thing though. It protects spawning fish and keeps healthy populations of rainbow and brown trout in Lake Tahoe.

While kokanee are abundant in September when the creek is open to fishing, they aren't into chasing bait or lures when they are in spawning mode. Once they kokanee enter the creek they are concerned with reproducing, not feeding. You can fish Taylor Creek during the summer months for the small resident rainbows and the occasional brown trout, but there are far better opportunities other places. Leave Taylor Creek for fish viewing rather than catching.

If you plan to make the trip, supplies are available in Lake Tahoe. Taylor Creek is closed to fishing from October 1 through the last day in June.

Also nearby is Fallen Leaf Lake.

Directions: From the junction of Highway 89 and 50 in South Lake Tahoe, drive north on Highway 89 past Camp Richardson to the right turnoff for the Taylor Creek Visitor Center. Turn right and follow the signs to the viewing area.

Kokanee viewing is a must at Taylor Creek during the fall when kokanee spawn in the clear water.

Rating: 10

Species: Lake Trout, Brook Trout, Rainbow Trout, Brown Trout, Largemouth Bass, Smallmouth Bass, Channel Catfish, Bullhead, Crappie, Bluegill, Goldfish, Carp and Kokanee

Stocked with rainbow trout by the Nevada Division of Wildlife.

Facilities: Fish Cleaning Stations, Restrooms, Boat Launches, Boat Rentals, Boat Tours, Fishing Piers, Bait & Tackle, Gas, General Stores, Lodging, Restaurants, RV Hookups, Campgrounds, Vista Points, Picnic Areas and Casinos

Need Information? Contact: Cave Rock Fishing Guide Leonard O'Mally (775) 588-4102, South Lake Tahoe Fishing Guide Mike Neilson (530) 544-1526, The Sportsman (South Lake) (530) 542-3474, Tahoe Visitor Center (530) 543-2674, Tahoe Fishing Company 888-340-1121

It was June of 1999 and my experiences at Lake Tahoe had just begun. I spent several days on water that spring, surveying many guides without letting them know I was a writer. My goal was to find the best guides the lake had to offer. My pal Blake Lezak and I flipped through every fishing magazine in the state and made countless phone calls to book guides. We fished out of big boats, little boats, off the west shore, east shore, south shore and north shore. By the end of the month we had been on more than a dozen guided trips, yet I still had no idea how to approach writing about Tahoe's fishery.

Situated partly in California and Nevada, Lake Tahoe is a natural lake with water so deep that many standard fish finders can't locate the bottom. It's a huge lake that is enjoyed by anglers, water skiers, swimmers, kayakers and boaters. Tahoe is the state's most diverse coldwater fishery, but it's not easy to fish. It's almost a guarantee that first time anglers will get blanked. Tahoe is a fishery that needs to be learned. Its gin clear water keep trout wary at all times. Fish are always on the move in Tahoe. Knowing where to find them when conditions change is vital to angler success.

Tahoe holds three freshwater angling records. In 1911, a 31.8-pound cutthroat was caught, followed by a 37.6-pound lake trout in 1974 and a 4.13-pound kokanee in 1973. That June, I became hooked on Tahoe forever.

Fishing the South Shore with Mike Nielsen of Tahoe Topliners Guide Service has become a favorite pastime of mine. That cold June morning is one I'll never forget. We were fishing for trophy lake trout when our left rod popped off the downrigger. Nielsen jumped to grab it, hooking the fish before it had a chance to wiggle its' way off the hook. I knew immediately it wasn't a big fish. Nonetheless, I didn't want to lose my turn reeling it in. Neither did Lezak. Nielsen handed me the rod first and told me just to reel it in so we could unhook the fish and get the lure back down to the bottom.

Unenthused, I reeled the fish in. My counter read 50 yards when I unexpectedly felt a sharp jerk on the rod. Maybe this wasn't a dinker? All the sudden this lake trout wasn't messing around. It had peeled off 100 yards of line and was headed for the bottom when I tightened the drag and began to pump the rod to try and get control of the fish. After 20 minutes we got our first glimpse of the trout, roughly 30 feet under the boat. Nielsen is used to catching trophy fish. He was positive this one was better than 30 pounds. We were careful not to bring the fish in too fast.

Five more minutes had passed. We were even able to film the fish with our video camera! Nonetheless, seconds later the rod went limp. Nielsen and I looked at

Lake Tahoe

each other in disbelief. How could that fish have got away? We did everything right. Oddly enough, there was still something swimming with my lure. I reeled it in and 10 feet from the boat the 30 pounder swam towards the fish I still had hooked and tried to eat the fish for the second time. Unfortunately, he saw the boat, got spooked and darted to deep water.

(Top) Mike Nielsen with a wild Tahoe rainbow.
(Bottom Right) Lake Tahoe's scenic shoreline

We examined the three-pound lake trout that was still hooked. It had teeth marks all over its side. Sure enough, the small fish we hooked originally was chomped on by a larger lake trout after we hooked it. This is part of the great mystique of Lake Tahoe's fishery. While there are tons of small lake trout, there are also fish better than 30 pounds. You never know what you are going to catch! When it comes to rainbow, brown and lake trout, you're chance of catching a state record from Lake Tahoe is better than anywhere else in the state.

For beginners, Tahoe's lake trout are challenging to catch. Unlike Donner Lake, Tahoe's fish aren't concentrated. They have more than enough space to roam and make anglers work to catch them. At 120,000 acres and a maximum depth of 1,640 feet, there are more fishing holes on Tahoe than there are gopher holes in one million old vacant dirt lots!

Mike Nielsen (Left) and Blake Lezak with an average Tahoe brown.

Tahoe used to be commercially harvested. The lake was gill-netted through the Twenties before commercial fishing was outlawed. Back then, there were mostly brook and cutthroat trout. When commercial fishing was banned, lake trout were introduced and have since become the lake's dominant species.

Lake trout were taken from Lake Michigan and introduced into Tahoe. Tahoe has since become one of the most popular lake trout fisheries in the West. There's no doubt it's the best in California. The number of lake trout is staggering. Even with anglers harvesting tens of thousands of lake trout each year, the population remains in tact.

Despite the over-fishing, Tahoe remains one of the state's top cold water fisheries. It offers trophy rainbow, brown and lake trout, but with extremely clear water, you have to downsize to have a chance at the record books. Many guides know how to catch a state record lake trout. Unfortunately, they are all illegal. Trolling a live kokanee or rainbow trout would do the trick most definitely. If you can find an artificial lure that resembles a rainbow trout or kokanee close enough, you may get your wish. There are many on the market, but knowing how to run them is another ballgame.

Tahoe's fish survive on kokanee, crawdads, minnows and what's flushed in via the lake's tributaries, not to mention the practice of cannibalism. There isn't a lot of reproduction going on because there aren't enough grass beds on the lake's bottom to sustain an organic fish diet. There's a false perception that minnows are abundant on the south shore and not of the north shore because there are lots of grasses on the south shore for the minnows to spawn in. Nevertheless, minnows use the grass to hide in, not to spawn in. They spawn in gravel, which is abundant on both shores. Crawdads do extremely well on both sides of the lake.

Above all, the most important ingredient to the lake trout's diet is freshwater shrimp. Miscies shrimp were taken from Waterton Lake in Canada from 1964-68 and have become a main food source for trout. They were planted to bridge the gap of the lake trout's food source between the small plankton trout feed on when they are young and the minnows they eat when they grow older.

Tony Abel with a Tahoe brown

The success of the introduction of shrimp was two-fold. The shrimp did provide more food and faster growth rates. On the other hand, they also sent lake trout into deeper water, making them more difficult for anglers to catch. Here's why. The shrimp don't like sun. During the day, the shrimp swim down 300-400 feet in search of darkness. The lake trout simply follow their food source. The exception comes at night when shrimp return to the surface. Unfortunately, lake trout are not available to anglers because Tahoe is closed to night fishing. Ironically, the shrimp population peaked in the Seventies when the record kokanee was caught.

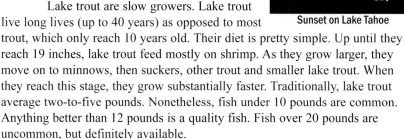

Sunset on Lake Tahoe

Lake trout are slow growers. Lake trout live long lives (up to 40 years) as opposed to most trout, which only reach 10 years old. Their diet is pretty simple. Up until they reach 19 inches, lake trout feed mostly on shrimp. As they grow larger, they move on to minnows, then suckers, other trout and smaller lake trout. When they reach this stage, they grow substantially faster. Traditionally, lake trout average two-to-five pounds. Nonetheless, fish under 10 pounds are common. Anything better than 12 pounds is a quality fish. Fish over 20 pounds are uncommon, but definitely available.

While there are too many fishing guides on Tahoe (more than several dozen to be exact), lake trout got a boost in the late-Eighties when the daily limit was lowered from five to two fish. Sport fishing and over-harvest is still a big problem. Catch and release would help the fishery. Nonetheless, with guides working for pay they feel it necessary to allow anglers to bring home their catch, rather than releasing it. Please take pictures and release the fish if you aren't going to eat them. More fish are removed each year. Tahoe's lake trout population is still intact, but could be better if anglers would practice catch and release.

Fishing for lake trout can be done more ways than you could ever imagine. Each guide practices their own methods, including deep and topwater trolling, jigging, still fishing, live bait and fly-fishing from float tubes.

Jigging is exceptional when the lake is calm. If there's any breeze, good luck. It's nearly impossible to hold your boat over schools of fish. When you are jigging, be sure to tip your lure with a minnow. Set out a minnow trap with dog food (for bait) close to shore, come back in a few hours and you should have a few. Only take what you need.

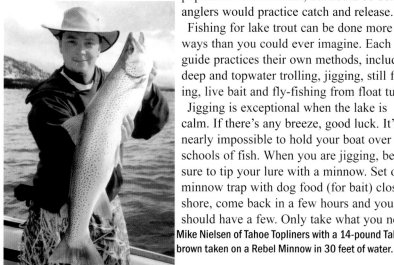

Mike Nielsen of Tahoe Topliners with a 14-pound Tahoe brown taken on a Rebel Minnow in 30 feet of water.

Uncle Ron Shaffer with a 5-pound Tahoe brown caught and released in Emerald Bay in the fall.

The minnow population is being depleted because so many people are trapping them.

Lake trout are in transition mode from May through June. They move from relatively shallow to deeper water. Trollers can find action in 80-130 feet of water with Rebel Holographic Minnows, Storm Thundersticks and Bomber Long A's. Anglers looking to jig should target 70-140 feet of water with three-and-four-ounce pearl and pearl and green Megabait Live jigs and Crippled Herrings.

Summer is the busiest time for guides on Tahoe. Fishing isn't necessarily the best, but more tourists mob the basin in the summer months than any other time of year. The downfall to the summer bite is that fish are deeper. Downriggers are mandatory, unless you opt to jig. Some guides fish deeper than 250 feet, but most lake trout will be found in 150-200 feet of water. Eight to 10-pound test is standard. For smaller lake trout, a nickel Sep's Pro Dodger in front of a minnow or night crawler, a size U20 FlatFish or silver, frog, pearl and rainbow pattern floating Rapalas in sizes seven to 11 are best. Keep your boat speed between 0.8-2.0 mph.

For the larger fish, the same lures work; however, you'll need to up the sizes. For FlatFish stick with the T 50's and 60's rainbow-patterned Rebels and silver and black and silver and blue J-Plugs.

There are dozens of quality areas on the south shore that harbor lake trout. You'll find fish on nearly every shelf. Basically, if you take out a lake map with a depth chart you'll find hundreds of shelves, ridges, flats and drop-offs that hold trout. All of them harbor fish.

Lake trout spawn between October and December. Throughout this period you'll find some lake trout in pre-spawn mode, others spawning and some in post-spawn mode. Locating the lake trout can take some work, but when you find them, expect to find large schools. Most lake trout will be found in 160-240 feet of water. Within that zone most fish will be between 120-220 feet. Because the fish are schooled up, jigging tends to produce better catch rates than trolling in the fall. Lake trout don't appear to want to chase baits or leave spawning areas.

The winter months see little angling pressure. Most visitors come to

Christian Perez (Left) and Blake Lezak with a Tahoe lake trout taken on New Year's Day.

Tahoe to ski, not to bundle up and fish for lake trout. On the other hand, anglers who brave the cold can experience outstanding catch rates. In the winter, it's best to slow down and downsize. Because the water is colder, lake trout are less active and tend to hit smaller baits. Troll Needlefish and Krocodiles pasted with Pautzke Gel Krill. Try running baits 80-120 feet. The great thing about fishing in the winter is that you can catch large lake trout on the surface.

A spawning kokanee

While only available seasonally, kokanee are a big hit in the summer on the south shore. Each fall, kokanee put on a show when they spawn up Taylor Creek to lay their eggs. There is a kokanee viewing area along Highway 89 to see this. It's a big tourist attraction.

During El Nino, in 1998, the Taylor Creek channel was expanded by rushing water, boosting its' carrying capacity to nearly 18,000 spawning fish. Prior to the influx of water, only 9,000 kokanee could file into Taylor Creek. On the other hand, at one time, biologists have recorded nearly 40,000 kokanee trying to squeeze into the creek. Kokanee also spawn in Third and Incline Creeks.

Kokanee used to spawn on the West Shore (between Meeks Bay and Tahoe City) where proper spawning gravel was found. However, during the drought years of the late-Seventies and early Eighties, the water dropped so low that kokanee couldn't even reach the gravel to spawn in. As many as 10,000 kokanee spawned each year on the West Shore. Those spawns no longer take place.

Traditionally, kokanee are found from Taylor Creek, north to Rubicon Point. Some years they can be found down the east shore as well. In early July, look 50-70 feet deep for kokanee. By August you'll find them in 70-85 feet. Kokanee average 10-11 inches.

Trolling and jigging are applicable for catching kokanee. Trolling is almost exclusively done with a dodger and a Kokanee Bug or some kind of small kokanee lure. Stick to pink and orange. A Macks Imperial Trolling Spoon in fluorescent orange and a red Needlefish are common. If you plan to jig, try a silver or white Crippled Herring or Megabait Live jig. You can get away with much lighter jigs than you'd use for lake trout because you are fishing in much shallower water.

(Top) This decomposed kokanee came out of the mouth of a lake trout. (Bottom) A Swimbait

Tahoe is one of the best brown trout lakes on the West Coast. However, prime time to target them is when anglers are on the slopes. Trolling for the browns is imperative. Eagle Point, Emerald Bay and Camp Richardson are hot spots along the south shore with Bomber Long A's, Rebels and Storms being a must. Cave Rock is also a great area to target browns. They frequent shallow waters to feed on stocked rainbows.

Brown trout are fall spawners. They tend to leave the lake and swim up tributaries when water temperatures are between 45-50 degrees. Unfortunately, many of Tahoe's tributaries don't have enough water for the browns to spawn in. Former California Department of Fish and Game Tahoe biologist Russ Wickwire told me when he surveyed Taylor Creek (one of the larger tributaries), he saw only 26 browns spawning. With the lack of sufficient tributaries, Wickwire's theory is browns have adapted to their environment and begun to spawn in the lake.

Nonetheless, there is a stable population of browns. Most of Tahoe's browns run three-to-six pounds. But, that's not to say there aren't larger fish available. While many anglers will argue the point, Tahoe likely has the best chance to kick out a new state record brown. This may sound odd considering that anglers don't consider it a brown trout lake. But, look at things this way. Tahoe is known as a lake trout fishery. A few anglers know of the great brown trout fishery, yet they keep it to themselves. Tahoe's browns aren't maintained by stocking, rather natural spawning. They are a delicate breed. If not released when caught, it could do serious harm to the fishery.

Tahoe's browns aren't easy to catch. They are the toughest species to target in the lake. If you fish during sunny days, catch rates will likely suffer. It's best to fish when there's a good chop on the water or under wintry conditions. Tahoe's biggest browns are hooked when it's cold, snowing and windy.

Browns show best in winter and early spring. Toplining shallow water areas, across points and flats are best. Most browns are taken from 30 feet and shallower. Many anglers drag a night crawler and flashers or minnows behind a dodger in 40 feet of water year round and catch browns, but action can be slow.

The biggest browns are taken on swimbaits. The key is to find one with a bill. Unfortunately, you can't troll swimbaits without a bill. An eight-inch Castaic Soft Bait or Megabait Charlie are some of the best baits on the market. On the other hand, don't discount fishing Rebels, lighted J-Plugs and Bomber Long A's.

There is also an

This 10-pound lake trout grabbed a J-Plug in Emerald Bay.

abundance of wild rainbow trout in Tahoe. They can be caught year round except in April and May when they are spawning in the lake's tributaries. Rainbows start up tributaries when the water hits about 45 degrees. However, once the bows get big, they don't need to spawn every year. Some remain in the lake. On a positive note, regulations prohibit fishing these tributaries during the spawn.

The California Department of Fish and Game no longer plants rainbow trout. The last plant took place in 1997. Prior, 10,000 half-pound trout were planted. Near Cave Rock, the Nevada Division of Wildlife (NDOW) plants 40,000 rainbows a year. Tahoe isn't a great planter lake, but anglers trolling Kastmasters and Krocodiles in front of Cave Rock, along Incline Beach and Sand Harbor can catch limits of small trout.

For the most part, shore fishing at Tahoe can be slow. Don't get me wrong, there are several areas where anglers can catch rainbows from shore, but the overall success rate isn't great. Try Cave Rock, Emerald Bay, Sand Harbor and Kings Beach. The same baits that catch browns work on rainbows. Most of the bows run two-to-four pounds, but fish to 12 pounds have been noted. Nielsen is the lake's expert rainbow and brown trout angler. If you want to learn how to catch big rainbows and browns, book at trip with him. He's one of the best in the country. Nielsen tracks the fish daily throughout the year. Trolling can be great, however, you have to be at the right depth, which changes drastically with the time of day and water temperature.

Skilled Tahoe trout anglers know the secret to catching the big bows: finding pollen on the surface in the middle of the lake. Most anglers, however, don't take the time to locate the pollen. Those who do are often successful catching large silver side rainbows. The rainbows feed heavily on the pollen.

Tahoe's cutthroats were last seen in 1939. While efforts have been made to reintroduce the fish, all have failed. The CA DFG planted 700,000 fingerling cutts in the early Sixties, yet not one was ever caught, seen or heard of. From 1956-62, more than one million fingerling and yearling cutts were introduced. The most detrimental event to hurt the cutthroat fishery was the instillation of Derby Dam on Pyramid Lake in Nevada and Lake Tahoe's Dam

in Tahoe City. The cutthroats used to spawn between the two lakes. and were no longer permitted to do so.

There are still brook trout near many of the lake's inlets. However, they refuse to enter the main body of the lake, probably terrified that they will be eaten by the lake trout. I don't blame them. Don't expect to catch a brook trout.

The Tahoe Keys has

An eight-pound wild rainbow from Lake Tahoe.

581

become a prime bass fishing area. In fact, all warm water species have done well here. All of these species were illegally introduced and luckily haven't left The Keys to take over parts of the main lake where they would compete with the trout. Because the water in the main body is too cold, the warm water fish stay in the Keys. Also, there are more nutrients. The Keys are loaded with largemouth bass to five pounds and more crappie and bluegill than you'd want to catch. Fish a night crawler below a bobber near any of the docks and you'll do fine.

Sometimes equipment must be sacraficed in the name of research. Sadly, this Suburban left us in Lake Tahoe.

If you plan to make the trip, supplies are available in dozens of cities around the lake. A California license is required on California shoreline and a Nevada license from Nevada shore. Either is acceptable on boat. Use caution when launching a boat when there are white caps on the lake. The lake can look like an ocean minutes after winds kick up and becomes very dangerous for boaters. Only four-stroke engines are permitted.

Also nearby are Truckee River, Cascade Lake, Eagle Lake and Sawmill Pond.

Directions: *From Sacramento, Lake Tahoe can be reached by traveling east on Highway 50 to South Lake Tahoe or east on Interstate 80 to the Highway 89 south or Highway 267 Kings Beach turnoff.*

Sunrise at Lake Tahoe

TRUCKEE RIVER (MAIN STEM)

Rating: 9

Species: Rainbow Trout, Brown Trout, Brook Trout and Cutthroat Trout

Stocks: Cutthroat are planted periodically.

Facilities: Picnic Areas, Restrooms and Campgrounds

Need Information? Contact: Truckee River Outfitters (530) 582-0900, Reno Fly Shop (775) 825-3474

The Truckee River is one of the better fly fishing waters in California. The river is lush with rainbow trout and offers some of the largest brown trout found in any river system in California. It's not uncommon to catch five-to-10-pound browns in the fall if you know what you are doing. The wild trout portion of the river unofficially stems from River Ranch to the Nevada state line, however, the best fishing is found from Truckee downstream. There's less water and too many rafters upstream of Truckee which keeps angling more productive downstream.

This section of the Truckee is managed as a wild trout stream. It is rich with insects and forage fish, helping rainbows and browns grow faster than they would in most systems. The Truckee is governed by special regulations and is the ideal water for spin fishermen and fly anglers.

Spring can be tough to predict. Action leans heavily on water and weather conditions. The amount of snowmelt dictates where fish will be in the water column, when hatches occur and how difficult fishing may be due to high water levels. Traditionally, June is a prime month for anglers to cash in on several hatches, including little yellow stoneflies, yellow stoneflies, various caddis and pale morning dunns.

Applying scent to lures and flies can increase catch rates

By early June, anglers in the know watch for the green drakes. The green drakes provide the best dry fly fishing on the river. Again, depending on the weather, the hatch may occur in June or early summer. During summer, nymph fishing is productive. Hairs ears, prince nymphs and the smallest midge pattern you can find will do the trick.

By late summer and into fall, crawdad patterns are standard for the big browns. When water levels drop, you'll find the big browns resting on the bottom. A size 10-12 crawfish pattern offers your best chance at browns that can breach 10 pounds. Anglers using an indictor and fishing big crawdad patterns in deep holes near the bottom will be in the strike zone.

Since the turn of the century, the US Fish & Wildlife Service has made an effort to reintroduce cutthroat to the Truckee. Sadly though, the stocks have

gone to waste as anglers see no sign of fish in the system. In reality though, the cutts have done a great job allowing the browns to grow to trophy sizes quicker. Rainbows (many trophy size) are the most common catch. Browns are available to anglers who specialize in fishing the deeper holes.

If you plan to make the trip, supplies are available in Truckee and Reno. The Truckee River is closed to fishing from November 16 to the last Saturday in April. For updated closures, bag limits and gear restrictions, please consult updated sportfishing regulations.

Also nearby are Lake Tahoe and Donner Lake.

Directions: *From Sacramento, drive east on Interstate 80 to Truckee. Access can be found off Highway 89 south, in the town of Truckee and at various locations further east along Interstate 80. Consult a local map for more in depth details.*

584   Rainbows like this one caught by Christopher Crawley are common at nearby Donner Lake, but not in the Truckee River.

MARTIS CREEK RESERVOIR

Rating: 7

Species: Rainbow Trout, Brown Trout, Cutthroat Trout and Green Sunfish

Stocked with 270 pounds of fingerling cutthroat trout.

Facilities: Campgrounds and Restrooms

Need Information? Contact: Truckee River Outfitters (530) 530-0900

Martis Creek Reservoir was once known as one of the premier wild trout fisheries in Northern California. Prior to the mid-to-late Seventies, Martis was an excellent brown trout fishery. However, the fishery has gone through astronomical changes in the last few decades.

The California Department of Fish and Game chemically treated the lake in the mid-to-late Seventies. The concept was to remove all non-native gamefish and restore Lahonton cutthroat, a fish that is native to the drainage. The treatment was successful, but only for a limited time. The cutthroat fishery excelled for a few years. Unfortunately, the non-native fish returned. The CA DFG has two theories: anglers illegally transported the fish into Martis or some of the non-natives avoided death by swimming up the lake's tributaries. Nonetheless, within five years the browns were again in charge.

Still, Martis is a productive reservoir. The reservoir is choked with nutrients and small fish. Lahonton redside minnows, Tahoe suckers and green sunfish provide rapid growing pills for the trout. In the Eighties, the CA DFG changed their management plan to include rainbows. At the present time there are rainbows, browns and cutthroat in the lake, but new issues have arrived.

The smaller fish help and hurt the trout. What happens is the smaller, non-game fish provide a good food source for the trout,

A Martis brown trout

but at the same time tie up nutrients the trout would normally consume.

Furthermore, the CA DFG believes that rainbows and cutthroat aren't spawning in Martis Creek as they did in the past. The population of trout is now supplemented with fish plants. Roughly 6,000 fingerling cutts were planted in 2003.

Soon, Martis may have even more to deal with. The Army Corp of Engineers has had trouble with Martis Dam. Due to leakage, issues they have to keep the lake at a minimal pool, which affects water quality issues. Water temperature, a decrease in nutrients and development in the region has been devastating to the fishery. Much of the water is being diverted off Martis Creek and used for ski resorts, golf courses and homes. In addition, activists are

A Martis rainbow trout

pushing for the removal of Martis Dam altogether.

For now, Martis can be an awesome fishery for fly anglers and spin casters. You have to use barbless hooks, but I've had days where I've caught and released more than 50 trout in an evening on a Panther Martin. Float tubers and those with waders or a car top boat have a big advantage over shoreline anglers.

If you plan to make the trip, supplies are available in Truckee. All fishing is catch and release. Only artificial lures with barbless hooks may be used. Martis Creek Reservoir is closed to fishing from November 16 to the last Saturday in April.

Also nearby are Lake Tahoe, Truckee River and Donner Lake.

Directions: *From Interstate 80 in Truckee, take the Highway 267/Kings Beach exit and continue to the left turnoff for the reservoir.*

Sunset at Martis Reservoir

Rating: 6

Species: Rainbow Trout, Brook Trout and Brown Trout

Stocked with 200 pounds of rainbow trout.

Facilities: Restaurant, Gas, Lodging, Bait & Tackle, Restrooms and Raft Rentals

Need Information? Contact: River Ranch (800) 535-9900

The Truckee River in the Tahoe Basin is known for four things: Fanny Bridge, Lake Tahoe's outlet, calm family style rafting opportunities and lastly, fishing. While fishing used to be a huge hit, the days when the California Department of Fish and Game planted nearly 50,000 trout annually are long gone. Today, budget cuts have limited the number of allotted fish to less than 500. Coupled with the number of vacationers that fish in this heavily used summer tourist trap, most planted fish are caught within a day or two of the stock.

Fanny Bridge is the bridge located just downriver of Lake Tahoe. The fame stems from giant rainbow and brown trout that tourists feed all day, nearly every day of the year. There are roughly 100 lunkers between three and 20 pounds between the bridge and Tahoe's dam. Unfortunately, these fish are protected. No fishing is permitted from the dam to 1,000 feet downriver.

From the bridge to River Ranch, (the same stretch of water that is planted by the CA DFG) rafters mob the river from 10 a.m. to 5 p.m. daily. Rafts are available for rent in Tahoe City. It's not uncommon to see hundreds on the river daily. The trip is a calm, relaxing drift complete with Class I and II rapids. Anglers may find it helpful to use it as a 3.5-mile ride to learn the river. Bring along a mask and snorkel, make a few pit stops and take a dip. Quickly, you'll notice that the river harbors large, deep pools complete with planted and wild trout. In fact, some huge browns inhabit this section.

A limit of trout from the Truckee River

If you plan to make the trip, supplies are available in Tahoe City. The Truckee River is closed to fishing from November 16 to the last Saturday in April.

Also nearby is Squaw Valley Ski Area, Donner Lake and Derby Pond.

Directions: *From the junction of Interstate 80 and 5 in Sacramento, drive east on I-80 to the junction with Highway 89 south. Exit, Highway 89, turn right and drive 11 miles to River Ranch.*

OLD CALTRANS QUARRY POND

Rating: 4

Species: Rainbow Trout

Stocked with 5,000 pounds of rainbow trout.

Facilities: Restrooms, Campgrounds and Picnic Areas

Without a substantial and appreciated effort from members of the city of Truckee, the Old Caltrans Pond located inside Donner State Park would be barren of fish. In order to give back to the community and provide children the opportunity to catch trout with little effort, the Bob Tilton Family, Truckee Rotary Club and the Nevada County Fish and Game Commission host a kids only fishing derby annually at the pond.

For the last decade the Tilton Family solely funded the derby. Bob Tilton used to own and operate a specialty fishing tackle shop in Truckee and was a local fishing guide before closing his business down because of too much competition. Tilton vied to keep the spirit of fishing alive and well in the community and came up with the idea of the derby.

The Old Caltrans Quarry Pond was formed when Interstate 80 was being built over Donner Pass. The pond ended up filling with water during a flood nearly a half-century ago. Recently, the Rotary Club and Fish and Game Commission have taken on much of the payment for the fish. The Tilton family pays for 50 trophy fish from five-to-10 pounds. In all, Mt. Lassen Trout Farm delivers about 5,000 pounds of rainbow trout a few weeks before the derby. Some years, the California Department of Fish and Game also plants fish. The actual derby is for children 12 and younger and is held sometime in July. Catch & release is discouraged. Because the pond is small and gets fairly warm by mid-summer, if the trout aren't caught they eventually will be found floating on the surface. To catch the trout, fish within a few weeks of the derby with bait, spinners or spoons.

Directions *and trip info for Donner Creek also apply to Old Caltrans Quarry Pond.*

A Brown Trout caught and released at Donner Ponds

A Brook Trout

DONNER STATE PARK PONDS

Rating: 8

Species: Rainbow Trout, Brown Trout, Brook Trout and Cutthroat Trout

Stocked with 10 pounds of fingerling cutthroat trout.

Facilities: None

If you pull out a map and slide the tip of your finger across the paper looking for Donner State Park Ponds, chances are you'll have trouble finding it. In fact, I can guarantee it. On a map, it's likely the ponds will show up as gravel quarries. Located near Cold Creek, these ponds are sandwiched between Donner Lake and the Southern Pacific Railroad tracks on the grounds of Donner Memorial State Park. The ponds were created during the construction of Interstate 80. Gravel was taken from this area for the freeway.

When heavy floods occurred in the Fifties, Cold Creek overflowed and filled in the gravel pits. Along with the water came rainbows, browns and brooks. The fish entered Cold Creek by migrating up from the Truckee River.

The ponds are referred to as food baskets. Because there is so much feed available, the trout grow fast. All species reach the three-to-four-pound class. Recently, the California Department of Fish and Game planted brooks, rainbows and browns. Since 1997, the CA DFG has also attempted to introduce sub-catchable cutthroat trout, but they've yet to take to the environment as they are likely being eaten. The CA DFG's idea is to one day use the ponds as a brood stock fishery. The eggs would be used to aid in the Lahonton cutthroat recovery plan.

Donner State Park Ponds used to be on private land, but California State Parks purchased the property in the mid-Nineties, opening them for public use. Fly-fishing is great. A float tube is best though. There is great shoreline access. Try tossing large Panther Martins or float night crawlers off the bottom. To locate the ponds pick up a map at the entrance kiosk. Springs help keep the ponds fresh with water year round, but they do freeze in the winter.

Directions *and trip info for Donner Creek also apply to Donner State Park Ponds.*

David Savage used a Thomas Buoyant to trick this fat brook trout at Donner State Park Ponds in the fall.

DONNER CREEK

Rating: 4

Species: Rainbow Trout and Brown Trout

Stocks: None

Facilities: Restrooms, Campgrounds and Picnic Areas

Need Information?
Contact: Donner State Park (530) 582-7892

For a few months out of the year, Donner Creek can be a great place for anglers to target huge browns. However, for most of the year Donner Creek holds few fish. The big browns can be found in March, April and May when they leave the Truckee River and swim up Donner Creek. While there aren't many, browns to eight pounds are common. Oddly enough, few anglers fish this part of the stream, located between Highway 89 and Donner Lake.

From its' outlet at Donner Lake to the Truckee River, Donner Creek stems 2.5 miles. Most anglers stick to fishing near the dam where some small stocked rainbow trout get flushed in. Every so often the California Department of Fish and Game dumps an extra load of fish into the stream. With easy access, most of the fish get caught fast. Any color of Power Bait or small spinner will prompt these stockers to bite. For the big browns, use a big bait.

If you plan to make the trip, supplies are available in Truckee. There is a fee to enter Donner State Park. Donner Creek is closed to fishing from November 16 to the last Saturday in April.

Also nearby are Old Caltrans Quarry Pond, Donner Lake and Donner State Park Ponds.

Directions: *From the junction of Highway 89 and Interstate 80 in Truckee, exit south on Highway 89 and drive two-tenths of a mile to Donner Pass Road. Turn right and continue one mile the entrance to the state park on the left.*

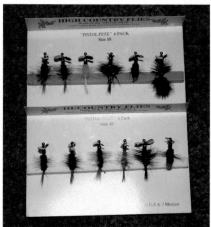

DONNER LAKE

Rating: 9

Species: Rainbow Trout, Brown Trout, Kokanee and Lake Trout

Stocked with 27,000 pounds of rainbow trout, 145 pounds of fingerling lake trout and 297 pounds of fingerling kokanee.

Facilities: Lodging, Boat Rentals, RV Sites, Campgrounds, Swimming Area, Picnic Area, Fishing Piers, Boat Launch, Restrooms, Fish Cleaning Stations and a Playground

Need Information? Contact: Mountain Hardware (530) 587-4844, Donner Lake Marina (530) 582-5112

Donner Lake's fishery can be looked at two ways. From Memorial Day through Labor Day, Donner is one of the most crowded high mountain lakes in the state. Thousands of tourists and locals swim, fish, water-ski, wake board and walk the shoreline of this 960-acre lake. It's crowded, definitely not ideal for fishing.

Fishing is best when tourism sags, however. After Labor Day, Donner becomes a ghost town. At 6,000 feet in the Tahoe National Forest, Donner is an incredible top of the line trophy lake trout and brown trout fishery, but it's not for everyone. You have to be an avid angler to catch the big boys because it's cold when they bite best.

Lake trout get huge here! Huge! The recipe for a possible state record lake trout includes a well balanced diet of stocked rainbows, kokanee, minnows and crawdads. Caught in June of 2000 on a green Apex, the lake record stands at 34 pounds, but it may not last long.

The comparison between Tahoe and Donner is an endless debate. Tahoe has a greater quantity of large fish. However, Donner's fish are more concentrated, making them easier to target (not necessarily to catch). Donner's lake trout also have an easier time corralling their prey, thus requiring them to expend less energy feeding. Donner's lake trout grow faster than Tahoe's. You'll notice Donner's have small heads and large bodies, a sign that they are growing fast.

Donner is a deep lake (262 feet), it's three-quarters of a mile long and has great structure for fish. The key to catching the lake trout is to follow the thermocline. Easier said than done though. The locals sure aren't going to give you information that would risk making these big dogs venerable! Only a select few who have proven they know how to fish the lake and practice catch and release know the secret. As a hint, keep in mind that traditionally J-Plugs have produced the biggest lake trout here. It is also important to find out what the lake trout are feeding on and to use a lure that resembles the food source.

Let's touch on the obvious; lake trout feed on stocked trout in the summer and whatever insects get flushed in with spring runoff from Donner Creek. If you can figure what patterns and minnow imitations they feed on in the fall, you'll be in business.

On average, Donner know-hows catch 12-pound lake trout in the fall, with 15-25 pounders caught weekly. Beginners, on the other hand, are custom to smaller four to six pounders before they learn the secrets of the masters.

Jigging can also be good if the wind is down, but it's a more subtle method than used in Tahoe. Some odd years, Donner can freeze in the winter.

Summer is a nightmare for anglers on boats. Wakeboarders and water-skiers are extremely careless out here. I have an old friend who said it gets so bad that he keeps a paintball gun on his fishing boat to discourage waterskiers from tipping his old boat over with a big wake! In the summer, you need to shorten your lines or risk having them cut off by careless boaters.

Donner is also a great planter lake. It boasts spectacular shoreline access on the north shore. There are rocky shores, fishing piers, docks and flat dirt openings between pines. The California Department of Fish and Game spills more than 52,000 half-pound bows into the lake.

Prior to the Nineties, Donner used to support kokanee as well. Unfortunately, the kokanee fishery is now far below average. Kokanee are available, yet an eight- to 12-inch average is too small to prompt anglers to fish for them. To catch them, hit the lake in June or July trolling Hum Dingers and Needlefish in 60 to 70 feet of water. From August through September target them in 30-50 feet. The CA DFG planted 47,520 fingerling kokanee in 2003.

Donner's browns can be enormous. Big browns are seldom caught, but anglers dragging Bomber Long A's, Rebel holographic minnows and YO-Zuri's from mid-October through December have the opportunity to nab a few monsters. March and April are also good months to target the browns.

If you plan to make the trip, supplies are available in Truckee. There is a day-use launching fee in the summer and all services are closed down in the winter (even the restrooms). Ice and snow are common on the launch ramp during the winter.

Also nearby are Donner Creek, Derby Pond and Donner State Park Ponds.

Directions: From the junction of Highway 89 and Interstate 80 in Truckee, exit south on Highway 89 and drive two-tenths of a mile to Donner Pass Road. Turn right and continue one mile to the lake.

Donner Lake

PROSSER RESERVOIR

Rating: 7

Species: Rainbow Trout, Brown Trout and Smallmouth Bass

Stocked with 8,000 pounds of rainbow trout and 250 pounds of fingerling rainbow trout.

Facilities: Restrooms, Boat Launch and Campgrounds

Need Information? Contact: Tahoe National Forest (530) 587-3558, Mountain Hardware (530) 587-4844

Prosser Lake is one of the best and most consistent ice fishing lakes in Northern California. At 5,711 feet in the Tahoe National Forest, this 734-acre reservoir typically freezes over in late December and can stay frozen as late as mid-April. While most of the fish landed are pan size, catch rates can be staggeringly high.

As soon as the ice melts away and the road to the lake is plowed, Prosser turns into one of the best stocked lakes in the region. For trollers and bank anglers, fishing is superb. Most of the trout are put in at a half-pound and tend to be about a pound by the time they are landed. There are also thousands of holdovers up to three pounds. It's unfortunate; however, that reproduction seldom occurs.

Float tubers do well fishing the Prosser Creek inlet in the spring. The area is too shallow for boats and can be difficult to fish because of hoards of tree stumps and bushes. For trollers, work the area near Lakeside Campground and the dam. Shore anglers do well fishing off the dam and the points near the Prosser Creek inlet. With 15,400 half-pound rainbow trout and more than 50,000 fingerlings planted each year, there's always good opportunities to be had.

Smallmouth bass were illegally introduced a while back and have since begun to flourish. Word on the street is that a few local bass enthusiasts caught the fish in Almanor and drove them to Prosser. The smallies tend to be in the one-to-three-pound class and are caught near tree stumps by the Prosser Creek inlet in the spring and off the dam in the summer as they try to capitalize on crawdads that reside in the rocks there.

If you plan to make the trip, supplies are available in Truckee. In winter and spring, call ahead for road conditions. The roads to the lake may be closed due to snow. Call the Forest Service in advance to make sure the ice is safe enough to walk on.

Also nearby are Stampede Reservoir and Boca Reservoir.

Prosser Reservoir freezes in the winter

Directions: From Interstate 80 in Truckee, exit Highway 89 north and drive 3.8 miles to the Prosser Reservoir turnoff. Turn right and drive one mile to the campground and lake on the left.

SAGEHEN CREEK

Rating: 6

Species: Rainbow
Trout, Brown Trout and
Brook Trout

Stocks: None

Facilities: None

Need Information?
Contact: Truckee
River Outfitters
(530) 582-0900

Sagehen Creek is an interesting water in the greater Truckee region. It is a small, seldom fished spring-fed mountain stream where you'll run into easily spooked fish. Its complexity is broken up by Highway 89 Bridge which divides the creek in separate areas. Downstream is governed by general fishing regulations where any legal bait can be used and five fish may be taken. On the other hand, upstream is set aside for the wild trout project and is on a catch and release basis only.

In the special regulations area you'll find exclusively fly fishermen. The stream is rigged with mostly browns, but some rainbows and brooks. The browns run in the seven-to-10-inch class, with a few larger ones mixed in. As you move towards the headwaters though, you'll discover that brook trout own the stream.

Sagehen Creek

If you plan to make the trip, supplies are available in Truckee. To reiterate, Sagehen Creek is governed by special regulations from the Highway 89 Bridge to the east boundary of the UC Sagehen Creek Field Station. Sagehen Creek is closed to fishing from November 16 to the last Saturday in April.

Also nearby are the Upper Truckee River, Stampede Reservoir and Coldstream Creek.

Directions: From the junction of Highway 89 and Interstate 80 in Truckee drive north on Highway 89 to the Sagehen Creek crossing.

BOCA RESERVOIR

Rating: 6

Species: Rainbow Trout, Brown Trout and Kokanee

Stocked with 9,000 pounds of rainbow trout and 47,520 fingerling kokanee.

Facilities: Boat Launch and Restrooms

Need Information? Contact: Tahoe National Forest (530) 587-3558, Mountain Hardware (530) 587-4844

Ice fishing in Northern California is a concept that many anglers have been unable to grasp. Living in the West, most folks don't consider ice fishing a viable option. They are scared that the ice isn't thick enough to venture out on and are unfamiliar with the basic techniques required to fish.

At 5,600 feet in the Tahoe National Forest, Boca is a top choice in the Tahoe-Truckee Region for ice fishing. The ice is safer than many nearby lakes because Boca is shallower and the ice freezes faster and gets thicker.

Boca is one of the easiest lakes to ice fish in the Tahoe region. Unfortunately, it's not always a guarantee. Boca can be dependable for ice fishing one day and unsafe the next. Varying weather in the Truckee region can freeze and thaw Boca several times during the winter. Traditionally, the lake is fishable through the ice on and off from late December through March.

When Boca is frozen and safe, a ice auger and night crawlers fished near the dam can fill your creel in a matter of minutes. Oftentimes, fishing can be good for a few days and then shuts off. Because you can drive to the dam heavy pressure is common. The area can get fished out fast.

Fishing the 980-acre lake right after ice out is your best shot at catching a limit of trout. Unfortunately, at this time, usually early March, the launch ramp is unavailable because the lake is down so low its a few hundred yards out of the water. The only way to launch a boat is on the lake's east shore right off the dirt. It can be difficult to launch boats over 15 yards; however, four-wheel drive vehicles usually don't have a problem. The reward for

Big Todd McLean with a bow caught through Boca's ice 595

launching here is you can see your car at all times (there's been a recent problem with break-ins) and the low water levels keep the fish concentrated and easier to target. Trolling the shorelines and crisscrossing the middle of the lake with Krocodiles and Needlefish produces limits of 10-12 inch bows and a few lucky anglers nab a big brown.

Each year a few lunker browns are taken from the lake, yet the number of browns doesn't promote anglers to target them. Rainbows, on the other hand, are plentiful. The California Department of Fish and Game dumps 17,100 half-pound fish into the lake each year.

Kokanee fishing changes year by year. In the summer months look for the kokanee near the dam. However, these fish are much smaller than those at Stampede. The kokanee average 12-13 inches. Each year, 47,520 fingerling kokanee are planted. Summer is marked by evening trout anglers fishing bait off the bottom and trollers fighting for space with water-skiers.

If you plan to make the trip, supplies are available in Truckee. In early spring and late summer call ahead for launching conditions. The lake may be too low to launch. Always check the thickness of the ice before venturing out on it.

Also nearby are Stampede Reservoir, Truckee River, Prosser Reservoir and Martis Creek Reservoir.

Directions: From Interstate 80 in Truckee, drive east to and exit north on Stampede Meadows Road. Continue 1.5 miles to the reservoir.

Boca Reservoir is a great ice fishing reservoir when the ice is thick enough to permit angling.

LITTLE TRUCKEE RIVER

Rating: 8

Species: Rainbow Trout, Brown Trout and Kokanee Salmon

Stocks: None

Facilities: Picnic Areas and Restrooms

Need Information? Contact: Truckee River Outfitters (530) 582-0900

This lower section of the Little Truckee River, between Stampede and Boca Reservoir, is a classic tailwater fishery with excellent results for fly anglers and spin casters. The Little Truckee hasn't always been a great trout fishery though. Prior to the late Nineties, the river was governed by general fishing regulations which allowed anglers to toss Power Bait and keep a bag limit of five. Luckily, in the late Nineties the California Department of Fish and Game adopted new regulations.

From the Stampede Reservoir Dam downstream to Boca Reservoir, only artificial lures with barbless hooks may be used. The bag limit is two with the maximum size limit of 14 inches in total length. No longer are trout planted in this section. However, many planted fish swim upriver from Boca Reservoir to spawn each year, some of which become resident fish.

The new regs have paved the way for the river to act like a wild trout stream. The quantity and quality of the fish has increased gradually since the new regs were put in place. Before the new regs, a limit of five trout could be lifted out of the system on opening day. Now those fish are kept in the system and allowed to grow larger.

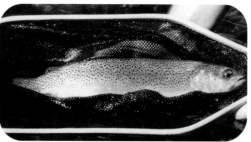

A Little Truckee rainbow

Split between Sierra and Nevada Counties, the Little Truckee is a medium size river in a dry, sage terrain. It has an abundance of plant life on the bottom, which in turn attracts insects and creates a healthy food source.

During the summer, heat can put a damper on the bite. The best action is during early morning and late evening. Fortunately in the fall, action lasts throughout the day. Try fishing a big terrestrial on the surface with a 5x tippet.

You may get lucky and nab a five-pound brown. There are both resident rainbows and browns available. PMD's, caddis and blue wing olives also work. You can almost always catch fish on dry flies. Don't discount green drakes or a stonefly grasshopper imitation.

On the other hand, nymphing can be great too. Drifting a size 16 San Juan worm is likely your best option. Many anglers use droppers: a size 18 copper john or a flashy pheasant tail is a good bet.

If you are fishing the Little Truckee for big fish, fall is the best time to arrive. During the fall, many big browns swim out of Boca and up the river to

feed on spawning kokanee and their eggs. Browns to eight pounds are common in the system during this time of the year.

If you plan to make the trip, supplies are available in Truckee. The Little Truckee River is closed to fishing from November 16 to the last Saturday in April. Check updated sport fishing regulations.

Also nearby are Stampede Reservoir and the Truckee River.

Directions: *From Interstate 80 in Truckee, drive east and exit north on Stampede Meadows Road. Continue 1.5 miles to Boca Reservoir. Ignore the left turnoff for the dam and continue straight. You'll drive along Boca's shoreline and then parallel the Little Truckee River. It will be on your left.*

Chris Evison caught and released this fat rainbow trout in the Little Truckee River in June of 2002.

STAMPEDE RESERVOIR

Rating: 9

Species: Rainbow
Trout, Largemouth
Bass, Smallmouth Bass,
Kokanee, Lake Trout
and Brown Trout

Stocked with 3,000
pounds of brown trout,
286 pounds of
fingerling kokanee,
140 pounds of
fingerling lake trout and
4,000 pounds of
rainbow trout.

Facilities: Boat Launch,
Campgrounds and
Restrooms

Need Information?
Contact: Fishing Guide
Keith Kerrigan
(530) 582-5689,
Mountain Hardware
(530) 587-4844

In the last decade, Stampede Reservoir has gone from an average trout fishery to one of the most productive and diverse fisheries in the state. There is no shortage of species to target. Lake trout, brown trout, rainbow trout, kokanee and small and largemouth bass inhabit the lake, and all but the largemouth have developed stable populations. At 3,450 acres, Stampede, which is located in a high desert environment about 20 minutes from Truckee, has enough room for all species.

The most heavily targeted fish is kokanee. Stampede has developed into one of the premier kokanee fisheries in the state and that sure isn't a secret. The number of anglers that show up to catch them is staggering. From 4:30 a.m. to 10 a.m. the lake looks like a boat show. Hoping to get in on the action anywhere from 25-75 boats will circle the area where the kokanee have stationed themselves. It reminds me of Southern California's Lake Skinner when striper fishermen target the boils. It's too crowded for me, but those who enjoy kokanee fishing love it. Kokanee are abundant in the lake, most of which are 15-19 inches, however, they can and do reach 22 inches.

Action begins in May and lasts through September. The kokanee start in May at the west end coming out of the Little Truckee and Sagehen Arms in 15-35 feet of water. As summer arrives they'll begin to work towards the dam, clustering up to prepare to spawn. Once they near the dam the bite begins to slow, as the fish no longer focus on feeding. The kokanee then return to the inlets to spawn, which typically occurs in the end of September and October.

In May, experienced kokanee fishermen can expect to land 25-30 fish a day if fishing in 35 feet of water. As summer approaches the heat begins to put a damper on the bite and the fish relocate to deeper water. In June, the fish are found at 50 feet in the early morning and as soon as the sun hits the water, they dive down to 60-65 feet. By the time August rolls around kokanee move into 80-90 feet. At the start of the kokanee season use a green dodger with a purple and pink bug. If that doesn't work, experiment. It can be a matter of trial and error. Switch colors and vary your depth five-to-10 feet. Nearly 50,000 kokanee are planted each year.

If the kokanee bite is off, the rainbow trout bite seldom suffers. It can provide staggering catch rates for those trolling the shorelines and in coves. The California Department of Fish and Game unloads 6,400 half-pound rainbows and yet few anglers target them. Some of the planters get swallowed by the lake trout and others by the browns. However, most remain untouched and wait for anglers to troll small spoons or float Power Bait off the dam.

Stampede commonly freezes over in January until early April. As soon as the ice thaws though, the browns go on the prowl, and there are some big ones to be caught. The CA DFG plants 8,700 sub-catchable browns annually. An unofficial lake record is said to be more than 20 pounds. Those tipping the scales over 10 pounds are common after ice out. Nevertheless, they still aren't targeted. Most anglers are frightened by the strong winds and cold weather, staying away this time of year. Additionally, the road isn't plowed. If there is snow on the road it can be tough to get a boat on the water.

As for the lake trout, they are relatively new to the lake. Lake trout were introduced in the mid-Nineties. Their population has yet to explode, but is definitely on its' way. The fish have matured to where they can spawn. The first spawn took place in 2000 and there are some 10-20 pounders in the lake, however, most of them are still on the small side. The lake record is 22 pounds. The missing element that would enable the lake trout to grow to enormous proportions is shrimp and the CA DFG is debating whether or not to introduce them. Roughly 49,000 fingerling lake trout are stocked.

The improved smallmouth bass fishery has many kokanee anglers worried. Smallmouth were illegally brought in from Lake Almanor. At the present time crawdads are thick in the lake, however, if the smallmouth continue to grow in numbers and feed on the crawdads, the lake's water quality will decrease. Crawdads keep the bottom clean and if they disappear poor water quality would devastate the kokanee fishery. As you may have guessed, the kokanee anglers would love to remove the bass out of the lake.

If you plan to make the trip, supplies are available in Truckee. Winds pick up at Stampede each day around noon, about the same time the water-skiers hit the lake.

Also nearby are Prosser Reservoir, Boca Reservoir, the Little Truckee River and the Truckee River.

Directions: *From Interstate 80 in Truckee drive east to Stampede Dam Truckee Road and exit north. Drive 10 miles to Forest Service Road 19N69 and turn left. Drive across the dam to the campground and boat launch.*

Keith Kerrigan caught this monster kokanee at Stampede Reservoir

Region 21

Grouse Ridge Region

Milton Reservoir
Jackson Meadows Reservoir
Catfish Lake
Tollhouse Lake
Meadow Lake
Weaver Lake
Mc Murry Lake
Bowman Lake
Sawmill Lake
Faucherie Lake
Lindsay Lake (Lower)
Lindsay Lake (Middle)
Colbertson Lake
Rock Lake (Lower)
Rock Lake (Upper)
Carr Lake
Feely Lake
Lily Pad Lake
Little Island Lake
Island Lake
Long Lake
Round Lake
Milk Lake
Rucker Lake
Fuller Lake
Spaulding Reservoir
Lake of the Woods
Independence Lake
Little Truckee River (Upper)
Coldstream Creek

MILTON RESERVOIR

Rating: 7

Species: Rainbow Trout
and Brown Trout

Stocks: None

Facilities: None

Need Information?
Contact: Truckee River
Outfitters
(530) 582-0900

There's a big difference between waters people think are secret and actual secret waters. While many anglers think Milton Reservoir is top secret, it's on the radar scope of nearly every fly fishermen that has ever fished the Truckee region. Designated a wild trout water, Milton is a quality brown trout fishery that shouldn't be overlooked.

Milton is a 70-acre tailwater fishery set at 5,700 feet in the Tahoe National Forest, just downstream of Jackson Meadow Reservoir. At one time, Milton held tons of browns between five-and 10 pounds. Nevertheless, things are different now. The lake had issues with bullhead and was consequently poisoned to remove them. Then in 1993, it was drained to repair the dam and remove silt. The California Department of Fish and Game used this as an opportunity to add fish habitat before restocking Milton with a few strains of browns and browns taken from Jackson Meadow Reservoir.

Currently, Milton is the only lake in the wild trout project that has a maximum size limit. The word on the street is that the limit is set to keep the bullhead population in check. Big browns eat bullhead. There are still big browns in Milton, but not as big as they used to be. There are also rainbows in lesser numbers.

With good hatches and good vegetation, this shallow water reservoir is

Rattlesnakes are prevalent near Milton Lake during the fishing season.

an ideal pick for 16-19 inch browns. The most well-known local fly fishing guru, Andy Burke, has landed 27-28 inch browns. However, he's seen one fish that was 10-11 pounds. Milton is a technical fishery as far as presentation goes. These browns are wary fish; attributed to a combination of shallow water, angler pressure and fear of natural predators such as osprey.

Browns reproduce in Milton in the fall, rainbows in the spring. Both species use the Middle Fork of the Yuba River to spawn. When is the best time to fish? Good question. It depends on snow pack. There will be years where you can't get into Milton until May. It's safe to say late June and July, and again in late September, are best. Midge fishing can be tremendous. Try a little midge pupa in rusty orange, olive, black or gray, size 18-22.

If you really want to be impressed, keep a close eye on the forecast. The flying ant hatch is amazing. Although it's only a two-day event, it's the best fishing Milton offers. This hatch typically occurs the first day it hits 78-80 degrees. Then, you'll want to throw size eight and 10's. There are some huge carpenter ants in this neck of the woods.

If you plan to make the trip, supplies are available in Truckee. In spring call ahead for road conditions. The road may be closed due to snow.

Also nearby are Jackson Meadow Reservoir and Independence Lake.

Directions: *From Interstate 80 in Truckee, exit Highway 89 and drive 17.5 miles north to Forest Service Road 07. Turn left and drive 17.3 miles to an unsigned dirt road on the right for Milton Reservoir. Turn right and drive two miles to the lake.*

Milton Reservoir

JACKSON MEADOWS RESERVOIR

Rating: 7

Species: Rainbow Trout and Brown Trout

Stocked with 8,000 pounds of rainbow trout, 300 pounds of fingerling rainbow trout and 48 pounds of fingerling brown trout.

Facilities: Campgrounds, Picnic Areas, Restrooms and a Boat Launch

Need Information? Contact: Mountain Hardware (530) 587-4844, Tahoe National Forest (530) 587-3558

Jackson Meadows Reservoir is a perfect planter lake. The California Department of Fish and Game has a two-fold management plan. Each year they plant 18,600 half-pound rainbow trout, 60,000 fingerling rainbow trout and 10,704 fingerling brown trout intended for a put-and-grow fishery. The plan has proved successful, as anglers looking to catch pan-size fish are almost never disappointed.

Catching these planters is easy for trollers, float tubers and shoreline anglers. The only downfall to Jackson Meadows is size. Other than a few lunker browns there are few trophy size fish. The majority of fish caught weigh from a half-pound to three-fourths of a pound. Don't get discouraged though, not all the fish are dinkers. There are thousands of holdover trout from one-to-three pounds and some big browns .

Jackson Meadows is a 1,000-acre lake at 6,000 feet in the Tahoe National Forest, but you don't need a big boat to fish it. We were successful in a canoe with an electric trolling motor, fishing in front of the dam. The bigger fish are typically found in deep water in the summer, however, toplining orange Cripplures, silver Kastmasters and white Phoebes produce easy limits. If you have a boat trolling can be extremely productive. The use of downriggers near the dam is an option, as well as trolling the shoreline from the dam to Woodchuck Campground, near the Middle Yuba River inlet and near Jackson Point. Float tubing and shoreline fishing Pass Creek Cove and along the dam is another option.

If you plan to make the trip, supplies are available in Truckee. The road to the lake closes in the winter. Jackson Meadows also freezes over.

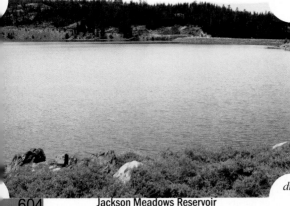

Also nearby are Webber Falls, Lake of the Woods and Independence Lake.

Directions: *From Truckee at the junction of Interstate 80 and Highway 89, drive 14.9 miles north on Highway 89 to Forest Service Road 7. Turn left and continue 16 miles to the left turnoff for the boat launch or drive 17.3 miles to the dam.*

CATFISH LAKE

Rating: 3

Species: Brown Bullhead

Stocks: None

Facilities: None

Catfish Lake is one of the least popular drive-to lakes in the Tahoe National Forest. The lake offers pretty campsites, however, few fish keep anglers from coming here. The California Department of Fish and Game stopped planting the lake with brook trout in 1988 due to winterkill issues. There are no trout left, however, a few small bullhead do remain. Unfortunately, the lake's name can be misleading. There are absolutely no catfish here.

The brown bullhead present are stunted. The largest fish you'll catch will stem no longer than five inches. A small chunk of chicken liver or a piece of a night crawler will catch you as many as you desire. Because of its' remote location at 6,460 feet in a heavily wooded section of the forest, coupled with the fact that the roads to the lake are rough, few anglers and campers come to Catfish. Leave this place off the list if you are coming to fish. Swimming and camping, on the other hand, are excellent.

Trip info for Meadow Lake applies to Catfish Lake.

Directions: *From Truckee drive 14.9 miles north on Highway 89 to Forest Service Road 7. Turn left and drive 10.4 miles to the turnoff for Meadow Lake (Road 86) on the left. Turn left and drive 11 miles to Meadow Lake. (The first part of the road is paved and then it turns to dirt. Several roads veer off the main road. Stay on Meadow Lake Road.) At the end of Meadow Lake there's a junction. Veer away from Meadow Lake, stay right and drive 8.7 miles past Meadow Lake to Catfish Lake on the left.*

Catfish Lake

TOLLHOUSE LAKE

Rating: 3
Species: Rainbow Trout
Stocks: None
Facilities: None

Tollhouse's remoteness makes it one of the most sought after lakes in the Tahoe National Forest. At 7,050 feet, the lake is at a high enough elevation that it's extremely forested and is remote enough that many people don't know about it. Others simply don't want to take the time to drive the rough dirt roads to fish it. Situated between Meadow Lake and French Reservoir, it's a long, slow drive to Tollhouse.

Unfortunately, if you are coming for the fish it's not worth it. Prior to the stoppage of fish plants due to the US Fish & Wildlife Service's mandate with frogs, Tollhouse held a nice population of rainbows. However, the California Department of Fish and Game hasn't been allowed to stock the lake since 1999 when 1,000 fingerling fish were planted. Sadly, no spawning has occurred and that last load is near the end of their cycle. Let's face it, by now there are either no or few trout left. There is hope that fish will once again be planted. If we are lucky, the allotment of 1,000 fingerling rainbow trout every other year will be reinstated. As for now come to swim and camp, not to fish this tiny pond size lake.

Grayling were once stocked in Tollhouse Reservoir (Above)

Trip info for Meadow Lake also applies to Tollhouse Lake.

Directions: *From Truckee, drive 14.9 miles north on Highway 89 to Forest Service Road 7. Turn left and continue 1.5 miles to Independence Lake Road. Turn left and drive 10.4 miles a turnoff for Meadow Lake (Road 86) on the left. Turn left and drive 11 miles to Meadow Lake. (The first part of the road is paved and then it turns to dirt. Several roads veer off the main road. Stay on Meadow Lake Road.) At the end of Meadow Lake there's a junction. Veer away from Meadow Lake, stay right and drive 2.5 miles past Meadow Lake to Tollhouse Lake.*

MEADOW LAKE

Rating: 9

Species: Cutthroat Trout and Rainbow Trout

Stocks: None

Facilities: Campgrounds and Restrooms

Need Information? Contact: Tahoe National Forest (530) 587-3558

Meadow Lake is one of the most successful put-and-grow cutthroat trout fisheries in the state. Hands down, the cutthroat are in excellent condition. A rough dirt road to the lake keeps many anglers from coming, therefore the lake should remain quality for years to come. Unfortunately, the California Department of Fish and Game is being forced to suspend fish plants while the US Fish and Wildlife Service determines the endangered mountain yellow legged frog inhabits the area. If the frog is found at Meadow, no more fish will be planted and the lake will turn barren of fish. Cutthroat trout cannot natural reproduce here.

As for now, cutthroat flourish. Meadow is a gorgeous lake rich with food. At 7,287 feet in the Tahoe National Forest, cutthroat have adapted well. Being so shallow, the lake gets warm in the summer, but it doesn't seem to bother the fish. Historically, Meadow was managed by the CA DFG as a rainbow trout fishery. However, the CA DFG gill-netted the lake to remove all rainbows in 1986-87 and restocked the lake with cutthroat. Catchable rainbow trout were planted through the early Eighties. There are still some rainbows in the lake, but they are not stocked and are greatly outnumbered by the cutts.

As its' name warrants, Meadow used to be a lush meadow. In the 1800's, miners constructed a dam in the meadow to create the lake. It has been enjoyed by recreationists ever since. Shore anglers and trollers can do well. From shore, simply toss out an inflated night crawler off the dam or off one of the points where you can reach deeper water. Because bald eagles commonly pick them off when they venture into shallow water, the cutthroat tend to stay in water deeper than 10 feet.

Trolling can be excellent; however, few anglers bring medium and large boats. We did, but I don't recommend it. The road is rough, borderline a four-wheel drive road. We should have never dragged a 17-foot boat with a 90 horsepower Honda on it, but in order to do a proper write-up we deemed it necessary. Car top boats and canoes are ok, but you'd be insane (like us) to drag a boat with a big motor to the lake.

A Meadow Lake cutthroat

Nonetheless, trolling can be phenomenal. Our arsenal included an orange Cripplure, an orange Pro Secret trolled behind a Sep's nickel dodger and a silver Needlefish with a red stripe down the middle. Meadow isn't that deep. At full pool you may be able to find one spot that reaches 40 feet deep. Most of the lake averages 12-19 feet.

For best results, drag your lures down the middle of Meadow and troll figure eights near the dam, but beware of an underwater steel line that goes from the dam out towards the middle of the lake. The dam area is ideal for snags. There's also a point near the boat launch (well what can be made into a boat launch, it isn't paved, just dirt) that juts up fast. It quickly goes from 28 to nine feet. If you can manage to stay on the downside of the shelf, you'll be successful. If you can find 25 feet, you'll find fish no matter what time of year.

Most of the cutts are eight to 12 inches, yet fish to 16 inches aren't uncommon. Meadow is situated in a heavily forested area brimming with bald and golden eagles. We found this out quickly by releasing a few cutthroat that were nabbed by bald eagles less than 20 feet behind our boat, as they were preparing to head back to deep water. Also, keep the wind in mind. Normally, the wind stirs up around 10 a.m. in the summer and will die down about an hour before sunset. The campsites around the lake are primitive, but have vault toilets so you don't have to worry about finding a tree to squat behind.

If you plan to make the trip, supplies are available in Truckee. In the winter and spring, the road to Meadow Lake is commonly closed due to snow. Call ahead for updated conditions. And, remember the road is rough. I warned you!

Also nearby are Tollhouse Lake, Catfish Lake and Jackson Meadow Reservoir.

Directions: *From Truckee, drive 14.9 miles north on Highway 89 to Forest Service Road 7. Turn left and continue 1.5 miles to Independence Lake Road. Turn left and drive 10.4 miles a turnoff for Meadow Lake (Road 86) on the left. Turn left and drive 11 miles to Meadow Lake. (The first part of the road is paved and then it turns to dirt. Several roads veer off the main road. Stay on Meadow Lake Road.)*

Cutthroat develop vibrant colors at Meadow Lake.

WEAVER LAKE

Rating: 7

Species: Lake Trout, Brook Trout, Rainbow Trout and Brown Trout

Stocked with 1,000 pounds of rainbow trout.

Facilities: None

Keeping Weaver Lake a quality fishery has been a labor of love for the California Department of Fish and Game. The CA DFG has battled budget cuts over the last decade in attempt to keep trout in Weaver. For now though, they've lost the battle. For starters, the lake was removed from the allotment list near the turn of the century when studies were conducted to find out if the endangered mountain yellow legged frog lived near the lake. It was determined the frog didn't and Weaver was then allowed back on the allotment sheet. However in 2004 when a 30-percent budget cut was implemented, Weaver was first on the chopping block.

Nevertheless, Weaver isn't expected to go fishless. In 2005 and until the CA DFG implements plants again, the lake will be planted with 1,000 pounds of rainbow trout funded by a local sportsman's club. Those fish will join self-sustaining populations of lake trout and brook trout. Brooks tend to do well here because they are able to utilize the many springs in the lake for spawning. Historically browns have also been present, but with insufficient tributaries for spawning, the population has dwindled.

The lake trout fishery isn't in danger of extinction either. Weaver is deeper than 100 feet and offers plenty of food and space for lake trout to endure successful spawns and to grow well. Interestingly enough, though, few lake trout ever grow larger than four pounds here. The most successful method to catch these fish is trolling near the bottom with half-ounce Krocodiles and Rebel Minnows. However, trolling isn't easy to accomplish. The dirt road to Weaver is long and especially rough over the last few miles. The last few miles require a high clearance or four-wheel drive vehicle. Small car top boats, canoes and float tubes are best.

Without a boat, action can still be had. Try bringing a float tube with a small fish finder to spot the lake trout and then drop a Megabait Live Jig to the bottom and you'll be in business. The lake trout tend to school up within a few feet from the bottom. Rainbows and brooks can be caught from shore.

Weaver Lake is an interesting high mountain lake. Located near Bowman Lake, Weaver is a large water surrounded by tall pines in a seldom visited portion of the Tahoe National Forest. The lake has no services, but does offer primitive camping. It's actually a popular destination to the small group of people who know about it. There's also a private lodge set aside for club members, with access to motorboats and cozy accommodations.

Trip info for Bowman Lake also applies to Weaver Lake.

Directions: *From Interstate 80 in Truckee, drive west for roughly 24 miles to the junction with Highway 20. Exit, drive 4.3 miles and turn right on Bowman Lake Road. Continue 14.8 miles to an unsigned left turnoff along the shoreline of Bowman Lake. Turn left and continue 1.2 miles to Weaver Lake.*

McMurray Lake

Rating: 3
Species: Brook Trout
Stocks: None
Facilities: None

McMurray Lake is an ideal destination for someone looking for a spot they can have all to themselves. Situated between Weaver Lake and Bowman Lake, McMurray is a small, shallow pond at 5,832 feet in the Tahoe National Forest that isn't overwhelmed by visitors. There's a small campground on the shore of McMurray that boasts lakeside views and prime access for folks to enjoy.

Unfortunately, fishing isn't good. The lake is no longer stocked by the California Department of Fish and Game, but that's not to say it's barren of fish. The lake used to be planted with brook trout, and for those who know brook trout, you are well aware that it's nearly impossible to remove them completely from a system. There are still brooks, but most anglers head home empty handed.

McMurray is a very rich lake that is teeming with food, yet there's only a small section that is deep for the brookies to lie in. If anglers can wade or use a canoe to access that deep section then success can be had, otherwise you are wasting your time. Most of McMurray has the characteristics of a meadow, not a lake.

Trip info for Bowman Lake also applies to McMurray Lake.

Directions: *From Interstate 80 in Truckee, drive west for roughly 24 miles to the junction with Highway 20. Exit, drive 4.3 miles and turn right on Bowman Lake Road. Continue 14.8 miles to an unsigned left turnoff along the shoreline of Bowman Lake. Turn left and continue six-tenths of a mile to McMurray Lake.*

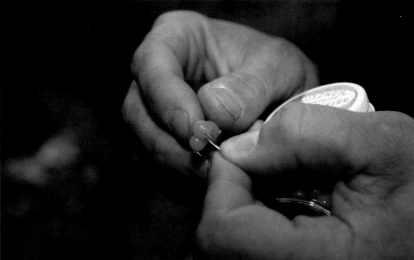

Fishing salmon eggs can be productive at McMurray if you can find the right hole to cast them in.

BOWMAN LAKE

Rating: 8

Species: Brown
Bullhead, Rainbow
Trout, Brown Trout and
Kokanee

Stocked with 20,140
fingerling rainbow trout
and 25,350 fingerling
kokanee.

Facilities:
Campgrounds and
Restrooms

Need Information?
Contact: Tahoe National
Forest (530) 587-3558

Knowing the history of Bowman Lake is extremely important to becoming a successful angler here. Bowman Lake is actually two lakes. The old Bowman Lake and the new Bowman Lake. The old lake was flooded when the new dam was constructed.

Knowing where the old basin sits is vital information to brown trout anglers. Browns tend to hold tight in this area. The old basin sits on the south side of the river channel where Old Bowman Lake was. The old lake is a natural basin that was inundated by the new reservoir.

Bowman is a large system with a ton of room and opportunity for trout to do well. Bowman's trout benefit from an enhanced influx of water entering the lake. Prior to the construction of the Milton-Bowman Tunnel, the lake was fed by only natural runoff. However, the excess water rushing in through the tunnel created a larger than normal nutrient system allowing trout to grow bigger, faster. The lake also has Lahonton red side minnows for the trout to feed on.

Bowman has excellent structure for trout. Nonetheless, shore angling isn't the top choice here, as Bowman doesn't offer great shoreline access. Aside from fishing near the inlets, bank anglers can expect to do well on the south side opposite the road near Canyon Creek. Look for large boulders off the points. It's no secret that when the canal is turned on to increase water levels in the reservoir, fishing can be exceptional near the inlet.

For now, the California Department of Fish and Game manages the lake as a put-and-grow kokanee, rainbow and brown trout water. The lake is planted yearly with more than 20,450 fingerling Eagle Lake strain rainbow

Bowman Lake

trout. While the return to creel on these fish isn't that good, there are many rainbows to be caught. Most often they are caught by trollers working the shorelines with night crawlers and flashers or small spoons. For rainbows, Bowman can be a hard reservoir to fish. The trout tend to scatter all over the lake rather than staying in one specific area. Rainbow fishing is often good near the inlet for anglers casting small spinners. Tossing bait off the dam can also be worthwhile.

Browns aren't typically caught by shoreline anglers. Mostly trollers working the old basin within the reservoir get into the browns, which have been known to peak over 10 pounds. Stick to fishing Rebel Minnows and J-Plugs in the fall and early spring. Also look for many browns near the inlet and canal spawning in the fall.

Bowman's kokanee aren't heavily targeted, yet do surprisingly well. The idea in planting kokanee here was to provide anglers with an easy fish to catch. While browns and rainbows scatter all over the lake, the kokanee can be found schooling up, thus are easier to target for trollers. Many anglers target the inlet for small kokanee in the spring. Kokanee also benefit from a good zooplankton population.

If you plan to make the trip, supplies are available in Truckee. In winter and early spring call ahead for road conditions. The road may be closed due to hazardous conditions. The launch ramp is a dirt ramp, however, suitable for boats to 18 feet. Larger boats can be launched with four-wheel drive vehicles.

Also nearby are Weaver Lake, Faucherie Lake and Sawmill Lake.

Directions: *From Interstate 80 in Truckee, drive west for roughly 24 miles to the junction with Highway 20. Exit, drive 4.3 miles and turn right on Bowman Lake Road. Continue 14.5 miles to the lake.*

Bowman Lake

SAWMILL LAKE

Rating: 4

Species: Rainbow Trout and Brown Trout

Stocks: None

Facilities: Campgrounds and Restrooms

Need Information? Contact: Tahoe National Forest (530) 587-3558

Sawmill Lake is another rich lake in the Tahoe National Forest with good growth rates on trout that are planted as fingerlings. No catchable size trout are planted. The California Department of Fish and Game plants only fingerling fish and operates a successful put-and-grow fishery.

With a plentiful population of Lahonton red side minnows, the rainbows often grow to 16 inches. Unfortunately, their numbers aren't staggering. Roughly 2,000 fingerling rainbow trout are planted. However, because of endangered frog issues, trout were last planted in 1999 and may not be planted again.

While Canyon Creek and South Fork Creek do enter the lake, the creeks don't offer sufficient habitat for spawning. But even when fish plants don't occur, rainbows and browns find their way out of Canyon Creek and into Sawmill. The lake gets little fishing pressure.

Trolling and bait fishing can be good; however, don't bank on launching a boat over 15 feet. Keep your offerings small, anything bigger than a Sep's Pro Secret is too big. For bank anglers toss night crawlers off one of the many points or off the dam.

Trip info for Bowman Lake also applies to Sawmill Lake.

Directions: *From Interstate 80 in Truckee, drive west for roughly 24 miles to the junction with Highway 20. Exit, drive 4.3 miles and turn right on Bowman Lake Road. Continue 16 miles to the end of Bowman Lake and a split in the road. Take the fork signed for Faucherie and Sawmill Lake. At the next signed turnoff, turn right and continue to Sawmill Lake.*

Sawmill Lake

FAUCHERIE LAKE

Rating: 6

Species: Rainbow Trout and Brown Trout

Stocked with 23 pounds of fingerling brown trout and four pounds of fingerling rainbow trout.

Facilities: Boat Launch, Restrooms and Campgrounds

Faucherie Lake is one of the prettiest lakes in the Sierra, yet the fishing can be horrendous if you fish anytime other than the fall. I was skunked the first time I fished the lake in July, as were all the other anglers I interviewed. The most striking statement came from an older gentleman who said he comes to the lake each summer to swim and canoe. He told me has snorkeled the lake's entire shoreline and has never seen a fish longer than six inches. I assure you - they are here. You can't snorkel at 50 feet deep!

If you fish Faucherie anytime other that the fall, the fishery can cause you to never want to come back. However, fish during the fall and you'll never want to leave! Faucherie has been actively managed as a rainbow and brown trout fishery since the early Twenties. From 1945-70 the lake was planted with only fingerling rainbow trout. Then from 1970-86,

Faucherie Lake Falls

catchable rainbow and brown trout were planted. Since 1986, the California Department of Fish and Game has switched over to planting fingerling rainbows and browns. Rainbows are allotted each year and browns are planted every three years. The management has proved to be a success. In 2003, 5,129 fingerling browns and 3,000 fingerling rainbows were stocked.

Fall fishing for browns and rainbows can be excellent. Browns tend to average one to 2.5 pounds, but the rainbows are a bit smaller. At times, browns to eight pounds are landed. Trout do well for several reasons. Faucherie is a deep, clear body of water and at 6,132 feet in the Tahoe National Forest, fishing pressure is low due to horrible dirt roads that must be taken to reach the lake. Faucherie's water is highly conducive to maintaining a strong population of Lahonton red side minnows, which the browns and rainbows feed on.

The only downside is that in most cases, browns can't spawn. There are few wild fish. Faucherie Falls, on Canyon Creek, prohibits any travel upstream out of the lake. The lake has four other seasonal inlets that don't provide any spawning habitat. There is a small chance the rainbows can spawn on the springs in the lake, yet that hasn't been proven.

Faucherie's structure is good for trout, but can be difficult to fish. The lake has numerous deep pockets of water and narrow, yet deep, canyons. It can be hard to troll effectively. Clear, emerald-like water has a visibility of at least 25 feet (if not 40). You have to use four-pound test or lighter to be successful. The structure can be impossible to fish for beginner trollers. In one area the lake jumps from 25 to six feet in only a few yards, in another, from 107 to 60. There are sections where open water can be found. However, most trout key in on the structure.

It's best to focus on the structure and to fly line a night crawler on four-pound test down to the bottom. Here's where to go: directly in front of the dirt launch ramp and dam is an island that has steep drop-offs. If you veer to the right after launching, you'll find much deeper water. Because of its' remote location, little to no fishing pressure occurs. The lake is a great place to bring a canoe and camp on the island. It's one of the most peaceful places in the Sierra. An added bonus is Faucherie Lake Falls. The waterfall is hidden behind the island on Canyon Creek and can be stunning throughout the summer.

Trip info for Sawmill Lake also applies to Faucherie Lake.

Directions: *From Interstate 80 in Truckee, drive west for roughly 24 miles to the junction with Highway 20. Exit, drive 4.3 miles and turn right on Bowman Lake Road. Continue 16 miles to the end of Bowman Lake and a split in the road. Take the fork signed for Faucherie and Sawmill Lake and continue to the boat launch.*

The shallow portion of Faucherie

LINDSAY LAKE (LOWER)

Rating: 4

Species: Brown
Bullhead and Brook
Trout

Stocks: None

Facilities:
Campgrounds and
Restrooms

Need Information?
Contact: Tahoe National
Forest (530) 587-3558

Before the illegal introduction of golden shiners and brown bullhead, Lower Lindsay Lake was an exceptional brook trout fishery. However, since those fish were introduced, a competition for food has taken away Lindsay's put-and-grow fingerling trout program. The California Department of Fish and Game has concluded that because there are too many golden shiners and brown bullhead, planting fingerling brook trout is no longer the way to go.

For now, the CA DFG has stopped fish plants. There are, however, still brook trout available. Prior to the Nineties, the lake was planted with catchable size trout. Because of endangered frog issues, no longer are trout being planted. They may never be planted again. On the other hand, brook trout naturally reproduce. They spawn in the lake, not in the inlet.

At 6,236 feet in the Tahoe National Forest, Lower Lindsay has a dam to retain water and can get quite warm during the summer months. Anglers who bring canoes and troll down the middle of the lake or fish out of a float tube do best. Oftentimes, anglers using bait have a tough time on the brooks because the brown bullhead chow on the worms before brooks have a chance. The bullhead are stunted. Unfortunately, a four-inch fish is a full grown adult.

Lower Lindsay is the only lake on the loop that offers lakeside camping. It can get crowded in the summer. Swimming is also an option.

If you plan to make the trip, supplies are available in Truckee. The road to the lake is closed in the winter and early spring. Call the Forest Service for updated conditions.

Also nearby is the Carr Lake Loop.

Directions: *From the junction of I-80 and Highway 89 in Truckee, drive west on I-80 for 23.1 miles to Highway 20. Exit east on Highway 20 and drive 3.7 miles to Road 18 (signed for Discovery Trail). Turn right, drive 8.3 miles to Forest Road 17 and veer right. Drive 2.5 miles and veer right on Road 17-0. Continue 1.4 miles to a split in the road. Veer left and continue to the end of the road and Lindsay Lake.*

Lower Lindsay Lake

Lindsay Lake (Middle)

Rating: 3
Species: Brown Bullhead and Brook Trout
Stocks: None
Facilities: None

The same sad saga told at Lower Lindsay Lake applies to Middle Lindsay. Prior to the unauthorized introduction of golden shiners and brown bullhead, Middle Lindsay yielded some nice brook trout. "Used to" is the key phase. Middle Lindsay still maintains a brook trout fishery, yet it's nowhere near as good as it used to be.

At 6,436 feet in the Tahoe National Forest, Middle Lindsay can be best fished right after ice out and in the fall when temperatures cool. Arrive during the warmer months and you'll have to out-compete the weeds and moss to have any shot at trout. In summer you have a better chance at catching aquatic snakes than trout. On the other hand, toss out a chunk of bait and you can catch as many four-inch bullhead as possible. When fall arrives, plan on dragging a float tube in. Anglers who fish the deeper sections of the lake do best.

To reach Middle Lindsay from Lower Lindsay, walk through the gate at Lower Lindsay and follow uphill on the wide, dirt access road. It's three-quarters of a mile from the locked gate to Middle Lindsay's dam.

Directions and trip info for Lindsay Lake (Lower) also apply to Lindsay Lake (Middle).

Middle Lindsay Lake

CULBERTSON LAKE

Rating: 6

Species: Rainbow Trout and Brook Trout

Stocks: None

Facilities: None

Culbertson Lake has what the other lakes in the Lindsay Lakes Loop don't, namely deep and cold water. Culbertson is situated in a cirque basin and has depths to 90 feet. It's the largest lake in the basin and oftentimes yields the largest fish.

Culbertson Lake is a natural lake. At 6,442 feet in the Tahoe National Forest a small dam was built here to increase storage ability. The lake is managed by the California Department of Fish and Game as a rainbow trout fishery. Because the lake is so rich the CA DFG has chosen to plant the fish as fingerlings and allow them to grow in the lake, rather than in a hatchery. The concept saves the CA DFG money, while at the same time creates a better looking trout.

Culbertson Lake

For best results, fish the upper end of the lake, targeting it in late August and September. Fly fishing in the evenings is best. Unfortunately, because of mountain yellow-legged frog issues the lake hasn't been stocked since 2000. If plants don't resume soon the lake could go void of fish. It's unclear if natural spawning occurs.

To reach Culbertson from Middle Lindsay continue on the wide dirt access road. In roughly 20 yards a road breaks off to the right and heads to Upper Lindsay. Stay left for Culbertson. Shortly you'll pass a small, shallow and barren pond. Ignore it. Keep walking. You climb up a small hill and enter a flat area smothered with elephant ears. At the end of the open field you'll drop down to the lake. At first, you'll pass a few cabins on the right. Continue on until you see the Culbertson's dam on the right. There's a small pond below the dam that offers good fishing, but it only holds a few fish.

Directions and trip info for Lindsay Lake (Lower) also apply to Culbertson Lake.

618

ROCK LAKE (LOWER)

Rating: 1
Species: None
Stocks: None
Facilities: None

Depending on who you are, reaching Lower Rock Lake can be an easy slow drive or a short 2.5-mile hike. Those who own property along the Lindsay Lake Loop, Forest Service rangers and dam keepers for PG&E are fortunate enough to have a key that lets them through the gate at Lower Lindsay Lake. However, all others have to walk or get lucky and catch a ride like we did.

At 6,622 feet in the Tahoe National Forest, Lower Rock Lake is barren of fish. The California Department of Fish and Game has deemed the lake ideal for winterkill. Consequently, the lake isn't planted. Resident rattlesnakes it does have. We ran into an angry timber rattlesnake while spending time at the lake with Ted Sanford, a PG&E dam keeper. Old Ted wasn't bothered by the snake. "What are you worried about," he said to me. "They are all over the place here. You don't bother them, they don't bother you." Point taken. Just don't unexpectedly bother them.

Lower Rock Lake

As for the lake, once in a while a brook or brown trout will swim out of Upper Rock Lake and down into Lower Rock, but the chances are slim. You're better off taking a dip rather than fishing. To reach Lower Rock Lake from Culbertson, continue on the route you came in on. In one-tenth of a mile you'll cross Culbertson's outlet stream before coming to a junction. The left fork will take you to Bullpen Lake. Stay straight on the wide dirt road for three-quarters of a mile to the lake on the right. There's a 230-foot elevation gain.

***Directions** and trip info for Lindsay Lake (Lower) also apply to Rock Lake (Lower).*

ROCK LAKE (UPPER)

Rating: 6

Species: Brown Trout and Brook Trout

Stocks: None

Facilities: None

When the California Department of Fish and Game first began managing the Grouse Ridge region, their idea was to stock each lake in the basin with a different species of trout to provide anglers with a variety of fish to catch. For nearly a century they succeeded. However, since the mountain yellow-legged frog issue came up in the late Nineties, the CA DFG has been forced to halt plants. Fish remain in the lakes, however, their populations are dwindling fast. With little to no spawning grounds in the rugged, mountainous region, trout fishing, which was excellent for more than a century, could soon turn sour.

For now, anglers who show up to fish Upper Rock Lake in the fall can expect to do well on brown trout and have an outside shot at brook trout. At 6,710 feet in the Tahoe National Forest, Upper Rock Lake is the only lake on the Lindsay Lakes Loop that was planted with browns. Fishing can be horrible in the spring and fall. Nonetheless, 12-18 inch browns can be common to "know hows" in the fall. Little fishing pressure can be found, but you'll need to work a bit to get to it. It's nearly a three-mile hike in from the locked gate at Lower Lindsay Lake. From Lower Rock Lake, reaching the upper lake isn't tough. Walk to the inlet of Lower Rock Lake and follow the faint trail at the inlet upstream to Upper Rock Lake roughly 100 yards ahead.

Directions *and trip info for Lindsay Lake (Lower) also apply to Rock Lake (Upper).*

Upper Rock Lake

CARR LAKE

Rating: 3

Species: Brook Trout

Stocks: None

Facilities:
Campgrounds and
Restrooms

Need Information?
Contact: Tahoe National
Forest (530) 587-3558

Carr Lake was named properly. While it is a hike-to lake, the hike is short enough to where you can practically drive your car to it. The walk from your car to the water is fewer than 50 yards. And as you might have guessed, Carr Lake gets crowded, real crowded, especially on weekends. There are two things that make Carr a popular place: fishing and camping. Although you have to walk your tents, coolers and stoves to your campsite (which is situated on the shoreline of the small lake in the Tahoe National Forest) the campsites fill fast.

As for the fishing, it doesn't get the same attention the camping does. Few anglers fish for brook trout, and if you don't access deep water from a float tube, you probably won't do well. Casting from shore, it's harder to reach the deeper water where most of the brookies lie. The ideal situation would be to drag a canoe with a trolling motor to the lake. Catching fish is simple for trollers, yet few make the effort. No fish are planted, but there is a self sustaining population.

Carr Lake

If you plan to make the trip supplies, are available in Truckee and Colfax. The road to the lake is closed from November 16 to May 15, sometimes later depending on the snowpack.

Also nearby are Feeley Lake, Island Lake, Long Lake, Round Lake and Milk Lake.

Directions: *From the junction of Interstate 80 and Highway 89 in Truckee, drive west on I-80 for 23.1 miles to Highway 20. Exit east on Highway 20 and drive 3.7 miles to Road 18 (signed for Discovery Trail). Turn right and drive 8.3 miles to Forest Road 17 and veer right. Drive 2.5 miles and veer right on Road 17-0. Continue three-tenths of a mile to a trailhead sign for Carr Lake and a locked gate.*

FEELY LAKE

Rating: 3

Species: Brook Trout
and Rainbow Trout

Stocks: None

Facilities: None

Feely Lake is a natural backcountry lake that was enlarged by a dam for water storage purposes. The majority of anglers who are successful are those who make the effort to haul in a canoe or float tube along the quarter-mile trail to the lake.

Shore fishing is a possibility. Unfortunately, catching fish from shore isn't likely unless you have a fishing pole that can cast as far as a water balloon launcher can let a balloon fly. The problem with shore fishing is you have to be able to cast at least 30 yards to reach the zone where the fish hang out. The first 20 yards from shore on towards the middle of the lake is too shallow to hold fish in the summer. Your best bet is to focus on the middle of the lake.

Feely's fish population isn't enormous, but there are plenty of rainbow and brook trout. The lake isn't heavily fished, so those who take the time to drag that canoe in, and more importantly bring along a small electric trolling motor, can fool the fish easily. Fly-fishermen casting from float tubes can also do well. At 6,724 feet in the Tahoe National Forest, Feely can be reached by continuing roughly 50 yards past Carr Lake on the Carr-Feely Lake Trail.

Directions *and trip info for Carr Lake also apply to Feely Lake.*

Feely Lake

LILY PAD LAKE

Rating: 5
Species: Brook Trout
Stocks: None
Facilities: None

Some anglers have a false perception of what size lakes big fish can inhabit. A lake doesn't have to be huge to hold large fish, however, if it lacks size, it must compensate for that lack of space with a good source of food and water quality. I've fished small ponds that hold three-to-four 10-plus pound browns in them. These ponds carry a tremendous amount of feed.

At roughly one-acre, Lily Pad rests at 6,875 feet in the Tahoe National Forest. Surprisingly, it's home to some one-to-two-pound brooks, which are much larger than those found in most other lakes in the Grouse Ridge area. Most people take a pass on fishing Lily Pad because it's so small and shallow. In fact, few anglers think there are any fish.

The lake is loaded with brookies. While it may be difficult to fish because of all the lily pads, if you carefully cast into open water, let your lure sink for a few seconds and follow up with a slow retrieve, you'll have a blast, landing more brooks than you'd ever dreamed of. I figured that because of the lake's size, using a larger spinner would spook the fish. However, I couldn't even get a bite on a Panther Martin. It wasn't until my fishing partner Blake Lezak began casting a Thomas Buoyant that the brooks began to feed.

To reach Lily Pad from the trail junction at the east end of Feely Lake, stay to the right and walk uphill for about 150 yards to Lily Pad Lake on the right.

Directions *and trip info for Carr Lake also apply to Lily Pad Lake.*

A Lily Pad Lake brookie

LITTLE ISLAND LAKE

Rating: 3

Species: Brook Trout
and Rainbow Trout

Stocks: None

Facilities: None

Sometimes lakes are so darn pretty that anglers don't necessarily need to catch a fish to be satisfied with the outdoor experience. At 6,860 feet up in the Tahoe National Forest, Little Island Lake is one of those places. Surrounded by pines and mountain peaks, this dark blue colored lake is one of the prettiest in the region. If you don't mind a swim, you can always enjoy the view from the lake's lone island, which rests about 20 yards from the shore.

For those who want to fish there are fish to be caught, mostly brookies, mixed in with a few rainbows. Because angler harvest is fairly high, the fish tend not to grow more than 10 inches, yet there are enough brooks and rainbows to warrant a few casts. Try tossing small spinners towards the island and in the lake's coves.

To reach Little Island from Lily Pad Lake, continue fewer than 100 yards past Lily Pad to Little Island on the left.

Directions *and trip info for Carr Lake also apply to Island Lake.*

Little Island Lake

ISLAND LAKE

Rating: 4

Species: Rainbow Trout

Stocks: None

Facilities: None

Although it used to be stocked with rainbow trout by the California Department of Fish and Game, Island Lake is more of a tourist trap than a fishing lake. When I arrived at this backcountry water, I had difficulty finding a spot on shore to cast from. This pretty lake, at 6,875 feet in the Tahoe National Forest, reminded me of a Saturday afternoon at Zuma Beach near Los Angeles. It was jammed. Lined with rocks, grass and pines, the entire shoreline was packed with hikers who had walked the 1.25 miles to the lake for various reasons, most of which included sleeping, picnicking, camping, swimming and reading books. I didn't see one person with a fishing pole though.

I asked many of these nature lovers if this lake is always crowded, and I was told if you arrive on the weekend during the summer you better get here early or risk not finding a spot. The hikers said there are only a few other places in the region that are as peaceful and pretty as Island Lake.

What are fishermen to do if their shoreline access is all used up by nappers? Well, if you are keen to the idea of dragging in a float tube (which would solve all your problems) then you'll have to show up really early in the morning or late in the evening when the hikers are on the trail back to their car or in commute. Otherwise, you'll be forced to compete with swimmers. Despite few anglers, there are plenty of rainbows to go around, especially when the fishing pressure is as low as it is. But, generally, fishing is poor. An interesting side note: Chinook salmon were planted here in 1978. As far as we know there are none left.

To reach Island Lake from Little Island, continue on the trail which will travel over one small hill and then descend to Island Lake on the left. Total distance is about one-tenth of a mile.

Directions *and trip info for Carr Lake also apply to Island Lake.*

Island Lake

Long Lake

Rating: 3
Species: Brown Trout
Stocks: None
Facilities: None

Of the handful or so Long Lakes in California, the Long Lake in the Tahoe National Forest near Grouse Ridge would be the one to let slip from your mind. This long, narrow, shallow lake, nestled at 6,870 feet in a wooded and granite forest, doesn't gleam well with anglers. At the present time, stocking has paused momentarily while efforts to study a possible frog population take place.

Personally, I fished Long thoroughly and didn't get a single bite, nor did I see any fish in the clear water. I made a few phone calls to folks who fish this area pretty hard and the responses I received weren't exciting. The California Department of Fish and Game biologist and Tahoe National Forest Fisheries biologist both told me the fishery isn't worth a dime. For me, that was all I needed to close my investigation. With few fish seen (and even less caught), don't waste your time casting and retrieving here. You'd have a better chance hooking a lake trout using dog food for bait in Lake Tahoe.

While the fishing is the pits, the scenery is worth the short hike. To set up a picnic along Long's shore, follow the directions to Island Lake. The path winds above Island and within a quarter mile you'll see the tail end of Long on the left.

Directions *and trip info for Carr Lake also apply to Long Lake.*

Long Lake

ROUND LAKE

Rating: 5

Species: Rainbow Trout
and Brown Trout

Stocked with one pound
of fingerling rainbow
trout.

Facilities: None

Each lake on the Carr-Feeley Loop has its' own unique characteristics. When it comes to Round Lake, what stands out most is its' depth. As opposed to the other lakes in the drainage, which are typically shallow, Round is deep. Its' steep drop-offs and clear water make visibility high. Subsequently, it makes angling more difficult, as Round's fish are easily spooked. Therefore, you need to downsize your line to be successful.

The inconvenience of fishing ultralight tackle may sound like hard work, but it's warranted. Round is the only lake on the loop that is situated off the main trail. Hence, it's less fished, which means the fish aren't yanked out before they can grow to respectable sizes. There are both rainbow and browns, although the browns are rare. For best results, try using a silver Krocodile or some form of spoon that will sink sufficiently. Most fish are landed within 15 yards of the shoreline. Try to cast out in the middle of the lake and then retrieve slowly to cause less spooking.

Getting to Round Lake from Long Lake is a synch. From Long continue on the trail for one-tenth of a mile to a junction on the left for Round Lake. Veer left and continue to the lake.

Directions *and trip info for Carr Lake also apply to Round Lake.*

Round Lake

MILK LAKE

Rating: 4

Species: Rainbow Trout

Stocks: none

Facilities: None

Because of its' scenic surroundings, Milk Lake is one of the most heavily traveled to backcountry lakes in the Tahoe National Forest. At 6,997 feet, Milk is home to a stable population of pan size rainbow trout. Due to heavy pressure the lake receives, the California Department of Fish and Game mercifully plants 5,000 fingerling rainbows each fall to provide anglers with opportunities for the following seasons. (Unfortunately, these plants were stopped in 2003. It is unclear when they will resume.)

Milk is a pretty lake with a different setting than most lakes on the Carr-Feeley loop. As opposed to timber and granite backdrops found at the other lakes, Milk offers grassy shorelines dappled with wildflowers, butterflies and an abundance of insect life. Most people come to Milk to picnic. In the spring, however, the rainbow trout fishery can be promising. Your best bet is to attempt matching the color of the most recent insect hatch. Also, use caution when tossing hardware, there are a lot of fallen trees and aquatic life to get snagged on. As summer progresses, Milk's fishing begins to slow. Arrive early, or go home unhappy.

To reach Milk Lake from Long Lake, continue past Long and beyond the trail junction for Round Lake that splits off to the right, a mere one-tenth of a mile ahead. Ignoring the junction, push forward for a short two-tenths of a mile to the junction for Milk Lake. Veer right and continue one tenth of a mile to the lake.

Directions and trip info for Carr Lake also apply to Milk Lake.

Milk Lake

RUCKER LAKE

Rating: 3

Species: Rainbow Trout and Brown Trout

Stocks: None

Facilities: Campgrounds and Restrooms

For the California Department of Fish and Game, Rucker Lake has been an experimental water. It's not uncommon for Rucker's surface temperatures to warm into the mid-Seventies in the summer. In response, decades ago the CA DFG stocked the lake with redband trout because redband were more likely to survive warm temperatures than most rainbows and browns. At times the redband did well, but no longer does the CA DFG have redband available to stock, nor were they a perfect match for Rucker as some die offs did occur.

Rucker isn't an ideal fishery. Located in the Tahoe National Forest, this small drive-to lake serves two functions. On one side you have summer homes with waterfront property and on the other there is a walk-in campsite offering lakeside camping.

Rucker is a pretty, high mountain lake located in a quiet, heavily forested area. There is no boat launch, yet many anglers and day users do bring canoes, kayaks and float tubes. Unfortunately the fishing is just fair. The CA DFG stopped planting trout many years ago and for now has no immediate plans to restock. Nevertheless, the CA DFG has verified that locals have illegally transported brown trout from nearby lakes. There aren't many browns though. There are a few rainbows that still remain. These fish are descendants from previous fish stockings. Some fish do spawn here from time to time.

As for catching fish, don't come expecting to catch a limit. In fact, you'll be fortunate to catch any. There are few fish in Rucker, but you'll likely have to get wet to have a chance at catching anything because the water near the shoreline is very shallow. You need to be offshore in order to put your bait or lures in front of trout. It's best to have a canoe or float tube, but no gas-powered motors are permitted. There are several deep holes in the lake and these spots obviously harbor most of the trout.

Trip info for Bowman Lake also applies to Rucker Lake.

Directions: From Interstate 80 in Truckee, drive west for roughly 24 miles to the junction with Highway 20. Exit, drive 4.3 miles and turn right on Bowman Lake Road. Continue 4.7 miles to the right turnoff for Rucker Lake (Road 18-06). Turn right, drive four-tenths of a mile and veer right. Continue three-tenths of a mile to the parking area.

FULLER LAKE

<table>
<tr><td>

Rating: 7

Species: Rainbow Trout and Brown Trout

Stocked with 4,250 pounds of rainbow trout and 2,000 pounds of brown trout.

Facilities: Restrooms

</td></tr>
</table>

Fuller Lake is a tourist's lake; a quiet, pretty, forested lake where anglers from the greater Sacramento region venture to for good shoreline and float tube fishing. While rainbows and browns inhabit the lake, lunkers are almost never caught. By planting 7,600 rainbow trout and 5,800 browns, the California Department of Fish and Game does its' best to reward these anglers for their long drive to this 69-acre lake at 5,340 feet in the Tahoe National Forest.

For the most part, anglers remain satisfied with these half-pound trout, particularly the float tubers who launch near the dam and have a field day fly-fishing the lake. While there aren't trophy size fish, holdover trout to two pounds are frequently caught. Fuller also has excellent shoreline access. For anglers who soak Power Bait and float night crawlers off the bottom, I'd focus on the dam area to obtain limits of trout.

Trip info for Bowman Lake also applies to Fuller Lake.

Directions: *From Interstate 80 in Truckee, drive west for roughly 24 miles to the junction with Highway 20. Exit, drive 4.3 miles and turn right on Bowman Lake Road. Continue 3.5 miles to Fuller Lake.*

Fuller Lake

SPAULDING RESERVOIR

Rating: 8

Species: Rainbow
Trout, Brown Trout,
Chinook Salmon and
Mountain Whitefish

Stocks: None

Facilities: Boat Launch,
Restrooms and
Campgrounds

Need Information?
Contact: Tahoe National
Forest (530) 587-3558

Some anglers don't understand the importance of structure in a lake. Whether it be fallen logs, drop-offs, trees, boulders or underwater caves, even the slightest bit of structure can allow a fishery to flourish. Fish use the structure as protection, for spawning and to hide from anglers. A 675-acre lake at 5,000 feet in the Tahoe National Forest, Spaulding Reservoir is a perfect example of a lake that has benefited from great structure. Spaulding has underwater caves, hundreds of dead trees both submerged and sticking out of the water, giant granite outcroppings that extend into the lake and boulders along the lake bottom.

While such structure has allowed the lake's browns to grow to trophy sizes, the rainbows haven't faired as well because they are typically caught soon after being planted. The California Department of Fish and Game stock rainbows most years. They are caught fairly quick by those trolling the dam area and shorelines, as well as anglers floating night crawlers off points.

What anglers don't realize is that there are also chinook salmon to fish for. They were planted in 1994 to utilize abundant forage species in the lake. Boat anglers can expect to land 18-20 inch chinook if trolling from August through October in 20-30 feet of water. However, to cash in on the action use your sonar to locate schools of pond smelt. Chinook school up in open water.

Squawfish often fool anglers who think they've hooked large browns at Spaulding Reservoir.

Trollers who can locate pond smelt slam the chinook as they round up smelt. In 2002, 39,000 fingerling Chinook were planted.

The browns weren't introduced into Spaulding, rather they migrated out of Fordyce Creek and the South Fork of the Yuba River into Spaulding. An abundance of food and shelter have allowed browns to grow better than five pounds. There are several large browns in the lake, yet most aren't caught by anglers targeting them. They are landed accidentally by those fishing for rainbows.

When trolling Spaulding, beware of underwater obstacles in the back of the lake near the Fordyce Creek inlet. There are hundreds of submerged trees that will easily snag your line. Also, many of the coves here can't be trolled because of the trees, but to catch the browns you need to concentrate on these arms. If you take your boat into one of these coves and turn the fish finder on, it will light up with fish. Try fishing these areas with a float tube and you should do extremely well.

If you plan to make the trip, supplies are available in Cisco Grove. Some winters Spaulding can freeze over. There is a 35-mph speed limit, so water-skiers are common in the summer.

Also nearby are Bowman Lake, Fuller Lake and the South Fork of the Yuba River.

Directions: From the junction of Interstate 80 and Interstate 5 in Sacramento, drive west on I-80 for to the Highway 20 turnoff. Exit and drive two miles to the right turnoff for Spaulding Reservoir. Turn right and continue to the lake.

Spaulding Reservoir

LAKE OF THE WOODS

Rating: 4

Species: Rainbow Trout
and Brown Trout

Stocks: None

Facilities: None

Need Information?
Contact: Tahoe National
Forest (530) 587-3558

Lake of the Woods is a small, shallow lake at 7,427 feet in the Tahoe National Forest. It's surrounded by pines and seldom used by anyone other than a few locals with float tubes.

While the lake is often overlooked by out-of-towners, opportunities for float tubers and trollers in canoes couldn't be better. The lake is small enough to deter power boaters and with only electric trolling motors allowed, it stays quiet enough to provide serenity.

Browns do well at Lake of the Woods. Weed growth along the shore makes for great breeding grounds for mosquitoes in the spring, which means more food for fish and better growth rates. While the browns average 10-12 inches, fish to 18 inches are not uncommon for know-hows. In 2002, the California Department of Fish and Game stocked 3,000 fingerling brown trout. For some reason, they didn't plant the lake in 2003. This could hurt the brown trout population in the future.

Due to the weeds, the lake only offers so-so shoreline fishing. However, float tubing and canoe fishing are excellent. That is, when the winds aren't blowing. If the forecast in Truckee calls for winds greater than 15 mph, then expect the lake to be blown out by noon. For the best catch rates, try to match your flies and spinners with the most recent insect hatch. When trolling, move as slow as your electric motor will allow you to go and keep your lures in the top 10 feet of water.

If you plan to make the trip, supplies are available in Truckee. The road to Lake of the Woods is typically impassible due to snow through June. Call the Forest Service for updated conditions.

Lake of the Woods

Also nearby are Webber Falls and Independence Lake.

Directions: *From Interstate 80 in Truckee, exit Highway 89 and drive 17.5 miles north to Forest Service Road 07. Turn left and drive 6.5 miles to the turnoff for Lake of the Woods on the right. Turn right and drive 2.2 miles to the lake.*

INDEPENDENCE LAKE

Rating: 8

Species: Rainbow Trout, Brown Trout, Cutthroat Trout and Brook Trout

Stocks: None

Facilities: Boat Launch, Restrooms and a Campground

Need Information? Contact: Tahoe National Forest (530) 587-3558

Special Note: At press time, a private individual was in the process of purchasing the property around Independence Lake. This would leave no public fishing access. Call the Forest Service for updated information.

I'll give you one important piece of advice. When you read the sign that says "Rough Road" on the way to Independence Lake, you should take it seriously. If you don't have four-wheel drive or a high clearance vehicle, you might not want to continue. If you are planning to visit prior to late June, don't bother. Portions of the road will be covered in snow. I found this out the hard way.

The road starts out smooth, but as soon as you drive through Independence Creek, (through, not over) it becomes rough. There are boulders, trees fallen halfway onto the road, snow, ice, water and wild turns. Once you think you can put your foot on the gas, reality sets in. Only 5 mph

Brown trout are common at Independence Lake

seems safe. The woods are thick and you need to also keep an eye out for deer that play chicken darting across the road. Even many with topo maps get lost finding the lake. The road splits off a few times and there are no signs to point you in the right direction. Make sure you bring a reliable map.

Once you reach the lake though, you won't be disappointed. Located

634

about an hour from Truckee, this high mountain lake is split between Sierra and Nevada Counties and rests at 6,952 feet in the Tahoe National Forest. Fishing pressure is usually non-existent, but for anglers who know how to fish it, catch rates can be staggering. Independence is a fishery only for hardcore anglers. This trophy fishery is pretty much preserved by special regulations and a poor access road to it.

There are many hot spots in the lake. However, most are closed to fishing. The Upper Independence Creek inlet is the best spot; unfortunately, no fishing is permitted within 300 feet of all tributaries. Only artificial lures with barbless hooks may be used. Due to the difficulty of towing a boat to the lake, most people try their luck tossing spinners from the shore, but shore fishing isn't likely to fill your stringer. You need a boat to be successful. Trolling is the key. Troll the shorelines and down the middle of the lake with spoons and stickbaits.

The lake holds mostly cutthroat, rainbow and brown trout, but a few brook trout work their way down Upper Independence Creek into the lake. The Department of Fish and Game used to stock cutthroat trout, but stocks have since ceased because of public access issues. Years ago, cutthroats were taken from Independence and attempted to be introduced into Stampede. Also, at one time there were plans to construct a Disney theme park on the site.

If you plan to make the trip, supplies are available in Truckee. The road to the lake closes in winter.

Also nearby are Webber Falls, Jackson Meadows Reservoir, Lake of the Woods, Webber Lake and the Little Truckee River.

Directions: *From Truckee, drive 14.9 miles north on Highway 89 to Forest Service Road 7. Turn left and continue 1.5 miles to Independence Lake Road. Turn left and drive 6.5 miles to the lake.*

Independence Lake

LITTLE TRUCKEE RIVER (UPPER)

Rating: 5

Species: Rainbow and Brown Trout

Stocked with 700 pounds of rainbow trout.

Facilities: Campgrounds and Restrooms

Need Information? Contact: Tahoe National Forest (530) 587-3558

Depending on what time of year you arrive, the upper portion of the Little Truckee River can look like an actual river or a small stream. From late May through June, this upper section flows fast and furious as tributaries pump snowmelt into the river. However by the first week of July, the Little Truckee runs out of stream and becomes, "little". When this occurs, the California Department of Fish and Game shows up with the fish planting truck and unloads buckets of half-pound trout in the two campgrounds along Highway 89.

The stocks are purely for recreation. Roughly 1,400 trout are taken out of the allotment for Jackson Meadows Reservoir and spilled into the river to provide campers with a fishing opportunity. The trout are best caught in one of the many pools along the river. Fortunately, Power Bait and small spinners work well.

If you plan to make the trip, supplies are available in Truckee. The Little Truckee River is closed to fishing from November 16 to the last Saturday in April.

Also nearby are Independence Lake, Webber Falls, Prosser Reservoir and Jackson Meadow Reservoir.

Directions: From the junction of I-80 and Highway 89 north in Truckee, exit north on Highway 89 and drive 11 miles to the Little Truckee River Bridge.

Little Truckee River

COLDSTREAM CREEK

Rating: 4

Species: Rainbow Trout and Brown Trout

Stocked with 200 pounds of rainbow trout.

Facilities: Campgrounds and Restrooms

Need Information? Contact: Tahoe National Forest (530) 587-3558

The "new" Coldstream Creek was made possible in 1885 by a diversion on the Little Truckee River near the Little Truckee Summit. The diversion sent water into Sierra Valley and transformed the creek from a small, spring fed seasonal brook into a year-round trout stream. A grandfather clause allows for 400-acre feet of water to be pumped out of Webber Lake, into the Little Truckee River and then diverted into Coldstream with the ultimate goal of adding water into the Feather River (North Fork) and catering to the needs of the residents of Sierra Valley. It is one of the few out-of-basin water diversions in the region.

Each spring and early summer, the California Department of Fish and Game drops roughly 390 half-pound trout into the small, overgrown stream in the Tahoe National Forest. High and rapid flows can make angling tough through June. However, by early summer the flows subside and pools begin to form. If you concentrate your efforts near Cold Creek Campground there are plenty of trout available. This is an excellent Pautzke salmon egg stream. Brush and trees make for difficult spin casting conditions.

If you plan to make the trip, supplies are available in Sierraville. Coldstream Creek is closed to fishing from November 16 to the last Saturday in April.

Also nearby are Independence Lake and the Little Truckee River.

Directions: *From the junction of Interstate 80 and Highway 89 in Truckee, exit north on Highway 89 and drive 18.7 miles to Cold Creek Campground on the left.*

Rainbows are common at Coldstream Creek

For Lake Tahoe lake trout please see pages 574-582

To learn more about catching topwater bass in Folsom Lake, please visit pages 209-212

Region

22

Interstate 80 Corridor

Oxbow Reservoir
French Meadows
Hell Hole Reservoir
Sugar Pine Reservoir
Morning Star Lake
Halsey Forebay
Bear River
Rollins Reservoir
Scotts Flat Reservoir
Deer Creek Forebay
American River (North Fork)
Drum Forebay
Putt Lake
Huysink Lake
Salmon Lake
Lock Leven Lakes (3)
Long Lake
Cascade Lakes
Kidd Lake
Serene Lakes
Yuba River (South Fork)
Lake Valley Reservoir

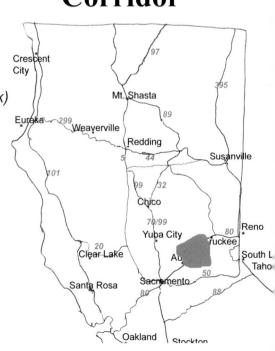

OXBOW RESERVOIR

Rating: 3

Species: Rainbow Trout
and Brown Trout

Stocks: None

Facilities: Picnic Areas
and Restrooms

Need Information?
Contact: Tahoe National
Forest (530) 543-2600

To be frank, Oxbow Reservoir is a mere widening in the Middle Fork of the American River. It's not an angler's dream by any means. On the other hand, there was once a time when the fishery flourished. Back in the Eighties, drought caused the flows to recede enough to enable the fish to live in the 30-foot wide river without struggling to battle torrent currents. At times, the river got so low it was more of a stream.

However, those instances are rare. Fed by the Rubicon and Middle Fork of the American Rivers, this place is like a massive toilet that is constantly flushed. Water is rushed thought this section to create hydroelectric power downstream. The fish are sucked out and spit out downstream and rarely spend much time at Oxbow. The California Department of Fish and Game hasn't bothered managing the fishery because the water is too unstable and the angler pressure is minimal. This place has great scenery, but it lacks cover for fish. For the die hard angler, there is a chance of catching fish. Rainbows and browns are constantly flushed through the system, but your chances are scarce. There are plenty of other waters in the region. Play it safe and try one of them.

If you plan to make the trip, supplies are available in Foresthill.

Also nearby are Grouse Falls, Mad Canyon Falls and Hell Hole Reservoir.

Directions: *From Sacramento, drive east on Interstate 80 and exit Foresthill Road. Drive east for 19 miles to Foresthill. In Foresthill, turn right on Mosquito Ridge Road and continue to the turnoff for Oxbow Reservoir on the right.*

Oxbow Reservoir

FRENCH MEADOWS RESERVOIR

Rating: 7

Species: Rainbow Trout and Brown Trout

Stocked with 5,000 pounds of rainbow trout.

Facilities: Boat Launch, Campgrounds and Restrooms

Need Information? Contact: Tahoe National Forest (530) 367-2224

If you live in the Sacramento area and you are looking for a spot where you can catch trout without battling crowds, French Meadows Reservoir would be the perfect spot for you. Even though it's only a two-hour drive from Sacramento, few anglers fish this remote reservoir. Why? Great question. The most likely answer is that folks don't enjoy the 27 miles of slow, winding road from Foresthill to French Meadows.

Nonetheless, French Meadows is a great trout reservoir for those looking to soak bait or troll. The 1,400-acre reservoir at 5,200 feet in the Tahoe National Forest is planted with 9,700 rainbow trout each year by the California Department of Fish and Game, many of which remain in the reservoir for several years. Most fish run 10-12 inches, yet 12-16 inch trout are common.

This is simple fishing. The great thing about French Meadows is that you don't need downriggers or leadcore to catch fish. Even during the warmest months you can find trout on the surface early and late in the day. It's best to troll small spoons or flashers and night crawlers. There's no need to run big plugs or stickbaits. It makes no difference where you troll either. Any of the shoreline is productive. One tip would be to use light line. I use four-pound test. There's no need for anything heavier.

French Meadows Reservoir

The water at French Meadows is extremely clear. Oftentimes, shoreline anglers fishing near the dam or off points can spot trout cruising the area. Any traditional trout rig will get the job done from shore.

If you plan to make the trip, supplies are available in Foresthill. In winter and spring, call ahead for road conditions. The road to the lake isn't plowed and is commonly closed due to snow.

Also nearby are Hell Hole Reservoir and Grouse Falls.

Directions: *From Sacramento, drive east on Interstate 80 to the Foresthill exit. Drive 17 miles to Foresthill and turn right on the signed road for French Meadows. Continue 36 miles to the reservoir.*

HELL HOLE RESERVOIR

Rating: 8

Species: Lake Trout, Kokanee, Rainbow Trout and Brown Trout

Stocked with 3,000 pounds of brown trout and 130 pounds of kokanee.

Facilities: Boat Launch, Campgrounds and Restrooms

Need Information? Contact: El Dorado National Forest (916) 333-4312

Hell Hole Reservoir. Sounds like a great place, doesn't it? Hell Hole Reservoir is a long drive on what many would call a hellish road, especially for folks who like to drive fast. Located in a remote section of El Dorado National Forest, Hell Hole is a haul from Auburn on slow, winding roads. If you drive the speed limit and allot for the many 15 mph turns, it would take roughly two hours from Sacramento to get here. Is the drive worth it? Most anglers would nod, yes.

Hell Hole is a diverse fishery that doesn't get overwhelmed by angling pressure. It's one of the region's most consistent kokanee fisheries, although it doesn't always yield trophy fish. From June through July, kokanee anglers fishing Sep's Pro flashers and dodgers in front of kokanee bugs, Needlefish and other lures tend to do well.

Hell Hole isn't like your traditional reservoirs, which offer great shoreline access and easy boating. It's a long, deep lake. In reality, it's a dammed portion of the Rubicon River that receives an influx of water in the spring and early summer and releases water from summer through fall. In fact, by mid summer oftentimes it can be so low that launching anything other than a car top or small boat can be challenging.

A few know-how's will tell you that the next state record lake trout will be caught here. The California Department of Fish and Game plants fingerling lake trout each year. Considering that these fish are rarely bothered and have plenty of food to eat, it's not uncommon to catch lake trout over 20 pounds. The downfall is locating them. Unlike Tahoe and Donner, there aren't groups of anglers constantly following these fish, nor are there any sporting goods stores or guides to call, so it can take some time to learn Hell Hole's fishery before success is easy to achieve.

If you are targeting the lake trout, you'll either want to troll or jig. Trollers that are running their lures near the bottom do best with Rebel Minnows and Bomber Long A's. If you are going after suspended fish, try a J-Plug or half-ounce Krocodile.

Hell Hole isn't planted with rainbows, but they are available. Browns, on the other hand, are planted and do well. Stories of huge browns being caught are true. Unfortunately, you have to arrive just after ice out (when roads are closed due to snow) or late in the fall to get in on the action. Trolling larger stickbaits are the best way. It's best to work the shorelines and have your bait in the top 15 feet of water, but this also poses a danger of getting snagged. Hell Hole is known for its' submerged granite slabs and boulders. It can take some time to learn the lake regardless of the species you are targeting. In the end though, it's worth it.

Trip info for French Meadows Reservoir also aplies to Hell Hole Reservoir.

Directions: *From Sacramento, drive east on Interstate 80 to the Foresthill exit. Drive 17 miles to Foresthill and turn right on the signed road for French Meadows. Continue 36 miles to French Meadows Reservoir. After driving across the dam, turn right on Road 22 and drive 6.5 miles to a split in the road. Turn left on Road 2, drive eight-tenths of a mile, veer right and drive eight more miles to the reservoir.*

Sugar Pine Reservoir

Rating: 6

Species: Rainbow Trout, Brown Trout, Smallmouth Bass and Sunfish

Stocked with 5,200 pounds of rainbow trout and 62 pounds of fingerling rainbow trout.

Facilities: Boat Launch, Campgrounds, Picnic Areas, Swimming Area and Restrooms

Need Information? Contact: Tahoe National Forest (530) 367-2224

With so many great trout fishing reservoirs nearby, Sugar Pine Reservoir definitely gets overlooked. At 160 acres and a 3,500-foot elevation, the lake holds the same fish as nearby Hell Hole and French Meadows Reservoirs, yet fishermen tend to pass on fishing Sugar Pine because lunkers rarely get pulled from the lake.

Sugar Pine is run as a put-and-grow and put-and-take fishery. To invest in the future the California Department of Fish & Game plants 25,358 fingerling trout, hoping they will grow to catchable sizes. Keeping anglers happy, another 8,820 fish weighing one-third of a pound are also planted from May through July.

Most of the rainbows are caught by trollers working the dam area or along points. No specific lures are needed, but keep to the small side. There's no point in running a large Rapala when there are few trophy trout to hit it. Bank fishermen do well fishing off the dam, in coves or off one of the many points. Although not targeted there are a sprinkle of browns and smallmouth bass in the lake.

If you plan to make the trip, supplies are available in Foresthill. There is a day-use fee. There is a 10 mph speed limit.

Also nearby are Mary Star Lake, Hell Hole Reservoir, North Fork American River and Mineral Bar Falls.

Directions: *From Sacramento, drive east on Interstate 80 and exit Foresthill Road. Drive east for 19 miles to Foresthill. Continue past Foresthill for nine miles to Sugar Pine Road (Forest Service Road 10). Turn left and follow signs to the lake.*

Sugar Pine Reservoir

Morning Star Lake

Rating: 7

Species: Rainbow Trout, Largemouth Bass and Channel Catfish

Stocked with 5,000 pounds of rainbow trout.

Facilities: General Store, Boat Launch, Campgrounds, RV Sites, Restrooms, Showers and Picnic Areas, Swimming Area and Pedal Boat Rentals

Need Information? Contact: Morning Star Lake (530) 367-2129

On some maps, Morning Star Lake is named Big Reservoir. So which name is correct? Here's a little history lesson I was told by a woman who claimed she owned Morning Star: The lake was built a long time ago. What has always been in question was who owned the rights to the land. The US Forest Service and De Anza Gold Mining Company each thought it was theirs. A long court battle ensued and thinking she was going to lose the battle to the Forest Service, the woman who owned the lake blew up the dam with dynamite. De Anza won the battle and the lake's dam was rebuilt in 1980.

Morning Star Lake is now run as a quality put and take trout fishery. Since the lake is privately owned no fishing license is required and no plants from the California Department of Fish & Game take place. The lake stocks 5,000 pounds of trout from Kimo Trout Farm near Jackson. While camping, swimming and hiking are also popular, fishing tends to get the most attention, probably because the action remains hot at the 80-acre surrounded by pines.

Although non-gas powered boats are permitted, the best way to fish the lake is with a float tube. Whether trolling down the middle of the lake, tossing Power Bait or night crawlers from shore or casting small Kastmasters from a float tube, catching fish usually comes quick.

Most anglers concentrate on catching trout, but those who fish for the catfish do well too. As a cold water reservoir catfish don't grow to huge proportions, but there are many cats in the one-to-three-pound range. Try putting two night crawlers on a single bait hook.

If you plan to make the trip, supplies are available at the lake and in Forest Hill. No fishing license is required. There is a fishing fee. No gas-powered boats are permitted. Morning Star is closed from November through April.

Also nearby are Sugar Pine Reservoir, North Fork American River, Rollins Lake and Hell Hole Reservoir.

Directions: *From Sacramento, drive east on Interstate 80 and exit Forest Hill Road. Drive east for 19 miles to Forest Hill. Continue past Forest Hill for nine miles to Sugar Pine Road (Forest Service Road 10). Turn left, drive three miles and turn right onto Road 24. In one mile Road 24 breaks off to the left. Stay right and follow signs to the lake.*

HALSEY FOREBAY

Rating: 5

Species: Rainbow Trout

Stocked with 4,000 pounds of rainbow trout.

Facilities: Restrooms

Need Information? Contact: Tahoe National Forest (530) 543-2600

Sometimes the worst thing to do is follow directions. Take Halsey Forebay for example. I followed published directions from the California Department of Fish & Game that tell you to exit Placer Hills Road to reach the lake. I did just that and then drove around a five mile radius for three hours looking for the lake. It was breakfast time so I pulled into a drive-through coffee and bagel shop in nearby Colfax. I showed the owner the instructions I was given and he too pondered over the directions. By reading the directions he was unclear where the lake was, but was darn sure than it wasn't near Colfax. He phoned his wife who had lived in the area her whole life. Sure enough, she knew were it was, but it was nowhere near where I was. She gave me better directions, and I quickly learned it was a lot to go through to get to little Halsey Forebay.

It's difficult to tell if the Forebay, located a few miles north of Auburn, was worth all the trouble to find it. The 18-acre pond-like reservoir is definitely worth it to a few locals who spend their weekends and time after work fishing for the 7,330 rainbow trout that the CA DFG plants from May through August. Most anglers fish near the intake, casting night crawlers and Power Bait from the railing above the concrete wall that separates the parking lot from the water. Others cast lures from the rock wall dam.

If you plan to make the trip, supplies are available in Auburn.

Also nearby are Bear River, Rollins Lake, Deer Afterbay and Folsom Lake.

Directions: *From Sacramento, drive east on Interstate 80 (past Auburn) to Dry Creek Road. Turn left, drive one-tenth of a mile (over the freeway) to a stop sign. Turn left, drive one-tenth of a mile to Christian Valley Road and turn right. Drive one-mile to Bancroft Road and turn right. Continue two-tenths of a mile to the lake on the left.*

Halsey Forebay

BEAR RIVER

Rating: 4

Species: Rainbow Trout
and Brown Trout

Stocked with 400
pounds of rainbow
trout.

Facilities:
Campgrounds, Picnic
Areas and Restrooms

Need Information?
Contact: Big 5 Sporting
Goods (530) 887-8326

The Bear River is a popular camping spot in the hills between Colfax and Auburn. Too bad the same can't be said for the fishing. Fishing is poor along the river, especially near the campgrounds. Only 800 trout are planted by the California Department of Fish and Game each year. Consequently, there is a small population of trout. Located upstream from Lake Combie, the river holds a few rainbow and brown trout that have been washed out of Rollins Reservoir, which is located a few miles upstream.

Signs near the river warn visitors of fluctuating water levels. Take the warning seriously. As soon as the decision is made to release water from Rollins, the river can become fast and swift in a matter of seconds. When water isn't being released, Bear spans roughly 20-30 feet wide and less than two feet deep. Most of the river is made up of long, slow moving sections and shallow pools.

If you are fishing with Panther Martins and don't spend too much time at any one pool. Make a few casts and if you don't get any hits, move on.

If you plan to make the trip, supplies are available in Colfax. Bear River is closed to fishing from November 16 to the last Saturday in April.

Also nearby are Rollins Reservoir, Halsey Forebay and Sugar Pine Reservoir.

Directions: From Sacramento drive east on Interstate 80 (past Auburn) and exit Placer Hills Road. Turn left at the stop sign off the freeway and drive one-tenth of a mile to a sign for Auburn/Placer Hills Road. Turn left, drive over the freeway and in one-tenth of a mile you'll come to a "t" intersection. Turn left on South Auburn Road and drive seven-tenths of a mile to a stop sign. Turn left onto Placer Hills Road and drive seven-tenths of a mile to Plum Tree Lane. Turn right and drive 1.9 miles to the river.

Rollins Reservoir

ROLLINS RESERVOIR

Rating: 6

Species: Rainbow Trout, Channel Catfish, Crappie, Bluegill, Largemouth Bass, Red Ear, Brown Trout, Smallmouth Bass, Carp and Kokanee

Stocked with 8,000 pounds of rainbow trout and 2,000 pounds of brown trout.

Facilities: RV Hookups, Campgrounds, Picnic Areas, Boat Launches, Gas, Café, Full Service Marinas, Boat Rentals, Restrooms, Swimming Area and Showers

Need Information? Contact: Long Ravine Campground (530) 346-6166

It's estimated that from June through August, 300,000 people visit Rollins Lake's 26 miles of shoreline. Those numbers are good for the local economy and while many would think it could hurt the fishing, it doesn't. Most of the tourists are, in fact, water-skiers and jet skiers. Fortunately, there are so many coves and 5 mph zones that there is room for everyone: fishermen, campers, swimmers and those who enjoy water sports. At Rollins, there is something for everyone.

At 2,170 feet in Gold Country above the town of Colfax, the 840-acre lake is a diverse fishery with great amenities, including four full-service campgrounds. No single species stands out at the lake. Fishing for each is productive at different times of the year. Surface temperatures can reach 75 degrees in the summer. The lake is 280 feet deep at full pool. With pine trees on the shoreline the lake is quite pretty. On the other hand, as soon as they start drawing it down the reddish soil becomes exposed, extracting from Rollins' beauty.

The most stocked fish is rainbow trout. The California Department of Fish & Game stocks 11,100 rainbows, just under a half-pound each, and also 5,400 brown trout.

Toplining just about any lure catches fish up until May. When trout move to deeper water, leadcore or downriggers are needed. At times, anglers fishing for rainbows with Rebels are surprised when they catch brown trout. Most of the browns are one-to-two pounders, but some to five pounds are caught each year. Kokanee were introduced to the lake in the mid-nineties, but didn't fair well and haven't been restocked since. Word is they are all gone.

As soon as the trout move to deeper water, the bass bite turns on. There are small and largemouth bass. When I last visited, an angler told me that when he was fishing in a cove the previous week, a huge bass surfaced and swallowed a baby duck. Too bad ducks are illegal to use for bait!

When the bass bite slows in late June, the crappie and bluegill begin to feed. The best area for panfish is in the Greenhorn Creek Arm, near the inlet.

If you plan to make the trip, supplies are available at the lake. There is a day-use fee.

Also nearby are Scott's Flat Reservoir, Bear River and Halsey Forebay.

Directions: From Sacramento, drive east on Interstate 80 to the Rollins Lake exit. Follow signs to the lake.

Scotts Flat Reservoir

Rating: 7

Species: Rainbow
Trout, Brown Trout,
Kokanee, Smallmouth
Bass, Largemouth Bass,
Bluegill and Catfish

Stocked with 84 pounds
of kokanee and 6,000
pounds of rainbow
trout.

Facilities: Restrooms,
Campgrounds, Boat
Launches, Fishing
Piers, General Store,
Bait & Tackle, Marina
and Picnic Areas

Need Information?
Contact: Scotts Flat
Recreation Area
(530) 265-5302

Scotts Flat Reservoir has several aspects that allow it to shine. To me, its' best trait is the exceptional handicap access it offers disabled people. The lake is one of the few Sierra destinations that has wheelchair access and flat ground.

Scotts Flat is a diverse fishery that combines a coldwater and warmwater program. While the lake is planted with roughly 25,000 kokanee each year, they aren't on top of the list of desired species, likely because they aren't as abundant as in Tahoe, Stampede and other nearby lakes.

While not heavily targeted, browns are available to determined anglers. The browns are likely to be found in creek inlets, especially Deer Creek. Also, target the impoundments where old hydraulic sites can be found. These pits were inundated when the banks were flooded years ago. A lake record 17-pound brown was caught in 1995.

In the spring and again in fall the bass fishery can be productive on mostly smaller fish. In the spring fish plastics shallow. Look for coves, stumps and submerged trees. The bite again picks up in the fall after lagging during the summer. Planted rainbow trout (8,600 in all) are an attraction for shoreline anglers and trollers. Downriggers or leadcore line is vital to success after mid-June.

Scotts Flat Reservoir

If you plan to make the trip, supplies are available in Nevada City. There is a day-use and boat launch fee.

Also nearby is the South Fork of the Yuba River.

Directions: *From Highway 20 in Nevada City drive east five miles to Scotts Flat Road. Turn south and drive 4.3 miles to the lake.*

DEER CREEK FOREBAY

Rating: 6

Species: Rainbow Trout and Brown Trout

Stocks: None

Facilities: None

Need Information?
Contact: Tahoe National Forest (530) 587-3558

The most difficult thing about fishing Deer Creek Forebay is finding it. Dozens of roads veer off Remington Hill and Deer Creek Roads, very few of which are signed. For some people it's easy to get lost. Follow the directions below precisely and you should be ok. The rule of thumb I like to use on these back roads is to stay on the road with tire tracks indented in it, and the wider road. One thing to consider is that Pacific Gas & Electric Company needs to use the main roads daily to access their facilities, so the main roads are pretty easy to spot. The roads which break off from the main roads are most likely logging roads.

Because the Forebay isn't stocked, chances are you won't find many people fishing it. The only way I discovered that rainbow and brown trout inhabit this one-acre pond was because on my first time trying to locate the Forebay I got lost and needed to ask a few loggers how to get there. "Big Jim" told me he catches a lot of rainbows out of the hole, sometimes a brown. Water enters the Forebay from the South Yuba Canal, bringing rainbow and brown trout along with it.

The Forebay is extremely small. You can cast across the entire lake with a decent rod and reel. The trout caught are wild. I wouldn't use Power Bait. Try casting small spinners where the water comes in the lake or out near the middle. Floating night crawlers off a bobber seems to work well too.

If you plan to make the trip, supplies are available in Grass Valley and Soda Springs. Due to snowy and muddy conditions, the roads to the Forebay may be inaccessible from December through April. Call the Forest Service for conditions.

Deer Creek Falls is near Deer Creek Forebay

Also nearby are Deer Creek Falls, Bear River Falls and Bowman Lake.

Directions: From Sacramento, drive east on Highway 50 for approximately 40 miles and exit Highway 20. Continue on Highway 20 for 10.8 miles and turn left on Remington Hill Road. (Remington Road is just past the Omega Lookout Point.) Continue 1.4 miles and veer right on Deer Creek Road (signed 32-07). Continue 2.8 miles to the Forebay on the right.

AMERICAN RIVER (NORTH FORK)

Rating: 7

Species: Rainbow
Trout, Brook Trout and
Brown Trout

Stocks: None

Facilities: None

Need Information?
Contact: Truckee
National Forest
(530) 587-3558

The North Fork of the American River is one of the state's top wild trout rivers. However, poor access coupled with butt-kicking hikes required to reach the river keeps many anglers from fishing this remote section of the North Fork. Rewardingly, the anglers who endure the descent, and the grueling climb out, stumble upon hundreds of opportunistic trout.

A wild and scenic river, the North Fork is a catch and release water from Palisade Creek to the Colfax-Iowa Hill Bridge, a distance of 37 miles. From its' headwaters at Mountain Meadow Lake, the North Fork is roughly 50 miles long, dumping into the Middle Fork of the American River near Auburn.

There are two main sections of the river. The upper portion above the Colfax-Iowa Hill Bridge is a hike-to stretch and the lower section, downstream of the bridge has drive-to access. With a mix of some hefty browns, the North Fork is a fine rainbow trout fishery which also includes some brook trout in the upper sections. Low fishing pressure allows the rainbows to average 10 inches. With the river's habitat in excellent shape, in addition to crystal clear and clean water, along with fairly deep pools the prognosis for the fishery's future remains good.

Fishing this wide and fast flowing river sounds like a blast, however,

The North Fork of the American River

reaching it isn't. Many of the trails to the river require a steep, and as much as a 3,000-foot descent to its' banks. The river can be reached via dirt roads off Foresthill Road and a network of roads leading to trailheads near Soda Spring and Donner Pass.

The California Department and Fish and Game last surveyed the river in 1994 where they calculated 800 trout per mile in the stream. These estimates are on the low end because electrofishing and snorkeling are difficult sampling tools in rivers with deep holes. Therefore, the numbers of fish per mile in the steam is expected to be substantially higher. A priceless tip on fishing this river is to arrive anytime after late summer and throughout the fall. Any earlier and the swift currents dictate your presentation, not you.

If you plan to make the trip, supplies are available in Foresthill and Soda Springs. In winter and spring call the Forest Services for updated road conditions. Many of the roads are closed during the wet season. For more specific trailhead information, contact the Forest Service. The North Fork of the American River is closed to fishing from November 16 to the last Saturday in April.

Also nearby are Cascade Lake, Kidd Lake and Lake Valley Reservoir.

Directions: From the junction of Highway 89 and Interstate 80 in Truckee, drive west for 12.7 miles to the Soda Springs exit. Turn left and drive nine-tenths of a mile to Pahatsi Road. Turn right and drive 2.8 miles to Kidd Lake. Drive 1.4 miles past Kidd Lake to the Cascade Lakes Parking Area and the Palisade Trailhead.

The North Fork of the American River

DRUM FOREBAY

Rating: 6

Species: Rainbow
Trout, Brown Trout,
Channel Catfish and
Smallmouth Bass

Stocks: None

Facilities: None

Need Information?
Contact: Tahoe National
Forest (530) 543-2600

The California Department of Fish and Game and Pacific Gas & Electric Company do not stock Drum Forebay with fish, therefore someone decided to take it upon themselves and add a few into the small holding pond. As the story goes, smallmouth bass and channel catfish were stocked and according a few locals, who asked to remain nameless, the fish are doing well. Maybe too well. The locals swear by seven-to-nine pound bass, however, most of the smallies stick to the one-to-three-pound average.

Fishing isn't easy though. Drum's water is so clear the bass can be spooked easily, and without a boat, they are extremely difficult to catch from the shore. The locals I was lucky enough to chat with have an "in", which you won't. They either have buddies who work for PG&E who allow them to use float tubes (no watercraft is allowed) or they said they know when to show up when no one is patrolling the lake. Even if you do manage to get on the water, success isn't eminent. You still have to overcome the fish's lethargic habits. The water is pumped in from Spaulding Reservoir. It's cold and bass' metabolism is kept slow. Try using plastics and grubs. The slower the presentation, the better.

Because water from Spaulding is pumped in there are a few rainbows and browns, but like the catfish they are seldom caught. Stick to trying to fool the bass.

If you plan to make the trip, supplies are availble in Truckee. No watercraft is permitted on the Forebay.

Also nearby are Fuller Lake and Lake Valley Reservoir.

Drum Forebay

Directions: *From the junction of Interstate 5 and 80 in Sacramento, take I-80 east for 62.6 miles and exit Drum Forebay Road. Turn left, cross over the freeway and drive four-tenths of a mile to a split in the road. Stay left on the dirt road and drive a half-mile to another split in the road. Staying on Drum Forebay Road, veer right and continue six-tenths of a mile to the spillway and lake.*

PUTT POND

Rating: 7

Species: Channel
Catfish, Bluegill and
Smallmouth Bass

Stocks: None

Facilities: None

Need Information?
Contact: Mountain
Hardware
(530) 587-4844

It's a mystery to many anglers how fish ended up in ponds along Interstate 80 near Donner Summit. The California Department of Fish and Game has only a few recorded accounts of plants in any of them. However, records from the late 1800's and early 1900's give us a hint towards how these fish arrived.

In the early days, anglers could fill out an application to petition the California Department of Fish and Game Commission for fish to stock their favorite body of water. If granted, the CA DFG would ship the fish in milk cans on the Southern Pacific Railroad. Anglers would pick up the fish at various train stops, however they didn't always plant the fish in the lakes they filled out applications for. Over time, anglers walked and carried fish on horseback to nearly every pond and lake along Interstate 80, which was obviously not around when all this was taking place.

Because of winterkill, predators, overfishing and other outside elements, not all the populations of have survived more than a century. The smallmouth bass and bluegill in little Putt Pond, however, have. The lake is brimming with these timid and skittish fish. There are some lunkers to be caught, some which climb into the five-pound class. To catch them, a pair of waders is a must, in addition to green and salt-and-pepper grubs. Be sure to use light line, nothing bigger than six-pound test in this shallow, clear and weedy water. Catfish are rarely landed because they aren't targeted. But abundant, bite-size bluegill are a great learning tool for youngsters eager to catch pan fish. Small pieces of night crawlers are all you need.

Putt Pond

If you plan to make the trip, supplies are available at the gas station off Nyack Road. The lake freezes in the winter.

Also nearby are Spaulding Reservoir and Lake Valley Reservoir.

Directions: From the junction of Interstate 5 and 80 in Sacramento, take I-80 east for 68.2 miles to the Nyack Road exit. Turn right and make an immediate right into a parking area. Drive through the lot and veer left on dirt road. Continue to the pond on the right.

HUYSINK LAKE

Rating: 3

Species: Brook Trout, Smallmouth Bass and Sunfish

Stocks: None

Facilities: None

Need Information?
Contact: Tahoe National Forest (530) 587-3558

Located near Lake Valley Reservoir in the Tahoe National Forest, when I first visited Huysink Lake, there were no trespassing signs posted so I refrained from fishing it. (I always obey the posted signs.) However, I was a bit concerned when I looked on the California Department of Fish and Game's stocking list and found Huysink on it. The CA DFG only stocks waters where public access is permitted. Now it definitely seemed odd that there were no trespassing signs at the roadside pond. Additionally, I looked on the Tahoe National Forest map only to find that the Huysink was surrounded by green, indicating that this was in fact national forest land. Still unsure of why this place was posted, I headed to the Big Bend Visitor Center where I again found that the pond was open to the public. They assured me they would head up there and clear things up.

While Huysink listed as 2.5 acres and 20 feet deep, don't get all revved up over fishing this tiny body of water; it's a small pond, not a big lake. The CA DFG does plant 500 fingerling brook trout (these plants are on hold now), but the lack of depth and space for them to hide in allows few fish to grow big. There are also largemouth bass, but not in great numbers. While the posted signs kept me from fishing the lake, I did see a few adult bass swimming around near the tules.

As for now concentrate on tossing spinners from the shore or dunking Power Bait. If you run into posted signs contact the Forest Service. Don't take the law into your own hands.

If you plan to make the trip, supplies are available in Truckee. The road to the Huysink is closed from winter through early spring. Call the Forest Service for updated conditions.

Also nearby are Lock Leven Lakes, Lake Valley Reservoir and Salmon Lake.

Huysink Lake

Directions: From the junction of Interstate 5 and 80 in Sacramento, take I-80 east for 72.3 miles to the Yuba Gap exit. Turn right off the ramp on Lake Valley Road and drive two-tenths of a mile. Staying on Lake Valley Road, veer right. The road splits in 1.1 miles. Stay left and drive four-tenths of a mile to a sign for Silvertip Picnic Area and Boat Ramp. Veer left and drive 3.7 miles another split. Veer left and drive 1.3 miles to the lake on the left.

SALMON LAKE

Rating: 3

Species: Rainbow Trout

Stocks: None

Facilities: None

Need Information?
Contact: Tahoe National
Forest (530) 587-3558

Salmon Lake? A backcountry lake loaded with salmon? That's sure what it sounds like. However, words can be deceiving. In actuality, there are no salmon in Salmon Lake. Ironically, I couldn't locate any fish. While the California Department of Fish and Game used to plant 500 fingerling rainbow trout each year, they don't seem to be showing up in anglers' creels. Since there is no inlet or outlet the trout can't leave, so either they are being caught so fast that their numbers never have a chance to build up or the stocking plant missed the lake completely.

At 6,700 feet in the Tahoe National Forest, Salmon Lake is a small, shallow, non-productive lake with rocks partially submerged on one side and steep drop-offs on the other. It's a poor fishery with well-shaded campsites. If you do want to give it a try, float a night crawler off the bottom near the middle of the lake or run a small spinner near the drop-offs. But, don't bet all your money on the bite.

From the Salmon Lake Trailhead, Salmon Lake is a mere one-mile away. The path begins on fairly flat ground before passing by a small and shallow pond. It then winds roughly 100 feet up the mountain over the rest of the mile. At this point, a spur on the right breaks off to Salmon Lake a short five-minute trot ahead.

If you plan to make the trip, supplies are available in Truckee. The road to the trailhead is closed from winter through early spring. Call the Forest Service for updated conditions. The lakes can also be reached via the Big Bend Trailhead.

Also nearby are Loch Leven Lakes.

Salmon Lake

Directions: *From the junction of Interstate 5 and 80 in Sacramento take I-80 east for 72.3 miles to the Yuba Gap exit. Turn right off the ramp on Lake Valley Road and drive two-tenths of a mile. Staying on Lake Valley Road, veer right. The road splits in 1.1 miles. Stay left and drive four-tenths of a mile to a sign for Silvertip Picnic Area and Boat Ramp. Veer left and drive 3.7 miles to a split in the road. Veer left and drive 3.3 miles to the trailhead.*

LOCK LEVEN LAKE

Rating: 6

Species: Rainbow Trout and Brook Trout

Stocked with

Facilities: None

I had a rough outing when I fished the chain of Lock Leven Lakes in the Tahoe National Forest. Not finding any other anglers to chat with, I looked to the local Forest Service office for some insight on the fishing. The man working the counter at Big Bend Visitor Center told me the fishing is always bad. The reason he gave me, however, was comical. He told me that the chain of lakes used offer great backcountry fishing, but an encounter with a swimmer has sent the fisheries into the dungeon.

A few years back a swimmer was sunbathing in the shallow water of High Lock Leven Lake when the California Department of Fish and Game stocking plane flew overhead and dropped a load of fish. As the story goes, the fish landed on his head and the angry swimmer filed a complaint with the CA DFG. As a result, the man told me that the lake hasn't been stocked since.

Lock Leven Lake

The man swears by his story, though I've yet to find an authorative figure to verify the event. I spoke with CA DFG pilots who said they'd never heard anything about the issue, nor had the fisheries biologist for the Tahoe National Forest or anyone else I contacted. There was no documented complaint either. Interestingly the lakes have been stocked the last few years, so there's an obvious cork in the story.

The fishing can be good at times. Brook and rainbow trout inhabit many of the lakes and because of their shallowness, swimming can be enjoyable in the summer. The lakes are set in a pined forest with large boulders populating their shoreline. No specific techniques are necessary. Just make sure you have a few spinners in your pack. Hardware works better than bait.

There are two routes to the lakes. The most popular start is from the Big Bend Trailhead. On the other hand, the less traveled route from the Salmon Lake Trailhead is much easier on your knees and less traveled. The path begins on fairly flat ground before passing by a small and shallow pond and then winds roughly 100 feet up the mountain over the first mile. At this point a spur on the right breaks off to Salmon Lake. Ignore it and continue another mile to Lower Lock Leven Lake. At the lake there's a junction. The left fork descends to the Big Bend Trailhead. For Middle Lock Leven make a right and continue a quarter mile. High Lock Leven Lake is only three-fourths of a mile from the Middle Lake.

Directions *and trip info for Salmon Lake also apply to Lock Leven Lake.*

LONG LAKE

Rating: 5

Species: Rainbow Trout

Stocks: None

Facilities: None

Need Information?
Contact: Tahoe National
Forest (530) 587-3558

There is no drive to access to Long Lake and for that reason many anglers overlook it without thinking twice. While the lake is planted with 2,000 fingerling rainbow trout each year, swimmers best utilize this small and shallow body of water at 6,620 feet in the Tahoe National Forest.

Because of its' depth, the water is comfortable to swim in by early summer. Most anglers don't complain about the swimmers because they don't fish it. Long Lake is a short 10-minute walk from the Palisade Trailhead at Cascade Lake; however, few anglers tend to give the lake a chance. With more than a mile of wooded shoreline, swimming conditions are ideal. I brought along a rod and after feeling the water I opted to swim to the lake's island and get a tan, rather than work to catch the resident eight-to-nine-inch rainbow trout (2,000 fingerlings were planted last by the California Department of Fish and Game in 2002), which are attainable by dangling a night crawler off the bottom or tossing red and gold Panther Martins from shore.

If you plan to make the trip, supplies are available in Soda Springs. The road to the trailhead is closed from winter through early spring. Call the Forest Service for updated conditions.

Also nearby are Kidd Lake, Serene Lakes and Cascade Lake.

Directions: *From the junction of Highway 89 and Interstate 80 in Truckee, drive west for 12.7 miles to the Soda Springs exit. Turn left and drive nine-tenths of a mile to Pahatsi Road. Turn right and drive 2.8 miles to Kidd Lake. Drive 1.4 miles past Kidd Lake to the Cascade Lakes Parking Area and the Palisade Trailhead.*

Long Lake

CASCADE LAKES

Rating: 3

Species: Brook Trout

Stocked with one pound of fingerling brook trout (Lower Cascade Lake).

Facilities: None

Need Information? Contact: Tahoe National Forest (530) 587-3558

Over the past decade, the California Department of Fish and Game have surveyed thousands of lakes in the state to determine what effect stocking has on the body of water. It was discovered that many lakes had self-sustaining populations of trout and no longer needed plants to maintain adequate numbers of fish. Along the Interstate 80 corridor between Truckee and Highway 20, Upper and Lower Cascade Lake rests in a basin of several lakes that have self sustaining populations of brook trout. They don't receive heavy use by anglers. Kidd, Long and Upper and Lower Cascade Lakes were all planted with brooks at one time, but it's been determined that planting is no longer needed. Except for Lower Cascade.

Because of the fishing pressure received at Cascade (which is surrounded by pines and steep dirt drop-offs) the lake is supplemented with 1,000 fingerling brook trout some years. While the fishing never turns heads, brooks are abundant to the 10-inch range. There are larger holdovers, however, only a few locals know how to catch them and those secrets aren't for sale.

For starters, you have two options. The first and most common, is spot fishing, where you trot along the shoreline with polarized glasses and cast a small spinner when you see fish. The second option is to get in a float tube and fish the deeper sections of the lake. I would jig a silver Crippled Herring spoon out towards the middle or hang a night crawler. Many anglers wait until late fall when the lakes are drawn down to low pool and the fish are more concentrated. On the other hand, with less oxygen the trout are more sluggish than they are in the spring.

Cascade Lake

If you plan to make the trip, supplies are available in Soda Springs.

Also nearby are Kidd Lake, Long Lake and Serene Lakes.

Directions: *From the junction of Highway 89 and Interstate 80 in Truckee, drive west for 12.7 miles to the Soda Springs exit. Turn left and drive nine-tenths of a mile to Pahatsi Road. Turn right and drive 2.8 miles to Kidd Lake. Drive 1.4 miles past Kidd Lake to the Cascade Lakes Parking Area and the Palisade Trailhead.*

KIDD LAKE

Rating: 3

Species: Brook Trout

Stocks: None

Facilities:
Campgrounds and
Restrooms

Need Information?
Contact: Camping
Reservations
(916) 386-5164

Kidd Lake is one of those odd waters. There is no day-use whatsoever. To use the lake you must have reservations by reserving a campground. There are just four sites and a campground host who told me she once heard there are fish in the lake, but has never seen one herself.

The real story is simple. There are fish in the lake, but none are stocked. The fishery relies on a self-sustaining population of brook trout. From 1952-93 the lake was planted yearly with brook trout, however, budget cuts in the California Department of Fish and Game required those fish to be transferred to other waters.

This 89-acre lake with a maximum depth of 54 feet suffers from drawdowns. It gets so harsh that by the time water is done being released only 26 acres are left for the brooks. While fishing pressure is almost non-existent, at times, brooks up to two pounds are landed on Panther Martins tossed from the shore. On the other hand, no gas-powered motors are allowed, so your fishing options are limited to electric trolling motors or bank fishing.

If you plan to make the trip, supplies are available in Soda Springs. The road to the lake is closed in the winter and spring.

Also nearby are Cascade Lake, Long Lake and Serene Lakes.

Directions: *From the junction of Highway 89 and Interstate 80 in Truckee, drive west for 12.7 miles to the Soda Springs exit. Turn left and drive nine-tenths of a mile to Pahatsi Road. Turn right and drive 2.8 miles to Kidd Lake.*

Kidd Lake

SERENE LAKES

Rating: 5

Species: Rainbow Trout

Stocked with rainbow trout periodically by the lake association.

Facilities: Lodging, Restaurant, Canoe and Kayak Rentals, Swimming Area and a Boat Launch

Need Information? Contact: Ice Lakes Lodge (530) 426-7660, Serene Lakes Property Owners Association (530) 426-3778

If you look on a map it could be difficult to find Serene Lakes. Formerly known as Ice Lakes their name was changed to attract a real estate market. Unfortunately, what used to be a gorgeous high mountain lake has been littered with wall-to-wall houses. While it's great for anyone who owns property, it's a waste of space for non-landowners. There is little public access as only about 100 yards remains.

Anglers who don't own property aren't welcomed with opened arms by the residents and for an understandable reason. The Serene Lakes Property Owners Association pays for fish to be planted each year. Roughly every two years they stock 1,000 fish, half of which are half pounders and the others about a pound. Rainbow and brook trout have been planted. According to a story I was told by a member of the association, Fitz William Redding Jr. was the first to stock the lake in the mid-1800's. The fish were taken from either the North Fork of the American River or Donner Lake. There are no known recollections of fish being planted from 1867-1999.

While fishing takes a back seat to swimming, canoeing and kayaking there are some fish to be caught. Trout grow as large as three pounds. Being that the lake is shallow (max depth is 15 feet) you don't need expensive gear to catch fish.

Public boats can also be launched. Directions to the launch are as follows: from Ice House Lodge backtrack a half-mile to Sierra Road and turn left. Continue to the launch. Restrictions permit only electric motors which keeps things quiet. Additional access can be found at the beach near Ice Lakes Lodge.

Before the dam was built, Serene Lakes used to be three small lakes, Sybil, Dulzura and Serena. At 6,872 feet in the Tahoe National Forest the lakes are now known as Serena and Dulzura. The association implemented an "honor system" catch & release policy. Adults are required to release their catch. Children can keep fish.

If you plan to make the trip, supplies are available in Soda Springs.

Also nearby are Long Lake, Kidd Lake and Cascade Lake.

Directions: *From the junction of Highway 89 and Interstate 80 in Truckee, drive west for 12.7 miles to the Soda Springs exit. Turn left and drive six-tenths of a mile to Soda Springs Road. Turn right and drive 2.1 to Ice House Lodge.*

YUBA RIVER (SOUTH FORK)

Rating: 7

Species: Rainbow Trout
and Brown Trout

Stocked with 1,500
pounds of rainbow
trout.

Facilities:
Campgrounds and
Restrooms

Need Information?
Contact: Tahoe National
Forest (530) 587-3558

From Sacramento to Reno, the South Fork of the Yuba River is one of the few stream fishing options anglers have to choose from along Interstate 80. Fortunately, it's a 20 to 30-foot wide river with deep pools and long runs. It gets planted with 3,000 rainbow trout by the California Department of Fish and Game to ensure decent catch rates in the spring and early summer.

Planted along a seven-mile stretch, the South Fork has plenty of good access points for anglers and enough space to give each their own fishing hole. However, flows are only consistent from May through June. Arrive any later and the river begins to look like a small stream. After June, most anglers simply pass it by. While the plants are minimal there are thousands of wild rainbow and brown trout in the river, yet most fail to reach any length longer than pan size. Don't get me wrong there are some big browns in the river. Unfortunately, only a few are caught each year. At 5,700 feet in the Tahoe National Forest, most of those lunkers are caught under the large granite boulders that line portions of the river.

The reason for such small fish is the lack of cold water in the system. When the dam was breached at Lake Van Norden in the mid-Eighties, cold water could no longer be released in the summer to help the fishery. Now the water is warm, flows are low and oxygen content is down. Bad sign for the fish.

If you plan to make the trip, supplies are available in Truckee. The Yuba River (South Fork) is closed to fishing from November 16 to the last Saturday in April.

South Fork Yuba River

Also nearby are Spaulding Reservoir, Putt Pond, Serene Lakes, Kidd Lake and Long Lake.

Directions: *From Interstate 80 in Truckee, drive 17 miles west to Kingvale. Access sites to the river are found from here to Eagle Lakes Road.*

LAKE VALLEY RESERVOIR

Rating: 6

Species: Kokanee, Rainbow Trout and Brown Trout

Stocks: None

Facilities: Boat Launch, Restrooms, Campgrounds and a Picnic Area

Need Information? Contact: Tahoe National Forest (530) 587-3558

The California Department of Fish and Game often attempts to introduce multiple species into the state's lakes, however, not all fish do well in their new homes. In 1972, lake trout were stocked into 312-acre Lake Valley Reservoir. It was an odd plant because the lake is only 32 feet deep. Lake trout typically do well in deep, large lakes. Nonetheless, the lake trout never took. However, the CA DFG learned that because the lake is rich and shallow, rainbows would do well. There is so much feed that they've chosen to stock the bows as fingerlings and let them do their growing in the lake to give them more wild characteristics.

Lake Valley Reservoir is not located on Forest Service land. It falls on private land. Pacific Gas & Electric Company operates the lake and its' dam. Few anglers fish it, but there is a paved launch ramp to this fairly large reservoir that has the capacity to harbor holdovers. Up until 2003, the CA DFG spilled 30,000 fingerling rainbow trout each year. Don't plan to catch browns. They aren't stocked yearly, only when hatcheries have an excess amount of fish. In 2000, 20,600 fingerling brown trout were planted. Kokanee will be introduced in 2005.

Lake Valley Reservoir

The reservoir is a great family spot. By summer the coves are warm enough for kids to swim in, rainbow trout can be caught by trollers and bank anglers and it stays quiet enough to read a book under a pine tree along the shore. However, there are also a few drawbacks, mainly low water levels. The drawdown pattern allows the lake to reach 320 acres in the spring and is progressively drained to a mere 30 acres by fall.

If you plan to make the trip, supplies are available in Soda Springs. The lake is closed in the winter and early spring.

Also nearby are Lock Leven Lakes and Salmon Lake.

Directions: *From the junction of Interstate 5 and 80 in Sacramento, take I-80 east for 72.3 miles to the Yuba Gap exit. Turn right off the ramp on Lake Valley Road and drive two-tenths of a mile. Staying on Lake Valley Road, veer right. The road splits in 1.1 miles. Stay left and drive four-tenths of a mile to a sign for Silvertip Picnic Area and Boat Ramp. Veer right and continue one-tenth of a mile to the lake.*

Region

23

Desolation Wilderness

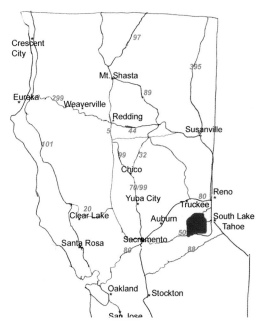

GROUSE LAKE

Rating: 6

Species: Rainbow Trout
and Brook Trout

Stocks: None

Facilities: None

Need Information?
Contact: El Dorado
National Forest
(530) 644-6048

Many fathers want to take their sons into the wilderness and get them started on backpacking at a young age. However, most of the hikes are too long and strenuous for children. The hike to Grouse Lake, near Wrights Lake in the El Dorado National Forest, is somewhere in the middle.

At 2.2 miles, it's not too long, but accompanies some challenge: the route gains 1,200 feet along the way. Yikes! To me this is a great test hike to see how far your kids can go. It's not too short to bore them. Nor too long to tire them out. If taken slowly, it's a great hike through a heavily forested wilderness area. What more could you ask for? Not much. At 8,145 feet in the Desolation Wilderness, Grouse blends its' beauty and mirror-like reflections with good fishing.

Catch rates are staggering and while the fish seldom grow larger than what fits in a skillet, you don't have to worry about getting skunked. We caught and released more than 20 fish in 15 minutes. Some are brooks, other rainbows, but all were willing to attack any Panther Martin.

Do you have to worry about targeting specific areas? No way. The lake is too small, but if you need some ideas, here you go. Rock-hopping to the large boulders that stick out of the water near the outlet stream is a sure way to catch fish, as is fishing the inlet and inlet stream for brooks.

Getting to Grouse Lakes will make you huff and puff a little bit, but if you take a few shore breaks you'll be fine. Begin at the signed trailhead. The path can be misleading early on as it leaves the parking area and bends around Wrights Lake's shoreline on fairly flat ground. The path crosses the lake's inlet and gradually ascends. Four-tenths of a mile in comes a trail junction. The left fork is a loop trail around Wrights Lake. Following signs for Twin, Island, Grouse, Hemlock and Smith Lakes, stay right and continue to climb. In another 1.1 miles you'll come to a second junction. The left fork heads to Twin Lake, Boomerang Lake and Island Lake. Stay right. Take this part of the trek slow. There's a lot of uphill on the last seven-tenths of a mile. Fortunately, there are also great views to consume while catching your breath. Wrights

Lake and Beauty Lake can be seen in their entirely. On clear days, Ice House Reservoir can also be seen.

If you plan to make the trip, supplies are available in Pollack Pines. The path to the lakes is commonly not snow-free until sometime in late May or early June. Call ahead for updated conditions.

Also nearby are Smith Lake, Hemlock Lake and Wrights Lake.

Directions: *From South Lake Tahoe at the junction of Highway's 50 and 89, drive west on Highway 50 for 20.9 miles to the Wright's Lake turnoff on the right. Turn right and drive 7.8 miles to Wrights Lake. At Wrights Lake Visitor Center veer right and continue to the trailhead.*

Grouse Lake

HEMLOCK LAKE

Rating: 3

Species: Brook Trout

Stocks: None

Facilities: None

Prior to the mid-Nineties, Hemlock Lake was a good put-and-grow brook trout fishery. At 8,400 feet in the El Dorado National Forest, this tiny backcountry water was stocked each year with brook trout. It's no longer planted. Regrettably, the brooks have seemed to disappear. There are some left in the lake, yet few anglers have any luck catching them.

Hemlock is a small lake with deep holes; however we found fishing to be poor. The California Department of Fish and Game planted 250 fingerling brook trout each year, until 2002. Unfortunately, we couldn't find any of them. The typical inlet and outlet areas were barren of fish, nor did we see any surface on the lake. Could be just coincidence, but I don't think there are many fish in Hemlock. Better spend your time at either Grouse or Smith Lake.

Once you do all the work getting to Grouse Lake, reaching Hemlock is a breeze. Gaining 250 feet, the path steadily climbs for a quarter-mile from Grouse to Hemlock.

Directions *and trip info for Grouse Lake also apply to Hemlock Lake.*

Hemlock Lake

SMITH LAKE

Rating: 4

Species: Brook Trout

Stocks: None

Facilities: None

Stumbling on a dammed lake in the high country is mind boggling. How did this dam get here? Why was it constructed in an area set aside for wilderness? Wouldn't the dam take away from the water's original state, which the wilderness was created to protect? These are all good questions. Whatever answers you are given when the question arises, keep one thing in mind; these dams do take away from the natural and prehistoric state. Also, the dams can block fish spawning; however proponents argue they increase the amount of surface acres and storage.

Most backcountry waters where you find dams are indeed natural lakes. The idea is to increase their capacity by building small stonewalls mended by cement. It can hurt spawning fish, but it keeps fish in the lake.

At 8,700 feet in the El Dorado National Forest, Smith Lake's three-foot dam is which keeps a small population of hungry brook trout in its' deep water. These fish rarely attain a length of more than nine inches, but they can be seen cruising the shoreline in search of insects or food and are easy to catch . Panther Martins work well; however, this is a great fly-fishing lake. Because three-fourths of the lake has no cover, i.e. trees, casting is made simple and any fly is appreciated by the brookies.

Reaching Smith Lake from seldom fished Hemlock Lake isn't a struggle. Continue ascending 270 feet over one-third of a mile to the back of the basin. For an outstanding view of the entire drainage and Lyons Lake on the other side, scramble up to the top of the pass while using caution not to slip on the loose rock. The view is unforgettable.

Directions *and trip info for Grouse Lake also apply to Smith Lake.*

Smith Lake

LYONS LAKE

Rating: 4

Species: Brook Trout

Stocks: None

Facilities: None

Need Information?
Contact: El Dorado
National Forest
(530) 644-6048

There are two ways to get to Lyons Lake: by trail or cross-county travel. Standing on the ridge above Smith Lake, a friend and I were overwhelmed by the rugged, rocky scenery that lay a few hundred feet below at Lyons Lake. The climb down from this vantage, however, is a steep one and only recommended for experienced off-trail hikers. The other route (which is described at the end of this write-up) is much easier, yet gains more than 1,500 feet over 4.7 miles.

The question is whether the fishing is worth the hike. To me, no. But, you can catch small brookies without having to compete with many other anglers. Brookies are no longer planted. Fortunately, they are so evasive that the California Department of Fish and Game would have great difficulty trying to remove them. Anglers can plan on casting spoons and spinners from shore and catching small brooks for years to come, even under extreme fishing pressure.

To reach Lyons, begin at the Lyons Creek Trailhead, which starts a short skip up from Forest Service Road 4 and runs for 1.5 miles before meeting up with the Bloodsucker Trail. Ignoring that turnoff, stay to the right and continue 2.7 miles to a final junction. The right fork takes you to Sylvia Lake. Stay left and continue one-half mile to Lyons Lake, which rests at 8,380 feet in the Desolation Wilderness.

Trip info for Grouse Lake also applies to Lyons Lake.

Directions: From South Lake Tahoe at the junction of Highway's 50 and 89, drive west on Highway 50 for 20.9 miles to the Wright's Lake turnoff on the right. Turn right and continue to the right turnoff for the Bloodsucker Trail.

Lyons Lake

TWIN LAKES

Rating: 7
Species: Brook Trout and Rainbow Trout
Stocks: None
Facilities: None

Every few years the California Department of Fish and Game tries to send a team of biologists and scientific aids into the backcountry to set gill nets, perform snorkeling samples and fish to determine how populations of trout are doing and what changes, if any, need to be applied to the fishery to ensure fish populations are healthy and stable. When they last sampled Twin Lakes in the early part of the 21st Century, they found that the lakes were loaded with brook trout, rather than rainbows. It was thought rainbows were the dominant fish because that was what was being planted. However, the brooks have taken over in both the upper and lower lake. With plants no longer taking place, it's likely the rainbows will die off. Spawning conditions are poor.

Twin Lakes is a set of two lakes. Each lake differs drastically. The lower lake is extremely shallow. You'll probably have to fish deeper water to be successful. Try casting spinners and spoons. The upper lake, on the other hand, is deep. At times, brookies can be found feeding on the surface, other times you'll need to use heavier spoons to pull them from deeper water. There are several points that provide good angling opportunities.

Reaching Twin from the junction with the turnoff to Grouse Lake is a short hike, but can be confusing if you lose the route. This path breaks left, rather than right and immediately climbs up slabs of granite. Through most of the route there are trail markers to aid your journey. Be sure to keep an eye on them. After you climb over the first ridge the trail becomes more level and you'll near Twin's outlet stream. Push forward. You'll pass a small pond on the left. There's no fish. Then you'll break left and within a few short minutes you'll find yourself on the shoreline of Lower Twin. For Upper Twin continue around the lake.

Directions *and trip info for Grouse Lake also applies to Twin Lakes.*

Twin Lakes

ISLAND LAKE

Rating: 7

Species: Rainbow Trout and Brook Trout

Stocks: None

Facilities: None

Island Lake is the farthest lake anglers can fish on the Twin Lakes Trail in the Desolation Wilderness. Typically, lakes that are at the end of trails have better fishing than those that are closer to trailheads. Most hikers would rather fish the first lake they come to rather than passing several lakes that harbor fish before stopping. Island is worth the extra few miles though.

It's not to say that fishing is better in Island Lake than it is in Twin Lakes (which is a shorter hike). It is true, though, that there is a fair number of fish in Island. At 8,133 feet, Island marks the end of the basin. It's loaded with brook trout and offers a sprinkling of rainbows. The fish aren't huge, but would be a perfect fit for a small skillet.

Island is as advertised, a lake fit with islands. Most anglers fish where the trail ends at the beginning of the lake. However, with more than 1.25 miles of shoreline, anglers who do a little walking are often rewarded. The brooks aren't picky. When the bite is on you could catch them on a penny with a hook in it. Try to fish off points or towards deeper water and don't feel bad about taking a limit of brooks. By taking some fish out of the system you'll help create a larger average size fish.

From Boomerang, reaching Island is an easy trip. You'll first walk up a small hill and then pass a fishless pond before ascending another hill and dropping down to Island Lake. Total trip time is fewer than five minutes.

Directions *and trip info for Grouse Lake also applies to Island Lake.*

Island Lake

UMPA LAKE

Rating: 1	
Species: None	
Stocks: None	
Facilities: None	

I call Umpa Lake a honeymooner's lake. It's surely not a fishermen's lake! Historically, before many of us were born, Umpa did hold fish. It's now fishless and has been for decades. Barring a sudden change in management there will never be fish swimming in Umpa again.

At 7,900 feet in the Desolation Wilderness, Umpa is a hard lake to find. There is no trail leading to it, nor any signs acknowledging its' whereabouts. This is what makes it such a great destination for honeymooner's or couples; it's almost guaranteed you'll have the place to yourself.

Umpa is one of the smallest lakes in the Desolation Wilderness. Plus there is enough room on Umpa's shoreline for setting up a tent and camping. You could cast across its' width and length and hit rock on the other side. It's also shallow, probably too shallow to swim in. Instead of thinking about fishing or swimming, plan on quality time with a loved one or watching mallards swim in circles. (They are much more exciting than the fish or the lack there of.)

From where the Twin Lakes Trail passes through a small meadow along the shoreline of Lower Twin Lake, you'll spot a faint trail spur that takes off to the left. For Umpa, break left and follow it uphill. You'll climb through a saddle and in fewer than five minutes be standing atop a great view of Umpa in front of you and Twin Lakes at your back. Drop down the ridge to Umpa.

Directions *and trip info for Grouse Lake also apply to Umpa Lake.*

Umpa Lake

BOOMERANG LAKE

Rating: 1

Species: None

Stocks: None

Facilities: None

In the case of Boomerang Lake, size does matter. Because it's smaller and shallower than its' neighbors Twin Lakes and Island Lake, Boomerang doesn't have the same excellent brook trout fishery. Boomerang suffers from winterkill, endangered frogs and a lack of cover. Unfortunately, trout which were once abundant at this lake are no longer available.

Frog issues forced the California Department of Fish and Game to abandon their stocking program in the entire drainage. Unlike many other lakes in the region that had brookies, the ones that resided in Boomerang didn't become self-sustaining. When the brookies were all caught several years ago they were deemed gone for good. Boomerang has been fishless for several years.

At 8,060 in the Desolation Wilderness, Boomerang is easily reached from Twin Lakes. From Lower Twin continue on the well-graded path up a small ridge to Boomerang. The walk should only take a few minutes.

Directions *and trip info for Grouse Lake also apply to Boomerang Lake.*

Boomerang Lake

AVALANCHE LAKE

Rating: 4

Species: Rainbow Trout and Brook Trout

Stocks: None

Facilities: None

Need Information?
Contact: El Dorado National Forest (530) 644-6048, El Dorado National Forest Supervisors Office (530) 543-2600

Some hikers seek challenges. We were part of that rare core when we decided to make a day trip to Avalanche Lake. Taking the trailhead from Echo Lake, Big Todd McLean and I knew we'd be testing our luck to make it to Avalanche in a day. There was a possibility, we thought, of trying to hike from the Horsetail Falls Trail over the waterfall via a cross country route.

For those of you who have hiked to Horsetail, you know how rugged this area can be. Truthfully, rugged is being kind. We decided to go light, packing just enough water, granola bars, film and fishing gear to get us through the day, while still allowing us to be mobile and agile. Our plan looked realistic for the first half-mile as we followed the established trail as far as we could before going astray. Recognizing the cliffs ahead presented what looked to be a near vertical ascent, we decided to forge our own trail. Studying the contour of the hillsides, we discovered what looked to be a small saddle we could possibly navigate.

We weren't prepared for the battle that ensued. This was like hiking in parts of Alaska where there are no trails, rather untouched ground that is difficult to pass through. We did fortu- nately manage to climb, jump, crawl and scrape our way through decades of decaying trees, leaves, brush and

Avalanche Lake

steep granite outcroppings. It took us more than an hour to climb a quarter-mile and reach the saddle we had seen from below. Instead of continuing up the ridge, we opted to traverse the ridgeline and head towards Horsetail Falls. While exhausting, this route proved easier. Used toilet paper and trail makers led us to believe others, too, had the same idea. We proceeded to follow the footsteps of our predecessors.

Another hour had passed when I saw a husband and wife team walking up the steep ridge near the brink of the falls.

"You have got to be kidding me," I thought looking at Todd, who had blood dripping down his legs and sweat raining off his eyelashes.

"Where are you headed," I asked the man, wearing a backpack and carrying a bottle of water. "We came up the trail. We are headed to the top of Horsetail Falls, to Avalanche Lake."

I paused.

Trail? There's a trail?

"Yah, do you know where the trail that takes you to the waterfall is?" he said. "If you keep following that it heads right up the mountain. Yah, and there are orange arrows spray painted on the rocks to show you where to go."

My topo map sure didn't show a trail. Personally, I though the route was too steep to scramble, but we learned on our way back there was a route. It's not maintained, not for the faint of heart, but doable. It's steep, dangerous and not advised by the Forest Service. The granite ranges in size from a softball to a Honda Accord and many are at a constant teeter. If you take this route, use caution and watch every step carefully.

This route may be risky; nonetheless, it's an experience many hikers see as a must. The route gives you hundreds of birds eye views of Horsetail Falls and spits you out at the outlet of Avalanche Lake, a gem itself. At 7,500 feet in the Desolation Wilderness, Avalanche is a chore to reach, a two-mile hike with a 1,400 foot elevation gain is necessary, but its' pristine still waters and willing trout make it worth the trek. (We later discovered this route is taken often.)

Avalanche isn't a large backcountry impoundment, rather a small widening of Pyramid Creek that harbors tiny rainbow and brook trout and offers several excellent picnic spots. The lake is complete with several small islands and a fiesta of small channels that feed it.

When fishing, you'll want to stick to something small. A small Panther Martin, Kastmaster or a fly and bubble combo, like a Pistol Pete, work great. Target the outlet pool, deepwater channel (it's only five feet deep) and the many inlets for fish that likely won't grow larger than eight inches.

If you plan to make the trip, supplies are available in Meyers. In winter and spring call ahead for trail conditions. Snow and avalanche danger can close the trail through June in some years.

Also nearby is the North Fork of the American River, Echo Lake and Lake Tahoe.

Directions: *From South Lake Tahoe, drive south on Highway 89 to Highway 50. Drive west on Highway 50 for 15.9 miles until you reach Twin Bridges. Pull into the dirt pullout on the right side of the road and walk across the bridge to the trailhead.*

Avalanche Lake

PYRAMID CREEK

Rating: 3

Species: Rainbow
Trout, Brown Trout and
Brook Trout

Stocks: None

Facilities: None

There are some backcountry streams that hold thousands of fish per mile. Pyramid Creek isn't one of them though. It's possible at one time that Pyramid Creek possessed them, however with aerial fish plants no longer taking place at the lakes in this drainage, the number of fish in the creek has plummeted.

It's true that some rainbows, brooks and browns naturally reproduce in the drainage, unfortunately their numbers are far fewer than in the past. The creek is also home to pan size, and smaller, trout. You aren't going to find any fish greater than 10 inches.

Pyramid Creek can be broken up into three sections, all of which differ drastically. The lower section runs mostly through the El Dorado National Forest. The middle section begins at the top of Horsetail Falls and ends at Ropi Lake. The third extends from American Lake to Desolation Lake.

The lower section doesn't get planted with fish, but it has a few wild rainbows. This portion is found from the bridge on Highway 50 to the base of Horsetail Falls. The trout that are found swim upstream from the American River, mostly to spawn.

From the top of the falls to Ropi Lake you'll find a decent population of mostly rainbows and brookies. This section always holds trout because the fish swim out of Avalanche and Pitt Lake and into the stream. In a sense, the creek is used as a highway for the fish to migrate between the lakes. Unfortunately, most trout run six-to-eight inches. They can be found in the small ponds, pools and riffles between Avalanche and Ropi Lake.

The top section holds the least fish, primarily because there is little creek itself. The creek spends most of its' time running between American and Channel Lakes and in Desolation Lake. In these areas you'll find predominately brook trout, but their numbers can be depleted with fish plants no longer taking place.

No matter which section you fish, make sure to use small hardware. Tiny Mepps spinners, drifting flies and Pautzke salmon eggs are best.

***Directions** and trip info for Avalanche Lake also apply to Pyramid Creek.*

Pyramid Creek

PITT LAKE

Rating: 5
Species: Rainbow Trout and Brook Trout
Stocks: None
Facilities: None

Pitt Lake is on the borderline of being called a lake. In reality, it's more of a widening of Pyramid Creek. In fact, with little effort you could fish your way around Pitt's shoreline in less than an hour. At best, the lake is 25 yards wide and 100 yards long. Regardless of its' size, Pitt offers consistent action on both rainbows and brookies. Fed by Pyramid Creek and another inlet from Lake of the Woods, Pitt's waters remain well aerated and also offers sufficient spawning grounds to overcome the lack of air stocking in recent years by the California Department of Fish and Game.

You aren't going to catch big fish at Pitt. This tiny pond holds mostly six-to-eight-inch trout. However, a skillet full of fish is attainable for backpackers. There's really no trick either. Target the inlet and outlet with small spinners, spoons or flies and you'll be in business. Most likely you'll find small trout rising.

At 7,515 feet in the Desolation Wilderness, Pitt is a combination of rocky shorelines and soft meadows split by small channels, creek beds and islands. It's pretty, yet intriguing to many anglers who opt to explore the interesting topography rather than fish.

To reach Pitt from Avalanche, follow Pyramid Creek upstream for roughly 10 minutes to Pitt Lake.

Directions *and trip info for Avalanche Lake also apply to Pitt Lake.*

Pitt Lake

ROPI LAKE

Rating: 7
Species: Rainbow Trout, Brown Trout and Brook Trout
Stocks: None
Facilities: None

Compared to neighboring lakes (Avalanche, Pitt, Osma and Gefo lakes), Ropi is huge. It's not just Ropi's size that attracts anglers though. The lake has several islands, tall rugged mountains and doesn't get crowded. Additionally, Pyramid Creek impressively cascades into Ropi, as well as several other small waterfalls originating from Toem and Pyramid Lakes.

In the Pyramid Creek Drainage, Ropi also offers what the smaller lakes don't: the chance at landing quality fish. At 7,615 feet in the Desolation Wilderness, browns, rainbows and brookies inhabit the lake. Additionally, each has proven they can grow to desirable sizes. While many pan size trout are also caught, larger 10-14 inch trout can typically be found in creels.

Ropi isn't the kind of lake you stop at to make a few casts and move on. Fishing can be a full day event. There's a lot of water to cover. It could take a few hours to thoroughly fish the shoreline. And it's worth it, too.

There are several ways to target Ropi's trout. The easiest technique is to cast spinners and spoons towards surfacing trout. Conversely, you can't always find fish on the surface. What you can always count on is finding trout near the lake's several inlets and in the outlet channel. Personally, I saw the most success tossing quarter-and-half-ounce Little Cleos. It was experimental to use much larger than normal lures for backcountry waters, but I ended up doing quite well on rainbows from 12-15 inches.

To reach Ropi from Pitt, simply walk up Pyramid Creek for one-third of a mile to Ropi's outlet. On the way you will pass many pools harboring brookies and bows. Try fishing below the small waterfalls and in pools.

Directions *and trip info for Avalanche Lake also apply to Ropi Lake.*

Ropi Lake

OSMA LAKE

Rating: 1
Species: None
Stocks: None
Facilities: None

Osma Lake has fallen victim to the mountain yellow-legged frog. Several years ago Osma was a sure bet for anglers looking to nab a half-dozen small brookies with little effort, but the stakes have changed. Osma no longer receives plants of any trout from the California Department of Fish and Game. And, barring a massive change in management, it will likely remain this way for the rest of our lives.

Osma has gone from a good fishing destination to a pretty lake with no fish. At 7,667 feet in the Desolation Wilderness, Osma is situated a few feet from Toem Lake. While the odds are against it, it would be possible for trout to swim out of Toem and into Osma during the spring when Osma's outlet flows into Toem. Fish do commonly use seasonal streams as highways; however, it's not likely the fish would remain in Osma for long periods of time. Don't bother fishing it.

To reach Osma from Ropi, continue around the west end of Ropi Lake on the faint dirt path. You'll see a small spur break off to the left. Take it. Passing a small primitive campsite, the route winds over a small ridge and drops you out at Osma. This route can be difficult to find. Don't attempt it without a good map.

Directions *and trip info for Avalanche Lake also apply to Osma Lake.*

Osma Lake

TOEM LAKE

Rating: 6

Species: Rainbow Trout, Brook Trout and Brown Trout

Stocks: None

Facilities: None

Will the fish stay or will they go? That's the big question at Toem Lake. It's likely that for at least the next decade, if not several, Toem Lake won't be planted with a single trout. Unfortunately, endangered frogs were found in the drainage, halting fish plants to try and save the species.

Nevertheless, thus far the trout have survived. In fact, Toem has some of the largest trout in the Pyramid Creek Drainage. While they haven't been planted since the 1950's, brown trout are available and can grow as large as 10 pounds. There aren't many of them, but they are visible from the shoreline in late fall. Rainbows are also present, but they aren't the main focus. If one species survives the lack of plants it's expected to be the brookies, which I found to be the smallest fish in the lake. Brooks can spawn even under poor water conditions.

Toem Lake

Toem is a medium size backcountry lake with clear water, shallow, narrow granite channels and steep drop-offs. At 7,627 feet in the Desolation Wilderness, the lake rests in the same basin as Ropi, but receives less fishing pressure. Hopefully, things remain that way. Heavy fishing pressure could be detrimental to the trout. At the present time, they are finding a way to spawn in the seasonal tributaries. The amount of trout available could plummet if anglers put too many fish on a skillet.

At Toem, several fishing methods work. I find angling to be best in the fall, when rainbows and browns sun themselves in the small, shallow backwaters. They are aggressive or annoyed by small spinners and spoons, and will likely take them. Otherwise, you'll want to fish the main body with large spoons. The lake is deep enough to where you can let your lure sink for 10 seconds and you won't snag bottom. You may need to experiment with several depths to find the fish during the summer.

From Ropi it's an easy walk to Toem. If you are standing on Ropi's dam, facing the lake, walk to the left around Ropi to Toem, which will be visible on your left in roughly 10 minutes. There is a faint path along the way.

***Directions** and trip info for Avalanche Lake also apply to Toem Lake.*

GEFO LAKE

Rating: 1
Species: None
Stocks: None
Facilities: None

The Desolation Wilderness is packed with lakes that are seldom visited. Gefo is one of them. While a manageable daytrip for many hardcore hikers, others are intimidated by the stiff elevation gain and rugged terrain before reaching Gefo and choose to go elsewhere. Gefo would be an excellent place for a great fishery. The key word is "would," or better yet, "was".

Gefo was a great trout fishery. It received plants from the California Department of Fish and Game's aerial stocking program when necessary and provided a good catch-and-keep fishery for many backpackers. Avalanche, Pitt, Pyramid Creek, Ropi, Toem and Osma Lakes are all passed before reaching Gefo, which prompted few anglers to hike all the way to Gefo when they could walk a much shorter distance and catch bigger fish in closer lakes.

Now it makes no difference. Another victim of the endangered frog, Gefo will likely never see fish again. Too bad too. Gefo is a secluded destination in the wilderness that is a perfect spot for honeymooners looking for a chance to avoid day hikers. It's likely you'll have the lake to yourself.

The last leg of the trip to reach Gefo requires cross country travel. There is no trail. From Toem you'll have to walk to the far side of the lake where the inlet is. In late summer and fall it will be dry. Follow this inlet up the granite slabs for roughly a quarter mile to Gefo. In the spring, you'll follow a large waterfall. In late summer and fall, you'll find stagnant water rather than a flowing stream. A good map may be necessary if you don't have great route finding skills.

Directions *and trip info for Avalanche Lake also apply to Gefo Lake.*

Gefo Lake

DESOLATION LAKE

Rating: 3
Species: Brook Trout
Stocks: None
Facilities: None

How many fish does a lake need to warrant anglers to fish it? I guess none. While a few anglers spend time making casts in Desolation Lake that number has decreased drastically over the years. More and more anglers are learning the truth. That is, Desolation is barren of trout.

There may be fish in the system since some trout migrate out of lakes further up in the drainage. Most of the time though, there are no fish in Desolation Lake. If you recall decades ago when there was great fishing, you aren't wrong, rather outdated. The California Department of Fish and Game no longer plants Desolation Lake because of endangered frog issues. Don't count on plants ever returning.

At 7,965 feet in the Desolation Wilderness, Desolation is a widening of Pyramid Creek and still a great place for a picnic or to hike. The lake gets relatively little use compared to Lake of the Woods and Aloha Lake. It can be reached by cross country travel from Ropi or Lake of the Woods. From Ropi, follow Pyramid Creek up the granite slab to the lake. From Lake of the Woods you'll need a good map, but Desolation is only a five minute hike.

Directions and trip info for Avalanche Lake also apply to Desolation Lake.

PYRAMID LAKE

Rating: 3
Species: Brook Trout
Stocks: None
Facilities: None

Pyramid Peak is one of the most sought after destinations for hardcore hikers in the backcountry of the Desolation Wilderness. There is no trail to the peak. Nevertheless, that doesn't shake many anglers from trying the feat. There are several peaks that give life-lasting views of the Desolation Wilderness. Pyramid Peak is one of them.

Pyramid Lake, which rests in a small basin below the summit, used to provide anglers with a source of sport and food on the route to the peak. Prior to the discovery of endangered frogs in the lake, the California Department of Fish and Game planted Pyramid almost annually with golden or brook trout. Unfortunately, those plants have been discontinued.

Pyramid Lake

Hikers still have a viable overnight stay with Pyramid Lake. On the other hand, they'll have to work harder for their food. Much harder. No plants mean less fish. Nevertheless, anglers can expect the overall size of trout to increase. Golden trout haven't been planted in several years. In fact, most goldens have outlived their lifecycle. With fish no longer planted it's highly unlikely that anglers will catch goldens in the future.

Brooks are self-sustaining. At 8,655 feet in the Desolation Wilderness, brook trout may not be catchable with every cast, but they are available. Pyramid Lake isn't huge, yet it has a lot of shoreline. If you want to fish the entire perimeter, plan on putting in some time. Pyramid has a ton of small canals, points, ponds and islands along its' banks, all of which may hold brookies at one time, or another. Because of all the structure, stay away from using large spoons. It's better to fish with spinners.

Reaching Pyramid takes a good map. It's best to try and reach the lake from Gefo rather than Ropi. From Ropi you could possibly follow Pyramid Lake's outlet stream to the lake. But, the terrain is extremely steep and unsafe. From Gefo the trek is easier. Don't look for a route. You are going to make your own. Head north on the granite slabs. Staying between the steep ridge below Pyramid Peak and the canyon where the outlet stream is, you'll find the lake in 10-20 minutes.

Directions *and trip info for Avalanche Lake also apply to Pyramid Lake.*

WACA LAKE

Rating: 1
Species: Brook Trout
Stocks: None
Facilities: None

Waca Lake is one of the farthest lakes from the Horsetail Falls Trailhead in the Pyramid Creek Drainage. There is no longer a reason for anglers to hike this far though. While good fishing was once guaranteed, those days are long gone. The California Department of Fish and Game says there could be a few brook trout remaining in Waca, but it's highly unlikely. I fished the lake in fall of 2003 and failed to see a single fish.

Much of the lake is shallow and so clear you'd be able to see trout from the shore if they were here. At 8,185 feet in the Desolation Wilderness, Waca is located close to Pyramid Peak and Aloha Lake. Waca used to receive plants of either rainbow or brook trout. However, as with the rest of the Pyramid Creek Drainage, frog issues have put fish plants on the chopping block for good. You can fish Waca, but you shouldn't plan on catching anything. Those days are as common as drive-in movie theatres are now.

To reach Waca from Pyramid Lake, follow upstream along Pyramid's inlet for roughly five minutes. It's a short climb over granite slabs.

Directions *and trip info for Avalanche Lake also apply to Waca Lake.*

Waca Lake   The Desolation Wilderness

ALOHA LAKE

Rating: 6
Species: Brook Trout
Stocks: None
Facilities: None

Aloha Lake is an unusual backcountry water. While Aloha is the largest lake in the Desolation Wilderness, it didn't tackle that feat all on its own. At one time, several natural lakes known as Medley Lake could be found were Aloha now sits. However, that was more than a century ago, long before a 20-foot high dam was built to create a huge impoundment of water on Pyramid Creek. At 630 acres Aloha is allowed to fill in the spring and summer and then is gradually drawn down in the fall before it freezes.

Boasting more than 11 miles of shoreline, Aloha was once one of the most popular fisheries in the wilderness, famous for yielding some of the largest brook trout anywhere in California. However, those days are now few, as fish plants have been suspended and the fishery has suffered. While brookies can reproduce here, over fishing may take a deadly toll.

Don't get me wrong, there are still brookies and there will continue to be. But since the population is no longer supplemented, only the future will tell if the lake will continue to kick out quality fish. The California Department of Fish and Game is skeptical, as am I.

Aloha is one of the most heavily visited lakes in the region. Ironically, the anglers who do best here wouldn't be caught dead fishing from shore. Here, success comes to those who are willing to carry in float tubes and rafts. The longtime favorite way to catch a limit of brookies in the two-to-five-pound range is to troll small Needlefish, Dick Nite spoons or a flasher and a night crawler combo. Because it's too hard to carry in a trolling motor you'll end up doing the rowing to keep the troll, but the rewards can be exciting. Trolling is only an option prior to the major fall drawdowns. Once the water is released, you'll find fish trapped in dozens of small lakes surrounded by more than 100 islands. It's a much different look than the large backcountry water that anglers are used to seeing in the spring and summer.

There are several routes that reach Aloha Lake. Trails from Echo Lakes, Twin Bridges, Fallen Leaf Lake, Emerald Bay and the Bayview Campground are all options. For the one that best suits you consult a map.

Directions and *trip info for Avalanche Lake also apply to Aloha Lake.*

(Right) Aloha Lake

CHANNEL LAKE

Rating: 3

Species: Brook Trout

Stocks: None

Facilities: None

Determining whether Channel Lake will harbor trout when you get around to reading this book isn't an easy task. Channel Lake is almost an exact replica of American Lake, which lies a few yards upstream. As with American, Channel no longer receives air stockings of trout from the California Department of Fish and Game. Again, we must site the endangered frog for this.

Channel isn't a great fishery. I'd go as far as saying you shouldn't waste your time fishing it. Channel is a pretty lake set in a remote granite section of the Desolation Wilderness, while it isn't stuffed with trout. It's been proven the brooks have established themselves even during the absence of trout plants, but their success will take years to determine. Additionally, this lake receives heavy use for a backcountry water, which could take its toll on the brooks in the long run.

For now brookies to nine inches will be available. Most of the fish run seven-to-eight inches and are stunted. Springtime is best. Brooks are less active in the fall.

It's a rugged, rocky off trail scramble from Desolation Lake to Channel Lake. Basically, it's best if you follow Desolation's inlet upstream to Channel. The trip should only take five minutes.

Directions *and trip info for Avalanche Lake also apply to Channel Lake.*

Channel Lake

AMERICAN LAKE

Rating: 3
Species: Brook Trout
Stocks: None
Facilities: None

Discussion regarding the endangered frog doesn't warm the hearts of American Lake anglers. This frog has caused the California Department of Fish and Game to abandon fish stocking programs that have taken place in the Desolation Wilderness for generations. Anglers that have backpacked to the Desolation Wilderness since childhood sadly return to find fishless waters.

Although many of the lakes in the Pyramid Creek Drainage have gone fishless, the brook trout at American Lake have fought back. These pan size fish have found a way to reproduce naturally. Even if the CA DFG wanted to remove all fish from the lake it may be impossible. Once brook trout enter a system it can be tough to remove them. Brooks are good at avoiding methods of removal.

While there are bookies in American, they aren't that plentiful. In fact, you may have difficulty catching them. The CA DFG reports there are still fish in the lake. I failed to get a single bite in late fall, nor did I see juvenile fish or rising trout. Personally, I wouldn't bother fishing American, but there are fish to be caught.

American is located on Pyramid Creek, just downstream of Aloha Lake's dam. It's a narrow reservoir that is best fished from shore with a fly and bubble combo (Pistol Pete's work great) or a spinner. From Channel Lake it's an easy walk upstream along Pyramid Creek to American. It should take fewer than five minutes.

Directions *and trip info for Avalanche Lake also apply to American Lake.*

American Lake

FRATA LAKE

Rating: 1
Species: None
Stocks: None
Facilities: None

Frata is one of the smallest named lakes in the Desolation Wilderness. Unfortunately, it no longer has any significance to anglers. Frata did harbor trout in the last century, but since endangered frogs were discovered in the Pyramid Creek Drainage, the fish in Frata were destined to never return.

Frata wasn't affected by the widespread struggle between the balance of fish and frogs. The lake was removed from the allotment list by the California Department of Fish and Game decades ago because of low survival rates and winterkill. This lake is as shallow as a plastic backyard swimming pool you'd find for sale at Target. When the fish were planted, they were easy pickings.

Frata still has some use for anglers. On windy nights anglers can take refuge at Frata, which tends to be more protected than nearby Lake of the Woods. There are a few nice spots too. Just don't bother with the fishing!

Directions *and trip info for Avalanche Lake also apply to Frata Lake.*

Frata Lake

LAKE OF THE WOODS

Rating: 5
Species: Rainbow Trout and Brook Trout
Stocks: None
Facilities: None

With nearly three miles of shoreline, Lake of the Woods isn't your average backcountry water in the Pyramid Creek Drainage. While most lakes run much smaller, Lake of the Woods has an advantage when it comes to the survival of trout. This is important when you consider that the lake will no longer be planted with rainbow or brook trout due to issues with an endangered frog.

Fortunately, the rainbows have proven they can naturally reproduce, but what worries the California Department of Fish and Game is that heavy fishing pressure will catch up with no future supplemental plants. That hypothesis won't be answered for several years. Space is on the rainbow's side. With an abundance of shoreline, these trout aren't constantly being harassed by anglers and have a ton of cover to hide in. They aren't sitting ducks like fish in many of the smaller nearby lakes.

On the other hand, it's not difficult to catch fish. In the mornings and evenings, clear water allows anglers to spot cruising trout. Many of the trout make daily runs into small coves where anglers have no problem spotting them. Try using a large spinner or spoon so you can cast to deeper water rather than making short casts from shore. Anglers who drag float tubes or inflatable canoes often run into the best action. Expect most trout to run between 10-12 inches, although it's not uncommon to catch fish to 15 inches.

Reaching Lake of the Woods is possible from the Horsetail Falls Trailhead and Echo Lake. From Ropi Lake on the Horsetail Falls Trail, there is a path that climbs uphill to Lake of the Woods. From Echo Lake, you'll want to take the PCT to the left turnoff for Lake of the Woods in Haypress Meadow.

Directions and trip info for Avalanche Lake also apply to Lake of the Woods.

Lake of the Woods

GRANITE LAKE

Rating: 4
Species: Brook Trout
Stocks: None
Facilities: None
Need Information? Contact: El Dorado National Forest (530) 543-2600

Granite Lake is one of the easiest lakes to reach in the Desolation Wilderness. Although it's less than one-mile to the lake, the 800-foot elevation gain keeps few anglers from trying their luck here. The hike is short, sweet, will stiffen up your legs, make you sweat and overwhelm you at times.

It's not the switchbacks that engulf your heart, rather the teeming views of Cascade Lake, Lake Tahoe and Emerald Bay. The hike begins in Bayview Campground, close enough to Highway 89 to hear the diesel engines slowing down for the winding turns. The trail begins under the cover of heavy pines. Unfortunately, this section of the path is littered with dead trees, both standing and fallen. It's a prime candidate for a wildfire. Hopefully, the Forest Service will perform a controlled burn soon.

The trail wastes no time ascending. Basically, the entire hike is straight up. After the first 10 minutes you'll come to a relatively open area where you'll want to keep on eye out on the right for breathtaking views of Emerald Bay. From this vantage you'll see where Eagle Creek enters Lake Tahoe, the sandy beach at the back of the bay, Fannette Island, Eagle Point and the rest of Lake Tahoe. Many hikers are more than satisfied at this point and turn back. Those who

Granite Lake

continue have more climbing to Granite Lake. It should take only 10 minutes.

Granite isn't a great fishing lake from shore. While there are brookies, it takes a heck of a long cast to get them. The problem is a shallow shoreline with many fallen trees and stumps in the way. These stumps are visible and are a good landmark to use for anglers who want to catch fish. You'll need to cast at least 10 yards beyond these stumps to be successful. To have a real shot at catching fish, try bringing a pair of waders or a float tube.

If you plan to make the trip, supplies are available in South Lake Tahoe.

Also nearby are Lake Tahoe, Cascade Falls, Eagle Falls and Taylor Creek.

Directions: *From the junction of Highway 50 and 89 in South Lake Tahoe, drive north on Highway 89 to the Bayview Trailhead parking area near Emerald Bay.*

FLOATING ISLAND LAKE

Rating: 3

Species: Brook Trout

Stocks: None

Facilities: None

Need Information?
Contact: Tahoe National
Forest (530) 543-2600

Floating Island Lake was one of the great, easy to reach destinations where you'd likely find few visitors in the backcountry. However, that concept was botched years ago when the trail to Mt. Tallac (which overlooks Lake Tahoe) was constructed to blaze along Floating Island's shoreline. Unfortunately, even on a late spring or fall weekday you'll find hikers on the route. Rather than anglers having a nice wilderness experience while making short casts, they are interrupted by loud voices and heavy footsteps.

Fishing isn't great at Floating Island either. This small lake is extremely shallow. Most of the time all the fish are concentrated on the south end. The north end is so shallow you could walk across it and probably not have water climb higher than your knees. The north end isn't deep, just deeper. There are no deep spots, period. Fortunately, the water is clear allowing anglers to see many of the fish. There aren't, however, many catchable size fish in the lake. I did see thousands of fingerling fish, but was unable to determine if they were trout. It's likely there were minnows.

Floating Island Lake

The best way to fish is with spoons or spinners on the south end. Try and cast between the tall grass and the fallen tree limbs in the middle of the lake. You'll want to let your lure sink for three to five seconds, but no longer because there are many fallen limbs that you can get snagged on.

To reach Floating Island, begin at the Mt. Tallac Trailhead and follow the established path uphill. You'll follow a ridge along Fallen Leaf Lake to a lookout point on the left. Take note of great views of Tahoe and Fallen Leaf and leash your shoes up. More uphill brings you to the top of this ridge before dropping into a small canyon and working your final steps to Floating Island, which comes a few feet after passing the Desolation Wilderness sign.

Directions: *From the junction of Highway 50 and 89 in South Lake Tahoe, drive north on Highway 89 for 3.8 miles to the left turnoff for the Mt. Tallac Trailhead. Turn left and drive four-tenths of a mile to a split in the road. Stay left and drive seven-tenths of a mile to the trailhead.*

CATHEDRAL LAKE

Rating: 4

Species: Brook Trout and Golden Trout

Stocks: None

Facilities: None

Cathedral Lake is one of the smallest lakes in the Desolation Wilderness. It's so small that you could walk the shoreline in less than five minutes. Being on the path to Mt. Tallac, it's not a place to come to find serenity or to fish.

At one time golden trout and brook trout were planted in this tiny backcountry water. However in recent years no fish stocking has taken place. Some anglers swear by catching fish. Others, including the California Department of Fish and Game, believe the lake is barren. Personally, I didn't get a single bite or see a fish.

There are two ways from Fallen Leaf Lake to reach Cathedral, rather than a long backcountry loop. One begins at Fallen Leaf's west shoreline. Over 1.6 miles you climb more than 1,150 feet. The route does, however, give you exceptional views of Fallen Leaf.

The other route offers nearly the same elevation gain, yet it spreads over 2.4 miles so it's much more gradual. This route not only gives you exceptional views of Fallen Leaf, but Lake Tahoe, Casino Row, Heavenly Ski Area and Mt. Tallac. You also have the option to make a pit stop at Floating Island Lake.

From Floating Island Lake it's only a 15-minute hike to Cathedral. From Floating Island, the trail continues uphill though more inclined than from the trailhead to Floating Island. The first landmark you'll come across is Cathedral Creek, which may dry up by late summer. Shortly after the crossing comes a trail junction. The left fork heads to Fallen Leaf, while the right fork skirts to Cathedral Lake. Continue for another 10 minutes to the trail.

Directions *and trip info for Floating Island Lake also apply to Cathedral Lake.*

Cathedral Lake

Region

24

Sacramento Foothills
Crystal Basin
Georgetown Area

Bass Lake
Cameron Park Lake
American River, South Fork (Coloma)
Jenkinson Lake
El Dorado Forebay
Slab Creek Reservoir
American River, Silver Fork
American River, South Fork (Riverton)
Walton Pond
Stumpy Meadows Lake
Rubicon River
Ice House Reservoir
Union Valley Reservoir
Loon Lake
Gerle Creek Reservoir
Wrights Lake
Dark Lake
Beauty Lake

BASS LAKE

Rating: 3

Species: Largemouth
Bass, Bluegill and
Channel Catfish

Stocks: None

Facilities: None

Need Information?
Contact: Fisherman's
Warehouse
(916) 362-1200

Driving by Bass Lake, it might seem bizarre to see anglers fishing from the road and not along the shoreline. Fishermen have to cast their lines over the barbed-wire fence to fish the small lake. Most rest their poles against the fence, set up a lounge chair and wait for a bite. It's comical! Since no fishing is allowed from inside the fence, hardcore anglers fish from the other side of it. I figured it was illegal to fish the lake at all, however, anglers do it everyday and the El Dorado County Sheriffs that patrol Bass Lake Road never bother them.

It's difficult to fish Bass Lake from over the fence, and in my mind is not worth it at all, but the few anglers that deal with the hassle say they do pretty well. I'm not sure how they reel the fish out of the water and lift them up and over the fence. Personally, I've never tried it before, and with all the other lakes nearby I'm not so sure I'd spent my time here. The only way to fish for the bass, which are usually on the small side, is with night crawlers. Those going for catfish have more options: chicken liver, beef liver, mackerel and anchovies are usually the best.

If you plan to make the trip, supplies are available in Cameron Park. Remember, it is illegal to fish from inside the fence. No services are provided.

Also nearby are Cameron Park Lake, Folsom Lake and Lake Natoma.

Directions: *From Sacramento at the junction of Interstate 5 and Highway 50 drive east on Highway 50 for 28 miles to Bass Lake Road. Turn left, drive under the freeway and continue two miles to the lake on the left.*

CAMERON PARK LAKE

Rating: 5

Species: Largemouth Bass,
Channel Catfish, Crappie
and Bluegill

Stocks: None

Facilities: Swimming Area,
Restrooms, Tennis Courts,
Volleyball Court,
Concession Stand, Picnic
Area and Canoe and
Paddle Boat Rentals

Need Information?
Contact: Cameron Park
Community Services
District (530) 677-2231

Built specifically to provide residents of Cameron Park with a close, clean and quality recreational area, Cameron Park Lake is small park lake between Folsom and Placerville that can offer good bass fishing for fish from one-to-five pounds. What keeps the lake from being referred to as a "good" bass lake is that there are few trophy size fish. The lake is a perfect spot to learn to bass fish though. Because the bass aren't heavily targeted, the majority of them aren't wary of lures or spooked easily.

When I was a teenager I used to spend time each summer here with my uncle Ron Shaffer who lived in Cameron Park. I fished the lake daily. The best lure then and still now, is a salt and pepper plastic worm. Night crawlers work well too. Due to overgrown weeds, the use of crankbaits can be difficult. The west shore produces the most action.

Although the bass fishery is flourishing, the same can't be said for the catfish. The catfish population has struggled to develop, leaving fishing for the species slow. There are a lot of bluegill and a sprinkle of crappie in the lake. Then again, few are larger than hand size.

If you plan to make the trip, supplies are available in Cameron Park. There is a day-use fee.

Also nearby are Bass Lake and Folsom Lake.

Directions: *From the junction of Interstate 5 and Highway 50 in Sacramento, drive east on Highway 50 for 30 miles and exit Cambridge Road. Turn left and drive 2.4 miles to the lake entrance on the right.*

Cameron Park Lake

AMERICAN RIVER, SOUTH FORK (COLOMA)

Rating: 7

Species: Rainbow Trout and Brown Trout

Stocked with 2,600 pounds of rainbow trout.

Facilities: Restrooms, Picnic Areas and a Visitor Center

Need Information? Contact: Marshall Gold Discovery State Historic Park (530) 622-3470

John Sutter is one of the most important figures in California history. It was at Sutter's Mill that John Marshall discovered gold in 1848, which prompted the largest gold rush in California. Located on the shores of the South Fork of the American River, this popular tourist trap is known as Sutter's Mill and is now the site of the Marshall Gold Discovery State Park. Few tourists know that the river is stocked with trout along the same stretch where gold was discovered.

Every other week from mid-April through mid-July, the California Department of Fish & Game stocks half-pound rainbow trout, totaling 4,780 each year. The plants are from Lotus Road in Coloma, upriver through the state park. Since the river is so wide, this section of the American can be difficult to fish without waders, unless you don't mind chest deep cold water. Although spin casters do well tossing Panther Martins, fly-fishermen tend to do best.

The South Fork near Coloma

Take a moment to ponder what it would have been like to fish here more than a century and a half ago when the Gold Rush occurred. I'm sure the river was too crowded with miners to fish, but remember, during this period there were no dams along the American so salmon and steelhead could be caught here.

If you plan to make the trip supplies are available in Coloma. There is day-use fee to enter the state park.

Also nearby are Walton Pond, Stumpy Meadows Reservoir and Rubicon River.

Directions: *From the junction of Interstate 5 and Highway 50 in Sacramento drive east on Highway 50 for approximately 42 miles to Highway 49. Turn left on Highway 49 and drive 8.1 miles to Marshall Gold Discovery State Park on the right.*

JENKINSON LAKE

At 3,500 feet near the town of Pollock Pines, Jenkinson Lake is the ideal location for a weekend family camping trip. Especially if you live in the Capital Region, look no further. Commonly referred to as Sly Park Lake, Jenkinson has it all, including campgrounds, picnic areas, hiking, biking and horse trails, swimming areas, water-skiing and of course, good fishing. It's difficult to get bored at this 640 acre lake!

Under the jurisdiction of the El Dorado Irrigation District, Jenkinson is a good warm and cold water fishery. During winter and spring, anglers focus on rainbow, brown and lake trout. While most of the catches are small, each year browns weighing more than seven pounds and lake trout over 10 pounds are caught, keeping the thrill of catching a trophy size fish fresh in anglers minds. While there are some big fish in Jenkinson, most anglers aren't lucky enough to catch 'em.

Rainbow trout are the most abundant fish in the lake. In addition to 10,704 fingerling brown trout and 5,610 sub-catchable rainbow trout, the California Department of Fish and Game stocks 8,250 pound-size rainbows from February through May. The bite on rainbows is phenomenal for anglers slow-trolling red and gold Thomas Buoyants, orange Cripplures and silver Kastmasters along the shorelines, the dam and Hazel and Sly Park Creek inlets. For bank fishermen, tossing Panther Martins off points or soaking Power Bait work well too. To catch larger fish, troll half-ounce spoons and Rebel Minnows. However, it may take a while to get a bite.

Although their population is small, the majority of anglers aren't aware that there are also lake trout in Jenkinson. Nonetheless, they aren't easy to catch. Locating the fish is typically easy, but

downriggers or leadcore is required to have a chance at catching them. The lake trout generally be seen on fish finders 75-150 feet deep near the dam or down the lake's main channel. Even when presenting a lure perfectly, they aren't always inclined to bite. We trolled Rapalas right in front of their faces and couldn't buy a bite in four hours of fishing. Despite the low catch rates, a few diehard anglers have caught lake trout to 15 pounds. Here's a valuable tip: There is one hole that reaches 153 feet and the lake trout tend to stack up in it. All you have to do is find it and you're in business. The CA DFG stocks 15,120 fingerling lake trout each year.

With the warmer weather in May and June, trout move into deeper water and focus changes to the bass and bluegill population. Most of the bass are in the one-to-three-pound range and are best caught on white spinnerbaits off points. During March and April, switch over to fishing coves. In the heart of summer, the evening catfish bite is fair on anchovies and nightcrawlers.

If you plan to make the trip, supplies are available in Pollock Pines. Boat rentals are only available from May through September. There is a day-use and boat launch fee.

Also nearby are Slab Creek Reservoir, El Dorado Forebay, Ice House Reservoir, American River, South Fork (Riverton) and Bridal Veil Falls.

Directions: *From Sacramento, drive east on Highway 50 (past Placerville) to Pollock Pines and exit Sky Park Road. Turn right and drive four miles to the lake entrance on the left.*

Jenkinson Lake

EL DORADO FOREBAY

Rating: 5

Species: Rainbow Trout

Stocked with 500 pounds of rainbow trout.

Facilities: Restrooms and a Picnic Area

Need Information?
Contact: El Dorado National Forest
(530) 644-6048

Set at 4,000 feet in the town of Pollock Pines, El Dorado Forebay is truly a place fit for locals. Partially because they don't know the fishery exists and also due to its' small size, few out-of-towners come here, and that keeps the locals happy. Off Highway 50 between South Lake Tahoe and Placerville, Pollock Pines is a popular pit stop area. There is a Taco Bell, pizza joint, grocery store and a few gas stations that get bombarded by tourists daily. The forebay is a different story.

El Dorado Forebay allows locals to escape all the commotion and catch a few fish. Every other week from April through July, the California Department of Fish & Game put smiles on anglers' faces by dumping rainbow trout, totaling 1,125 each year. At 23 acres, catch rates remain high for those tossing small Panther Martins off points or soaking Power Bait near the picnic area.

If you plan to make the trip supplies are available in Pollock Pines.

Also nearby are Slab Creek Reservoir, American River, South Fork (Riverton), Ice House Reservoir, Union Valley Reservoir and Loon Lake.

Directions: *From Sacramento, drive east on Highway 50 (past Placerville) to Pollock Pines and exit Sky Park Road. Drive north and continue to Pony Express Road. Turn left, drive one-tenth of a mile and turn right on Forebay Road. Drive nine-tenths of a mile to the El Dorado Forebay on the left.*

El Dorado Forebay

SLAB CREEK RESERVOIR

Rating: 4

Species: Rainbow Trout, Brown Trout and Mountain Whitefish

Stocks: None

Facilities: Primitive Boat Launch

Need Information? Contact: El Dorado National Forest (530) 644-6048

I've never had such a hard time trying to locate boating regulations as I did with Slab Creek Reservoir. I contacted four Forest Service offices, talked with more than 15 employees, and still couldn't get an answer. "I don't know what to tell you, sir. I can't answer that question. Why don't you try this number? Maybe someone over there will be able to help you." Dealing with the Forest Service all the time, I'm used to this kind of thing. Instead, I decided to head back down to the reservoir and ask the anglers if they knew. (The Forest Service never did provide me with an answer.) Out of luck, none of the anglers knew what the regulations were either. Nor did they seem to care. They told me they've never seen anyone patrol the area, nor were any restrictions posted, so they launch their boats and have fun. "There's a launch ramp here, so I guess the lake is meant to have boats in it," said one angler, from the driver's seat of his 20-footer.

Because the fishing isn't great, the road to the reservoir is narrow and winding and the launch ramp is sand and gravel, few anglers choose to use the reservoir. Set in a canyon north of Pollock Pines, Slab Creek Reservoir is a narrow, dammed portion of the South Fork of the American River. No plants are made. The trout here are mostly planters that have been flushed downstream from the Camp Sacramento area.

Most anglers end up catching mountain whitefish, but there are wild browns and rainbows scattered in the reservoir. The mountain whitefish looks like a suckerfish and is abundant. They'll hit lures or bait, and weigh up to eight pounds. Due to extremely steep shorelines, Slab Creek is only accessible to boaters, unless you fish at the mouth where the river comes in (and where the boat launch is). By allowing you to cover more space in a short period of time trolling the shoreline is best for trout. Small Krocodiles work best.

If you plan to make the trip, supplies are available in Pollack Pines.

Also nearby are Ice House Reservoir, El Dorado Forebay, Jenkinson Lake and the American River, South Fork (Riverton).

Directions: From Sacramento, drive east on Highway 50 (past Placerville) to Pollock Pines and exit Sky Park Road. Drive north and continue to Pony Express Road. Turn left, drive one-tenth of a mile and turn right on Forebay Road. Drive nine-tenths of a mile to the El Dorado Forebay and reset your odometer. In three-tenths of a mile Forebay Road splits. Stay to the right and drive 6.8 miles to a bridge across the American River. After crossing the bridge veer left and continue two-tenths of a mile to the launch ramp.

AMERICAN RIVER (SILVER FORK)

Rating: 7

Species: Rainbow Trout
and Brown Trout

Stocked with 3,800
pounds of rainbow
trout.

Facilities:
Campgrounds and
Restrooms

Need Information?
Contact: El Dorado
National Forest
(530) 644-6048

There are few places along the American River where serenity can be found and the sounds of roaring engines along Highway 50 aren't heard. Silver Fork is one of them. A short distance away from Highway 50, the Silver Fork of the American River can provide that wilderness feeling associated with high mountain streams; it's shadowed by pines and blessed with the scent of campfires and burnt pinecones.

Roughly an hour drive from Sacramento and 30 minutes from Lake Tahoe, the Silver Fork remains quiet even when bumper-to-bumper traffic along Highway 50 frustrates motorists. Fishing is also enjoyable. With its headwaters at Silver Lake off Highway 88, the 10-to-20-foot wide river has a sufficient amount of water in it year-round to sustain fish. In addition to an abundance of wild rainbow and brown trout, the California Department of Fish and Game stocks 7,345 rainbow trout each year from late April through July. At 4,500 feet in the El Dorado National Forest, anglers do well fishing Power Bait in various pools near the campground. For wild trout, walk upstream of China Flat Campground and use small spinners or flies.

If you plan to make the trip supplies are available in Kyburz. The American River (Silver Fork) is closed to fishing from November 16 to the last Saturday in April.

Also nearby are Icehouse Reservoir, Union Valley Reservoir and Loon Lake.

Directions: *From South Lake Tahoe at the junction of Highway 50 and 89 drive west on Highway 50 for 26.8 miles to Silver Fork Road on the left. Turn left and drive 2.4 miles to China Flat Campground.*

The Silver Fork of the American River near China Flat Campground

AMERICAN RIVER (RIVERTON)

Rating: 7

Species: Rainbow Trout and Brown Trout

Stocked with 3,850 pounds of rainbow trout.

Facilities: Restrooms, Campgrounds, Picnic Areas, Lodging, Gas, General Store and Restaurant

Need Information? Contact: El Dorado National Forest (530) 644-6048

The 26-mile stretch of the American River from the Icehouse Reservoir turnoff to Camp Sacramento has gone through hell over the past few decades. First, a flood ravished the river. Then once the river and the residents who lived among its shores recovered from the flood, a fire raced through the drainage, destroying homes, trees and ravishing the land's beauty. Remnants of the fire still exist, however, the river and its inhabitants have returned to normal life.

Located between Placerville and Lake Tahoe, along a winding stretch of Highway 50, this section of the American River is easily accessed by anglers. With the California Department of Fish and Game showing up often in spring and early summer to toss approximately 7,660 rainbows, the fishing can be good. In the spring the river can reach up to 30 yards wide, but it recedes to a mere five yards by fall.

While plants commence in late-April, it's best to fish the river sometime after mid-June when flows begin to subside. At this time any method of fishing can be productive, including spin casting, the use of Pautzke salmon eggs, Power Bait and fly-fishing.

If you plan to make the trip supplies are available in Kyburz. The American River (Riverton) is closed to fishing from November 16 to the last Saturday in April. Most of the access to the river can be found via picnic areas and campgrounds. There is a lot of private property along the shore. Please keep off posted land.

Also nearby are Icehouse Reservoir, Echo Lakes, Wrights Lake, Dark Lake and American River, Silver Fork.

Directions: *From the junction of Interstate 5 and Highway 50 in Sacramento drive east on Highway 50 for approximately 59 miles to Ice House Road. The river is stocked from this point to Camp Sacramento.*

The American River is a common place for gold panning.

WALTON POND

Rating: 4

Species: Rainbow Trout

Stocked with 600
pounds of rainbow
trout.

Facilities: Picnic Areas

Need Information?
Contact: El Dorado
National Forest
(530) 333-4312

Almost no out-of-towners know about little Walton Lake. Stocked with rainbow trout only once a year (for free fishing day in June), this four-acre lake receives little to no pressure from even the locals, except perhaps the week it's stocked. It's as easy as fishing in a swimming pool during that time. The California Department of Fish & Game trucks in 1,150 half-pound rainbow trout for the occasion. On that free fishing Saturday in June, the lake can get crowded, but catch rates are high. Come any other month and most likely there won't be anyone fishing, or many fish swimming.

With most of the fish being caught in June, don't bother coming to fish the rest of the year. However, it would be a good idea to plan a picnic. The lake is heavily shaded by pines and remains quiet, making for a great family destination.

If coming right after the stock, don't worry about using a specific lure or color of Power Bait, as the majority of them will work. Being able to cast across the four-acre lake makes using lures a good choice, too bad the shoreline will most likely be too crowded to cast. If it is crowded, Power Bait, marshmallows or night crawlers will do the trick.

If you plan to make the trip supplies, are available in Georgetown. After snowstorms the road to Walton may be inaccessible. Call the Forest Service for updated conditions.

Also nearby are Stumpy Meadows Lake, Rubicon River, Hell Hole Reservoir and American River, South Fork (Coloma).

Directions: *From the junction of Interstate 5 and Highway 50 in Sacramento, drive east on Highway 50 for approximately 42 miles to Highway 49. Turn left on Highway 49, drive eight-tenths of a mile and veer right on Highway 193. Continue 14 miles and turn right on Main Street in Georgetown. Continue 4.5 miles (Main Street becomes Wentworth Springs Road) and turn right on Balderston Road. Drive two-tenths of a mile to the lake on the left.*

Walton Pond

STUMPY MEADOWS LAKE

Rating: 8

Species: Rainbow Trout and Brown Trout

Stocked with 5,600 pounds of rainbow trout and 800 pounds of brown trout.

Facilities: Boat Launch, Picnic Area, Restrooms and Campgrounds

Need Information? El Dorado National Forest (530) 333-4312

Whether casting from a float tube, a boat or from shore, Stumpy Meadows Lake is a great place to fish. Additionally, the lake provides spectacular scenery (it's surrounded by pine tree covered mountains). At 4,200 feet in the El Dorado National Forest, the lake is roughly an hour and a half drive from Sacramento a journey well worth it.

Although not a trophy trout fishery, Stumpy Meadows, sometimes referred to as Edson Lake, is an ideal place to learn to fish. A direct response to heavy stocking, the lake yields high catch rates. Beginning in May and ending in late August, the California Department of Fish & Game releases a total of 10,000 half-pound rainbows and 2,320 half-pound browns. Even more attractive to anglers, no special techniques need to be performed.

Anglers who keep it simple do the best. For trollers, no leadcore or downriggers are needed. Trout typically stay in the top 20 feet of water throughout summer. There are several trolling patterns that work, including across the dam, down the middle of the lake, around the shoreline and off the points. If fishing from a float tube stick near the dam, off points or in a cove. Be sure to stay out of the boater's way. As there are steep drop-offs near the parking area, try fishing off the rocks near the railing. The best methods are to fish a nightcrawler about 10 feet down from a bobber or to soak Power Bait.

Every so often someone catches a brown in the four-to-five-pound class, but most of the fish caught are rainbows just under a pound.

If you plan to make the trip, supplies are available in Georgetown. The road to Stumpy Meadows isn't plowed during the winter and is usually inaccessible from January through March. Call the Forest Service for updated road conditions.

Also nearby are Rubicon River and American River, South Fork (Coloma).

Directions: *From the junction of Interstate 5 and Highway 50 in Sacramento, drive east on Highway 50 for approximately 42 miles to Highway 49. Turn left on Highway 49, drive eight-tenths of a mile and veer right on Highway 193. Continue 14 miles and turn right on Main Street in Georgetown. Continue 16.1 miles (Main Street becomes Wentworth Springs Road) to the lake.*

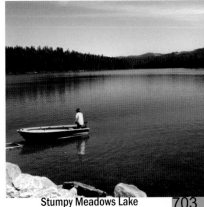

Stumpy Meadows Lake

RUBICON RIVER

<table>
<tr><td>

Rating: 6

Species: Rainbow Trout
and Brown Trout

Stocks: None

Facilities: None

Need Information?
Contact: El Dorado
National Forest
(530) 333-4312

</td></tr>
</table>

The Rubicon River is an odd wild trout stream. In fact, it's one of the few wild trout waters that aren't governed by special regulations. The California Department of Fish and Game doesn't plant trout in the Rubicon. Nonetheless, a healthy population of wild rainbow and brown trout exist. The downfall to the Rubicon is that there are few trophy trout available. A trout longer than 12 inches is almost unheard of.

The lack of trophy trout keeps the Rubicon from being exposed to thousands of anglers, which is fine and dandy for the few who fish of the river. This river is loaded with six-to-10-inch rainbows and browns that can be taken on spinners, night crawlers and flies.

One nice trait of the Rubicon is that it's an easy river to fish and you don't need to able to read water extensively to find success. The Rubicon isn't turbulent water, rather a series of deep pools and long runs. The water is extremely clear, but for some reason the trout aren't as skittish as you'd expect.

Personally, when I fish the Rubicon, I bring along a night crawler fished on a single barbless hook, an assortment of one-eighths, three-eighths and quarter-ounce Panther Martins and standard nymphs, such as pleasant tails and prince nymphs. From spring through summer, you can always find trout in the deep holes and at the tops of long runs. Also, it's effective to fish where tributaries enter the river. Don't bother fishing much slow moving water.

Access is good, although chances are you'll have a rough time crossing the river through early summer. There is a well graded trail on the north side of the river that makes for great access. The further upriver of the bridge you walk, the fewer anglers you'll run into, but the fishing doesn't necessarily get better.

If you plan to make the trip, supplies are available in Georgetown. The Rubicon River is closed to fishing from November 16 to the last Saturday in April.

Also nearby are Stumpy Meadows Reservoir and Walton Pond.

Directions: *From the junction of Interstate 5 and Highway 50 in Sacramento, drive east on Highway 50 for approximately 42 miles to Highway 49. Turn left on Highway 49, drive eight-tenths of a mile and veer right on Highway 193. Continue 14 miles and turn right on Main Street in Georgetown. Continue 22.1 miles (Main Street becomes Wentworth Springs Road) to the signed turnoff for the Rubicon River. Turn left and continue 4.7 miles to a dirt road on the right, just after crossing the bridge. If you have a high clearance vehicle turn right and drive three-tenths of a mile to the river. Smaller cars should park alongside the road and walk the rest of the way. The road is extremely rough.*

ICE HOUSE RESERVOIR

Rating: 7

Species: Rainbow Trout and Brown Trout

Stocked with 10,000 pounds of rainbow trout, 48 pounds of fingerling brown trout and 1,700 pounds of brown trout.

Facilities: Picnic Areas, Launch Ramp, Restrooms and a Campground

Need Information? Contact: El Dorado National Forest (530) 644-6048, Icehouse Resort (530) 293-3321

It was mid-April on a Friday when I was forced to leave Lake Tahoe early because word had come over the radio that a surprise powerful winter storm was headed to the Tahoe Basin in less than an hour, possibly closing Interstate 80. I needed to make sure I wouldn't be stuck at Tahoe. Tomorrow was to be a big day. My boat and I were headed to Sacramento so my uncle Ron Shaffer and I could go striper fishing. The bite on the river was reportedly terrific. The stripers had begun to school up from Rio Vista to Colusa.

The snow began to stick as I headed over Donner Pass. Descending into the Sacramento Valley, the snow turned to rain. Nearing the Metropolitan area, the rain began to fall harder and harder. A small stream flood warning had been issued for the foothills of the Sacramento and El Dorado Counties. That meant the river was going to muddy and swell. I was worried we wouldn't be going striper fishing. We didn't.

Saturday's forecast was for morning showers in the valley and snow in the mountains. The weather wasn't going to keep us from fishing. After catching a seven-pound brown with fishing guide Mike Neilsen in Lake Tahoe earlier in the week, I wanted my uncle to get the same experience. Nielsen told me there was a good chance at catching a large brown this time of the year in Icehouse Reservoir, just over an hour east of Sacramento off of Highway 50.

Because the reservoir was located at 5,500 feet in the El Dorado National Forest we decided not to leave until 9 a.m., hoping some of the snow from this off-season storm would melt. When we left the Capitol, chains were still required to get into the Tahoe Basin. Fortunately for us, Ice House Road, which had a few feet of snow on its banks, was plowed.

However, we weren't so lucky when we arrived at the launch ramp, which was hidden under a foot of snow and ice. Our vehicle had four-wheel drive and we were sure we could get the boat in the water, but pulling it out was doubtful. The ice was too thick, even for snow tires.

I wasn't concerned with the poor launching conditions. Somehow we were getting the boat in the water. After chatting with another angler, who was also determined to launch, I grabbed a snow shovel out of the back of his truck and began scooping snow off the ramp. Ten minutes later I had completed three of the 100 yards I needed to clear to be able to launch. This was going to take a long time!

I then heard what sounded like a bulldozer coming into the parking lot. It was a snowplow, with "SMUD" written on its side. SMUD? That was

Plowing the launch ramp after a winter storm at Ice House Reservoir

Sacramento Municipal Utilities District. What was it doing all the way up here? We were in El Dorado County, he was way out of his region, but no one seemed to mind. The man with the other boat bribed the driver with $20 to plow the ramp. He didn't take it. He plowed the ramp to make some fishermen happy.

We were the first anglers on the lake. Blanketing the lake's rocky shorelines, there was two feet of snow on the ground, snow was falling from the pines trees that surround the lake, the water was glassy, and as usual the weather forecast was wrong; there wasn't a cloud in the sky.

Just as we put our lines in the water, an osprey swooped down from its' nest and snatched a fish from the lake. While another osprey soared above a cove looking for lunch, a flock of Canadian geese honked continuously as they hovered two feet above the water heading towards the dam. Two mallards basked in the sun off one of the points. It couldn't have been a more beautiful day!

Unfortunately I couldn't say the same for the fishing. It stunk! We were the only two on the lake that caught any fish at all. Of the 12 other anglers, no one else had caught anything, and we weren't about to show off our two nine-inch rainbows and 11-inch brown.

The drop in the barometer the night before and its' sudden rise that day had shut off the bite, but the fabulous scenery had overshadowed the poor fishing. Whether it's ice fishing in the winter, trolling the lake in the spring or soaking Power Bait from shore, Ice House Reservoir normally provides its' visitors with great action. The stocking of 16,400 half-pound rainbow trout, 4,390 browns and 10,704 fingerling browns keeps the lake full of fish year-round.

Methods differ depending on the season. While fishing through the ice can be the only way to go in the winter, the best time to catch the bigger fish is right after ice out, usually in early April. (Some years it won't freeze.) The problem is that launch ramp may not be accessible until late April or even May. For roughly the first two weeks after the ice clears, fishing for Icehouse's larger browns is phenomenal. Most of the browns caught are from two-to-four pounds, some larger. Trolling Mini Speed Traps in front of the dam works best. There is a shelf on the south side of the dam that produces good results.

After the initial few weeks after ice out the big browns move into deeper water and attentions turns to the smaller rainbows and browns. Anglers trolling red and gold Thomas Buoyants do best. Fishing from a float tube out in front of the dam is equally as effective. Bank fishermen aren't left out. Setting up near the dam, boat launch or on one of the many points and casting out Power Bait or night crawlers should catch you fish.

It's a good idea to fish the South Fork of Silver Creek inlet from April through June. The channel is deep enough to get your boat near the inlet. There is also a trail the loops around the lake, allowing shore fishermen in on the action too.

If you plan to make the trip, supplies are available a few miles down the road at Ice House Resort. In winter call ahead for road conditions. Chains may be required. The campgrounds are closed during the winter.

Also nearby are Wrights Lake, Union Valley Reservoir, Loon Lake, the American River, South Fork (Riverton) and Jenkinson Lake.

Directions: From the junction of Interstate 5 and Highway 50 in Sacramento, drive east on Highway 50 for approximately 59 miles to Ice House Road. Turn left and drive approximately 10.5 miles to the Ice House Reservoir turnoff. Turn right and continue 1.2 miles to the launch ramp.

A sheet of ice on Ice House Reservoir in March

UNION VALLEY RESERVOIR

The Crystal Basin Recreation Area offers something for everyone. So does Union Valley Reservoir. Union Valley Reservoir is the largest lake in the basin and offers a diverse coldwater fishery that is also enjoyed by boaters. Union Valley isn't a secret. From Memorial Day through Labor Day, the lake gets bombarded by Sacramento area residents.

Unfortunately, access at the reservoir doesn't always cater to fishing. Typically, during the winter the lake is inaccessible due to snow. Nonetheless, some years the reservoir is so low that the launch ramp will be 200 yards out of the water. Other years, water will run over the spillway. To be safe, call ahead to check on launching conditions.

Union Valley Reservoir is turning into one of the Northern California's popular kokanee fisheries. While kokanee don't get huge, they definitely are abundant. Troll near the dam, off points and in the cove near Sunset Campground. More than 25,000 fingering kokanee are

Jason McLean with a Union Valley Reservoir kokanee taken in June of 2003.

planted.

Due to Union Valley's size and depth, a quality lake trout fishery has also developed over the last few decades. There are nowhere near the amount of lake trout as Lake Tahoe, Donner Lake or Fallen Leaf Lake. However, there are some big fish to be caught. Many lake trout know-hows believe the next state record lake trout will be caught here, but that statement is highly debated. The ingredients are definitely present, yet it remains to be seen how big these lake trout can grow. Throughout the summer, Union Valley's lake trout tend to hug the bottom closely, except during first light when they suspend to feed. Roughly 10,000 fingerling lake trout are planted each year.

Rainbow trout are also available. They are stocked by the California Department of Fish and Game with the purpose of being caught. More than 33,000 three-to-the-pound rainbows are planted annually, in addition to 26,520 sub-catchable rainbows. Those which aren't picked off by browns and lake trout are usually caught by trollers in the spring. The lake does have a population of holdover rainbows, but rarely do you see one over two pounds.

Browns are hard to come by. Occasionally, someone dunking a night crawler in one of the fingers will catch a huge brown, but the chances of that happening are slim.

Union Valley Reservoir is heavily used. It's a good idea to make camping reservations ahead of time. We arrived on a Friday night and had to sleep in the back of a 17-foot boat because all of the campsites were taken. Don't make the mistake we did.

Trip info for Loon Lake also applies to Union Valley Reservoir.

Directions: *From the junction of Highway 89/50 in South Lake Tahoe, drive west on Highway 50 for 26.1 miles to the Ice House Reservoir turnoff on the right. Turn right and drive 15 miles to the Sunset/Foshada and Union Valley Reservoir turnoff on the left. Turn left to the lake.*

Union Valley Reservoir in late winter of 2002.

LOON LAKE

Rating: 7

Species: Rainbow Trout and Brown Trout

Stocked with 10,000 pounds of rainbow trout.

Facilities: Campgrounds, Picnic Areas, Restrooms and a Boat Launch

Need Information? Contact: El Dorado National Forest (530) 644-6048, Icehouse Resort (530) 293-3321

A lot like Lower Blue Lake near Carson Pass, Loon is the ideal lake to learn how to troll, to introduce kids to fishing, to catch limits and most importantly, to experiment. The rainbow trout love to bite at this 6,378-foot lake resting below the Desolation Wilderness in a remote and picturesque granite setting known as the Crystal Basin Recreation Area.

Loon is a good choice for a weekend family camping trip. There are good camping facilities and lots more to do than just fish. Several hike-to lakes rest a short distance away in the Desolation Wilderness, swimming can be refreshing and the lake is one of only a few that offers boat-in campsites.

The fairly large lake in the El Dorado National Forest has no boating restrictions and is heavily used by Sacramento area residents. However, the California Department of Fish and Game combats the crowds with 19,700 half-pound rainbow trout each year. Limits are common. Even beginners catch plenty of fish. The lake has a stable population of holdovers, yet few manage to push more than a pound. Catching a two-pound trout would give you bragging rights.

Because of the lake's contour, Loon is a great place to bring children. Access is exceptional. The boat launch is a paved, two-laner and the lake is easy to troll. Also, bait dunkers have plenty of drive-to access. There's a picnic area near the boat launch, rocky shorelines to fish near the dam, hike-in spots on the backside of the lake and campgrounds with walk-to fishing access.

Techniques at Loon vary, but all work. The quickest way to nab an easy limit is trolling. Year-round, both toplining and downriggers work. I like to do both at the same time. Run two toplines, one off each side and two other lines on a downrigger. Set the downriggers to 47 feet and 32 feet. Top producers at Loon were the orange Cripplure, a red Sep's Pro Secret behind a nickel dodger, a silver Needlefish with a red tip and a silver Kastmaster.

There is one rule to follow on

710 Jason McLean caught this Loon Lake bow on a Cripplure in the spring of 2003.

Loon. Stay slow. You can catch fish trolling up to 3 mph, however, you'll fool dozens of more fish if you can maintain a speed of 0.5-1 mph.

Your best bets are to troll from the boat launch to the cabin (while staying roughly 50 yards offshore), near the dam and in the channel between Loon and what was formally known as Pleasant Lake. A lot of fish are at the north end of Loon (the area which used to be called Pleasant Lake), but because of submerged structures and dozens of small islands, this area can be hard to troll.

Typical shoreline techniques work as well. Keep things simple. Part of the reason Loon's bait dunkers do well is because even the top few feet of water remains cool enough in the summer to harbor rainbows. For best results, cast out an inflated night crawler or a marshmallow/mealworm combo. Tossing lures from the shore provides only fair catch rates.

One downfall to Loon is the wind. Winds kick up daily and can create hazardous conditions for those with small boats. The typical wind comes from the west, therefore most anglers start by fishing the east end so they can have calm water longer.

If you plan to make the trip, supplies are available in Pollack Pines. In winter, call ahead for road conditions. The road is plowed to the lake, however, at times snow accumulates on the shore and the lake becomes difficult to reach.

Also nearby are Gerle Creek Reservoir, Union Valley Reservoir, Ice House Reservoir and Union Valley Reservoir Falls.

Directions: *From the junction of Interstate 5 and Highway 50 in Sacramento, drive east on Highway 50 for approximately 59 miles to Ice House Road. Turn left and drive 6.5 miles to a split in the road. Stay right and continue 17.9 miles to another split in the road. Stay right and continue 4.5 miles to the Loon Lake Recreation sign. Veer right and drive four-tenths of a mile to the day-use area. For the dam, veer left at the Loon Lake Recreation sign.*

Loon Lake

GERLE CREEK RESERVOIR

Rating: 5

Species: Brown Trout

Stocks: None

Facilities: Fishing Pier, Restrooms and Campgrounds

Need Information?
Contact: El Dorado National Forest
(530) 644-6048

Gerle Creek is one of only a few reservoirs in California where wild brown trout are the sole inhabitants. The California Department of Fish and Game doesn't plant any fish, however, they are actively managing the lake to protect the wild brown trout population. The browns are part of a resident self-sustaining population of browns that successfully spawn in Gerle Creek each fall.

Gerle Creek Reservoir is home to mostly 10-15 inch fish. Nonetheless, a good number of larger browns also inhabit the lake. Unfortunately, summertime isn't reserved for anglers. A campground along the shore draws big crowds. Most people make a day out of swimming and floating on rafts instead of fishing. Few anglers fish in the summer. At 5,206 feet in the El Dorado National Forest, Gerle warms enough in the summer to make swimming comfortable.

If you plan to make the trip, supplies are available at Ice House Resort. In winter call ahead for updated road conditions. The road may be closed due to snow.

Also nearby are Union Valley Reservoir, Loon Lake and Union Valley Falls.

Directions: *From the junction of Interstate 5 and Highway 50 in Sacramento, drive east on Highway 50 for approximately 59 miles to Ice House Road. Turn left and drive 6.5 miles to a split in the road. Stay right and continue 17.9 miles to another split in the road. Stay left and drive 2.9 miles to Gerle Creek Campground on the left.*

Gerle Creek Reservoir

WRIGHTS LAKE

Rating: 6

Species: Rainbow Trout, Brown Trout and Brook Trout

Stocked with 800 pounds of rainbow trout and 800 pounds of brown trout.

Facilities: Restrooms, Picnic Areas and Campgrounds

Need Information? Contact: El Dorado National Forest (530) 644-6048

For many California anglers, Wrights Lake is a typical weekend camping destination. Roughly an hour and 15 minutes from Sacramento and 45 minutes from South Lake Tahoe, this calm and quiet lake doesn't get much fishing pressure. The 65-acre lake is more attractive to those who fish a few times a year for stocked fish. Things never get rowdy. No gas-powered boats are allowed so tranquility can be expected. Seasonal cabins cover much of the lake's shoreline. There is still plenty of public access though.

Much of Wrights is shallow, yet float tubers and shoreline anglers share success. Bringing 1,600 rainbow trout and 2,000 browns, the California Department of Fish and Game supplies the fish that cruise the lake in search of Power Bait, gold Kastmasters and silver Panther Martins.

Wrights Lake at sunset

At 7,000 feet in the El Dorado National Forest, there are brooks here too. However, rarely do they leave the lake's only major tributary. Don't expect any big ones. Seldom does a fish more than 14 inches get caught. Fishing takes a backseat to the overall wilderness experience. If you are looking for a place where you won't get run over by boaters and can enjoy the heavily forested setting than it can't be beat.

If you plan to make the trip, supplies are available in Pollack Pines. Call ahead for road conditions. During winter chains may be required.

Also nearby are Dark Lake, Beauty Lake, Grouse Lake, Hemlock Lake, Smith Lake, Icehouse Reservoir, Loon Lake and Union Valley Reservoir.

Directions: From South Lake Tahoe, at the junction of Highway's 50 and 89 drive west on Highway 50 for 20.9 miles to the Wright's Lake turnoff on the right. Turn right and drive 7.8 miles to Wrights Lake.

DARK LAKE

Rating: 4

Species: Rainbow Trout
and Brown Trout

Stocked with 400
pounds of rainbow trout
and 400 pounds of
brown trout.

Facilities: None

Need Information?
Contact: El Dorado
National Forest
(530) 644-6048

Fishing at little Dark Lake in the Wrights Lake Recreation Area is almost solely practiced by homeowners who reside in cabins tucked under the pines towards the back of the lake. Without pressure on the California Department of Fish and Game from those residents, it's almost certain that this shallow, silt bottom lake would be wiped off the stocking list. The lake sees little fishing pressure and almost none from non-residents.

Aside from the 800 rainbow trout and 1,000 brown trout the CA DFG plants each year, there are no other fish. The trout are limited to pan size. No trophy fish are available. Situated in the El Dorado National Forest, Dark Lake is in fact dark, most likely because of the silted bottom. Wooded shorelines keep much of the access to float tubers and those with non-gas powered boats. Any common trout rig will work here, but for the most part anglers overlook this waterhole.

Trip info for Wright's Lake also apply to Dark Lake.

Directions: *From South Lake Tahoe at the junction of Highway's 50 and 89, drive west on Highway 50 for 20.9 miles to the Wright's Lake turnoff on the right. Turn right and drive 7.8 miles to Wrights Lake. Continue three-tenths of a mile past Wrights Lake Visitor Center to the Maud Lake Trailhead on the right.*

Dark Lake

BEAUTY LAKE

Rating: 1

Species: None

Stocks: None

Facilities: None

Need Information?
Contact: El Dorado
National Forest
(530) 644-6048

To most fishermen Beauty Lake's beauty goes unappreciated. Anglers who are frustrated when their bait remains untouched, even after hours of fishing, often overlook the lake's fascinating wooded scenery while contemplating why fishing is so bad. The explanation is concise and simple. There is about as many fish in Beauty as there is an Arrowhead water bottle. There are no fish here!

The most likely reason plants don't take place is because Beauty is extremely shallow, (fewer than five feet deep), and is a prime candidate for freezing solid in the winter. Yet, what Beauty's splendid scenery is good for is relaxation. Even on weekends, this easy to reach hike-to lake remains crowd-free. To reach Beauty, begin at the Maud Lake Trailhead and walk the fairly flat path for a half-mile to the lake in the El Dorado National Forest.

Trip info for Wrights Lake also apply to Beauty Lake.

Directions: *From South Lake Tahoe at the junction of Highway's 50 and 89, drive west on Highway 50 for 20.9 miles to the Wright's Lake turnoff on the right. Turn right and drive 7.8 miles to Wrights Lake. Continue three-tenths of a mile past Wrights Lake Visitor Center to the Maud Lake Trailhead on the right.*

Beauty Lake

Region

Carson Pass
& Hope Valley

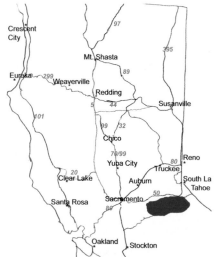

25

Granite Lake
Silver Lake
Kirkwood Lake
Caples Lake
Woods Lake
Winnemucca Lake
Round Top Lake
Lost Lakes
Upper Blue Lake
Lower Blue Lake
Tamarack Lake
Twin Lake
Meadow Lake
Sunset Lakes
Wet Reservoir
Carson River (West Fork)
Red Lake
Scotts Lake

GRANITE LAKE

Rating: 2

Species: Brook Trout

Stocks: None

Facilities: None

Need Information?
Contact: Plasse's Resort
(209) 258-8814

If you don't have good directional skills, stay away from Granite Lake. Just finding the trail to Granite Lake can take some work if you aren't careful. Unfortunately, the rewards at Granite Lake aren't worth much either. Fishing has hit rock bottom. The California Department of Fish and Game abandoned the lake's high country stocking program a few years ago and the lake has never recovered. Yes, we are referring to another endangered frog issue. In the past brook trout were planted as fingerlings, but with heavy fishing pressure they didn't last long. Some say there are a few brook trout left in the lake though. My last visit in summer of 2002 yielded no fish. Nor did I see one. Unless stocking resumes, don't come to fish.

The scenery, on the other hand, makes the hike worth it. As its' name implies, the lake is located in granite country and can be beautiful, even if the fishing isn't so hot. At 7,581 feet in the El Dorado National Forest, Granite Lake is best suited as an easy day-hike from Silver Lake.

Park in the dirt lot next to Plasse's Resort and then walk back on the dirt road you came in on. Walk roughly 50 yards and take a right at the sign for the campground. There's a wooden footbridge to aid in crossing the creek. Continue on the dirt road through the campgrounds to the poorly signed trailhead for Granite Lake/Camp Minkalo. Don't be surprised if you miss it. We did. Paralleling Silver Lake, the road turns to a single track path. Within 15 minutes you'll come to a split in the trail. Heading uphill, stay right. The left fork continues around the lake. After another 15 minutes of a gradual elevation gain, there's a junction. Stay right again. In fewer than 10 minutes you'll come to a small pond. Continue on the path for another five minutes to Granite Lake.

Trip info for Silver Lake also applies to Granite Lake.

Directions: *From the junction of Highway's 50 and 89 in South Lake Tahoe, drive south on Highway's 50/89 for 4.7 miles to Meyers. In Meyers, turn left on Highway 89 and drive south for 10.9 miles to Highway 88. Turn right and drive 21.3 miles to the Plasse's Resort turnoff. Turn left and continue one-mile to the resort and parking area.*

Granite Lake

717

SILVER LAKE

Rating: 7

Species: Brook Trout,
Rainbow Trout, Brown
Trout and Lake Trout

Stocked with 2,400
pounds of brown trout
and 9,100 pounds of
rainbow trout.

Facilities: Restrooms,
Boat Launch, RV
Hookups,
Campgrounds, Boat
Rentals, Lodging, Bait
& Tackle

Need Information?
Contact: El Dorado
National Forest (209)
295-4251, Kay's Silver
Lake Resort (209) 258-
8598, Kit Carson Lodge
(209) 258-8500,
Plasse's Resort
(209) 258-8814.

Silver Lake's fishery may go through a drastic change in the next few years. Prior to the year 2000, Silver Lake had no way to generate hydroelectric power. Typically, the lake was rarely taken down more than a few feet from full pool. However, in 2001, work began on a hydroelectric facility near the dam. This is not good news for fishermen. Owned by the El Dorado Irrigation District for decades, the lake was sold to the Pacific Gas & Electric Company. Silver will now be able to produce power. It's expected that the lake will be drawn down drastically in the future, which can be detrimental to the fishing.

While the lake has yet to be drawn down, the fishing remains fair year-round. The lake doesn't receive a ton of fishing pressure, but it is heavily stocked. The California Department of Fish and Game dumps 5,760 browns, 18,810 rainbows and fingerling lake trout, keeping the bite consistent on mostly pan-sized fish. To keep anglers interested larger rainbows and browns are planted each summer by Alpine County.

At 7,200 feet in the El Dorado National Forest, Silver freezes in the winter. One downfall is that water-skiing is allowed on this 525-acre reservoir. Just a few miles from Caples Lake, Silver is situated in granite country and unlike Caples, it has a lot of deep holes and drop-offs, although the deepest spot in the lake is roughly 60 feet. Also, when the wind is howling at Caples, it is often much calmer at Silver.

Fishing for rainbows and browns can be good for those who toss Power Bait from the shore, and exceptional for trollers toplining Needlefish and Mini Speed Traps around the lake's shorelines. While the lake trout fishery has yet to receive a lot of attention, a few fish over 20 pounds prompts some anglers to target them, but the overall population has yet to flourish. Lake trout can be caught trolling brown trout patterned Rebels in deeper water.

If you plan to make the trip supplies are available at the lake. There is a boat launch fee.

Also nearby are Caples Lake, Bear River Reservoir, 4th of July Lake, Frog Lake, Woods Lake and Winnemucca Lake.

Directions: *From the junction of Highway's 50 and 89 in South Lake Tahoe, drive south on Highway's 50/89 for 4.7 miles to Meyers. In Meyers, turn left on Highway 89 and drive south for 10.9 miles to Highway 88. Turn right and drive 19.7 miles to Silver Lake.*

KIRKWOOD LAKE

Rating: 4

Species: Rainbow Trout

Stocked with 800 pounds of rainbow trout.

Facilities: Campgrounds and Restrooms

Need Information? Contact: El Dorado National Forest (530) 622-5061

Every skier in the Sacramento and Stockton region has heard of Kirkwood, which is home of one of the most popular ski areas of the state. On the other hand, few, if any, know of little Kirkwood Lake and there is a good reason for it. Kirkwood is a small lake that doesn't allow gas-powered motors, nor does it offer even fair fishing. At 7,670 feet in the El Dorado National Forest, Kirkwood is more of a camping lake, which is shaded by pines and has a Girl Scout Camp on its' south shore.

Frozen in the winter, Kirkwood stays quiet in the summer when a few anglers arrive in attempt to catch some of the 1,680 trout that are planted by the California Department of Fish and 'Game. Most anglers are unsuccessful; however, anglers who have the patience to soak night crawlers off the bottom catch a few small trout. The best method would be to troll the lake with a canoe and an electric trolling motor, but many anglers don't waste their time, not with Caples and Silver Lake a short distance away.

If you plan to make the trip supplies are available in Kirkwood.

Also nearby are Caples Lake, Woods Lake and Silver Lake.

Directions: *From the junction of Highway's 50 and 89 in South Lake Tahoe, drive south on Highway's 50/89 for 4.7 miles to Meyers. In Meyers, turn left on Highway 89 and drive south for 10.9 miles to Highway 88. Turn right and drive 14.6 miles to the Kirkwood Lake turnoff on the right. Turn right and continue to the lake.*

(Left) Kirkwood Lake

CAPLES LAKE

Rating: 8

Species: Rainbow Trout, Brook Trout, Brown Trout and Lake Trout

Stocked with 8,200 pounds of rainbow trout, 2,200 pounds of brown trout, 3,400 pounds of brook trout and 162 pounds of fingerling lake trout.

Facilities: General Store, Bait & Tackle, Boat Launch, Boat Rentals, Lodging, Gas, Restaurant, Campgrounds, Restrooms and Picnic Areas

Need Information? Contact: Dale's Foothill Fishing Charters (530) 295-0488, Caples Lake Resort (209) 258-8888

At 620-acres and 7,800 feet in the El Dorado National Forest, just west of Kit Carson Pass, Caples Lake is an ideal put-and-take fishery. The California Department of Fish and Game spends a lot of time stocking fish into the lake and anglers happily take them out. Caples is extremely easy to fish and to the satisfaction of anglers, catch rates remain high. The CA DFG plants 14,920 rainbows, 5,780 brooks and 5,280 browns each year, in addition to 1,000 pounds of fish paid for by the Alpine County Chamber of Commerce.

Caples is operated by the El Dorado Irrigation District, which has no means of creating hydroelectric power so they don't need to draw down the lake, at least not yet. Plans to do so are in developmental stages. So, when many other lakes in the region have barren shorelines from receding water levels, Caples is sparkling clear and surrounded by a pine forest.

Trolling and still-fishing is great from spring through fall. Caples offers good shoreline access near the dam and spillway. Anglers who float night crawlers or Power Bait off the bottom go home with smiles on their faces. For boaters, the lake isn't very deep (60 feet at most) so toplining is the rule. Downriggers and leadcore aren't necessary, even in the summer. The most consistent method is trolling night crawlers behind a set of Sep's Pro flashers, but just about any spoon will work. Concentrate on the dam area and towards the back of the lake. The Emigrant and Woods Creek inlets are good area, but they are too shallow to troll in.

A Caples brookie

California residents from the Stockton area and Nevada residents from Reno fish Caples, yet it never gets too crowded. Typically Caples freezes over from December through early April and is known as one of the best ice fishing spots in the state. Caples Resort stays open year round and sometimes rents ice fishing equipment.

Caples is likely California's most consistent ice fishing lake. Due to its elevation, it's often the first to freeze and the last to thaw. Ironically, few anglers ice fish. On the other hand, anglers fishing near the spillway, dam or off points can take quick limit drowning live bait through the ice.

Caples also harbors lake trout and while they aren't heavily targeted, a few lunkers, like a 26-pound fish caught in April of 2001, are caught each year after ice out. Most of the lake trout are

Guide Dale Daneman with a trout taken on a Sep's flasher.

two-to-four pounds and are hooked by anglers trolling the dam area with Rebel Minnows. The CA DFG stocks 30,080 fingerling lake trout each year.

There are two downfalls: the lake is susceptible to winds, and the launch ramp doesn't open until 7 a.m., so unfortunately you can't get a boat on the lake for the early morning bite.

If you plan to make the trip, supplies are available at Caples Resort. There is a boat launch fee. There is a 5 mph speed limit. Keep an eye out for submerged rocks near the surface toward the creek inlets. They are hazardous to boaters.

Also nearby are Silver Lake and Woods Lake.

Directions: *From the junction of Highway's 49 and 88 in Jackson, take Highway 88 east for approximately 62 miles to the lake.*

Caples Lake is one of the most popular ice fishing destinations in the Sierra Nevada Mountains.

WOODS LAKE

Rating: 7

Species: Rainbow Trout
and Brown Trout

Stocked with 1,000
pounds of rainbow
trout.

Facilities: Restrooms,
Picnic Areas and
Campgrounds

Need Information?
Contact: El Dorado
National Forest
(530) 622-5061

Woods Lake is a drive-to lake with a backcountry feeling. Just west of Kit Carson Pass, this 16-acre lake is tucked into a small basin bordering the Mokelumne Wilderness. If the brisk, cool mountain air and forested settings don't hook you, the possibilities for pan-sized trout will keep you coming back year after year.

With powered boats prohibited, Woods Lake can provide that serene feeling, but crowds do develop. At 8,000 feet in the El Dorado National Forest, there are a few places the fish congregate, particularly at the back of the lake where its largest inlet is. This unnamed stream comes from Round Top Lake and keeps the oxygen at high levels in the spring and early summer, thus prompting trout to be active. Directly across from the inlet there are two huge rocks which mark the second best fishing spot. Here, there are steep drop-offs allowing you to cast and retrieve lures and soak Power Bait.

Although there are plenty of fish (2,125 are planted annually), size is a downer. Rarely are fish over 10 inches caught. Keep in mind though; coming to Woods is for the beautiful surroundings, not for trophy fishing. In the spring, also keep an eye out for Woods Lake Falls. It announces itself by spilling down the jagged cliffs at the back of the lake and can be quite striking at peak flow.

If you plan to make the trip, supplies are available at Caples Lake. Woods Lake Road is often closed in the winter and spring. Call the Forest Service for updated conditions.

Also nearby are Caples Lake, Carson River (West Fork) and Blue Lakes.

Directions: *From the junction of Highway's 50 and 89 in South Lake Tahoe, drive south on Highway's 50/89 for 4.7 miles to Meyers. In Meyers, turn left on Highway 89 and drive south for 10.9 miles to Highway 88. Turn right and drive 10.8 miles to Woods Lake Road. Turn left and continue to the lake.*

Woods Lake in late summer with a near dry Woods Lake Falls in the background.

WINNEMUCCA LAKE

Rating: 5

Species: Brook Trout and Rainbow Trout

Stocks: None

Facilities: None

Winnemucca Lake is one of the few backcountry lakes that I'd refrain from backpacking to. Don't get me wrong, the lake provides exceptional scenery and decent fishing, but an influx of day-use hikers and families takes away from the woodsy experience. Near Kit Carson Pass and ultimately draining into Caples Lake, at 8,980 feet Winnemucca Lake in the Mokelumne Wilderness is a hike suitable for all ages. The California Department of Fish and Game lists the lake as being planted with fingerling rainbow trout, yet my fishing partner and I failed to see any signs of them. The brooks, however, own this hike-to lake.

There are several methods to catch trout. Unfortunately, none of them work simultaneously. Tossing small Panther Martins and Kastmasters from shore near the inlet and outlet can be productive. Nonetheless, this side of the lake is shallow.

During the day it's best to cast a spoon as far towards the middle as possible, let it sink and then reel it in slowly. Sometimes, bait is best. Casting out Power Bait is probably the least effective method. The brookies can't resist flies. Elk hair caddis work remarkably. The largest concentrations of fish can be found near the steep drop-offs on the far side of the lake. While trout up to a pound are caught, don't expect to catch many over eight inches. Pan-size brookies are a majority.

Winnemucca Lake

Park in the Woods Lake day-use or the wilderness parking area and locate the trailhead sign for Woods Lake. It can be found near the outlet of Woods Lake. Immediately cross Woods Creek and follow the path as it parallels Woods Lake for nearly a quarter-mile. This is where the hike starts to get fun. As you walk, clusters of red, green, yellow and orange wildflowers paint the landscape. Winnemucca Creek emerges on your right. The heavily forested area gives way to open meadows as more wildflowers and awe inspiring views of Carson Pass can be seen in the distance. Gradually gaining elevation, you'll walk three-quarters of a mile from Woods Lake to where you'll meet up with, but won't cross, Winnemucca's outlet stream. Push on. The lake is a tad more than a quarter mile ahead.

Directions and trip info for Woods Lake also applies to Winnemucca Lake.

ROUND TOP LAKE

Rating: 4
Species: Brook Trout and Rainbow Trout
Stocks: None
Facilities: None

Just a short walk from Winnemucca Lake, Round Top Lake is a great destination for a day hike, yet heavy day use can take away from a backpacking experience. The trip to Round Top Lake allows for an exceptional loop trip, beginning and ending at Woods Lake, while spending a few hours at both Round Top and Winnemucca Lakes. The trip fits well in a day. It's not too long or too short. The fishing may be just ok. Nonetheless, the high country scenery is exceptional.

Round Top is much shallower than Winnemucca and at 9,341 feet in the Mokelumne Wilderness, if you use a large spoon you are bound to get snagged. While Round Top rests right on the path it doesn't get that much fishing pressure, most likely because the fishing isn't that good. Expect all fish to be pan-size and most to be caught in the outlet area. Fly fishing elk hair caddis works best.

From Winnemucca Lake, continue on the signed path for nearly nine-tenths of a mile to Round Top. Along the way you'll be overwhelmed by the view of 9,536 feet Fourth of July Peak and Carson Pass. The view is much better than the fishing. Taking the route back to Woods Lake drags you past an old mine, which you are forbidden to enter. The path is clearly marked and easy to navigate. Set aside at least a half-day for this loop trip. And, don't come for great fishing, rather a chance to perhaps catch fish and enjoy to the scenery.

Directions and trip info for Woods Lake also apply to Round Top Lake.

Round Top Lake

LOST LAKES

Rating: 5

Species: Brook Trout
and Golden Trout

Stocks: None

Facilities: None

Need Information?
Contact: The Sportsman
(530) 542-3474

The significance of the Lost Lakes deals with water. These small and fairly shallow lakes mark the headwaters of the West Fork of the Carson River. Lost Lakes aren't heavily fished, yet they are a good destination for anglers who don't mind a long drive on a dirt road to a drive-to lake where they can avoid crowds. You'll likely see a family camping on the shore of the upper lake, but few others. Any more people and it would be considered crowded.

Upper and Lower Lost Lakes differ drastically. At 8,620 feet in the Toiyabe National Forest, the lower lake is loaded with brook trout. To keep the population stable, the California Department of Fish and Game airlifts some 1,500 fingerling brooks each year. (No plants took place in 2003 or 2004.)

On the other hand, at 8,660 feet, the upper is commonly barren of fish. Because it's shallow, the lower lake is a good candidate for winterkill. Trout don't do well. The CA DFG does restock the lake with fingerling golden trout in most years, but they fail to show up in angler's creels. One CA DFG biologist told me he surveyed the lake for more than 20 years and never found a fish. The CA DFG attempts to plant 1,500 fingerling golden trout annually. (No plants took place in 2003.)

Lost Lakes

Don't bother bringing a motor boat, as the lakes are too small. A float tube would be helpful, however, shoreline fishing remains your best bet. Use caution not to get snagged. There are a lot of dead trees in the lake. Quarter-ounce Panther Martins work best.

Trip info for Lower Blue Lake applies to Lost Lakes.

Directions: *From the junction of Highway's 50 and 89 in South Lake Tahoe, drive south on Highway's 50/89 for 4.7 miles to Meyers. In Meyers, turn left on Highway 89 and drive south for 10.9 miles to Highway 88. Turn right and drive 2.3 miles to Blue Lakes Road (Road 015) and turn left. Continue 10.3 miles to a split in the road. Stay right and drive one mile to Lower Blue Lake. At a fork in the road at Lower Blue Lake, stay right and drive 2.7 miles to Upper Blue Lake. From Blue, continue 3.7 miles to the Lost Lakes turnoff on the right.*

UPPER BLUE LAKE

Rating: 9

Species: Rainbow
Trout, Brown Trout and
Cutthroat Trout

Stocked with 5,800
pounds of rainbow
trout.

Facilities:
Campgrounds and
Restrooms

There are 10 drive-to lakes that can be reached via Blue Lakes Road. All offer good fishing, yet only one has a diverse fishery that provides a chance to hook into trophy size fish. At 344 acres, Upper Blue Lake is deep and large enough to sustain trophy fish and a large population of smaller fish, keeping anglers who aren't keen on spending the entire day trolling around for that shot at catching a big one happy. (Fishing has declined a tad recently though. The road to Blue was paved bringing more anglers to the lake.)

Upper Blue is visited by a variety of different anglers, including those trolling for stocked rainbows, shore fishermen, float tubers, trollers who use downriggers to catch cutthroats and specialty fishermen who arrive in June and October for that chance of landing a big brown. There is no shortage of options at Upper Blue.

There easiest way to catch fish is to target the stocked bows. The California Department of Fish and Game plants 12,400 rainbows weighing a half-pound each. If trolling, stay 10 to 30 yards offshore. Also, there is a rock jetty near the dam that the fish love to take cover in. Troll as close to the jetty as possible. Be sure to use caution in this area though. There's a lot of shallow rocks to get hung up on. No downriggers are needed, simply topline for the planters. From the shore, soak Power Bait or float night crawlers off the bottom. If fishing from the jetty, tossing Kastmasters can provide good action.

As for the cutthroat, there are many in the lake. Most years, 10,000 fingerling cutthroat are planted. However, they are seldom caught without downriggers or leadcore. Throughout the summer the cutthroat stay in 30-50 feet depths and are willing to hit gold Kastmasters and Cripplures. The north and east shorelines usually provide the most consistent action. Each season cutthroats from six-to-eight pounds are landed, but most are one-to-two pounds.

Those who come for the browns don't always go home happy. Not a lot of browns are caught because they aren't targeted. In the summer they dive down deeper than 100 feet. The time to target the browns is in the fall when they come up to the surface to feed and bulk up for the winter before the lake freezes. Browns to 10 pounds are landed each fall, but most aren't reported. No browns are stocked, yet there are a stable population of wild browns.

Trip info for Blue Lake (Lower) also applies to Blue Lake (Upper).

Directions: *From the fork in the road at Lower Blue Lake, veer right and drive 2.7 miles to Upper Blue Lake.*

LOWER BLUE LAKE

Rating: 7

Species: Rainbow
Trout, Brook Trout,
Brown Trout and
Cutthroat Trout

Stocked with 4,600
pounds of rainbow trout
and 17 pounds of
fingerling brook trout.

Facilities:
Campgrounds and
Restrooms

Need Information?
Contact: El Dorado
National Forest
(530) 644-6048

Lower Blue Lake is the perfect place for an angler to learn how to troll for rainbow trout. With the California Department of Fish and Game spilling 9,400 rainbows into the 198-acre lake, the trout bite stays hot from June through October. And best of all, no trolling experience is needed. There are, however, a few items you will need, such as light line (four-pound test is best), a small lure (just about anything will work, yet gold Kastmasters and red and gold Thomas Buoyants did well for us) and you must keep a slow troll. Where should you troll? Start near the dam and troll either side of the lake, staying between 0.8 and 1.8-mph. It's best to remain roughly 15-30 yards offshore. On the other hand, fish are all over the lake. You don't have to follow a path religiously.

There are a few places you should get a bite every time you pass them, the hottest spot being a small island on the north side of the lake (if the lake is too low the island won't exist. The dam and points on the south shore are also prime spots. Because there are a lot of stumps and large boulders to get snagged on, play it safe and don't troll the inlet area. Most of the rainbows are in the eight-to-10-inch class. Due to a high harvest rate, few grow to larger proportions. Shoreline fishing can also be exceptional for those tossing Panther Martins and soaking night crawlers off the dam and points along the north end.

There is a small population of cutthroat, but most of them tend to stay in deep water and are seldom caught or targeted by anglers. In 1997, the CA DFG planted fingerling brooks. In 2003, 5,000 fingerlings were stocked.

There is one problem with trolling Lower Blue Lake, however. There is no maintained or paved boat launch. Launching car top boats and canoes is a synch. If you have a four-wheel drive vehicle you should be able to launch just about anything. We had no problem launching our 17-footer.

If you plan to make the trip, supplies are available in Meyers. Call ahead for road conditions. Blue Lakes Road is closed from the first snowfall in winter into late spring.

Also nearby are Twin Lake, Wet Reservoir and Upper and Lower Sunset Lake.

Directions: *From the junction of Highway's 50 and 89 in South Lake Tahoe, drive south on Highway's 50/89 for 4.7 miles to Meyers. In Meyers, turn left on Highway 89 and drive south for 10.9 miles to Highway 88. Turn right and drive 2.3 miles to Blue Lakes Road (Road 015) and turn left. Continue 10.3 miles to a split in the road. Stay right and drive one mile to Lower Blue Lake.*

TAMARACK LAKE

Rating: 4

Species: Brook Trout
and Cutthroat Trout

Stocks: None

Facilities: None

While most lakes found off Blue Lakes Road offer great trout fishing, the same can't be said for Tamarack Lake. If you arrive in June or early July, Tamarack appears to be a great looking lake to fish. However, after mid-July, Tamarack takes on a whole different look.

As the summer progresses the lake loses nearly 90 percent of its water as agriculture allotments are met downstream. Tamarack's fish don't have much of a chance, especially when they are planted as fingerlings. Up until 2002, the California Department of Fish and Game airlifted 3,000 fingerling cutthroats in each fall. Unfortunately, by fall Tamarack no longer looks like a lake. At 7,873 feet in the Toiyabe National Forest, this lake turns into two ponds. In reality it's what's left of the water near the lake's two dams.

Don't get me wrong there are fish to catch, but it takes the sport out of it when they are so concentrated. The lack of water also keeps the fish size down. Pan size is the limit. Both brooks and cutthroat are common. When the water gets low, don't be too picky on baits. Any small Panther Martin or night crawler will do.

Trip info for Blue Lake (Lower) also applies to Tamarack Lake.

Directions: *From the junction of Highway's 50 and 89 in South Lake Tahoe, drive south on Highway's 50/89 for 4.7 miles to Meyers. In Meyers, turn left on Highway 89 and drive south for 10.9 miles to Highway 88. Turn right and drive 2.3 miles to Blue Lakes Road (Road 015) and turn left. Continue 10.3 miles to a split in the road. Veer left and drive one mile to the lake on the left.*

Cutthroat are common at Tamarack Lake

Tamarack Lake

TWIN LAKE

Rating: 8

Species: Cutthroat
Trout and Brook Trout

Stocked with six
pounds of fingerling
cutthroat trout and three
pounds of fingerling
brook trout.

Facilities: None

Sometimes, practicing illegal methods pays off. In the case of Twin Lake, the introduction of a non-native food source paved the way for the region's best, least-known quality fishery. Unknown to most anglers an old California Department of Fish and Game warden acquired freshwater shrimp from Heenan Lake and strategically placed them in his favorite waters in the region without the approval of CA DFG biologists.

Luckily, the illegal transportation paid off and didn't backfire. The introduction of shrimp into Twin gave the fish a sufficient food source to enable them to grow to satisfactary sizes. The shrimp have adapted well to their new environment, especially in a shallow, grassy lake like Twin where they can hide and evade the trout. They can maintain their population by using the grass as shelter without becoming forage, which in turn allows the shrimp to be a major food source for the trout. The consequences of adding shrimp into Twin's ecosystem have been phenomenal.

Planting 3,000 fingerling brooks and 6,000 fingerling cutthroat trout, the CA DFG treats Twin as a put-and-grow fishery. And growing they do well. Many of the cutthroat and brooks reach two-to-four pounds.

Ironically, the fishing pressure at Twin is low. Because of flat shorelines at 8,145 feet in the El Dorado National Forest, Twin is a great place to bring a canoe,

Twin Lake

float tube or small car top boat. Trolling is most productive with small spoons. Fortunately, shoreline anglers can also get in on the action by tossing spinners.

Trip info for Blue Lake (Lower) also applies to Twin Lake.

Directions: *From the junction of Highway's 50 and 89 in South Lake Tahoe drive south on Highway's 50/89 for 4.7 miles to Meyers. In Meyers, turn left on Highway 89 and drive south for 10.9 miles to Highway 88. Turn right and drive 2.3 miles to Blue Lakes Road (Road 015) and turn left. Continue 10.3 miles to a split in the road. Stay right and drive one mile to Lower Blue Lake. At Blue, veer right and continue eight-tenths of a mile to Twin Lake.*

MEADOW LAKE

Rating: 5
Species: Cutthroat Trout and Brook Trout
Stocks: None
Facilities: None
Need Information? Contact: The Sportsman (530) 542-3474

Meadow Lake is often overlooked by anglers due to the lack of drive to access. Anglers can drive close to Meadow, but withouth a hardcore four-wheel drive jeep, you can't drive all the way to the shoreline. This keeps many anglers from visiting, but also helps keep a stable population of trout in the reservoir.

At 7,774 feet in the El Dorado National Forest, the California Department of Fish and Game governs Meadow as a put-and-grow fishery. Each year 15,000 fingerling cutthroat trout are airlifted into this deep lake in steep granite country. (These plants didn't take place in 2003-04.) Without a road leading down to its' shoreline, some walking is required to reach Meadow. The trek isn't long, no more than a half mile, but it's a bit steep and could be rough if you chose to drag a boat in with you. Unfortunately, you pretty much need a canoe or float tube to be successful except for shoreline fishing, which isn't typically productive. Additionally, Meadow gets dawn down each year and drains into the Mokelumne River.

The ideal scenario would be to bring a canoe and poles with leadcore line. This would allow you to reach depths where the cutthroat lie. Most of the brook trout stay closer to shore. Try trolling silver Kastmasters or Needlefish as slow as you can. Work on getting your lures down 20-50 feet. While the lake is deep, the fish rarely peek above a pound because there isn't enough food. Some freshwater shrimp enter the lake via Twin Lake's outlet stream. However, it's not enough to allow the population to grow to trophy proportions.

Trip info for Lower Blue Lake also applies to Meadow Lake.

Directions: *From the junction of Highway's 50 and 89 in South Lake Tahoe, drive south on Highway's 50/89 for 4.7 miles to Meyers. In Meyers, turn left on Highway 89 and drive south for 10.9 miles to Highway 88. Turn right and drive 2.3 miles to Blue Lakes Road (Road 015) and turn left. Continue 10.3 miles to a split in the road. Stay right and drive one mile to Lower Blue Lake. At Blue, veer left and drive 2.5 miles to the Meadow Lake overlook. Park and walk down to the lake.*

Meadow Lake

SUNSET LAKES

Rating: 8
Species: Brook Trout, Rainbow Trout and Cutthroat Trout
Stocks: None
Facilities: None

The Carson Valley Irrigation District has altered many natural ponds in the Carson River Drainage to allow for more water storage. Sunset Lakes are an example, nonetheless the lakes hold some large brook trout.

Sunset is managed three-fold. The goal of the California Department of Fish and Game is to provide a trophy fishery, manage it for recreational harvest and to offer a diverse fishing experience. They've done well with all aspects. The fish in Sunset definitely leave an impression, and a good one for that matter! At 7,850 feet in the Toiyabe National Forest, the lakes hold brook, rainbow and cutthroat trout.

The fisheries could be some of the best put-and-grow lakes in the Sierra, however, each year the water levels drop extremely low. Some years the upper lake dries up completely. Fortunately, the lower consistently maintains enough water to sustain fish.

For best results bring along a float tube or small car top boat paddle out to the middle and jig a small Kastmaster, Megabait Live Jig, Crippled Herring or dangle a night crawler near the bottom.

Trip info for Blue Lake (Lower) also applies to Sunset Lakes.

Directions: *From the junction of Highway's 50 and 89 in South Lake Tahoe, drive south on Highway's 50/89 for 4.7 miles to Meyers. In Meyers, turn left on Highway 89 and drive south for 10.9 miles to Highway 88. Turn right and drive 2.3 miles to Blue Lakes Road (Road 015) and turn left. Continue 10.3 miles to a split in the road. Veer left and drive 2.9 miles to a split in the road. Stay left and drive four-tenths of a mile to Lower Sunset. For Upper Sunset, backtrack one-tenth of a mile to a dirt road on the right. Turn right and drive two-tenths of a mile to the lake.*

Sunset Lakes

WET MEADOWS RESERVOIR

Rating: 10
Species: Brook Trout
Stocks: None
Facilities: None

Wet Meadows Reservoir is the best, least fished, drive-to reservoir in the greater Tahoe region. It's one of the few drive-to reservoirs that specializes in trophy size fish, yet remains mostly free of crowds even on weekends. The fish you'll catch are mind boggling, but to find out how big, you'll need to head out to the Toiyabe National Forest, near the border of the Mokelumne Wilderness to find out. I'll give you one hint. We are talking five pounds plus!

It isn't a huge planting schedule that makes Wet Meadows such a great lake. Ironically, the California Department of Fish and Game doesn't stock fish. The lake is home to a self-sustaining population of brook trout, many so large that that locals attempt to hide the fishery by telling anglers that it goes dry each year and subsequently, has no fish. Well, that tale is two fold. Wet Meadow does, in fact, nearly dry up each year as water is sucked out to maintain household needs downstream in Nevada, but there is always enough water for the brookies to maintain their population.

The CA DFG doesn't know how these fish grow so fast and to such large proportions. On the other hand, they aren't going to complain. There's the old saying: "If it aint broke, don't fix it," and they are sticking with that attitude. No stocking has proved to be the best management.

So how do you catch these trophy size brookies? It all depends on the time of year. The reservoir is inaccessible do to snow from December through June, but it does remain fairly full through early summer. This is when non gas-powered car top style boats greatly increase your odds. Trolling Kastmasters gives you the advantage of covering much more area than shoreline angling. For bank anglers, set up camp on one of the sandy beaches and either dangle a night crawler off the bottom or toss large Krocodiles from shore.

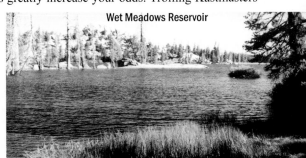

Wet Meadows Reservoir

Trip info for Blue Lake (Lower) also applies to Wet Meadows Reservoir.

Directions: *From the junction of Highway's 50 and 89 in South Lake Tahoe, drive south on Highway's 50/89 for 4.7 miles to Meyers. In Meyers, turn left on Highway 89 and drive south for 10.9 miles to Highway 88. Turn right and drive 2.3 miles to Blue Lakes Road (Road 015) and turn left. Continue 10.3 miles to a split in the road. Veer left and drive 2.9 miles (you'll pass Tamarack Lake in one mile) to a split in the road. Veer right. From the sign for Wet Meadows Reservoir it is nine-tenths of a mile to the lake.*

CARSON RIVER (WEST FORK)

Rating: 8

Species: Rainbow Trout, Brown Trout, Brook Trout and Cutthroat Trout

Stocked with 12,500 pounds of rainbow trout and 620 pounds of fingerling cutthroat trout.

Facilities: Restrooms, Picnic Areas and Campgrounds

Need Information? Contact: The Sportsman (530) 542-3474

Without the West Fork of the Carson River, the region corresponding to Blue Lakes Road and Hope Valley couldn't be considered a top-notch weekend camping trip. The river, more the size of a stream, completes this area by giving anglers a great place to stream fish.

Unfortunately, crowds are common at the West Fork. Fortunately, there is good access along an eight-mile stretch of the stream, which tends to disperse the crowds. The California Department of Fish and Game tosses 17,160 half-pound rainbow trout and 8,060 fingerling cutthroat. There are wild trout, however, they are far less abundant than the planters. The Alpine County Fish and Game Commission dumps 3,800 pounds of fish from the American Trout and Salmon Company, 1,900 of which are trophy three-to-eight-pound fish. To attract more anglers, the Alpine County Chamber of Commerce adds 500 pounds of trophy fish.

To be successful on this 10-15 foot wide stream in the Toiyabe National Forest stick to tossing Power Bait and Panther Martins in these areas: where the river crosses under Blue Lakes Road, Hope Valley Campground, where the river crosses under Highway 88 and 89, Kit Carson Campground, Snowshoe Springs Campground, access points along Highway 88/89 and at Crystal Springs Campground.

Stick to fishing the river from opening day through late July. If you arrive any later the water begins to recede, fish get trapped in pools, the river ceases to flow in many places and only the mosquitoes are happy. There are also larger browns in the river near Hope Valley. However, these are wild fish and wary of hardware. You'll need to fly fish to nab 'em.

If you plan to make the trip, supplies are available in Woodfords and South Lake Tahoe. The West Fork of the Carson River is closed to fishing from November 16 to the last Saturday in April. Snow keeps Blue Lakes Road closed until June in most years. Call the Forest Service for updated conditions.

Also nearby are Caples Lake, Upper and Lower Blue Lakes and Burnside Lake.

Directions: From the junction of Highway's 50 and 89 in South Lake Tahoe, drive south on Highway 50/89 for 4.7 miles to Meyers. In Meyers, turn left on Highway 89 and drive south for 10.9 miles to Highway 88. Access to the river is available here, off Blue Lakes Road and along Highway 88/89.

RED LAKE

Rating: 7

Species: Brook Trout
and Cutthroat Trout

Stocked with 5,000
pounds of brook trout,
153 pounds of finger-
ling cutthroat trout and
555 pounds of cutthroat
trout.

Facilities: Restrooms

Need Information?
Contact: The Sportsman
(530) 542-3474

While there are many quality trout lakes along Highway 88 and the Kit Carson Pass corridor, Red Lake is one of a handful that doesn't require any hiking or a long, slow, winding drive on a dirt road to reach it, nor do crowds develop often. Within rock throwing distance of Highway 88, Red is a quality brook and cutthroat trout lake with good access.

Winter and spring are the best times to target the brooks. Springtime fishing is rewarding for anglers who toss small spinners or float night crawlers off the bottom. Winter brings ice fishing to Red, one of the few easily accessible ice fishing spots in the Sierra. After the 4th of July, Red begins to be drawn down. With less water coming into the lake from the three unnamed streams that feed it, oxygen levels decrease. Consequently, the trout become lethargic and are less inclined to feed. Each year the California Department of Fish and Game plants 7,500 half-pound brook trout, 3,050 fingerling cutthroat trout and 222 brood stock cutthroats in the 85-acre lake at 8,000 feet in the Toiyabe National Forest.

If you plan to make the trip, supplies are available in Meyers and at Caples Lake. In winter call ahead for road conditions. Chains may be required. No motorized boats are permitted.

Red Lake

Also nearby are West Fork of the Carson River, Scotts Lake and Blue Lakes.

Directions: *From the junction of Highway's 50 and 89 in South Lake Tahoe, drive south on Highway's 50/89 for 4.7 miles to Meyers. In Meyers, turn left on Highway 89 and drive south for 10.9 miles to Highway 88. Turn right and drive 6.5 miles to the lake on the left.*

Scotts Lake

Rating: 5

Species: Rainbow Trout and Brook Trout

Stocks: None

Facilities: None

Need Information?
Contact: Toiyabe
National Forest
(775) 882-2766

Sometimes road signs can be deceiving. The posted sign at the base of Highway 88 to Scott Lake is one of them. The sign says the road is for "Off Road Vehicles Only" followed by a picture of a passenger car with a sticker across it that reads, "Not recommended." Most of the time these signs are right, but it this case we'll have to make an exception.

If your car has any clearance at all, you'll make it with no problem. The road is well graded and with the exception of two small gullies about halfway to the lake, even a Honda would survive. As expected, that sign scares off a lot of people, which means not many people come to Scotts Lake. Additionally, there is no sign on Highway 88 to let visitors know the lake exists, so Scotts is primarily only visited by locals.

Located at 8,011 feet in the Toiyabe National Forest, there are primitive campsites and fire pits built along the shore. The lake is surrounded by pines and harbors rainbow and brook trout, none that amount to much size. There are dozens of dead trees that poke out of the water all around the lake. Try casting near the trees or use a float tube to reach deeper areas of the lake. Unfortunately, fish stocking no longer takes place. Action is scarce.

If you plan to make the trip, supplies are available in South Lake Tahoe. The road to the lake is closed in the winter.

Also nearby are the West Fork of the Carson River and Red Lake.

Directions: *From the junction of Highway's 50 and 89 in South Lake Tahoe, drive south on Highway's 50/89 for 4.7 miles to Meyers. In Meyers, turn left on Highway 89 and drive south for 10.9 miles to Highway 88. Turn right and drive 1.5 miles to an unsigned dirt road on the right. Turn right and continue 2.8 miles to the lake.*

Scotts Lake

Region

26

Ebbetts Pass
Markleeville

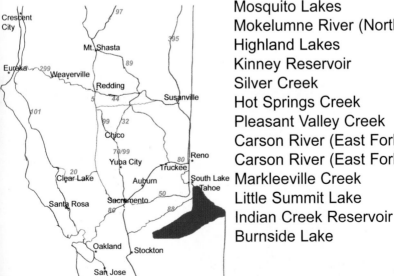

Spicer Meadow Reservoir
Union Reservoir
Utica Reservoir
Elephant Rock Lake
Lake Alpine
Mosquito Lakes
Mokelumne River (North Fork)
Highland Lakes
Kinney Reservoir
Silver Creek
Hot Springs Creek
Pleasant Valley Creek
Carson River (East Fork)
Carson River (East Fork, Lower)
Markleeville Creek
Little Summit Lake
Indian Creek Reservoir
Burnside Lake

SPICER MEADOW RESERVOIR

Rating: 8
Species: Rainbow Trout and Brown Trout
Stocked with 584 pounds of fingerling rainbow trout.
Facilities: Restrooms and Campgrounds

Spicer Meadow Reservoir is a large reservoir in remote granite country. It has several islands, many submerged outcroppings, and offers a great deal of bank fishing access. Even in this secluded area of the Stanislaus National Forest, there is a paved boat launch. The California Department of Fish and Game manages Spicer as a put-and-grow fishery. A one time, up to 250,000 fingerling Eagle Lake trout were planted annually. (The actual number varies by year.) On average 50,000 fingerlings are planted. The number was reduced as the productivity of the lake decreased. If productivity continues to fall, catchables may need to be planted. For now though, 10-14 inch rainbows are more than satisfying.

Spicer Meadow Reservoir

In the late Sixties, cut-bows were planted. While this stain of a hybrid rainbow and cutthroat is no longer planted, it has managed to maintain its' population by successfully spawning in Highland Creek and other tributaries. It's not uncommon to catch 18-20 inch cutt-bows.

Spicer Meadow is a trollers' lake. At up to 300 feet deep at full pool, anglers with a downrigger can cover more water than bank fishermen soaking Power Bait and worms. Your best bet is to drag a Yo-Zuri Crystal Minnow, Rebel, Bomber or a night crawler and flasher combo. Troll the entire shoreline, near the inlet, around the islands, by the dam and down the middle of the lake. Expect trout to be on the surface in May and June and from 20-50 feet deep for the duration of summer.

Trip info for Alpine Lake also applies to Spicer Meadow Reservoir.

***Directions:** From the junction of Highway 4 and the 99 Freeway in Stockton, drive east on Highway 4 for 46.6 miles to the junction with Highway 49. Turn right and drive for 1.5 miles on Highway 4/49 to the turnoff for Highway 4 on the left. Turn left and continue 42.4 miles to Spicer Reservoir Road. Turn right and drive 8.1 miles to the Spicer Meadow Reservoir turnoff on the right. Taking the turnoff continue 1.7 miles to the dam.*

UNION RESERVOIR

Rating: 6

Species: Rainbow Trout and Brown Trout

Stocked 1,000 pounds of rainbow trout.

Facilities: Restrooms and Campgrounds

At one time Union Reservoir was a sour apple. After providing anglers with a good put-and-take fishery the allotment of trout to be stocked by the California Department of Fish and Game was suddenly pulled because of a lack of public access. Following a battle to create public use, the allotment was reinstated. Once again Union thrives as a put-and-take lake. Don't expect to reel in any hogs though. On average, the fish stocked are caught soon after the truck pumps them in.

For a remote lake set in granite country crowds can get heavy. Anglers tend to catch and keep many trout the week they are planted. Motorboats are permitted, allowing anglers to troll as well as dunk bait from shore. If bait fishing, seek deeper, cooler water. Union has a problem with a booming population of black bullhead. If you like bullhead soup, don't feel bad about keeping and eating hundreds of them at a time. An eight-inch fish is a trophy!

Trip info for Alpine Lake also applies to Union Reservoir.

Directions: *From the junction of Highway 4 and the 99 Freeway in Stockton, drive east on Highway 4 for 46.6 miles to the junction with Highway 49. Turn right and drive for 1.5 miles on Highway 4/49 to the turnoff for Highway 4 on the left. Turn left and continue 42.4 miles to Spicer Reservoir Road. Turn right and drive 8.0 miles to the turnoff for Union and Utica Reservoirs on the left. Turn left and drive seven-tenths of a mile to a split in the road. Stay right for Union Reservoir and drive 1.1 miles to the lake.*

Union Reservoir

UTICA RESERVOIR

Rating: 2
Species: Rainbow Trout, Brown Bullhead and Brown Trout
Stocks: None
Facilities: Restrooms and Campgrounds

Utica Reservoir used to offer a decent trout fishery for summertime anglers. That time has long since passed. Utica was pulled from the allotment list more than 20 years ago when the California Department of Fish and Game decided that too many trout were being killed in the winter when the lake froze. While Utica is a good size, it is still just too shallow. Its' link to Union Reservoir, however, allows some trout to inhabit the lake. Unfortunately, it's not a place to expect to catch them.

Bullhead, on the other hand, are abundant. To cash in on the action, toss in a piece of a night crawler on a small hook and you'll catch as many as you want. The lake is overpopulated with bullhead!

When I visit Utica I leave my rods in the car and put on my swimming trunks. The comfortable summer water makes for a better experience than the poor fishing.

Schools of small catfish are seen at Utica.

Trip info to Alpine Lake also applies to Utica Reservoir.

Directions: From the junction of Highway 4 and the 99 Freeway in Stockton, drive east on Highway 4 for 46.6 miles to the junction with Highway 49. Turn right and drive for 1.5 miles on Highway 4/49 to the turnoff for Highway 4 on the left. Turn left and continue 42.4 miles to Spicer Reservoir Road. Turn right and drive 8.0 miles to the turnoff for Union and Utica Reservoirs on the left. Turn left and drive seven-tenths of a mile to a split in the road. Stay left for Utica Reservoir and drive one mile to the lake.

Utica Reservoir is pretty, but not a great place to catch rainbow trout.

ELEPHANT ROCK LAKE

Rating: 3

Species: Rainbow Trout and Black Bullhead

Stocks: None

Facilities: None

Need Information?
Contact: Stanislaus National Forest
(209) 795-1381

Elephant Rock Lake has all the characteristics of a backcountry lake, yet a dirt road winding around its' shore keeps it from being classified in that category. At one time, the small pond-size lake was planted with 400 fingerling rainbow trout each year. Unfortunately, those plants were pulled in 2000 when endangered frogs were found along the shoreline. Most likely the lake won't be planted anytime in the near future.

There are, however, tens of thousands of black bullhead to be caught. Yet, at a full length of five inches, they can be impossible to catch. With no future scheduled plants of trout, the California Department of Fish and Game isn't bothered by the bullhead problem. In fact, they've pretty much dropped the lake from their management list.

Elephant Rock is set aside for swimmers who come to avoid crowds. One-fifth of the lake is covered in lily pads while the rest of the lake is open water. Elephant Rock Lake yields grandeur views of Elephant Rock, just not good fishing.

Trip info for Alpine Lake also applies to Elephant Rock Lake.

Directions: *From the junction of Highway 4 and the 99 Freeway in Stockton, drive east on Highway 4 for 46.6 miles to the junction with Highway 49. Turn right and drive for 1.5 miles on Highway 4/49 to the turnoff for Highway 4 on the left. Turn left and continue 42.4 miles to Spicer Reservoir Road. Turn right and drive 8.1 miles to the Spicer Meadow Reservoir turnoff. Ignoring the right fork to the reservoir, continue straight and drive 4.0 miles to the lake on the left.*

LAKE ALPINE

Rating: 8

Species: Rainbow Trout and Channel Catfish

Stocked with 11,200 pounds of rainbow trout.

Facilities: Campgrounds, Picnic Areas, Boat Launch, Boat Rentals, Restrooms, Lodging, RV Hookups, Restaurant, Bait & Tackle, Showers and a General Store

Need Information? Contact: Lake Alpine Resort (530) 753-6358

Lake Alpine is undoubtedly the biggest tourist attraction in the Ebbetts Pass area. This 179-acre lake is the most heavily planted water along Highway 4 from the low-lying foothills of the Central Valley to its' junction with Highway 4 near Markleeville. The California Department of Fish and Game pumps some 15,280 half-pound rainbow trout into this scenic lake at 7,320 feet in the Stanislaus National Forest. To attract more anglers, the Alpine Chamber of Commerce plants 1,000 pounds of trophy fish, as does the Alpine County Fish and Game Commission. All the trophy fish weigh between three-and-eight pounds and come from the American Trout and Salmon Company. The commission also plants 1,000 pounds of half-pound fish.

So with all these plants, how good is the fishing? Pretty good. Shoreline bait dunkers and trollers can equally cash in on the action. As with all planted lakes, Power Bait is the mostly commonly tossed bait, with rainbow and Captain America producing the highest catch rates. Trollers working the shorelines, dam area or down the middle fool the fish with Sep's trolling flies set 16 inches behind a Sep's Pro dodger in watermelon color. For the larger fish, try slow trolling mid size Rebel Minnows. Brown trout patterns work best.

Alpine is more than an angler's lake. With granite shorelines shaded by pines and small islands to lay out on, this man-made lake is an excellent family destination. A lot like Pinecrest Lake to the south along Highway 108, Alpine offers excellent camping and full amenities, not to mention a great place to take the kids.

One thing to consider is the lake is highly susceptible to winds. When the winds kick up be sure to get off the lake.

If you plan to make the trip, supplies are available at the lake. In winter and early spring call ahead for road conditions. The road may be closed due to winter conditions.

Also nearby are Mosquito Lakes, Kinney Reservoir, Highland Lakes, Mokelumne River North Fork and Spicer Meadow Reservoir.

Directions: *From the junction of Highway 4 and the 99 Freeway in Stockton, drive east on Highway 4 for 46.6 miles to the junction with Highway 49. Turn right and drive for 1.5 miles on Highway 4/49 to the turnoff for Highway 4 on the left. Leaving Highway 49, turn left on Highway 4 and drive 49.1 miles to the reservoir on the right.*

MOSQUITO LAKES

Rating: 6

Species: Rainbow Trout

Stocked with 2,160 pounds of rainbow trout.

Facilities: None

Need Information? Contact: Stanislaus National Forest (209) 795-1381

Situated in a high country setting at 8,000 feet in the Stanislaus National Forest, Mosquito Lakes are two small and extremely shallow lakes that aren't heavily fished, but are heavily planted. These four-acre roadside waters make for good bait fishing, but can yield mixed results for spin fishermen because of exposed and hidden stumps, and thick weeds. Experienced fly-fishermen can experience high catch rates in these still waters near the brim of the Pacific Grade Summit on Highway 4, 732 feet below Ebbetts Pass. The upper lake is best fished with bait, while the lower lake, which is thicker with weeds, is best fished with a fly rod.

Natural reproduction doesn't occur, but with 2,071 half-pound rainbows spilled into each of these ponds, catch rates can be promising. Both lakes are nearly identical and only separated by a small rock-built dam. At times, the ponds, which freeze over in the winter, are also planted with trophy three-to-five-pound brood fish by the CA DFG and also the Alpine County Fish and Game Commission. The ponds mark the headwaters of the North Fork of the Stanislaus River and are also one of the most scenic drive-to areas in the state.

Trip info for Alpine Lake also applies to Mosquito Lakes.

Directions: From the junction of Highway 4 and the 99 Freeway in Stockton, drive east on Highway 4 for 46.6 miles to the junction with Highway 49. Turn right and drive for 1.5 miles on Highway 4/49 to the turnoff for Highway 4 on the left. Leaving Highway 49, turn left on Highway 4 and drive 55.7 miles to the reservoir on the right.

Right (Mosquito Lake)

MOKELUMNE RIVER (NORTH FORK)

Rating: 5

Species: Rainbow Trout

Stocked with 740
pounds of rainbow
trout.

Facilities:
Campgrounds and
Restrooms

Need Information?
Contact: Stanislaus
National Forest
(209) 795-1381

The North Fork is not your typical river. You can rock hop across it, there's no way a boat would float and the maximum depth is three feet. If I named it, I'd call it a stream. The North Fork is roughly five feet wide, maybe 10 in some places and doesn't have a lot of volume. Why is it called a river then? My guess it because of its' length. The river spans more than 65 miles and flows year-round. What matters most to us is, yes, there are trout. The California Department of Fish and Game plants 1,230 rainbows annually.

The North Fork can be a solid early season fishery. Unfortunately, things peter out fast. By July, flows can subside greatly, causing fish plants to be cancelled until the next season. The North Fork consists of a high alpine terrain. Beginning at Highland Lakes some 8,884 feet in the Stanislaus National Forest, the area you should be concerned with fishing stretches two miles. Action is never hot, however, planters and small wild fish makes for decent action for Power Baiters. The best areas to fish are along Highland Lakes Road (especially in Bloomfield Campground) and in the meadows of Hermit Valley along Highway 4.

The North Fork of the Mokelumne River

Trip info for Alpine Lake also applies to Mokelumne River (North Fork).

Directions: *From the junction of Highway 4 and the 99 Freeway in Stockton, drive east on Highway 4 for 46.6 miles to the junction with Highway 49. Turn right and drive for 1.5 miles on Highway 4/49 to the turnoff for Highway 4 on the left. Leaving Highway 49, turn left on Highway 4 and drive 62.7 miles to Highland Lakes Road on the right. Turn right and drive 3.3 miles to the Mokelumne River crossing.*

HIGHLAND LAKES

Rating: 5

Species: Rainbow Trout

Stocks: None

Facilities:
Campgrounds and
Restrooms

Prior to the mid-Nineties, Highland Lakes was a prospering put-and-grow brook trout fishery. The California Department of Fish and Game planted fingerling brooks each year which provided anglers with pan size brookies the following summers. Things have changed since the late-Nineties though. CA DFG survey teams located the Yosemite toad in the lake's drainage and subsequently stopped planting fish.

While brookies aren't as abundant as they once were opportunity still remains. The brooks have established a self-sustaining population and will be available as long as the lake isn't poisoned, which wont happen. At best expect eight-to-10-inch trout.

Highland Lakes are two small lakes ideal for anglers who want to get away from it all without enduring a long drive on a dirt road. It's a mere five mile drive from the highway to the high meadow atmosphere. The lakes come wrapped in breathtaking views of mountain peaks, sparkling clear water and colorful panoramas of wildflowers. The lakes are a great place to launch a canoe and troll down the middle with a Dick Nite spoon or wait till evening to nab rising fish on small spinners or flies.

Trip info for Alpine Lake also applies to Highland Lake.

Directions: *From the junction of Highway 4 and the 99 Freeway in Stockton, drive east on Highway 4 for 46.6 miles to the junction with Highway 49. Turn right and drive for 1.5 miles on Highway 4/49 to the turnoff for Highway 4 on the left. Leaving Highway 49, turn left on Highway 4 and drive 62.7 miles to Highland Lakes Road on the right. Turn right and drive 5.1 miles to Lower Highland Lake and 5.9 to Upper Highland Lake.*

Highland Lakes is a poor fishery, but offers great scenery.

KINNEY RESERVOIR

Rating: 5

Species: Rainbow Trout

Stocked with 1,000
pounds of rainbow
trout.

Facilities: None

Need Information?
Contact: Tioyabe
National Forest
(775) 822-2766

Don't confuse Kinney Reservoir with Kinney Lakes. The lakes are consistent produces of cutthroat trout; however the reservoir holds no cutthroat. Also, the reservoir is a roadside water, while the lakes are in the backcountry. The lakes are natural, but as for the reservoir, it is manmade and in low water years can be sucked dry by late summer.

That is one of the reasons why the Alpine County Fish and Game Commission doesn't plant it. The California Department of Fish and Game stocks fish sparingly. Only 2,000 half-pound rainbows are planted annually. The best opportunity occurs near the dam where bait dunkers experience decent catch rates with Power Bait and inflated night crawlers.

Unfortunately, trophy fish don't reside at the 33-acre reservoir at 8,353 feet in the Tioyabe National Forest, just below Ebbetts Pass. Nor are there any services or restrooms! So you have to balance the easy access and lack of trophy fish with the few crowds that arrive and decide if you'd rather fish here or one of the nearby lakes with trophy fish.

If you plan to make the trip, supplies are available in Markleeville. In winter and spring call ahead for road conditions. The road may be closed due to snow.

Also nearby are Lake Alpine, Silver Creek and Raymond Meadow Creek Falls.

Directions: From the junction of Highway 4 and the 99 Freeway in Stockton, drive east on Highway 4 for 46.6 miles to the junction with Highway 49. Turn right and drive for 1.5 miles on Highway 4/49 to the turnoff for Highway 4 on the left. Leaving Highway 49, turn left on Highway 4 and drive 65.2 miles to the reservoir on the left.

Kinney Reservoir

SILVER CREEK

Rating: 5

Species: Rainbow Trout
and Brown Trout

Stocked with 1,200
pounds of rainbow
trout.

Facilities:
Campgrounds, Picnic
Areas and Restrooms

Need Information?
Contact: Toiyabe
National Forest
(775) 882-2766

Silver Creek is a small, high gradient stream between Ebbetts Pass and Markleeville, on the leeward side of the Sierra. Anglers need to be aware of the drastic changes the stream undergoes over its nine-mile stretch beginning at 8,500 feet at Lower Kinney Lake and terminating at the East Fork of the Carson River some 2,600 feet below.

The upper stretch is rocky with few pools, where as the lower stretch becomes less sloped and begins to show off more and deeper pools. The lower stretch is the easiest and most productive section of the stream and contains the most trout. Fortunately for anglers, there is a lot of drive-to access. The stream, which runs through the Tioyabe National Forest, parallels Highway 4. Best access points are where the highway crosses the road, at Centerville Flat and in Silver Creek Campground.

Silver Creek is well stocked. In addition to 300 pounds of trout planted by the Alpine County Fish and Game Commission, the California Department of Fish and Game stocks 2,190 half pound rainbow trout. The commission plants about 200 three-to-six-pound fish each year to attempt to attract anglers to fish this stream. The majority of the fish are caught on Orange Deluxe Pautzke salmon eggs. There are few pools suitable for the use of spinners. For the more experienced angler, try using white trout jigs in the deeper holes to target the browns.

Silver Creek

If you plan to make the trip, supplies are available in Markleeville. Silver Creek is closed to fishing from November 16 to the last Saturday in May.

Also nearby are the East Fork of the Carson River and Kinney Reservoir.

Directions: *From the junction of Highway's 50 and 89 in South Lake Tahoe, drive south on Highway's 50/89 for 4.7 miles to Meyers. In Meyers, turn left on Highway 89 and drive south for 10.9 miles to Highway 88. Turn left and drive six miles to Woodfords. Turn right on Highway 89 and drive 6.5 miles to Markleeville. Continue on Highway 89 for approximately six miles to the junction with Highway 4. Veer right onto Highway 4 and drive 2.3 miles to the stream. The road parallels the river.*

HOT SPRINGS CREEK

Rating: 5

Species: Rainbow Trout and Brown Trout

Stocked with 550 pounds of rainbow trout.

Facilities: Campgrounds, Picnic Areas and Restrooms

Need Information? Contact: Grover Hot Springs State Park (530) 694-2248

Whether it be dramatic waterfalls, coastal redwoods, giant sequoias, pristine rivers, rugged mountain ranges, fields of wildflowers or flocks of birds, California's state parks were created to showcase and preserve many of our great treasures. In most cases, the state parks have done a great job, but in the case of Grover Hot Springs State Park, I believe their goal was missed. Some of the natural hot springs in the park no longer flow through their wild range. The hot springs have since been channeled into a concrete swimming pool to allow visitors to enjoy the natural phenom in a safe environment.

There are, nonetheless, still hundreds of acres of unchanged countryside for sightseers to cherish,

Hot Springs Creek

including Hot Springs Creek, several miles of hiking trails and fields that burst with wildflowers. Hot Springs Creek has a strain of wild rainbow and brown trout that inhabit the stream, but to enhance the fishery and make it more attractive to anglers, the Alpine County Fish and Game Commission has opted to plant rainbow trout. The California Department of Fish and Game doesn't plant any fish.

The planted fish are trucked in from American Trout and Salmon Company. Both trophy and pan size fish are stocked; 250 pounds of three-to-six-pound fish and 300 pounds of smaller half-pound trout are planted throughout the spring and summer. Unfortunately, there are few large pools to fish, so you'll have to rock hop up and downstream with either Gold Label Pautzke salmon eggs or mini night crawlers.

If you plan to make the trip, supplies are available in Markleeville. There is a day-use fee. Hot Springs Creek is closed to fishing from Nov. 16 to the last Saturday in April.

Also nearby are Markleeville Creek and Pleasant Valley Creek.

Directions: *From the junction of Highway's 50 and 89 in South Lake Tahoe, drive south on Highway's 50/89 for 4.7 miles to Meyers. In Meyers, turn left on Highway 89 and drive south for 10.9 miles to Highway 88. Turn left and drive six miles to Woodfords. Turn right on Highway 89 and drive 6.5 miles to Hot Springs Road. Turn right and drive 3.6 miles to a stop sign. Turn right, drive through the entrance kiosk and park near the bridge over the creek.*

PLEASANT VALLEY CREEK

Rating: 7

Species: Rainbow Trout

Stocked with 1,000
pounds of rainbow
trout.

Facilities: None

Need Information?
Contact: Pleasant
Valley Fly
Fishing Preserve
(530) 542-0759

At 5,600 feet in the Toiyabe National Forest, Pleasant Valley Creek has gone through a series of changes through the years. From 1928-49, it was used as a fish hatchery by the California Department of Fish and Game. The CA DFG leased the land around the creek from the landowner for $5 a year while they raised rainbow trout. The ranch has been owned by the same family since 1868. Up until the late Nineties it was open to the public, however misuse closed its' waters and shoreline to anglers.

The closure might sound like a bad thing. Pleasant Valley Creek, however, is in better shape now than before. In 1998, the creek was renamed Pleasant Valley Fly Fishing Preserve and has been deemed a fly fishing only stream. Catch & release is the law. Only barbless hooks may be used. The rainbows are fairly new. As a result of the New Years Day flood in 1997, all the fish planted by the CA DFG were either swept downstream or killed. Each year Alpine Fly Fishing stocks the creek with 1,000 pounds of trout from the American Trout and Salmon Company.

The creek drains into Markleeville Creek and many of the planted fish end up downstream each year. Fortunately, the creek is fed by a large watershed (Tamarack, Wet Meadows, Upper and Lower Sunset and Hellhole Lake) and fails to dry up. This allows for trout to naturally reproduce. With rainbows up to four pounds, the fishing can be good. In the flood, much of the insect population was killed off. In 2001, signs of a good caddis hatch came back to life helping trout grow more rapidly. Check with Alpine Fly Fishing for seasonal fly patterns.

If you plan to make the trip, supplies are available in Markleeville. A quota of five anglers per day is implemented on the creek. The creek is open to the public providing you pay the fishing fee, of $95 per day. Pleasant Valley Creek is closed to fishing from November 16 to the last Saturday in April.

Also nearby are Hot Springs Creek, Markleeville Creek and Carson River (East Fork).

Directions: From the junction of Highway's 50 and 89 in South Lake Tahoe, drive south on Highway's 50/89 for 4.7 miles to Meyers. In Meyers, turn left on Highway 89 and drive south for 10.9 miles to Highway 88. Turn left and drive six miles to Woodfords. Turn right on Highway 89 and drive 6.4 miles to Markleeville and turn left on Hot Springs Road. Continue one mile to Pleasant Valley Road and turn left. Drive seven-tenths of a mile to where the road turns to dirt. Continue two miles to the stream.

CARSON RIVER (EAST FORK)

Rating: 7

Species: Rainbow
Trout, Brown Trout and
Cutthroat Trout

Stocked with 8,800
pounds of rainbow trout
and 150 pounds of
cutthroat trout.

Facilities:
Campgrounds,
Restrooms and Picnic
Areas

Need Information?
Contact: Tahoe Fly
Fishing Outfitters
(530) 541-8208

They are many differences between the East and West Fork of the Carson River. While both hold rainbow, brown and cutthroat trout and flow year round. Their main dissimilarity deals with topography. Sporting the high country feeling (low and high gradient stretches, meadows, pined covered shorelines and rocky and sandy banks) the West Fork is eye appealing. In contrast, the East Fork can be eye damaging (a little exaggerating here, but you get the point). That high mountain feeling and crisp mountain air is replaced by a hot, dry and arid desert landscape, which many anglers choose to pass up. On the upside, there are fewer anglers and I've found that the East Fork holds more fish! Yes!

Those who can overloook the bland surroundings and lose themselves in the current of the 10-20 foot wide, fast-flowing river can expect to do well. The river is heavily planted by the California Department of Fish and Game, the Alpine County Chamber of Commerce and the Alpine County Fish and Game Commission. The CA DFG dumps 17,450 half-pound rainbow trout, while the Fish and Game Commission plants 3,200 pounds of fish from the American Trout and Salmon Company, half of which are 14-16 inches and the others four-to-eight pounds. The Chamber of Commerce plants 1,000 pounds of fish each year. Fish are scattered along a six-mile stretch of Highway 89/4 and while small Panther Martins and silver Kastmasters fool fish best, just about anything will work. Another plus, due to a larger watershed the East Fork has a consistent flow year round. Low water levels aren't a problem traditionally.

If you plan to make the trip, supplies are available in Markleeville. The Carson River (East Fork) is closed to fishing from November 16 to the last Saturday in April. Fishing downriver of Hangman's Bridge is governed by special regulations.

Also nearby are Indian Creek Reservoir, Silver Creek and Markleeville Creek.

The East Fork of the Carson River

Directions: *From the junction of Highway's 50 and 89 in South Lake Tahoe, drive south on Highway's 50/89 for 4.7 miles to Meyers. In Meyers, turn left on Highway 89 and drive south for 10.9 miles to Highway 88. Turn left and drive six miles to Woodfords. Turn right on Highway 89 and drive 7.8 miles to Hangman's Bridge. Access is available from this point on upstream to Wolf Creek.*

CARSON RIVER (EAST FORK, LOWER)

Rating: 7

Species: Rainbow Trout, Brown Trout and Cutthroat Trout

Stocks: None

Facilities: None

Need Information?
Contact: Alpine Fly-Fishing Guide Jim Crouse (530) 542-0759

The East Fork of the Carson River is a true success story. In an effort to block a proposal to place a dam along the East Fork of the Carson River, anglers petitioned the California Department of Fish and Game to add the river to the list of the state's wild trout waters. In 1984, an 11-mile section of the river was added to the list, preserving its' free flowing waters. Then in 1998, special regulations were implemented, forcing anglers to catch and release all fish caught from Hangman's Bridge on downstream to the Nevada state line. The regulations have helped to make the river more of a quality trout water. The East Fork contains predominately rainbow trout, although there are a few lunker browns and some cutthroat in the system.

At 5,000 feet in the Toiyabe National Forest, near the town of Markleeville, this lower section of Carson differs greatly in its' appearance from the stocked section of the East Fork. The wild trout section has a higher gradient, there's a longer distance between pools and the landscape is conquered by pinyon pines and sagebrush, taking on more of a desert feeling. The lower East Fork isn't a roadside water.

While most anglers fish near Hangman's Bridge, the best fishing is found roughly 1.5 miles downriver near the confluence with Markleeville Creek. Rather than a ton of pan size fish, like the ones that were abundant from 1984-98, the average size is now 12 inches. Trout to 20 inches are common.

Early season flows can be high making fishing tough, however, as long as flows remain below 700 cfs the river will be fishable. In the early part of the season the fish will be down on the bottom and off to the side, just out of the current. Use a weight to catch more fish. In mid-June or July, the dry fly season begins and the fish start feeding on the top. For the best results use a Zonker streamer, Woolly Buggers or nymphs like Hares Ears or AP Black.

The Lower East Fork of the Carson River

If you plan to make the trip, supplies are available in Markleeville. The Lower East Fork of the Carson River is closed to fishing from November 16 to the last Saturday in April. Only artificial lures with barbless hooks are permitted. Fishing is catch and release only.

Also nearby are Markleeville Creek and Pleasant Valley Creek.

Directions: *From the junction of Highway's 50 and 89 in South Lake Tahoe, drive south on Highway 50/89 for 4.7 miles to Meyers. In Meyers, turn left on Highway 89 and drive south for 10.9 miles to Highway 88. Turn left and drive six miles to Woodfords. Turn right on Highway 89 and drive 7.8 miles to Hangman's Bridge.*

MARKLEEVILLE CREEK

Rating: 7

Species: Rainbow Trout
and Cutthroat Trout

Stocked with 750 pounds
of rainbow trout.

Facilities: Restrooms,
Lodging, General Store,
Campgrounds, Picnic
Areas, Bait & Tackle and
Restaurants

Need Information?
Contact: Alpine Chamber
of Commerce
(530) 694-2475

Walking through the Markleeville General Store, you get the feeling some big fish are caught each year in Alpine County. The walls are covered with Polaroids of anglers posing with five-to-10 pound trout as if they are caught daily, well they are. What boggled me the most was that these fish were all caught out of Markleeville Creek, a little dribble of water across the street from the general store on Highway 89.

I didn't believe there was any way these lunkers could be caught in that 10-20 foot wide stream. When I walked down the bank though, my opinion changed drastically. I was positive the clerk was telling me fish tales to get me to buy some fishing tackle. He wasn't fibbing! These fish were stacked up in two pools.

It turns out the Alpine Fish and Game Commission plants the fish to bring tourists to the area. The South Lake Tahoe Public Utilities District pays for the fish and the Commission does the stocking. Each year 1,150 pounds of Eagle Lake rainbow trout (550 pounds are between four-and-eight pounds) are purchased from the American Trout and Salmon Company and dumped into the same two pools in Markleeville Creek. The CA DFG adds 1,380 dinker rainbow trout. The Commission plants roughly 18,000 pounds of trout in Alpine County yearly. The program began in the early Seventies, with the trophy aspect being added in 1998.

When fishing Markleeville Creek, try to be a commando. The trophy fish are planted across the street from the general store. Catchable size fish are planted downstream to Markleeville Campground. Because so many anglers fish for the big boys these fish have become familiar with what anglers look like. If they see you they aren't going to bite. Live bait seems to be the hot ticket, with inflated night crawlers soaked in Pautzke Liquid Krill and Power Bait taking the most fish.

Trip info for Carson River (East Fork) also applies to Markleeville Creek.

Directions: *From the junction of Highway's 50 and 89 in South Lake Tahoe, drive south on Highway's 50/89 for 4.7 miles to Meyers. In Meyers, turn left on Highway 89 and drive south for 10.9 miles to Highway 88. Turn left and drive six miles to Woodfords. Turn right on Highway 89 and drive 6.4 miles to Markleeville. The stream flows through town on downstream along Highway 89.*

Markleeville Creek

LITTLE SUMMIT LAKE

Rating: 6

Species: Brook Trout, Brown Trout, Rainbow Trout and Cutthroat Trout

Stocked with 1,000 pounds of rainbow trout.

Facilities: None

Need Information? Contact: Markleeville General Store (530) 694-2448

The Alpine County Fish and Game Commission chose to make Little Summit Lake a quality fishery. With the California Department of Fish and Game opting not to plant the lake, the Commission decided to use 1,000 of the 16,000 pounds of fish they plant in Alpine County each year to plant Little Summit. Situated near Indian Valley Reservoir, Little Summit sees minimal crowds. Other than a few locals, this pond remains deserted.

Some years Summit even goes dry. The lake is fed by snow runoff and two springs. On a clear day you can see the springs in the lake. At full pool the lake's deepest point is 16 feet. The Commission first planted it in 1990, one a year after the lake went dry. Now only rainbows and a few browns are planted, including some trophy fish. The fish average 14-16 inches with the lake record being an eight-pound brook. Snails and shad provide a stable food source to keep the fishery solid (according to the commission).

Trout can be taken on the fly, with spinners or by soaking bait. The lake is so small each method can be employed to discover which technique works best on that particular day.

If you plan to make the trip, supplies are available in Markleeville.

Also nearby are Hot Spring Creek and Markleeville Creek.

Directions: *From the junction of Highway's 50 and 89 in South Lake Tahoe, drive south on Highway's 50/89 for 4.7 miles to Meyers. In Meyers, turn left on Highway 89 and drive south for 10.9 miles to Highway 88. Turn left and drive six miles to Woodfords. Turn right on Highway 89 and drive 3.7 miles to Airport Road. Turn left and drive approximately one mile to the left turnoff for the lake. This dirt road may be locked, forcing you to park and walk in.*

Pleasant Valley Creek (above) is a short drive from Little Summit Lake

INDIAN CREEK RESERVOIR

Rating: 7

Species: Rainbow
Trout, Brown Trout and
Cutthroat Trout

Stocked with 650
pounds of sub-catchable
rainbow trout.

Facilities: Restrooms,
Boat Launch and
Campgrounds

Need Information?
Contact: The Sportsman
(530) 542-3474

The most integral part of Indian Creek Reservoir's downfall stems from a population boom in Nevada. Since the reservoir is so close to the state's border, more people are frequenting Indian Creek and catching easy limits. Thus as time progresses, the big holdovers that were custom are becoming less available. Additionally, the lake's popularity skyrocketed when Alpine County began planting trophy fish into the system. While there is a lot of feed in Indian Creek, the increased fishing pressure isn't allowing the fish to stay in the system long enough to grow big.

Additionally, poor water quality and low oxygen levels have caused die-offs in the past. Specifically, low and warm water, high PH levels and elevated alkalinity levels have put added stress on the fish, resulting in slower growth rates. Nevertheless, trout can still be caught regularly.

Indian Creek Reservoir is loaded with quality rainbow trout.

A large stocking program has kept anglers smiling. The California Department of Fish and Game plants some 5,160 sub-catchable rainbow trout, while the Alpine County Fish and Game Commission pays the American Trout and Salmon Company to stock 4,000 pounds of rainbow trout, half of which are trophy four-to-eight-pound fish.

The rainbow trout fishery is twofold with elements of both put-and-grow and put-and-take practiced. The fish are planted as sub-catchable, so they can do part of their growing in hatchery runs and the rest in the lake. The trophy element is provided by the holdovers. The put-and-grow aspect is made possible by an abundance of feed, mainly the Tahoe tui chub, red-sided suckers, freshwater snails and threadfin shad.

Unfortunately, the suckers became a problem. They became so prolific that Alpine County planted 10,000 sub-catchable browns in 2000 to combat the problem. Browns are caught occasionally. The locals refer to the browns as "pigs". Anglers don't target browns though. It's called luck when you land a big one.

Contrary to popular belief, cutthroat are available. The CA DFG plants about 200 brood fish each year, although recent budget cuts may forbid this from occurring in the future. The fish are spawned out so they don't reproduce in the lake. It's estimated that only five to 10 percent of the cutts make it through their first year. The rest are caught or die of old age. They do, however, respond well to the high ph levels and alkaline conditions.

As for angling, it all works, especially in the winter when most other fisheries in the region are closed, frozen or inaccessible. In winter and spring, trolling and bait fishing is popular. This 160-acre lake near Markleeville gets fished hard after a plant, so arrive early. It doesn't matter what you troll as long as you troll slow. Any spinner or small spoon will work. As summer arrives, the algae bloom becomes terrific and while the bait anglers get annoyed with it, fly fishermen do fantastic capitalizing on the big fish that feed in these areas.

If you plan to make the trip, supplies are available in Markleeville.

Also nearby are Markleeville Creek, Hot Springs Creek and the East Fork of the Carson River. Indian Valley Reservoir may freeze during the winter months.

Directions: *From the junction of Highway's 50 and 89 in South Lake Tahoe, drive south on Highway's 50/89 for 4.7 miles to Meyers. In Meyers, turn left on Highway 89 and drive south for 10.9 miles to Highway 88. Turn left and drive six miles to Woodfords. Turn right on Highway 89 and drive 3.7 miles to Airport Road. Turn left and drive 3.6 miles to the lake.*

Indian Valley Reservoir

BURNSIDE LAKE

Rating: 5

Species: Rainbow Trout and Brook Trout

Stocked with 470 pounds of rainbow trout.

Facilities: None

Need Information? Contact: Toiyabe National Forest (775) 882-2766

It's funny how anglers toss around rumors. When I arrived at Burnside Lake, two teenagers who said they lived in Gardnerville, Nevada, told me that they had been fishing Burnside for years, but everyone else fishing was trespassing because they didn't get consent from the owner. They said that during the previous summer they met a man who told them that he owned Burnside and pays the California Department of Fish and Game to stock it with fish. As a kind deed, the man let respectful anglers fish the lake if they asked him nicely. Some con artist did a great job with these kids!

I checked with the local Forest Service office in Carson City and they assured me the lake is on public land. The CA DFG does stock it, but the funds come from taxpayers, not some man who wants his "private lake" stocked.

As for Burnside, this seven-acre lake at 7,500 feet in the Toiyabe National Forest is a no brainer to fish and freezes over in winter. Most anglers arrive and set up shop along the dirt shoreline, toss out Power Bait and inflated night crawlers and wait patiently for a pan size rainbow or brook trout to swim by and take a nibble. Tossing spinners can also be productive, just remember, to keep them on the small side. These fish (the CA DFG dumps 980 rainbows, to meet the resident brook population) rarely exceed 10 inches. As for a boat, a Sea Eagle Paddleski would work well, but lake isn't deep or big enough to put a larger boat on it. A float tube would be helpful to fish the weedy areas, however, it's not necessary.

Burnside Lake

If you plan to make the trip, supplies are available in Meyers and Woodfords. The road to Burnside typically closes in late October and remains closed until late May.

Also nearby are the West Fork of the Carson River, East Fork of the Carson River and Markleeville Creek.

Directions: *From the junction of Highway's 50 and 89 in South Lake Tahoe, drive south on Highway's 50/89 for 4.7 miles to Meyers. In Meyers, turn left on Highway 89 and drive south for 10.9 miles to Highway 88. Continue straight onto a dirt road and drive nine-tenths of a mile on Road 019 to a fork. Stay on Road 019 for 4.6 more miles to the lake.*

TOPAZ LAKE

Rating: 8

Species: Largemouth Bass, Rainbow Trout, Cutbow Trout and Brown Trout

Stocked with 1,500 pounds of cutbow trout, 625 pounds of sub-catchable rainbow trout and 34,960 pounds of rainbow trout.

Facilities: Campgrounds, Picnic Areas, RV Hookups, Café, Lodging, Casino, Boat Rentals, Launch Ramp, Restrooms and Bait & Tackle

Need Information? Contact: Topaz Marina (775) 266-3236, Douglas County Recreation Area (775) 266-3343

Prior to 1997, Topaz Lake was considered one of the best trophy trout lakes in California, but the flooding of the West Walker River dealt the lake, a blow it has yet to fully recover from. Here's what occurred: On New Years Day in 1997, the West Walker River flooded its' banks and destroyed 13 miles of Highway 395. The river, which feeds Topaz, carried debris into the lake, including propane tanks, dirt, mud and trees. A dark brownish color (the same color as the mountains that surround the lake) formed in the water. Much of the vegetation and organisms that lived in the lake were killed off, giving the fish little forage. The fishery suffered tremendously.

Before the flood however, rainbows in the four-to-eight-pound class were common. Luckily, Topaz has poised to make a strong comeback. In a natural process the vegetation has reestablished itself, organisms again flourish, and other forage, including crawdads and minnows, have allowed the lake to again produce fish in the one-to-four-pound range. Barring future floods, Topaz is on its way to regaining its game as a trophy fishery.

The lake is governed by Nevada and California, resting half in half respectively. On the north side, in Nevada there is a casino and restaurant that overlooks the lake. The Nevada Division of Wildlife wishes to keep the lake open year-round. On the other hand, the California Department of Fish & Game prefers to close Topaz to fishing six months out of the year in accordance with the laws that govern other waters in Mono County. So the agencies came to a compromise, closing the lake for three months, October, November and December.

The CA DFG plants 10,000 sub-catchable trout and 15,013 five-to-the-pound rainbows. NDOW stocks 60,000 rainbow trout. Fishing is hottest from the opener through March, when easy limits are picked up by trollers toplining Rapalas or by shoreline anglers floating night crawlers off the bottom.
As the water warms in April, the trout move into 20-25 feet. Those using deep diving lures still have a chance at catching fish toplining. However, downriggers and leadcore work better. Depending on fluctuation, maximum depth ranges from 60-120 feet. To irrigate Scotts Valley downstream the lake is drawn down each year.

With summer come water-skiers. Most anglers choose to write off the lake until winter. Those that do fish it anchor in deep water and drift night crawlers off the bottom to catch bigger fish. Most of the trout caught are rainbows, but there is also stable population of wild brown trout. Each year a few more than 10 pounds are landed. The Nevada DOW also plants 3,800 cutbow trout.

There is one major downfall to fishing Topaz. At 5,000 feet on the eastern slopes of the Sierra Nevada, the winds can get treacherous in a hurry, making fishing miserable and water conditions dangerous.

If you plan to make the trip supplies are available at the lake. The lake can be fished with either a California or Nevada fishing license.

Also nearby are West Walker River, East Walker River and Walker Lake.

Directions: *From Highway 395 in Bridgeport, drive north for 45 miles to the lake on the right.*

Topaz Lake

About The Author

The founder of the "Definitive Guides" to California outdoors, award winning author Chris Shaffer has spent the last decade of his life exploring, investigating and documenting more than 1,500 lakes, rivers, streams, ponds and waterfalls throughout California. The California native is a graduate of Cal State Northridge and Crespi High School in Encino.

Shaffer has taken an active role reporting on and photographing California outdoors. Currently in print, *The Definitive Guide to Fishing in Southern California, The Definitive Guide to Fishing Central California* and voted book of the year by the Outdoor Writers Association of California in 2004, *The Definitive Guide to the Waterfalls of Southern* and Central California, are to be joined by *The Definitive Guide to Fishing in Northern California* in early 2005. A former LA Times sportswriter, Shaffer is currently working on several other outdoor related titles. More than 800 of Shaffer's photographs have been printed in newspapers and magazines worldwide.

Shaffer's work extends far beyond the book business. Aside from running a publishing company and writing books, he is a regular guest on California Sportsmen radio, Northwest Wild Country radio with Joel Shangle and other local radio shows. Shaffer also is a columnist and regular contributor for Fishing and Hunting News and The Sportsman's Series, Salmon & Steelhead Journal, Salmon, Trout & Steelheader, Game & Fish and a freelance consultant for the California Department of Fish and Game and Pautzke Bait Company.

Shaffer has performed seminars at Fred Hall Fishing Shows in the past and is a regular speaker and host at International Sportsmen's Exposition

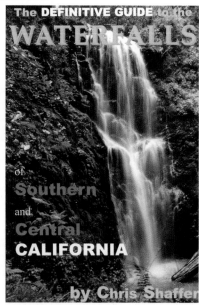

shows. Shaffer also is a full time product tester for several companies in the fishing industry including Sea Eagle, Panther Martin, Luhr Jensen, Pautzke Bait Company, Rebel, Bomber, Yakima Bait, Silver Thread, Heddon, Cotton Cordell, Megabait, Optimum, Castaic Soft Baits, YUM, Pistol Pete, Smithwick, Castaic Soft Baits, Costa Del Mar, Excalibur, Creek Chub, Lowrance, St. Croix, Thomas Buoyant, Canon, Sep's Pro Fishing, Shasta Tackle Company, Powell Fly Rods and Lamiglas.

A member of the Outdoor Writers Association of California, Outdoor Writer Association of America and Western Outdoor Writers, Shaffer also contributes to several newspapers and magazines, including the Los Angeles Daily News, Fish Taco Chronicles, Fish Alaska Magazine, Ojai Valley News, San Gabriel Valley Tribune, Florida Game and Fish, Oregon Game and Fish, Washington Game and Fish, California Game and Fish, ESPN.com Outdoors and Outdoor California magazine.

Shaffer's expertise as a freshwater fishing expert has taken him to Prince of Wales Island, Alaska, Yukon Territory, Canada, Ireland, Kitimat, British Columbia, Everglades National Park and countless destinations in the Pacific Northwest and the Northeast. Shaffer has caught and released more than 37 species of freshwater fish in Northern America.

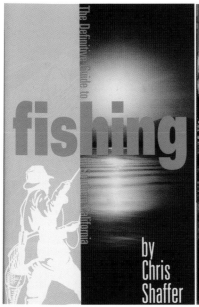